Praise for the Osborne New Testament Commentaries

"With this new series, readers will have before them what we—his students—experienced in all of Professor Osborne's classes: patient regard for every word in the text, exegetical finesse, a preference for an eclectic resolution to the options facing the interpreter, a sensitivity to theological questions, and most of all a reverence for God's word."

—**Scot McKnight**, Julius R. Mantey Chair of New Testament,
Northern Seminary

"The Osborne New Testament Comm  lifetime of serious study and teaching insights in a highly accessible, spiritu dous resource that will serve a new ge to come. Highly recommended!"

—**Andreas J. Köstenberger**, founder, Biblical Foundations; senior research professor of New Testament and biblical theology, Southeastern Baptist Theological Seminary

"Grant Osborne has spent his entire professional career teaching and writing about good principles for the interpretation of Scripture and then modeling them in his own scholarship, not least in commentaries on numerous New Testament books. The Osborne New Testament Commentaries, therefore, are a welcome new series by a veteran New Testament scholar determined to spend as much time as God gives him in his retirement years distilling the conclusions of the finest of scholarship without bogging down the reader in detailed interaction with all the various perspectives that have been suggested. If all the volumes are as good as this inaugural work on Revelation, the series will become a most welcome resource for the busy pastor or teacher."

—**Craig L. Blomberg**, distinguished professor of New Testament,
Denver Seminary

"Like many others in the church and academy, I have greatly benefitted from the writings of Grant Osborne over the course of my professional career. Grant has a gift for summarizing the salient points in a passage and making clear what he thinks the text means—as well as making it relevant and applicable to believers at all levels of biblical maturity. I especially commend the usefulness of these verse-by-verse commentaries for pastors and lay leaders."

—**Stanley E. Porter**, president, dean, professor of New Testament, and
Roy A. Hope Chair in Christian Worldview, McMaster Divinity College

"For years I have found Grant Osborne's commentaries to be reliable and thoughtful guides for those wanting to better understand the New Testament. Indeed, Osborne has mastered the art of writing sound, helpful, and readable commentaries and I am confident that this new series will continue the level of excellence that we have come to expect from him. How exciting to think that pastors, students, and laity will all be able to benefit for years to come from the wise and insightful interpretation provided by Professor Osborne in this new series. The Osborne New Testament Commentaries will be a great gift for the people of God."

—**David S. Dockery**, president, Trinity International University

"One of my most valued role models, Grant Osborne is a first-tier biblical scholar who brings to the text of Scripture a rich depth of insight that is both accessible and devotional. Grant loves Christ, loves the word, and loves the church, and those loves are embodied in this wonderful new commentary series, which I cannot recommend highly enough."

—**George H. Guthrie**, Benjamin W. Perry Professor of Bible, Union University

"Grant Osborne is ideally suited to write a series of concise commentaries on the New Testament. His exegetical and hermeneutical skills are well known, and anyone who has had the privilege of being in his classes also knows his pastoral heart and wisdom."

—**Ray Van Neste**, professor of biblical studies, director of the R.C. Ryan Center for Biblical Studies, Union University

"Grant Osborne is an eminent New Testament scholar and warm-hearted professor who loves the Word of God. Through decades of effective teaching at Trinity Evangelical Divinity School and church ministry around the world, he has demonstrated an ability to guide his readers in a careful understanding of the Bible. The volumes in this accessible commentary series help readers understand the text clearly and accurately. But they also draw us to consider the implications of the text, providing key insights on faithful application and preaching that reflect a lifetime of ministry experience. This unique combination of scholarship and practical experience makes this series an invaluable resource for all students of God's Word, and especially those who are called to preach and teach."

—**H. Wayne Johnson**, associate academic dean and associate professor of pastoral theology, Trinity Evangelical Divinity School

LUKE

Verse by Verse

LUKE

Verse by Verse

GRANT R. OSBORNE

LEXHAM PRESS

Luke: Verse by Verse

Osborne New Testament Commentaries

Copyright 2018 Grant R. Osborne

Lexham Press, 1313 Commercial St., Bellingham, WA 98225
LexhamPress.com

Print ISBN: 9781683592389
Digital ISBN: 9781683592396

Lexham Editorial Team: Jeffrey Reimer, Elliot Ritzema, Danielle Thevenaz, and
    Sarah Awa
Cover Design: Christine Christophersen
Typesetting: ProjectLuz.com

CONTENTS

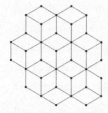

SERIES PREFACE

There are two authors of every biblical book: the human author who penned the words, and the divine Author who revealed and inspired every word. While God did not dictate the words to the biblical writers, he did guide their minds so that they wrote their own words under the influence of the Holy Spirit. If Christians really believed what they said when they called the Bible "the word of God," a lot more would be engaged in serious Bible study. As divine revelation, the Bible deserves, indeed demands, to be studied deeply.

This means that when we study the Bible, we should not be satisfied with a cursory reading in which we insert our own meanings into the text. Instead, we must always ask what God intended to say in every passage. But Bible study should not be a tedious duty we have to perform. It is a sacred privilege and a joy. The deep meaning of any text is a buried treasure; all the riches are waiting under the surface. If we learned there was gold deep under our backyard, nothing would stop us from getting the tools we needed to dig it out. Similarly, in serious Bible study all the treasures and riches of God are waiting to be dug up for our benefit.

This series of commentaries on the New Testament is intended to supply these tools and help the Christian understand more deeply the God-intended meaning of the Bible. Each volume walks the reader verse-by-verse through a book with the goal of opening up for us what God led Matthew or Paul or John to say to their readers. My goal in this series is to make sense of the historical and literary background of these ancient works, to supply the information that will enable the modern reader to understand exactly what the biblical writers were saying to their first-century audience. I want to remove the complexity of most modern commentaries and provide an easy-to-read explanation of the text. I have read nearly all the recent literature and have tried to supply a commentary that sums up the state of knowledge attained to date on the meaning and background for each biblical book.

But it is not enough to know what the books of the New Testament meant back then; we need help in determining how each text applies to our lives today. It is one thing to see what Paul was saying his readers in Rome or Philippi, and quite another thing to see the significance of his words for us. So at key points in the commentary, I will attempt to help the reader discover areas in our modern lives that the text is addressing.

I envision three main uses for this series:

1. **Devotional Scripture reading.** Many Christians read rapidly through the Bible for devotions in a one-year program. That is extremely helpful to gain a broad overview of the Bible's story. But I strongly encourage another kind of devotional reading—namely, to study deeply a single segment of the biblical text and try to understand it. These commentaries are designed to enable that. The commentary is based on the NIV and explains the meaning of the verses, enabling the modern reader to read a few pages at a time and pray over the message.

2. **Church Bible studies.** I have written these commentaries also to serve as guides for group Bible studies. Many Bible

studies today consist of people coming together and sharing what they think the text is saying. There are strengths in such an approach, but also weaknesses. The problem is that God inspired these scriptural passages so that the church would understand and obey *what he intended the text to say*. Without some guidance into the meaning of the text, we are prone to commit heresy. At the very least, the leaders of the Bible study need to have a commentary so they can guide the discussion in the direction God intended. In my own church Bible studies, I have often had the class read a simple exposition of the text so they can all discuss the God-given message, and that is what I hope to provide here.

3. **Sermon aids.** These commentaries are also intended to help pastors faithfully exposit the text in a sermon. Busy pastors often have too little time to study complex thousand-page commentaries on biblical passages. As a result, it is easy to spend little time in Bible study and thereby to have a shallow sermon on Sunday. As I write this series, I am drawing on my own experience as a pastor and interim pastor, asking myself what I would want to include in a sermon.

Overall, my goal in these commentaries is simple: I would like them to be interesting and exciting adventures into New Testament texts. My hope is that readers will discover the riches of God that lie behind every passage in his divine word. I hope every reader will fall in love with God's word as I have and begin a similar lifelong fascination with these eternal truths!

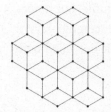

INTRODUCTION TO
THE GOSPEL OF LUKE

In many more liturgical Christian churches, the congregation sits for general Scripture readings but stands when the Gospels are read. This is because the Gospels tell the life story of Jesus the Christ, Son of God and Lord of all. When we read the Gospels, we learn of the life of God made flesh, the most significant being ever to appear on planet Earth. And Luke is the most comprehensive of the four, telling us more about Jesus than any other. It contains an unbelievable collection of stories not just about Jesus but also about the Twelve, and the relevance for the life of the church today is incredible.

Yet I think Luke is probably the least popular Gospel of the four. Matthew has always been the quintessential Gospel, famous for the Sermon on the Mount and the Olivet Discourse. People are drawn to Mark because of its dramatic, fast-moving pace and the clarity of its presentation. John is the spiritual Gospel, famed for its high **Christology**[1] and its clear presentation of the

---

1. Terms in bold type are discussed in the glossary (page 585).

gospel message. Luke gets kind of lost in the shuffle, but it does not deserve to be. As you will see as you read this commentary, it contains a rich collection of stories, every single one filled with relevance for the Christian life today.

AUTHOR

All four Gospels are anonymous—that is, none name their authors. On the other hand, the earliest witnesses, the church fathers, are clear and nearly unanimous that the titles in our Bibles—Matthew, Mark, Luke, and John—correctly identify the authors. In fact, Luke's authorship of the Gospel that now bears his name was universally affirmed until the critical scholars of the nineteenth century. The earliest witnesses are from the second century, with the manuscript 𝔓75, the Muratorian Canon (AD 170), the Anti-Marcionite Prologue (175), and Irenaeus (185) all confirming Luke, a physician and coworker of Paul, as the author of both Luke and Acts. Over the next two centuries Tertullian, Clement of Alexandria, Origen, Eusebius, and Jerome all attest to Luke as having written the third Gospel. This doesn't *prove* Luke wrote it, but it does show that the ancient church unanimously believed he did. These witnesses should be taken seriously.

The internal evidence backs up the external witness for Luke as the author. Here too I consider Luke-Acts as a united set, beginning with the prologue of Luke 1:1-4, which claims that its material was "handed down" by "eyewitnesses." This shows, first, that the author was not himself a disciple who had seen them unfold; and, second, that the stories were told to him by those who were present as they took place. This would fit Luke well: he was a Gentile convert who had to do extensive research.

Paul tells us that Luke was a physician (Col 4:14), and this may be the reason that the author of this Gospel had a special interest in healing miracles. It contains the healing stories of Mark and Matthew as well as several others (Luke 7:11-17; 13:10-17; 14:1-6; 17:11-19; 22:51). In addition, the author often used medical terms

(4:38; 5:12; 6:18; 8:44; and others). Again, this does not prove Luke the physician was the author, but it does support the possibility.

The "we" passages of Acts, where the author speaks as one who was present, are critical in determining the authorship of Luke-Acts (Acts 16:10–17; 20:5–16; 21:1–18; 27:1–28:16). There we see the author was indeed a companion of Paul who traveled extensively with him. Attempts to make the "we" a fictional device rather than an indication that the author was a historical participant fail to account for writing in the ancient world. This kind of fictional device was simply not used by ancient writers; it would have been seen as fraudulent by readers in the first century. Further, the "we" sections do not occur at especially critical sections of Acts. It is unlikely they are strategically placed but rather are simply there because these were the times when the author accompanied Paul on his journeys. They begin at Troas, in western Asia Minor, and carry through the Gentile ministry of Paul, further making Luke the likely author. In short, I believe Luke is far and away the most likely choice as author of the Third Gospel.

DATE

There are three major views for dating the Gospel of Luke, but most recent scholars believe there is too little evidence for preferring one over the other. Still, it is not an inconsequential issue. Here are the options: (1) Luke was written in the early 60s, which is where the book of Acts ends, with Paul in prison in Rome (AD 60–62); or (2) if Mark was written in the mid- to late 60s, as many suppose, then Luke, which used Mark extensively, would have been authored in the 70s; or (3) it was written at a date near the turn of the century, perhaps the 90s. Most opt for one of the first two, with the majority choosing the 70s (option two). It is common to suggest a date in the mid-70s or later on the basis of chapter 21, where Jesus describes the destruction of Jerusalem, which happened in AD 70, but that is unnecessary. This suggestion is predicated on the supposition that the destruction had to have already taken place for all that detail to be known, but that ignores the fact (in my opinion) that it is a prophecy on the part of Jesus.

My proposal is to take seriously the place where Acts ends as a marker for dating the series. If this is the case, Luke is writing Luke-Acts while Paul is in prison in Rome, AD 60–62. This is the most likely scenario, and in the Mark commentary in this series I will be arguing that Mark was written in the mid-50s. This makes best sense of the data.

It is impossible to know much about the place where Luke wrote his Gospel. Several suggestions have been made at various times, like Antioch, Caesarea, or Asia Minor (modern-day Turkey). The most likely would be Rome, especially if this Gospel was written while Paul was in prison there. But no hints are given in either book, and it is of little consequence where Luke composed them.

PURPOSE

Few books have a single purpose behind them, and Luke is no exception. The purposes for his writing are closely linked to the theological themes he develops in his two-volume work.[2] The primary purpose is found in the prologue (1:1–4). He is producing a definite history of the life of Christ and the launching of the church and its mission. He writes an eyewitness account (an "orderly account," 1:3), the product of his interviewing many who participated in the events themselves. Moreover, he wants to develop as comprehensive a history as he can. This Gospel has the largest number of stories of any of the four and is the longest of them.

Still, Luke's primary goal is not to produce the most material but to accurately convey stories. He wants his readers to realize that all these things really took place in human history. Throughout Luke as well as Acts, he emphasizes that everything was witnessed and can be attested (see Luke 1:21–22; 2:32; 5:32;

---

2. See "Major Theological Themes" below.

10:39; 13:31). History is salvation history, for God has brought his salvation through Jesus the Son of God into this world, and God's salvation has been acted out in the life and death of his Son. Jesus has fulfilled prophecy and in this way has summed up the message and purpose of the Old Testament in himself.

Luke in this sense builds on Paul and presents the good news, the gospel of the grace of God extended to sinful humanity in the life and death of Jesus as a salvific act, a working out of salvation. The three concepts (see especially 24:47-49) are repentance, forgiveness of sins, and the proclamation of this good news to the nations. Luke presents Jesus seeking and saving the lost (19:10), and this evangelistic purpose is especially central in Acts.

In this sense Luke has a twofold purpose: to encourage believers that they are part of a divine movement that is bringing God's reign into this world, and to convince unbelievers that Christ is truly Lord and Savior of this world. He wants to strengthen the church and to reach the lost.

SOURCES

The question of how the first three Gospels relate to each other is called the "**Synoptic** problem." The current consensus is called the "four-source hypothesis," that Mark is the first Gospel and the primary source of the other two. In addition to Mark, they used Q (see below) as well as special sources peculiar to Matthew (M) and Luke (L). This means that the primary source for Luke is the Gospel of Mark, with about 40 percent of Luke's material drawn from Mark. Luke frequently follows Mark not only in wording but often in the order of his stories (for instance, 4:31-6:19). In fact, in general Luke follows Mark's organization of the material.

Also, there is what is known as Q material (from the German *Quelle*, "source"). This material consists of stories or especially sayings found in both Matthew and Luke but not Mark. These passages are alike verbally but are often in different places in the two Gospels. About one-fifth of Luke stems from this material. My personal view is that there is no evidence that Q was a written document. Rather, it was likely a common oral tradition that circulated in the early church—not something that was written down.

After Mark and Q, the rest of the material in Luke's Gospel was derived from the stories Luke drew from various eyewitness accounts and is found only in his Gospel. Many of the eyewitnesses who told these stories to Luke are probably named in his Gospel. For instance, Cleopas, the disciple named on the road to Emmaus (23:13–35), may have been the source of that story. The women named in 8:1–3 and 24:10 may have been sources for other stories found in this Gospel.

OUTLINE

It is always difficult to determine the outline for any book because so many decisions are involved at every level. Scholars always differ on the details, and it is doubtful whether there are any two works that agree down the line. All we can do is our best, and that is what I have done. I can honestly say that an immense amount of thought has gone into this finished product, and so this is my contribution to the possible structure of the Third Gospel.

I. The infancy narratives (1:1–2:52)

    A. The prologue (1:1–4)

        1. Previous witnesses (1:1–2)

        2. Luke's current work (1:3–4)

    B. Announcement of John the Baptist's birth (1:5–25)

        1. A priestly couple who are childless (1:5–7)

        2. Zechariah in the temple (1:8–10)

        3. The appearance of the angel (1:11–12)

        4. The angel's message (1:13–17)

        5. Zechariah's part in this (1:18–23)

        6. Prophecy fulfilled: Elizabeth's pregnancy (1:24–25)

    C. Announcement of Jesus' birth (1:26–38)

        1. The appearance to Mary (1:26–27)

        2. The message of the angel (1:28–33)

3. Reassurance by the angel (1:34–38)
D. Mary's visit and Elizabeth's witness (1:39–45)
    1. Mary's trip to visit (1:39–40)
    2. The result of the greeting (1:41–45)
E. Mary's song of praise: the Magnificat (1:46–56)
    1. Introductory praise (1:46–47)
    2. God's saving power (1:48–49)
    3. The divine reversal (1:50–53)
    4. God's faithfulness to Israel (1:54–55)
    5. The final three months (1:56)
F. The birth of John the Baptist (1:57–66)
    1. The birth of John (1:57–58)
    2. The presentation and naming of John (1:59–66)
G. Zechariah's song of praise: the Benedictus (1:67–79)
    1. Introduction: filled with the Spirit (1:67)
    2. Praise for messianic redemption (1:68–75)
    3. The future ministries of John and Jesus (1:76–79)
H. The growing maturity of John (1:80)
I. The birth and presentation of Jesus
    1. The birth of Jesus (2:1–20)
        a. The historical circumstances (2:1–2)
        b. The journey to Bethlehem (2:3–5)
        c. The birth of Jesus (2:6–7)
        d. Shepherds led in worship by the angels (2:8–14)
        e. The worship of the Christ child (2:15–20)
    2. The presentation of Jesus in the temple (2:21–40)
        a. The circumcision and naming of the baby (2:21)
        b. The trip to Jerusalem (2:22–24)
        c. Simeon's witness (2:25–35)
        d. Anna's witness to Jesus (2:36–38)
        e. Conclusion: return to Galilee and Jesus' maturation (2:39–40)
    3. Jesus in the temple at twelve (2:41–52)
        a. The setting (2:41–42)

3. The parable of the lamp (8:16–18)

4. Jesus' true family (8:19–21)

5. Authority over nature and the cosmic powers (8:22–56)

    a. Power over nature: the stilling of the storm (8:22–25)

    b. Power over the cosmic forces: the Gerasene demoniac (8:26–39)

    c. Authority over sickness and death (8:40–56)

F. The training of the Twelve (9:1–50)

1. The mission of the Twelve (9:1–6)

    a. Passing on authority (9:1–2)

    b. Instructions for the Twelve (9:3–5)

    c. The mission takes place (9:6)

2. Herod shows interest in Jesus (9:7–9)

3. The feeding of the five thousand (9:10–17)

    a. The return of the Twelve (9:10–11)

    b. The dilemma: feeding the crowd (9:12–14a)

    c. The feeding miracle (9:14b–16)

    d. Results and aftermath (9:17)

3. Peter's confession and the passion prediction (9:18–27)

    a. Jewish speculation about Jesus (9:18–19)

    b. Peter's confession (9:20)

    c. Sayings on suffering and discipleship (9:21–27)

4. The transfiguration (9:28–36)

    a. The setting on the mountain (9:28)

    b. The appearance and heavenly witnesses (9:29–31)

    c. The disciples' confusion (9:32–33)

    d. The divine affirmation (9:34–45)

    e. Aftermath: their silence (9:36)

5. Healing the demon-possessed child (9:37–43a)

6. The second passion prediction and rivalry (9:43b–48)

    a. Prediction and failure to understand (9:43b–45)

    b. Rivalry over greatness (9:46–48)

7. Conflict over rival exorcists (9:49–50)

MAJOR THEOLOGICAL THEMES

Each Gospel has a distinct set of theological messages it wishes to communicate to readers. These themes tie the Gospel together, and they emerge when we consider the narrative flow from one episode to another. In Luke's case, these mega-themes both unite the Gospel and carry over to the book of Acts. Luke is a historian, but he is also a theologian and cares deeply for the truths Christ has taught and that guide the church.

SALVATION

The new age introduced by Christ is the age of salvation. The reason Christ came to earth was to die for the sins of humankind, to become the atoning sacrifice on the cross so that sinners could repent, believe, find salvation, receive forgiveness of sins, inherit eternal life, and enter the kingdom of God. All of this language is endemic to Luke-Acts and together describes the gospel, the good news he intends to proclaim through his writings.

Jesus' saving purpose was evident from the beginning. At his birth, the angelic host told the shepherds that "a Savior has been born to you; he is the Messiah, the Lord" (2:11). Then when Zacchaeus came to faith, the scene was summarized as, "For the Son of Man came to seek and to save the lost" (19:10). The spread of the good news throughout Luke constitutes the message of salvation going out into the world. Then in Acts 5:31 when Peter and the apostles refused to desist in their witness, they told the authorities, "God exalted him to his own right hand as Prince and Savior that he might bring Israel to repentance and forgive their sins."

The theme of salvation in Luke-Acts is summed up in Luke 24:47: "Repentance for the forgiveness of sins will be preached in his name to all nations." Each concept sums up a major emphasis of Luke's writings. Jesus died for the sins of humankind, who participate in God's salvation by repenting or turning from their sins to God (Luke 5:32; Acts 13:3-4; 15:7-8; 16:30; 17:3-4), receiving the judicial results of that repentance: forgiveness of sins (Luke 1:77; 3:18; 4:18; Acts 2:38; 5:31; 10:43; 13:38; 26:18). In the missions of Luke 9-10 and often in Acts, preaching is the means by which the message of salvation goes out to the nations.

CHRISTOLOGY

Jesus is the core not only of Luke's Gospel, as is expected, but also of the book of Acts. In a real sense, the primary question Luke wants us to ask is, "Who is this?" (5:21; 7:49; 8:25; 9:9). At the announcement of Jesus' birth he is presented as "the Son of the Most

High" who will inherit David's throne and establish a never-ending kingdom (1:32–33). At his birth the angel of the Lord proclaims him to be Savior, Messiah, and Lord (2:11). Throughout the infancy narratives he is revealed as the greater prophet (than John the Baptist) who will inaugurate the new era of salvation.

There is a great stress on lordship in Luke, for the Suffering Servant becomes the risen Lord of all. His power over nature (8:22–25; 9:10–16) and disease (4:38–40; 5:12–16; 7:22), indeed, over death itself (7:11–17; 8:51–56) and the cosmic powers of darkness (4:1–13, 36, 41; 8:26–39; 10:17–20), shows him to be Lord over all. He is not only prophet and royal Messiah; he is God's Son and sovereign over all creation.

God's Reign over History

Luke places great stress on salvation history, that is, God's rule over human affairs as he controls history and brings salvation into this world. The divine "must" (Greek: *dei*) is predominant in Luke, meaning that God has sovereignly predetermined his moves in this world to accomplish his purposes. So Luke in his writing is proclaiming the contours of God's plan as it is worked out in Jesus and the church. The coming of Christ, his ministry to the world, and the results of his coming are all ordained by God and are acted out according to his will (4:43; 9:33; 19:5), especially his death and resurrection (9:22; 17:25). The plan of salvation is also part of this divine "must" (Acts 4:12).

Holy Spirit

For Luke the Holy Spirit is the point of continuity between the life of Jesus and the mission of the early church. The Holy Spirit is a central figure, appearing seventeen times in this Gospel and forty times in Acts. The Spirit was active at every part of Jesus' birth (1:35; 2:25–27; 3:22) and again at his resurrection. Jesus promised the coming of the Spirit in his resurrection appearance and defined his coming as "power from heaven" (24:48–49).

So the disciples in the upper room in Acts 1 constituted a nascent movement waiting for that power the Spirit would bring (Luke 24:48; Acts 1:8), and when that empowering presence arrived, he launched a world-changing force.

THE MESSIANIC COMMUNITY, THE CHURCH

When Jesus chose the Twelve (Luke 6:12-16), he was establishing the new Israel, the messianic community of the last days, intended by divine decree to populate the kingdom of God and take the world into the new covenant age. The disciples were characterized by misunderstanding and failure during Jesus' lifetime, but he patiently led them into understanding, consummated in his resurrection appearances. When the Spirit arrived at Pentecost, he inaugurated a messianic movement that traversed the world with the gospel. In Acts the church moves from evangelizing the Jews (chs. 1-7) to evangelizing the Samaritans (ch. 8) and then the nations (chs. 9-28). Paul guided the church and provided the impetus for its messianic mission, using not just witness but even opposition as evangelistic devices to energize the mission to the world. The more the Jews and Romans persecuted the church, the more powerfully the gospel went forth into the world.

PRAYER AND WORSHIP

Luke may be called "the theologian of prayer," since he shows Jesus at virtually every major event in his life deep in prayer—for instance, at his baptism (3:21), his choice of the Twelve (6:12), Peter's confession and the first passion prediction (9:18), and the transfiguration (9:28). His death on the cross flowed out of his Gethsemane prayer (22:41-42) and featured three prayers and answers to prayer (23:34, 43, 46). In a very real sense, Luke turns the crucifixion from a scene of horror into a scene of worship. The key passage on prayer is 11:1-13, containing the short form of the Lord's Prayer and the parable of the friend at midnight, which tells us how committed God is to answering our prayers. Then the

parable of the persistent widow (18:1–8) extols believers to persevering prayer.

THE MARGINALIZED: THE POOR AND WOMEN

In showing that the gospel is intended for all peoples, Luke especially singles out the forgotten social groups of this world, in particular the poor and women. The theme passage for Jesus' ministry,
drawn from Isaiah 61:1–2, states that the Spirit has anointed Jesus
to "proclaim good news to the poor" and liberate the oppressed
(Luke 4:18–19). This establishes a pattern of social concern for the
entire Gospel. Jesus was born as one of the poor, and he demands
that true disciples will seek to bring not only spiritual salvation but
also use their worldly resources to alleviate suffering everywhere
they can. The way to eternal reward is to use earthly resources to
"gain friends," that is, to give to the poor to help them, and that
will be banked in heaven and come back to you as eternal reward
(16:9). Discipleship demands a proper balance between the earthly
and the heavenly, and that means that worldly wealth must never
be allowed to dominate our lives. When God allows us to be rich,
he mandates that we use our resources to help the poor. In other
words, possessions must become a means of ministry to others.

In addition, Luke emphasizes the place of women in the church.
Three-eighths of the names in Luke are those of women, and
women are patrons of the apostolic band (8:1–3) and official witnesses of the death, burial, and resurrection of Jesus (23:49, 55–56;
24:10). In the Jewish and even Roman worlds, women were for the
most part restricted to the home and had little public persona or
impact. But in both Luke and Acts, they had a great impact on
the messianic community, the church. They are clearly important resources for ministry among God's people and in God's mission to the world.

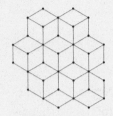

THE INFANCY NARRATIVES:
TWO BIRTHS FORETOLD
(1:1–38)

Luke makes it very clear in his prologue (1:1-4) that he is writing most of all a historical work on the life of Jesus of Nazareth that covers his life systematically. But this is not your everyday historical work, for the story he is telling is of the most unique person history has ever seen. This is made clear in the infancy narrative (1:1–2:42), in which Jesus is compared to the other dominant figure of that period, John the Baptist. The Baptist was the first prophet to appear in four centuries, and had an Elijah-type ministry among the Jewish people. Yet it is clear that Jesus overshadowed him at every point, in the announcement of their birth (1:5-38), in the births themselves (1:57-66; 2:1-7), and in the presentation of Jesus in the temple (2:22-40). John is the great prophet; Jesus, the greater prophet and king.

PROLOGUE: LUKE INTRODUCES
HIMSELF AS A HISTORIAN (1:1-4)

Luke begins with one of the great sentences in Scripture, a single, well-balanced Greek sentence of high prose, placing his work carefully within **Hellenistic** history writing. Luke wants his readers to understand he has carefully researched and produced a biography that his readers can trust. However, we must realize that the standards it follows are from the first century rather than the twenty-first. For instance, it does not follow the exact chronological order of events in Jesus' life. Ancient historians were free to move events around in order to give an accurate portrayal but not a chronological one, and this can be seen by comparing the structures of the four Gospels. This would not be allowed today but was fine by ancient standards.

Previous Witnesses (1:1–2)

Luke wants it known that he was nowhere near the first "to draw up an account of the things that have been fulfilled among us." There are two points in this. First, he was building on his predecessors ("many"). It is difficult to know who these are. He was certainly aware of Mark's Gospel, but most would also include what we call Q as well as Luke's own interviews with eyewitnesses.[1]

I do not believe Luke intends to critique the earlier works or that he thought them inadequate. Rather, he wants to produce the whole story and show how Jesus inaugurated the age of the Spirit and brought the people of God into the divine task of bringing God's salvation to a lost world. These earlier witnesses were not insufficient, for they too were chronicling "the things that have been fulfilled among us." The fulfillment of Old Testament prophecies is a major emphasis of Luke (1:20, 57; 2:6, 23; 4:21; 9:31; 21:22; 24:7, 26, 44), but the emphasis is also on their fulfillment "among us," Jesus' followers participating in the events. These events constitute not just history but salvation history, the entrance of God's salvation into human history through Jesus and his messianic community.

Moreover, those who compiled the accounts were "eyewitnesses and servants of the word" (1:2), meaning they were

---

1. See "Sources" in the introduction.

first-generation followers of Christ, many of whom became apostles, all of whom served God by the accounts they assembled and
disseminated (compare Acts 26:16). Luke was not one of them;
he was probably converted on Paul's second missionary journey
(Acts 16:6–10), but he used their material. Luke is saying that the
reader can test the accuracy of his account by going to the original
eyewitnesses of the events to corroborate what they are reading.

LUKE'S CURRENT WORK (1:3–4)

Luke now provides his purpose in writing as well as his creden-
tials for undertaking such a task. His is an organized and well-
investigated work: he has carefully read and followed everything
he could get his hands on. I believe he did this research while Paul
was in prison in Rome, gathering, comparing, and coming to understand the eyewitness reports, then putting them together into an
"orderly account" and publishing them around AD 62, when the
imprisonment ended.[2]

As I said above, this is not "orderly" in terms of chronological exactness but in terms of a carefully constructed and coher-
ent compilation of the material. It is accurate history. "From the
beginning" means the beginning of Jesus' story, not the beginning
of Luke's involvement. His research and writing went back to Jesus'
birth and produced an "orderly account" of the infancy narratives
as well as of Jesus' adult ministry. As I have said, it is especially salvation history that is in Luke's mind. He is tracing not just human
history but also the extent to which in Christ God's salvation has
entered human history and transformed it.

We do not know who Theophilus was, but he was probably a
wealthy believer of high social standing who was the patron of this
work and perhaps helped distribute it. It does not seem that more
than this opening paragraph was addressed to him in particular,

---

2. See "Date" in the introduction.

and the rest of the Gospel and Acts were certainly written generally for all readers.

The purpose (1:4) is that Theophilus (and others) "may know the certainty of the things you have been taught." There is a strong apologetic air in this, indeed in all of 1:1-4. The words "know" and "certainty" frame the verse, emphasizing again the trustworthiness of his Gospel. Some think this refers to a potentially hostile reception of Luke's work, as if he were writing to counter slander and false rumors about the church. I find this unlikely and believe that Luke writes to give Theophilus and other readers confidence about the truths he will be presenting in these pages. The "things you have been taught" probably refers to Christian teaching and preaching both to believers and unbelievers. Luke has both an evangelistic and a teaching interest in writing his Gospel.

JOHN THE BAPTIST'S BIRTH IS ANNOUNCED (1:5-25)

The two scenes announcing the births are given in parallel episodes that establish the basic thrust of the whole, for they are followed by the meeting of the two mothers-to-be and Mary's thanksgiving (1:39-56); the two births, also in parallel (1:57-2:21); and finally by the postbirth events (2:22-52). John the Baptist and Jesus provide a transition from the old to the new, and in this transition there are four contrasts pointing to the overwhelming glory of Jesus the Christ. The Baptist has a wondrous beginning, for he like Jesus is announced by an angelic herald, named by that selfsame angel, and called to a ministry fulfilling God's purposes. The key is that this divine ministry is that of forerunner to the expected Messiah of Israel. The emphasis is not on his inferiority, for he too is prophesied in Scripture, and the new age begins with him. The real importance of John the Baptist to history simply shows even further the infinite importance of Jesus the Christ.

A PRIESTLY COUPLE WHO ARE CHILDLESS (1:5-7)

Both Zechariah and Elizabeth came from priestly families, demonstrating the pedigree of their son. Luke includes Zechariah's family line to emphasize this background, specifying that this event took place "in the time of Herod king of Judea," undoubtedly to contrast the false earthly king with the true "King of Judea" soon to be born. This Herod is Herod the Great, made king of Judea by Rome, an earthly privilege not extended to his sons. Since Herod died in 4 BC, this places the events here somewhat earlier, say about 6 BC. Luke mentions earthly rulers (also Caesar Augustus and Quirinius in 2:1-2), but they play little role here except to situate these God-driven events within human history.

While the priesthood was quite corrupt at that time (especially at the top), Zechariah and Elizabeth were "righteous in the sight of God, observing all the Lord's commands and decrees blamelessly." The term "righteous" refers both to spiritual and ethical righteousness. They were right with God in both their lives and their behavior. Moral righteousness is uppermost, as seen in the added "observing ... blamelessly." There is a marked similarity to Abraham and Sarah, who also were both blameless and childless. This shows that God had a purpose for their childless state; it was not judgment for sin. That purpose comes up here. The three descriptions in verses 6-7—righteous, childless, elderly— all parallel Abraham and Sarah as well as Elkanah and Hannah in 1 Samuel 1:1-20. The parallel with Hannah will come to the fore in Mary's song in 1:46-56.

ZECHARIAH IN THE TEMPLE (1:8-10)

There were about eighteen thousand priests at this time, divided into twenty-four divisions (named after Aaron's descendants, 1 Chr 24:1-31), each one with several orders consisting of eight or nine families each. Each priestly division was responsible for supplying the priests in the temple complex for two weeks a year. Those who served were chosen by lot (Luke 1:9). Zechariah was chosen to serve in the holy place, and it is likely that this was the only time in his life (due to the thousands of priests) he had been privileged to do so. He is burning incense during the afternoon offering, called the *Tamid*. Incense was offered on the altar of incense in the holy place during the morning and evening sacrifices at nine in the morning and three in the afternoon.

Zechariah brings burning coals into the holy place from the altar of burnt offering and gets ready to burn the incense on the altar of incense in front of the veil before the holy of holies. The people are outside, participating in the sacrifices, praying as the priest with two assistants takes the coals into the sanctuary to burn the incense. The assistants then leave Zechariah alone. As the worshippers are praying in the court of Israel (1:10), he lays the incense on the altar and prostrates himself before it. The incense signified prayer, a sweet-smelling offering to the Lord.

Zechariah is about to receive the heraldic angel and the message from the Lord at the most sacred moment of his life.

The Appearance of the Angel (1:11–12)

While Zechariah is placing the incense on the altar, an angel appears. It is debated whether the Greek *ōphthē* (meaning "to see" or "appear") refers to an actual appearance or a vision. However, this verb is used in Luke's writings to indicate a supernatural event (Luke 24:34; Acts 2:3; 7:30, 35; 9:17; 16:9), and that would be the case here. Angels often in the Old Testament announce the birth of significant people (Gen 17:15–19; 18:10–15; Judg 13:3–21).

The angel stands "at the right side of the altar of incense" between it and the menorah, or golden candlestick. The right side signifies God's favor, and it is fitting that God's temple is the place where the events are set in motion that will end with the births of the messianic forerunner and the Messiah himself.

Zechariah is "startled and ... gripped with fear." This is the common reaction in the Bible to encounters with God and his angelic heralds (Exod 16:15; 2 Sam 6:9; Isa 6:5; Luke 2:9; 9:34; Acts

5:5, 11). The verb for "startled" is *etarachthē*. Like *epepesen phobos* (gripped with fear) it also indicates great fear; together they could be translated "troubled and afraid." He knows he is unworthy and wonders if the angel has come to judge him for his sins (as we all would in such a situation).

THE ANGEL'S MESSAGE (1:13–17)

There is no need for Zechariah to be "gripped with fear" (1:12), for (*dioti*, "because") God has heard his prayer. We don't know for sure what prayer this is, perhaps a request for a son or for God to deliver Israel (a major focus of the evening offering prayers). Several scholars believe the focus is on both, and that makes sense in light of the messianic significance of the infancy narratives. The birth of John the Baptist will initiate the process of deliverance that will move from John to Jesus to redemption not just for the nation but for all humanity.

The angel announcing the good news here reminds us of the message to Abraham and Sarah that God would grant them a son in their extreme old age (Gen 16:11 to Hagar; 17:15, 19, to Abraham and Sarah). The angel even tells Zechariah what name he should call his son. The name "John" (*Iōannēn*) means "Yahweh is gracious" and means their son will be the means by which God's gracious mercy will pour down on his people.

The angel then tells the effects of John's birth (1:14), first on the parents and then on the nation: "joy and delight." This rejoicing will be personal for Zechariah and Elizabeth, and it will be corporate and **eschatological** for those who respond among the Jews. *Polloi* (many) does not mean all in Israel will find joy, for only a few will respond positively to the salvation message John and Jesus will bring. Still, the emphasis here is on the positive side, the rejoicing that will flow out of the Baptist's ministry as many are made right with God.

There are three terms for joy in this context, all of them used frequently in Luke-Acts for the exultation caused by God's salvation poured out on the nation—*chara* (joy) in 2:10; 8:13; 15:7, 10; *chairō* (rejoice) in 1:28; 10:20; 15:5, 32; and *agalliasis* (exultation) in 1:44; Acts 2:46; 11:28. This introduces a theme that will flow throughout Luke's two-volume work, the rejoicing that will come as God's mercy is felt through John and Jesus throughout the land.

The angel in verses 15–17 turns from John's effects on others to his own demeanor. His life will be dominated by God. The angel begins with an incredible prophecy that sums up the whole: "He will be great in the sight of the Lord." What every one of us wouldn't give for this to be said of our future when we were born! This points to 7:28, where Jesus will testify, "among those born of women there is no one greater than John." His greatness is seen both in who he is and what he does. His righteous character and his ministry as messianic forerunner both set him apart from those around him. He is the first prophet to appear in four centuries. Still, his greatness is not in his stature or accomplishments but in his obedience to God's will for his life and ministry, in particular, as the messenger who prepares the way for the Messiah (Luke 7:27; see Mal 3:1).

There are five areas in which his greatness will be measured: (1) a disciplined life that refuses "wine or other fermented drink." This is more than priests fulfilling their duties (Lev 10:9); it is more like the permanent vow of the Nazirites (Judg 13:4–7). This may be an allusion to Samuel, who took such a vow as the first prophet in Israel (1 Sam 1:11).

(2) He was "filled with the Holy Spirit" even before he was born, referring to his lifelong prophetic role under the control of the Spirit. The Spirit is the major figure, superintending the infancy stories and behind every detail. His empowering presence is a permanent fixture in John's life and ministry.

The last two are closely connected, referring to religious and social revival. His is a ministry of reformation. (3) He will "bring back" (*epistrepō*, "return") many Israelites to "the Lord their God" (1:16), rescuing the people of God from apostasy and divine judgment. This was Elijah's ministry (Mal 2:7; 3:1; 4:5–6), and as the Elijah-like prophet, it is John's as well.

(4) His prophetic role is to "go on before the Lord, in the spirit and power of Elijah" (1:17). He will be the great spiritual reformer like Elijah was, and his ministry in this light occurs in Luke 3. In Malachi 4:5–6 Elijah is prophesied as being sent by God "before that great and dreadful day of the LORD comes." The arrival of Jesus the Messiah is part of that coming. The Baptist is fulfilling that role, to "turn the hearts of the parents to their children and the disobedient to the wisdom of the righteous" (alluding to Mal 4:6). This refers to social reform, as families will be reunited (the horizontal relationship), as well as spiritual reform as disobedient children are made right with their parents and a disobedient nation returns to God and his wisdom (the vertical relationship). The "wisdom of the righteous" would be those in the nation who are following the way of the Lord. This is an all-embracing revival with restoration taking place in every area of life, the human family progressing to the family of God.

(5) Summing up the above, John's God-given ministry as the messianic forerunner is "to make ready a people prepared for the Lord." John's ministry fulfilled Isaiah 40:3: "Prepare the way for the LORD; make straight in the desert a highway for our God" (see Luke 3:4). This is the corporate side of that task. When he prepares the highway to Zion, he first will make the nation ready for the coming of the Messiah and then will ready the people for spiritual revival. A prepared nation (see Exod 19:10–11; 2 Sam 7:24) is filled with reformed people who are living out their messianic destiny as the messianic community.

ZECHARIAH'S PART IN THIS (1:18–23)

A critical part of this first chapter is the contrast between Zechariah's doubt and Mary's simple faith (1:34, 38, 45). His doubt provides another parallel with Abraham (Gen 15:8), who also doubted due to his and Sarah's old age. The request for a sign was quite common, as seen in the stories of Gideon (Judg 6:30–40) and Hezekiah (2 Kgs 20:8–11). The angel tells him God is going to answer his prayers, but he has stopped believing it could happen.

The angel responds by identifying himself: "I am Gabriel. I stand in the presence of God" (1:19). He and Michael are the only two angels named in Scripture (Dan 8:16; 9:21). His name means "God is my warrior/hero," and he is the one who gives the prophecy of the seventy weeks in Daniel 9. Extrabiblical literature names several archangels who stand in God's presence (seven in 1 Enoch 20, four in 1 Enoch 40), and this makes Gabriel significant indeed. Here he is "sent to speak to you and to tell you this good news." He acts as God's herald, making an announcement from the very throne of God. This would be like the president sending the chairman of the Joint Chiefs of Staff to give the orders to a lowly corporal.

Zechariah's sign is fitting in light of his doubt and unbelief (1:20): "And now you will be silent and not able to speak until the day this happens, because you did not believe my words." Since he is unable to believe the promise from God, he will be rendered speechless. He will not be allowed to participate in the process until it is over, when the "words ... will come true at their appointed time." God is faithful even when Zechariah is not. God is in charge, not him, and all promises will be "fulfilled" (*plērōthēsontai*, NIV: "come true") or come to completion as God in his sovereignty has designated.

The people are confused by the lengthy time Zechariah has taken to offer the incense in the holy place, and they are "waiting ... and wondering" what is going on with him (1:21). Normally, this time passed quickly, and the priest on exiting the holy place would give a final blessing. The sanctuary was a fearsome place, and a delay could mean divine judgment, so the people were understandably anxious.

When Zechariah exited, he was unable to give the priestly blessing; "he kept making signs to them but remained unable to speak." The onlookers conclude from the parallel in Daniel 10:15–16 that he must have seen a vision; Luke's Greek term here, *optasian*, can be used of a vision or of a supernatural appearance (see Luke 24:23, which uses this term to describe the women at the tomb seeing angels). The crowd assumes the former; Luke's readers know it is actually the latter. Furthermore, the crowd thinks the muteness a positive thing—God granting a vision—but we know it is a punishment caused by Zechariah's failure to believe.

He finishes his "time of service" in 1:23, his week-long tour of duty in the temple (see 1:8–9). Zechariah and Elizabeth lived in "a town in the hill country of Judea" (1:39) south of Jerusalem. We know little about his home circumstances. Many priests had a secular job to make ends meet, but we know nothing of this in their case.

PROPHECY FULFILLED: ELIZABETH'S PREGNANCY (1:24–25)

The angel's prediction comes to pass, and Elizabeth conceives. Unlike her husband, she is a model of faithfulness. It is difficult to know why she goes into seclusion for five months. The law did not demand it. Some think it is because of public disgrace from a barren woman conceiving, but that does not fit the context. Others think the opposite, that it is personal time for worship and praising God. I think this is closer to what is going on here. In the literary context, this provides a segue to her time with Mary and with verse 25 provides time for her to reflect on God's graciousness.

In verse 25, Elizabeth realizes that the Lord has done two things for her: "shown his favor and taken away my disgrace among the people." It is hard for us today to understand just how much reproach she had endured for being childless all those years. Rachel cried out to Jacob in Genesis 30:1, "Give me children, or I'll die!" And when in 30:23 she gave birth to Joseph she said, "God has taken away my disgrace." The self-image and public persona of women in the ancient world was caught up with the number of sons God gave them, and to be childless was to be cursed from God. Elizabeth was filled with relief as well as joy.

JESUS' BIRTH IS ANNOUNCED (1:26-38)

The positive counterpart to the announcement to Zechariah is now found in the angelic promise to Mary. In spite of the contrasts between him and Jesus, we must be careful not to denigrate John the Baptist too much. John is one of the greatest of the prophets, and it is his greatness that Luke uses to demonstrate the infinite glory and wonder of Jesus the Messiah. John in all his faithfulness to God and his calling from God was the forerunner sent to prepare the way for the Messiah (1:17), and his supernaturally endowed birth and life make Jesus and his arrival all the greater.

One of the most interesting parallels between John and Jesus is at the social level. The narrative of John's annunciation speaks of his high status—a temple setting, the announcement by the archangel Gabriel in the holy place itself, the father a priest offering incense. Jesus' annunciation is set in a small, poor village, to an unknown young woman of no consequence. This theme will carry through Luke's Gospel, as God chooses the lowly to bear his greatness.

THE APPEARANCE TO MARY (1:26-27)

Gabriel is God's herald not only to Zechariah but also to Mary. The mention of this being the "sixth month" of Elizabeth's pregnancy ties the two very closely together and means the five-month seclusion was meant to prepare Elizabeth for her encounter with Mary and the baby. When Mary arrived, the time of hiddenness ended.

Gabriel is specifically stated to be sent "from" (*apo*, not translated in the NIV) God, stressing the heavenly origin of the message. Heaven directly involves itself in the affairs of earth, and the birth that all of history has been awaiting is about to be announced. The place to which he is sent is a small town of no consequence, as seen in Nathanael's response in John 1:46, "Nazareth! Can anything good come from there?"

The angel is sent to a young virgin girl, Mary, from that village (v. 27). By mentioning *parthenos* (virgin) twice before naming her, Luke prepares for the unprecedented nature of the virgin birth. Unlike Matthew (see 1:23), Luke does not mention the virgin-birth prophecy of Isaiah 7:14, but his use of this word shows his awareness of that extraordinary prediction.[3] He does stress her situation as "pledged to be married to a man named Joseph." In the first century, marriages were almost always arranged, and Mary was likely about fourteen years old, with Joseph an older man, possibly a widower, chosen to be her husband. The marriage was at its first stage, involving the payment of the dowry or bride price. The betrothed girl legally belonged to her husband but would not move in with him until the wedding ceremony about a year later.

Joseph is identified as "a descendant of David," also emphasized in 1:32, 69; 2:4, 11; 3:31. Already the child is revealed as the Davidic Messiah.

THE MESSAGE OF THE ANGEL (1:28–33)

There are two parts here, the greeting of Mary (vv. 28–30) and the message proper (vv. 31–33). Elizabeth came to realize she had been greatly favored by God (1:25), but Gabriel makes it clear to Mary in the very greeting, "Greetings, you who are highly favored!" Gabriel had to announce himself to Zechariah, and he does so in order to rebuke his unbelief (1:19). This is not needed with Mary, who is told that God both greatly favors her and is with her. In every sense she could be called the most favored woman in all of

---

3. The people of Isaiah's day did not realize this to be the case, thinking the passage was speaking about a "young woman" and referring to the birth of King Hezekiah. But with the birth of Jesus to Mary, his followers realized it prophesied the virgin birth.

history, for she has been chosen to bear the Messiah. It is impossible to be more special than that.

"The Lord is with you" promises God's continuous presence in her life. Of course, God is present in all our lives, but this is a special promise, paralleling the angel's greeting to Gideon, "The LORD is with you, mighty warrior" (Judg 6:12). For Mary it means that God will be especially present throughout her life's calling of raising the Messiah and watching over all that God is going to do with and through him.

Mary is "greatly troubled" at the implications of this, wondering "what kind of greeting this might be" (1:29). It is interesting that she is not shocked by the coming of Gabriel but rather at what he implicates in his greeting. Some have said it is because males did not greet females in the Jewish world, but I find that doubtful. It is the meaning that vexes her, not the fact of the greeting itself. This state of confusion will continue throughout her interaction with Gabriel, and it is perfectly natural. Nothing like this had happened in centuries, and how could she not be in shock? To hear language that places her in exalted company with the heroes of the Old Testament would perplex anyone.

The angel soothes her troubled spirit: "Do not be afraid, Mary; you have found favor with God" (1:30). This repeats the message of verse 28, assuring her that God is thoroughly pleased with her. She feels quite unworthy, as we will see in her "Magnificat" of 1:46–55, but God wants her to know his special grace and mercy in her life. The "favor" she has in the Lord's eyes will be seen in the incredible task he has entrusted to her, bearing his Son and Messiah. God's gracious choice of individuals is found often (Gen 18:3; Judg 6:17; 1 Sam 1:18), and she needs to realize how special she is.

The task is now given her in verses 31–33, encompassing six items. In every way this should be called the greatest privilege found anywhere in Scripture. (1) She will "conceive and give birth to a son" like no other in all of history. This is a common pattern of announcement in Scripture (Gen 16:11; Judg 13:5; Isa 7:14). The

Isaiah passage is especially important for this passage, for it also entails a virgin birth. Once more (1:13) the child's name is a heavenly decision, and he is to be called Jesus, as Matthew 1:21 adds, "because he will save his people from their sins." The name Jesus (*Iēsous*) is the Greek equivalent of the Hebrew *Yehoshua/Yeshua*, which means "Yahweh saves." Since in the ancient world the names given children reflected the parental hopes for the child, this shows God's messianic intentions for the child.

(2) His effect on this world is told next: "He will be great." John would be "great *in the sight of the Lord*," referring to the effects of his chosen task as messianic forerunner. Jesus will be "great" (also Titus 2:13) because he will partake of the greatness of God (Deut 10:17) and through him "all people will see God's salvation" (3:6).

(3) Therefore, as God's emissary he will be called "the Son of the Most High," an exalted form of "Son of God," which itself is one of the major titles of God (Gen 14:18-20; 2 Sam 22:14; Ps 7:17). Luke uses this title often (1:35, 76; 6:35; 8:28). Parallels with **Qumran** (4Q246) show that this title has kingly overtones and points to this child as royal Messiah. As with "Son of God" there are also overtones of divinity. He is Messiah yet more than Messiah.

(4) As royal Messiah he is to be given by God "the throne of his father David," recalling the Davidic covenant and pointing to his messianic reign as king (2 Sam 7:13-16; Pss 2:7; 89:27-29). Luke will stress this house/throne-of-David imagery (1:69; 2:4, 11). The fact that Jesus fulfilled the Davidic Messiah expectations of the Old Testament was very important to the early church for obvious reasons.

(5) This messianic reign means the child will "reign over Jacob's descendants forever" (1:33). This reflects Isaiah 9:7 ("he will reign on David's throne") and the prophecies of the eternal reign of David in 2 Samuel 7:13-16; Psalms 89:3-4; 132:11-12; Isaiah 9:6-7; Daniel 7:14. "Jacob's descendants" is literally "the house of Jacob," a circumlocution for Israel. This promise of an eternal throne did not come to pass literally, for the house of David no longer ruled

the nation. It was the messianic expectation that kept the Davidic promises alive, and thus the coming of Christ is the actual meaning and fulfillment of the prophecies concerning David.

(6) Concluding the list is the summary promise that "his kingdom will never end," especially fulfilling the promise of Daniel 7:14 that "his dominion is an everlasting dominion that will not pass away, and his kingdom is one that will never be destroyed." The eternal rule of the Messiah is a major feature of Lukan theology.

REASSURANCE BY THE ANGEL (1:34–38)

Mary's question reflects her natural doubts—since she is an unmarried virgin, she sees no way she could possibly conceive. Yet her question does not contain the same disobedience as Zechariah's in 1:18. She says, "How *will* this be?" while he had doubted God, saying, "How *can* this happen?" Still, it seems unnecessary, since she was soon to be married. Some think it is purely literary, preparing for the stress of the next verse. However, it is better to see this historically; Mary is thinking of her immediate situation. For her to conceive in the immediate future, it would have to be a virginal conception. All of the Old Testament women had been married, so hers would be the first such birth. John's birth would be incredible; Jesus' would be miraculous.

The answer of Gabriel further stresses the supernatural origins of Jesus' birth (1:35–37). The Holy Spirit normally plays a prophetic role, inspiring wisdom. Here he joins the Father and the Son in his trinitarian role as the active source of the new creation: the Holy Spirit will "come on" and "overshadow" Mary with the "power of the Most High." It is divine, not human, agency that will bring forth this child. Some have tried to read a sexual connotation into the two verbs, but neither carries any such idea. Mary is a passive vessel for the activity of the Spirit, and the verb "to overshadow" (*episkiasei*) carries the Old Testament concept of the **Shekinah** presence of God in the tabernacle (Exod 40:35). It is God's presence via the Spirit that will produce the child. The "power of the

Most High" in the Spirit will descend on Mary, and the Christ child will be the result.

The two descriptions of the child are both vertical, showing his relationship to the Godhead, rather than horizontal, relating to earthly concerns. This child will be "holy"; this connotes that he will be set apart for God more than that he will simply live a holy life. Everything he does will relate to his relationship to God, and so there is a hint of his divine status in his holiness. He is set apart in a special way as the Son of God.

His status as Son of God restates Luke's words in 1:32 that "he will … be called the Son of the Most High." The title speaks of the special filial relationship of the Son to the Father. He is the Davidic Messiah, but he is also much more. While not an ascription of divinity, it has connotations of such and moves in that direction. So this is a promise of virgin birth as in Isaiah 7:14, but it is also a **christological** masterpiece, telling us also what kind of divinely produced child this Jesus will be.

Mary probably was unaware of Elizabeth's pregnancy, since the latter had hidden herself away, but now the angel tells her, and relates her own conception to that of her cousin (1:36-37). The angel mentions this to comfort Mary that she is not alone. She is remarkably young, but Elizabeth is remarkably old to bear a child, and that same power has overtaken her. Her pregnancy is six months advanced, and so God's power is already established and proved. Old age and the childless state are no obstacles to the power of the Most High, and neither is Mary's virginal state.

The conclusion is quite fitting: "No word from God will ever fail." The supernatural power of the "word of God" is well established in Scripture. God spoke, and creation came about. Nothing is impossible or beyond God's power to accomplish.

Mary's total surrender to the Lord's will sets her apart from Zechariah (1:38). She first identifies herself as "the Lord's servant," using *doulē*, a slave wholly subservient to her Master. "The Lord's servant" is almost a title, used of Joshua (Judg 2:8) and David (Ps

35:1), so Mary is in reality accepting an exalted place in God's plan. She doesn't understand all that is to happen, but she places herself wholly under God's will, saying, "May your word to me be fulfilled." Whatever God has in store—and there could be personal pain (disgrace and rejection as an unwed mother)—she is willing to allow God's purposes to be brought to completion. When "the angel left," this plan was put into motion, and Mary accepted his will completely.

———

The prologue of 1:1-4 is the most detailed apologetic defense of the historical trustworthiness of the biblical stories. Luke (and the other authors, see John 19:35; 2 Pet 1:16) always sought eyewitness accounts and very carefully told the details the way they took place. Accuracy deeply mattered to them, and we can therefore trust what we are told.

The appearance of the angel Gabriel and the announcement of John's coming birth (vv. 5-17) take place at the most sacred moment of Zechariah's life, when he is chosen to perform the duties and burn the incense in the holy place in the temple. As he is praying for the nation, God is answering the prayers of him and Elizabeth for a child, and that child will be the most extraordinary one born in Israel in four centuries, the great prophet who will prepare the way for the Messiah. John will be the one coming in "the spirit and power of Elijah" to fulfill the prophecies (Isa 40:3; Mal 3:1) and introduce the final age of salvation. Can any of us imagine such an overwhelming privilege? Even two thousand years later we fall on our knees and thank the Lord for the coming of John the Baptist.

Still, Zechariah is human, and by this time he had completely given up hope for having children (vv. 13-18). So even though the angel Gabriel visited him with a promise from God, he couldn't believe it was true. Here is the great contrast with Mary. He had biblical precedent for the miracle (Abraham and Sarah), but Mary's situation demanding a virgin birth had never happened before, yet she believed. So God judged him and struck him dumb until the birth occurred, and he dropped out of the action for the next nine months, unable to participate.

The action shifts to Elizabeth and then Mary, who exemplify faith and joy in God in spite of difficult circumstances. This is a terrific model for us, for we are often asked to trust in God through hard times. Elizabeth goes into a five-month seclusion as she works through the mercy and grace God has shown to her (vv. 24-25), and Gabriel now appears to Mary, who demonstrates the faith that Zechariah lacked. Mary is floored but accepts the favor God is showing here. For centuries Jewish women have wondered who will be privileged to bear the Messiah, and she now finds out she is the one (vv. 26-33), and that her child will not only be the Messiah but also the Savior (the very meaning of the name Jesus). All of history has waited for this moment, and she is overwhelmed yet at the same time humbly accepting of this astounding privilege.

Once more it is the Holy Spirit who will bring this to pass (v. 35). In every single section of the infancy narrative, he makes it possible for these unbelievable events to take place. Luke will feature the Spirit's enabling presence throughout both Luke and Acts, and the message to us is clear. This selfsame Spirit is also with us and will empower us in the very same way to carry out the mission God has for us.

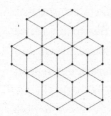

THE INFANCY NARRATIVES: MEETING AND BIRTH
(1:39–80)

The first half of this passage could be labeled "the testimony of two mothers": 1:39-45 is the witness of Elizabeth and her baby to the coming of the Christ child, and 1:46-56 is Mary's witness to the same. The two announcements of the herald Gabriel combine into a single testimony and hymn to the action of God in initiating the messianic era. With John and Jesus, God's salvation has descended into this fallen world. In a real sense, John the Baptist's witness to Jesus surpassing him begins in the womb, and this is the actual first time they connect, not at Jesus' baptism. So Elizabeth becomes a prophetess and joins her son, who while still unborn accepts his God-ordained role as the prophet who is to prepare the way for the Messiah to come and deliver the nation.

MARY VISITS AND ELIZABETH WITNESSES (1:39-45)

MARY'S TRIP TO VISIT (1:39-40)
Once she learns of Elizabeth's pregnancy, Mary travels to "the hill country of Judea," eighty to a hundred miles (a three- to four-day journey), to see her cousin. This parallels 1 Samuel 1:1,

41

where Elkanah the husband of Hannah is from the hill country of Ephraim. The fact that she hurries there is not due to any sense of shame with her pregnancy but due to her desire to please and obey God and to congratulate Elizabeth and to share her own good news with her. When Mary enters and greets Elizabeth, the latter's seclusion comes to an end, and the two can rejoice together. It is wonderful to imagine the excitement and joy not only of the two women but of heaven itself as the two rushed and hugged one another.

The Result of the Greeting (1:41–45)

There are two immediate results: First, the baby leaps for joy (v. 44) in Elizabeth's womb, and second, Elizabeth is filled with the Holy Spirit and pours out a blessing on Mary. Zechariah is still mute, and so we don't know how much Elizabeth knows about the details of Gabriel's visit. This is not just a baby stretching its limbs, for the infant made its strong move at the precise moment it heard Mary greeting his mother, clearly reacting to Mary and her child. In Genesis 25:22 the term "leaped" is used of Jacob and Esau jostling for position in Rebekah's womb. The struggle there is reversed in this instance as the infant is excited and filled with joy. In 1:15 Gabriel had said John would be filled with the Spirit even before he was born, so this pictures the unborn baby John as the vehicle of the Spirit's witness to the significance of the baby Jesus.

Now it is Elizabeth's turn to be filled with the Spirit, and she continues the Spirit's witness through her unborn baby. Some think that 1:42–45 is a hymn, but it lacks a poetic air and is more likely an exclamation of joy. The primary form of her joyous response is a twofold beatitude she addresses to Mary and the baby Jesus (vv. 42, 45), which frames her speech. She begins with a blessing addressed first to Mary and then to her baby (v. 42). We are not told how Elizabeth knew Mary was pregnant; most likely the Spirit made her aware of it. The baby's leap of joy and her exclamation of blessing were both Spirit reactions to the baby Jesus. All of heaven would be filled with excitement as the deliverance of fallen humanity drew nigh. This is the first beatitude in Luke and could hardly be more apt. *Makarios* does not just mean the person is "fortunate" or "happy." In this spiritual context it nearly always means "God's great blessings are upon you" and describes a divine outpouring of blessedness and joy.

Mary is "blessed ... among women," probably with a superlative thrust ("most blessed"). How could it be otherwise since she was chosen by God to bear his Son and Messiah? Jewish women had been waiting and hoping for centuries to be chosen for that blessing. To be God's elect vessel for bringing the Savior and deliverer of the nation into this world would be the greatest privilege imaginable.

If Mary is blessed, how much more her child. No one in all of history would deserve more glory and blessing than he. "The child you will bear" translated literally is "the fruit of your womb," similar to the cry of the unknown woman in 11:27, who said (literally), "Blessed is the womb that bore you and the breasts from which you nursed," to which Jesus replied, "Blessed rather are those who hear the word of God and obey it." Mary is the faithful bearer of the Christ child, but it is the Messiah himself who carries the true blessing. Still, Elizabeth is celebrating the fact that God has now through her and Mary inaugurated the new age of salvation, a true blessing indeed.

The deeper reason for the incredible blessing is that Mary is not just the future mother of a great prophet or even of the Messiah. She is to be "the mother of my Lord" (1:43), the Lord of all. This is the very first time *kyrios* is used of Jesus in Luke, and like "Son of God" it highlights the special relationship he will have with Yahweh. It is hardly that Elizabeth knows he will be deity, and she definitely says more here than she knows. She meant this in a messianic sense, and Luke brings in a higher **Christology** than she could have known. But she did realize his incredible significance and how unworthy she was to be a part of it.

In 1:44 she explains how she knew all of this the moment she laid eyes on Mary. It was because when Mary greeted her, "the baby in my womb leaped for joy." Still, it was the Spirit who told her it was more than just the normal movement of a baby. The Baptist without ever having taken a breath still was aware he was in the vicinity of his Messiah. So the babe in the womb recognized the truth of the situation before Elizabeth herself did, and he conveyed his joy by leaping in the womb. "Joy" translates the Greek *agalliasei*, the same term as in 1:14, referring to messianic joy.

Elizabeth closes with another beatitude in 1:45. This is the strongest contrast yet. Zechariah was struck mute because of unbelief, while Mary is especially blessed because she "has believed that the Lord would fulfill his promises to her." There is one disputed particle, as *hoti* could designate the reason for her belief (she believed "*because* the Lord was faithful") or its content (she believed "*that* the Lord would be faithful"). Both make sense, but the latter is slightly better here. Her faith was strong enough to encompass an event that had never happened in history, a virgin birth. Mary is an incredibly deep young lady, as seen in the term *teleiōsis*, meaning God would fulfill his promises in the sense that he would "bring them to completion" in her. God is absolutely faithful, and every single thing he promised would be fulfilled.

MARY SINGS A SONG OF PRAISE: THE MAGNIFICAT (1:46–56)

Mary reacts to the high emotions of the moment by breaking into a hymn of praise and thanksgiving. It is called the "Magnificat" because of the first word in the Latin translation of Jerome's Vulgate for "exalt" or "glorify." It is built on Hannah's song in 1 Samuel 2:1–10, extolling the mercy of God and his revolutionary reversal of the prevailing social situation, both in Hannah's day and Mary's. This becomes a major theme in Luke—God's reversal of the fortunes of the lowly in Jesus.

There has been quite a lot of discussion regarding the origins and authenticity of this hymn. Several critical scholars think it is a free composition by Luke himself. Others consider it a Jewish hymn or perhaps a Jewish-Christian praise song that originated elsewhere and is incorporated here. This is a possibility but is unnecessary, for there are no hints of elements that don't fit this context. It makes great sense right where it is. There is no reason why Mary could not have composed it herself, for it fits the situation quite well. Considering the poetic culture of the time (to this day Semitic children make up poems on the spot for fun), and factoring in the inspiration from the Spirit, there is no reason to doubt that Mary composed this herself. If there was ever a right time for such a composition, this was it.

There is also debate whether there is a two-part (vv. 46–50, 51–55), three-part (vv. 46–49, 50–53, 54–55), or four-part (vv. 46–47, 48–49, 50–53, 54–55) structure to the hymn. I will adopt the four-part structure as slightly better for Mary's message.

INTRODUCTORY PRAISE (1:46–47)

There is poetic parallelism between "my soul glorifies" and "my spirit rejoices" in verses 46 and 47, as Mary's emotions[1] bridge from praise to exultation over the Lord himself. The motif of the leading women of the Old Testament crying out their praise to God is continued here, building on Miriam in Exodus 15, Deborah in Judges 5, and especially Hannah at the birth of Samuel in 1 Samuel 2:1–10.

The parallelism in this opening praise is obvious, between "my soul / my spirit" and "Lord/God." Elizabeth praises Mary, but Mary praises her Lord. The movement occurs when she "glorifies" her Lord, which gives way to wondrous joy. Hannah expressed her joy and delight at the outset of her hymn (1 Sam 2:1), and Mary does likewise.

---

1. The textual variant, with three Old Latin versions reading, "and Elizabeth said," is extremely doubtful. Mary is the focus and is central throughout.

The stress here is on the Lord God as "my Savior," celebrating the fact that the Christ child has come to deliver the people of God and produce salvation, a theme drawn from several passages like Psalm 25:2; Isaiah 12:2; Micah 7:7; and Habakkuk 3:18. So this opening contains gratitude and praise for God, who has allowed her to be the vessel bearing the promised Messiah and deliverer of the nation.

GOD'S SAVING POWER (1:48–49)

Mary turns from praise for the saving presence of God to his loving concern for her own lowly state. As so often in Scripture, God has used the humble rather than the powerful to perform his mighty deeds. In the Old Testament it was the oppressed and powerless Israelites who became the people of God; now it is a young and unknown daughter of Israel chosen to bear the Messiah. Mary's "humble state" refers not to her modesty but to her lowly social status and background. She is far removed from the leading people of Israel and is merely a "servant" of the Lord.

Her joy is centered on God's being "mindful of" his humble servant and exalting her above anything she could ever even dream about. God has looked beyond the beautiful and powerful people at the top of the chain and chosen her out of those at the bottom to be his exalted vessel of deliverance. Israel was the lowliest of the nations, and Mary was the lowliest among Israel's daughters, so the parallels are exact. God once more elevates the least favored to the highest place in order to demonstrate his mercy and glory, and he has done so once more.

The turning point is verses 48b–49, as Mary confesses that "from now on all generations will call me blessed, for the Mighty One has done great things for me." She who was heretofore ignored by all around will from this moment be seen as especially blessed, as Elizabeth just recognized (1:42, 45). She has become the great exemplar of divine reversal, from the unnoticed to the most blessed among women. Moreover, this is not a temporary thing but will extend to "all generations" in the distant future, for it is the Messiah she bears. Thus God's past practice of elevating the lowly now will control future generations because of God's choice of her.

The next verse establishes the theme for the rest of the hymn—the "Mighty One" (Zeph 3:17, the warrior who delivers) accomplishing "great things" for Mary, not referring to her personally but to what he is going to accomplish through her. The glory goes to God, not Mary. The "mighty" deeds of the Lord began with the "power of the Most High" coming upon Mary and her conception of Jesus (1:35). The Mighty One is the Divine Warrior who fights on behalf of his people and delivers them from the powers of darkness.

Thus Mary adds, "holy is his name," for the saving deliverance seen in the birth of Jesus is the supreme act of a holy God. His attributes—his might, his holiness, and his mercy (vv. 49–50)—come up again and again in verses 28, 30, 35, 37, 45, to stress God's covenant faithfulness and favor in the events at the births of John and Jesus.

THE DIVINE REVERSAL (1:50–53)

Here we are at the heart of Mary's incredible hymn. She sees herself as fulfilling the type of Hannah, who bore the first great prophet of the people, Samuel. As in her day, God's "mercy extends to those who fear him, from generation to generation." God's might comes down via his mercy, the active side of his holiness. The past generation after Hannah and Samuel provided the model for the future generations after Mary and Jesus, recipients of God's mighty mercy. The key is to "fear him," bridging from fear of displeasing such a merciful God to reverence for all the mighty things he has done. The stress on fearing God is a common theme in Luke (12:5; 18:2; 23:40; Acts 10:2, 22, 35; 13:16, 26) and is the only viable reaction of those who have experienced his mercy.

The next three verses (vv. 51–53) are justly famous, describing this great revolutionary reversal of the social order by God's mighty acts. Mary's words feature three areas of this sinful world—a moral revolution (v. 51), a political revolution (v. 52), and a social revolution (v. 53). All of these are the "mighty deeds" he has performed "with his arm," a common image of God as Divine Warrior in Scripture (Exod 6:1; Deut 7:19; 2 Kgs 17:36; Isa 30:30).

The Greek verbs in these verses are in the aorist tense, and a great deal of discussion has attended their force here: (1) They could refer to God's past deliverance of Israel, as God won victory after victory for his people. (2) The acts may be the deliverance of God's people in the time of the author, that is, redeeming the poor in the church. (3) They could be gnomic, telling what God normally does for his people. (4) They might be prophetic aorists, stressing the certainty of God's future actions leading to Christ's ultimate victory at his return. (5) They could be ingressive, pointing to the beginning of God's mighty deeds with the coming of the Christ child.

I prefer this last option, the ingressive, as Mary is celebrating the new stage of God's redemptive work with the gift of the Christ child. These are sweeping promises and seem to encompass all of God's redemptive actions, from the deliverance of Israel to the redemption of humanity under Christ. First, there will be a moral revolution, as God scatters "those who are proud in their inmost thoughts." His mighty arm will disperse those who think too highly of themselves. The proud are enemies of God and his people throughout Scripture. Pride, the elevation of self over God, could almost be a definition of sin, which deifies self as God. Down deep inside, the arrogant think only of themselves. They have no awareness of God and no concern for others.

The other two revolutions look at it both ways. In the political revolution God "has brought down rulers from their thrones but has lifted up the humble" (1:52). The term *dynastas* is behind the English "dynasty" and refers to the passing of throne-rule from father to son down through the ages. These powerful ruling families (certainly Caesar would be in mind) will be removed from their seat of power by the mighty arm of God. In contrast, the "humble," those whom the rulers have mistreated and persecuted, will be "exalted" (*hypsōsen*). Their oppression will be totally reversed by the Messiah. All at the top of the social scale will be brought low.

The social revolution takes place as God has "filled the hungry with good things but has sent the rich away empty" (1:53). This reverses the order of the previous and places God's people first.[2] This is another frequent theme in Scripture, God's deep concern for the poor (1 Sam 2:5; Pss 107:9; 146:7; Luke 6:21; 11:13). "Hunger" is more than just lack of food but stands for deprivations of all kinds (4:2; 6:3, 25). The problem of wealth and poverty is one of the great needs of every age. The depravity of humankind is nowhere more evident than in this area.

God is promising here that his Messiah will right these terrible wrongs, that he will not allow the rich to continue to steal the very livelihood from the poor of this world. We will be discussing this issue several times in Luke-Acts, for it is everywhere. These latter two areas are intertwined. The powerful and the wealthy believe the world belongs to them, and they can do whatever they like with the powerless and the poor. The sad truth is that in this evil world they can do that and more. However, God is promising that his Son will reverse these terrible injustices, but on this issue the attention does indeed go to the **eschaton** (the "end" of all things), for this will not occur until the second coming.

GOD'S FAITHFULNESS TO ISRAEL (1:54–55)

At the end of her song, Mary returns to the theme of divine mercy from verse 50, framing the second half of her hymn of joy with this theme. God's faithful vigilance for the messianic community of the future is anchored in his watching over and taking care of his covenant people in the past. He has "helped" his people

---

2. The result is a **chiasm** for literary effect: A brought down rulers; B lifted up the humble; B' filled the hungry; A' sent the rich away empty-handed.

throughout their history, and his covenant mercies will continue to do so in the time to come. The verb *antilambanō* means to "come to the aid, support the needs" of others, and this is a promise that what characterized God's dealings with Israel will continue to be felt with new Israel.

Israel is his "servant" (*pais*), his people and part of his family, often emphasized (Isa 42:1; 44:21; 45:4; 49:3), and God has in the past and will faithfully continue in the future to care for her needs and protect her. Yet there is a warning aspect in this as well, for only those who are faithful to him will continue to be a part of Israel. While not explicit here, there is an implicit extension of this to the new Israel of Jesus and Paul. The apostate nation will not be considered part of Israel, but those grafted into the olive tree (Rom 11:17–21) of the covenant people will become true Israel. Mary is celebrating the deliverance of God's Israel as he remembers his mercy from the past and extends it into the future for his (true) covenant people.

Especially in mind is the Abrahamic covenant, embracing the promises "to Abraham and his descendants forever." In the opening scene of that original covenant God promised, "I will make you into a great nation, and I will bless you" (Gen 12:2), and at the covenant ceremony he told him, "Look up at the sky and count the stars … so shall your offspring be" (Gen 15:5). This is how God "promised our ancestors," and Mary is celebrating those continued blessings through her child. Mary sees in the events soon to transpire the fulfillment of the covenant promises, and for her that binds the two parts of salvation history, the old covenant and the new, into a single, united movement. There is continuity rather than discontinuity between the two aspects of God's covenant with his people.

THE FINAL THREE MONTHS (1:56)

In the nine-month period of her pregnancy, Elizabeth spent the first six months in seclusion (1:24, 26), and in the last three months

Mary "stayed with" her and "then returned home" after the birth of John. We are told neither why she stayed nor what they did during that period. The basic point is that through their mothers the two primary figures in the messianic drama are united. The new era of history, the age of salvation and age of the Spirit, is inaugurated with the unborn babies in seclusion together. The two miracles, the one to be born to a mother long past the age of conception, the other born to a virgin in fulfillment of Isaiah 7:14, are together. The stage is set for the single most important period of time history will ever know.

JOHN THE BAPTIST IS BORN (1:57-66)

Zechariah had not responded to Gabriel's announcement with faith in the miraculous intervention of God and as a result had been struck dumb. For nine months, a time in which Elizabeth basked with joy in the wondrous news, he had been in a far worse seclusion than she had, a time in which he had to live and work through his failure. Yet that time had clearly worked, and he had found the faith that had been missing. When John is born, he will find the joy as well. His hymn of praise parallels Mary's, and this time there will be no contrast between her triumph and his defeat. He will join her in messianic exultation, and he too will celebrate the coming deliverance.

The earlier events, the announcement to Mary and her greeting by Elizabeth, led to and were interpreted by a hymn. Here again, the birth and naming of John are also followed by and explained via a hymn. At the same time, as Gabriel's appearance to Zechariah is paralleled by his appearing to Mary, the birth of John is paralleled by the birth of Jesus. The basic message is the same: as John is the great prophet sent by God and appointed for this time, Jesus is the greater prophet and the Messiah to whom all of history has been pointing. John has been born to prepare the world for the greatest birth of all.

THE BIRTH OF JOHN (1:57-58)

The birth itself is told very simply, the language echoing the birth of Jacob and Esau in Genesis 25:24. His mother had spent months in seclusion, the last three of which were with her cousin Mary and the unborn baby Jesus. Now her time had come, and John arrived into the world. Since she had not shared any of it publicly with her neighbors, it probably came as something of a surprise. Gabriel's prophecy had indeed come to pass, and her neighbors were overjoyed when they heard how "the Lord had shown her great mercy."

Gabriel had predicted the birth would be "a joy and delight" (1:14), and that certainly is the case here. This is a dominant theme throughout the infancy narrative (1:14, 58, 64; 2:10, 14, 28) and actually flows throughout Luke-Acts. The verbal "shown great mercy" is actually "magnified [*emegalynen*] his mercy." As Mary "magnified/glorified the Lord" in 1:46, God has done the same to Elizabeth at the birth of John. She has been glorified by the Lord in being given the incredible privilege of bearing the messianic forerunner, the first great prophet in four hundred years.

THE PRESENTATION AND NAMING OF JOHN (1:59-66)

The circumcision of a Jewish male on the eighth day after his birth is a covenant sign (Gen 17:9-14; Lev 12:3), which took precedence even over the Sabbath (John 7:22-23). At that ceremony they had decided to name the child. Normally the naming took place at birth (Gen 4:1; 25:25-26). Some think this is following **Hellenistic** practices, but I think it was more likely due simply to the extenuating circumstances of Zechariah's mute state. Since he could not speak, the family was in process of naming him after Zechariah himself (it was fairly common in their culture to name a child after the father or grandfather) when Elizabeth spoke up forcefully.

Since Zechariah was unable to voice his opinion, the family and friends did not know what Gabriel had said (1:13). Likely he had communicated this to his wife, so she corrected the serious error about to be made, crying out, "No! He is to be called John."

The passive "is to be called" is a divine passive, meaning God's will was for him to be called John. The name John (*Iōannēs*), as I noted in 1:13, means "God is gracious" and is a testimony to the grace and mercy of God in sending John to initiate these incredible events.

The family and friends are not ready to surrender their decision. The father normally named the child, and it was quite unusual to give a child a name from outside the family (1:61). She is breaking custom and speaking outside her husband's will, so they demand that Zechariah signal his decision. It seems his judgment by God made him deaf as well as dumb, for the signals must go both ways. Undoubtedly, they expect him to concur and consent to their decision.

They are rather shocked when he concurs with the "wrong" person, his wife. As they ask his intentions, he asks for a writing tablet so they can get his intentions in writing: "His name is John" (1:63). Both Zechariah and God have made their desires completely clear. He could not have known what his wife said, as he clearly was not there. So God must be behind it all.

The terms of Gabriel's judgment have now been fulfilled (1:20, the birth and naming of John), and Zechariah has overcome his unbelief and come to faith in God's plan. So "immediately his mouth was opened and his tongue set free" (1:64). As his new-found faith found full expression, "he began to speak, praising God." He has come full circle, and the result will be his own hymn of praise (vv. 67–79).

The neighbors who have been a part of all the action now add their own "fear" (*phobos*), rightly translated "filled with awe" by the NIV (1:65). This is not terror but religious wonder, the normal response in Scripture to the transcendent actions of God when perceived by the people (1:12; 5:26). The second result is fame, as people in all the hill country of Judea "were talking about all these things." Thus John's renown has its beginning with his very birth and naming. At the start of it all, he has already become the subject of discussion far and wide.

Still, the true wonder, as it should be, centers not on John but on God. The people ponder these events deep in their hearts and begin asking, "What then is this child going to be?" and the reason is clear: The "Lord's hand was with him" from the very start (1:66). The "what" they are asking has to do with what God is going to accomplish in the life of this child. It is clear to all that greatness awaits him, for "the hand of God" is the same as his "mighty arm" (1:51) and always performs wondrous deeds of deliverance (Exod 13:3; 15:6; Isa 31:3).

ZECHARIAH SINGS A SONG OF PRAISE: THE BENEDICTUS (1:67-80)

Both Mary's and Zechariah's praise songs become literary devices used to give perspective and meaning to the events surrounding them. They share the primary theme of the section: God's covenant faithfulness in sending his messianic deliverer at this key moment in history. In fact, all the theories of literary origin proposed for Mary's hymn (see the introduction to 1:46-56) are also proposed for this hymn. One difference between them is that Mary's hymn was more personal, celebrating God's hand in her life, while Zechariah's is more national, celebrating God's hand in the history of Israel. There are two parts—praising God for sending his messianic redeemer, the Davidic king (vv. 68-75), and the prophetic promise regarding John's part in preparing the way for that messianic event (vv. 76-79).

INTRODUCTION: FILLED WITH THE SPIRIT (1:67)

Zechariah during his own personal nine-month seclusion, when he could not communicate with others, had come to an enormous understanding of the significance of the events in which he was taking part, encompassing not only his son but the baby Jesus as well. His hymn in one sense responds to the neighbors' question in verse 66, "What then is this child going to be?" and Zechariah is telling them his son will be fulfilling Isaiah 40:3 as the one who prepares the way for the Messiah.

The way he was able to work this out is also made clear. He "was filled with the Holy Spirit." His hymn is also a prophecy regarding what is to transpire through these events. The Spirit is said to be behind all of the praise songs of the infancy narratives—Mary in 1:35, Elizabeth in 1:41, Zechariah in 1:67, Simeon in 2:25. When Zechariah found faith, the Spirit found him and turned him from a priest into a prophet.

PRAISE FOR MESSIANIC REDEMPTION (1:68–75)

There is a different term for "blessed" here, *eulogētos*, from which we get "eulogy" in English, and it connotes praise to God. Zechariah has been made aware by the Spirit that in the birth of his son a messianic process has been initiated in which "the Lord, the God of Israel," has acted in a new way to bring national redemption to his people. These two titles are especially apropos when discussing the salvation of God's chosen people, connoting Yahweh, the covenant name of God, and stressing his special relationship with his covenant people as their God.

That this Lord God has "come to" or "visited" (*epeskepsato*) refers to the grace and mercy of God, who has descended to his people so as to deliver them both socially and spiritually (Gen 50:24–25; Exod 3:16; 13:19; Ps 80:14; Isa 23:17). The Old Testament imagery of national redemption is certainly in mind in the statement that the Lord God "has come to his people and redeemed them." He will come via the arrival of his Messiah: the first coming will mean spiritual salvation, and the second coming will bring full salvation, combining the spiritual with the political and social realms via the destruction of the enemies of God and his people.

Israel's Redeemer will provide holistic deliverance that will encompass every area of life. Some have narrowed this to a purely spiritual deliverance, but with verses 51–53 the broader sphere is almost certainly in mind. In 1:71–74 national deliverance from their "enemies" is the thrust; and in 1:75–78, spiritual deliverance. Zechariah certainly does not understand how all this will transpire, and his prophecy is presented in the most general terms. He undoubtedly thought Jesus would fulfill the political as well as the spiritual spheres in his first coming.

To describe this he uses language of national deliverance: God "has raised up a horn of salvation" (1:69), taking this from Psalms 18:2; 89:17–24; 132:12; and 2 Samuel 22:3, where the horn image depicts military prowess often used of the house of David (Ps 132:17; 2 Sam 7:26). So this is a reference to the Christ child as the Davidic Messiah/deliverer.

Zechariah wants to anchor all this in the past promises of God through the prophets (1:70). Zechariah says God spoke "through the mouth [omitted by the NIV] of the prophets"; the singular "mouth" stresses the united voice of all the prophets behind these divine promises. These are the "holy prophets" of old who speak for a holy God, and he is celebrating the fact that his son and Mary's son are the fulfillment of the whole prophetic witness as they come.

This "salvation" (*sōtērion*) will entail especially a political deliverance "from our enemies and from the hand of all who hate us" (1:71). This is the militaristic side of "the horn of salvation," looking at the Messiah as the Divine Warrior who will destroy the enemies of his people, perhaps an allusion to Psalm 106:10, "He saved them from the hand of the foe; from the hand of the enemy he redeemed them." Some have read this as spiritual warfare against the satanic forces of evil, but "those who hate us" are human opponents. Cosmic war is likely found in verse 79 but not here.

In verses 72–75, a series of infinitives demonstrates the purposes or goals of God's deliverance that has now come. Verses 72–73 look at God's past actions, and verses 74–75 at his present purposes. In the past God kept his promises to his covenant people and showed them mercy by forgiving their trespasses and watching over them so as to protect them from their enemies. Probably those who take this first infinitive as result are correct. God's faithfulness to his covenant promises has resulted in his show of mercy throughout the history of Israel. In so doing he has remembered "his holy covenant" as he has again and again delivered his undeserving people from their enemies. These are his holy people, set apart for his purposes, and God is vigilant over them.

Likely, both the Abrahamic and Davidic covenants are in view in the hymn as a whole, but Zechariah centers on the Abrahamic promises in 1:73, because they stressed God's watching over his people and ensuring their success (especially Gen 12, 17, 22, 26). Zechariah defines the goals from the Abrahamic covenant in 1:74. Rescue from Israel's enemies especially recalls the exodus event but includes the return from exile as well. In fact, the entire history of the nation involved one rescue after another. The "enemies" are primarily the Romans but would include all who stand between them and God. For the messianic community that will follow, enemies would include apostate Jews who persecute the church.

The second clause, "to enable us to serve him without fear," is the result of the first. God rescues his covenant people so they can fulfill their covenant and serve him. For Zechariah as a priest, serving God would refer to the priestly duties in the temple and among the Jewish people. Here it reaches beyond that to the service of God (Greek *latreuō*) in general. "Enable" is *tou dounai* (to give, grant); when God rescues his people, he grants them the privilege of serving him. In this way, service for the Lord is another spiritual gift. In another way, every aspect of our lives can be viewed as serving him.

THE FUTURE MINISTRIES OF JOHN AND JESUS (1:76–79)

The tone shifts here from the aorist tenses of the first half of the hymn (vv. 68–75) to future tense (vv. 76–79). Most therefore consider this a prophecy, for it looks to the future work of John and Jesus as the messianic age unfolds. John is labeled "the prophet

of the Most High," paralleling Jesus as "the Son of the Most High"
(1:32). He is not only the first prophet in four centuries but also
the greatest of the prophets as the messianic forerunner, himself
fulfilling prophecy (Mal 3:1; 4:5) and preparing for 7:26–35, where
his prophetic ministry will be laid out for us.

His prophetic office will be to "go on before the Lord" and "prepare the way" for the Messiah, drawn from Malachi 3:1 and Isaiah
40:3. It is difficult to decide whether "the Lord" here is God or
Jesus. God the Most High will send him on his mission, and as it
progresses he will be laying the groundwork for Jesus to become
Lord of all. Still, as the NIV translation makes clear, the first half
of the verse ("prophet of the Most High") centers on God, and
the second half ("prepare the way for him") on Jesus. If we were
to decide God is the focus, we would retranslate, "You will go on
before the Lord [God] to prepare his ways." However, the whole
context refers to the highway to Zion constructed for the coming
of God's Messiah, so I believe the NIV is correct.

Most likely Malachi 3:1 built on Isaiah 40:3, and the Gospels
echo both prophecies. God was constructing his highway to a
restored Zion and removing all obstacles in the path of the coming
of his Messiah. The passage from Isaiah was central to the community at **Qumran**, who wrote down the Dead Sea Scrolls. This community viewed itself as the channel through which the messianic
age would arrive (1QS 8:13–14), and the early church did the same.
In fact, the Christians first named themselves "the Way" (Acts 9:2;
19:9, 23). They believed both the exodus and the return from exile
were fulfilled in Jesus, and that John was the wilderness voice proclaiming the arrival of God's salvation in Jesus the Messiah.

With verse 77 we turn from social revolution (vv. 71–74) to spiritual salvation, and the restoration comes via repentance and the
forgiveness of sins (also 1:17; 3:3). The deliverance of God's people
from their enemies (vv. 71, 74) now turns to "knowledge of [spir-
itual] salvation" or deliverance from the far greater enemy, sin.

This is the second "gift" from God after "enable us to serve" in 1:74. In fact, this is the great "gift of salvation" that makes serving God possible. God's place for John is twofold, to prepare the way for Jesus (v. 76) and with his prophetic preaching to enable the people to understand that God's salvation has now come in an entirely new way (v. 77), perhaps referring to the new covenant of Jeremiah 31:31-34. "Knowledge" here does not just speak of intellectual comprehension but more the actual spiritual experience of God's salvation through the forgiveness of sins. This in fact will be the meaning of John's ministry, "preaching a baptism of repentance for the forgiveness of sins" (3:3). These were two interdependent aspects of a single mission, bringing God's new-covenant salvation into this world and inaugurating a new era of salvation. The barriers making it impossible for sinful humanity to come to God were about to be removed, and John's message and his messianic ministry were the two things that prepared for that wondrous event.

In the last two verses of the hymn Zechariah turns from John's part in the salvation drama to God's central role. The basis of everything in this chapter is the "tender mercy of our God." Every blessing and redemptive gift flows out of it. In Mary's praise song the mighty deeds of God are defined as "his mercy [extending] to those who fear him" (1:50), especially God's "remembering to be merciful to Abraham and his descendants forever" (1:54). Elizabeth further designated the birth of John as the Lord's "great mercy" (1:58), and Zechariah's song has already celebrated the "mercy" shown as God remembered "his holy covenant" in sending his salvation once more to his people (1:72). This is all summed up in the "tender mercy" noted here. The coming of Christ and beginning of the new age of salvation were not deserved or earned; they stem from God's "compassion" (*splanchna*) and mercy to an unworthy people.

Especially resulting from God's compassionate mercy is the coming of the Messiah, here pictured as "the rising sun" that "will come to us from heaven." The term *anatolē* literally means "to spring up" and could refer to the messianic "branch" that was to sprout up (Jer 23:5; Zech 3:8; 6:12) but more likely connotes a star rising up and shining from heaven, as seen in the following imagery of God's light shining on the people dwelling in darkness in the next verse. Still, many see a double reference, with the shoot of David (Isa 11:1–3) also being depicted here. In the person of the Messiah, the Branch, the light of God has shone down from heaven.

The messianic light has a twofold mission here, to shine on those in darkness and to guide the feet of those who respond (1:79). This is likely an allusion to Isaiah 9:2 (quoted in Matt 4:15–16), "The people walking in darkness have seen a great light; on those living in the land of deep darkness a light has dawned." In Isaiah these were Jews living in pagan Galilee, but here these are Jews living in spiritual darkness, and "the shadow of death" is spiritual rather than physical. Sin has imprisoned them in darkness, but now as a result of his compassionate mercy God has shone his light of salvation on those caught up in darkness.

The result of this light from heaven is the revelation of a new path out of the morass. The Messiah will "guide our feet into the path of peace." In their sin they could only stumble in darkness, with "the shadow of death" alluding to Psalm 23:4, "though I walk through the valley of the shadow of death" (KJV). The unbelievers spend their life living within that shadow, but God has provided a path out from it, called here "the path of peace." Peace in Scripture is a life in harmony with God and the tranquility that results from it. Clearly God's peace is synonymous with salvation here, with forgiveness, the removal of the chaos of sin, the path that leads to peace. John prepares the people for that path, and Christ leads them on it to discover that inner tranquility of soul.

THE GROWING MATURITY OF JOHN (1:80)

Luke covers the growing years in a single verse (like Isaac in Gen 21:8 or Samuel in 1 Sam 2:21, 26), including his wilderness sojourn when he followed the development of the wilderness prophet Elijah. His entire childhood is covered by the phrase "grew and became strong in spirit." "In spirit" could be the Holy Spirit but in this verse is more likely his inner growth as a person. He matured not just physically but spiritually as well.

His time in the wilderness has led many to postulate that John was a follower of the Qumran community, but there are too many differences between John's outlook and theology and that of the Essenes at Qumran.[3] There were similarities (an asceticism, a view of themselves as preparing the way for the Messiah), but the Essenes were a monastic movement that stayed apart from others while John ministered openly to the nation. The Essenes at Qumran viewed the temple and Jewish priesthood as apostate, while John came from a priestly family. They both centered on water rites, but John's baptism was radically different from Qumran's purification rite.

John's wilderness life is not described in the Gospels, but it is clear he was readying himself to call the nation in a new exodus to repentance and getting right with God. In a sense, John's seclusion in the wilderness followed his mother into a seclusion that prepared him for his public ministry to come. In the literary development of Luke it is necessary that John disappear from view while Jesus enters the picture in full view.

———

This chapter centers on the witness of the two mothers-to-be regarding the messianic events that are unfolding (vv. 39–45). The predominant themes are joy and a sense of wondrous blessing from God. A beautiful scene is when Mary walks through the door and baby John "leaps" for joy in the womb, sensing that his

———

3. Qumran is the name of the community and especially the library in the Dead Sea area. The movement that populated Qumran is that of the Essenes.

Messiah is near, the focus of his coming life and ministry. The three-month sojourn of the two women with each other would have been an incredible time.

This section of the book centers on the two hymns, with Mary's focusing on God's blessing in reversing her situation and Zechariah's on the messianic events unfolding for the nation. Mary's praise song (vv. 46–55) is the theme of their time together, as they celebrate the joy of God reversing the evils of this world through the Messiah. Mary praises her God both for elevating her place in this world and for turning the social situation around to favor the poor and the hungry, elevating his covenant people and delivering them from their oppressions. There is an important lesson in this, for spiritual evangelism must always include social concern. Converting sinners has to involve alleviating their suffering as well. The Messiah is living proof that you cannot have the one without the other.

Zechariah's praise song (vv. 68–79) centers on national redemption and moves from the social/political deliverance of the nation in verses 71–74 to spiritual salvation in verses 75–78. The spiritual side would be the immediate effects of the Christ, who would become the atoning sacrifice for their sins. The social deliverance would await the second coming, when Christ would return and destroy the powers of evil for all eternity.

John's coming (vv. 76–79) introduced both aspects of the messianic work but especially the redemptive side. In preparing the way, he would make possible the forgiveness of sins, and as we will see in chapter 3 his ministry of baptism focused on exactly that aspect of the messianic age, the bringing of salvation.

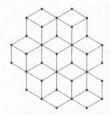

THE BIRTH AND PRESENTATION OF JESUS

(2:1–52)

Luke has built his infancy narrative around the John-Jesus parallel, first in the announcement and then in the birth of the two
figures. At the end of chapter 1 John is born and named, and now
Jesus is born and presented in the temple. There are two parts to
the birth story, first the historical and earthly side (vv. 1–7), and
then the involvement of the heavenly powers (vv. 8–20). The story
of John's birth was simple, just one verse (1:57), while that of Jesus
is filled with drama. The contrast is significant: the earthly circumstances are lowly and humble (the manger, the shepherds, the
barn), and yet all the glories of heaven are focused on his birth.
The very choirs of heaven are praising the humble Christ child in
this central event of history.

JESUS IS BORN (2:1–21)

THE HISTORICAL CIRCUMSTANCES (2:1–2)

The powerless nature of the coming of the Messiah is evident
from the first, as the census of Caesar Augustus makes the trip
to Bethlehem possible and allows Joseph and Mary to fulfill the
prophecy of the Messiah's birth from Micah 5:2. Herod the Great

and his death provide the key to the question of when Jesus was born. He slaughtered boys two and under just before his death (Matt 2:16), and he died in 4 BC, making Jesus born about 6 BC. Caesar Augustus, Julius Caesar's nephew and heir, with the birth name Gaius Octavius, was on the throne. After his uncle's assassination, he ruled with Marc Antony for a while, but that dissolved and ended in civil war. He defeated Antony in a naval battle at Actium in 32 BC, and the Roman senate named him *Augustus* (which in Latin means "Majesty") in 27 BC, making him emperor of the new Roman Empire. Caesar was his adopted family name, but beginning with him it came to be used as a title for the emperor. He reigned from 31 BC to AD 14.

We know from other ancient sources that Augustus reorganized the empire into provinces, eventually numbering ten (= the "ten kings" of Rev 17:12). The censuses they took of the provinces were for the purpose of taxation, which explains the enrollment here. Herod had been king of Judea, and his son Archelaus reigned after he died. Archelaus was deposed in AD 6, and the Romans decided to turn to a Roman governor for the province, Quirinius, who began his time in office by taking a census.

The problem is that this does not fit the timeline here, for the birth of Jesus demands a census twelve years earlier, in 6 BC. Some solve this by translating Luke 2:2, "This registration happened before Quirinius was governor of Syria." This would remove the chronological contradiction, but does that really solve much, when the registration would then be twelve years before the actual census?

A better solution comes from the fact that we do know Quirinius led several military forays in that region under the aegis of Syrian Roman rule, and it is likely he did so in some official capacity. Moreover, "governor" could simply refer to a ruling position, not necessarily as legate of the region. Thus we could translate, "while Quirinius was governing in Syria." Since he administered a census in AD 6, this would be the first of two under Quirinius. This is not overly unusual, for the Romans conducted a census every fourteen years in Egypt. With an ever-changing political climate and fairly constant military action taking place, this would make sense.

Luke says all this in order to make a very important point. The Jews chafed under Roman rule, and the census drove that point home: Rome did not just rule over their land but controlled their finances as well. Everything they had actually belonged to Rome. The Jews longed for the Messiah to give them freedom, and Luke is saying that God is in the process of doing just that. Caesar rules over his small part, but in reality a much greater king is about to be born, and the *Pax Romana* (the pretentious "Roman Peace") is soon to be replaced with God's greater (and eternal) peace.

The Journey to Bethlehem (2:3-5)

Joseph and Mary comply with the official demands and become part of the "everyone" who goes "to their own town to register." We are not to picture hundreds of people coming on a certain weekend. Rather, at some time during the year of the census they were to come long enough to register. Moreover, this performs another divine purpose, that of fulfilling Scripture. Joseph and Mary were of the house of David, and so their ancestral town was Bethlehem (1 Sam 16:4; 17:15), thus fulfilling the birth of the Messiah in Bethlehem (Mic 5:2) as well as the promise to Mary that God will "give him the throne of his father David" (1:32).

Mary would have been required to accompany Joseph because in the Syrian region women were also liable to the poll tax and so would need to be enrolled. The town of Bethlehem was about five miles from Jerusalem. It would be a grueling trip for a woman expecting soon, as it was ninety miles from Nazareth. The traditional picture of Mary riding a donkey makes a lot of sense.

Luke tells us also that they are "pledged to be married" and that the marriage has not as yet been consummated. The fact that she is at this time "expecting a child" underscores once more the virgin birth. There is a slight discrepancy with Matthew 1:24-25, which relates that Joseph had taken "Mary home as his wife." But he did not consummate their marriage until she "gave birth to her first-born, a son" (2:7). Yet Luke says they were betrothed here. Most likely they are living together as husband and wife but still technically "betrothed" because they had not consummated their marriage. This would be another part of the reason they both traveled to Bethlehem.

Through Joseph Jesus "belonged to the house and line of David," stressing again the ancestral line of the family. One unexpected thing for ancient readers would be to read "the town of David" beside Bethlehem rather than Jerusalem, since the latter was called "the city of David" so often in Scripture (2 Sam 5:7; 1 Kgs 8:1; 9:4; 1 Chr 11:7; 13:13; and countless others). In 1 Samuel this was also unexpected as David's birthplace, for it was a small town of no importance otherwise, and that was still the case in the time of Jesus. This is another time in which God chooses the insignificant things of the world to make his greatness known (Mic 5:4).

THE BIRTH OF JESUS (2:6–7)

As throughout this story, the emphasis is on the lowly and humble beginnings of the Christ child. Very few of the traditional details— the animals present, the barn setting, and the feeding troughs— are highlighted, nor some of the apocryphal stories about birth pangs while they traveled. We are told simply that the time of delivery arrived and the baby was born, wrapped in cloths, and laid in a manger, a humble but still stable setting (no pun intended).

Luke points out that he was a "firstborn son" (*prōtotokos*), which is intended to ready us for 2:23–24 and possibly to set him apart from Mary's later children (Mark 6:3; Luke 8:19–20) as the son of David and heir of David's throne (2 Chr 21:3), thus to highlight his messianic significance. While not obvious in the narrow context, everything that preceded and will follow prepares us for a messianic reading of this detail.

Mary wraps her newborn in swaddling cloths, the normal practice of Jewish mothers. These are lengthy strips of cloth bound
around the child to keep the limbs straight and still. The purpose
was to keep them secure and provide stability. The emphasis is
on the normality of the Messiah's beginning, as all babies experienced this.

The fact that the Christ child was "placed ... in a manger" sets
him apart, for it is a feeding trough for animals. One question is
where this trough was found. The key is the following, "because
there was no guest room available for them." Traditionally this was
translated "no room in the inn," but this is not the Greek word for
an inn (compare 10:34). The word is *katalyma*, better seen as a guest
room in a house (as in 22:11). The average home then often had a
separate room for guests, and animals would reside for the night
in a lower level of the living room, with the feeding troughs there.

So they weren't residing in a barn with animals their only
company. They would have been treated as normal guests, staying in a home either of a relative or someone in the community.
They would likely have been downstairs because a closer relative
was visiting in the normal guest room. The cloths and the manger
are to be signs for the shepherds (2:12), showing that the child is
socially at their level, a humble baby. This child will be the lowly
Messiah for lowly shepherds.

SHEPHERDS LED IN WORSHIP BY THE ANGELS (2:8–14)

God's choice to include shepherds specifically in this messianic
birth is significant at two levels: Jesus is the lowly king coming
especially to raise the lowly and exalt them; and as David was the
messianic shepherd, so also will Jesus be.

The shepherds "keeping watch over their flocks at night" is an
idyllic picture of the people of God living their regular lives. They
become the focal point for the messianic glory of God revealed
to humankind. The message is that the downtrodden are to be

elevated (1:51-53). Shepherds would need to take turns being vigilant to guard against thieves and predators, so this picture fits the original scene well. God chooses lowly shepherds to be the first witnesses not only for the birth of the Messiah but also for the celebration of the angelic realm at his birth. This parallels his choice of women as the first witnesses of the resurrection (24:1-8).

So while they are on their lonely vigil, "an angel of the Lord appeared to them, and the glory of the Lord shone around them" (2:9). The stress is on the **Shekinah** glory once more descending on our world, as it did during the exodus (Exod 13:21-22), at Sinai (Exod 24:16-17), and with the tabernacle and temple (Exod 40:34-35). This is the third of four appearances of angels (1:11, 26; 2:9, 13). Angels are mentioned fifteen times in the first two chapters, demonstrating the supernatural nature of this event. The terror of the shepherds is the normal human response to the transcendent realm of God throughout Scripture. At times it is awe (like Zechariah and Mary in 1:12, 29, or the three disciples at the transfiguration in 9:34). While Luke's description includes both here, terror is definitely more predominant at the incredible glory of God displayed around them.

The angel calms them down: "Do not be afraid" (2:10), and then tells them the incredible message: "I bring you good news that will cause great joy for all the people." Fear is to be replaced with great joy, and that joy will be universal on all Israel. The language and tone would fit the birth announcement of a new emperor, and that is exactly what this is, but one that extends far beyond the confines of the Roman Empire or even of the first century. This will be the King of kings and Lord of lords.

There is great emphasis on the fact that "today in the town of David a Savior has been born to you" (2:11). The word "today" (see 4:21; 5:26; 19:9; 23:43) stresses the fact that it is on this very day but also that this is the turning point of the ages, when all the "yesterdays" have been fulfilled and the new-covenant era inaugurated. The "town of David" (again, Bethlehem rather than Jerusalem) announces further that this is the new messianic age being initiated in fulfillment of Micah 5:2.

Moreover, it means the coming of the "Savior" in keeping with his name, Jesus (see 1:31). He is the One who will deliver the people from their sins. This Savior is both "Christ and Lord," both Messiah and cosmic Lord of all. God is Savior in 1:47, and Jesus partakes of both aspects of God's nature, his Saviorhood and his lordship. This is unique language here (literally, "a Savior who is Christ Lord"), found nowhere else in the New Testament, and is incredibly high **Christology** for a birth announcement!

The final aspect of the angelic announcement (2:12) gives the shepherds "a sign," building on biblical precedent (Exod 3:12; 1 Sam 2:34; Isa 37:30), that will confirm the reality of a truth. When they arrive in Bethlehem they will find an infant (*brephos*) or newborn baby, and this baby will be "wrapped in cloths and lying in a manger." He will be able to identify with them in their lowliness and help lift them out of their humble state. The incongruity of the security (the cloths) and the lowly circumstances (an animal trough) provides confirmation for those who could appreciate such a paradox.

The refrain for the worship scene is provided by the heavenly choir (2:13-14). In the Old Testament the "heavenly host" also refers to the armies of heaven who surround God for worship and to help his people (1 Kgs 22:19; Jer 19:13). The contrast with Rome is found at every point of this passage. Rome's armies controlled the world, but with the sword, not the "good news," and they prided themselves on having established the *Pax Romana*, their version of peace, which meant doing exactly what the Romans tell you to do. Here the angelic hymn began with "Glory to God in the highest heaven," the reminder that true splendor and glory is not an earthly thing centered on the so-called glory of Caesar but a heavenly reality centered on the Most High God (*hypsistos*, 1:32, 35, 76). Here the same term is "the highest heaven," the habitation of the Most High God.

The second half of the praise song details what the highest
heaven is doing for earth: bringing "peace to those on whom
his favor rests." Again, this is not the false peace of the Romans,
which is nothing more than total submission to their will, but
true peace, that complete tranquility with God that produces the
same peace with the people around us. This is peace "to those" on
whom his favor [*eudokias*] rests," understood by most as meaning they are chosen by God and under his favor (as in 12:32). The
idea of messianic blessings for Christ followers flows through the
infancy narratives.

THE WORSHIP OF THE CHRIST CHILD (2:15-20)

The heavenly host having returned to heaven, the shepherds are
left pondering what to do in response to the angels' message. So
they decide to do three things: they go to Bethlehem, they see
the baby, and they tell everyone what had happened in the sheep
fields. The key to it all is their realization that "the Lord has told
us about" the birth event and its significance. They could hardly
ignore anything as important as that or keep quiet about it. If we
could go crazy over a World Series victory or an NBA champion-
ship, how excited should we be about the coming of God's Messiah?
The angels did not tell them they had to go, but that didn't matter.
They had to go, and with as much "haste" as possible, for they had
just been participants in history's greatest event so far.

When they arrived, they "found Mary and Joseph, and the baby,
who was lying in the manger" (2:16). They now take the place of
the angels and proclaim to all and sundry "the word concerning
what had been told them about this child" (2:17). Like Mary, they
believe what the angels have told them and respond immediately to
its urgent message—the Messiah has come; he is here! It is the perfect scene—Mary, Joseph, and the Christ child together in the guest
room. The shepherds told everyone they met what had happened to
them and what had been told to them. This is evangelism at its best;
the first mission team in all of history has just made its appearance.

The result is just as expected—"all who heard it were amazed at what the shepherds said to them" (2:18). These next two verses build on each other with the corporate reaction of the onlookers and the private reaction of Mary herself. Everyone who hears their story is filled with wonder, as is the case in many of these episodes (1:21, 63; 2:18, 33). They are rightly in awe at the implications it held for them all, but they go no further. We never hear from them again, and we don't know how many became followers. The one exception is the shepherds (see v. 20 below), but we hear nothing from the townspeople (who will become the "crowds" later in Luke). The message for us is that excitement and wonder are not enough. Too many churches in our day opt for the spectacular and try to entertain the people more than touch their lives. This is a huge mistake.

Mary's response (2:19) has a deeper reaction, with serious reflection and meditation continuing in her life. This is the proper response, and she is the model of discipleship, as she "treasured up all these things and pondered them in her heart." The imperfect tense *syntērei* (kept on treasuring) and the present-tense participle *symballousa* (was pondering) stress the ongoing nature of her meditation on the separate events as a divinely sanctioned whole. She in a sense becomes the systematic theologian of the birth events as she is both thrilled over them and thinking long and hard about them.

This does not mean that her serious contemplation gave her full and final understanding. It is likely that she understood at this time, but Mark 3:20–21, 31–35, show that she later failed to maintain this level of understanding. There she with her other sons had concluded, "He is out of his mind," most likely meaning Jesus was overworked and close to a nervous breakdown. She was finite, and even though she knew he was the Messiah (her other sons at that time were unbelievers) she was capable of thinking on the earthly plane and misreading a situation. Still, she was the first to understand the true implications of this miraculous birth.

The shepherds had also attained a deep faith and realization regarding what they had just seen (2:20). They returned to their flocks and their home true believers and followers and continued their virtually evangelistic work, "glorifying and praising God for all the things they had heard and seen." What truly astounded them was that all these incredible things took place "just as they had been told." Every single thing the angels had told them came true, and you can almost see their eyes bright and big with excitement as they told people all this for a long time to come. The two terms here, "glory" and "praise," have been central concepts throughout these two chapters, so this verse functions as a virtual summary of the atmosphere throughout the infancy narratives. Theirs is to be our response as well, for the glory of the coming of the Christ child still overwhelms us. For many of us, Christmas is our favorite time of the year, but the glory of Christ himself is the true highlight of the Christmas season, much more than the lights and the tinsel and the other bright and loud elements, as much fun as they are. We must combine the awe of verse 18 with the praise of verse 20. Mary and the shepherds show us the true and proper reaction to the Christ event.

JESUS IS PRESENTED IN THE TEMPLE (2:21-40)

Jesus' birth story centers far more on obeying the law than it does on obeying Rome. (The law is mentioned three times in verses 22-24.) Torah observance is critical (vv. 22, 39), so seven days after his birth the baby Jesus is circumcised (2:21). At the same time, Mary was unclean for seven days, and that too ended at Jesus' circumcision. Still she was to stay at home until the fortieth day, when she would offer sacrifices for her purification and present Jesus in the temple. Two ceremonies are combined, Mary's purification and the presentation of the firstborn to the Lord. At the same time, John's place in the narrative has ended; he does not appear in the second chapter. The Messiah has arrived, and all the attention is on him.

THE CIRCUMCISION AND NAMING OF THE BABY (2:21)

Paralleling the naming of John in 1:59-63, Jesus too is circumcised on the eighth day and named, as commanded in Genesis 17:12; 21:4; Leviticus 12:3. The circumcision signified they were now one of the covenant people, Israel, and the naming gave the babies their sense of destiny and calling from God. The choice of a name embraced the parental hopes for the child. This section/event/etc. functions as the conclusion of the birth story and prepares for Jesus' presentation in the temple. Jesus' destiny has been clear from the start: he is Jesus, Savior and Lord, as Gabriel had said in 1:31. This will guide the rest of the Jesus story as told by Luke. Jesus will fulfill and complete his destiny from God.

THE TRIP TO JERUSALEM (2:22-24)

Mary waited until the fortieth day, as the law required (Lev 12:1-6), and then they were to travel to Jerusalem for the purification rite. These verses are arranged **chiastically** around the two ceremonies:

> A Purification (22a)
>   B Presentation of Jesus (22b)
>   B′ Scriptural basis of the presentation (23)
> A′ Scriptural basis of the purification (24)

Even though the purification ceremony centers only on the mother, Luke calls it "*their* purification" (omitted by NIV) to stress that they did so as a family. They also decided to combine it with the presentation of Jesus as the firstborn, based on Exodus 3:2, 12, 15, as cited in verse 23.

The purification ceremony involved the offering of "a pair of doves or two young pigeons" (2:24; from Lev 12:8). They were a poor family and could not afford to sacrifice a lamb. However, Luke is silent regarding the redemptive payment from Numbers 18:16 (five shekels), and some think that this means Jesus is being equated with Samuel as being already holy and consecrated to the Lord, not needing to be "redeemed" for everyday life. This is quite viable and thereby stresses the sacred nature of Jesus and his consecration to God. It is part of his very nature, and his parents recognize that fact by not paying the redemption price.

Luke presents Joseph and Mary as faithfully observing the law, assiduously following its precepts, and as very pious and obedient to the Lord.

SIMEON'S WITNESS (2:25-35)

Two prophetic-type figures are at the center of this episode, Simeon and Anna. He is described as "righteous and devout," like Zechariah and Elizabeth (1:6). He is likely a layman, though later tradition labeled him a 112-year-old priest (Gospel of Pseudo-Matthew 15:2). We don't know his age, but he speaks of his readiness to die (v. 29), so he probably was elderly. The main thing is his deep piety and Spirit-filled nature.

The hallmark of his spiritual condition is his deep hope, "waiting for the consolation [*paraklēsis*] of Israel." The restoration of the nation and the defeat of her enemies is a feature of Isaiah (40:1; 49:13; 51:3; 61:2; 66:13). This consolation was to be accomplished by the Servant of Yahweh (Isa 52–53), and it would not take place until the Messiah arrived and instituted the messianic age. So Simeon was especially waiting for the Christ child to appear and thought that day had now arrived.

He was also a Spirit-filled prophet. "The Holy Spirit was on him" is probably a general statement, but the inspiration of the Spirit relates entirely to the significance of this child being presented to the Lord. This is the subject of 2:26–27. First the Spirit had "revealed" to him that "he would not die before he had seen the Lord's Messiah," the one who would indeed restore Israel. This promise had come sometime in the past and had defined his life, making possible his going home to be with the Lord.

The implication is that Simeon had been waiting for this day for a long time, possibly years. His coming to the temple this day was instituted not by him but by the Holy Spirit. One can only guess at the anticipation and excitement he felt as he walked through the gates of the temple, knowing the Spirit was momentarily going to show the Christ child to him. He was waiting when Joseph and Mary arrived, and undoubtedly the Spirit revealed to him at that very moment that they were the ones.

As the sacred couple proceed through the court of the Gentiles into the court of women (Mary could go no further), they are intercepted by a very excited man with a prophetic air about him. He is probably not a priest, but he performs a priestly act as he takes the baby in his arms and pours out his thanks and praise to God on his behalf. The parents are doing so much more than just presenting their child to God. They are initiating a messianic sequence that will mean the restoration of Israel, indeed of all humanity.

He utters the third hymn of this narrative, called the Nunc Dimittis (again, the opening words of this passage in the Latin Vulgate). It is composed of three couplets (vv. 29, 30-31, 32) centering on (1) thanksgiving for fulfilling the promise, (2) thanksgiving for the salvation that has come, and (3) thanksgiving for the universal overtones of the consolation.

The praise is offered to the "Sovereign Lord," which is *despotēs* or "Master," with himself as the "servant" of his Lord. God is the sovereign solely in charge, and Simeon has relinquished all to him. God had promised Simeon he would see the Messiah before he died, and that the restoration of the nation would thus begin. That promise had now come to pass, and so he is "now" ready to be "dismissed" or "released in peace," a euphemism for death (Gen 15:15; Num 20:29). His prophetic task is now complete and his life fulfilled, so he is ready to go. Many have pictured him as a sentinel or watcher who has now fulfilled his duty and announced the arrival of the deliverer.

The second couplet (2:30–31) celebrates the "salvation" or "consolation" that has now come. There is double meaning in "my eyes have seen your salvation," since the baby's name, Jesus, means "Yahweh saves." Simeon has physically looked on Jesus/salvation, and in so doing he has spiritually seen God's salvation arrive in this world. It is the baby Jesus who will bring this salvation and restore Israel to its intended destiny (though it will mainly be the new Israel who experiences "the consolation of Israel").

God has "prepared" this salvation "in the sight of all nations." The idea of seeing God's salvation prepared before the nations stems from Isaiah 40:3–5 (cited in Luke 3:4–6) and is echoed in Isaiah 52:10, "all the ends of the earth will see the salvation of our God." The actual phrase is "in front of all the people" and extends Simeon's original "consolation of Israel" into a universal promise for all the people of earth, not just the Jews. All humanity is included in the new age of salvation inaugurated by the coming of the Messiah, and the Abrahamic covenant (Gen 12:3) will now be fulfilled as well.

These universal overtones are the subject of the third couplet (2:32), which expands the meaning of "prepared [for] all nations." This messianic salvation (2:30) will bring the disparate nations that are now in enmity against each other together, in particular the Gentiles and the Jews. God's salvation is the one antidote to racial prejudice that will work. This, in fact, is a major theme in Isaiah, the universal effects of God's salvation on all the nations of earth, as the Messiah is to bring about (and Israel participate in) "a light for the Gentiles, that my salvation may reach to the ends of the earth" (Isa 49:6; see also 42:6; 51:4–5). In Zechariah's hymn (1:78–79) the Messiah brings God's new dawn to the nations to shine his light on the darkness of sinful humanity and bring the peace of God.

This light that illumines the Gentiles is at the same time "the glory of your people Israel." God's covenant people will share his glory through the coming of the Messiah. Here is truly the "consolation of Israel" that was the focus of Simeon's hope (2:25). From the very time of the Abrahamic covenant, Israel was meant to be the channel of God's blessing to the nations (Gen 12:33; 18:18; 22:18; 26:4; 28:14). So Israel was not only meant to share God's glory but also to be the means by which it was shared with the nations.

Joseph and Mary are filled with wonder at all that is being said (2:33), continuing the amazement that characterizes everyone who comes in contact with the baby Jesus (1:21, 63; 2:18, 33, 47; see also 4:22; 8:25; 9:43). Mary knew of Jesus' destiny from the beginning through Gabriel's message (1:28–33), but to hear the details and realize more thoroughly what all this entailed would be overwhelming. We all share that wonder and awe. Even after two thousand years, it never gets old.

However, Simeon is not finished. There is a negative side to the Messiah's coming (2:34–35). The Spirit has revealed to him the rejection and opposition that the Messiah will face as he changes salvation history. The image of Israelites "falling and rising" likely stems from the "stone of stumbling" in Isaiah 8:14 and 28:16 that will cause many to fall. This messianic image depicts the Servant of Yahweh forcing all in Israel to take sides, resulting in spiritual failure as well as victory.[1] The apostasy of the nation was a continuous problem throughout the history of Israel, and it would be no different in the messianic age.

In this way Jesus the Christ will be "a sign that will be spoken against," probably building on Isaiah 8:18, where Isaiah and his children become signs of rejection and judgment to an apostate nation to call it back to God. In all of this the sign is God's faithfulness in spite of judgment. Still, many in Israel will "speak against" or reject the sign and turn away from God's Messiah. That is the prophecy here. Jesus is not only the Savior but also the Suffering Servant.

---

1. Some have said that this pictures one group, Israel, which as a whole will fall only to rise again. While that would fit the history of the nation, that does not fit the context here, which is one of division and foment.

Verse 35 has two parts. The first half continues to describe Jesus' ministry to the nation of Israel as he reveals "the thoughts of many hearts," that is, forces people to make a faith-decision that will bring them spiritual victory or defeat. There will be no neutrality when we encounter Jesus, and there will also be no hypocritical pretending when we are not right with God. The hearts of all will be evident. This will be the Spirit's work as he convicts every person (John 16:8–11).

The second half turns to the personal effects all this will have on Mary herself: "A sword will pierce your own soul too." This most naturally refers to her many sorrows, especially being present at the crucifixion of her son (John 19:25–27). However, other interpretations have often been held, like a reference to her own personal doubts, her rejection and persecution as a Christ follower, the personal tests and difficulties she endured, her pain at watching all her son and his followers went through. The most natural understanding is likely best, that this refers to her life of sorrow and pain not only as the mother of Jesus but also as a follower of the Christ. This all culminated in the cross. So she is the archetype of the faithful follower who experiences "participation in his sufferings" (Phil 3:10).

ANNA'S WITNESS TO JESUS (2:36–38)

The second prophetic testimony is provided by Anna, an elderly woman who had been widowed just seven years into her marriage and then lived eighty-four more years. If she had been married at age fourteen (the normal age), she would now be 105 years old, the same age as Judith in Jewish tradition (Judith 16:23). She is also considered a prophetess like Miriam (Exod 15:20), Deborah (Judg 4:4), Huldah (2 Kgs 22:14), Isaiah's wife (Isa 8:3), or the daughters of Philip (Acts 21:9). This means she too was inspired by the Spirit like Simeon (2:25).

She spent all of her time worshipping in the temple. The text reads, "She never left the temple but worshiped night and day," but it is doubtful that we are to read this literally to mean she slept and ate her meals in the temple, probably living in a spare room of the temple (allowed at times). Rather, it is a euphemism for constant worship, also paralleling Judith, a widow who was constantly in the temple (Judith 8:1–8; 11:17). So she like Mary is also a model of the faithful follower. The mention of constant fasting as well as prayer shows the depth of her commitment to the spiritual needs of the nation. Every aspect of Jewish life, laborers like the shepherds, priests and prophets, pious men and women of all stripes, rejoiced at the coming of God's Messiah.

In verse 38 she joins the others, especially the shepherds and Simeon, in both giving thanks to God and witnessing "to all who were looking forward to the redemption of Jerusalem." This stems from Isaiah 52:9 and parallels Simeon's "consolation of Israel" (2:25). Needless to say, the redemption of Jerusalem means the salvation that comes only through Jesus Messiah. Anna culminates the list of those in these chapters who celebrate the new age of salvation the Christ child is bringing with him.

Conclusion: Return to Galilee and Jesus' Maturation (2:39–40)

Jesus' childhood and years to adulthood are covered in a brief comment. The family remains faithful to the Torah at all times, staying in Jerusalem as long as needed to do "everything required by the Law of the Lord." The point is Jesus' pious upbringing by his parents. When that duty was finished, they returned to their hometown of Nazareth in Galilee, and Jesus was brought up there as the carpenter's son, and then when Joseph died, as the village carpenter (Mark 6:3). Luke says nothing about the material from Matthew like the magi, the slaughter of the innocents by Herod, and the flight to Egypt not because he didn't know of them but because they did not fit his purposes here. His attention is entirely on witnesses to the significance of the Christ child.

Verse 40 covers at least the next thirty-plus years of Jesus' life until he begins his public ministry and messianic work. There are three aspects to Jesus' growth. First, he physically "grew and became strong," meaning normal development from infant to child to maturity. The second two relate to the spiritual side. He was "filled with wisdom," relating to his knowledge of the ways of God and his ability to use that knowledge in living for God. As wisdom-filled, then, "the grace of God was on him." In this he is like his mother, who was "highly favored" by the Lord (1:28, 30). This wisdom and grace will be characteristic of Jesus for the rest of his life and shown clearly in the narratives of this Gospel. His first thirty years of life were the perfect preparation for his extraordinary messianic ministry in the last years of his life.

JESUS GOES TO THE TEMPLE AT TWELVE (2:41–52)

This episode is thought by many to be a fictitious legend modeled after similar stories about great men like Moses, Cyrus, Alexander, and Buddha. But it is much more restrained compared to legendary creations, with no miracles or great deeds. It has all the earmarks of a historical story. Luke intends it to serve as an illustration of Jesus' incredible wisdom and favor with God as found in verse 40. It exemplifies the close relationship between Jesus and his Father that characterized his adolescence. We also see Mary continuing to "ponder" who Jesus is (2:51; compare 2:19). This is the first contact between Jesus and the temple officials. This first one is quite positive, but it will soon turn decidedly negative.

THE SETTING (2:41–42)

Passover was one of three pilgrimage festivals (with Pentecost and Tabernacles), and pious Jews like Jesus' family were expected to attend one of them each year (Exod 34:23 and Deut 16:16). Women and children were not required to make the journey, so this showed how faithful they were. Moreover, their family did so nearly every year, and this story stems from the festival when Jesus was twelve years old, on the verge of adulthood (which began at age thirteen[2]). It was an eighty-mile journey, which would have taken over three days, so the trip demanded real sacrifice.

Especially at Passover (the primary festival) Jerusalem would swell from a population of about seventy thousand (Rev 11:13) to over a quarter million, and people would be everywhere. This helps explain the chaos that allowed his parents to lose sight of Jesus as they started the return journey.

Jesus Goes Missing (2:43–45)

The family remained at the festival the whole eight days (combined with the Feast of Unleavened Bread). They were only required to stay for the first two days, so again, their piety is commendable. The normal practice was to travel in a caravan for protection from brigands on the roads. So they did not miss Jesus, probably thinking he was with "relatives and friends" in the group. They did not notice until that first night that he was not with the group at all.

People have speculated that Jesus or his parents were at fault for the situation, but neither is necessary. Jesus simply "stayed behind in Jerusalem," expecting his parents to understand. He was undoubtedly a precocious child and already had an in-depth understanding of Torah. Normally, this would lead to special training, perhaps, like Paul, becoming a disciple of a leading rabbi when he reached thirteen. So he almost certainly expected his parents to realize this when he wasn't with them.

Amazing the Teachers in the Temple (2:46–47)

It took Jesus' parents three days to find him—the first day returning to Jerusalem, the second looking for him, and the third finally discovering where he was. Some think that this looks forward to the resurrection, but that is doubtful. The parallels simply are not there. He is in the temple courts sitting with the scribes and

---

2. Bar mitzvah, the Jewish ceremony for celebrating the transition of young men into adulthood, was not practiced then but stems from a later time.

rabbis and in normal fashion (this is how rabbis taught) engaging in dialogue with them.

It has been common to think Jesus was accepted as one of the rabbis, perhaps even lecturing them. That is overstating what Luke says. He has Jesus among the teachers "listening to them and asking them questions." His posture is that of disciple rather than teacher at this point. The question-and-answer format was actually the teaching method by which rabbis operated. Still, however, the maturity and knowledge that were evident behind everything he said "amazed" them. He already showed his dexterity in matters of Torah, and this will become evident throughout the rest of Luke's Gospel, for instance, the way he bests Satan in 4:3-8. Of course, we are not surprised, for he is the God-man and the final interpreter of Torah. But here he is, twelve years old and already wondrously filled with wisdom.

CORRECTING HIS PARENTS (2:48-50)

After three days of worry and searching, Joseph and Mary are understandably upset and rebuke Jesus as a thoughtless child: "Son, why have you treated us like this?" As with any parent, their anxiety had grown and grown as the days began to pile one on top of the other. Jesus is surprised that they are even "searching for" him. They should have known. Mary had complained, "Your father and I have been anxiously searching," and so he asks, "Didn't you know I had to be in my Father's house?" He had two fathers, and if he wasn't with the one, they should know he would be with the other one, and where else but in *his house*, the temple.

The Greek actually states, "I had to be in the _____ of my Father," and we have to supply the missing term on the basis of context. So some have seen this as "my Father's business" (KJV), referring directly to his mission from God; and a few have interpreted this "my Father's teachers." Neither fits as well, for his parents were looking in places for him, and so Jesus was telling them where they should have looked for him.

The emphasis in Jesus' reply is on *dei*, "must, had to be," the particle of divine necessity. Luke often uses this of God's chosen plan for Jesus as his ministry and mission unfold (4:43; 9:22; 13:33; 17:25). On the verge of manhood, Jesus was beginning his God-ordained mission a little early and expected his parents to understand. So in a sense both thrusts are present. They should have looked in the temple, where Jesus would be initiating his messianic ministry.

The sonship language in "my Father" and in the implied "house" is profound. Jesus is Messiah but much more than Messiah. He has a special and incredibly deep relationship with his Father that penetrates everything he does. Note the three levels here: Jesus remained in the temple to initiate his earthly ministry in the temple; this involved a sense of his messianic calling, entailing what he "must" do to fulfill his office; and above all, he had to begin all this in his "Father's house," as part of a Son's response to his Father's will.

Surprisingly to Jesus, his parents still "did not understand" his explanation (2:50). In spite of the angels' message in 1:32 and Jesus' explanation here, they still experience the same wonder (v. 48) and confusion (v. 50) that all humans do. So this is part of Mary's learning process. While confused, she wisely doesn't give up and stop there, as we will see in 2:51. What they fail to understand is not just why Jesus remained in Jerusalem but also the nature of his messianic mission as he had explained it to them. Luke wants his readers to realize how difficult it is even for those closest to Jesus to understand who he is and what he does. The key is that we like Mary need time and must continue to reflect and pray to the Lord for wisdom.

CONCLUSION: RETURN HOME AND REACHING MATURITY (2:51–52)

Back home in Nazareth, Luke covers the next couple of decades in two verses, centering on Mary and then Jesus. Due to the possibility that some readers might wrongly interpret Jesus' actions in Jerusalem as disobedience, his obedience to his parents is stressed. Even as the Son of the heavenly Father, he does not shirk his earthly duty to be submissive to them as well. There is even the hint that he continued to submit as an adult, for the comment covers the entire period before Jesus began his earthly ministry while in his early thirties.

We then see that his mother continues to ponder and that she "treasured all these things in her heart" (v. 51b, see 2:19). She was truly a spiritual giant and throughout this Gospel is seen as the perfect model of the Jesus follower as well as his mother. If this characterized Mary herself, how much more should it be seen in us.

The description of Jesus in 2:52 repeats the list in 2:40 and frames the Jerusalem episode with this glimpse of his development both on the earthly and the heavenly planes. His physical, intellectual, and spiritual growth were easily observable by all who had contact with him. In fact, this verse could be labeled the theme of the Jerusalem event. His wisdom amazed the teachers, and the favor he received from everyone in the temple at that time was obvious. This also leads into chapter 4, when this would all be put to the test by Satan.

———

The comparison of John with Jesus continues in the birth narrative. John's birth was only a verse long (1:57), while Jesus' is twenty verses and filled with drama. At the outset their humble earthly situation is emphasized, as they are an insignificant family submitting to the Romans and coming to register for the Roman census in Bethlehem. Yet that is where God glorifies their situation, for in doing so they fulfill Micah 5:2 and bring the Messiah into this world. What is nothing in the eyes of the authorities becomes the most significant event in human history.

The birth itself typifies the paradox of Christianity, bringing together the lowly and humble (the manger, the shepherds) with the grand and glorious (the worship of the angelic choir) to demonstrate how God has taken the insignificant things of earth (his people) and elevated them above any other earthly thing. The circumstances of Jesus' birth are as low as one could imagine, and yet all of heaven is agog at the majesty of the scene. This is a perfect picture of who we are as Christ followers, the humble of this world made glorious by God's Son.

Note the three levels of response to the birth announcement, from Mary's deep contemplation to the shepherds' excited witness to the awe (yet few results) of the townspeople. It is not enough to be a mere onlooker at a major event. We must respond carefully and ponder deeply, allowing the event to change us. The townspeople had no ongoing reaction, and as a result this stupendous event in the end became meaningless to them, to their detriment.

The presentation of Jesus in the temple stresses Joseph and Mary's deep piety and faithful observance of Torah. Jesus has authority over Torah and yet submits to it in his family and life. The two prophetic witnesses here, Simeon and Anna, provide prophetic perspective for the meaning of all this. Simeon highlights the effects of Jesus' birth for "the consolation of Israel," as the Messiah has arrived and the last days begun. Through his witness, the significance of all we have been told is made clear. Anna repeats what Simeon has said, that with this child the redemption of Israel has arrived.

The incident in Jerusalem (vv. 41–52) typifies Jesus' adolescence and shows how prepared he was for his mission and ministry that were yet to come. It also demonstrates how difficult it is to fully comprehend Jesus, even for his parents. If anyone should have known, it would be Mary. But she is blindsided, and Luke wants us to identify with her and learn to submit our minds as well as our hearts to Jesus and the Spirit. Even at age twelve, he amazed the learned rabbis of his day. We must listen to him and follow his wisdom every bit as much as Mary and Joseph did.

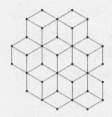

PREPARATION FOR
JESUS' MINISTRY

(3:1–38)

John, as we have seen, has been raised under the guidance of the Lord to be the messianic forerunner. This is the purpose of 3:1–4:13, to show how the Baptist's ministry prepared for the unveiling and initiation of the Messiah. In 3:1–20 he proclaims the "way of the Lord" from Isaiah and conducts a new ministry in salvation history, "a baptism of repentance for the forgiveness of sins" (3:3), revealing also a new ethics that will demonstrate this. Then he baptizes Jesus in the Jordan, commissioning him for his messianic ministry (3:21–22). The genealogy of Jesus that follows (3:23–38) traces his origins back to "Adam, the Son of God," and shows that he is indeed the God-man, identified both with all of humanity and especially with God himself as "the Son of God." Finally, the testing in the wilderness by Satan (4:1–13) shows that Jesus begins his ministry with a complete triumph over the powers of evil, defeating them with the power of the word of God.

JOHN MINISTERS IN GALILEE (3:1–20)

THE HISTORICAL CIRCUMSTANCES (3:1–2)

Luke continues his policy of setting key salvation-historical events like the birth of Jesus (2:1–2) and the ministry of John the Baptist in the context of world history. God's salvation has entered this world and its history, and he is in utter control of both. So the word of God coming to John in 3:2 is every bit as significant as the empire created by Caesar Augustus and now policed by Tiberius Caesar. The events Luke relates in his Gospel were completely ignored by the world rulers listed here but would have far more impact than anything they would accomplish.

The "fifteenth year of the reign of Tiberius Caesar" could be from his co-regency with the emperor Augustus in AD 11/12 (so 26/27), but it is generally preferred to calculate from the date of the death of Augustus in AD 14, so AD 28/29. This would place the date of the beginning of John's and Jesus' ministries at AD 28, with Jesus' death in 30. So Jesus would have been about thirty-four years old when he began his ministry.

The rest of the rulers named were governing regions that Herod the Great had formerly ruled on his own. Pontius Pilate was actually the least significant of these as prefect of the territory of Judea. Prefects were financial administrators for collecting taxes and maintaining peace and were less important than legates—military men who ruled through the Roman army. Herod Antipas, son of Herod the Great, was tetrarch or regional governor of Galilee and Perea from AD 4 to 39. Philip, the half-brother of Antipas, ruled Iturea and Trachonitus in the northern area on the east side of the Jordan from AD 4 to 34. Lysanius, an unimportant figure, ruled Abilene, a territory northwest of Damascus, but we know virtually nothing about him. Luke mentions all these to situate John's and Jesus' ministries historically. The very fact that virtually none of us modern-day readers can organize all these names and territories in our minds is exactly the point—they are all eclipsed by what God is going to be doing in the ensuing years through these two, John and Jesus.

After situating the action in the Roman world, he situates it in the Jewish world, "during the high-priesthood of Annas and Caiaphas." There was only one high priest at a time, and he was

to occupy that position for life. So something is off with this statement, for Luke uses the singular "high priest" and then names
them both. This had become a political position, appointed by and
under the control of the Romans. Annas was actually high priest
from AD 6 to 15, and his son-in-law Caiaphas from AD 18 to 36. Both
were deposed by the Romans when they fell out of favor. Moreover,
Annas established a dynasty, with five sons who served as high
priest at different times. It is Annas who interrogates Jesus at his
trial in John 18, and Caiaphas in the other Gospels. In actuality,
Jesus was first brought to Annas for preliminary questions and
then taken to Caiaphas for the Sanhedrin trial.

The point is the same with both the Roman and the Jewish
list of rulers. John came into a world under the control of secular
forces (including the Jewish leaders) who had all the power. But
"the word of God came [not to them but] to John." John and Jesus
would change the world, and all these others would be nothing but
footnotes in history. This is *rhēma theou* rather than *logos*, and it
refers not to Gospel or biblical content but to a specific command
or message given by God, here the commissioning of John to his
prophetic ministry. John is neither rabbi nor scribe but a prophet
proclaiming God's message to his people.

The word came to him "in the wilderness," where John had
been preparing for his ministry (1:80). The wilderness of Judea is
not a parched desert land but a sparsely populated region where
John had gone to prepare in isolation, just him and God. He was
deliberately modeling himself after Elijah and other wilderness prophets (compare 2 Kgs 2:4–11). Mark stresses this when
he describes John wearing "clothing made of camel's hair, with a
leather belt … [eating] locusts and wild honey," paralleling Elijah in
2 Kings 1:8 (Mark 1:6). In addition, this builds on the positive side
of the wilderness experience of Israel when God redeemed them
from slavery in Egypt and brought them through to the promised
land, thereby establishing the pattern for the restoration of God's

people in the return from exile and now through the coming of the Messiah.

JOHN'S MINISTRY (3:3)

John's ministry began in the Jordan region and was primarily a prophetic preaching ministry, and baptism was a prophetic acted parable to illustrate the necessity for spiritual cleansing. His was a call to repentance similar to Elijah's and Isaiah's, telling the nation that they have strayed away from God and must return to him for forgiveness of sins. For John radical sorrow for sin and repentance are the path to renewal and restoration. In the other Gospels his baptism is central, while here his preaching is central, and baptism is a metaphor to illustrate the message of repentance.

Repentance in Luke is a major term for salvation, entailing not only a turning from sin to God but also an ethical mandate for living God's way (3:10–14). The Jews had little awareness of a need to repent. For them baptism was simply spiritual cleansing in a general sense, for they were the covenant people and by national heritage basically right with God. So John's baptism meant their Judaism was no longer sufficient. Forgiveness of sins was the judicial result of repentance, and the Jews did not really feel they needed it. All they needed to do was perform the external rite of presenting sacrifices and offerings to remain right with God.

John's baptism was a brand-new entity. For the Jews it meant general cleansing from the detritus of life, allowing them to worship in the temple. For John it was radical repentance, a new beginning with God, and a one-time event rather than a daily occurrence. There is a difference of opinion as to the antecedents of John's baptism. (1) Some see it flowing out of Jewish washings for cleansing, but while this supplies several parallels and more general background, John is doing something more. (2) Several scholars see it as emulating **Qumran**'s daily immersion that signifies separation from the evils of this world. However, John's was a once-for-all initiation into a new relationship with God and much more than Qumran's practice. (3) Jewish proselyte baptism was also a one-time event and an initiation rite, but it was only for Gentiles, and there is some question as to whether it existed this early. The earliest evidence for this rite is later in the first century.

Most today believe John's baptism was unique to him, a rite ordained by God, which he led John into utilizing. As such it signified the arrival of the messianic age and a new beginning with God. As a "baptism of repentance for the forgiveness of sins" it was *sui generis*, a brand-new phenomenon. So John's choice of baptism for his generating metaphor was a Spirit-inspired decision and undoubtedly quite shocking for most Jews. But he was popular from the start, and people flocked to him from everywhere.

PROOF FROM ISAIAH (3:4-6)

Isaiah 40:3-5 was quite well known among Jews in the first century. It was used also at Qumran (1QS 8:13-14) to justify that community's monastic study of Torah and separation from the rest of Judaism, considering them an apostate people and the temple an abomination to God. It is also the perfect passage for Luke's purposes, picking up several themes from earlier material—the wilderness (1:80; 3:2-3), preparation (1:16-17), the way of the Lord (1:17, 76, 79; 2:31).

Luke sees this passage fulfilled in John the Baptist's ministry (as do the other Gospel writers—Mark 1:2-3; Matt 3:1-4; John 1:23). The early church even drew their title for their movement from John's words in this passage—the Way (Acts 9:2; 19:9, 23; 22:4; 24:14, 22). They viewed themselves as the messianic sect among the Jews, establishing the "way" to meet God and find renewal. Isaiah 40 is the turning point of that prophetic book, moving from the prediction of the exile (39:5-6) to God's promise to "comfort" (40:1) and restore his people. This was to be accomplished in the return from exile. In the new covenant initiated by John and Jesus, a new return from exile would be accomplished, and the first step was taking place in the Baptist's ministry of repentance and his preparation for the coming of Jesus.

John himself is the "voice crying in the wilderness," fulfilled in 1:80 and John's own preparation in his wilderness sojourn. He may have gone there in the first place in order to fulfill this text, but he also wished to relive Elijah's wilderness ministry. The Jews believed the final messianic renewal would begin in the wilderness. "The way for the Lord" is seen here as the highway to Zion, the path to the messianic return from exile that Christ alone can bring about. This is a construction metaphor picturing John removing natural obstacles that stand in the way and produce roadblocks to getting right with God.

This in fact is the meaning of verse 5 (Isa 40:4), describing how God will respond to his people and level the difficult terrain, building that highway to messianic renewal (see Isa 57:14–17; 62:10). This will be a supernatural act, as the valleys, mountains, and crooked roads will all be smoothed. The path will be constructed so apostate Jerusalem can become godly Zion once more when the Messiah comes. This may well be a two-way street. First, the highway is cleared and constructed for the King of kings to come and rescue his people, and then God's people can traverse that road to renewal and revival under their Lord.

Luke is picturing the coming of the Messiah to bring salvation or deliverance to his people. This is found in the closing summary, "And all people will see God's salvation" (3:6). As John and the faithful clear the obstacles, the people of God are enabled to "see" the Messiah come and "God's salvation," which he brings. The Masoretic text (the Hebrew text) of Isaiah 40:5 has "the glory of the Lord will be revealed." Luke reflects the **Septuagint** (the Greek text) instead. Some think Luke did not see God's glory brought about in Jesus' earthly ministry, but that is doubtful. More likely he wished to stress the messianic salvation that came through Jesus. The stress is on "all people," which would include Gentiles as well as Jews. This is a primary message of the two-volume Luke-Acts, that in the coming of Jesus the Abrahamic covenant (Gen 12:3) would finally be fulfilled and salvation brought to "all people." This in fact is how he closes Acts, quoting Isaiah 6:9-10 and then saying, "God's salvation has been sent to the Gentiles, and they will listen!" (Acts 28:26-28).

THE PREACHING MINISTRY OF JOHN (3:7-14)

This ensuing section demonstrates the content of John's preaching, centering on ethical renewal in light of imminent divine judgment on the nation. He begins quite harshly, calling his listeners "you brood of vipers" (literally, "sons of snakes") to highlight the destructive evil (like the serpent in the Garden in Genesis) that has overtaken the nation. This picture is often used of Israel's enemies (Isa 14:29; 59:5; Jer 46:22), and to use it here of Israel itself is a powerful rebuke. Unless swift changes are made, they are headed for the wrath of God. It is time to stop their complacency and "flee" from what they have become. They cannot escape "the coming wrath" merely by going through the motions of the sacrificial system or even of baptism without true repentance. Throughout this passage, language of the Day of the Lord predominates, when God's wrath will descend on a profligate nation. It is time to heed the warnings.

The proper form that renewal must take is first the repentance of verse 3, and it will lead to "fruit in keeping with repentance" here (3:8). A new God-centered ethics is necessary to demonstrate that revival has truly taken place, proved by concrete "fruit" in their daily lives. Moreover, they must stop trusting their national heritage, signified by the claim, "We have Abraham as our father." Proper ancestry will not keep them from the wrath of God. When one is living apart from God, ancestry no longer matters. So John warns them, "Out of these stones God can raise up children for Abraham." God determines who are his children, not national heritage. This image stems from Isaiah 51:1: Abraham is "the rock from which you were cut." That no longer matters when the nation has gone apostate.

So warning is necessitated, for "the ax is already at the root of the trees," a powerful threat of imminent judgment. Several have labeled this "fire and brimstone" preaching. The image is that of fruitless trees that must be cleared out of the way so there is room for the good trees to grow. This is similar to the vine-and-branches metaphor of John 15:1-6, where the branches that have stopped bearing fruit are "picked up, thrown into the fire and burned" (15:6). So here every single fruitless tree "will be cut down and thrown into the fire." These are divine passives; God the Divine Warrior and Judge is the figure swinging the ax. The tree will be destroyed down to its very roots, with fiery judgment the primary biblical image for divine wrath. The wrath of God is a destructive force, and God demands not just verbal adherence but also a lifestyle change observable in ethical living. It is fruit-bearing that counts.

Three groups are central in verses 10-14: the crowds (vv. 10-11), the tax collectors (vv. 12-13), and the soldiers (v. 14). All have the same response from the warning of verse 9: "What should we do?" This is the practical side of repentance. They are properly terrified of the extreme judgment they are facing and realize John has said that repentance must be seen in practical results. Anyone who took the warning at all seriously would have this question first and foremost.

John answers that the crowds should share their possessions with the less fortunate. Concern for the needs of others and social justice are at the heart of the ethics God requires. Possessions and the greed for more are one of the greatest signs of a life dedicated to sin and self. The *chiton* was a sort of undergarment worn under the coat, and the image is that the other person has nothing to cover their nakedness. The reason to wear two is to protect from the cold, and John's demand is to keep the bare necessities and use all excess to help others. The Baptist is using clothes as an illustration of a greater obligation, to refuse to center on material possessions in general, and to use everything we own for the benefit of others.

Let me attempt a covering rule for biblical ethics: Everything we own is a gift from God and given to us primarily to provide us a ministry of helps. All our possessions are meant to be enjoyed, but that pleasure is a two-way street. We receive them from God, and in the words of Ecclesiastes we should "eat and drink and find satisfaction" by accepting and using them as his gift to us (Eccl 2:24). That is completely valid but is the lesser purpose. Primarily, he is giving us a calling to use those possessions to enhance the lives of those around us. That is the greater enjoyment, to be used by God through the possessions he has given us to make other people's lives better. We are to keep those two purposes of our worldly possessions in balance, but the more God gives us the more the balance should shift to almsgiving and helping others. We will come across this principle again and again in our journey through Luke.

The tax collectors now come to John with the same question (vv. 12–13). His answer is quite simple: "Don't collect any more than you are required to." Rome did not collect taxes but instead farmed out the privilege to collectors who bid for the office and then collected extra amounts to make a profit. The temptations were enormous, and collectors were generally called "robbers" by the people (most of them were). Consequently, they were one of the most despised groups in the land. There were two levels of taxation: the direct or poll tax, the amount required for each adult by Rome, and indirect taxes like the sales tax or customs duty when purchasing things. Both were subject to abuse, so Jesus tells them not to defraud when collecting taxes. As we will see with Zacchaeus in 19:1–10, those at the top could get quite wealthy. This is a call to honesty and fairness.

The final response comes from a company of soldiers (v. 14), actually Jewish mercenaries recruited by Herod Antipas (along with tax collectors the most despised group in the land), for they were the sword-arm of the hated Roman Empire. They rarely fought on behalf of the Jewish people but used their power to subjugate them. The foot soldiers were paid very little, so they regularly robbed the people to supplement their income. Rome allowed this to keep them content with their low pay. John's reply assumes this problem, "Don't extort money and don't accuse people falsely—be content with your pay." These were the two means they mistreated civilians, taking money and possessions via the sword, and by fraud (accusing falsely to extort money).

JOHN'S WITNESS TO THE CHRIST (3:15–17)

The excitement and confusion of the crowds in light of John's powerful preaching is completely understandable. Messianic fervor was at an all-time high, and they naturally wondered if he himself was the one and not just the forerunner. In light of Roman intimidation and foreign control, they longed for a deliverer who would redeem them from this terrible oppression. Their expectant waiting went beyond the times to the person who was prominent and provided answers—could he be the one? They sincerely hoped so—the sooner the better! Yet they were uncertain, for John had made no moves in that direction.

So in 3:16–17 the Baptist sets the record straight. He uses his primary metaphor, baptism, as the means of doing so, contrasting his water baptism with the Spirit baptism Jesus the Christ will bring with him. His practice of immersion with water is merely a type of the greater immersion in the Spirit that is coming. The emphasis is on his feeling of utter unworthiness for the messianic task.

"One who is more powerful than I" is virtually a title referring to Jesus' incredibly greater ministry and personhood (on which see 2 Sam 22:33; Isa 11:2). His "coming" is not a reference to his birth but to the beginning of his public messianic ministry. John is saying that his ministry is preparatory, making the way ready for Jesus' arrival. In comparison, he is nothing, not even fit for the lowliest task of all. Not even a slave could be required to untie the straps of a sandal, since a person's shoes collected all the dirt and dust of life and lowered anyone who did so. So John is saying he is not even worthy to be Jesus' slave.

Jesus' baptism is also inordinately superior, for he will baptize
not with water but "with the Holy Spirit and fire" (see also Matt
3:11). Baptism in the Holy Spirit stems from Isaiah 11:2 ("The Spirit
of the LORD will rest on him"); Ezekiel 36:25-27 ("I will put my
Spirit in you"); 39:29 ("pour out my Spirit"); and Joel 2:28 ("I will
pour out my Spirit on all people"). This looks forward to the fulfilment of these prophecies in the coming of the Spirit to inaugurate the new age and in the entrance of the Spirit into the believer
at conversion (Rom 8:14-17).

The added "and fire" could add the idea of the Spirit purging
the people of God to that of salvation, building on Isaiah 4:4-5
(the messianic Branch will cleanse the people) and Zechariah 13:9
("refine them like silver"). It could also add the image of judgment,
with those who reject Messiah and Spirit thrown to the wind like
chaff (Isa 41:16; Jer 4:11-12; Ezek 13:11-13; Luke 3:17). It is likely that
both are present, with humankind divided into those who find
God's salvation and are honed in the purging fire, and those who
reject and are thrown into judgment.

These images are further enhanced in 3:17, the image of Christ
with the "winnowing fork ... in his hand," a pitchfork used to throw
the grains of wheat into the air at harvest time, allowing the wind
(of judgment) to blow away the useless chaff. The good grain will
fall to the ground to be gathered into the barn, while "he will burn
up the chaff with unquenchable fire." Thus all humanity is divided
into the saved and the unsaved at the final Harvest, when Christ
returns, and the consequences are eternal. The emphasis is not
only on the destruction of the useless chaff but also the purging
of the saints on the "threshing floor," that is, the process of cleansing or purging the saints so they are pure "grain."

CONCLUDING EVENTS (3:18-20)

Luke concludes with a summary statement (v. 18) and a final historical footnote (vv. 19-20) that culminates John's ministry. For

the rest of John's earthly ministry he performed the twofold duty of exhorting the Jewish people and proclaiming the good news to them. The exhortation was primarily admonition and warning, for John saw the nation disintegrating into the people of Isaiah's and Elijah's time. He had to warn them of impending judgment, but he also "proclaimed the gospel" (euangelizetō) to them. This is exactly the thrust of gospel preaching in our day. We need as many Johns as we can find in our world, for this combination of warning and promise is always desperately needed.

The story of how his ministry to the Jewish people ended is covered much earlier here than in the others (Matt 14:3-4; Mark 6:17-18). Luke wished to show that the Baptist's ministry ended just before Jesus' began. It is slightly out of order, since the baptism of Jesus clearly occurred before John was arrested. But his message is correct at any rate. Mark 1:14 echoes the point: "After John was put in prison, Jesus went into Galilee, proclaiming the good news of God." Luke's set of comparisons is complete—John leads to Jesus in the announcement of birth, in the birth itself, and now in their ministries. John is indeed the messianic forerunner.

Luke tells the story simply, without all the detail of Mark 6:14-29 or Matthew 14:1-12. John again relives the story of Elijah, this time in his opposition to the wicked deeds of Ahab and Jezebel (1 Kgs 21:1-28). He goes up against Herod Antipas, tetrarch of Galilee, for his adulterous liaison and marriage of Herodias, former wife of his half brother Philip. So it was both adultery and incest (Lev 18:16; 20:21). Luke then adds a note not in Mark or Matthew, that he also condemned Herod for "all the other evil things he had done." Since his opposition was public, he became a real threat to Herod, and as a result Herod "locked John up in prison" and eventually beheaded him. This is the same Herod who questions Jesus during his trial before Pilate (23:7-12), so his career is primarily known for his opposition to everything Christian. Like Pilate, he is vastly eclipsed by the very ones over whom he has earthly power.

JESUS IS BAPTIZED (3:21–22)

The next two sections (the baptism and genealogy) flow together by centering on the revelation by the heavenly witness of God (vv. 21–22) and the earthly witness of ancestry (vv. 23–38) that Jesus is actually not just Messiah but also Son of God. As with the Baptist's arrest, Luke has a truncated version compared to Matthew 3:13–17, not even telling us that John is the one who baptized him. He presents Jesus almost as just another person baptized by John (v. 21a, "when all the people were being baptized"). Here his immersion into the waters of divine anointing/commissioning is secondary to the heavenly witness that follows. Grammatically, all of verse 21 consists of subordinate clauses modifying the heavenly voice of verse 22.

By submitting to John's baptism Jesus identified with the human dilemma (Matt 3:15, "to fulfill all righteousness"), which caused consternation among many church fathers at the idea of his identifying with sinners. But he is identifying himself as the solution for sin, the answer to fallen humanity's need to repent. In addition, his baptism is an anointing of itself, a commissioning to his messianic ministry.

Luke highlights four aspects: (1) Jesus is a man of prayer. Luke will stress his prayer life throughout his account, and his communication here is a two-way street. Jesus here reaches up to heaven via prayer, and God responds by reaching down to earth via heavenly testimony. Jesus will be in prayer before every single major event in his ministry (e.g., 5:16; 6:12; 9:18, 28; 11:1; 22:41).

(2) "Heaven was opened." This imagery usually depicts a major biblical event as heaven enters our world in a new way. It is an **eschatological** image for divine revelation (Isa 64:1; Ezek 1:1; John 1:51; Rev 4:1). In Mark 1:10, heaven opens as Jesus is coming out of the water; here, as Jesus is praying. When Jesus prays it is a world-changing event. Likely the entire event was seen by the early church as a cataclysmic intersection of heaven with earth. God is pictured as intervening to create a new world order.

(3) The Holy Spirit descending on him in bodily form like a dove. Only Luke tells us the onlookers actually saw a dove coming down. This is not a vision but the actual sighting of a dove. Numerous suggestions have been made as to the meaning of this. One is that it refers to the dove that went out after the flood in Genesis 8:8–12 and showed that the earth was once more habitable. Another identifies it with the *bath qol*, "the daughter of the voice" in Judaism, an epithet for the rabbinic interpretation of Scripture. The best option is to combine Genesis 1:2 (the Spirit of God hovering over the waters at creation) with the Spirit as a symbol of Israel (Hos 7:11), thus the inauguration of the new age with the coming of the Christ, God's Son. There is a new reality, a new creation, entering this world.

(4) The heavenly voice declares, "You are my Son, whom I love; with you I am well pleased." This sentence combines Psalm 2:7 ("You are my Son; today I have become your father") with Isaiah 42:1 ("Here is my servant, whom I uphold, my chosen one in whom I delight"). Jesus as Messiah is both Son of God and Servant of Yahweh. The heavenly witness affirms him and his ministry at the very start of his public work. The voice is speaking both to Jesus ("you are" in Mark and Luke) and the onlookers ("this is" in Matthew). I think each group actually heard it addressed to them.

Luke's highlighting of the Father's words stresses three aspects: the witness to Jesus as Son of God, the notation of the deep love in which he is held by God, and the great pleasure he gives his Father. The heavenly Father is giving a ringing endorsement to his special Son and wants to make certain everyone realizes it at the very beginning of Jesus' ministry. From Psalm 2:7, God is saying that Jesus is the Chosen One for all three reasons. No one is better qualified to represent his Father and conduct a heavenly ministry on the earth. Jesus is clearly the God-man, whom God has sent to initiate the age of salvation.

LUKE PROVIDES JESUS' GENEALOGY (3:23-38)

This section begins with the comment that "Jesus himself was about thirty years old when he began his ministry." As I said in my comments on 3:1-2, Jesus was born about 6 BC, and he entered his public ministry (along with the Baptist) in the fifteenth year of the reign of Tiberius Caesar (3:1), or about AD 28, so he would have been thirty-four. Luke says "about thirty years old" because that was the age of David when he began his reign (2 Sam 5:4) and the age when a priest would began his service (Num 4:3). The point is that Jesus entered his messianic office at the proper age for beginning ministry.

Luke's genealogy is quite distinctive from Matthew's. The latter begins his Gospel on the note of Jesus' Abrahamic and Davidic ancestry and proceeds upward from Abraham to Jesus, organized in three groups of fourteen names. Luke's of course comes at the beginning of Jesus' public ministry and proceeds via seventy-seven quite distinctive names in the opposite direction, from Joseph down to "Adam, the son of God." Many construct eleven groups of seven names each, but there are no natural lines of demarcation for such an organization.

While some have tried to argue that Luke provides Mary's line and Matthew Joseph's line, that does not fit the lists themselves. Genealogies always proceed from the father, and that is the case in both lists. It begins, "He was the son, so it was thought, of Joseph." This means that Jesus was not the natural-born son of Joseph, since he was born of a virgin. Still, he was the official adopted son and heir. This is a legal line rather than a bloodline, and that was perfectly sufficient.

Matthew's names are primary dynastic figures to stress Jesus' royal ancestry, while Luke's are unknown and common names for the most part to stress Jesus' humanity and identification with all the peoples of earth. The emphasis is not on identifying the people but on their common humanity with Jesus—all are sons of Adam, and all are completely dependent on Jesus to find salvation. He is the Savior of the world (John 4:42) and not just of the Jews.

The most identifiable portion of the list occurs at the unique Lukan material from Abraham to Adam. From the patriarchs (Judah, Jacob, Isaac) and from Abraham to Shem (3:34b–36a), the names come from the genealogy of Shem's family line in Genesis 11:10–32. Then from the final list of names, from Shem down through Adam in 3:36b–38, the names are taken from Genesis 5, the genealogy of the family tree from Adam to Noah. Where Matthew and Luke cover the same period, namely, from Joseph to David (3:23–31a) and from David to Abraham (3:31b–34a), we do not know the source of nearly half of the names. Though the others are paralleled in Scripture, we know nothing about nearly all of them, with a few exceptions (like Nahum and Zerubbabel). These names may be drawn from family records existent at the time, for most families of note, especially those in the Davidic line, had such family lists.

Some scholars say there is little or no emphasis on Adam, but that view is very difficult to maintain. In fact, that is one of the three primary emphases: (1) Jesus as Son of God, with God publicly proclaiming him as the beloved Son on the one side and Satan testing his sonship on the other side. (2) Jesus as the archetypal representative man, the second Adam, identifying with the whole human race and summing up humanity as it should be in himself. (3) Jesus as son of David, the quintessential messianic figure, and as the child of Abraham's line, true Israel. Luke does not stress his royal messianic origins, for he has Nathan rather than King Solomon as "the son of David" (3:31). David's heirs were a disgrace and came under divine judgment. The promise of the Davidic covenant that God would "establish the throne of his kingdom forever" (2 Sam 7:13) was fulfilled through the Davidic Messiah rather than through the bloodline, for the royal line ceased due to sin. In Luke's genealogy the kingly Messiah came through the common line of David, not through the royal line.

It is terrific to meditate on a comparison between the world rulers of verses 1-2 and the peasant prophets John the Baptist and Jesus. To the world they were nothing, not worthy even of a glance. Yet no two figures in history have ever had a greater impact. Even secular historians recognize the impact of these two.

John deliberately spent several of his years leading up to his ministry in the wilderness, modeling himself after wilderness prophets like Elijah. His was an austere prophetic message (like Elijah's), calling the nation to repentance while there was still time. As he entered his ministry, he preached a message of repentance centered on a brand-new kind of baptism, a one-time anointing that signified a radical repentance and ethical renewal (vv. 3-6). This was an exciting innovation that was intended to bring revival to the Jewish people. This has since become a basic Christian belief, but we need to get back to these fundamentals and rediscover John's exciting message for a church that too often resembles the cold people John was trying to revive. We need that same revival in our time.

We also desperately need to rediscover John's ethical mandate (vv. 7-14). Too many half-hearted church members have grown complacent, and many preachers today ignore material on divine judgment for sin in favor of more positive messages, forgetting that such material is false when directed at people living in sin. We are reenacting the people of John's day. The "ax is already at the root of the trees" (3:9) for us as well, and we had better wake up. All three groups in verses 10-14 had the same problem: greed. That characterizes a consumer society like ours even more than John's original audience.

The rest of the chapter centers on Jesus, presented by John as the far more important one sent by God. John's water baptism was in reality preparation for the Spirit baptism of Jesus, which would become a holy fire purging and cleansing the saints and a fiery judgment on those living apart from God (vv. 16-17).

The baptism of Jesus by John is an anointing for ministry, signifying both his identification with the human condition and need for redemption and the messianic work by which he will bring that redemption to pass. The emphasis is on the descent of the Spirit, inaugurating the age of salvation, and the testimony of God as to the true significance of his beloved Son. His baptism is so much more than a commissioning at the hands of John. It is a trinitarian act.

Luke's genealogy (vv. 23-38) is unique, not a royal genealogy like Matthew 1:1-7 but Jesus' human ancestry, showing his common roots with all humanity, Gentile as well as Jew. He is Messiah, but Luke does not emphasize him as royal Messiah so much as the Redeemer of all people. Primarily, he is Son of God, with his special filial relationship with the heavenly Father making him uniquely prepared for his messianic work. He is also the second Adam, the one who is uniquely able to bring all humanity to God. His scope is not restricted to Israel. His genealogy shows he is sent to comprehensively unite all the peoples of the earth and provide redemption for them.

THE TESTING OF GOD'S SON
(4:1–13)

This is regularly called "the temptation narrative," but that is not quite correct. Temptation only covers Satan's part, and that is not even the main point of the story. In reality, Satan is a tool of God, and he accomplishes God's purposes here. It is the Spirit who leads Jesus into the wilderness, and God is testing his Son before he embarks on his mission. Throughout Luke God and the Spirit are the prime movers, and in the immediately preceding episode the Spirit descended on and God testified about Jesus, God's Son. This is a trinitarian section, and these are trinitarian events. Jesus the Christ is announced by his Father, empowered by his Spirit, and is victorious over Satan at the very start of his mission. Note the progress of the **Synoptics**—"sent" by the Spirit in Mark 1:12; "led" by the Spirit in Matthew 4:1; and, a twofold thrust here, both "led" and "full of" the Spirit.

It is common for critical scholars to label this a **midrashic** legend, but that is a worldview problem, not a literary conclusion. If one accepts that there is a God and a demonic realm of evil, there is no reason to deny Jesus telling his followers of just such an attack by Satan. The cosmic war with Satan informs the entire New Testament and permeates every level of it. It is very important that we not only accept the reality of this scene but that we reorder our lives accordingly and conduct ourselves in light of our own spiritual warfare against the demonic powers of darkness.

Jesus as Son of God is highlighted in the baptism, the genealogy, and the testing narratives, a unique feature of Luke's contribution to the Jesus story. He undergoes the very testing that Israel experienced in the wilderness and throughout the Old Testament. God tested Abraham in the "binding of Isaac" episode (Gen 22), Moses in the wilderness of Midian (Exod 2–3), and Job throughout his story. Now God is testing Jesus in the wilderness to prove his faithfulness and obedience, and he will succeed where Israel failed.

Typology is at the heart of this narrative in three ways. First, Jesus is the second Adam, and similar to Romans 5:12–21 he succeeds where Adam failed and provides the strength to overcome. Second, he is the new Moses, with "the high place" (3:5; Matt 4:8, "very high mountain") recalling Moses on Mount Nebo (Deut 34:1–4), and Satan showing Jesus the world's kingdoms reflecting that passage where God showed Moses the surrounding lands. Jesus' forty-day fast in 4:2 recalls Moses in Exodus 34:28. Third, he is true Israel, the central theme here. Jesus' three responses to Satan are all drawn from Deuteronomy 6–8, where Israel failed the same three tests (see below). Jesus as the Son of God is the antitype of Israel, God's Son (Exod 4:22; Jer 31:9; Hos 11:1). Jesus suffers the same hunger and misfortunes as Israel and endures the same testing as God's Son. As God's Messiah as well as Son, he overcomes and shows the way to victory when following God.

LUKE INTRODUCES THE SETTING (4:1–2)

The Spirit has descended on Jesus (3:22), and as a result he is "full of the Holy Spirit." His trip into the wilderness is not conducted on his own, but he is "led by the Spirit into the wilderness," undoubtedly to emulate Israel, Moses, and Elijah as he is tested by God. In his test he will take on his cosmic adversary, Satan, and as the Divine Warrior he will begin his ministry by defeating Satan in open combat. The Spirit has been central, filling Elizabeth (1:41), Zechariah (1:67), John (1:15, 80), and Simeon (2:25-27) in the infancy narratives, and now descending on (3:22) and launching Jesus with power as he prepares for his own mission.

In Mark the Spirit forcefully "impels" or "casts Jesus out" (*ekballei*) into the wilderness, while in Luke the Spirit "guides" or "leads him" as he goes into the wilderness. The Spirit both empowers and directs him as he passes through God's tests. The wilderness is the perfect arena for these tests, and virtually every test in the Old Testament (Israel, Moses, Elijah) took place there.

Luke notes two particular tests in verse 2. First, Jesus went through a forty-day temptation at the hands of the devil, emulating Israel's forty years in the wilderness (Deut 2:7; Num 14:34) and Moses' forty-day fast (Exod 34:8; Deut 9:9). Second, and connected to the first, he "ate nothing during those days," like Moses above and Elijah (1 Kgs 19:5, 8). There is double meaning in *peirazō*, both "tempted" by Satan and "tested" by God. By the end of that time, Jesus "was hungry" and like Israel more susceptible to the temptation. The key is that while Israel failed her test, Jesus will succeed and point the way to victory for us. Jesus will prove his worth as the Son of God, overcome the failures of Adam and Israel, and demonstrate for Luke's readers how to find victory. This latter point is secondary here but still part of Luke's larger purposes. Primarily, Luke is stressing that at the beginning of his ministry Jesus is completely victorious over the powers of evil.

JESUS IS TEMPTED THREE TIMES (4:3-12)

There is some question about order, for Matthew and Luke reverse the second and third temptations. Most believe Matthew preserves the original order, following a geographical/spatial progression from the wilderness plain to the pinnacle of the temple and then the high mountain. Luke wishes to climax with the temple temptation, fitting his emphasis on Jerusalem as the goal of Jesus' ministry. He follows the order of the Deuteronomy material (8:3 followed by

6:13, 16, with the latter two reversed in Matthew), and also in Psalm 106, with the bread temptation following 106:13-15 (the manna and quail), the temptation to worship Satan corresponding to 106:19-23 (the golden calf incident), and the temple scene corresponding to 106:32-33 (Meribah).

The book of Deuteronomy provides the theological heart of the story, encompassing a series of homilies proclaimed by Moses on the plains of Moab as Israel was about to enter the promised land. He reinterprets the Torah and stresses how the daily conduct of Israelites must reflect God's laws. He demands covenant renewal in light of the failures that have kept the nation in the wilderness. The faith of earlier times must be reproduced and transmitted to later generations. In particular Deuteronomy 6-8 provides the backdrop here, with the three citations taken from 8:3; 6:13; and 6:16 in order.

The chapters progress from the necessity of loving the Lord your God and proving it by obeying his instructions (ch. 6) and then by driving out the opposing Canaanite nations. In other words, chapters 6-7 list internal problems and external problems to following the Lord. Then chapter 8 returns to the internal life of the people and stresses the danger of forgetting the Lord. The three citations of Jesus identify specific areas where Israel failed the test and Jesus, as true Israel, will pass the test.

THE FIRST TEST: TURN STONE TO BREAD (4:3-4)

The devil waits until Jesus is quite hungry and then strikes: "If you are the Son of God, tell this stone to become bread." *Peirazō* has double meaning here. As the antagonist, the devil's task is to "tempt" Jesus, but as the tool of God it is to "test" Jesus. Jesus, filled with the Spirit, must rely on God to help him withstand the pressure. Satan does not doubt Jesus' status as "Son of God" as proclaimed by Gabriel (1:32, 35) and attested by God himself (3:22).

The devil's "If you are the Son of God" uses a condition-of-fact *ei* ("if") that assumes the reality of the statement, thus saying in effect, "I know you are God's Son, and you know you are God's Son; now prove it to everyone around you." The temptation is subtle but clear, telling him to use his office selfishly and perform a miracle just to satisfy his hunger. The devil wants him to ignore his obedience to his Father and center on his own desires. Like many wealthy and powerful people in our day, he is tempted to assume his privileges and go beyond the wilderness miracle of manna by turning the rocks themselves into bread. It would not be a God-performed miracle but a selfish act.

Jesus' response is drawn from Deuteronomy 8:3 and the typological representation of Jesus as true Israel. In that chapter Moses challenged the nation to remember past failures and avoid them as they enter the promised land. Here Jesus uses the verse "Man shall not live by bread alone" to tell Satan he is fully aware of what he is doing—that tactic worked with Israel; it will not work with Jesus. Unlike Israel, he will not allow life's situations to determine how he responds to God's will. The saying is not just a practical principle but an oracle from God ("it is written"). Israel's hunger led to rebellion and complaints (Exod 15:24; 16:2–3). Jesus is typologically reenacting that conflict, but as true Israel he refuses to allow "bread alone" to define his existence. He will not ignore his father in favor of his earthly needs. Submission to his Father and his mission has absolute priority.

THE SECOND TEST: WORSHIP SATAN (4:5–8)

Here the devil tries to seduce Jesus into idolatry by promising to give him early what would one day be his anyway. In Matthew 4:8 the setting is on a "very high mountain," evoking imagery of Sinai. In Luke the devil leads "him up to a high place," possibly so the pinnacle of the temple will be the highest point (4:9). There he shows Jesus all the world's kingdoms "in an instant," pointing to a vision. It becomes a comprehensive offer of worldly power, with Rome and the other world powers at stake. The scene is reminiscent of Deuteronomy 34:1–4, where, just prior to his death, Moses climbs to the top of Mount Nebo across from Jericho and is shown "the whole land" by God.

Satan's promise is to give Jesus "all their authority" as well as their "splendor," in other words, universal power over this world. He arrogantly claims that "it has been given to me, and I can give it to anyone I want to." But does the devil actually have this authority? Paul calls him "the god of this world" (2 Cor 4:4) and "the ruler of the kingdom of the air" (Eph 2:2), and in the Gospel of John Jesus calls him "the prince / ruler of this world" (John 12:31; 14:30; 16:11). His offer is for temporary, earthly power rather than eternal authority. It is God's world, not Satan's, but God has allowed Satan certain dominion over it (Dan 10:13, 20–21), as seen in the divine passive "it has been given to me" = "God has given this to me." He is offering Jesus political rule in exchange for allegiance to him. Jesus would then become a political Messiah, virtually the antichrist/beast of 1 John 2:18; Revelation 13.

God had promised Jesus universal dominion (Dan 7:13–14; Rev 11:15) as well as "all authority in heaven and on earth" (Matt 28:18), but that would come after his second coming. This way he could have it early without having to endure the cross. He would surrender being the Suffering Servant and get to be King of kings immediately, but to do so he would have to switch his loyalty from his Father to the devil in a way similar to Absalom's rejection of David. He would have to "worship" Satan (4:7) by bowing down and giving obeisance to him as Jesus' new god, always Satan's final goal (as in Rev 13:4, 8; 14:11; 16:2; 19:20). Idolatry was the terrible primary sin of the apostate Jews, seen in the first commandment, "You shall have no other gods before me" (Deut 5:6–8); or in Deuteronomy 6:10–15; 8:11–17, warning God's people not to forget him or follow other gods.

Jesus' response in 4:8, "Worship the Lord your God and serve him only," has all this in mind, and specifically Deuteronomy 6:13. Israel is there reminded not to commit rebellion and idolatry as they did at Massah and Meribah (Deut 6:15–16, from Exod 17) and

at the golden calf (Exod 32). Idolatry never failed to bring tragedy to Israel, and Jesus was not about to accede to this horren-
dous proposal.

THE THIRD TEST: CAST SELF FROM PINNACLE (4:9–12)

The movement of the three temptations has been from the plains
to a high place and now to the pinnacle of the temple. There have
been several suggestions as to which part of the temple this was.
Perhaps it was a balcony over one of the temple gates, or the roof
of the temple, but most likely this was the royal portico on the
southeastern side with a 450-foot drop down to the bottom of the
Kidron Valley, so steep that people would get dizzy looking over
it (Josephus, *Antiquities* 15.411–12). The devil challenges Jesus to
prove his divine Sonship by casting himself down. No spectators
are present, so this is a personal rather than corporate test.

This seems a ridiculous challenge at first glance, but Satan then
quotes Psalm 91:11–12. Jesus has twice corrected the devil by quoting Scripture, so Satan now turns the tables on him. This is part of
a threefold series of psalms (90–92) at the beginning of book 4 of
the Psalter on the tragedy of the exile, with this psalm celebrating God as "my refuge and my fortress" (91:2) and petitioning him
for protection from the vagaries of life. So this promise of divine
protection is the heart of Satan's test, asking Jesus to prove that
the angels will indeed "guard you carefully" and "lift you up in
their hands, so that you will not strike your foot against a stone."

Again, Satan is misusing the promise because in reality Psalm
91 centers on the responsibility of the faithful to depend on the
Most High God while the devil wants Jesus to perform a self-centered act and use God for his own ends. Several have noted a further irony in the **Septuagint** version of the psalm (Ps 90 LXX), in
which the "pestilence that stalks in the darkness" (v. 6) is defined
as "the noonday demon," referring to deliverance from the powers
of darkness. So Satan is using a psalm that in Jewish tradition is
directed against him and his fallen angels.

Jesus' response in 4:12, "Do not put the Lord your God to the test," is taken from Deuteronomy 6:16. This was directed at the necessity of Israel's fearing God and serving him only, lest his wrath "burn against" them (Deut 6:15a) again as it did at Massah when the people had "tested" God and were destroyed (6:15b–16). Once more Jesus succeeds where Israel failed, reenacting Israel's test and determining not to repeat Israel's failure. He is the obedient Son, passing his test by refusing to test God.

THE TEMPTATION IS CONCLUDED (4:13)

The devil was now "finished" with "all this tempting," utterly defeated by the superior force and greater moral power. He is out of options and is forced to leave Jesus and wait "until an opportune time" once again arises. He had exhausted all his ammunition, with nothing at all to show for it, for the Divine Warrior had deflected every salvo. Nothing remained but ignominious retreat and admission of total failure. In Luke, the devil only appears occasionally (10:18; 11:18; 13:16) until the passion events, when he will become aggressive again (23:3, 31, 53). Jesus has proved the adage, "Resist the devil, and he will flee from you" (Jas 4:7). Yet the point here is not that we do this in our own strength. Rather, it is that Christ has done it for us, and our victory comes when we completely depend on the Triune Godhead and draw strength from him.

———

There are two errors in the way people have used this story. Many have thought the main point is discipleship, that like Jesus we can defeat Satan by resisting him. Others have reacted and gone too far by saying this is entirely **christological**, telling how Christ began his ministry by completely defeating Satan. The truth is in the middle: Jesus is true Israel demonstrating how to defeat Satan for the new Israel (the church) by obedience and faithfulness to God. He proves himself as Son of God and the Divine Warrior (the primary thrust), showing us how we can win the victory as well (the secondary thrust).

There are two themes in this. The primary theme is that the Divine Warrior has engaged the devil in open combat and won an absolute victory in a "war of words" centered on the "double-edged sword" of the word of God (Heb 4:12). In doing so, he has begun his messianic ministry by proving he is the Son of God. This scene is a true "combat myth" similar to Revelation 13 between two heavenly powers, with Jesus emerging as *Christus Victor*. He conducts his ministry from this moment as a "binding of Satan," an authority that he will pass on to us (Mark 3:15; 6:7). The secondary theme is that Jesus is the true Israel, modeling spiritual victory for the new Israel (Christ followers). Jesus as the last Adam has reversed the failure of not only Israel but also Adam (Rom 5:12–21), enabling believers to find victory over human frailty and the tendency to sin (1 Cor 10:13). He saw himself also as true Israel reenacting the wilderness temptations so that we as new Israel could rise above the same temptations that defeated the wilderness generation in their forty-year sojourn in the desert. By yielding ourselves completely to him, we become overcomers.

The three temptations here fit the three types in 1 John 2:16— "the lust of the flesh [the stones into bread], the lust of the eyes [showing Jesus the kingdoms of the world], and the pride of life [forcing the angels to protect him]." These were also the three temptations that defeated Eve in the garden in Genesis 3:6: the fruit as "good for food" (lust of the flesh), "pleasing to the eye" (lust of the eyes), "desirable for gaining wisdom" (pride of life). In other words, these are the archetypal temptations we all experience, and Christ here has shown us how to find "a way out" (1 Cor 10:13).

Jesus has passed the test, been approved by God, and begins his ministry at this point with an initial victory over Satan. In the Gospels, V-day occurs at the beginning of the war.

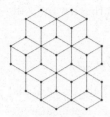

JESUS' EARLY MINISTRY IN GALILEE
(4:14–44)

Jesus' ministry in Galilee (4:14-9:50) builds on Mark's outline. More and more believe that the actual chronology of Jesus' public ministry is found in John, and that in reality Jesus regularly went to Jerusalem for the festivals (as John 1-11 shows). The coverage in the **Synoptic** Gospels likely begins about nine months to a year after he began, and those early months are found in John's Gospel. We cannot know why it is this way, but most speculate that Matthew, Mark, and Luke want to center on Jerusalem as the place where Jesus yields his life as the atoning sacrifice and so omit those other aspects.

Luke like the others concentrates on Jesus' Galilean ministry as he works with his disciples and challenges the crowds to follow him. Jesus the Christ is Lord and Savior but also Teacher as he reveals himself step by step to those he encounters. Coming to Jesus involves believing, confessing, and emulating him in one's life. The first half of this section (4:14-6:49) centers on the assembly of his apostolic band and their training via the Sermon on the Plain (6:7-49), Luke's equivalent to Matthew's Sermon on the Mount. A critical side note is the growing rejection and opposition he receives from the leaders, the counter-note to the symphony on discipleship. The rest of the material traces the call to faith and confession, centering on Jesus' authority and call to discipleship.

JESUS RETURNS TO GALILEE (4:14–15)

Jesus was conceived by the Spirit (1:35), filled with the Spirit at his baptism (3:22), and empowered by the Spirit as he faced Satan in his time of testing (4:1). The "power of the Spirit" continued to galvanize him as he returned home. As we move to his public ministry, there is movement from the Spirit working through the prophetic ministry of others (Simeon, Anna, and John) to Jesus' direct, inspired teaching throughout his ministry. The power of the Spirit is with him every step of the way. As Jesus' ministry is launched under the power of the Spirit, so will the church in Acts find their ministry initiated by the Spirit (Acts 2).

Jesus was already becoming famous ("news" here is *phēmē* = English: "fame"), as reports about him began to spread everywhere. Mark 1:28 tells us this came about because he demonstrated an entirely new depth of authority in word and deed (1:22, 27). He quickly gained a following. The truth is that gifted speakers in the first century provided the major entertainment for people, as evidenced by the "soapbox" speakers in the marketplaces of every city. Yet Jesus had so much more, and his spiritual depth and power to work miracles as well as his speaking ability mesmerized all around him.

In his case, it was not in the marketplace but the synagogue where he made his reputation. This is in keeping with the Jewish way of life, seen in the synagogue teaching by rabbis. Jesus quickly became one of the most popular "rabbis," as he was regularly labeled (interestingly, not in Luke, but compare Mark 9:5; 10:51; John 1:38, 49; 3:2). It says here that "everyone praised" his synagogue messages. So the first thing we learn about this speaking is the prowess he brought to it. This tendency to speak in the synagogues will continue in Acts with Stephen and Paul. The synagogue practice was not like churches today. They did not have regular officials whose task was preaching. Rather, they asked well-known leaders (often visitors) to speak, and that's what Jesus did. He became renowned very quickly.

JESUS GIVES HIS INAUGURAL ADDRESS IN NAZARETH (4:16-30)

The tone that will dominate Jesus' public ministry is established here. The themes introduced here will be seen again and again: Jesus as the Spirit-inspired fulfillment of Scripture, his message of liberation for the oppressed in the new age of salvation, the Jewish rejection of him, and his turning to the Gentiles. Many consider this a Lukan creation, but the parallel incident in Mark 6:1-6 and Matthew 13:54-58[1] provides corroboration for the view that it actually happened. It has all the earmarks of a realistic narrative, and there is little reason to think it a product of the imagination.

THE SETTING (4:16-17)

Jesus had already moved to Capernaum (a more central city) and become well known, so as he returns to his hometown, he is asked as a highly respected teacher/rabbi to read the Scripture lesson and comment on it in the local synagogue. Nazareth was a small village with about four hundred inhabitants and only dirt roads, but like all places with at least eleven males (the traditional number demanded for a synagogue), it had a synagogue. Like his parents, Jesus was quite pious and attended the synagogue regularly. Upon visiting his hometown, he would naturally go to the synagogue in which he had grown up. In fact, in Acts the Jewish believers continued to attend synagogue, and it became a major center of evangelistic activity.

Services included the singing of a psalm, opening prayer, the confession of the Shema (Deut 6:4-9), further prayers, and

---

1. It is hard to know whether these are the same event or two separate and similar events. I tend toward the latter, but either is possible.

readings from the Law and the Prophets. Some have posited a regular liturgical cycle of Scripture readings, but there is no real evidence of this, and probably Jesus chose which passage he wished to read and comment on. The reading would be from the Hebrew, then an Aramaic translation (called the Targum; people no longer spoke Hebrew), followed by an exposition on the text by the one who had read it. At any rate, the Isaiah scroll was handed to him. Each Old Testament book had its own scroll. Synagogues would only have as many scrolls as they could afford, and most were unable to purchase all the scrolls. Jesus turned to Isaiah 61 and read the first two verses to the congregation, then commented on their meaning.

The Passage Chosen (Isaiah 61:1–2) (4:18–19)

The first three lines follow Isaiah faithfully. While not one of the Servant Songs, this chapter is still closely linked with Isaiah 42:1–4, and Jesus clearly sees himself as the Servant of Yahweh and as the Spirit-inspired prophet (the major emphasis of Luke's first four chapters) who is introducing the Spirit as bringing about the new age of salvation. The Spirit then has "anointed" Jesus (= his baptism in 3:21–22), and as *Christos* means "anointed one," this is the very essence of his person. This was a messianic anointing, and his public ministry was a messianic act.

The mission the Spirit has given him is threefold, all interrelated: to "proclaim good news to the poor ... freedom for the prisoners ... recovery of sight for the blind." The three terms describing the content of the preaching build on each other: freedom and recovery of sight depict the salvation results of the good news. With this the age of the Spirit has indeed come into this world. The same is true of the recipients of this gift of salvation. The prisoners and the blind further describe the "poor" for whom Christ has come.

Christ does not have in mind just the economically poor but all whom society has marginalized and ignored. They do not just consist of those imprisoned in Roman jails but those chained and mistreated in general in an evil world, and the blind are not just those who cannot see but those blinded by the darkness of sin. Christ is promising true spiritual liberation from the shackles of sin and of the social injustices that characterize this evil world. We will be commenting in the miracle stories that follow that in healing people's diseases Jesus is proclaiming "freedom for the prisoners" of the evil effects of sin in this world.

Several differences accrue between Isaiah and what Christ reads here: (1) Jesus omits "to bind up the brokenhearted," the second item in Isaiah, possibly because the point is made again in the following "freedom for the prisoners." The result is greater emphasis on Jesus' mission "to proclaim good news to the poor" as the governing idea here. (2) Jesus inserts Isaiah 58:6, "to set the oppressed free," which serves as a composite summary for the social and spiritual results of his mission. The actual verb is "to release the oppressed," an important verb for describing Jesus' ministry of release and liberation. (3) He omits "the day of vengeance of our God" after "the year of the Lord's favor," probably to center on God's salvation and liberation.

The final note, "to proclaim the year of the Lord's favor," brings in imagery from the Year of Jubilee, that year after forty-nine, or seven sevens, described in Leviticus 25 as a harbinger of the final age in which all wrongs are made right and all transgressions forgiven. Christ means that "the year of the Lord's favor" has come with the dawn of the messianic age, the coming of salvation and of the Holy Spirit. In this new age, people will be set free and made right with God, inheriting eternal salvation. While there will be a social dimension to it, it primarily refers to spiritual reform and rejuvenation. Jesus is speaking of deliverance not from Rome but from Satan and the evil powers.

Jesus' Teaching (4:20–21)

Following synagogue practice, Jesus rolls up the scroll and hands it to the attendant. His sitting down was not to end the reading but to begin the teaching. Rabbis sat down to teach (Luke 5:3; Mark 4:1; Matt 23:2), so when he does so, everyone readies themselves to listen, using a strong term *atenizontes*, "intensely fastened on him." For the rest of this section, the reaction of the people will spiral downward from amazement and doubt (v. 22) to anger (v. 28) to an attempt to kill him (v. 29). This too will become almost a standard set of reactions as the people marvel at the power of both his words and his deeds and yet reject the messianic content.

He begins by proclaiming, "Today this Scripture is fulfilled in your hearing." He sees himself as the subject of Isaiah's prophecy, and "today" (*sēmeron*) stresses the "now-ness" of salvation (compare 2:11; 5:26; 12:28; 19:5, 9; 23:43). He is virtually announcing the initiation of the messianic age. "In your hearing" means that in the very exposition Jesus was at that moment giving, the age of fulfillment was in process of coming to pass. His very words were themselves a completion of the true meaning of Isaiah's prophecy. In Jesus and his message God's salvation has arrived.

REACTION AND RESPONSE (4:22–27)

Jesus' neighbors begin with a positive reaction. Obviously, his exposition was much more extensive than Luke's single comment in verse 21, and the people are "amazed" at his rabbinic gifts and at the "graciousness" of his words about Isaiah 61. One of the things I can't wait to do when I get to heaven is listen to sermons like the one Jesus preached here. It was almost certainly one of the truly blessed messages of history, and the result is that everyone "speaks well of him."

Their added comment "Isn't this Joseph's son?" is often misread by commentators because it is interpreted in light of the parallel in Mark 6:3, where, "Isn't this the carpenter? Isn't this Mary's son?" indicates rejection due to the fact that he had grown up in Nazareth and couldn't be the rabbi and miracle worker he had become. Some go so far as to retranslate "speak/testify well of him" as "testify against him." But this ignores the added "at the gracious words," which tells us they were pleased with him at this stage.

So "Joseph's son" should not be taken negatively as a rejection of Jesus for being just a village youth at one time. It is just the opposite at this initial stage (though it later becomes negative). They are here filled with wonder and actually filled with pride as well that the son of the village carpenter who himself followed in his father's footsteps could become such a gifted rabbi. It is with Jesus' response that they turn angry and oppose him.

Jesus' response is surprising in light of the "gracious words" he had spoken earlier in his exposition. It is this that causes the reversal in their attitude toward him. The key to the change in approach is seen in their demands he quotes in verse 23. Jesus had said that the Isaianic promises were coming true in him, but he has not yet shown that in his deeds in Nazareth. They had heard reports of the miracles he performed in Capernaum, and they want to see that for themselves in Nazareth. So by telling them that they will "doubtless" say, "Physician, heal yourself," Jesus points out that they will demand that he prove by his deeds what he says he is. They are not satisfied with just "gracious words"; they are demanding miracles. Several interpreters think they are showing skepticism about the reports from Capernaum, and that makes sense here. They doubt him and are saying in essence, "Put your money where your mouth is."

So Jesus in 4:24–27 responds to their skepticism with a strong rebuke. He begins with the first *amēn* saying in Luke (also 12:37; 18:17, 29; 21:32; 23:43). These sayings provide divine self-attestation to the truth of a solemn saying and can be translated, "I am telling you the exact truth." *Amēn* means "so be it" and is also used to confirm the truth at the end of a prayer, meaning, "May it be so." His statement is an important maxim confirming the rejection of a prophet by "his hometown," namely, the apostate nation that is rejecting God along with the prophet. So Jesus turns their demands around on them and accuses them of opposing God's prophet in league with the Israel of old.

He then gives two examples of prophets rejected by their own people, Elijah and Elisha (vv. 25-27). Both had similar ministries to the Baptist and Jesus, calling the nation from its sins back to God, and both had no success until they were sent to two Gentiles, the widow of Zarephath (Elijah) and Naaman the leper (Elisha). The first story took place in 1 Kings 17-18, during Ahab's evil reign when God cursed Israel with a severe three-and-a-half-year drought and famine. There was such evil that God led Elijah outside Israel to Sidon and a Gentile widow, who alone was receptive to Elijah. The parallels to Jesus' rejection in his own hometown are obvious.

The second incident with Elisha parallels the first (4:27). In 2 Kings 5:1-14 he is sent outside Israel to the Gentile commander of the army of Aram, Naaman, who has leprosy and again alone is open to the work of God. So the Gentile is healed but no one from Israel, for they are opposed to Elisha. Jesus is making two points: when the people of Israel reject God and oppose his prophet, they likewise are rejected by God. Also, God will then turn to the Gentiles for a people who will respond to his prophet. So this too points to the Gentile mission.

REJECTION OF JESUS (4:28-30)

The implications are quite clear: Jesus is equating the people of Nazareth with the apostate Israel of Elijah's time. They respond with fury at the obvious implications. The implicit prophecy that Jesus would turn to the Gentiles caused even more intense anger, similar to what will later happen to Paul when he tells the people of Jerusalem that God in his Damascus road vision was sending him to the Gentiles (Acts 22:21-22).

Somehow they construe his severe rebuke as blasphemy (4:29) and decide they must put Jesus to death. Probably they thought that any rebuke of them constituted rejection of God. The Romans did not allow subject nations to execute people, though the Jews did get away with it in the stoning of Stephen (Acts 7:58–59). They would undoubtedly decide it wasn't worth the effort, much as with Stephen's murder. This was much more of a lynching even than with Stephen,[2] for in Acts 7 it was at least the biblical punishment for blasphemy (Lev 24:13–16). Still, in Deuteronomy 13:5 it says a person who "incites rebellion" should be put to death. Some could have been thinking of that. At any rate, they "cast him outside" (*ekballō*, the verb for casting out demons; NIV: "drove him out") the city (anticipating Jesus' crucifixion "outside the city," Heb 13:12), to the top of a hill with the intention of throwing him to his death. Clearly to them Jesus is a false prophet deserving of death.

In verse 30 Jesus simply "walked right through the crowd" and goes about his business. This is reminiscent of John 7:30, 44; 8:20, 59; 10:39, where no one could seize him "because his hour had not yet come," that is, the hour of his God-appointed destiny on the cross. That is certainly the implication here as well. As Moses and the Israelites passed through the waters of the Red Sea, so Jesus passed through the teeming, hostile crowds. It is also possible (as some surmise) that Luke wants us to see this as a foretaste of the resurrection, with God rescuing Jesus from death, here through miraculous escape, there through the even greater miracle.

JESUS TEACHES AND PERFORMS MIGHTY DEEDS IN CAPERNAUM (4:31–44)

Summary: Teaching with Authority (4:31–32)

These verses describe the "news" that spread everywhere in 4:14. Capernaum was the primary city of that section of Galilee (likely about 1,500 inhabitants) situated on the lake and a trade center for fishing and agriculture. Like the region, the archaeological site shows no evidence of wealth. Still, it was a natural site for Jesus'

---

2. Some think their intention was to throw Jesus down and then stone him, but we cannot know for sure.

headquarters in Galilee, and he (and possibly his team) took up residence there. It is often thought he had not yet begun assembling his apostolic band, but that is unlikely because John 1:35–51 has him calling Simon and Andrew and Philip and Nathanael soon after his baptism when he spent a few days with his cousin the Baptist.

Luke begins with synagogue ministry. Interestingly, "Sabbath" is actually plural "Sabbaths" (*sabbasin*) and could be summarizing ministry on several Sabbaths. However, the plural can act as a singular, as in 4:16 above, and the setting here is more likely his ministry on one particular Sabbath. Either way, the emphasis is on the effect his teaching had on the townspeople. They reacted with shock and awe, for Jesus' "authority" (*exousia*) was so much more evident than with the average rabbi. Scribes and rabbis (as in the later Talmud) would teach by following tradition and summarizing various interpretations, while Jesus "told it like it is" and revealed the actual meaning of the texts. Undoubtedly, he was also an excellent orator who galvanized the people, much like John the Baptist had done.

The Exorcism of a Demon (4:33–35)

The next four episodes draw out the events behind the "news" of 4:14, and Luke takes them from Mark 1 (1:23–28 = 4:33–37; 1:29–31 = 4:38–39; 1:32–34 = 4:40–41; 1:35–38 = 4:42–43). The authority of Jesus' deeds follows closely on the authority of his words. Mark and Matthew center on a demon-possessed person in the Capernaum synagogue. The Gospels often call demons "unclean spirits" to stress their evil nature; there is nothing good or pure about them. They are also "spirits" because they are not human and have no physical body.

Whenever demons have any contact with Jesus, their reaction is always immediate and severe. They recognize him for who he is and realize that cosmic war has now come to them. They also recognize a superior force and must fight for their very place in this world. So this scene is one of spiritual warfare from beginning to end. The demon "cried out at the top of his voice," as if the volume of his cry is a weapon to be used against Jesus.

The opening particle *ea* could be an interjection like "Hey!" or "Ah!" but is better seen as an imperative of rejection like the NIV, "Go away!" The demons want nothing to do with Jesus. They know they cannot defeat him, so they just want him to leave them alone. The phrase that follows (*ti hēmin kai soi*) literally means "What is it to us and to you" and is used in the Old Testament (Josh 22:24; 2 Sam 16:10; 1 Kgs 17:18) and by Jesus (John 2:4) as a distancing mechanism to mean, "We have nothing to do with this" or "Why bother us?"[3] The plural "us" recognizes that this is a "world war" taking place, with the entire demonic realm involved. Some think "us" also includes the man, who could also be destroyed in the battle, though I find that somewhat doubtful since Jesus (and the demon knows this) was going to liberate the man by casting out the demon. The true danger to the man is if the demon is allowed to remain in control.

A battle is taking place, for the demons a war of words. They realize Jesus' intention and so say it outright, "Have you come to destroy us?" Demons cannot be killed; they are eternal beings. But they can lose their place of power and be cast out. The tactic for avoiding this and defeating Jesus in this skirmish is for the demon to reveal the true essence of Jesus and by uttering this to gain power over him. As some describe it, as with ancient magical rites and incantations the name of the god or demon can be a means of discovering the hidden essence of a person (encased in their name) and thus of gaining the upper hand and forcing the supernatural being to do your will. So here by uttering, "I know who you are — the Holy One of God," a name of Jesus revealed by Gabriel in 1:35, the demon thinks he can force Jesus to do his bidding. But in his

---

3. The NIV translation, "What do you want with us?" is a little weak. It should be more some sense of "Leave us alone; we have nothing in common."

holiness Jesus is the antithesis of this evil, impure being. As the Holy One, Jesus is filled with the Holy Spirit, and the demon's ploy cannot possibly work.

The binding of Satan (Mark 3:27 = Luke 11:21–22) begins in verse 35. The demon is seen prattling on and on, trying to find some formula that will allow him to regain the advantage. Jesus makes two simple commands, "Shut up" and "Come out," and the demon is immediately overpowered and has to leave. There are none of the complicated formulas uttered by Jewish (and later Christian) exorcists. Jesus doesn't need such things, and later (Mark 3:15; 6:7) neither will his followers. His word is law, and the demon has to obey. The demon was not trying to tell others who Jesus was, only gain power over him. So those who say Jesus did not want his name publicized are probably wrong. This is a power game, not a public-relations battle.

The demon can no longer shriek like he did in verse 33; he has been struck mute by Jesus. So all he can do as a final act of defiance is throw the man down unhurt and now clean of impurity. There are several such exorcisms in the Gospels, and all are in a sense a "show and tell" of the binding of Satan. With Jesus' arrival, the power of the dark forces is broken, and Satan's hold as "god of this age" (2 Cor 4:4) begins to unravel. Our task is to wake up a slumbering church and make them aware that this process has just begun, and we fight real battles with the cosmic forces of evil every day. We spend all our time on earth's battles, and as one of my colleagues once put it, are "pragmatic atheists when it comes to Satan," knowing he exists but living as if he is not around. That is the source of all too many spiritual defeats, as C. S. Lewis makes clear in *The Screwtape Letters*.

REACTION AND RESULTS (4:36–37)

The amazement we have seen in virtually every scene (1:21, 63; 2:18, 33, 48) continues here, as people say, "What words these are!" It is interesting that they center on what Jesus said more than on what he did. Still, it is his authority and power in both word and deed that causes the wonder. They were used to demons overpowering people, and suddenly with seemingly little effort Jesus drives the evil power far away. For him to command the "unclean spirit" effortlessly, and the immediate submission that they saw on the demon's part, shocked them. He has broken the power of Satan's realm once and for all. The present-tense "commands" and "come out" mean this is not a single act on one occasion but an ongoing power of Jesus over the powers of darkness. Things will never be the same.

The result of this is fame, as the reports spread "throughout the surrounding area," meaning all of Galilee. This is a major theme in Mark 1 and is also emphasized in Luke (4:15, 32, 40, 42). As with the Baptist, people cannot get enough of Jesus. They flock to him from everywhere. In Mark 1:45 we are told that the crowds were so great that he "could no longer enter a town openly but stayed outside in lonely places," where crowds could more easily gather.

ITINERANT MINISTRY IN GALILEE (4:38–44)

Peter's mother-in-law healed (4:38–39)

This is the first appearance of Simon Peter in Luke, and Luke assumes his readers will know who this later major Christian figure was. We know Peter had joined Jesus' team very early and been with him from the start (John 1:40–42). Peter had grown up in nearby Bethsaida (John 1:44), but probably Capernaum was his current residence, and Jesus may have made his home his own residence as well.

First Corinthians 9:5 tells us Peter was married, and his wife often accompanied him on his mission trips. His mother-in-law, who probably also lived there, had fallen ill "from a high fever." In those days that would be quite serious. It was also believed that such illnesses were a sign of divine displeasure (Deut 28:22), so some may have read this as a spiritual as well as a medical problem. They had often seen Jesus perform mighty works, so it was natural

they ask him "to help her." This was the same Sabbath day as the
casting out of the demon, so this is a healing on the Sabbath, but
probably because this is early in Jesus' ministry and takes place
in a private home, it does not produce the negative reactions that
will occur later.

As before Jesus is in complete sovereign control of the circumstances. He simply "bent over" her and "rebuked" the disease,
using the same verb, *epetimēsen*, as in the "rebuke" of the demon
in 4:35 (NIV: "said sternly"). The language actually continues the
language of demon possession, with the fever in control and Jesus
rebuking it so that it "left her" like the demon did the man in 4:35.
Luke isn't saying this too is an exorcism, but he is connecting the
two incidents.

She is immediately well, arises from the sickbed "to wait on
them." She is fully restored and shows her gratefulness by caring
for Jesus and his disciples.

Multiple miracles (4:40–41)

This is now the evening of that Sabbath day, and in 4:31–41 Luke
follows Mark in tracing Jesus' multifaceted ministry on a single
Sabbath at the start of his public work. Due to the "news" that had
spread everywhere (4:14), people from all around brought their
sick to him, and as sunset arrived he was suddenly confronted
with a multitude of different ailments, including more demon
possession. Jesus' compassion is seen in the fact that he devoted
individual attention to each one.

Luke writes that in healing them he was "laying his hands on
each one," a frequent practice (Mark 5:23, 41; 6:5; 7:32; 8:23, 25; 16:18;
Luke 13:13). Interestingly, it was not practiced much in Judaism
but was in **Hellenistic** circles. Probably, Jesus saw it as a helpful
practice, for it made his intimate concern for the sick that much
clearer. Physical contact was an aid to healing.

There were also several demon-possessed people brought to
him, and there the atmosphere was not personal care but violent

confrontation. In keeping with the screaming of 4:33, the demons nearly always shrieked as they fought to gain some power over Jesus. There the demon called him "the Holy One of God"; here they go more deeply into his divine essence and call him "the Son of God," still trying to gain some control over him. Needless to say, nothing works, for Jesus is the absolute Sovereign over the underworld as well as this world.

Luke adds that Jesus "would not allow them to speak, because they knew he was the Messiah." The reality of his messianic office is the theme of all four of these early chapters. Jesus does not want that made known by the demons. In regard to Mark scholars have called this "the Messianic secret," his desire that his true nature not yet be made known. Everything the demons did was to obstruct rather than enhance his messianic work. There were only two things to be done with the fallen angels: silence them and cast them out.

Concluding aspects of his ministry (4:42-44)

As Luke brings this early part of Jesus' ministry to a close, he concludes with two aspects of Jesus' work: his desire for regular private times (Mark 1:35—with his Father in prayer) and his determination to reach the Jewish people with the good news of the new era he is introducing. There are two poles of his ministry, private and public.

John came out of the wilderness with his message of repentance. To Jesus as well, the wilderness was a place of retreat and divine comfort, so he now goes there for some private R & R. The crowds (ochloi, almost a technical term for the "people" who flock after him). In the parallel Mark 1:35-37 it is the disciples who come and get him, but Jesus in Luke has not yet called them and formed his team. As stated above, many of them have been chosen, but they have not yet been assembled as a band of disciples. Their motivation is in direct contrast with the people of Nazareth and their violent rejection of Jesus—they are trying "to keep him from leaving them." So his Capernaum ministry begins on a positive note. Still, this doesn't mean they are what we would call "seekers." They were interested in his mighty works more than with his words of salvation.

Jesus establishes right here the contours of his ministry (4:43). Again he centers on the divine necessity (*dei*, "must"; see 2:49— the term occurs eighteen times in Luke). God has ordained him not to be a local prophet but to be a worldwide proclaimer of good news. Luke highlights two aspects of that task. First, he "was sent," *apestalēn*, a divine passive that means God commissioned and sent him to preach the gospel. He is not in control of his mission; God is, and thus he must travel to "other towns" with his God-given mission.

Second, he is proclaiming "the kingdom of God," a term that occurs thirty-seven times in Luke-Acts. God's reign has entered this world, and it has arrived with the coming of Christ. At the same time, it is a future entity that has not yet come with finality. It will be consummated at the second coming. Here it is inaugurated. God's reign has begun and is in process of initiating his salvation in this world. This message encapsulates the preaching of Jesus and of the apostolic preaching in Acts (8:12; 19:8; 20:25; 28:23, 31).

His ongoing ministry from this point on is "preaching in the synagogues of Judea" (4:44). He cannot remain in one place, for his is a universal mission of bringing salvation to all Jews and indeed to the whole world, as we will see throughout Luke-Acts. It is strange that Luke has "Judea" rather than "Galilee," as in Mark 1:39. Jesus in Luke does not go to Judea until he enters Jerusalem for passion week. Still, in Luke the term "Judea" is often used for all the territory of the Jews, Galilee as well as Judea (6:17; 7:17; 23:5; Acts 10:37; 26:20). Jesus is commissioned by God to begin a universal mission to all peoples.

We now see Jesus' messianic ministry unfolding, and he begins with an inaugural synagogue sermon in his hometown of Nazareth (4:16–30). He chooses Isaiah 61:1–2 because it defines the goals of his ministry, to alleviate the suffering of the poor and liberate those held captive by the results of sin in the world. These themes define his miraculous ministry as a whole, for they include all three areas—captivity to Satan, to physical illness, and to spiritual sin.

Things begin well but rapidly go south. The people of Nazareth are pleased at the "gracious words" of his sermon and proud that "Joseph's son" had done so well for himself as to become a famous rabbi. But everything turned poorly when Jesus rebuked them for their demands that he perform miracles to prove he was God's prophet as well as a rabbi. Their desire was not to follow him but to see spectacular deeds, and there was no faith or belief involved. They set the tone for future confrontations throughout Galilee by trying to put him to death for blasphemy. So strong a reaction so early in Jesus' ministry is shocking, but it will typify future reactions as well. In fact, it sets the tone for the rest of the church age. We too will experience the reaction of the people of darkness to the light of Christ in us (see John 3:19–20). Darkness hates light and will always seek to eradicate it.

The casting out of the unclean spirit in the Capernaum synagogue is another programmatic event, establishing the contours of spiritual warfare not just for Jesus' ministry but for the life of the church in every age. These fallen angels have one major desire, to defeat God's people and take them into bondage. Jesus sets the standard for all of us. We cannot tolerate demonic activity but must oppose it wherever we encounter it. Christians must stop pretending all is well and ignoring the signs around us. That almost got us defeated in both world wars, and the effects will be even more devastating in the cosmic war. The fact is that Jesus has already bound Satan, and all we have to do is rely entirely on him and the Spirit's empowering presence to have victory in our lives as well.

The rest of Jesus' early ministry (4:38-44) centers on both proclamation and action in several venues, homes, synagogues, and open-air ministry. His is a ministry of power, exhibiting a God-given authority in word and deed and accompanied by the presence and power of the Spirit. The demons are cowed in his presence, and a mere word from the Lord overpowers them. This is the beginning of a worldwide, not just local, phenomenon.

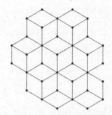

DISCIPLESHIP AND CONFLICT
(5:1–6:11)

This material combines a story from Luke's L material,[1] namely, 5:1–11, with four conflict narratives taken from Mark 2:1–3:6. All of these episodes begin with the literary notation *egeneto*, "it came to pass" (NIV: "one day," 5:1, 12, 17; 6:1, 6, 12), which links these together as a single larger unit. Luke's purpose is to show how Jesus began his ministry by choosing disciples and confronting the leaders, who are increasingly offended when Jesus keeps taking liberties with their traditions (see below). Some think all of this section concerns discipleship, but apart from the calling of Levi, 5:12–6:16 centers more on the controversies with the Jewish leadership. So this section weaves together the positive reactions of Jesus' followers (5:1–11, 27–28; 6:12–16) with controversy stories (5:12–16, 17–26, 29–32, 33–39; 6:1–5, 6–11) to show the breadth of reactions to Jesus that will characterize his ministry to the people of Israel.

JESUS CALLS HIS FIRST DISCIPLES (5:1–11)

Luke has replaced Mark 1:16–20 with this story of the miraculous catch of fish and then placed it later in the narrative because he

---

1. One of the scenes Luke uncovered, investigated, and used. See Luke 1:3 and "Sources" in the introduction.

wished to continue the parallels with John the Baptist and show
Jesus' ministry before followers joined his team. In this way there
are now five parallel scenes: the announcement of the two births
(1:5–25, 26–38), the songs of praise (1:46–56, 67–79), the births themselves (1:57; 2:1–20), the presentations (1:59–66; 2:21–40), and the
Galilean ministries (3:1–20; 4:14–44). In all of them, John is the
great prophet called by God to initiate the new era, while Jesus is
the greater prophet and Messiah called by God to fill the new era
with its salvation content.

Jesus has established his own ministry and been incredibly successful, and now he invites disciples to join his team. While there
are similarities with Mark 1:16–20 (the lake scene, the call of disciples, the phrase "fish for people," the disciples leaving everything),
the differences in the fishing scene and the miraculous catch are
sufficient to make it likely this is a separate story Luke borrowed
from his special sources (1:1–4).

THE SETTING (5:1–3)

Jesus' popularity continues to grow, and a crowd mobs him, "listening to the word of God," a favorite Lukan phrase for the proclamation of the gospel and Scripture (see 8:11, 21; 11:28; Acts 4:29,
31; 6:2, 7; 8:14; 11:1). This is the first step to discipleship, but in itself
it is not enough, for hearing without obedient response gets us
nowhere with God. Jesus is teaching by "the Lake of Gennesaret,"
the local name for the Sea of Galilee, named for the region south-
west of the lake. It is a fertile lake known for its fishing, and is
about thirteen miles long and seven miles at its widest.

As the crowd grows, Jesus looks for help and spies two boats
at the water's edge that had just come in from a night of fishing.
The fishermen were "washing their nets," scraping the seaweed
off them and cleaning them up so they wouldn't dry out and crack.
A boat from that period recently discovered was 25.5 feet long, 7.5
feet wide, and 4.5 feet deep, with four oars and a capacity of ten

people. These fishermen had two to a boat, so room for a lot of fish. They had caught none that night.

All four were disciples of Jesus, and he chose Simon's as a make-shift pulpit for his preaching of the good news. In verse 3 we have Simon's preliminary obedience, the next step to discipleship. We must remember that he and the others had been fishing all night and undoubtedly were exhausted, simply wanting a good sleep. To say yes to Jesus' request to row him out a way so he could teach the crowd was certainly the last thing Simon wanted to do. His willingness to do so was pure sacrifice on his part. Jesus sat in the boat to teach, the normal position when rabbis taught.

RADICAL OBEDIENCE AND MIRACULOUS RESULTS (5:4–7)

Simon and the others were professional fishermen, and Jesus was a carpenter. Yet he commandeers the boat for a ridiculous adventure, saying, "Put out into deep water, and let down the nets for a catch." Everything about this command was wrong. You fished at night, not during the day, because when the sun came up and the water started to get warmer, the fish went deeper. Not only that, but for this "deep-sea" fishing they used a heavy trammel net that would need both boats and all four fishermen. Such a large net would be easily seen and avoided during the day. Still, this was a very deep lake, and the nets could not go deeper than twenty feet or so. They had caught nothing that night even at the good time for fishing. Every little detail spelled failure, and they would have been justified to laugh at Jesus' request. The first command ("Put out") is singular, addressing Simon alone, but the second ("let down the nets") is plural, addressing all of them and both boats. This is really about discipleship, and the focus is on the fishermen who will become disciples rather than the crowds.

Simon hints somewhat at the problematic command in verse 5, saying, "Master, we've worked hard all night and haven't caught anything." He realizes, needless to say, that the command is not at all practical. Not only that, but if they throw out the nets again, they will have to go through the tedious task of washing the nets a second time. Who knows when they would get to bed! But that is exactly Jesus' purpose. This is all about obedience rather than about fishing. Their fishing is a metaphor for ministry (as we will see in v. 10), and their radical obedience is the key to this story. What they do in their own strength (fishing all night) ends in failure, but when they respond in obedience to their Master, it turns into amazing success. It is mainly the disciples who acknowledge him as Master (8:24, 45; 9:33, 49), and it typifies their surrender to his sovereign authority.

What Simon says in the rest of the verse is the center point of this story: "But because you say so, I will let down the nets." Recognizing Jesus is his Master and submitting to what seems a ridiculous order are the true key to discipleship. God asks us to surrender completely to him, even when it does not seem logical. The leading of the Spirit is an essential component of success in ministry.

The results (5:6–7) are immediate and beyond the disciples' wildest imaginations. It would have been amazing to catch anything at all, but they "caught such a large number of fish that their nets began to break." I doubt if that had ever happened before. This episode could be called "The ones that didn't get away!" The number of fish, in fact, is so great that the disciples have to call out to the other boat on shore to come and help them. When they arrive and both boats are filled to the very top, the weight of fish is so great that both boats begin to sink. When we get to heaven and are talking to Simon and the others, I guarantee that they will all say that in their many years as professional fishermen, they never came close to as great a pair of catches as the two here and in John 21. Jesus' omniscience was in full view; he knew exactly when and where to throw the nets. Moreover, God put the fish there at exactly the right time.

The theme for us is quite clear: when we totally surrender to God, wondrous things will happen.

DISCIPLESHIP AND RADICAL HUMILITY (5:8–10A)

The astounding miracle makes Peter spiritually aware. He now sees Jesus for who he truly is, and it overwhelms him. He "fell at Jesus' knees and said, 'Go away from me, Lord; I am a sinful man!'" His reaction demonstrates Jesus' words in John 16:10 regarding the Spirit's convicting the world "about righteousness, because I am going to the Father, where you can see me no longer." The Spirit confronts us with the supreme righteousness of Jesus and our unrighteousness.[2] Peter no longer felt worthy to be in Jesus' presence. In fact, every great leader has to go through just this kind of epiphany and confess their utter sinfulness in order to get right with God, like Moses (Exod 3:5–6), Isaiah (Isa 6:5), and John the Baptist (Luke 3:16). So Peter sees in a new way the lordship of Christ and fully surrenders to him.

The basis of this astonishment (a primary theme, see 2:18, 47–48; 4:22, 32, 36) is "the catch of fish they had taken" (5:9). They are filled with awe at the demonstration of Christ's power over nature. We can only imagine how, as people who had spent their lives on the lake, they had dreamed of such an event since they had been small children. And it was this carpenter/rabbi who had made it come to pass. They realize the compassion and mercy of Jesus and his Father and can only react by falling at his feet. As with Moses and Isaiah this is a virtual commissioning of Peter for the ministry that would dominate for the rest of his life.

The other two members of the "inner circle" of the disciples are now introduced. These three will be present at the transfiguration and other major events, so this is the core of the apostolic band.

---

2. This is the only time in Luke his full name will appear. Peter is the name Jesus was to give him as a prophecy that he would become the "rock" (the meaning of Cephas/Peter) of the church (see John 1:42; Matt 16:17–18).

Andrew was probably also present (as he was in Mark 1:16–20); he would have been part of the "we" in verse 5a but is not named here because Luke wished to focus on the inner circle of three. They are all called "partners" here (Greek: *koinōnoi*, the word for "fellowship"), meaning the two boats were part of a fishing business.

THE CALL TO A NEW FISHING ENTERPRISE (5:10B–11)

They are about to sign a contract for a new fishing business never before contemplated on planet Earth, and they will have a much larger group of "partners." Jesus first calms their fears, as Gabriel did to Zechariah, Mary, and the shepherds in 1:13, 30; 2:10. The miracle takes on the cast of a theophany (a manifestation of God) as it reveals Jesus as the God-man who controls nature; and as always when God is revealed in all his glory, the people present are filled with terror (here seen in Peter's reaction, 5:8).

The commissioning of Peter[3] to his new "business" is quite imaginative, a wonderful way to couch the task of evangelism. Jesus is saying that as of that very moment ("from now on") the disciples' old life is over and a new life has been initiated. This parallels Isaiah 6 and Ezekiel 1–2 as an anointing to office. The wording is different from Mark 1:17, "fish for people." The verb *zōgreō* here means to "capture alive," as in "you will catch people alive." So this is a new kind of fishing and a new catch of fish, reversing the Old Testament metaphor for judgment (Jer 16:14–16; Ezek 29:4–5) and switching to a hunting image for rescuing people from danger and death. So they will be engaged in an entirely new kind of fishing in which they will turn people from the death of sin to the new life of Christ.

Their response is the final step to discipleship. When they got to shore, they "left everything and followed him." Theirs was a radical commitment to Christ, and they surrendered "everything" to

---

3. The verbal idea is singular, centering on Peter, but the others are implied in the context.

follow him. All four fishing partners entered the new partnership with one another and Jesus, and it involved a universal mission, for the whole world became an ocean of "fish" to net for God and rescue from eternal death. These former professional fishermen, as several interpreters have pointed out, now become "amateur fishermen" who now must sit at the feet of the Master and learn this whole new way of netting people for God.

We must also carefully qualify the meaning of "left everything." This is not meant in an absolutely literal way, akin to St. Francis of Assisi's rejection of every earthly possession. Peter owned his own home, and John 21 tells us they kept their boats and continued to fish when not engaged in ministry. We will be discussing the issue of possessions many times in this commentary, for Luke has a special interest in this issue. According to Luke, Jesus has complete priority over our possessions, and while we enjoy the material blessings God brings our way, they are primarily meant to be shared with others, not consumed just for personal pleasure. Still, when Zacchaeus, a very wealthy tax collector, came to faith, he gave away half his possessions (19:8), meaning he still kept a fortune. Wealth is not a yoke around our necks; it is an opportunity to serve God and others with our largesse.

JESUS HEALS A LEPER (5:12-16)

Jesus' authority and power continue, and he follows Mark 1:40-45 closely in this story. Leprosy in the first century covered a large number of skin diseases like lupus, ringworm, or psoriasis. Hansen's disease, what we call leprosy today, was just one of many. In Leviticus 13:2 "leprosy" is described as any "swelling or a rash or a shiny spot on their skin," so a lesion or swollen area would have been considered leprosy. This was seen in the Jewish law as defiling the person, and everyone they touched also became unclean (Lev 14:46). So when the individual went anywhere, they had to cry "unclean, unclean" so people could make sure they didn't inadvertently make contact and themselves become defiled. It was a debilitating disease, physically and socially, for the person was ostracized (Lev 13:45–46) and often had to live outside the town (Exod 4:4; Num 5:2–3). It was considered an extreme punishment from God and could only be healed by God.

THE HEALING (5:12–14)

You can see the man's desperation in his reaction to Jesus, falling face first to the ground and begging, "Lord, if you are willing, you can make me clean." Priests and rabbis were obviously not required to cure a leper, and Jesus could have refused to help. Probably others did refuse, because again no one dared touch the man. It took courage for the man to come to Jesus, because everyone expected him to avoid all such contact, and anyone who noticed would vilify him. He also believes completely in Jesus, for he is the second person to address Jesus as "Lord" (after Peter in 5:8) and says, in effect, "If you want, you can do it." In light of the seriousness of leprosy, this is an amazing confession of faith. He clearly sees that Jesus wields the power of God in his healing ministry. The only question is whether Jesus wants to do it, not whether he can do it.

Jesus' response shows his awareness of the man's faith: "I am willing. ... Be clean!" Note that he is not just healing the man; he is pronouncing him "clean" of defilement as well. Jesus truly has the authority of God behind him, dealing with the physical and the spiritual/religious at the same time. In the Old Testament God often stretches out his hand as well (Exod 3:20; 7:5; Deut 4:34; 9:29; Ps 136:12), which signified the power to do wondrous things. As in 4:40 Jesus uses touch to heal the sick, not caring that that was supposed to render him unclean as well. As God's Son and Messiah, he was impervious to such things.

As with Peter's mother-in-law (4:39), the man was "immediately" healed. Jesus then orders that he tell no one (as in Mark 1:44) until he sees a priest and can be officially declared clean and able to reenter society. There are probably two reasons for the silence:

the legal demand to see a priest and Jesus' desire that his ministry not become a circus with people constantly wanting spectacular miracles. This kept taking place throughout his public ministry and was a major distraction.

Instead of publicizing the miracle, Jesus wanted him to follow
Torah injunctions by getting a priest to declare him clean and
then offering the required sacrifices from Leviticus 14:3–7. He
would bring two birds and sacrifice the one. Then he was to dip
the other with scarlet yarn and hyssop in the blood of the one sacrificed, sprinkle the blood seven times on the one who had been
healed, and release the bird. The defilement would fly off with
the freed bird.

REACTIONS TO THE HEALING (5:15–16)

Mark 1:45a tells us the man disobeyed and spread the news everywhere, but Luke simply says in general that "the news about him
spread all the more," repeating the notes from 4:14, 37, regarding his growing fame. The point in both Mark and Luke is that
when the healing power of Jesus removes all sickness and infirmity,
you simply cannot keep quiet. You have to tell everyone you meet
about the wondrous thing God has done for you. As in Mark 1:45b
the result is that the crowds flocking after him become so large
that Jesus has to withdraw. There it was to minister in the wilderness area, where there was room for the multitudes to gather.
Here it is for times of prayer with his Father. Jesus' prayer life will
become another major emphasis of Luke, and we will see Jesus
praying before every major event in his life (6:12; 9:18, 28; 11:1;
22:41; 23:34, 46).

JESUS HEALS A PARALYZED MAN (5:17–26)

It is common for critical scholars (for instance, the Jesus Seminar)
to doubt the historicity of this event, since it combines the miracle
with Jesus' authority to forgive sins. That, however, is hardly necessary, for Jesus' awareness of himself as both authorized for God's

mission and as the Servant of Yahweh would naturally include the authority to forgive sins. Everything we have seen in Luke thus far leads to this; it is the next viable step in Jesus' ministry, and the opposition of the Pharisees shows the realistic nature of the scene.

THE SETTING (5:17–19)

We are now introduced to two other major groups in the Jesus drama, the Pharisees and the scribes or teachers of the law. The next several episodes center on controversies over the law, and with each one the opposition to Jesus grows more intense. In Mark especially but also in Luke there is a strong contrast between Jesus' popularity with the crowds and his rejection by the leaders. This all begins here.

The Pharisees were a lay order that developed out of the *Hasidim* (pious ones) of the Maccabean period and consisted of strongly orthodox Jews who took a particular interest in protecting the law from pagan influences. They called this "building a fence around the law," which made it easier for people to keep it. As a result, they developed an "oral Torah" or set of traditions to guide the general populace in keeping the law. The teachers of the law were the lawyers of their day, experts in the Torah and mainly Pharisees who were recognized for their knowledge. For them the law was not a theoretical entity but a practical one, so they interpreted the regulations in terms of everyday life. They were especially strong on Sabbath rules and the purity laws. They had developed thirty-nine rules (calling them "forty-minus-one") for keeping the Sabbath holy. Several of them are featured here.

They were watching Jesus closely, suspecting that he would be a false prophet and teacher. So they were looking for things to criticize, and they quickly found them. They had come from all over the Jewish world to listen to Jesus and hear what he had to say, but they were far more interested in indicting him than in learning from him.

Luke stresses that "the power of the Lord was with Jesus to heal the sick," and this is a perfect lead-in for the paralyzed man on a mat. So once more his authority in word is interwoven with his authority in deed. It is God who is behind Jesus, and woe to those so-called religious experts who rise up against him.

Mark 2:3 relates that four men carried the paralytic on the sleeping mat, undoubtedly one on each corner. The problem is that there are so many gathered around Jesus, both officials and people from the crowds, that they couldn't get to him through the number crowded around the house. The answer was very simple. Homes back then had flat roofs consisting of mud and clay with thatch packed on top of boards or tree limbs. Moreover, the stairway up was in the back and on the outside rather than the inside of the house. The roof would even become a living room or dining room at times. So they just went around the back of the house, up the stairs, dug through the dirt roof, and removed a few boards, then lowered him to Jesus.

Luke says they "lowered him on his mat through the tiles into the middle of the crowd, right in front of Jesus." Tiles were used in Greek homes, and Luke could have been simply using a term that would be more easily understood in a Greek setting. Or this could be a Greek home. We simply cannot know for certain. Luke's main thrust is the faith of these men, and their ingenuity in getting through to Jesus.

The Controversy and Healing (5:20–24)

Jesus deals with the spiritual side before the physical. Note the faith is not just with the crippled man but with those who brought him as well ("*their* faith"). This does not mean that Jesus assumed his illness was the result of sin. Still, this is how the people around him would have understood it. In one sense this is true, for sickness and death are the result of sin entering this world. At any rate, the faith in Christ of the crippled man and his friends who bore him meant they were also dealing with their relationship with God, and so Jesus declares, "Friend, your sins are forgiven."[4] When Luke said God's power to heal came on him (5:17), it meant spiritual healing as well as physical. As in Psalm 103:3, God is a compassionate Lord "who forgives all your sins and heals all your diseases."

This caused a great deal of dissension with the Pharisees and scribes, who said to each other, "Who is this fellow who speaks blasphemy? Who can forgive sins but God alone?" (5:21). Since forgiveness is an essential component in salvation, it is very serious indeed, and the Jews believed forgiveness could not come from the priest or any person but from God alone. People receive forgiveness when they perform rituals such as sacrifices, and priests can pronounce that it has occurred, but only God can actually declare a person forgiven. So Jesus was making himself equal with God and was thus a blasphemer, which in Judaism entailed mocking or defiling the name of God. Jesus did so by taking on himself what only God could do, thus reviling the glory of God, and that constituted blasphemy.

Jesus was fully aware of what they were thinking (another example of omniscience) and so decided to fulfill 2:35 and "reveal" their thoughts (5:22–23). He challenges their reasoning; he is the prophet, not them; he has the mind of God in this. He asks, "Which is easier?" (*eukopōteron*, "the easier work" or "easier to do"). It is a little difficult to understand the reasoning behind this, for on the surface one would think truly forgiving sins is the harder thing to do. The key is the difference between saying and doing. It is easier to talk the talk than to walk the walk. So Jesus does the harder and heals the man as evidence that he can truly proclaim the man's sins forgiven. He is both miracle-working prophet and the Son of God.

The healing then follows as proof of his authority over both the physical and spiritual realms (5:24–25). The language "But I

---

4. For some reason, though the faith is with them all, Jesus addresses only the man as forgiven. He may have meant his companions as well by implication.

want you to know" (Greek: "That you might know") is drawn from Moses' confrontation of Pharaoh on behalf of God (Exod 7:17; 8:10, 12; 10:2), especially in Exodus 9:14, which adds, "so you may know that there is no one like me in all the earth." These Pharisees and scribes, like Pharaoh, are going against God and will soon learn just what they are up against.

This is the first instance of the Son of Man title in Luke, which is the most common title Jesus uses for himself in the Gospels (eighty-three times in all, twenty-five in Luke). He likely preferred it for its ambiguity and freedom from political considerations. It could be seen in its Ezekiel background, where it is used ninety-three times for "mortal human," or its use in Daniel, where it is a glorified quasi-divine title with overtones of majesty and universal dominion (Dan 7:13-14). It has both aspects in the Gospels and so is perfect for Jesus as the God-man. Here it especially concerns his God-given authority to perform miracles and forgive sins.

The Baptist in his preaching and actions centered on his baptism as a metaphor for repentance, which brought forgiveness of sins. As such he pointed forward to Jesus, who here assumes that mantle, and under authority from God as Son of Man, he forgives sins. That is the goal of both ministries and the result of the new era of salvation Christ has inaugurated through his ministry of salvation. Jesus is the God-man who is both incarnate as a human and the presence of God on earth.

So as proof of the validity of this authority, he commands the man, "Get up, take your mat and go home" (5:24). This threefold command is concrete proof of Jesus' power from God. The man not only has the strength in his legs to rise off the mat, take it up, and take a few steps, but also to walk all the way home. He is completely normal. He has been utterly healed.

RESULT: THE PRAISE OF GOD (5:25–26)

After being healed, the man "immediately" obeyed, getting up and going home. The whole way home, he couldn't stop praising God.

The praise probably lasted for many days, even weeks. Everyone who had been present and everyone he told joined him in the celebration of praise. It became a festival of praise. Needless to say they were "filled with awe" and kept exclaiming, "We have seen remarkable [literally, 'unbelievable, inconceivable'] things today." Luke's account has been infused with wonder and amazement from the start (1:21, 63; 2:18, 33, 48; 4:36), and how could it be otherwise? We are at the most "remarkable" period in human history, hearing what is truly the greatest story ever told. I feel awe writing these paragraphs! The term *sēmeron* (today) is theologically important in Luke. He uses it often (2:11; 4:21; 12:28; 13:32-33; 19:5, 9; 23:43) to stress the now-ness of salvation, the moment of God-given destiny that has arrived with the new era. The crowds hardly caught this, but Luke wants us to see the deeper implications. Their joy is grounded in events far greater than they realize.

JESUS CALLS LEVI (5:27-32)

This passage blends themes: It is both a discipleship passage (with 5:1-11) and the second of five controversy narratives (with 5:17-26, 33-39; 6:1-5, 6-11). Jesus does not choose his disciples from the rich and famous, but, as God did throughout the Old Testament (for example, Abraham the wandering nomad, David the shepherd boy), he draws his apostolic team from the marginalized and the outcasts like this despised tax collector. In doing so, he manages to enflame the rigid religious sensibilities of nearly every Jewish official he comes across. Yet at the same time, in doing so he fulfills his declaration from Isaiah 61:1-2 (in 4:18-19) to proclaim the good news to the poor and bring liberation to the oppressed. With Jesus and the arrival of God's kingdom, social barriers have been taken away and the "dividing wall of hostility" between economic and ethnic groups has been destroyed (Eph 2:14). He gets in trouble with the scribes and Pharisees this time because he is extending fellowship to "sinners," completely unclean to them. He gets in trouble from both sides, for forgiving sinners (5:21) and now for associating with them.

LEVI CALLED AND FOLLOWS (5:27–28)

Capernaum is the main town in the northeastern part of Galilee, with the main trade route from the north passing through it and a fishing industry right there. So it is perfectly natural for Rome to have a custom booth there for collecting taxes, with tax collectors living there, Levi here and Zacchaeus in 19:1–10. There was no group more despised than they were, and it is shocking that Jesus chose one of them to be his disciple, in effect throwing the Pharisees' bias as a gauntlet right in their face. It didn't take them long to react.

Levi is not found anywhere else in the Gospels. The strong consensus is that he is also called Matthew, used in 9:9 of him and 10:3 of the tax collector who is a disciple. Like Simon Peter or Saul/Paul, people were often called by two names. Jesus "sees" Levi/Matthew sitting at the tax booth, with *theaomai* indicating he "observed" or "studied" him (collecting taxes on trade goods passing through) long enough to be impressed. Making another of his inspired lightning-quick decisions, he right there offers the challenge, "Follow me." Throughout the Gospels, *akoloutheō* is the primary verb for discipleship (as also in 5:11; 9:23, 59; 14:27; 18:22).

Levi clearly was able to make decisions just as quickly. He "got up, left everything and followed him" (5:28). Our head spins with these life-changing decisions coming at warp speed. The paralytic "got up" from his crippled state, and Levi "gets up" from his crippling sin, released as well from his captivity (4:18). At one level this is his conversion; at another level he joins Peter, James, and John (5:11) as a member of the apostolic band. The official formation of the team does not come until 6:12–16, but these are the preliminary stages. Many see a problem in his quitting his job and then paying for the lavish banquet that follows, but nowhere does it say he gave away all the money he had been earning as a tax collector (which was probably formidable). He probably used it to help support Jesus and his fellow disciples in their ministry.

THE BANQUET (5:29)

In honor of his life change, and to introduce Jesus to all his friends, Levi hosts "a great banquet for Jesus at his house," which must have been quite large as befits an important person in the community. Of course, all his former friends were fellow tax collectors and other "sinners." We will see this often in Luke, where table fellowship (sharing meals, a phenomenon we will see often in Luke) is both a focus for fellowship and a means of evangelism. This is why the Pharisees are so upset: in sharing a meal with such sinners, Jesus is both accepting and identifying with them. A maxim that illustrates this is "to share a meal is to share a life." Those you ate with became your circle of friends, and you shared everything with them. That is what is going on here. Levi is introducing them not just to Jesus but to the new life he has embraced.

THE CONTROVERSY (5:30–32)

Needless to say, the scribes and Pharisees began to grumble and complain. This does not mean they were attending the celebration. They would never demean themselves with such untouchables (literally, for to touch them was to be defiled by them). It is hard to know whether they made the comments while it was going on (such banquets were fairly public—they hardly had gated communities back then) or afterward. The verb for "complaining" (*gongyzō*) was used in the Old Testament **Septuagint** for Israel's grumbling against God (Exod 15:24; Num 14:26–35; 17:6), but there was a viable aspect to it as well, as they tried to help their fellow Israelites keep the law faithfully.

As said above, "eating and drinking" with "sinners" meant sharing in their practices and thus branded you as a sinner too. For Jesus sinners were the focus of his ministry, and his purpose was to bring salvation to them. To the Pharisees these people would tarnish not just their reputations but their very relationship with God. The term "Pharisee" means "a separated person," and they lived up to their name.

Tax collectors, as we noted in 3:12, were particularly despised because their greed and fraud were well known and their bad reputations well deserved. At the same time, the fact that they came so frequently to John and Jesus shows that many of them longed for a better life and wanted to get right with God. My guess is that there were quite a few converts from that group. To the Pharisees they were doubly unclean and outcasts, for they both broke the law regularly and constantly associated with Gentiles. There was hardly another group they despised more.

Many have thought "sinners" to be not just a general description but a specific group, the 'am ha'aretz, or "people of the land," Jews who were not scrupulous about keeping the law. There is little evidence for this here, however, and it is more likely these were people of low repute like gamblers and prostitutes. But certainly the "sinners" would include nonobservant Jews here. Matthew would have had many friends from these different walks of life.

The primary message here is the breadth of the church's mission, as Jesus and his followers try to befriend and bring all kinds of "sinners" back to God. The point of it is not fellowship but salvation, and the message for us is that no one is excluded, even those who have chosen a lifestyle that is despicable to us. God "so loved the *world*" (John 3:16), not just those who fit our comfort zone.

Jesus answers the scribes and Pharisees with an aphorism that they could understand: "It is not the healthy who need a doctor, but the sick" (5:31). The Pharisees are wrong when they restrict their work to those who don't need it. Jesus is the true physician who goes where the sick are to help them directly. As a result, the Pharisees are hypocrites who reject the very people who need their help and to whom God wants to send them. The sick are calling to them, but they refuse to respond. Jesus does the opposite: he does not wait for the call but directly seeks out the sick sinners and goes to them to bring spiritual healing.

So Jesus defines his ministry in the light of this aphorism: "I have not come to call the righteous, but sinners to repentance" (5:32). This could be paraphrased, "I have not come to call those who think they are righteous to repentance, but rather those who know they are sinners." He is not ministering to the self-righteous Pharisees but to the honest sinners who admit to their true stance with God. This hardly means God is not interested in the Pharisees—Nicodemus and Joseph of Arimathea both came to Christ.

Jesus means he is focusing on those who are open to the gospel rather than those who are hardened and closed to it. So he is totally reversing the ministry philosophy of the Pharisees. No wonder he and the Baptist are so popular while the Pharisees had few followers. They avoided the very people who needed them. The goal of ministry is clear: repentance (see 13:3, 5; 15:7, 10; 16:30; 24:47), not conformity to legal regulations like the Pharisees, but the forgiveness of sins and getting right with God.

JESUS DEBATES THE PHARISEES
OVER FASTING (5:33–39)

The same group of Pharisees and scribes who disputed with Jesus and his disciples over eating with sinners now question him about fasting. They were bested in the previous dispute and now try to regain the offensive. We have no idea whether this all took place on the same day. Probably it was sometime later, for it seems a separate setting.

THE PHARISEES' QUESTION (5:33)

Clearly Jesus and his followers in light of the new kingdom reality did not adhere to the same lifestyle or set of regulations followed by the Pharisees. Even the Baptist followed the strict practice of fasting and prayer observed by the Pharisees, while Jesus' followers were libertines in comparison, "eating and drinking" freely.

The major required fast was on the Day of Atonement (Lev 16:29–34), and fasting normally one day. However, fasts could last three days (Esth 4:16) or even a week (1 Sam 31:13), though the fasting was done during the day and ended at dusk (2 Sam 3:35). There was a four-day fast to mark the destruction of Jerusalem. The forty-day fasts in which Moses (Exod 34:28), Elijah (1 Kgs 19:8), and Jesus (Luke 4:2) consumed nothing at all were unusual and highly significant religious events. Fasting was often done at traumatic times in the life of Israel (Zech 7:5; 8:19, both connected to the exile). The Pharisees fasted twice a week, on Monday and Thursday, and John's followers probably did the same. Fasting was a practice well known by the Jews, associated with repentance and sorrow for sin. The hope was that by combining fasting with prayer, God would respond more readily. So the question was completely valid.

Jesus' Response (5:34–35)

Jesus' coming is marked by joy, not sorrow, so he uses the metaphor of a wedding celebration to illustrate his point. So long as the bridegroom is present, it is time for celebration, not gloom. There is no place for fasting. This is a metaphor often used of the messianic age (Isa 54:5–6; 62:4–5; Ezek 16; Hos 2:16–25), and the wedding feast is an apt image for the "eating and drinking" the Pharisees had asked about. Since fasting indicates mourning and sorrow, it is not apropos for Jesus' ministry. Certainly sorrow for sin is a critical aspect of repentance and forgiveness, but Jesus centers on the joy of the forgiven former sinner.

Still, Jesus recognizes there is a place for fasting. That is for the future rather than the present of his ministry: "The time will come when the bridegroom will be taken from them; in those days they will fast" (5:35). Obviously, the "time" when Jesus is taken away refers to his passion and death. As several scholars have commented, the time after the resurrection was characterized by joy (24:41, 52) and featured several meals (24:42–43; John 21:10–13).

This verse is important historically because it shows his realization that he was destined to die. It is likely that Jesus means that, in the interim period between his death and the final resurrection at his second coming, fasting will once more become appropriate. That fits the place of fasting in the early church. The complete and final restoration of humankind will not come until Christ returns and eternity begins (Rom 8:18-22; 1 Cor 15:20-28). Fasting is an important part of Christian experience until then.

TWO KINGDOM PARABLES ON THE OLD AND THE NEW (5:36-39)

Jesus illustrates his point in verses 34-35 with two parables, both metaphors contrasting the old covenant with the new. The literal point would be a commonsense principle drawn from everyday life. But as spiritual metaphors they are quite profound. A parable is an extended metaphor, often a mini-story or an illustration that explains a spiritual truth. In this case both parables are about something new that is inserted in something old and the effects that result, stressing the incompatibility of the new covenant Jesus has brought when forced into the old covenant of Moses. The first parable (5:36) is about an old garment that has torn and a piece of a new garment sown into it as a patch. The old garment has already shrunk and is dried out and inflexible. The new patch that was sown into it will shrink when washed. When that happens, the thread will tear both the old garment and the new, destroying both.

The second parable (5:37-39) has the same basic plot, this time new, unfermented wine poured into old, brittle wineskins. At first, leather wineskins are soft and flexible, but as they age they become dry and brittle. New wine is unfermented, and while in the old wineskin it will ferment and expand, causing the brittle skin to crack and then break. Both the wineskin and the wine are destroyed as the wine "runs out" of the ruined wineskin onto the ground. Jesus this time provides the solution—only pour new, unfermented wine into new, flexible wineskins (v. 38) and let it age properly.

Both have the same message. Christ has initiated a new covenant between God and humanity, encased in his gospel message of salvation. The Pharisees are trying to force this new truth into the old, used-up structures of their rigid Judaism. The two cannot fit together, and in the end they will both be destroyed. The new freedom in Christ cannot be encased in the rigid rules of the oral traditions. The gospel truths cannot be forced into the old religious ways of Judaism. The new directives of Jesus must be allowed to be expressed in the new, fresh religious structures Jesus is developing. The new way is actually not brand new but that which fulfills the old. It is the gospel of repentance and forgiveness of sins, a new form of old truths that liberates the oppressed (4:18-19) and brings salvation in Christ.

The concluding verse (5:39) is difficult to understand.[5] On the surface it seems to admit that the old ways of the Pharisees are superior to the new ways of Jesus. What it actually admits, however, is that there will be many who prefer the old structures of Judaism and are not willing to embrace the new forms of relating to God. Christ demands new approaches and ways of living out the new covenant reality, but many simply cannot do so. The book of Acts will trace these challenges, and two groups come to mind. The negative example is the Judaizers of Galatians and Philippians 3, who demand that converts become Jews before they become Christians, thinking that the law must be explicitly obeyed by Christians. Paul shows that they were false teachers/heretics, tragically wrong. The positive example is the Jewish Christians of Romans 14-15, who continued to follow the old Jewish ways but not to replace the new with them. They are a viable form of Jewish

---

5. In fact, Codex Bezae and several church fathers (such as Irenaeus and Eusebius) omit this verse because it seems to say the old ways of Judaism are better. However, the manuscript evidence is overwhelming for its inclusion.

Christianity. This is also the Paul of Acts, who continued to offer sacrifices and observe the Jewish feasts.

Paul asks two things in these passages. On the positive side, Christians (especially Gentile Christians) must learn to understand and tolerate Jewish Christians, appreciating them for their love for Christ and their honest attempt to live for him. On the negative side, Christ followers must realize that many others will never accept the new approaches of Jesus and Christianity. Many Jews will utterly reject the new wine of Christ and Christianity; others like the Judaizers will fall into the error of these two parables and try to force the new wine of Christ into the old, rigid wineskins of their Judaism. They have destroyed both Judaism and Christianity and must be utterly opposed.

JESUS' DISCIPLES PICK GRAIN ON THE SABBATH (6:1-5)

These next two conflict narratives center on Sabbath controversies. At the same time the opposition intensifies. This is in keeping with the increased emphasis in Judaism during that time on Sabbath, food laws, and circumcision as signs of Jewish identity.

THE SETTING (6:1-2)

Roads in the ancient world did not skirt and go around property lines, and as a result they often would go right through a farmer's field. It is interesting that Jesus and his disciples are walking through a field on a Sabbath, for traveling on that day was also considered work and restricted to "a Sabbath day's walk" (Acts 1:12) or two thousand cubits (= eleven hundred meters; see m. Sotah 5:3; m. Shabbat 7:2). They were probably following this restriction, for there is no criticism of this.

Galilee had some of the best soil in the Mediterranean region and was famous for its farms. These were wheat fields that became ripe in March and April, and the crops would be growing right up to the road. As they passed by, his disciples "began to pick some heads of grain, rub them in their hands and eat the kernels."

Picking a few grains for a snack on someone else's property was allowed back then, but the problem was that this was the Sabbath. So the Pharisees rebuked Jesus: "Why are you doing what is unlawful on the Sabbath?" Exceptions were only allowed when a life was in danger, and that was not the case here. In actuality several Sabbath rules were being broken. The picking of the grain was reaping, and rubbing of the grain to clear the grain of husks was considered threshing. All this could also have been considered harvesting, and technically they were preparing a meal. That would be four rules broken, a formidable problem. It is not that they were forbidden to eat. Rather, the preparation was to be done on Friday, and the Sabbath was to be a day of rest. Though Jesus himself was not eating the grain, he would be guilty by association, for he was the rabbi in charge and was allowing it.

JESUS' RESPONSE (6:3-5)

Jesus answers their charge with an example from Scripture (6:3-4) and then a solemn pronouncement (6:5). His scriptural parallel begins with a mild criticism, "Have you never read?" assuming they knew the story but had missed an important point. The point is drawn from 1 Samuel 21:1-6, where David performed an even greater breach of Sabbath protocol. He was on the run from Saul and starving, so he stopped and asked Ahimelech the priest for some bread. The priest had only the sacred "bread of the presence" used in the tabernacle, so it was available only if David and his men had kept themselves holy. David responds that his men are holy "even on missions that are not holy" because they accompanied him, God's chosen one. David considered himself a higher law than the ceremonial law of the Torah, and rabbis said this was because he was a messianic figure.

Jesus is using a rabbinic hermeneutical principle here—from the lesser to the greater. It functioned on two levels, first in the bread (the lesser) versus David (the greater), and then David (the messianic type) versus Jesus (the Messiah himself). So if a Torah regulation could be overcome by David, how much more could it happen with Jesus, God's Son and Messiah. Note Jesus' point: by a strict interpretation of the law, David broke a very important Torah regulation, yet he was never criticized, for he was the future king and the prototype of the Messiah. If that is true, how much more is it the case with the Messiah himself—Jesus was equally free of guilt.

Jesus' conclusion is an incredibly bold pronouncement guaranteed to cause a reaction: "The Son of Man is Lord of the Sabbath" (6:5). As the Danielic Son of Man (Dan 7:13–14) with universal dominion (see 5:24), Jesus is also sovereign Lord over the Sabbath and its regulations. He is the final interpreter of the law and has complete authority to set aside Sabbath rules. In light of the importance of Sabbath rules in first-century Judaism, Jesus is making a shocking **christological** statement about the extent of his lordship. He has proved by his miracles that he has authority over creation, but now he states that he has authority over God's spiritual realm as well.

JESUS HEALS ON THE SABBATH (6:6–11)

Jesus has just stated that he is Lord of the Sabbath. Now he proves it with another act of power. Sabbath laws were equally strict about healing diseases and medical conditions on the Sabbath. Again, it was allowed only if a life was at stake, and that was not the case here. We do not know the cause of the man's shriveled hand, whether it was an accident or paralysis, but it was probably the latter, as it seems to be treated here as a medical situation. Shriveled hands were thought to be divine punishment for sin (1 Kgs 13:4–6; Ps 137:5), so we are dealing with a spiritual as well as physical problem.

The central question in the previous Sabbath healing (4:33–37) was not on the Sabbath issue but on Jesus' power over the unclean spirits. Here the Sabbath conflict comes to the fore, and the debate centers on the legality of breaking the Torah restrictions. So this final conflict is the key to the others, for in answering them Jesus is in effect questioning the Torah itself. His basic point is that on the Sabbath people have priority, not rules.

THE SETTING (6:6–7)

On another occasion (we don't know if this was the following week) Jesus is again teaching in the synagogue, likely the same one in Capernaum, and this time it is a man with an atrophied hand present at the service. He apparently is not suffering discomfort, but the fact that this was the "right" hand means his life was maximally disrupted, as he undoubtedly was right-handed. In the Gospel of the Nazarenes the man is a stonemason whose hand was paralyzed in an accident, and he was forced to become a beggar. There is no way to judge the truth of that story.

The critical fact for this story lies in the Pharisees and scribes. They are not interested bystanders simply attending the service but have become vigilantes waiting for Jesus to do something wrong so they can attack. Their animosity and the resulting desire to do Jesus serious harm will become a plot line that controls the rest of Luke's Gospel. Luke says they "watched him closely" (*paretērounto*), picturing them continually sneaking around and peering around corners trying to catch him breaking the law. Exodus 31:14 even says a Sabbath-breaker is worthy of death, and this is their goal, to see Jesus die.

JESUS' RESPONSE (6:8–9)

Once again Jesus' omniscience (see 5:7, 22; see also 9:47; 11:17; 24:38) intervenes, and he knows their thoughts. He also knows how best to counter their evil intentions, and so he tells the crippled man to "get up and stand in front of everyone." A "show and tell" is the best way to respond. It is one thing to verbally correct them, quite another to answer with a mighty deed that will demonstrate the truth he wishes to communicate.

Jesus had said in his first sermon at the Capernaum synagogue that the purpose of his ministry was to fulfill Isaiah 61:1–2 and free the prisoners from their bondage. His message here is that this is also the purpose of God's gift of the Sabbath. In light of this he asks, "Which is lawful on the Sabbath: to do good or to do evil, to save life or to destroy it?" The traditions of the Pharisees and all of their restrictions have placed God's people in bondage, and that is even more true for handicapped people like this man. For him the Sabbath is the one day of the week he cannot "rest," the only time he cannot be healed. How can that be right?

By their rigid rules this legal mafia has turned the Sabbath into an evil day that destroys. God's true intention in blessing his people with the Sabbath was for their "good" and to "save" lives. This latter verb is sōzō, the primary verb for salvation, used also for physical as well as spiritual deliverance. The Sabbath was supposed to allow people to regain their strength and worship God, but they had turned it into a day that allowed people to degenerate and their lives to worsen. This is counter to God's will. The answer to Jesus' query is obvious.

ACTION AND REACTION (6:10–11)

Jesus answers his own question by acting rather than speaking. The man acts as well. He does not demur and tell Jesus he is unable to comply. His immediate act of faith and obedience is rewarded with immediate healing, and as he thrusts his hand forward, his paralysis goes away and his hand is fully restored. Mark 3:5 tells us Jesus was both angry and distressed at their stubborn hearts, but Luke simply says Jesus "looked around" at them, centering on Jesus' mighty act more than his attitude. In so doing, Jesus shows the true nature of the Sabbath and the "good" it is meant to bring about.

There are important ramifications in this for Sabbath debates in our time as well. The question of Sabbath restrictions and the meaning of the "day of rest" were not solved in Jesus' day, and we still must ask how far such "freedom" can go on the Lord's Day. No

Christian doubts the twin aspects of rest and worship that should characterize the day, but some burden this with all kinds of dos and don'ts, while others turn it into just another secular weekend holiday. Eric Liddell in the movie *Chariots of Fire* illustrated it best. Can a little boy kick a soccer ball and play on Sunday, and what does God really want us to do? I can only give my opinions, but I think we should find balance with the "rest and worship" principle. It is "the Lord's" day, and we should spend time with God and with family and friends. As a former pastor and seminary teacher, I have spent my life in ministry on Sunday, but I try to curtail even commentary writing on Sunday, for that is my "work," and I want to have time with my family and others on that day. But I try not to be legalistic about it.

The reaction of the leaders (6:11) is critical and sets the tone for the rest of Luke. Luke softens Mark 3:6, in which they begin to "plot with the Herodians" to put Jesus to death. Luke has them "furious" and beginning a general discussion of "what they might do to Jesus."[6] They were completely stymied. It is one thing to counter what Jesus says, but how can they disprove what Jesus has done? Their only response to this can be blind rage. The picture is of anger and confusion. They know they want to get rid of Jesus, but they don't know how to counter even this one mighty act of his, let alone how to counter all he has said and done. You can almost picture them setting up committees and study groups to come at it from many different angles. The what is decided; the how completely eludes them.

———

6. There are a couple of reasons why Luke would generalize Mark's presentation of the leaders plotting Jesus' death. For one thing, he has already presented a scene of people trying to execute Jesus for blasphemy (4:28–30). For another, he wants to build tension more gradually in ensuing chapters.

These two chapters (5–6) introduce the major themes of the book. Chapter 4 began with Jesus' messianic mission to rescue the poor and liberate the captives, then moved to the opposition he was to face first from the satanic realm and his great victory in binding these forces. He truly freed the prisoners and brought healing and life to those who were lost. Chapter 5 begins with his choice of a team to go to war. This incredible scene (vv. 1–11) introduces the new kind of fishing to which he is calling them, and defines the life of surrender necessary to find success in this new enterprise. It demands a radical obedience that allows Jesus to guide their lives and promises a wondrous catch of fish to those willing to surrender to his leading (vv. 4–7). When radical obedience takes place, wondrous things begin to happen. God's work in and through us as we obey results in a radical humility and repentance that bring about a new life of discipleship (vv. 8–9) and a radical surrender that enables us to fish in this new way and bring life out of death (vv. 10–11). This is a story not only about discipleship but also about success in ministry.

Two healing miracles follow, the leper (vv. 12–16) and the paralytic (vv. 17–22). Both introduce not just Jesus' power over nature and illness but also the increasing intensity of opposition against him. The irony is shocking. Instead of wonder and gratitude, these Jewish leaders focus only on their precious and rigid traditions. In reality, Jesus cares far more about freeing the helpless and the captives (4:18–19) than he does about the petty rules of the religious elite. Compassion outweighs rule-bound religion every time. The lesson is important for us as well. Human beings, uncomfortable with Spirit-led freedom, always tend to make up rules.

The call of Levi (vv. 27–32) combines discipleship (Levi) with further evidence of the growing opposition to Jesus (the Pharisees and scribes). Levi, a despised tax collector and likely a formerly dishonest person, is one of the fish "caught alive" (5:10) by Jesus. He exemplifies the proper reaction and life-change of the true convert by hosting a banquet in which he introduces Jesus and the new life he offers to all his former friends. This is true "evange-lism explosion." The Pharisees are horrified at Jesus in his open-ness and acceptance of sinners. Theirs is an anti-evangelism in which they refuse to be sullied by the very people to whom God wishes to send them. No wonder they had little effect on people around them except to introduce a new level of negativity into Judaism. There are many like them in our churches today, and we must beware of a rule-bound Christianity.

The issue of fasting and the two parables that follow (vv. 33–39) are the center point of this section and explain the new era intro-duced by Christ and its relationship to the old covenant that it is replacing. Fasting belongs with the old era and has no place in the joyous atmosphere of Christ's new-covenant realm. For us fast-ing has value primarily as defined in sacrificing an earthly need like meals in order to open ourselves up to God's leading on an issue. As we fast we remind ourselves that God is what matters, not human desires and needs, and we center more completely on him in our lives.

The two parables explain this phenomenon more deeply. Christ has brought newness into this world, and we must allow him to develop the new structures by which we dissimilate this newness into our lives. We cannot force the new truths of the kingdom into the old religious ways, or both will be lost. This sets the tone for the rest of Luke, where Jesus will indeed be creating these new ways and teaching them to his followers. We are asked to be character-ized by openness and a willingness to embrace these new paths.

The final two conflict narratives (6:1–5, 6–11) go further into the question of the Jewish law versus Christ and the issue of ful-fillment. Jesus as Son of Man has authority over the law and is its final interpreter, but the Jewish officials adamantly oppose these messianic powers in Jesus. His right to ignore Sabbath laws inflames them, and their rejection intensifies. In our time, there are similar issues in many circles about eating out or shopping on Sunday, and so on. The same freedom Christ stresses here should characterize our time as well. We are to keep the Sabbath holy, but what defines that holiness and what is restricted are open for debate. My principle is to put family and worship of the Lord first over either too much restriction or too much freedom. Finding the balance is my goal.

The second and final episode (vv. 6–11) builds on and extends the first. The issue is still Sabbath regulations and the freedom of Jesus and his followers to ignore them in favor of ministry to the needs of people. Both hunger (vv. 1–5) and deformity (vv. 6–11) are reasons to bypass such human rules, for individual need outstrips external rules, and so often such rules hurt rather than help the very ones for whose benefit God gave us this Sabbath in the first place. We are meant to enjoy the day of rest, not just submit to it. Finally, this final scene also establishes the intense opposition to Jesus that has built for these five episodes and now will guide the reactions of the leaders for the rest of Luke's Gospel. There will be no respite in the complete focus of their machinations to rid themselves of Jesus.

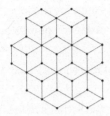

CALLING OF THE TWELVE AND SERMON ON THE PLAIN

(6:12–49)

I n this section Luke's discipleship emphasis comes to the fore-
ground, demonstrated first in Jesus choosing the Twelve and
second in the sermon Jesus addresses mainly to his disciples and
secondarily to the crowds. The scene is built around Jesus on a
mountain, reenacting Moses ascending and descending Sinai. He
goes up the mountain to pray and there chooses his twelve disciples, then goes down and preaches his second programmatic
sermon (after 4:16–30), announcing kingdom rules to his followers. Like Moses giving the original Torah (law), this can be seen
as the Torah of the Messiah. The other two commissioning narratives before this one (5:1–11, 27–32) have been preparatory, pointing forward to the final call and commission here.

JESUS CALLS THE TWELVE (6:12–16)

Another "it came to pass" (see 5:1, 12, 17; 6:1, 6) links this event with
the five episodes in Jesus' ministry in 5:1–6:11. It is Jesus' response
to the others and culminates them as he assembles the team that
will carry his mission further in Galilee. In light of the incredible escalation of hostility and plots against him, he needs a small
supporting network he can count on to carry out his messianic

directives. To prepare for that choice of the right men for the job, he emulates Moses and ascends a mountain in order to spend a night in prayer to his Father.

As I stated earlier in my comments on 5:15–16, Luke shows Jesus turning to prayer at every important event and turning point. This was an all-night prayer vigil, undoubtedly asking the Father's help in making the right choices and for blessing on the entire enterprise. This is the Father's choice as well as Jesus', and it is a true turning point in the battle against evil. Unlike standard rabbinic practice, where disciples chose which rabbi they wished to study under, this decision is entirely God's. Jesus is carrying out his Father's will, and the events that follow in verses 13–16 are the result of intense prayer and divine guidance.

The morning after the prayer vigil, while still on the mountain, he called a group of followers who had accompanied him and from them chose twelve to be his major team. We don't know how many others were there, but it sounds like a fairly significant number. The verb *eklegomai* is often used of divine election (see, for example, Mark 13:20; Acts 1:24), and that fits well in this context.

The choice of the number twelve is important, for it fits the twelve patriarchs and twelve tribes of Israel, signifying that the church is the new Israel and the twelve disciples in a sense the twelve patriarchs who will lead it. There is direct continuity between the two covenant groups. As Paul states in Romans 11:17–21, the church has not replaced the Israel of old but has joined it on the olive tree, and the Israels of the two covenants flow together into one. The joining of the Gentiles into that mix was always the intention, as the Abrahamic covenant showed (Gen 12:3).

Not only did Jesus choose them, but he also "named [*onomazō*, NIV: 'designated'] them apostles." In Acts this becomes a title identifying them as the official representatives of Jesus with authority from him.[1]

---

1. See, for example, Acts 1:2, 26; 2:37, 42, 43.

It is debated whether "apostle" is meant as a title here. Many think it entirely functional, that is, it indicates not so much their authority as their purpose as Christ's messengers to those outside. In itself the term refers to someone "sent" on a mission by another and given authority to represent the sender. I think the force here is a balance between the two poles, recognizing them as sent and commissioned by Jesus and thereby given Christ's authority as his representative. They were the leaders among Jesus' followers and were always meant to stand out. The Aramaic *shaliach* was used of a prophet or Jewish leader commissioned as a "sent one," God's envoy or agent, and this applies here. They have left their jobs and joined Jesus to be with him wherever he went.

The list of the Twelve is one of four in the New Testament (with Matt 10:2-4; Mark 3:16-19; Acts 1:13). In each list there are three sets of four, headed by Simon Peter, Philip, and James the son of Alphaeus. The first four are the same in all the lists (Peter, Andrew, James, and John), though not always in that order. Judas is always last, though he is omitted in Acts 1:13 because it lists the Eleven (he had committed suicide by that time). Other things to note: (1) Bartholomew is normally (and correctly) identified with Nathanael from John 1:45-49. (2) Simon the Zealot does not reflect the later AD 60s movement of Zealots, which advocated rebellion against Rome. This could have meant simply that he was zealous for God, but more likely he was a nationalist and follower of nascent groups that later became that movement. (3) Judas son of James is probably another name for Thaddeus in Mark and Matthew; second names were common then. (4) The name "Iscariot" in Judas Iscariot means either "man of Kerioth," a village twelve miles south of Hebron in Judea, or is a reference to the Sicarii (a group of assassins—quite unlikely), or could be an Aramaic term meaning "the false one." The first is the most likely; it designates his hometown in the same way that "the Nazarene" did for Jesus.

JESUS PREACHES THE SERMON
ON THE PLAIN (6:17-49)

Like the Sermon on the Mount, this has variously been called "the Torah of the Messiah" or "the new constitution of the messianic community." It is both, for it intends to set out the life and attitudes of the new Christ movement, the values of those who have become members of the new covenant. While some think the Sermon on the Mount and the Sermon on the Plain are separate sermons (for the Lukan form occurs somewhat later in the public ministry of Jesus), I think they are slightly different versions of the same sermon. Most of Matthew 5-7 occurs here or is scattered in various places in Luke.

After a note on the setting (vv. 17-19), the sermon contains three major parts: a set of beatitudes and woes addressing God's justice in pouring out his blessings on the poor and his judgment on the rich (vv. 20-26); a section of ethical exhortation commanding that we love our enemies and telling how to respond to those who persecute us (vv. 27-36); and a set of sayings and parables that illustrate how to avoid judgmentalism and live the way God wishes (vv. 37-49).

THE SETTING: TEACHING AND MIGHTY DEEDS (6:17-19)

Coming down from his prayer mountain, Jesus teaches "on a level place" or plateau on the mountain. As we have seen, people flock to him there from all around, and he addresses the diverse crowd. Thus, this would fit Matthew's setting as well. We could harmonize the settings by labeling it "the sermon on the plateau of the mount." We don't know where this mountain was in Galilee. There were several that would fit, and Galilee was small enough that any place could draw people from the northern and eastern sides (Tyre and Sidon) as well as the western portion (Capernaum). It could be anywhere.

Luke tells us the listeners consisted of "a large crowd of his disciples," demonstrating the success of Jesus' mission. Luke will speak of seventy-two disciples sent out in 10:1 and of a hundred and twenty disciples gathered in the upper room in Acts 1:15. Many of these were likely converted in this early period and have come to be taught by Jesus. In addition, there were great numbers of the uncommitted who came from as far south as Jerusalem in Judea or as far north as Tyre and Sidon on the coast of Syria. This shows the extent of Jesus' great popularity. It is a summary statement that says in effect that people came from everywhere to hear Jesus and see his mighty works. Many have brought their sick to be healed by him. It is quite a scene.

Verse 18 tells the two reasons they have come—to hear him and be healed by him. This has been seen in every section of Jesus' public ministry and is at the heart of his fame. Israel had not seen this combination of charismatic preacher, prophetic presence, and miracle-working power since the days of Elijah and Elisha, so all of Judaism is enthralled by him and simply cannot get enough.

The results of his ministry at this time are summarized in verses 18b-19. First, "those troubled by impure spirits were cured," indicating that a number of demons were cast out of people. As he did in 4:31-37, 40-41, Jesus adds action to his teaching, showing the truths he is proclaiming by putting them into practice through his deeds. It is fitting that acts of power proceed his extensive teaching in 5:20-49, for his powerful deeds proved his right to speak and showed that the Father was indeed behind everything he said. They also demonstrated the compassion for the needy that was behind everything he said.

Jesus had healed many by touching them (4:40; 5:13), and in verse 19 some reason that they could reverse the process and be healed by touching him. Jesus had shown on multiple occasions his power to heal virtually everyone who came to him (4:40). They had seen how "power was coming from him and healing them all," so how could they not flock to him? Mere contact could bring healing, and they were naturally astounded. Not even Elijah and Elisha were this prolific and continually powerful. The extent of his powers had never been seen before in history. Yet people are about to be shown an even greater power—Jesus' teaching.

BLESSINGS AND WOES (6:20-26)

Like Matthew 5 this sermon begins with a series of beatitudes. However, the Sermon on the Mount has a series of blessings while Luke's version has a matching set of four blessings and four woes. The result is an indictment of the rich and promises that God is watching over the poor. The emphasis is on the dichotomy between the rich and the poor and the assurance that divine justice will be done. While there are both outsiders and insiders in the group being addressed, these are on the whole meant for disciples, although the general categories (for example, the indictment of the rich) also apply to nonbelievers. The parallels are quite clear:

The Blessings	The Woes
The poor	The rich
The hungry	The well-fed
Those who weep	Those who laugh
Those rejected	Those spoken well of

To be "blessed" (*makarioi*) normally referred to the fortunate, those who had the good things in life and could remain happy with the way things were. However, this approach is inadequate here, and in this God-centered context "blessed" means that God's blessings remain on them. The message is not earthly happiness but divine blessings. These are eschatological promises. Moreover, they deal with biblical ethics, with how one reacts to life's difficult situations. The theme is God's reversal of roles, as the poor inherit God's world and the rich face God's judgment. Those facing the pain and anxiety that life's deprivations produce can take comfort in the grace of God, which will right all wrongs and reward those who suffer unfairly.

Jesus addresses the poor first (6:20), and this first category sets the tone for the others. The poor are featured in Luke. In 4:18 we saw that Jesus' ministry was meant to proclaim the good news to the poor (from Isa 61:1), and it is a socioeconomic category as well as a spiritual one. The "poor" in both testaments are those who are destitute and therefore must trust God to care for their needs. They are the marginalized in this world, and in the prophetic writings the poor are also the righteous remnant who remain loyal to Yahweh in the midst of a godless nation. They follow God even while persecuted.

Jesus now addresses them directly in the second person and presents their blessing of the kingdom in the present tense (the other three are in the future tense), thereby emphasizing the newness of divine blessing. The "kingdom of God" is not just the final kingdom that will arrive with the day of the Lord at the end of history but also the present reign that has begun with the arrival of Jesus the Christ. The present and the future are intertwined, and the kingdom blessings belong spiritually to Jesus' followers now and will culminate in the final and full blessings of eternity. As it says in Mark 1:15, "the kingdom of God has come near." Luke stresses throughout his Gospel what has come to be called "inaugurated **eschatology**," highlighting the tension between the "already" and the "not yet" in Jesus' teaching. Jesus' followers "already" have God's kingdom and are part of it, and they await its final consummation that is "not yet" here.

The poor are also the hungry (v. 21), a connection made often in the Old Testament (Job 24:4-11; Isa 58:6-10; Ezek 18:7). Hunger was widespread in the first century, and the vast majority of those hearing Jesus' words could identify. Food was an idiom for life's needs in general, and the "daily bread" in the Lord's Prayer referred to all the necessities of life. Once more, this refers to those who have no solution except to turn to God for help.

The hungry are promised that they "will be satisfied," and once again this is not only socioeconomic but spiritual and eschatological in force. This is a divine passive, promising that God would fill their needs. The imagery is drawn from the messianic banquet that is featured in Psalm 107:3–9; Isaiah 25:6; 49:10; 55:1–2; Luke 22:18; Revelation 19:9. God will pour out his plenty on those who have sacrificed so much for him, and their suffering will be over forever. While this is a future promise, it has present ramifications, for he will satisfy his people spiritually in the midst of their earthly deprivations.

Weeping is also a frequent experience of the poor (v. 21), and here it is caused not only by earthly suffering but also by the persecution of the next category. In fact, the injustice of it all may be primary here. The pain and suffering are in the present, and the joy will occur in the future. God will right all wrongs and vindicate those whose sad lives bring such sorrow. Life has turned against them, and the world has intensified the pain by mistreating them. Once more, the reversal has God's people in mind, for it is they who will laugh with joy in the end when God turns everything around. It includes present peace and joy in the sense that Christ followers experience God with them in their suffering, but the laughter indicated here is primarily future, as in Revelation 19:7, "Let us rejoice and be glad and give him glory! For the wedding of the Lamb has come."

The fourth beatitude is meant only for Jesus' disciples and refers to the intense persecution they will face, using several verbs: "Blessed are you when people hate you, when they exclude you and insult you and reject your name as evil, because of the Son of Man" (v. 22). Jesus sees this as a "fellowship of suffering" (Phil 3:10), for this has already been his lot in Luke 5, and he is now telling his disciples that it will become theirs as well. The Gospel of Luke tells of opposition against Jesus, and the book of Acts shows the intense rejection that will accrue for his followers as well.

This final beatitude takes a different form from the first three and acts as a conclusion. The first three described their state or condition as followers, while this tells how they will be treated by the world around them. The fourfold description moves from attitude (hate) to the resultant mistreatment (exclude, insult, reject), with a growing intensity of persecution. "Reject your name" is singular, referring to their Christian identity rather than their personal names. The fact that they have taken the name of Christ will be seen as an indication of evil. This has come to pass in our day, when it is unpopular to evangelize or to restrict salvation to those who belong to Christ. The time may be near when Christianity will be virtually outlawed in the so-called land of the free.

The basis for this opposition and persecution is stated simply as "because of the Son of Man." It is our identification with Christ that is the basis of the mistreatment, as in 1 Peter 4:14–16, "If you are insulted because of the name of Christ, you are blessed." "Son of Man" was introduced in 5:24 and 6:5 and means we identify with the glorious and authoritative Lord of this world and of the realm of God. The world is rejecting Christ when they reject us, and we align ourselves with him.

The eschatological reversal of this in verse 23 is particularly strong, "Rejoice in that day and leap for joy." As the opposition intensifies, so does the joy, undoubtedly because of the privilege of participating in the Lord's suffering. This is stated very well in 1 Peter 1:10–11, which sets forth the principle that suffering is the path to glory. The more we share Jesus' suffering, the more we share his glory. As we suffer poverty, hunger, sorrow, and hatred for the sake of Christ, we fully rejoice as we realize how God is going to reverse all of that and pour out his blessings on us. Our suffering is temporary (1 Pet 1:6), but our glory and joy will be eternal. This means "that day" of rejoicing is not future but present; we have joy as we suffer hardship. "Leap for joy" recalls John in his mother's womb leaping for joy as Mary with Jesus in her womb drew near (1:41, 44).

There are two reasons for this joy. First, "great is your reward in heaven." The earthly joy is real, but the heavenly reward will be eternal. We will not only be vindicated and be given justice in the

present but rejoice even more in the promises to come. We don't
live for Christ for the reward we will get, but Christ still wants to
encourage us and tell us that reward will be there. A lot of debate
has taken place over the question of rewards in heaven. I personally think there will be rewards, but they will not be material (a
bigger crown or mansion in heaven) but spiritual. Everything we
do for the glory of God and to help others is recorded and banked
in heaven and will be returned to us when we arrive. I will talk of
this further in my comments on Luke 16:9–13.

The second reason is, "for that is how their ancestors treated
the prophets." This parallels Hebrews 11:35–38, which speaks of
prophets who were tortured, jeered, beaten, stoned (Jeremiah,
according to tradition), sawed in two (Isaiah, according to tradition), and killed by the sword. We will see this rejection of God's
messengers also in Luke 11:47–51 and elsewhere (Acts 7:51–52; Rom
11:3). Jesus here prophesies the future difficulties of God's people
and sees them fulfilling the experiences of the prophets. The
nation of his day is no different than the apostate nation in the
days of Isaiah and Jeremiah.

The false and temporary rejoicing of the worldly is in contrast
to the pain of the faithful saints. They have all the wealth of this
world and enjoy a life they don't deserve, but it is short-lived. In
verses 24-26, Luke parallels the four deprivations and God-blessed
lives with four woes on the rich and comfortable of this world.
Remember that there are not only disciples but unbelievers present among the crowd, so these woes are speaking directly to them
and are meant to inform and warn the disciples as well. There are
several woe passages in the Old Testament (Deut 27:15–26 [curses];
Isa 5:8–23; 65:13–16; Hab 2:6–20), so this was an established form.
The woes are not an expression of pity, as if Jesus is saying, "I feel
sorry for you." They are judgment oracles that mean, "God's wrath
will fall on you."

First, the rich (in contrast with the poor of v. 21) "have already
received your comfort" (v. 24). The rich are those who belong to

this world and live for the things of this world. Their god is their possessions, and they have accumulated more and more for their own pleasure. They have grown rich at the expense of the poor. They have taken for themselves what should have been shared with the unfortunates of this world, so they will pay the price for their greed. They have grown fat and comfortable, but all they will ever have is their earthly comfort in the here and now. God will reverse their situation, and in the next life they will have nothing. They have received earthly goods from God and spent them entirely on themselves, so their future will contain no comforts. Justice for them is the loss of everything.

It is critical to realize this is not an indictment on all the rich. There are wealthy followers of Jesus in this Gospel, like Zacchaeus and Joseph of Arimathea. But their wealth to them is a gift from God, and they serve him with it. It is not the fact of their wealth that renders so many of the rich guilty but what they do with it and what part God plays in it. Wealth should be seen as an opportunity to serve God in a new way, by using possessions to glorify him and help others.

The "full" or "well fed" (in contrast with the hungry of v. 21a) are those who have far more than they need of earthly goods (v. 25a). They have no needs, and everything the world has is already theirs. When God reverses their situation, they will be the ones who are hungry and have nothing in the next life. They have spent it all in the here and now, and nothing is left for them. The reversals of Mary's song in 1:51-53 describe them: the proud have been scattered, the rulers of this world brought low, the rich cast out empty-handed. They will have nothing, for they took it all now, shared with no one, and lived only for themselves. For eternity they will have nothing but themselves and will be bereft of all they once held dear. The story of Lazarus and the rich man in 16:19-31 describes them.

The same is true of those characterized by worldly laughter (in contrast with the weepers of v. 21b), describing their attitude toward life (v. 25b). This is not joy in the Lord but the laughter (*gelōntes*) of the Las Vegas lifestyle, all selfish pleasure and greedy gloating as they take everything for themselves. In the great reversal, they will be the ones who "mourn and weep." This is the judgment on the rich in James 4:9, "Change your laughter to mourning and your joy to gloom" and 5:1, "weep and wail because of the misery that is coming on you." They have had it all and laughed at the misfortunes of the poor that made their selfish living possible. At the final judgment they will pay for their sins, and that payment will be for eternity.

The popular people who are "spoken well of" by all around (in contrast with the hated and rejected of v. 22) will also see the loss of it all (v. 26). This refers both to the Pharisees in Jesus' day and the false teachers of the early church. They have lived to be liked by those around them rather than to be accepted by God. In our day this describes those who are guided by earthly reputation rather than living to please God. There are all too many Christians who are afraid to speak up for truth lest the pagans around them ridicule them, and seek the plaudits of this world rather than approval from God. Peer pressure is enormous, and Satan wields it with expertise, cowing Christian witness again and again.

Jesus links this woe with Israel's past, "for that is how their ancestors treated the false prophets." This is a serious and dangerous reality, for false prophets and teachers tell people what they want to hear, not what God wants them to hear (Isa 30:10; Jer 14:13–16; Ezek 22:23–31). In 2 Timothy 4:3 Paul labels this condition "itching ears," meaning an absence of desire for truth and a curiosity for titillating speech that will entertain. These people are not interested in substance, caring only for pleasure. They need serious exhortation that will lead them to God, but they both want and receive only flattery that allows them to continue on the path to destruction. I can't believe how much preaching in our time is characterized by this. It breaks my heart. To live your life according to the world's standards drives you further and further from God.

CHALLENGE TO A LIFE OF LOVE (6:27–36)

This section is a "paraenetic exhortation"—moral and ethical instruction that exhorts listeners to live in accordance with God's demands. This is primarily meant for Jesus' followers, to teach them the laws of the kingdom he is instituting, but it also is intended to show the crowds what they are missing in their continued failure to commit to Jesus. In fact, the crowds may contain many who will become the very enemies Christ is talking about here.

Jesus is depicting a whole new way to love and an entirely new depth of love. I would define love as "selfless giving," an attitude of complete selflessness toward others and the action of giving that results. There is a fourfold challenge here defining this most difficult concept regarding love, containing four descriptions of what constitutes an enemy and four verbs telling how to react to them:

1. The basic rule is to "love your enemies," a revolutionary concept, as there is little evidence for this in Jewish literature. In Leviticus 19:33–34 love for neighbor (19:18) is extended to the resident alien, and Proverbs 25:21 commands kindness toward enemies (also Exod 23:4–5; Job 31:29–30; Prov 17:5, 24:17, 25:21–22; Rom 12:14, 20). The **Qumran** community that wrote the Dead Sea Scrolls went so far as to extol loving each other but hating one's enemies (1QS 1:9–10).

2. Your enemy is defined as someone "who hates you," and love is not just an attitude but the action that results, namely "doing good" for others. These people show you only animosity and hostility, but for this you return to them good deeds (see also 1 Pet 3:9; Rom 12:20).

3. Further, your enemy "curses you," and for that you return "blessings." Insult and slander were one of the primary means of persecution (1 Pet 2:12–13, 23; 4:4). The blessings with which we respond begin with our prayers that God

pour out his favor on them, beginning with his Spirit to bring them repentance and new life (the greatest blessing we can bestow). Both Jesus and Stephen asked God to forgive those who took their lives (Luke 23:34; Acts 7:60). While certainly this does not negate prophetic warning, since conversion cannot take place without realizing one's sin, he mainly has in mind prayer for God's blessing on them.

4. Your enemy, finally, is one who "mistreats you," speaking of active persecution, and you return for that "prayer" rather than retaliation. I love the prayer of the rabbi in *Fiddler on the Roof*, "Lord, bless the czar and keep him (lengthy pause) far away." This command undergirds all the others. This prayer certainly can include a plea for vindication and justice, as in Revelation 6:9–11, where the martyrs under the altar cry out an imprecatory prayer, "How long, Sovereign Lord, holy and true, until you judge the inhabitants of the earth and avenge our blood?" However, this prayer is primarily for the enemies' conversion and for all that is good for them.

Jesus continues in verses 29–30 with four examples of the kind of love he intends followed by a summary conclusion, the "Golden Rule" (v. 31):

1. Turn the other cheek (v. 29a). As also in Matthew 5:39, this illustrates an openness to suffering and forgiveness that Christ exemplified himself and demands of his followers. In the first century, this would refer to a backhanded blow meant as a studied insult. The refusal to retaliate entails a willingness to accept a degrading and vulnerable situation. The Christ follower accepts dishonor rather than the personally satisfying but morally wrong act of reprisal. We refuse to demand our rights when that requires returning evil for evil. Instead, we forgive rather than seek revenge.

2. Give your shirt as well as your robe (v. 29b). People at that time often wore an inner shirt or tunic and an outward robe

or coat. This could refer to robbery, a legal lawsuit where the garment is in pledge of a loan, or giving to someone in need. Most think the parallel Matthew 5:40 ("sue you and take your shirt") refers to the legal situation, while this describes robbery, with the order here (coat, then shirt) depicting the thief stripping off first the outer coat and then the inner shirt. The point in both is a refusal to cling to earthly possessions and a willingness to maintain your witness over your earthly rights.

3. Give to the needy poor (v. 30a). This could refer to a beggar or a needy person who asks for alms or help. It could also be a loan (as in 6:34) or an outright gift. Commentators argue between these options, but there is a breadth here that must include them all. Jesus demands of his disciples a refusal to cling to earthly possessions and a willingness to share them with those less fortunate than themselves. We encounter this position several times in Luke, for the question of earthly possessions is a central feature of this Gospel.

4. Don't demand the return of your possessions (v. 30b). As above, this could refer to legal action, robbery, or giving to the needy. In the patron-client society of the Roman world, reciprocity was always expected, and giving was done not out of kindness but for prestige. Giving was a social strategy to cement power and authority in business or society in general. Jesus reversed all that. Giving was an act of love, and the goal was helping others rather than gaining power over them. There was no desire for attention or expectation of payback, only the intention to benefit others.

Jesus summarizes the list with the Golden Rule (v. 31), "Do to others as you would have them do to you," also found in Matthew 7:12, where it is found late in the Sermon on the Mount to summarize "the Law and the Prophets"—indeed, all the ethical content of the sermon. Judaism had the negative form of this, "Don't do to others what you don't want to see done to yourself" (Tobit

4:15; b. Shabbat 31a), but Jesus teaches a positive ethic. He wants his followers always to reflect on how they would like to be treated when making decisions regarding their treatment of others. He is demanding not just fair treatment of others but an attitude that always seeks what is best and most helpful for them.

To illustrate the Golden Rule, Jesus turns in verses 32–34 to three examples of the principle of reciprocity (**lex talionis**, "the law of retribution") that don't work by themselves. Simply to return love when loved or good deeds only to those who are good to us is insufficient for God's kingdom people. We live by a higher ethic, and more is expected of us. So he asks first, "Where is the credit in loving only those who love you?" This is what sinners do, and there is nothing special in that. Such reactions do not prove your moral and spiritual superiority. This credit is both with God and the world. God will not laud you, and the world will not be touched by such conduct, for they do the same. It is when we love those who dislike us that we stand out.

The action side of love comes next (v. 33). If the only time we do good is when we receive good in return, we are no different than the pagans. As I noted above, in the patron-client society of Rome, good is always a calculated act, designed entirely to get something in return. God will not bless such behavior, and the reward from the world is temporary at best. Worldly sinners live by this ethic, and there is very little credit in such behavior.

A specific example completes the set, as Jesus applies the Golden Rule to business ethics, in particular to lending and the laws of usury (v. 34). The expectation of being paid back is the heart of all business deals. It is just regular life in the world, and no credit accrues to such action, for it is expected. There is no reward from God, and no special attention from the world. Jesus could have in mind loans without interest, as mentioned in the Torah (Lev 25:35–37; Deut 23:19–20), but in the Judaism of Jesus' day interest was common in business deals, and he likely has that in mind here.

In verse 35 Jesus puts the section together in summary form to make his central point: "But love your enemies, do good to them, and lend to them without expecting to get anything back." The meaning and thrust of kingdom ethics flows out of this summary. God demands we live on a much higher plane than the world. For sinful humanity the law of reciprocity rules—they will merely respond, good for good and evil for evil. This is reversed for Christ followers, who ought to love when wronged and return good for evil. There is a single verbal idea behind "not expecting anything back," *mēden apelpizontes* (NKJV: "hoping for nothing in return"). In other words, you give without thinking of what you will get out of it. Your only concern is to help the other. No repayment is expected, and no thought of personal benefit enters the equation.

When there is no thought of reward in the earthly setting, then the reward from the heavenly setting will enter the picture. Jesus notes that then (and only then) "your reward will be great." In other words, the absence of concern for earthly reward will result in an even greater heavenly reward. You are trading the temporary for the eternal. The loan becomes a gift, and the profit becomes eternal reward. While many think there are not rewards in heaven (we all receive the crown of life), I disagree. As I said on 6:23, my view is that everything we do on earth for the glory of God and the benefit of others is immediately (so to speak) banked in heaven and will be returned to us by God as eternal reward. We receive God's *charis* (credit, favor), and he is pleased with us.

Moreover, we will have a new status in heaven and "be children of the Most High." In one sense, all Christians are the children of God (Rom 8:14–17), but there is a special sense here. "Child of / son of" is an idiom used in Semitic languages to describe the main characteristic of a person. Here it means that in a very special way Christians exemplify "the Most High" God in their attitudes and behavior. God is a God who "is kind to the ungrateful and wicked," and you have now joined him in your own behavior toward others.

Concluding by restating his basic point, Jesus gives his disciples their marching orders, "Be merciful, just as your father is merciful" (v. 36). Love, kindness, mercy—these attitudes and actions (they are both) demonstrate what it means to be "children of the Most High" and to live accordingly. Love and mercy define the character of God throughout the Old Testament, and the good news of Jesus flows out of this. God's mercy led Christ to the cross and brought salvation to an undeserving humankind. This mercy must now be exemplified by his followers. When we show mercy, we imitate the God of Scripture and truly become his people and members of his family.

KINGDOM RULES FOR THE COMMUNITY (6:37–49)

The refusal to judge others (6:37–42)

Jesus turns in verses 37–38 to the issue of judging others, and he uses the same fourfold pattern he did in verses 29–31. First, the opposite of mercy is judgment, so if God's people are merciful, they cannot be judgmental toward others. "Do not judge" in verse 37 is a present-tense prohibition, *mē krinete*, meaning either "stop judging" or, more likely, "don't judge at any time." We need to interpret the meaning of "judge" carefully. It is not referring to a court trial, nor is it general discernment and admonition of sin in another person's life. Evaluating right and wrong in each other is valid and important in the church and family (see 1 Cor 5:5; Phil 3:2; Gal 6:1; Heb 3:13; 1 John 4:1).

This refers to a judgmental attitude that looks down on others and enjoys condemning them with an attitude of superiority. It is being critical of others and enjoying it. An example of this kind of judging is gossip, which I call "passive slander." It turns judging others unfairly into entertainment, hurting their reputations just for the pleasure of passing on a juicy tidbit. There is no loving concern or humility in such an act. The missing component is love, caring for others enough not to allow sin to gain control of their life. It is the mercy of verse 36 that makes for proper judgment of others. Those who are judgmental in this way will themselves "be judged," a divine passive that means that person will be condemned by God for the lack of love and mercy shown to others. There is an inaugurated thrust in this. They will be judged now and will face final judgment in the future.

Second, judgmentalism always leads to condemnation. Judgment without love or mercy leads to serious sin against others and against God, and the Lord will return it back on our heads. The way God deals with us depends on how we deal with others. This is the proper law of reciprocity: God treats us the way we treat others. We cannot imitate Christ without emulating his attitudes and reaction to others. To be Christlike we must make certain that all our relationships seek to build others up and help them grow. If we take a superior attitude and condemn others, God will condemn us first for the sin of prejudice and then for beating down rather than building up those around us. Again, this does not mean we cannot admonish others and seek to get them right with the Lord. The issue is *how* we do so and our true purposes in pointing out sin in their lives.

In the final part of verse 37, Christ turns to the positive side. God will bless those who in challenging others do two things: forgive and give. Instead of berating others for their sins, we forgive their sins (6:37b). This is a key point. The judgmental attitude enjoys pointing out negatives and putting people down. The caring Christian seeks always to bring them to repentance so they can find forgiveness both from the Lord and from the people they have hurt. We must bring them back to the Lord to find forgiveness, and we must be willing to forgive to the extent that they have hurt us.

The spiritual side of forgiving sins leads in verse 38 to the social side of generous giving. We have seen this often in Luke, and it will continue to be emphasized throughout this Gospel (1:51–53; 2:12; 4:18–19; 6:29–31). True followers of Christ will never be enamored of possessions and luxurious living. The more they have, the more they will give away.

Jesus then illustrates this principle of giving with a saying about reward, using the picture of purchased grain poured into a container or measure to achieve a "good measure" being purchased. To get the maximum return for the payment, the grain is "pressed down [and] shaken together" so that it settles to the bottom of the container, and this keeps happening until it is "running over" the top of the container. The picture of this gift "poured into your lap" shows the grain poured out of the measure into the lap of the purchaser, who is wearing a robe with a bag in his lap to receive the grain.

The message is that God will pay back the maximum return to those who give to others. He will give us far more than we have given to others. When we are gracious and generous, as in verse 35, our "reward will be great." As before, this blends the already and the not yet. Our reward from God begins now as he pours his blessings into our lives, and it will especially be evident when we get to heaven.

In verses 39–42 Jesus uses three metaphors or parables (see comments on 5:36) to demonstrate his point. These are not what we normally think of as parables, though, for they don't have a plot or story line.

The blind who "lead the blind" in verse 39 are the Pharisees and scribes, blind guides who are attempting to lead the equally blind people of Israel. Both groups are blind to the true ways of God, but the Pharisees think that with their oral tradition they have insight into the things of God while in reality they have none. This is similar to John 9:39–41, where Jesus said, "For judgment I have come into this world, so that the blind will see and those who see [namely the Pharisees] will become blind," adding the indictment, "now that you claim you can see, your guilt remains." The Jewish leaders are blind to the reality of who Jesus is, so both they and their followers will "fall into a pit," that is, into absolute spiritual failure. In Judaism this image pictures suffering and catastrophe (Prov 22:14; Isa 24:18) and often the pits of Sheol, or Hades (Ps 31:17; Prov 1:12). There may be two levels to the warning: generally the fall into spiritual disaster, and specifically that they are heading for hell as they turn against Jesus and his ways.

The second extended metaphor (v. 40) depicts discipleship, both the negative example of the Pharisees and their followers and the positive example of Jesus and his disciples. In verse 39 the Pharisees are blind guides or teachers leading the people of Israel into more and more spiritual blindness. The message here is that students will not gain greater knowledge than their teachers; they will become more and more like their teachers.

The imagery of being "fully trained" means that in the process of training they will change their ways (the verb, *katartizō*, is used of "preparing" nets in Mark 1:19) and take on the lifestyle of their teacher. This will be negative with respect to the Pharisees and positive with respect to Jesus. The positive is uppermost here, so Jesus is talking about Christlikeness as the goal of discipleship. We could apply this saying to the false teachers of our own day. The teaching arm of the church is all the more important when we see teachers, both in politics and in the church, brainwashing their followers and turning them away from the ways of God. We must lead our people deeper and deeper into the truths of the word and the life of Christ.

The third saying (vv. 41-42) returns to Jesus' message about judging others. Self-righteous judges look down on their "brother" or fellow disciple for the "speck of sawdust" in their eye and ignore the huge "plank" or log in their own eye. The hypocrisy of ignoring your greater problems in order to pretend you are superior to others has always been a huge problem in the church. The solution should be common sense—deal with your problems first, then you can see clearly to help others.

We must all win the right to teach and correct others. Paul makes a similar point in 2 Corinthians 1:3-4. There, as we work through our personal hardships, we are enabled to help others as we "comfort those in any trouble with the comfort we ourselves receive from God." The same point is made here. As we work through our personal issues, we learn a lot that we can then share as we help others go through their own issues. We first deal with our problems and then with humility share the solutions with others going through similar problems.

A tree and its fruit (6:43–45)

Jesus continues to address discipleship in verses 43–45, this time from the standpoint of the teacher or leader who exemplifies the truths to those being trained. There are three aspects. First, like a good or a useless tree, your "fruit" will expose what you are truly like: "by their fruit you will recognize them" (Matt 7:20). By examining whether a tree bears figs or thorns you can determine its usefulness. This means that teachers must make certain their life proves the goodness of their message.

Second, a tree always bears the fruit that is in keeping with its actual nature (v. 44). Thornbushes will never produce figs. The message to hypocrites is, "Make very certain that you are who you say you are. Pretension only works for a short time, and the truth always comes out in the end. You may think you can get away with it forever, but God will right all wrongs, and you will pay the ultimate price at the final judgment."

Third, the key is to have a storehouse of good in your heart from which you can produce good things in your life and teaching (v. 45). What you say will in the end unmask who you really are. The message and life of a good person will eventually come to the surface, and the same is true of bad things emerging from an evil person. You can fool people for a while but not over the long haul, and you can never hide what you are from God. First be honest with yourself, and then you can change accordingly to produce only goodness.

Parable of the wise and foolish builders (6:46-49)

Jesus concludes his sermon by exhorting the audience to obey. The incredible results of obeying Jesus were shown earlier in the miraculous catch of fish in 5:4-7. One of the primary titles in Luke, "Lord," has been used of Jesus three times thus far, by Simon Peter in 5:8 after the catch of fish, by the leper in 5:12 as he asks for healing, and by Jesus as he speaks of himself in 6:5 as "Lord of the Sabbath." All three connote a very high **Christology** with overtones of deity, and "Lord, Lord" here picks up on that. To acknowledge Jesus as Lord is to recognize that he is much more than a rabbi or even a prophet. The presence of the double "Lord, Lord" here is very emphatic and emotive. To confess Jesus as Lord and fail to obey is a contradiction, taking what should be high worship and emptying it of meaning. The central part of the Great Commission is "teaching them to obey everything I have commanded you" (Matt 28:20). A pastor friend said it quite well: "For too many Christians the great omission in the Great Commission is the words 'to obey.'" May that not be true of any of us.

What should be happening as a result of this sermon is found in verse 47, in the one who "comes to me and hears my words and puts them into practice." This is the same sentiment as in James 1:22-23, describing the proper disciple as one who listens to the word and does what it says. In both Hebrew and Greek, the verbs for "hear" are closely connected to "obey." We have not truly heard until we have obeyed. As with all of Scripture, God's commands are at all times meant to be lived out in our daily lives. Jesus as Lord of all has the full authority of God—indeed, full authority *as* God.

The parable of verses 48-49 parallels Matthew 7:24-27, which ends the Sermon on the Mount. Matthew, writing for a Jewish audience, draws on background that would be familiar to an audience in Palestine, while Luke, with a more Gentile setting, contextualizes it with **Hellenistic** features. Matthew stresses winter rains unleashing a huge flood, while Luke doesn't mention rain but possibly overflowing creeks and rivers producing a flood. Luke also has more detail, yet the story is the same in both.

The purpose of the parable in both Matthew and Luke is to contrast the person who hears and obeys with one who listens but fails to put the teaching into practice, likening them to homes constructed on different foundations, building on a similar story in Ezekiel 13:10–16. The wise builder takes the time and expense to do it right—he digs the foundation deep into the very bedrock and anchors it in the rock. This home is probably built in a river delta that can flood fairly easily, so it needs to be very secure. Floods in Israel come very suddenly and can produce huge amounts of water. However, when the flood strikes this house, it is not shaken because it is so rock-steady.

The person who does not live Jesus' teaching is like a foolish builder who erects his house on the kind of clay soil that seems hard and sturdy until the water hits it. It soaks up the water and then becomes a sponge without substance. When the torrents strike that home, it collapses and is swept away, totally destroyed. Jesus' thesis is that those who practice what he says are grounded on God's foundation, anchored in divine truths that keep them safe and secure. The difficulties of life and false teaching cannot move them away from their faith in Christ, and they triumph spiritually. This is a serious warning to the hypocrite or half-hearted follower who isn't taking Jesus' teaching seriously. Such people are headed for disaster.

———

In this section we have now entered the ministry proper of Jesus. He both chooses his companions in his messianic mission and addresses them with his formative Sermon on the Plain, providing in a sense a constitution for the new community. As a second Moses he ascends a mountain and, after a night of prayer, chooses twelve "apostles" or official representatives of the new Israel to serve as his envoys or agents (vv. 12–16). This is their commission, and he will focus on them as leaders of his new movement.

After choosing his team, Jesus addresses them and the crowds with his greatest sermon, probably a truncated version of his Sermon on the Mount in Matthew 5–7. It is in a sense the Torah of the Messiah, the new rules for the kingdom age he is introducing. He begins with both beatitudes and woes (vv. 20–26), deepening his opening address of 4:18–19, where he used Isaiah 61:1–2 to show his major purpose of lifting up the poor and freeing the captives. These demonstrate that as God's people we must eschew the centrality of possessions in our lives and use our material blessings to lift up the marginalized and the poor. This also directly condemns those who live for the riches and pleasures of this world. The contrast is frightening. Those who have little now will have everything in heaven, and those who have grabbed it all for themselves here will be completely bereft for eternity. It is not wrong to be rich, but it is a serious sin to live for your riches, and all who do so will pay the piper.

Next is an important section on love of enemies (vv. 27–31), extolling the triumph of love over reciprocity and revenge. Even when hurt, the child of God turns the other cheek and returns blessing for dislike. God's people take their possessions and use them to help the unfortunate. Following this is a wonderful section on true reciprocity (vv. 32–36), exhorting us to give to others without concern for what we get in return. Our reward is the joy of knowing that we have truly changed another's life for the better. This is especially true when we do good to those who have turned against us and emulate God's love for sinners, namely his incredible love for us when he sent his Son to the cross for us who were his enemies.

In the next section, on judging (vv. 37–42), we see the importance of refusing to stand over others to judge and point out their sins and problems from our superior position. Instead, we must seek always to discern their needs and draw them closer to Christ.

We must find the humility to realize we are not better than anyone and that we have the privilege of true reciprocity—helping others so they can help us. We thus become like our teacher, Christ, as we love others and give of ourselves rather than condemn them.

Jesus concludes this wonderful Sermon on the Plain by presenting us with two metaphors. First, we must be fruitful trees who show by our works what we truly are by maintaining a storehouse of good in ourselves, from which we draw out that which will exemplify Christ through our conduct and treatment of others (vv. 43–45). Second, we must in every sense make Jesus Lord of our life and obey him (vv. 46–49). We must sink the foundation of our lives into the very bedrock so that we can stand firm when the floods of life try to bring us down. I wrote the first draft of this chapter on the day Hurricane Harvey hit Texas, pouring out sixty inches of rain over the next several days. Like people in the path of a hurricane, if we want to weather life's disasters we must be secure on solid ground, with our utter dependence on God and Christ. It is absolutely mandatory that we live lives of obedience and practice what we preach.

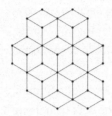

COMPASSIONATE MINISTRY AND GROWING POPULARITY

(7:1–50)

We now enter the ministry proper section of Luke, as Jesus encounters a broad assortment of people, including a Gentile centurion and two women, proving that he is indeed a Messiah who does not restrict himself to Israel but has come for all humanity. Moreover, his is a ministry of compassion and mercy, as he heals a Roman officer's servant and a widow's son and forgives a fallen woman's sins. His authority and power are at all times wielded for the benefit of hurting people. At the same time, these people exemplify saving faith. More and more, those reached by Jesus respond in faith as his popularity grows throughout the region. Framing the chapter are unexpected individuals—a centurion and a sinful woman—who show this faith and extend the definition of the people of God beyond Israel.

JESUS SEES A CENTURION'S FAITH AND HEALS HIS SERVANT (7:1-10)

THE SETTING (7:1-2)

After finishing his sermon, Jesus returns to his new home in Capernaum, and Luke emphasizes "the people who were listening,"

literally, "in the hearing of the people," looking back to the concluding teaching in 6:46–47 on hearing and obeying the words
of Jesus. Throughout this chapter we will see people responding
to him.

On this first occasion, we are told of the response of a Roman
centurion. Centurions are featured often in Luke-Acts (nineteen
of the twenty-three New Testament occurrences), with the centurion's confession at Jesus' crucifixion (Luke 23:47) and the conversion of Cornelius in Acts 10 especially prominent. A centurion
was in charge of ten platoons, or a hundred men, and was in some
ways the most important officer in the Roman army. This one was
a Gentile though probably not Roman; Galilee wasn't important
enough and had mainly auxiliary troops. He would have been a
mercenary but still important, and he was either a God-fearer or a
proselyte to Judaism. Centurions were moderately wealthy, earning a good living, and he had built one of the Capernaum synagogues (v. 5). He had a slave whom he "valued highly." The Greek
word for "valuable" (*entimos*) is not meant in monetary terms but
as "highly esteemed, very dear." This slave had a terminal illness
and was near death. The centurion had no recourse but to come
to Jesus, as he had undoubtedly heard a great deal about him and
his miraculous ministry.

The Testimony of His Jewish Friends (7:3–5)

It is hard to know why he doesn't come to Jesus himself; in Matthew
8:5 he does, but Matthew probably simplifies the story. He was
probably reluctant, being a Gentile and a soldier, thus with two
strikes against him.[1] Showing a remarkable humility, he asks some
of his Jewish friends to intercede for him. The use of go-betweens
was very common in the first century. Moreover, these are the
upper crust of Jewish society, "elders of the Jews," civic (and

---

1. Some think that as a military officer, he always sent "underlings" to do his
bidding, but that is not the atmosphere here.

probably religious) leaders and highly respected. They forward his request, which shows his deep faith that Jesus can "come and heal his servant" if he so wishes.

Their testimony of their affection for the centurion (7:4–5) is rather remarkable given the normal animosity Jews showed Gentiles, especially the military that was the basis of Roman oppression of the Jews. This in itself attests the religious sensitivity of the man and the extent to which he had proved himself to the Jews of Capernaum. They declare him completely "worthy," or deserving (*axios*), of Jesus' attention and give two pieces of evidence for this: "he loves our nation and has built our synagogue." This could mean he is a God-fearer rather than a proselyte, for one would expect them to say, "he loves the Lord God" if that were true. But we cannot be sure. This is a great example of an exception to the rule, for it shows that there were instances of high Roman officials who were more positive toward Israel. This in fact is important for Acts, which pictures a large group of God-fearers from whose ranks many converts to Christ came.

Jesus' Response and the Centurion's Deep Humility (7:6–8)

Jesus accedes to the request and is on his way to the centurion's house when the man sends others to meet him on the way, showing an incredible humility. As a centurion he could have made Jesus do anything he wanted, but instead he contradicts the testimony of the elders and in essence tells Jesus, "I don't deserve you coming to me." In fact, it is a double sense of unworthiness. He admits he had not come in the first place because he didn't feel worthy to stand in Jesus' presence, and he still feels that way.

His humility recalls that of Peter in 5:8, when he said, "Go away from me, Lord; I am a sinful man!" He like Peter recognizes the supreme holiness and righteous character of Jesus and his own unrighteousness in comparison. He too is a model for us as we come to grips with our sinfulness and deep need for God's grace and forgiveness. That is what he does, throwing himself on the mercy of Jesus. He knows Jesus has the power to heal from a distance. All he has to do is "say the word, and my servant will be healed." He is unworthy to stand in Jesus' presence, but he isn't asking for himself. His request is for his beloved slave, and he throws himself on Jesus' compassion.

To show why he is certain Jesus' mere word is sufficient, he uses his own authority as a centurion for an illustration (7:8), using a rhetorical technique called "from the weightier to the lighter." As a centurion in the Roman army, he has absolute authority over his ten platoons, and his word is law. Whether he tells his men to "go" or "come" or "do this or that," he knows he will be obeyed. Jesus, however, is in charge of heaven's armies, and his word is far weightier than a mere centurion can muster. He commands the cosmic forces of heaven and earth, and his word will absolutely be obeyed. With this far greater authority, Jesus can heal any way he decides.

FAITH AND HEALING (7:9–10)

Jesus' response is a major step to the universal mission to the Gentiles, which Luke will stress in the rest of Luke-Acts. Jesus, the Jewish Messiah, is "amazed" at the deep faith of a Gentile, saying to the crowd, "I tell you, I have not found such great faith even in Israel." Earlier in Luke it is always others who are astonished at Jesus, but now there is a complete reversal as Jesus is filled with wonder at this Gentile centurion. This Gentile exemplifies something not seen among the Jewish people, and he "turns" to the crowds specifically and emphatically to tell them about this.

Throughout his two-volume work, Luke shows the growing rejection of Jesus by his Jewish compatriots and the growing numbers of Gentiles who come into the kingdom in their stead. It is not just this man's faith in his miraculous power that so moves Jesus. It is saving faith, faith in Jesus himself as God's Messiah and the clear repentance that underlies it, that so overwhelms him. This man becomes a model for the new Israel Christ is establishing.

The actual healing is not described. Rather, we see the emissaries of the centurion returning home and finding his slave healed. The emphasis is on the man's great faith, and the healing is the aftermath brought about as a result of that faith. In fact, the Greek says that they found the slave "in good health." The healing is assumed. Complete healing has been effected. In many ways this is even stronger than other healing stories, because the man's entire body is cleansed of all disease and weakness.

JESUS RAISES A WIDOW'S SON (7:11–17)

In some ways these two miracle stories are complementary, in other ways quite distinct. The centurion is one of the more influential people in Capernaum, with money, authority, and power. The widow was a virtually nameless and powerless woman with no money and no family to care for her. The one is at the top of the social scale, the other at the bottom. Yet there are important parallels as well, as both are forced to throw themselves completely on the mercy of Jesus and both feel the effects of his incredible power.

John the Baptist has come in "the spirit and power of Elijah" (1:17), but John fulfills the preaching side of Elijah's ministry, and Jesus fulfills the wonder-working-prophet side. In particular, this miracle recalls Elijah raising the son of the widow of Zarephath (1 Kgs 17:17–24) and Elisha raising the Shunammite's son (2 Kgs 4:8–37). This also begins the process of revealing Jesus to the people, as the people acclaim Jesus as a "great prophet" (7:16), but it also launches a series of questions regarding his identity: "Are you the one who is to come?" (7:19). This will dominate in ensuing chapters.

THE SETTING (7:11–12)

Jesus was undoubtedly visiting his hometown and in the process visited the small village of Nain six miles from Nazareth and twenty-five from Capernaum. With him are his disciples but also a "large crowd." We don't know why, but most likely his growing popularity meant he pretty much went nowhere alone at that time. The point here is the confluence of two large crowds, for another one was part of the funeral procession in the next verse.

Since the Jews did not embalm people, funerals nearly always took place on the day a person died, usually at the end of the day. This young man was the only son of a widow, a real tragedy, as she would now be all alone with no one to take care of her. This begins a string of three only children (8:42; 9:38) to be raised or healed by him, proving his great compassion for the needy. The entire scene is engulfed with the sadness of this poor woman who is left with absolutely nothing and no one to help her. It seems there is nothing to be done but weep for her. But then God orchestrates the events and has the miracle-working Messiah happen by at just the right moment.

COMPASSION AND HEALING (7:13–15)

Once more Luke hints at the true significance of Jesus, calling him "the Lord" in a setting that magnifies his nature and person. This is actually the first time he has been labeled "Lord," initiating a string of such occasions (7:19; 10:1, 39, 41; 11:39; 12:42; 13:15; 17:5, 6; 18:6; 19:8; 22:61; 24:3). Luke is well known for this and shows that Jesus is not just the "great prophet" (7:16) but Messiah and Lord of all. He demonstrates the authority of Yahweh as he raises the dead and heals the sick. This exalted Lord is filled with compassion (*esplangchnisthē*, NIV: "his heart went out to her") when he sees this tragic scene. At the moment of death, this young man would have been anointed with fragrant burial oils, wrapped in a cloth, and placed on a plank (they didn't use coffins). Family, friends, and villagers would have gathered around, and that very same day they would have conducted a funeral procession outside the town to the burial site. Jesus would have come across the procession on the way to the burial. As with Lazarus in John 11:19–33, the crowd would have been quite noisy in their grief.

The next two verses (14–15) do not describe a resuscitation but a resurrection. Jesus' intention is obvious from his movements. He touches the funeral bier or plank, probably to stop the funeral procession, and gives a direct command to him. Note that Jesus is not defiled for touching a corpse; as the healing Messiah, he is impervious to defilement. In a real sense the young man actually isn't there, for his spirit is in heaven with God. So the command calls him back and in one fell swoop reunites spirit and body, "Young man, I say to you, get up!" The order is *egerthēti*, "Be raised up [by God]," as the God-man gives him his life back. He has authority over death, as he will for every believer at the end of history.

Three statements in verse 15 describe the effects of his command. The corpse ("dead man") sits up, starts to speak, and Jesus gives him back to his mother. The picture is the corpse coming to life and sitting upright on the funeral bier. Probably when he began to speak no one could hear what he said because everybody was screaming in shock and joy. Jesus' handing him over to his mother is heavily symbolic and a very touching scene, the most powerful picture yet of the captives being released by Jesus (4:18). This recalls 1 Kings 17:23, where Elijah gives the boy who was raised from the dead back to the widow of Zarephath.

THE AWE AND JOY THAT RESULT (7:16–17)

The reaction of the onlookers is normal for what is virtually a theophany or manifestation of the presence of God in Jesus, and they heap glory on both Jesus and his Father. Fear and awe as a result of demonstrations of Jesus' miraculous power are frequent in Luke (1:65; 5:25; 8:25, 37), as is praise (5:26; 18:43; 23:47). I cannot imagine what it would be like to be present when Jesus conquers death and raises the dead.

They also take a step forward in recognizing Jesus for who he is. The crowds in the rest of Luke are enamored of his performing miracles but hardly ever go the next step to belief. They are what we today call "seekers" and remain uncommitted. Here they confess him as a "great prophet" who has "appeared among us." Among the prophets, Elijah and Elisha were the two who regularly performed miracles, and the people here recognize the parallel. However, they fall short of affirming him as Messiah and the "prophet like Moses" who was yet to come. He is not "the" prophet (the direct article is missing here). So this is a huge step forward but not yet conversion to Jesus.

They also realize that "God has come to help his people," understanding the extent that God is behind Jesus' power. This definitely distinguishes them from the leaders who oppose Jesus. Seeing Jesus and his miracles as a divine visitation for the benefit of God's people is also a step closer to conversion. Jesus to them is a gift from God, a prophet from of old sent to show Israel that God still cares for them.

The result is a further note to 4:14, 37, that "news" or reports about him "spread throughout Judea and the surrounding country." His popularity continues to soar, moving far beyond Galilee. Judea here stands for all of Palestine, not just that one province. As we will see in the next scene, this means the Dead Sea area as well, where John the Baptist has been imprisoned by Herod in a fortress called Machaerus.

JOHN SENDS QUESTIONS TO JESUS (7:18–35)

It is natural after Jesus has performed such an extraordinary miracle that people ask, "Who is this?" No one in all of history has ever done so many astounding things, and he will not just continue but extend this wondrous activity in 8:22–9:56, when he will perform all four kinds of miracles—nature, exorcism, illness, and raising the dead! No wonder everyone is wondering (pun intended). In fact, we have similar questions in our day, so Luke has John ask the question everyone else has on their mind. While the crowd confessed that Jesus is "*a great prophet*," John now queries whether Jesus is "*the* one who is to come."

Jesus' Answer to the Baptist (7:18–23)

As the news spreads (7:17), disciples of the Baptist hear it and tell him all about the miraculous ministry of Jesus. Luke had earlier reported John's arrest and imprisonment when he denounced the immoral liaison between Herod Antipas and Herodias, former wife of his half-brother Philip. John would of course be anxious to keep up with news about Jesus. However, enough time has passed that he is starting to get discouraged and doubtful since Jesus seemingly is not acting like the Messiah John knows him to be. Machaerus, where John was imprisoned, was a Maccabean fortress east of the Dead Sea that Herod the Great restored and used as one of his palaces. So John sends two of his disciples to Jesus, probably as an official delegation on the basis of the demand in Deuteronomy 19:15 for two witnesses.

The importance of the question is seen in the fact that Luke, after having reported it in 7:19, repeats it in 7:20. It first occurs on the lips of the Baptist and then is asked directly of Jesus: "Are you the one who is to come, or should we expect someone else?" Luke wants us to ask this as well, and it culminates the events of the last two chapters, for it tells us this miracle-working prophet from Galilee is indeed the expected Messiah, the prophet like Moses who will change the world.

There is some debate as to why the Baptist, who had been called to be the messianic forerunner from birth, should ask this question. Some think this is due to John's imprisonment. If Jesus had indeed come to free the prisoners (Isa 61:1–2 in 4:18–19), why is John still languishing in prison? Others think John's doubts are due to the lengthy amount of time with little progress; he wants Jesus to act more decisively. A third possibility is that Jesus in his positive ministry of performing miracles did not fit the kind of Messiah John was expecting, one who would bring God's judgment on the apostate nation and pagan world. This third view makes the most sense as it fits the Baptist and his ministry well. I don't see him as concerned about his imprisonment or impatient of

Jesus' timing. He simply does not understand how and why Jesus is developing his ministry in the way he has. Like Jesus' disciples later, he wanted Jesus to be conquering King more than Suffering Servant and to bring about the end of history. He wanted "Onward Christian Soldiers," not "Gentle Jesus, Meek and Mild."

The idea of Jesus as the Coming One refers back to the Baptist's testimony in 3:16: "one who is more powerful than I will come." He now extends this to "the One Expected to Come" of prophecy, namely the prophet like Moses of Deuteronomy 18:15, as Jesus will say in 13:35, "Blessed is he who comes in the name of the Lord." John is confused and wonders if this is still true.

Jesus' response to the Baptist is found in verses 21–23. John's messengers arrived and asked his question at the very time Jesus was engaged in the very ministry John was questioning—curing the sick, casting out evil spirits, and restoring sight to the blind (v. 21). Being in prison and just hearing the reports, John did not realize how powerful a ministry Christ was actually conducting. So he does not simply answer the query with words but with powerful deeds. There is little meekness in these acts; they are all about power. Moreover, these two are official Deuteronomic witnesses, and it is important that they see these miracles being performed and not just hear about them. So they will report what they have actually *witnessed*.

Jesus begins his response with Isaiah 35:5–6 and 61:1 to show that in reality his miraculous ministry fulfills messianic prophecies (v. 22). These are not just prophetic miracles à la Elijah and Elisha but messianic miracles that demonstrate that the kingdom of God is entering this world and changing everything. Jesus mentions six miracles, and they parallel Isaiah well: the blind (both), the lame (both), lepers (only Luke), the deaf (both), the mute (Isaiah only), the dead raised (only Luke), the poor (both, this time Isa 61:1). In Isaiah these lists are describing the messianic age that is coming, and Jesus' message to John is that his miracles prove that this age has arrived with him. These were common messianic expectations, proved by such passages as **Qumran**'s 4Q521, which contains a list quite similar to this one. So the Messiah was indeed seen as a wonder-worker in Judaism. It also proves that as Messiah Jesus has indeed come as Isaiah's Servant of Yahweh. So John's militaristic expectation of a judging Messiah stands corrected; it is part of the not-yet rather than the already.

He concludes with a beatitude, "Blessed is anyone who does not stumble on account of me" (v. 23). The idea of "stumbling" (*skandalisthē*) stems from the stone passage of Isaiah 8:14, describing the Messiah as the chief cornerstone (Isa 28:16) and "a stone that causes people to stumble and a rock that makes them fall" (featured in Mark 12:10–11; Acts 4:14; Rom 9:33; 1 Cor 1:23; 1 Pet 2:8). The servant ministry of Jesus, anchored as it is in his messianic actions here, calls for decision and demands conversion. The nation as a whole, and John's followers in particular, cannot avoid this decision and dare not "stumble" or fall away.

Jesus' Witness about John (7:24–28)

The messengers return to John, and Jesus turns to the crowds and provides his own witness to the place of the Baptist in redemptive history. He begins with a series of options (vv. 24–25) and then provides his answer (vv. 26–27) with a surprising conclusion (v. 28). The two questions of verses 24–25 concern what kind of prophetic figure John was, and both expect a negative answer:

(1) "A reed swayed by the wind": This pictures cane grass on the banks of the Jordan gently swaying in the breeze and could refer to an irrelevant or trivial person easily swayed by others. More literally, Jesus is saying that people did not travel to the Jordan just to see the vegetation but to see a person of substance. John was known as a strong person with powerful convictions, so Christ is saying that a great prophet clearly attracted their interest, and they know it.

(2) "A man dressed in fine clothes": This contrasts John with Herod and his court. The point is that luxury and expensive clothes

are found in palaces. The answer is a clear "of course not," for
John was a wilderness prophet dressed accordingly (Mark 1:6). The
irony is that he was just then imprisoned in a palace fortress built
by Herod the Great. So in these two metaphors Christ is saying that
the Baptist is an important rather than meaningless figure, in no
way like the irrelevant sycophants of Herod's court.

Jesus responds strongly (7:26-27). John is a prophet and more
(see Luke 3:15; John 1:20; Acts 13:25). His father Zechariah prophesied that John would be "the prophet of the Most High" (1:76).
He like Elijah was a prophetic voice calling the nation to repentance. All Israel knew him in that guise. Yet he was also much
more; he was the forerunner of the Messiah, the one who fulfilled
Malachi 3:1 (and Isa 40:3). The citation of verse 27 is drawn from
the Malachi passage along with Exodus 23:20, literally saying, "I
am sending my messenger before your face." In Exodus it is the
angel going before Israel in the desert, but at a secondary level it
refers to a sacred forerunner to God's salvation via the Messiah.
The two together prophesy John as the divine herald commissioned
by God to prepare the "way" for Jesus Messiah.

There is quite a bit of debate as to whether the way is being
prepared for Jesus as Messiah or for Israel to accept him as the
coming Messiah. In a sense it is both, but what Jesus is prophesy-
ing is the "new exodus" that Jesus is bringing to the nation (and the
Gentiles). John is the **eschatological** prophet going before Jesus
Messiah to bring about the final exodus/deliverance and inaugurate the messianic age.

Jesus concludes his presentation by making an assertion that is
shocking in its depth of meaning (7:28). He begins with the highest praise possible: "among those born of women there is no one
greater than John." Thus he is the greatest man alive. No single
person has had a greater privilege than clearing the path for God's
Messiah to bring about the age of salvation. No high priest, no
Roman emperor, can match his importance to this world.

However, John is merely "preparing the way," while the "least important" (in this-world terms) convert is greater because they get to experience the kingdom reality directly. It is better to live in the age of fulfillment than to be the one inaugurating (but not experiencing) the kingdom of God itself. Peter in 1 Peter 1:10–11 told how the prophets "searched intently and with the greatest care," longing to experience the coming of the Messiah. John prepared for it, but every saint gets to live it out. So none in the old covenant period was as great as John, but everyone who is part of the new covenant era is greater than John.

The Rejection of John and Jesus (7:29–35)

In verses 29–30, we are told of the immense gulf between the Jewish people and the Pharisees vis-à-vis John. This is very emphatic—"all the people, even the tax collectors." The tax collectors, beginning with Levi and embracing those at the banquet in 5:27–32, were quite enamored of Jesus, partly because he accepted and welcomed them. Apparently quite a few had been baptized by John (3:12). Luke specifies them here to show how Jesus ministers to the marginalized and despised. The messianic community embraces all.

Again, the emphasis is on Jesus' words more than his deeds. Mighty works highlight the power of the kingdom truths, but his words tell how to enter the kingdom. The common people "acknowledged that God's way was right," meaning they heard and obeyed (6:46–47; 7:1). Most of those in this group "had been baptized by John," and now they are heeding John's plea from 3:16–18 and turning to Jesus, realizing he is the Messiah and that in both John and Jesus God's way had indeed been proved right. "Acknowledged that God's way was right" in the Greek is *edikaiōsan ton theon*, "justified God," meaning they recognized the righteous nature of God and decided to repent and obey the divine truths Jesus taught.

In complete contrast to the common people, the Pharisees and legal experts (the scribes) "rejected God's purpose for themselves," namely, that they repent and turn to Christ (7:30). These so-called leaders of Israel spend all their time in self-justification and ignore God's true purpose or plan (*boulē*). The emphasis on the baptism of John is quite interesting. His immersion ministry was "a baptism of repentance for the forgiveness of sins" (3:3) and so translated to Jesus and justification language very well. Those who submitted to John's baptism became believers and Christ followers, and those who rejected it became enemies of Christ and his church. This does not mean that John's followers were automatically followers of Christ, but the conversion to Christ was a natural step for them. We see in Acts 19:1–7 how one group of John's disciples had to turn to Christ.

The "people of this generation" in verse 31 are not those of verse 29 but the leaders of verse 30, those who "rejected God's purpose." They parallel the wilderness generation who were punished by God at the exodus (Deut 1:35; 32:5). Two questions arise from Jesus' words here: What was that wilderness generation like, and how does this generation of Jewish leaders parallel them? Jesus' argument is that the parallels are extremely close, and God's judgment is about to descend on the nation because of it.

So Jesus tells a parable to describe the problem (7:32). The sarcasm is evident as he likens the leaders to children playing and squabbling in the marketplace. The marketplace is the central square in any city where trade and civic leadership take place. With the mothers shopping, the children play a game, inviting another group of children to join them. They play music and tell the other group what game to play with that music. At first they create joyful music and try to pretend they are at a wedding (flutes were often featured at weddings), but the other group won't join them. So they switch and create sad music, a dirge, and try to pretend they are at a funeral. But the other group still won't join and play with them.

The parable is easy to understand, but Jesus' message in it is not. The first group could be God's messengers trying to get the Jews to follow John the Baptist with his ascetic message of judgment, and then to follow Jesus with his joyous message of salvation (he uses the bridegroom metaphor for himself in 5:34–35). The Jewish leaders are spoiled brats refusing to play the game God has sent with John and Jesus. Yet others have seen the first group as the Jews trying to force John and Jesus into playing their games, refusing to accept John's call to judgment or Jesus' call to salvation. Both options are viable, but to me the first option makes more sense. The Pharisees and scribes will not accept either message of judgment (John) or salvation (Jesus).

Jesus brings this out clearly in his explanation in 7:33–34, showing what their rejections entailed. John in his ascetic ministry "came neither eating bread nor drinking wine." Several see in this an allusion to God's sustaining Israel in the wilderness in Deuteronomy 29:6. John had his deeply effective ministry while living an ascetic lifestyle, yet he was taken care of by God in a way similar to the wilderness generation. Yet how did the leaders interpret his powerful ministry? "He has a demon," meaning not that he was demon-possessed but that he had lost his mind.

Jesus, on the other hand, had the opposite lifestyle, eating and drinking, referring to his table fellowship with people (5:29–30; 7:36–39; 10:38–42; 11:37; 13:26; 14:1; 19:5–7), an important part of his ministry. Their reaction is just as negative with Jesus, concluding he is "a glutton and a drunkard," which could have two possible allusions: Deuteronomy 21:20, where he is seen as a "stubborn and rebellious" son who should be stoned to death; or Proverbs 23:20–21, which portrays a foolish son on the wrong path in life. As a "friend of tax collectors and sinners," he is unclean and not worthy of being called a rabbi.

So the leaders reject both John and Jesus for opposite reasons, opposing John's austere lifestyle and Jesus' joyous lifestyle.

They have turned against God's envoys and thus have no place in God's kingdom.

In the concluding verse 35, "wisdom" is the wisdom of God, specifically seen in the kingdom messages of John and Jesus. It is the divine wisdom that has brought the new covenant era, the messianic age, and made possible the new age of the Sprit and of God's plan of salvation in Christ. The "children" of wisdom are those characterized by wisdom, John and Jesus especially but also their followers, who are part of God's plan and are proclaiming the new kingdom truths.

The faithful lives and witness of the Christ followers are placed in contrast to those who have accepted the lies of the Pharisees and scribes and joined them in rejecting John and Jesus. The irony is that it is the very outcast disciples of Christ and the despised tax collectors and sinners who are the wise while the religious elite, the leaders of Israel, are the fools.

Thus wisdom is "justified by" (*edikaiōthē*) or "proved right, vindicated" (see 7:29) as God's blessing lies on those who follow John and Jesus. Interestingly, in the parallel Matthew 11:19 it is "by her deeds," looking to the mighty works that led to John's query in the first place. Luke is stressing that the Christ followers are also the "work/deed" of God. They put Christ's wisdom into practice and by their faithful lives prove it right to the world. The fallen woman in the next episode is one of the "children of wisdom," showing in her gratefulness to Jesus the radical change that wisdom has made in her life.

JESUS IS ANOINTED BY A SINFUL WOMAN (7:36–50)

This passage illustrates the radical contrast between the wisdom of Jesus and the Pharisees in their reaction to sinners. This formerly fallen woman shows that sinners are now proving wisdom right by their response to the kingdom proclamation of Jesus. It introduces another major theme of Luke, the place of women in the wise plan of God. Women were greatly marginalized in Judaism, but this is the first of two successive episodes (with 8:1–3) showing how God is using women to further his kingdom plan. This is also a major example of Jesus eating and drinking, and thus identifying, with sinners (7:34) as he forgives their sins and brings them to God.

The Setting: The Anointing (7:36–38)

It is surprising that Jesus is here eating and drinking at the home of a Pharisee, implying that they too are part of the very sinners with whom Jesus is associating. He clearly wishes to examine Jesus for himself, but the placement of this right after the passage where the Pharisees denounce Jesus for this very activity is deeply ironic. Jesus proves further how open he is to sinners of all stripes by accepting and entering the lion's den in his desire to win all, even his enemies, to God. So at the outset this "Simon" (his name in 7:40) emulates Nicodemus in John 3:2 by calling Jesus "teacher" in 7:40; he is certainly not hostile like most of the other leaders, and apparently most of his Pharisaic guests feel likewise. Not all the leaders were blindly hostile to Jesus. "Reclining at the table" is the posture at banquets. The Jews at this time borrowed the practice of the Gentile world by lying on couches in a V pattern around the food as they partook of a meal. The meal was in honor of Jesus, a respected rabbi and possible prophet (7:39).

Into this scene a woman enters, not an invited guest yet also not an intruder. Several interpreters have pointed out that the doors at important banquets like this were left open so people could enter and listen to the conversation at the meal. She came entirely to see Jesus and is described as a notorious "sinner in the town" (NIV: "lived a sinful life"), a term often used of an immoral woman. Unbound hair (v. 38) was frowned on (1 Cor 11:5–6) and was associated with prostitution, and it is possible that she was such. She hears that Jesus is at the meal and decides to come. To show her love and appreciation, she brings with her "an alabaster jar of perfume." Alabaster was a soft white marble (or pure yellow or even red with impurities in it), often used as a container. The perfume in it was costly (*myron* was one of the more expensive perfumes) and quite fragrant, and her action was premeditated, perhaps indicating prior contact with Jesus.

She apparently enters and goes immediately behind Jesus, standing at his feet while he reclined on the couch facing the food. The language of verse 38 is quite dramatic, using imperfect tenses to picture her ongoing signs of affection and gratitude. It could be translated, "she kept wetting his feet with her tears then wiping them with her hair, kissing them and anointing them with the fragrant ointment." She wanted to express her gratitude and love to Jesus, but she quickly became so overcome with emotion that she could only weep continuously, her tears falling on his feet as she leaned over him.

This would have been a shocking scene. Some think she had intended to anoint his head, then her emotions gained control and she began just to cry out her tears. Luke does not indicate that, and the anointing of his feet would have been an indication of her great humility and sense of unworthiness, as when John the Baptist said in 3:16 he was not worthy even to untie the sandals on Jesus' feet. The accumulation of dirt on the feet symbolized the sin in a person's life. Jesus would have removed his sandals coming into the room, and so as she leaned over, her tears fell on his bare feet. It seems likely that she had met Jesus earlier, and he had forgiven her sins. Her sense of joy and gratitude caused her to break down, and she couldn't stop weeping with her deep emotions as she stood at his feet.

Her action of letting her hair loose and wiping his feet with it would have galvanized everyone and been quite scandalous (see above). Kissing his feet would have been even more shocking to those reclining with Jesus at the meal. Still, the kissing and anointing exemplify worship and reverence. Luke in writing this may have been thinking of Isaiah 52:7, "How beautiful on the mountains are the feet of those who bring good news." She like the woman in Matthew 26:6–13 was anointing him for his future ministry. Anointing the head was a kingly act; anointing the feet indicated future destiny. Luke's narrative indicates all this took some time, and it would have been a powerful scene.

CONFLICT OVER HER ACTIONS (7:39–43)

Needless to say, what the woman did took control of the conversation. The Pharisee who had planned the banquet is the first to respond. For some reason he doesn't vocalize it but thinks to himself, interpreting the scene on the basis of his Pharisaic prejudices that allowing the woman to touch Jesus would render him unclean. He has heard that Jesus was considered a great prophet (7:16), but he now strongly doubts that, using in the Greek a contrary-to-fact condition: "If he were a prophet (which he isn't) ... ?" If he truly were a prophet, he would "know who is touching him and what kind of woman she is—that she is a sinner." His Pharisaic bias would focus on her sinful past and ignore her repentant present. Her former lifestyle must have been well known in the community. He assumes Jesus should condemn her as well, and his forgiveness and acceptance of the woman (to Simon still a sinner) is repugnant to him.

Jesus again shows his omniscience (see 5:21–22) and responds to the Pharisee's ruminations (7:40). The language is quite respectful, with Jesus using his first name, Simon, and the man responding with a title of respect, "Tell me, teacher." This now becomes the primary title used by the crowds and leaders (8:49; 9:38; 10:25; 11:45; 18:18). In that culture "I have something to say to you" introduced a pointed comment correcting another person.

Jesus now uses a parable to show him the error of his ways and to illustrate the importance of forgiveness (7:41–42). It concerns a moneylender the like of whom has never been seen on planet earth. He had two debtors in particular. A denarius was the wages for a day's work by the average worker. So the one owed him nearly two years' worth of work, the other about a month and a half's worth.

Though the one owed ten times as much, they both had the same problem: an inability to pay the debt. Now comes the impossible part—the moneylender "forgave" the debts of both of them. The verb (*echarisato*) stresses the "grace" (*charis*) behind the act of forgiveness, making this an apt parable for the grace of God in forgiving sins. That is the intended meaning behind the symbolism.

Jesus' question ("Now which of them will love him more?") draws the proper answer out of the Pharisee: "I suppose the one who had the bigger debt forgiven" (7:43). He didn't want to answer ("I suppose") but could not avoid Jesus' query. It is crucial to realize that the question is not just about gratitude but about love. This points directly to the woman, who showed her love and devotion, not just her gratefulness. This is a perfect parable. The woman, in the Pharisee's eyes, would have had a far bigger debt of sin to God— an amount Simon was not willing to forgive. Jesus has forced him to indict himself and show his true colors.

The Application of the Parable (7:44–47)

There is double meaning when Jesus turns to the woman and asks Simon, "Do you see this woman?" The first is almost superfluous; he cannot miss seeing her there. The implied question, though, is, "Do you really see her as she truly is?" She is a former sinner now forgiven, and Simon cannot see that. The parable was simple, the implications profound. This is a perfect parable of God forgiving those—namely, all of us—who are not worthy. This is God's grace and mercy illustrated.

Jesus then contrasts his reception by the Pharisee with that of the woman (7:44–46). He failed to show common courtesy, as making water available for washing the feet made dirty by the dusty roads was normally done (as evidenced by the six water jars in John 2:6). Hospitality was critical in the ancient world, and guests were made to feel special. Simon's failure to show hospitality itself was scandalous, but this may not actually be the emphasis. There is some evidence that footwashing was not required of hosts and would have been regarded as special care. There is consider-able debate as to whether his failures (the washing of Jesus' feet, the kiss of greeting, the anointing of his head) should be taken as definite insults or just a failure to show honor. I think the latter, but this is not the point.

The emphasis is on the woman, who showed this and more to Jesus. All she did in verse 38 Jesus now repeats. The Pharisee did show common courtesy but no more, while she showed extraordi-nary love and devotion. The kiss of greeting was the one expected sign of respect, but the other two were not. The anointing of the head with oil was not a regular practice and if done would indeed would have shown exceptional honor. Hers were kisses of grati-tude and devotion, and she did not just use olive oil (the common oil when anointing the head) but an incredibly expensive per-fume. Again, I do not think Simon was guilty of deliberate prov-ocation and rudeness but rather did only what was customary at the most basic level (though many disagree), while she did more than one could ever expect.

Jesus' conclusion is found in verse 47. Jesus states, "I tell you, her many sins have been forgiven—as her great love has shown," a translation that demonstrates that Jesus had previously forgiven her, and her acts of devotion were the result of the joy and gratitude she felt as a result. The Greek would also allow that Jesus forgives her sins here and could be translated, "her many sins have been forgiven because [hoti] she has shown great love." But that would imply salvation by works, so the NIV is the better understanding.

THE MESSAGE FOR THE FORGIVEN WOMAN (7:48-50)

When Jesus says to the now-forgiven woman, "Your sins are for-given" (7:48), the verb is in the perfect tense (apheōntai), mean-ing she is now in a state of forgiveness (the perfect tense implies a state of being) and not just then being forgiven. He is encouraging her by confirming her relationship with God but also telling the guests at the banquet as well as the Pharisee that God has forgiven the woman, even if Simon has not. Note the contrast implied in verse 47b, "But whoever has been forgiven little loves little." Jesus is describing Simon, who refuses to forgive the woman. Now the contrast is between him and God. The compassionate Lord has forgiven her much because he loves her so deeply, completely opposite to the harsh and rigid Pharisee.

The guests ask the same question as in 5:21, when Jesus forgave the paralyzed man: "Who is this who even forgives sins?" In every sense this is greater than any of Jesus' miracles. Even the resurrection of the dead effects temporary change in an earthly way. Forgiveness is eternal and heavenly in its ramifications. So their question is natural. There was no hint in the Old Testament that even the Messiah could forgive sins. When prophets pronounced forgiveness (2 Sam 12:13; Isa 40:2) they were not speaking for themselves but directly with a message from God. Jesus speaks for himself not only as God's envoy but also as the God-man. He does not answer the question but demonstrates his response in the proclamation of verse 50. This issue will be a driving force in the chapters yet to come.

Jesus not only proclaims the woman's forgiveness but also her salvation, saying to her, "Your faith has saved you; go in peace" (7:50). It is critical to understand that her faith, not her actions of devotion, is what saved her. This was introduced in 7:9, the healing of the centurion's slave, and it will be seen several more times (8:25, 48; 17:6, 19; 18:8, 42). The verb "has saved," as the one in verse 48, is in the perfect tense, meaning she now exists in the state of having salvation and being right with God. God has recognized her faith, her sins have been forgiven, and now she can experience God's blessings and "go in peace." The turmoil of her life of sin is over, and she now has both peace with God and peace within herself. Now she must go and find peace with those she formerly hurt. Her story must have astounded people for the rest of her life.

All the people to whom Jesus ministers in this chapter display a deep humility and abiding faith. Moreover, they are all marginalized people, outcasts to the Jewish leaders. Thus, they exemplify the liberty for the oppressed people of Isaiah 61:1-2, whom Jesus spoke about in Luke 4:18-19. The first is a Gentile centurion, an important Roman officer and a God-fearer who loves Judaism. He believes everything he has heard about Jesus and sends a Jewish delegation to intercede and tell Jesus of his walk with God.

The Gentile centurion whose slave is healed exemplifies this perfectly. He is a powerful, wealthy individual who can have whatever he wants yet who recognizes in Jesus the only possible way his slave can be healed of his terminal disease. He comes to Jesus in abject humility and throws himself virtually at his feet in total dependence on him. This is a remarkable step to true faith, and Jesus is touched. The centurion is a model of what it means to give yourself completely to Jesus and demonstrates perfectly the path to repentance. The healing is a consequence of his deep faith, which is the true high point of the story.

The next miracle is accomplished on behalf of the social opposite to the centurion, a widow without support from family and friends. Yet she is personally the equal to the centurion, for she too is dependent on Jesus, this time to raise her son. This miracle is the greatest proof yet of Jesus as God's Messiah and Envoy. His power over death on behalf of a lowly widow and her son is perfect proof not only of his God-given authority as Lord but also of his deep and abiding compassion for the suffering multitudes. The reaction of the people also demonstrates their recognition that God has sent him as a "great prophet," yet not a confession that he is the prophet-Messiah. But it is a step in the right direction.

Next we see Jesus interacting once more with John the Baptist (vv. 18-35), now in prison. His own human doubts are seen. He has been locked up for some time, but Jesus has gone no further in bringing the end that John expects. He is the wilderness prophet, proclaiming the coming judgment, while Jesus is the joyous Messiah introducing the age of salvation. So he is not the kind of Messiah John expects, and the Baptist is an example of all the rest of us when Jesus does not meet our expectations. We too want Jesus to fit our model and act like we want him to act, so we have doubts like John does.

Christ then tells the crowd about what kind of person John actually is, a person of great substance, unlike the weak luxury-loving figures of Herod's court (vv. 24-28). He fulfills the prophecy of Malachi 3:1 as the messenger sent to be the forerunner of Jesus Messiah, and as such one of the greatest men of his day. Then Jesus makes a startling claim. The least in the kingdom that John and Jesus are introducing is actually greater than John is, for they have become the children of the kingdom.

Turning to the leaders (vv. 29-35), he contrasts them with the followers of the Baptist who are part of this kingdom reality. The leaders are like children playing a game and refusing to play wedding (the joyous ministry of Jesus) or funeral (the ministry of judgment of John). The leaders are completely outside the kingdom, without hope. They are very much like many religious leaders of our time who want little to do with the Jesus of the Bible because he won't fit their liberal ideas of the universal goodness of humankind.

The final episode (vv. 36-50) concerns a banquet a Pharisee held on behalf of Jesus and a startling intruder, a woman who wants to thank Jesus for forgiving her but breaks down and can only weep tears of gratitude and devotion to him. The Pharisee and his party are offended at Jesus' associating with sinners, and they condemn him and her. Jesus uses a parable to force this rigid religious leader to admit his prejudices and show his unwillingness to forgive in contrast to God's (and Jesus') willingness to do so. Jesus contrasts her deep gratitude and gracious shower of love and devotion to the basic courtesy but no more of the Pharisee (vv. 44-46). She, not he, exemplified God's grace and acceptance. The Pharisee was not willing to forgive, but Jesus in verses 48-50 assures her not only that she has been forgiven but also that "her faith has saved her," providing the kingdom message that will now dominate the rest of Luke-Acts.

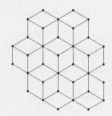

AUTHORITATIVE TEACHING
AND MIGHTY DEEDS
(8:1–56)

I n the last couple chapters Luke has inserted a great deal of material from a source he has in common with Matthew (from Luke
6:20-8:3), which scholars have labeled Q (see the introductory
chapter), and now he returns to the material from Mark 4-6 and
follows it in this chapter. This critical chapter draws together the
two primary aspects of Jesus' public ministry—his words and his
deeds. Luke begins with his first parable section, containing the
parables of the sower (vv. 1-15) and the lamp (vv. 16-21), and then
he moves on to a miracle section where he performs every type
of his miracles in order, demonstrating his power over nature
(calming the storm, vv. 22-25), over the cosmic powers (casting
out "Legion," vv. 26-39), over illness (the woman with the menstrual flow, vv. 43-48), and over death (raising Jairus' daughter, vv.
40-42, 49-56). At the same time, Jesus separates the sections with
two discipleship portions—the place of the women who served as
patrons of the band of disciples (vv. 1-3) and the disciples as his
true family (vv. 19-21). So this chapter has everything, a true summary and picture of his messianic work in this world.

This chapter also flows naturally out of chapter 7, which introduced Jesus' special ministry to the marginalized people like

Gentiles and women, with two stories of his acceptance and help to women, the widow of Nain and the sinful woman, preparing for the place of women in his ministry in the very first episode of 8:1-3. So this is a natural follow-up and summarizes the various ways his ministry worked. Then chapter 9 continues with a focus on the Twelve—their mission (vv. 1-6), their involvement in the feeding miracle (vv. 10-17), Peter's confession and the discipleship sayings (vv. 18-27), the transfiguration (vv. 28-36), and discipleship failure combined with Jesus' corrections (vv. 37-50). So all three chapters of which this is a part are strong on what we call ecclesiology, teaching on discipleship and the church, the messianic community Jesus is constructing.

LUKE INTRODUCES WOMEN WHO ARE PART OF THE BAND OF DISCIPLES (8:1-3)

This section begins with another summary of Jesus' itinerant ministry "from one town and village to another" (see 4:14-15, 43-44; 5:12). Galilee was a small province. Seventy by forty miles, it took only a couple of days to traverse it, but it contained 204 towns and villages (see Josephus, *Life* 235), and a preaching tour could take some time. His topic was the good news of the coming of the "kingdom of God," the new era of salvation Christ has inaugurated. The Twelve accompany him (see 6:12-16), probably not as participants quite yet but as observing and training for the task like all rabbinic disciples do. During this time Jesus undoubtedly both preached to the people and taught the disciples. They will participate fully in 9:1-6.

In addition, Luke tells us that a group of women also traveled with the mission team as patrons who supported them. There was likely a larger group ("many others," v. 3), but three are mentioned here, described as "cured of evil spirits and diseases." Matthew and Mark don't tell us this until late in the passion events (Matt 27:55-56; Mark 15:40-41), but Luke places it here to tell us once more how important the women were to Jesus' mission.

The first one mentioned (and possibly the leader of the women's ministry) was Mary Magdalene. She was not the sinful woman of the previous story (7:16-20), and so she was never a prostitute like tradition says; Luke would have told us if that were so. But she had been possessed by seven demons (see also the addition in Mark 16:9), and Jesus had cast them out, certainly converting her in the process. "Magdalene" means she came from Magdala, a town on the western shore of the Sea of Galilee. She is named first in the lists of those who were present at the crucifixion, burial, and resurrection of Jesus (Matt 27:56, 61; 28:1 and parallels), showing her importance (the order of names was always meaningful).

The other two were wealthy believers who used their means to support the team (Mary may also have been wealthy). They would have been called "patrons," and the Roman Empire was a patron-client society in which such wealthy people played important roles. Most of the others probably took care of the needs of the group, preparing meals and such, with these three among others helping pay the bills. We know next to nothing about Susanna, but Joanna was the wife of an important official in Herod's service, his "steward" or manager of his extensive estate (*epitropos*). So she would have been a rich aristocrat by marriage and quite able to help. She too was a witness of Jesus' resurrection (24:10). As a Herodian she probably faced some rejection from many Jewish believers, and we don't know how she and her husband worked out her time away from home and duties. In every way she sacrificed greatly for Jesus.

The women had a deep involvement in the ministry of the mission team. As patrons they would have had some kind of a leadership role, for patrons were at the core of the Roman socioeconomic system. Still, we cannot overplay this factor, for they operated under the Jewish system and so were primarily ministering to the needs of Jesus and the Twelve. In this they anticipated the total sharing of Acts 2:44-45; 4:32-35: "No one claimed that any of their possessions was their own, but they shared everything they had."

With both their time and their means they "supported" the team with all they had.

JESUS TELLS THE PARABLE OF THE SEEDS (8:4–15)

As always, Jesus is thronged with large crowds "from town after town." On this occasion he tells them another parable. These are always pithy stories and either extended metaphors (images without characters, like the vine and the branches of John 15) or stories (like the good Samaritan of Luke 10:29–37). This is the former, containing a powerful message embedded in the symbolism of the details. This is commonly called the parable of the sower, but the seed rather than the sower is central. Others see the harvest as central and focus on judgment and reward. This is also erroneous, for the key element is response to the seed truths, and the harvest is the result of this response. There is special importance to this seed parable (and the parable of the tares in Matt 13), for it is the only one explained in Luke. So it is especially critical, depicting the confrontation of the listeners by the kingdom "mysteries" or secrets (8:10), which demand response and commitment. This parable governs the others.

These are kingdom parables, illustrating the meaning of the arrival of God's new reign in this world that has come with Jesus. Each detail has symbolic value. The field is God's kingdom, the farmer or sower is Jesus, the seed is the kingdom truths he proclaims, and the four soils correspond to the groups in Israel to whom Jesus has been ministering: the hardened path (the leaders), the rocky and thorny soils (the crowds), and the good soil (the disciples). In Palestine sowing is done in the rainy season (October to December) and harvesting in the dry season (May to June). Certainly farmers would not throw seed on bad soil, but their normal practice was to place a seed bag over their shoulder and throw the seed onto the good soil. The wind would blow some seed onto the bad.

THE FOUR SOILS (8:5-8)

Galilee was well known for the fertility of its soil, and as a result much of it had been bought up by wealthy landlords from distant lands like Egypt or Babylon or Asia Minor. They owned large properties and broke them up into a series of tenant farms (see the parables of the shrewd manager [16:1-13] and the tenant farmers [20:9-19]). These farmers would raise the crops and give half to the landlord. Their method was to throw the seed on the soil and then plow it into the ground; sometimes the soil was also worked before the sowing of the seed. So Jesus is asking, "Which kind of soil are you?"

The first seed "fell along the path" (8:5). These were the roads of the ancient world, often walking paths, that did not skirt around properties like today but passed right through the middle of the fields, with the crops growing right up to the road itself. Farmers of course would never deliberately throw good seed onto the hard-packed road, but a few seeds would just fall or be blown onto the road. This seed could not take root and would be trampled on the top of the road as people walked over it.

The second seed "fell on rocky ground" (8:6). These are not pieces of rock embedded in the ground. Rather, in some places in Galilee (mainly in the hill country) there are layers of limestone and shale several inches below the surface that would trap the rain and keep it from penetrating the deeper soil. Harvest season had an early (autumn) and a late (spring) rain (see Deut 11:14; Jer 5:24), with mainly pure sun in between. The limestone would keep the rain near the surface, and as a result the plants would explode out of the ground at first, then wither on the stalks under the glaring sun. The limestone also kept the roots from growing deep, so as the hot sun sapped the moisture from the soil, the plants would wither and die.

The third seed "fell among thorns" (8:7). These are a type of weed with very strong roots that steal moisture from the soil and thereby "choke" the good plants. In the early weeks they also look like wheat and so are very difficult to weed out of the soil. Later they grow as high as six feet. There is a progression in these three bad soils, and the plant dies later in each instance.

The fourth seed "fell on good soil" (7:8), which actually describes most of Galilee. In Matthew 13:8 and Mark 4:8 Jesus describes each crop as getting progressively greater, with thirty, sixty, or a hundred other plants growing out of each plant. In Luke only the ultimate growth is depicted—"a hundred times more than was sown." Luke is stressing the growth of disciples who listen to and obey the truths of Jesus. God's word in him bears incredible fruit in the lives of his followers.

The parable proper ends with a challenge (8:8b): "Whoever has ears to hear, let them hear." This is the main point of it all, and Jesus essentially repeats it in 8:18: "Therefore consider carefully how you listen." As I have said often, one has not heard until they have responded with commitment and obedience (see discussions at 6:11, 46–49; 7:1, 8, 29). The challenge contains an essential message: If you are willing to listen, you had better do so while you can.

THE PURPOSE OF PARABLES (8:9–10)

His disciples are somewhat confused and ask him the meaning of the parable, meaning not the background details but the allegorical message behind it. They want to know what he is saying about the Lord and their relation to him. His answer loops the negative soils into a single category to describe those opposed to him and contrasts the uncommitted leaders and crowds to his disciples. Jesus' word encounters people and forces them to decision, thereby producing these two groups.

This takes place because God has given[1] his "kingdom mysteries" (mystēria, NIV: "the secrets of the kingdom of God") to them via Christ's teaching and parables. This is an **apocalyptic** term

---

1. "Has been given" is a divine passive, meaning God is the divine agent who gives the mysteries to his people.

and refers to the hidden truths God has not made known in the past but has now revealed to his people. It invokes understanding at both the mental and spiritual levels. Jesus has told these hidden things to the crowds and leaders as well, but couched in parables, and they are unable to grasp and accept these truths. This doesn't mean Jesus spoke only in parables, but the kingdom teaching is inherently parabolic and enigmatic, demanding careful reflection, spiritual insight, and openness to the new things God is just now revealing. The soil of the heart must be receptive and fruitful for this to take place.

Christ now turns to Isaiah 6:9–10, taken from the prophet's commissioning service, where Isaiah is given a message that apostate Israel is certain to reject. Jesus is saying that the Jewish people of his day are exactly like the people of Isaiah's time in their obduracy. This citation is introduced by the Greek particle *hina*, indicating both purpose and result, thus combining both the divine choice of God and the guilt of the people. Israel has rejected Christ's kingdom truths, and as a result God has turned against them. This is a particle of judgment, and it means he is now anchoring their rejection by rejecting them.

This divine condemnation is presented two ways, both seeing and hearing (thus with all their senses) what Christ is saying to them. The Isaiah text contains present-tense participles and main verbs which mean that the people of Israel continually see and hear these seed truths of Jesus, but because of their hardened hearts they never at any time perceive the reality of what Jesus is truly saying. Matthew 13:14–15 is even more harsh, introducing the Isaiah quotation with the causal *hoti* (because), stating directly that God's judgment has come "because" of their negative response to Christ. He then includes the rest of the Isaiah quotation, in particular, "Otherwise they might see with their eyes ... and I would heal them." God no longer wants them to repent. In Acts 28:26–28 this Isaiah passage leads to the conclusion "that God's salvation has been sent to the Gentiles, and they will listen!"

JESUS GIVES THE MEANING OF
THE PARABLE (8:11-15)

Only for his disciples, Christ now interprets the parable, in particular the spiritual truths embedded in the symbols. For nearly a century many scholars thought that parables originally had a single point centered on the presence of the kingdom and that the allegorical elements were added later. (Joachim Jeremias was a famous example of this.) This is now recognized as a serious error. Jesus presents multiple meanings, which flow out of the various details of this parable. The sower here is Jesus, and the seed that is sown is defined as "the word of God," meaning that Jesus' teaching originated from God and is now encased in Jesus himself, who speaks God's words. He then turns to the four soils and explains the spiritual truths behind them and the way he demands people respond to them.

The different soils represent the leaders, crowds, and disciples with their various levels of willingness to truly listen. The seed in the hard-packed path (8:12) represents listeners who hear only on the surface. The birds who devour the seed symbolize the devil, who "comes and takes away the word from their hearts." These are the leaders who listen from a prejudiced perspective and have already rejected Jesus' message even before they have heard it. Satan devours them even as they listen, and there is no possibility of conversion. They cannot "believe and be saved." In John 12:30; 14:30; 16:11 the passion itself is seen as a battle against Satan, and in 22:3-4 Luke says he "entered Judas" and guides him in betraying Jesus.

The rocky, limestone-filled soil (8:13) represents the crowds who at first "receive the word with joy" but have a short-lived happiness because of their mere shallow emotion rather than deep joy in Christ; "they have no root" and "believe for a while, but in the time of testing they fall away." The crowds are enamored of Christ and follow him everywhere but avoid any commitment. Their interest is in the spectacular, both in his stimulating messages and especially in his powerful miracles. They are actually shallow, and in the difficulties and tests that life forces on them they have insufficient depth to stay with Christ and simply fall away. In today's terms I would call them seekers who are interested but not ready to follow him.

The thorny soil (8:14) represents those who listen and like the rocky ground seem to respond for a while, but as time passes "they are choked by life's worries, riches and pleasures, and they do not mature." There is no spiritual growth, for there is little life in Christ, and they are what I would call carnal or quasi-Christians. The worries or anxieties of life are found in Philippians 4:6 ("do not be anxious about anything") and Matthew 6:25-34 ("do not worry about your life"). The true child of God learns to rely on him and not to allow the earthly side of life to gain control (see 5:11, 28; 6:20-26; 9:46-48; 11:39-44; 12:22-34). Riches and the pleasures of life are deadly temptations and ruin many spiritually.

The good soil (8:15) represents the Christ followers "with a noble and good heart," meaning they have the spiritual depth to hear and obey, as Jesus has been saying (6:11, 46-49; 7:1, 8, 29). They not only listen carefully to the word but also "retain it, and by persevering produce a crop." The Greek term for "retain" is *katechō*, to "hold fast" or "possess" something. It is a strong term for remaining faithful and refers to maintaining a firm grasp on your commitments. When they do this, they "persevere" or "endure" (*hypomonē*), an ongoing life of remaining true to Jesus' teachings. This is the basis of their fruitfulness as they "produce a crop" (see John 15:2-8).

JESUS TELLS THE PARABLE OF THE LAMP (8:16-18)

These three sayings are strung together with the theme of "light" as the word that is heard. Luke is following Mark but omits the other Markan parables, placing them elsewhere. Each saying occurs again in Luke: verse 16 in 11:33; verse 17 in 12:2; and verse 18 in 19:26.

Covering a lamp with a pot extinguished it without fumes getting into the air; to hide it under a bed was to keep the light from the room, though that is more dangerous because it might set the bed on fire. The only real purpose for a lamp is to place it on a lampstand, which puts it high enough to bathe the room with light. There are three possible understandings of this image: it could refer to discipleship and evangelism, to the fruitfulness of the proclaimed word, or to Jesus' teaching that illuminates the way to God. A growing number of interpreters opt for the third because of the stress here on Jesus' explaining the parables and challenging the listeners. Yet there is equal emphasis on the fruitfulness of discipleship and responding to the word. If we have the light of Christ we must show it to all the world.

The saying of 8:17 applies the parable of the lamp. The link is the term "hidden," which is probably drawn from the use of "mystery" in verse 10. The time of hiddenness and secret is the present time when Jesus is speaking in parables and mysteries. The time of disclosure and openness has three possible interpretations: (1) It could mean that those who reject the word (8:5-7) will be made manifest on the day of judgment. This is unlikely because of the positive thrust of verse 16. (2) It could mean the kingdom of God will be manifest at the return of Christ. This would fit 12:2 and Mark 4:22, but this passage doesn't have the same apocalyptic context and it does not fit well. (3) The truths of the kingdom are now hidden but are in the process of being revealed and made public. This is best in this context. The disciples are to proclaim openly what Jesus has told them in secret (v. 10). This makes a great deal of sense in light of the understanding of verse 16 above and the emphasis on light and hearing in verses 16 and 18, surrounding this verse.

Finally, Jesus expands the final challenge to have "ears to hear" in verse 8 (8:18). All the groups of 8:5-8 must "consider carefully how you listen." Christ has given the only eternal truths they will ever hear, and God will hold them accountable for how they respond. Their response will determine their eternal destiny, so it is nothing to trifle with. The warning is severe. Whoever has (knowledge of the kingdom mysteries in v. 10) will be given more (clear, direct knowledge of these now-revealed and open truths, v. 17). Whoever fails to have this knowledge will lose everything. "Even what they think they have will be taken from them." Those who reject Jesus in favor of the things of this world are living a life of ignorance and falsehood but don't know it; even those lives will be taken from them at the last judgment.

JESUS TELLS WHO HIS TRUE FAMILY ARE (8:19-21)

This event occurs before the parables rather than after in Matthew 12:46-50 and Mark 3:31-33. Luke places it here to portray the results of hearing and heeding the Word of God in Jesus as forming Jesus' true family. It provides a perfect conclusion for 8:4-18. Those who listen and put into practice what Jesus says (8:8, 15, 18) become his family.

Luke simplifies the story so it can form this conclusion. In Matthew and Mark it follows extended ministry, and in Mark Jesus' family think he has overworked himself nearly into a nervous breakdown. His brothers, who are unbelievers (John 7:5), think he has lost his mind. Luke simply focuses on their arrival so as to center entirely on Jesus' response.

When they arrive from Nazareth, they are unable to get to him because of the large crowd. Someone makes it through the scrum and tells him that "your mother and brothers are standing outside, wanting to see you." Some see them as outsiders as in verse 10, but that is very doubtful. The entire emphasis is on the next verse. He is not rejecting his family (see also on 14:25-26), but rather using the opportunity to challenge those gathered around him, especially his disciples.

So Jesus responds with a twofold characteristic of his "true" family. They "hear God's word," the basic thrust of the entire section (again, 8:8, 15, 18), which becomes a summary statement for the whole. Then they "put it into practice," obey it and live it out in their daily life (6:46-49). Again, mere listening for intellectual comprehension is not listening at all. It is false until it guides one's life. In this, Jesus has formed a new community, the true family of God. This became a major image for the church (Rom 8:14-17; Eph 2:19; 1 Tim 3:15), and Christ is in process of forming it here.

JESUS HAS AUTHORITY OVER NATURE AND THE COSMIC POWERS (8:22-56)

This section demonstrates Christ as Lord of all, showing his authority over creation, the cosmic powers, illness, and death itself. This world has been conquered by sin and death, but Christ is completely sovereign and in process of conquering the evil powers, including this fallen world, for the people of God. Luke has centered on Jesus' authoritative word (8:4-21), and now he focuses on his mighty deeds. So when he sends out his disciples on mission (9:1-6; 10:1-24), he commissions and sends them on the basis of his lordship over all creation.

POWER OVER NATURE: THE STILLING OF THE STORM (8:22-25)

"One day" (literally, "it came to pass on one of these days") during the period of Jesus' ministry in chapters 7-9, he decided to cross the lake with his disciples, and so they set out, probably in the same two boats four of them used to fish in 5:1-11 (Mark 4:36—"There were also other boats with him"). These two would be large enough to carry the Twelve plus the women of 8:1-3. From what follows, Jesus possibly wished for a brief time of rest and then to spend some time ministering among the Gentiles in the Transjordan region on the other side of the lake. As we have seen, Jesus has been extremely busy and obviously quite tired. He lies down on a pillow (Mark 4:38) in the middle of the boat, and falls asleep.

On the way across (it is seven to eight miles across the lake) they suddenly encounter a violent squall. This was not uncommon.

The lake is nearly seven hundred feet below sea level and ringed by small mountains with steep cliffs and several gorges that funnel heavy winds with cool air down and create storm conditions on the spur of the moment. This was apparently one of the worst, so severe that the boat is "being swamped, and they were in great danger." One would think the professional fishermen would be used to it, having spent their lives on this lake. But there were many in the boat who would not know what to do, and it was a quite perilous situation.

The most amazing thing is that Jesus sleeps through all this (8:24). I am totally jealous, a light sleeper who would have been awake at the first sign of trouble. As the wind whipped harder and harder and the water began filling the boat, he remained securely asleep. I picture him so settled in his God-awareness that even danger could not disturb him. What a model for us! They had to go and wake him up. They cry out, "Master, Master" (epistata), a term used often (5:5; 8:45; 9:33, 49; 17:13) for government officials and teachers, which indicates their dependence on him. Things have got bad enough that even the fishermen are terribly afraid and cry, "We're going to drown!" They are scared for their lives, and Jesus is fast asleep.

Jesus' response is immediate, even curt: "He got up and rebuked the wind and the raging waters." This echoes his "rebuke" (epetimēsen) of the demon in 4:35 and the fever of Simon's mother-in-law in 4:39. This personifies the scene as a confrontation with evil, but not an exorcism, for it is entirely portraying Jesus' power over nature.

His authority is supreme, and the storm stops abruptly, with complete calm taking over. This is the same control exercised over the natural elements by Yahweh in Psalms 89:9; 107:23–30; Isaiah 51:10; and of course in Jonah 1–2. Jesus subdues the forces of nature and places them under his control. He watches over his followers, protects them, and delivers them.

His rebuke of nature is followed by his rebuke of the disciples: "Where is your faith?" This is not as harsh as Mark 4:40, "Why are you so afraid? Do you still have no faith?" There is an assumption here that they have a little faith, but it is not strong enough to overcome their difficulties. The point is that they should have been able to trust God and Jesus to take care of the situation.

For their part the disciples are filled with "fear and amazement," the normal response to God's and Jesus' wondrous power (fear in 2:9; 5:26; 7:16; wonder in 1:65; 2:18, 33, 43, 47; 4:36). They ask, "Who is this?" It is the key query of these chapters, asked by all who feel the supernatural power of the God-man, Jesus the Christ (see 4:36; 7:49; 8:25; 9:9). This highlights the **christological** significance of the miracle and prepares for Peter's confession at Caesarea Philippi in 9:20. All of us who read this are expected to ask this same question. Is Jesus an ordinary prophet, or something more? No one, not even Elijah and Elisha, has ever done what he is doing, has had such command over all creation. He can be nothing other than not only Messiah but the God-man and Lord of all.

Power over the Cosmic Forces: the Gerasene Demoniac (8:26–39)

On the other side of the lake, Jesus is in the region of the Decapolis, the "ten cities" (the meaning of the Greek *Dekapolis*) that dominated the Transjordan and Syria. This is a Gentile region, as seen in the presence of pig farms, and this scene shows Jesus ministering to all the people of planet Earth, fulfilling the Abrahamic covenant and blessing the nations (Gen 12:3; 18:18; 22:18; 26:4). While Jesus has cast out unclean spirits previously (4:31–37, 41; 6:18), he has not shown the power he does on this occasion. This is a virtual army of demons ("Legion," 8:30), a seemingly invincible force of hostile powers of darkness. Yet they are completely helpless and subject to him.

After Jesus and the disciples had crossed the lake, they landed in the "region of the Gerasenes." The name of the exact place in verse 26 is a text-critical problem, for three different places are named in various manuscripts—Gadara (six miles southeast of the lake, the place in Matt 8:28), Gergesa (quite close to the lake), and Gerasa (the major town thirty-five miles southeast from the lake). Of these, the third is the best option, as it has better manuscript witness, combining both Western and Alexandrian readings. While the city itself was far inland, the wider "region of the Gerasenes" likely included the area east of the Sea of Galilee.

There they encountered a man who was in serious trouble (v. 27). The description of his plight is tragic. Luke highlights three introductory aspects to introduce the horror of possession. First, he is "demon-possessed," and in 8:30 we learn it is with multiple demons. An army of unclean spirits has taken over his body, and his true persona is lost somewhere in his mind. Demon possession most likely means the loss of individuality and of all that makes a person a thinking individual. However we define possession, it is horrible beyond belief. And it was not only a problem in the ancient world. It continues to occur, including in modern Western nations. Some think it isn't truly real; they are like the ancient Greeks, who thought all disease had a natural basis. But there is a spiritual realm, and there are evil spirits who torment people. There is simply too much evidence. The Bible doesn't say at all clearly whether a Christian can be possessed, and I think how one answers depends on one's theology. If Satan is in total control, the person is no longer a believer, so I think it depends on whether one believes a Christian can lose their salvation.

Second, the man went about naked. There was no longer any concern for hygiene or safety or even common decency. He had lost all sense of being human and had become virtually a wild animal (as evidenced in the demons possessing pigs, 8:33). The Jewish repugnance for nakedness, even in statues, makes this even stronger. He would have been looked on with absolute disgust.

Third, he lived in the tombs, the expected abode for demons in Jewish writings (b. Berakot 3b; b. Sanhedrin 65b). Everyone needs shelter from the elements, and he would not have been welcome anywhere near people. Gentile tombs were especially unclean places, not whitewashed or taken care of very well. Jewish tombs were much better but were still places of death, with decaying bodies. Yet the wealthier tombs were also perfect shelters, placed in the caves and burrowed into hills. They were family resting places, with an antechamber before the room with the body. Being unclean, tombs were shelters for lepers as well as demon-possessed people.

The power and authority of Jesus are evident from the start of the confrontation in 8:28–31. The demons' reaction is like a common person standing before the Roman emperor. There is immediate and total submission, as the demoniac falls to the ground at Jesus' feet. This doesn't mean they are giving up, just that they are stalling for time as they try to figure out how to get Jesus to leave them alone. They know they cannot defeat him, and they just want their freedom (ironically, their freedom to enslave the man). His reply is much the same as in 4:34 (and Mark 5:7), "What do you want with me" (ti emoi kai soi, "What is it to me and to you"), meaning "Go away, leave me alone, we have nothing in common."

As we see next, he knows who Jesus is: "Son of the Most High God," the strongest christological title in Luke (see 1:32, 35, 76). As I said in 4:34, this is not telling those around who Jesus is but an attempt to get at his hidden essence and gain some control, forcing him to leave them be. Their fear is evident as they "beg" him, "Don't torture me!" Clearly, the demons don't want Jesus to do to them what they have been doing to the man, and they plead with Jesus to leave. They can neither defeat him nor order him to do their bidding, so they become beggars at the side of the road.

Luke tells us that this occurred after Christ had "commanded the impure spirit to come out of the man" (8:29). The reason for Jesus' order is then provided, giving a further glimpse into the effects of this terrifying tragedy. The demons seemed not to seize

the man once and for all but to come and enter him again and
again in waves of horror, which could well be even worse. They
gave him supernatural strength, and neither chains nor guards
could detain him, for he broke the chains, and Mark 5:4 tells us
"no one was strong enough to subdue him." We also learn here that
the poor man was doubly imprisoned, not only by the demons but
also by his fellow Jews, who both bound him with chains and set
guards over him. To some extent this was done for his sake, so the
violent convulsions would not injure him. It is hard to fathom the
agony of soul and body he went through. Finally, after escaping
his chains, he was "driven by the demon into solitary places." The
desert was viewed as the proper home for demons, and this was
also convenient for the villagers, who didn't want the man around.

Somewhat unusually, Jesus asks his name (8:30). Most likely
he does not do this to find out the demon's name, as in the erroneous view in some circles today that you need to find out a demon's
name in order to exorcize it. This is the exception, not the rule. I
agree with those who say Jesus did it to awaken the man and get
him ready to be freed of the demon. It does not work yet, and the
demons respond, "Legion," to which Luke adds, "because many
demons had gone into him." It is probably not their name but an
evasive answer so they can avoid surrendering as long as possible.

A legion was the largest component of the Roman army, who
numbered their size by this designation (there were up to twenty-
one legions in the Roman army). A legion numbered 5,600 infan-
trymen and a couple of troops of cavalry. This hardly means there
were that many demons inside the man but rather an "army" of
hostile forces who occupied the man (like the Roman army occu-
pying Palestine). This is the real basis of the term "spiritual warfare." Satan and his fallen angels have declared war against us, and
this is the actual "world war" being fought today.

They knew what was at stake and "begged Jesus repeatedly not
to order them to go into the Abyss" (8:31). This image stems from
the bottomless depths of the ocean that in the ancient world was

too deep to be plumbed, often called "the great deep" (Gen 7:11; Ps 42:7; Isa 51:10). It became an idiom for the place of the dead (Pss 63:9; 71:20) and then as a "prison house" for unclean spirits (1 Enoch 10:4–6; 18:14). In 2 Peter 2:4 and Jude 6 these evil angels are "kept in darkness, bound with everlasting chains for judgment on the great Day." Some think this is simply a metaphor for this world as an actual prison for demons, while others think there may be two kinds of demons, some allowed to roam this world and others (perhaps more evil?) chained in the abyss. I prefer the former, but either is possible. They know Christ has the power to place them in chains in the place of eternal torment and beg him not to do so. He is absolutely sovereign.

By verse 32, the unclean spirits know the battle is over and they are at Jesus' mercy. So they pose an alternative option that will allow them to retain their freedom and avoid the chains: "a large herd of pigs ... feeding there on the hillside." They plead that he will allow them to enter and possess the pigs, much more apropos because pigs too were unclean animals (Lev 11:7). Mark 5:13 tells us there were two thousand of them.

This is highly offensive to many modern readers, as Jesus gives permission to destroy the animals, as he knew they would. Demons are all about destruction, and as soon as they enter the poor defenseless pigs they cause them to rush down "the steep bank into the lake" and the herd "was drowned." Yet we must keep in mind the first-century context. This scene proves two things—the complete evil and unclean nature of all unclean spirits, and their implacable purpose in this world. Anyone who plays around with the occult is a complete fool and brings ultimate destruction on themselves. Churches must make their people aware of the serious nature of spiritual warfare.

Christ's purpose in ministry is now complete, and another "prisoner" has been liberated (4:18). After another incredible demonstration of the power of God in Jesus, the report once again spreads like wildfire, and the "town and countryside" quickly hear all about what has happened (v. 34). The problem is that the results are not just spiritual victory over the forces of darkness but also economic disaster for many in the community, the loss of their livelihood. The primary attention, however, is on the positive side. As pretty much the whole town comes out "to see what had happened," they are treated to an incredible sight. In the rest of this section, the man from whom the demons had been cast out is mentioned three times.

In verse 35 he is "dressed and in his right mind." He has regained his dignity and returned to normal. He is "sitting at Jesus' feet," ready to listen to him teach and already in process of becoming a disciple (see vv. 38–39). The whole town is filled with fear, undoubtedly because of the supernatural power it took to do what Jesus did in conquering an entire "legion" of demons and restoring the most notorious demoniac any of them had ever seen.

So now the news spreads even faster as the enormity of the defeat of the cosmic powers becomes evident to all (8:36). It is not only the fact that it happened but "*how* the demon-possessed man had been cured." The overwhelming authority and godly might Jesus displayed galvanizes everyone. At this point the terror gets even greater and the people of the Gerasene region (not just the town but the entire area) ask him "to leave them, because they were overcome with fear" (8:37). My guess is that some of them thought Jesus might have been an evil sorcerer and were terrified that he might do other things to them. Most likely they also were more than aware of their economic losses with the drowned pigs and were afraid Jesus might do even more to them. This is evident in Mark 5:16, telling us that the onlookers "told about the pigs as well." So both reasons led to their request that he leave. He complies, and he and his disciples "got into the boat and left."

Just before they leave, one final yet significant thing happens (8:38–39). The man who had been set free from the demon's control and had been sitting at Jesus' feet now begins to beg "to go with him," clearly to become his first Gentile disciple. Jesus refuses, not because he doesn't want a Gentile disciple or finds him unworthy, but because he has something even better in mind for him. He sends him back to his hometown region, commissioning him to "return home and tell how much God has done for you." He is to become the first missionary to the Gentiles, long before Paul appears on the scene, and he will witness to everyone of the great things God has accomplished in him. Note that he immediately begins spreading "how much *Jesus* had done for him." God and Jesus have become one; to speak of God is to speak of Jesus.

Authority over Sickness and Death (8:40–56)

These two miracles complete the collage that proves Jesus is indeed Lord over creation by showing his power over every kind of miracle—nature, exorcism, sickness, and death. These final two are interconnected, as they occurred simultaneously and are told through a literary technique called "intercalation," or sandwiching, where one story is inserted into another. Yet this is not just literary, for the two undoubtedly took place just this way.

Still, by narrating it this way, Luke highlights five common elements: (1) Luke continues Jesus' interest in ministering to and including women; (2) faith is the central element in both and enables the women to experience spiritual as well as physical healing (also 5:20; 7:9, 50); (3) both undergo ritual defilement, yet Jesus is unconcerned and rises above the issue of uncleanness; (4) Jesus' mighty power is even more revealed to the people of Israel and once more proves his identity (see 7:22); (5) Jesus' compassion for the hurting is once more evident to all.

Jairus's impassioned plea (8:40–42a)

The Gentiles in the Gerasenes begged Jesus to leave, so he returns to the region of Capernaum, and the moment he touches shore a very important man, a synagogue ruler, comes and prostrates himself at Jesus' feet. He is a bereaved father about to lose his precious daughter and is beside himself with worry. Synagogue rulers were not religious officials but wealthy lay patrons (aristocrats) who strongly supported the synagogue and were placed in charge of planning synagogue services (including choosing the readers of Scripture) and maintaining discipline. There was also a synagogue assistant who did most of the work.

Jairus had heard of Jesus (who hadn't?) and so immediately came to him on behalf of his terminally ill daughter. It is startling that so high and dignified an official would throw himself at Jesus' feet, but he was desperate and obviously believed in Jesus' power and authority. He probably did not think of Jesus' power to heal at this distance, so he pleaded with Jesus "to come to his house" and help her. It does not seem that synagogue rulers followed the scribes and Pharisees in opposition to Jesus.

We learn that the ill young girl was twelve years old, which was on the verge of womanhood. Girls, like boys, were minors until they were thirteen, when they became adults and she became marriageable. As her father's only daughter, she was especially precious to him. Interestingly, her twelve years of age was exactly the amount of time the woman in the next part (v. 43) had been ill.

The woman with a hemorrhage (8:42b–48)

Jesus immediately leaves for the man's home, and on his way he encounters another tragic situation. Luke stresses the crush of the crowds that thronged him, probably to set the scene for the woman courageously working her way through them to get to Jesus. Only women can understand how debilitating her illness was, but it was far worse in the first century. The hemorrhage was menstrual flow, and menstruation rendered a woman unclean (Lev 15:19–30). Worst of all, she had been "subject to bleeding for twelve years" (8:43), the same length of time as the age of the terminal young woman in verse 42, and "no one could heal her" hints that this is lifelong and in a way "terminal" in the sense that she would never get better.

One can hardly imagine the serious complications, just with the physical side of it—the constant cramping, the weakness and debilitation caused by the blood loss and disposing of it. Still worse than this was the constant defilement the condition caused, for not only was she unclean but anyone who touched her became unclean. So she would have been banished from home and community, branded a virtual leper.

There is some question about the clause "and she had spent all she had on doctors," who were unable to heal her (included as a footnote in the NIV of v. 43). It is missing from several important manuscripts (𝔓75 B D), and it is likely that those who have it added it on the basis of its presence in Mark 5:26. Still, it was true and made her situation even more tragic, for she had lost everything she had to live on and would have been rendered a virtual beggar as a result.

She parallels Jairus in her belief that Jesus' touch could heal her and remove the defilement (8:44). This is an important point, for Luke mentions the touch four times. Belief in the transfer of power via touch was widespread (Acts 5:15; 19:12) and certainly true. It was a real act of courage for her to make her way through the crowd. If anyone had recognized her, she would have been made a pariah and forcefully ejected from the scene, since she defiled anyone she touched. In this she has more faith than Jairus, for she believes she can find healing just from touching him, and his conscious act is not needed. Perhaps she doesn't think herself important enough to bother him.

She in a sense sneaks up and touches "the edge of his cloak," perhaps the tassels on the four corners that were on the hem and represented God's commands and the importance of obeying them (Num 15:38–40). Her act of faith worked, and "immediately her bleeding stopped" for the first time in twelve years.

Jesus' power is under such control that he knows something unusual has taken place and so asks, "Who touched me?" (8:45).

With the jostling crowds undoubtedly touching him continuously, this is remarkable, and Peter responds accordingly: "Master, the people are crowding and pressing against you." However, this was the one occasion the touch involved healing power going out of him, and he felt it. As often in Luke, his omniscience is evident (see 5:21–22). So he reveals this and admits the basis, "I know that power has gone out from me" (8:46). Some speak of Jesus almost as an Eveready battery discharging power, but that is not it. As the God-man, he controls the power of God within him and knows when it is dispersed. This is not magic but miracle. He is fully aware of the woman and her need and here is trying to draw her out. His desire is that she be healed spiritually as well as physically. The latter has already happened, and it is time for the more important eternal touch.

The woman wants to remain anonymous; she has been shunted aside for her unclean state for twelve years and is terrified of social interaction. But she has no choice, as Jesus has commanded her to come forward. So she "came trembling and fell at his feet" (much like Jairus, 8:41). She is probably also filled with fear and awe at the power and authority of Jesus. What she cannot discount is that she has already been healed. The joy must be overwhelming. So she came forward and "told why she had touched him and how she had been instantly healed." Note the threefold emphasis on the immediacy of both the healing and the raising from the dead (vv. 44, 47, 55); Jesus' power is absolute. She like the Gerasene demoniac (8:38–39) becomes a witness to the community.

Jesus begins by calling her "daughter" to stress the new relationship. She is now part of God's family (8:19–21). His final words are significant and point to one of the primary thrusts of this story—the power of saving faith (8:48). "Your faith has healed you"; "healed" comes from the Greek *sesōken*, which has a double meaning—"saved" as well as "healed." Physical healing has become spiritual salvation through her faith. As we will see, her faith becomes a model for Jairus to emulate. Her faith is not the basis of the miracle; that would be salvation by works. Her faith allowed her to participate in the miracle and experience physical and spiritual salvation. Faith is closely linked with Jesus' miracles (5:20; 7:9, 50; 8:25). In fact, this is word for word what Jesus told the sinful woman who anointed him in 7:50. These words prepared for the Pauline gospel of Ephesians 2:8-9. His final "Go in peace" was the normal goodbye in the Jewish world, but here it is filled with spiritual promise and meaning. She is now at peace with God, herself, and all those around her.

The raising of Jairus's daughter (8:49-53)

At the very moment Jesus was saying his farewell to the healed woman, an emissary arrived from Jairus's home with terrible news, "Your daughter is dead." Apparently she died while Jesus was healing the woman. Note the contrast between the woman's faith and the man's lack of faith in his "Don't bother the teacher anymore." To him and everyone else there, it was assumed that the interruption as Jesus healed and then dialogued with the woman was fatal and that Jesus was now helpless to do anything. They believe Jesus is restricted in his power by lack of proximity to the young woman and now by her death. Apparently the news about the raising of the son of the widow in Nain near Nazareth (7:11-17) either never reached Capernaum (hard to believe) or was not considered by the grief-stricken people.

So Jesus corrects their misunderstanding and counsels, "Don't be afraid; just believe, and she will be healed" (8:50). The woman had this saving faith, but Jairus does not, and he needs to follow her example. This does not mean that God and Jesus cannot heal her until his faith unlocks their power. Rather, it means they want him to participate in the healing experience via belief. Fear of the power of death ("the sting of death," 1 Cor 15:55-56) must give way to the security produced by faith. Again, there is double meaning in *sōzō*—his daughter will be "healed," and they will experience God's "salvation" through faith.

They finally arrive at Jairus's home, where the corpse of his daughter rests (8:51), and Jesus restricts everyone from entering apart from the inner circle of his disciples (Peter, James, and John) and her parents. These three have been called **eschatological** witnesses, with Jesus at the major events (5:8–10; 9:28; Mark 13:3; 14:33). Gathered in the house are mourners, who are weeping inconsolably in grief. However, when Jesus says, "Stop wailing. ... She is not dead but asleep," he makes a play on words of one of the basic idioms for death, being asleep. In this case her death is as temporary as sleep.

At this their tears quickly turn to skeptical laughter (8:53). Mourning was a critical aspect of Jewish funeral rites; they even often hired professional mourners for greater impact. For Jesus to silence them would have shocked ancient funeral guests. They all knew death when they saw it and could not countenance what they thought of as disgracing the family in their grief. This echoes Abraham and Sarah's laughter when God told them he would give them an heir in their old age (Gen 17:17; 18:12), showing their shocked disbelief. However, in reality this is simply lack of faith. In a literary sense, this prepares the reader for the wondrous surprise of resurrection, as laughter is soon to be replaced by shock and a new kind of disbelief—"I can't believe he has the power to raise the dead."

The incredible miracle and aftermath (8:54–56)

Jesus takes over and in an instant changes the atmosphere. He doesn't rebuke them but simply reaches down, takes her hand, and commands, "My child, get up!" He had previously called the bleeding woman "daughter" (v. 48) and now calls this girl "my child," continuing the theme of the family of God. Touching a corpse caused a person's defilement, but Jesus is above that and as the Messiah he is unaffected. It is almost as if he is indeed her (spiritual) father and is waking her up from the "sleep" of verse 52. Luke omits Mark 5:41's Aramaic *Talitha koum* ("Little girl, I say to you, get up") because his Greek readers would not understand the touch.

The miracle is made apparent three different ways (8:55). First, "her spirit returned" to her. The Bible reveals that every person has a material (body) and a spiritual (spirit) side. At death, they separate, and the body rests in the grave while the spirit returns to God in heaven. Theologians call this "the intermediate state." As Jesus raises the young girl from the dead, her spirit returns from heaven and once more unites with her body. Second, "at once she stood up," continuing the emphasis on the immediacy of the miracles as they take place (8:44, 47). His power over his creation is absolute, and she responds in an instant. Third, Jesus commands that she receive nourishment, thereby proving to everyone there that she is really and truly alive. This is what Jesus will do after his resurrection to show the disciples that he has risen from the dead (24:30-31; John 21:12-13).

The parents, as elsewhere, are filled with wonder and astonishment at this stupendous miracle (8:56). But Jesus concludes the scene with a startling command "not to tell anyone what had happened." In Mark this is called "the messianic secret," where Jesus ordered those healed (and even his disciples) to remain silent about his miraculous power. He did this because the Jewish people expected a conquering king rather than a suffering servant, and he did not want that promulgated. Jesus does this with demons (4:41) and a leper (5:14), but he does not silence the widow and her son in 7:15-17, and he goes so far as to tell the restored demoniac to return home and tell what he had done (8:39). So why the command here? Many think it is judgment on the lack of faith shown by the bystanders and their scorn, but that was not the parents or Jesus' disciples. Perhaps Jesus did not want all the focus of people on the miracles rather than his teaching, and the silence allowed the deep mysteries of Jesus as sovereign over his creation to come to the fore (they are beyond human comprehension).

———

This chapter is absolutely essential to Luke, for it contains the very philosophy of Jesus' ministry. We first see those who are to be involved in this ministry, the women who serve as patrons and take care of the mission team (vv. 1-3), and then the true family of Jesus, those who hear and obey (vv. 19-21). To these followers as well as the crowds, Jesus directs parables that contain how they must respond to his teaching if they are to join God's family.

The parable of the sower (better, of the soils, vv. 5-15) addresses the question of response, what Jesus demands of those who wish to be God's people. The soils picture the different ways people "hear" or respond to Jesus: Those with an implacable refusal to heed his truths (the hard path) and who allow Satan to take away any possibility of true change; those who have a merely shallow interest easily crowded out by life's difficulties (the rocky soil); or those for whom what little life they have is choked out by desire for earthly pleasures and material possessions (the thorny soil). In contrast, the good soil depicts those who not only listen but also obey, growing incredibly in their spiritual life. Christ is the dispenser of the mysteries, those truths hidden and kept for this new age and now made available to all who will truly open their ears to God's truths and respond. But we are all responsible for what kind of soil we have become, and the question is, what kind of soil are you?

The parable of the lamp is closely connected, a series of sayings about the "light" of the world in Jesus and the demand that true disciples take these hidden truths that Christ has now revealed and proclaim them to the world. This mission is an essential part of being the family of God. When we truly listen and put Christ's teaching into practice, we truly become Christ's family (vv. 19-21).

The rest of this chapter (up to 9:17) turns to his mighty deeds and shows that when Jesus forms his messianic community he does so as the Lord over all creation. Every kind of miracle is performed here one at a time to demonstrate this unbelievable reality.

First, he has authority over nature as he stills a storm that is about to drown the disciples (vv. 22–25). When he immediately calms a super-powerful storm with just a few words, everyone asks the natural question, "Who is this?" All of Luke's Gospel is progressively revealing the answer to this. He is the God-man, creator and sovereign over his creation, able to control all of nature by his will.

Second, he is the absolute victor and sovereign over the cosmic powers. This is an evil world, under the influence of the powers of darkness, but they answer to Jesus. We see in the Gerasene demoniac a terrible picture of the effects of these unclean spirits on the people of this world (vv. 26–39). They have bound unfortunate victims to themselves and show their true colors by torturing and killing the very people who follow them. This poor man went through unbelievable suffering at their hands, but Jesus in his compassion and authority over them once again bends them to his will almost effortlessly. He allows them to enter and destroy the pig herds of probably several villages in order to show the world that they are unclean beings who live only to destroy living things. Yet he is completely victorious, and the former demoniac becomes the first missionary to the Gentiles. Jesus is in the process of restoring Israel and creating a new Israel.

Finally, two interconnected miracles complete his performing every kind of miracle there is. The woman with the twelve-year menstrual flow is another tragic character, and Jesus' compassion for her is evident throughout the scene. She has the faith and courage to work her way through the crowd and touch his garment, and the incredible miracle happens immediately, with her not only healed but also made clean by Jesus' miraculous power. Her faith then becomes the model for Jairus as his daughter is raised from the dead. Jesus has finalized his power over all of nature and finalized his messianic authority in the eyes of all around.

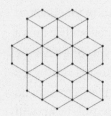

THE TRAINING OF THE TWELVE
(9:1–50)

This is the final chapter in Jesus' Galilean ministry (4:14–9:50) before Jesus sets his sights on Jerusalem and his passion there. His primary task is preparing his disciples for their leadership role as they will be charged with leading the church and continuing his ministry. So Jesus shifts his attention from the crowds to his disciples and immerses them in his person and ministry. The stress is on Jesus' authority, which is linked to his destiny as the Suffering Servant of Yahweh. His disciples, in order to become the future leaders, must be immersed not only in his authority but also in his suffering. He has just sovereignly controlled nature, cast out demons, healed the sick, and raised the dead. He has also proclaimed the arrival of the kingdom of God and the new age of salvation. He is now passing on both these aspects to his followers, immersing them in all aspects of his incarnate purpose in this world. They are being made ready for their postresurrection mission to the world.

JESUS SENDS OUT THE TWELVE (9:1–6)
Can you imagine the overwhelming wonder the disciples must have been feeling as Jesus commissioned them? Jesus had just demonstrated a greater power than anyone had ever shown in all of

history, and he is passing it on to his disciples. This is a sacred conclave if there ever was one, and as the Twelve gather as a commissioned team perhaps for the first time, they had to have been overcome with the enormity of it all as Jesus "gave them power and authority" to replicate his control over "all demons and to cure diseases." They now join him in having authority of word and deed in their ministry to both proclaim kingdom truths and perform mighty works. They are now truly envoys and agents ("sent ones"; see 6:13) of the kingdom. The themes of chapters 7–8 are here summed up and transferred to the disciples.

With this new authority Jesus officially "sent them out" with the twofold ministry mandate to "proclaim the kingdom of God" and "heal the sick" (9:2). The rest of this section provides detailed instructions for performing these tasks effectively and correctly. They are to focus not on their earthly comforts but also on their divine duties, and this will free them for what is truly important. They will depend on God, not on themselves. The presence of God's kingdom means that his reign has begun, and they are to tell the nations of this momentous event and call them to repentance and conversion.

In the **Hellenistic** world, itinerant philosophers were known for traveling in style and making an excellent living. Jesus would not have this be true of his followers. A concern for possessions and a luxurious lifestyle is inimical to spiritual life and ministry, so he commands here a minimalism in equipment taken along on the travels and a complete dependence on the Lord to care for one's needs along with the people to whom they are sent.

His general command is, "Take nothing for the journey." The goal is to proclaim the kingdom rather than enjoy the journey. Then he exemplifies what he means with five particulars—"no staff, no bag, no bread, no money, no extra shirt." These would be considered necessities by travelers. The bag was a kind of knapsack or backpack for food or extra clothes and served as a pillow when sleeping. A staff was needed over rugged terrain and climbing up the hills. The extra shirt would serve also as a blanket for sleeping.

There is some concern over a discrepancy in the Gospel accounts, as Mark 6:8–9 allows them to take a staff and sandals while Matthew 10:10 and Luke prohibit taking staff (9:3) and sandals (10:4). Some think there is no real problem, as these readings simply represent different ways of stating the same larger truth—dependence on God—and are examples of the evangelists' freedom in telling the story; but the contradiction still exists. Others think Mark has in mind the shepherd's hook for guidance while Luke and Matthew intend the club used for protection; the problem here is that it is the same Greek term in all three Gospels. Another view is to think Jesus said not to take an *extra* staff and sandals, but the text does not say this.

My solution is that Jesus sent them on more than one mission. Matthew and Luke follow Q, in which the disciples' mission is sacred; Jesus therefore used a temple motif, according to which staff and sandals are left at the door because it is holy ground (see also the burning bush in Exod 3:5). Mark used his own source, narrating a different mission that Jesus views as a new exodus like Israel's in Exodus 12:11, when the people were told to eat the Passover meal in haste, with staff in hand and sandals on one's feet. Here in Luke we are to reflect on the sacredness of the mission on which Christ is sending his followers.

On their mission, they were also to depend on the care of the people to whom they minister and remain satisfied with the lodging they receive (9:4), even if it means sparse accommodations. They must learn to be content with their situations and focus on preaching the gospel, not on the quality of the living arrangements. At a later time there were often false teachers and prophets who would take advantage of Christians by misusing their hospitality. This is mentioned in the second-century church document the Didache (ch. 12), where it said anyone who stayed more than three days should be treated suspiciously. There was to be no concern for profit-making in their mission.

Finally, Jesus gives instructions as to how to handle themselves when people reject them and their message (9:5). When Jews were leaving a Gentile area, they shook the dust from their feet (Acts 13:51) to rid themselves of particles that would render them unclean. So it implied defilement and was meant to tell those who rejected them that in reality God was rejecting those people and considered them nothing but unclean pagan Gentiles. They were no longer worthy of God's truths. This is not the unpardonable sin, for Jesus and the disciples returned to these towns later. It is saying that so long as they remain opposed to the gospel, they are unclean.

On this occasion Jesus and the disciples are completely successful on their itinerant ministry, probably throughout Galilee ("everywhere"). They perform both duties, preaching and performing miracles, and this is the first time the disciples exercise their new power and authority. This is a preview of their mission in Acts as they replicate Jesus' ability to heal the sick (and probably to cast out demons).

TROUBLE GATHERS AS HEROD SHOWS INTEREST IN JESUS (9:7-9)

Though the mission is successful, all is not rosy. Herod now joins the Pharisees in opposition to Jesus. Luke omits the flashback from Mark 6:17-30 and centers on his growing interest in Jesus (from Mark 6:14-16). He begins to hear all the rumors about Jesus and is "perplexed" by them. This is Herod Antipas, son of Herod the Great, tetrarch of Galilee and Perea from his father's death in 4 BC to AD 39, when he was exiled. So he ruled throughout Jesus' life. He wanted to be king like his father, but Augustus only allowed him to be tetrarch, a minor ruler of one-fourth of a Roman territory.

The speculation that Jesus was "John [the Baptist] ... raised from the dead" was one of the popular legends about Jesus in some

circles at that time. Jesus and his disciples had a preaching ministry similar to that of John, but such a rumor certainly represented ignorance about the birth, life, and even the age of Jesus.
He and his cousin were born about the same time, but Jesus' ministry took off after John's was virtually completed, which would
have contributed to the rumors. From Mark 1:14; Matthew 4:12 we
know John was arrested just before Jesus began his Galilean ministry. The imprisonment and beheading of John would have taken
place during Jesus' ministry in Galilee.

Luke mentions two other rumors in verse 8. Elijah of course
was expected to come back as the messianic forerunner (Mal 3:1;
4:5), and Jesus reenacted his miraculous ministry, so this is quite
natural. The exhortation to the nation to repent echoed both Elijah
and John. Finally, some thought that in Jesus "one of the prophets of long ago had come back to life," perhaps a reference to the
prophet like Moses of Deuteronomy 18:15. Matthew 16:14 mentions
Jeremiah as well. Obviously, Herod's confusion is caused somewhat
by the plethora of rumors swirling around.

So Herod's question echoes the basic one we have seen often,
"Who, then, is this?" (see 5:21; 7:49). It is one of the major questions
Luke wants all of his readers to ask. It is the key to everything,
and through it we realize that Jesus is indeed prophet, Messiah,
and God of very God. Herod has no idea what he is asking. He just
wants to know whether Jesus is any danger to him and will raise up
trouble for him. He has gotten rid of troublesome John and doesn't
know quite what do with this new upstart. As a result, Herod "tried
to see him" (also 23:8) and find out or himself.

JESUS FEEDS THE FIVE THOUSAND (9:10-17)

This is the only miracle found in all four Gospels, probably
because of its deep theological heritage. It links the miracle of
the manna (Exod 16) and Elisha's multiplication of twenty loaves
to feed a hundred people (2 Kgs 4) with, first, Jesus' Last Supper
and, second, the messianic banquet. Its basic message is God's

provision for his people, and it is especially related to the disciples, as Jesus involves them in every stage of the event. They must learn to leave life's anxieties with the Lord and trust him to care for them. Jesus is the new Moses and the Elisha prophet, indeed God's Messiah sent to launch the new realm of God and bring salvation to a fallen world.

THE RETURN OF THE TWELVE (9:10–11)

The mission of 9:1–6 is over, and the victorious disciples return and report to Jesus about their successful ministry. Jesus apparently decides that some rest and relaxation is needed, and they go from Capernaum around the northern edge of the lake to Bethsaida in Philip's territory of Gaulinitis, the hometown of Simon Peter and Andrew (John 1:44). They may wish to escape the clutches of Herod Antipas (vv. 7–9) for a while and at the same time have a desire for a time of rest and perhaps private training. This is short-lived, however, for the "crowds learned about it and followed him" (9:11). Jesus can never get away for long.

Jesus "welcomed them" and obviously changes his instruction from discipleship to evangelism, both discoursing about God's new reign and establishment of his kingdom on earth and, as he does often, anchoring it in a ministry of healing. Compassion is his hallmark, and he never turns away a needy person.

THE DILEMMA: FEEDING THE CROWD (9:12–14A)

It was getting late, and the disciples began to worry about the crowd and the evening meal. Dinner was normally eaten about sundown. The disciples want the huge crowd dismissed because they are in a "a remote place," probably somewhere outside Bethsaida. So there is reason for concern, and they want the people to "find food and lodging" before things get dangerous. The note about lodging is likely due to the fact that people have come to hear Jesus from far away. This reflects the Near Eastern concern for hospitality. Jesus is hosting a great crowd and so is responsible to provide for their nourishment and safety. The scene echoes Israel in the wilderness taken care of by God (Exod 16).

Jesus wants to involve the disciples, challenge their faith, and help them reflect on Jesus' true power to care for the needy. Seeing that they number five thousand men plus women and children,[1] he makes an impossible command: "You give them something to eat" (9:13). Their reply is the only possible one, for none of them have even brought any provisions along: "We have only five loaves of bread and two fish," and John 6:9 tells us even that was actually supplied by a small boy. They also can hardly afford to purchase enough food to feed the crowd. In John 6:7 Philip states that it would take two hundred denarii ("more than half a year's wages") to pay for that much food. The only recourse is to disperse them while there is enough time in the day for that many people to fend for themselves. The laws of hospitality must give way to simple common sense.

THE FEEDING MIRACLE (9:14B–16)

Jesus gives a peculiar command to "have them sit down in groups of about fifty each." Some think this recalls the division of Israel (Exod 18:21; Deut 1:15), but that is into "thousands, hundreds, fifties and tens" and may be a little obscure for this. Still, **Qumran** took this division of the people of Israel as a model for their community organization, and Mark 6:40 expands it into "groups of hundreds and fifties," perhaps indicating Jesus' formation of his messianic community into a new Israel. Personally, I think this may well be the symbolic purpose behind this new organization of the people. It also is probably an allusion to the messianic banquet, reflecting the division of a large group for a sumptuous meal.

---

1. Note the immense difference between the number here and Elisha's similar miracle with one hundred men and twenty loaves (2 Kgs 4:42–43). That was one loaf for five people, while this is one loaf for a thousand people—two hundred times as great a miracle!

The disciples comply and group the people, and they "reclined"[2] on the grass. Then Jesus assumes the place as host of the banquet (9:16). The language in his blessing of the meal ("looking up to heaven, he gave thanks and broke [the bread]") has overtones of the Last Supper (22:17, 19) and some think has eucharistic overtones. However, that is secondary to the main thrust: God's provision for his people in Christ. Again, note how involved the disciples are: they bring the food, group the people, distribute the food, and clean up the scraps. This is definitely a miracle with discipleship implications. The message is that when we allow Jesus to take over and surrender to him, we will participate in miraculous things (the same message as 5:1–11).

In all of this there are three primary themes: Jesus' great power and authority, his compassion and provision for the needs of his people, and the privilege of his followers to participate in his wondrous work in this world. The "multiplication" of the loaves and fish recalls the stilling of the storm—Jesus' great power over his creation. There have been numerous attempts to explain it away: the wealthy women patrons of 8:1–3 provided the food; the example of the young man's selfless sharing of his meal convicted the others, so they all began sharing the food they had brought; or it is a fictional legend made up by the later church. None of these work. The only reason to deny a supernatural event here is to reject the possibility of a supernatural God. God had performed this before in the miracles of the manna (Exod 16) and in Elisha's miracle of 2 Kings 4. There is no reason why he and his Son couldn't perform it again.

Results and Aftermath (9:17)

This was truly a sumptuous feast. We are told they "*all* ate and were satisfied"; the second verb (*chortazō*) means they "gorged themselves" on the food (as in Rev 19:21). The food of the poor (barley

---

2. NIV: "sat down"; reclining was the proper posture for banquets (see 22:14).

loaves and a fish paste) had been transformed into a true banquet. Everyone went away stuffed to the gills. Not only that, but there was a feast left over just from the scraps, twelve baskets in all. The term *kophinos* indicates a large basket, so this was a monumental amount of food Jesus provided for the people. There is some debate regarding possible symbolism in the number twelve, and many think it simply the historical amount left as signifying the huge meal provided. Still, with the seven baskets left over after the feeding of the four thousand (Mark 8:8), it seems to me that the early church had to see significance. At the least, the two numbers represent the perfect work of God in providing for his people.

PETER CONFESSES AND JESUS PREDICTS HIS PASSION (9:18–27)

This section is both the high point of the disciples' coming to awareness and the midpoint in Jesus' public ministry. Peter finally vocalizes for the Twelve their belief in Jesus as Messiah, and the tone of everything changes here. Here is the answer to the question everyone has been asking: "Who is this?" (see on 8:25; 9:9). At the transfiguration, God will expand on this and give the ultimate answer in 9:35. This is the true midpoint in Jesus' public ministry. The disciples have been on a journey with Jesus *up to* this point in their relationship, and with this Jesus now shifts his eyes to Jerusalem, and the action moves *down to* his passion in Jerusalem. His messianic destiny has led him to this point, and now it leads him to his ultimate appointment with his supreme sacrifice.

JEWISH SPECULATION ABOUT JESUS (9:18–19)

In Luke every major event in Jesus' ministry begins with prayer (see on 3:21). He treasured his time of privacy alone with his Father. He is the Messiah and God-man but still needs strength and comfort in his earthly journey to his moment of destiny. This is a critical moment and provides a transition from the feeding miracle to the confession of his followers. Again, he provides the model we must follow in our Christward journey. If he needs prayer at this critical juncture in his life, how much more do we at every important moment and event.

He has just drawn out his disciples through their participation in the multiplication of the loaves, and now he wants to draw them out again and make them aware of the extent of their understanding vis-à-vis who he is. So he asks them an initial question, "Who do the crowds say I am?" His purpose is not to discover something new (he already knows the answer) but to get the disciples to reflect more carefully on his identity as well as his ministry to the crowds and its effectiveness.

The answers reproduce Herod's speculations in 9:7–8—the Baptist, Elijah, or one of the prophets. All of them emerge from the view of the crowds that Jesus, like the Baptist, is in continuity with the Old Testament prophets. The basic premise is correct but incomplete and inadequate. He is not the Baptist returned from the dead, but he is the One the Baptist has come to introduce. He is not Elijah, but he like the Baptist has come in the spirit and power of Elijah. The Baptist reenacted the preaching of Elijah, Jesus the miracles of Elijah. He is "one of the prophets" but far more; he is the Messiah prophesied by the prophets.

PETER'S CONFESSION (9:20)

Now Jesus' primary purpose comes to the fore as he asks the disciples, "But what about you?" It is their answer that is the critical component. As usual Peter answers for the others, confessing, "God's Messiah." Each of the **Synoptic** Gospels has a slightly different response, with Mark 8:9 the simplest declaration, "the Messiah," and Matthew 16:16 the most detailed, "The Messiah, the Son of the living God." Yet all contain the central element that Jesus is the expected Messiah. Luke has "God's Messiah," with "God's" a genitive of purpose, meaning "Messiah from God" or "the God-sent Messiah." The Greek for "Messiah" is of course *Christos*, the "Anointed One." In Scripture the concept refers to the royal Messiah

descended from David. He is anointed and commissioned by God
(Ps 2:2; Dan 9:26) to inaugurate the new messianic era, the age of
salvation, with all the meaning spoken at Jesus' birth (1:31–33, 35).

SAYINGS ON SUFFERING AND DISCIPLESHIP (9:21–27)

Jesus' response in verse 21 is strange as he "strictly warned them
not to tell this to anyone." This is once again what in Mark is called
"the messianic secret" (4:41; 5:14; 8:56). The Jews expected a conquering king while Jesus has come to be a suffering servant. Only
after the cross can this be understood; he will come to finally defeat
the evil powers at his second coming. Jesus did not want this propounded until he had completed his mission. The disciples cannot
understand this any more than the crowds could, so Jesus wants
them to be silent about it. They must pass through his suffering
with him before they can be ready to speak.

Jesus' prediction of his passion and resurrection in 9:21b–22 is
in part a reason for the command to silence; they must realize he
is to be suffering Messiah before conquering Messiah. In fact, he
will conquer through suffering. This is the first passion prediction
(with 9:44; 18:31–33; see also 17:25) and adds the important nuance
of the suffering Son of Man (see on 5:24 and compare 6:5, 22; 7:34),
which will dominate from now on. He identifies himself with the
righteous suffering of the true people of God in Daniel 7:21–22
(universal dominion through suffering) as well as the Suffering
Servant in Isaiah 53:4, 11. The key is the redemptive results of messianic suffering. He is clarifying the true meaning of himself as
"God's Christ" and showing that his victory will come on the cross,
where he will become the atoning sacrifice and defeat sin once
for all. The "third day" theme became a primary creedal affirmation (1 Cor 15:40) and is linked with Hosea 6:2 ("on the third day
he will restore us").

There are five elements in the suffering motif: (1) the divine
"must" governs every part; this is his messianic destiny. (2) He
will "suffer many things," fulfilling the prophecies of the righteous

sufferer of Psalm 34:19 and the dying Messiah from Daniel 7;
Psalms 22, 69; and Zechariah 7–14 (especially 12:10, the "piercing"
of the messianic figure). (3) He will "be rejected by the elders, the
chief priests and the teachers of the law," the leaders of Israel who
made up the Sanhedrin. Luke has emphasized throughout (since
3:6) that the leaders more than the people are responsible for the
growing opposition to Jesus. (4) Another divine "must" says it is
a necessity that he "be killed," obviously pointing to his crucifixion as an atoning sacrifice for all people. Jesus came to earth in
order to die, and it will be the culmination of his messianic work.
(5) "On the third day be raised to life": his passion will end with
final victory over death, and he will be raised as the "firstfruits"
(1 Cor 15:20, 23) of our future resurrection.

The next few verses (23–26) are discipleship sayings that begin
with the requirements for discipleship: "Whoever wants to be my
disciple." The Greek is a condition of fact, "If [ei] anyone wants,"
which assumes the reality of the premise, "Of course they do." They
have committed themselves to Jesus; now they need to know what
that entails. The second half of this is also important; the NIV's
"wants to be my disciple" is in Greek actually "wants to come after
me," depicting discipleship as a journey to Christlikeness. The later
"follow me" is another way to say this. Being a Jesus "follower" is
not an individualistic walk with Christ in which we decide the path
we wish to take and do whatever we like. It is following Christ's
path and imitating him.

There are three steps on this road to discipleship: First, they
"deny themselves," a requirement unknown in ancient writings.
This is the basis of the other two and is clarified in 9:24—to save
one's life they must "lose" or surrender it. It means disciples refuse
to allow the "self" to control their life. Note the formula: to confess Christ we must deny self.

Second, they must "take up their cross daily," stressing the
ongoing nature of this—every day for the rest of their lives. The
image Jesus uses stems from the Roman practice of making the

condemned criminal carry the crossbeam to the execution site. Jesus carried his cross partway, and then Simon of Cyrene was conscripted to carry it the rest of the way (due to the scourging of Jesus, Luke 23:26). It signifies that you're already dead. There is double meaning in the metaphor here—it reinforces the meaning of the first requirement of dying to self: true discipleship involves a willingness to die for Christ if need be. When we follow Jesus, we embark on a road of rejection and hardship, a "participation in his sufferings" (Phil 3:10).

Third, they will "follow" Jesus all the way. As I said above, we are not free to make our own way and devise our own plan. To be a Christ follower is to live a life of servanthood and sacrifice as he did. "Follow" (*akoloutheō*) is the basic term in the Gospels for discipleship, involving imitation and obedience. It is only made possible by the first two steps and flows out of the denial of self and the process of dying to the things of the world.

The implications of this are fleshed out in the next three verses (24–26), which build on the gain-loss antithesis. To gain Christ demands the loss of self. Christ stresses here the futility of centering on self, and he states it both ways in verse 24. Those who wish to "save their life" by yielding to the ways of getting ahead in the world will ultimately "lose it." They will be lauded by the world and have temporary pleasure but lose Christ and the possibility of eternal life. On the other hand, "whoever loses their life for [Christ]" will in the end "save it." Losing one's life refers both to self-denial and to suffering and martyrdom. Embracing Christ's path of suffering and sacrifice will result in eternal reward.

To anchor this truth Jesus uses the image of profit and loss (9:25), saying in effect, "Where is the benefit or profit [*ōpheleō*] in gaining the whole world and yet losing or forfeiting [*zēmioō*] their very self?" They have temporary pleasure and plenty, but they suffer eternal loss. The gain is partial, the loss total. Moreover, the "loss" is forfeited at the final judgment, as the next verse makes clear. "Gaining the whole world" is not all it's cracked up to be.

The Roman emperors are perfect examples. They had control of the GNP (gross national product) of the entire Roman Empire for their personal pleasure, but they were virtually all unhappy people who died in misery. Caligula and Nero were insane.

Christ finalizes the choices in **apocalyptic** truth (9:26). The earthly choices in the end bring in the heavenly reality. This expands the theme of loyalty from verses 24-25 (and 12:8) and embraces two nuances. A preference for worldly gain and status ultimately involves a rejection of Christ and being ashamed of his life of service and sacrifice. Also, when one is suffering with Christ and experiencing persecution from the world, one can disown (= be ashamed of) him in order to be accepted by the world. These are not separate options but interconnected issues.

The judgment is another Son of Man saying (see 9:22), this time centering not on the suffering Son of Man but on his vindication and victory over his enemies at the last judgment. When Christ the exalted Lord is "ashamed," it takes on a much more dangerous hue, for it means he puts them to shame by pouring out eternal judgment on these who have become his enemies, here those who were "ashamed" of him. This is all anchored in his glory: "when he comes in his glory and in the glory of the Father and of the holy angels." This apocalyptic glory is threefold, all referring to his glorious second coming and then the final judgment that ensues, a judgment in which the holy angels will be involved as harvesters (Matt 13:39) and as witnesses in the heavenly court (Matt 16:27; 25:31). This stress on his glory recalls Daniel 7:13-14 as the glorious Son of Man enjoys universal dominion and becomes Judge of all.

Jesus' enigmatic saying in verse 27 both concludes the section on discipleship and introduces the transfiguration scene. In essence it promises that "some" of the faithful disciples "who are standing here" will be rewarded with glory in this life when they "see the kingdom of God" before they "taste death." There is quite a debate over its meaning: (1) On the basis of verse 26 it could be the final kingdom brought at Christ's return, but that would mean Jesus was wrong, and if so the early church would hardly have added this saying. Moreover, there would not be merely a few who would see Christ return. (2) It could refer to Pentecost, but that will not be the coming of the kingdom. (3) Some think it is the destruction of Jerusalem, but again that is not a kingdom event. (4) Many see this as the death and resurrection of Christ—that might be part of it but is unlikely to be the entire thrust.

The best is to see this as the entire chain of events in which the Son of Man is seen in his glory and inaugurates God's kingdom (present as well as future) on earth. This includes the transfiguration. The few are his disciples who will be there for all these events—the transfiguration as prefiguring Jesus' death and resurrection, his ascension to glory, Pentecost, the destruction of Jerusalem, and the successful mission to the nations. This is a promise that the disciples who share in his suffering will also share in his glory and see the kingdom progressively triumphing in this age and the age to come.

JESUS IS TRANSFIGURED (9:28-36)

This more than any other passage answers the question asked so often, "Who is this?" (5:21; 7:49; 9:9). It provides the second divine witness to Jesus (with 3:22) that he is the beloved Son and Messiah. It is an extraordinary event, as it proves him as preexistent Lord as well as present Son and future King. Critical scholars doubt its historicity, with many like Bultmann calling it an Easter story projected back into the life of Jesus. However, Peter, speaking of this event, made a specific point of stressing its historical worth: "we did not follow cleverly devised stories when we told you about the coming of our Lord Jesus Christ in power, but we were eyewitnesses of his majesty" (2 Pet 1:16). This should be taken seriously.

THE SETTING ON THE MOUNTAIN (9:28)

"Eight days" after Peter's confession differs from Mark 9:1 and Matthew 17:1, "after six days" (with a Sinai allusion, Exod 24:16) and is likely simply a time marker, "about a week later." Jesus left most of his disciples and took the inner circle with him up a mountain. As in nearly every event, his purpose is to spend time with his Father in prayer (see on 3:21), and his radiant countenance is the result of his deep prayer.

We don't know which mountain they ascended. Traditionally, it is Mount Tabor, but that is only 1,900 feet high and had a Roman garrison at its summit. Some think it was Mount Hermon, 9,232 feet high, but it was in Gentile territory; others prefer Mount Meron, the highest in Palestine at 3,926 feet. We cannot know for certain. Likely this is meant as a reenactment of Moses ascending Mount Sinai.

The Appearance and Heavenly Witnesses (9:29–31)

Luke takes a milder tack to describing Jesus' appearance, simply saying, "the appearance of his face changed," most think to avoid any link to pagan myths about magical transformations of the gods. Still, he adds, "his clothes became as bright as a flash of lightning." Here Jesus is not simply a new Moses, repeating the metamorphosis of Moses as he descended Sinai (Exod 34:29–35). He transcends Moses, whose face and clothes consisted of reflected glory from God while Jesus experiences the radiated glory of his Person. This echoes Ezekiel 1:4, 7, and Daniel 7:9 (God's glory on his throne). The "flash of lightning" shows Jesus' divine glory extending even to his garments, an image of a heavenly being.

The two witnesses (9:30; see Deut 19:15) are not your average people but two apocalyptic heralds and messianic prototypes, the prophet like Moses (Deut 18:15) and the forerunner of the Messiah (Mal 4:5). Moses represents the law, Elijah the prophets, so this sums up the messianic fulfillment expectation of the Old Testament. The "glorious splendor" of their garments parallels Christ and shows they are appearing from heaven. The "glory" of these two (NIV: "glorious splendor"; Greek: "appeared in glory") adds to the glory of God visible in Christ. Jesus has already been shown in Luke fulfilling both offices. The new age Jesus establishes is a new exodus (Moses), and his followers form the new messianic community of the last days (Elijah).

Only Luke tells us what they talked about: "his departure, which he was about to bring to fulfillment at Jerusalem" (9:31). This is explicitly identified as his *exodos*, looking at Jesus' exodus from this earth as a "departure" to God. It has been variously identified as his death, his resurrection and ascension, or perhaps the entire work of Christ from his death to his **parousia** (second coming) as an "exodus" event. Definitely the final resting place of Jesus in heaven is part of the imagery, though it is more difficult to determine whether Luke is thinking of the ascension or the parousia. I think it slightly more likely to be the latter, for apocalyptic imagery has predominated in this chapter.

THE DISCIPLES' CONFUSION (9:32–33)

It is hard to believe, but in the midst of all the transcendent events taking place, the disciples struggled and nearly fell asleep. Probably, they kept nodding off while Jesus was praying and missed quite a bit of the dialogue between Jesus and the two apocalyptic witnesses. This will happen again in Gethsemane when they will actually fall asleep, again while Jesus is at prayer (22:45).

Overwhelmed by the scene (and probably by the appearance of the two glorious figures), Peter tries to make the best of the situation. They had missed part of the dialogue, so he decides to try to get it extended longer so they can still have a part in it. Seeing "his glory and the two men standing with him" (at first, they saw only two people and didn't realize who they were), he wants to continue the experience, saying to the transfigured Christ, "Master, it is good for us to be here" (9:33). That is an understatement if there ever was one.

He sees these great men about to depart (9:33) and suggests, hardly thinking clearly, "Let us put up three shelters—one for you, one for Moses and one for Elijah." Out of the blue he tries to prolong the time with Moses and Elijah by suggesting that they celebrate the Feast of Tabernacles. At that festival, for seven days they would build three shelters or booths (calling them "tabernacles") out of branches and dwell in them for that period. It was a harvest festival and a time of great rejoicing and dancing as they celebrated God's provision for Israel in the wilderness. (Perhaps the recent feeding of the five thousand suggested it to Peter.)

Luke tells us that he said this because "he did not know what he was saying" and so blurted out the first thing that came to mind. Due to their being virtually asleep they had missed the chance to interact with their Old Testament heroes, and they were about to leave. This way they could have an entire week together (or at least an extended period). Peter could not be more wrong. First, in erecting one booth for each he makes Moses and Elijah equal to Jesus, a huge error. They are witnesses, not central figures, and they are there to initiate the new exodus as Jesus moves to his destiny in Jerusalem. Also, lengthening their time on the mountain would conflict with God's timetable, for everything was to move inexorably now to the passion events.

THE DIVINE AFFIRMATION (9:34-35)

The cloud overshadowing them is God's response to Peter's foolish suggestion. This is the **Shekinah** cloud from the exodus (Exod 13:21-22; 16:10; 19:16), which symbolized the presence of God's glory with his people. Here it signifies that the new exodus has started. It points forward to the cloud at the ascension (Acts 1:9) and at the return of Christ (Matt 24:30; Rev 11:12). Here it signifies God's **eschatological** presence with the scene and continues the Sinai imagery (the cloud covering the mountain, Exod 24:15; 34:5). As the three entered the cloud, they were filled with terror because they realized the significance, that this has now become a very powerful theophany with God and his glory literally present.

As at the baptism (3:22), God himself now speaks from the cloud (9:35) with a very similar message. He delivered the divine

imprimatur to Jesus ("You are my Son"), while here it is given to
the disciples ("This is my Son") with the same allusion to Psalm
2:7 (see that passage) and the same stress on Jesus as the royal
Davidic Messiah. The addition of "whom I have chosen" stems
from Isaiah 42:1 ("my servant ... my chosen one in whom I delight").
The emphasis now is on Jesus as the Suffering Servant of Yahweh,
preparing the way for his movement from this point to Jerusalem.
This in effect becomes a clarification to Peter's confession, telling
the three that as Messiah Jesus will walk the path of suffering, not
military conquest.

The final "Listen to him" echoes Deuteronomy 18:15, where
the "LORD your God" promises to raise up the prophet like Moses
and then commands, "You must listen to him." They are listening to the erroneous expectations of their Jewish background and
waiting for the messianic conqueror but must hear what Jesus is
saying and be ready for the suffering Messiah. The rest of their
time with Jesus will more and more center on that theme, and
they are not ready.

AFTERMATH: THEIR SILENCE (9:36)

In Matthew 17:9 and Mark 9:6 Jesus commands them to tell no
one what had just happened until after the resurrection. Luke
here states simply that the three "kept this to themselves and did
not tell anyone." They were likely so filled with awe at the whole
experience that they were virtually struck dumb. The hint is that
this was God's will, and it was not to be revealed until the proper
time in God's plan. As for them, they undoubtedly reflected on it
(and perhaps ruminated on it together) for the rest of the time on
the way to Jerusalem.

JESUS HEALS A DEMON-POSSESSED CHILD (9:37–43A)

This episode is quite abbreviated from Mark's lengthy narration
(Mark 9:14–29), yet it still contains the primary themes of demonic

torture of the child and the failure of the disciples to cast it out.
The emphasis is on Jesus' supreme authority and sets the stage for
his authoritative passion prediction "while everyone was [still]
marveling at all that Jesus did" (9:43b). Everything is now pointing to the cross, and the failure of the disciples to grasp this dominates the rest of this section (9:37-50).

The two parts (vv. 37-43a, 43b-50) belong together. Jesus is the
Messiah, the one chosen by God, the authoritative Lord of the universe, but at the same time he is the chosen righteous sufferer, and
his true destiny is the cross. He is filled with preexistent glory and
is the present Shekinah of God, but his primary purpose as the
incarnate one is to become the atoning sacrifice for sins and bring
salvation to sinful humankind.

As Moses descended from Sinai to face an Israel in the midst
of failure, so Jesus "came down from the mountain" to face the
inability of the disciples to use the authority he had given them
over the demonic realm. The presence of the "large crowd" continues his great popularity with the common people.

The horrific effects of demon possession are once again evident
(see also 8:27, 29) in this terrible description. This boy is the "only
child" (*monogenēs*, used of Jesus in John 1:14, 18; 3:16) and the man
begs Jesus to look into the boy's dilemma. These cosmic powers
desire only one thing—to torture and destroy anyone made in the
image of God. When they were cast out of heaven after their initial
rebellion (Rev 12:7-9) and imprisoned in this world, they landed
with an implacable hatred for God and his creation.

This demon uses a prior medical condition, epilepsy, to torment the child. It "seizes him and he suddenly screams; it throws
him into convulsions so that he foams at the mouth ... destroying
him." This is always the goal of demon possession. The old legend
of Satan helping his followers is a satanic lie. It is always destruction his minions are about. The unclean spirit takes the elements
of epilepsy, multiplies them, and enjoys the process of torture and
death as it consumes the child.

While the inner circle was experiencing Jesus' glory on the mountain, the rest of the disciples were experiencing massive failure down in the valley. They should not have been. Jesus had given them authority over the evil powers and disease (9:1), and they apparently were able to use that power on occasion (9:6).[3] We are not told why they could not do so here, but it most likely is because they had ceased to depend on the Lord's strength (Mark stresses their self-centeredness) and were almost showing off as they tried to cast it out.

Jesus' response is quite harsh. There is a question about the antecedent of "You unbelieving and perverse generation." It could refer to the unbelieving crowd, or it could be the faithless disciples in the midst of their failure. Most likely it is both of these but especially the disciples, for they are the nearest focus ("I begged your disciples to drive it out, but they could not"). Jesus is exasperated with the unbelief they were displaying, linking it with the "warped and crooked generation" of Israel in the wilderness (Deut 32:5, 20). He wonders, "How long shall I stay with you and put up with you?" The "how long" expresses his prophetic sorrow at their continued failure as well as his awareness of his imminent departure in Jerusalem. Will they ever be ready to carry on his mission to a fallen world? He does not have much longer to carry them.

The demon makes one more grand gesture to prove his animosity. As the boy is on his way to Jesus, the demon seizes him and throws "him to the ground in a convulsion." In Mark 9:21–24 there is a conversation with the boy's father about faith, but Luke skips this in order to center on Jesus' power over the demon. Again, his act of healing and exorcism is instantaneous, as he casts out the impure spirit and heals the epilepsy in one fell swoop. (Two

---

3. Luke never mentions that they cast out demons, but his positive portrayal of their healing could implicitly mean they were able to do so. Mark 6:13 states they "drove out many demons," and Luke would hardly have been unaware of that.

miracles for the price of one!) The moment he "gave him back to his father" must have been a triumphant scene, and the tears would have flowed. The amazement of the crowd is the typical response (4:32; 5:25; 7:16; 8:25). Their wonder is over "the greatness [or 'majesty'] of God" exemplified in Jesus.

JESUS PREDICTS HIS PASSION A SECOND TIME (9:43B–48)

There is both contrast and continuity between this passion prediction and the powerful miracle just completed (and the crowd's astonishment). Jesus' great power involves not just miracles but also his destiny to be the suffering and redeeming Messiah. Christ's greatest act of power is the cross, for that will bring life to all humanity, and that life will be eternal. So the miracles are **proleptic** anticipations of Jesus as Suffering Servant, who by sacrificing himself provides true spiritual healing and resurrection to eternal life.

The other major theme in this paragraph is discipleship failure. He could not have made his destiny any clearer, but the disciples are not only unable to comprehend what he is saying but actually contravene it with their self-centered desire for personal greatness. Luke draws this from Mark, where it is one of the primary themes of his Gospel as a whole. Jesus on his "new exodus" journey to Jerusalem involves his followers, for they are the focus of Jesus' efforts to prepare them not only for the passion events but also for their lifelong mission to the world that will follow.

PREDICTION AND FAILURE TO UNDERSTAND (9:43B–45)

The crowd is astonished at Jesus' wondrous power (v. 43a), and while they are still expressing that, Jesus makes an equally shocking pronouncement to his disciples (apparently not to the crowd). They undoubtedly expected him to talk about his majestic God-given authority over nature and Satan, but instead he tells them he is now going to face the world's hatred. Jesus' interest has shifted from

the uncommitted crowds to the committed but amazingly uncom-
prehending disciples. The crowds will from now on increasingly
be his adversaries, and with the focus now on the denouement in
Jerusalem, he realizes he has just a brief period to train the Twelve.

What Jesus is reminding them about in 9:44 (see 9:22 for the first
prediction) will dominate his trip to Jerusalem with the Twelve,
and everything will flow from it. So he begins with a critical command to "listen carefully to what I am about to tell you." It is impossible to overstate the importance of this prediction, for the salvation of humankind is tied to it. All of the astounding miracles were
merely a prelude to this, for they had only temporary effect, while
this announcement embraces that which has eternal repercussions.

The passion prediction itself omits the details on Jesus' death
and resurrection and centers on the complete reversal of the crowds'
interest in Jesus: "The Son of Man is going to be delivered into
the hands of men" (9:44). The verb (*paradidosthai*) speaks both of
delivery and betrayal. There is a question whether it is the specific
betrayal of Judas here or the general handing over of Jesus "into the
hands of" his enemies. The language strongly favors the latter, and
in fact the passive voice is probably a divine passive and means God
is soon to "deliver" Jesus to his God-given destiny of becoming the
atoning sacrifice for sin. As such it provides a commentary on the
true meaning of the "greatness of God" not merely providing miracles but more importantly providing redemption through suffering.

Two items are critical in verse 45. First, in spite of all Jesus
has said regarding his actual purpose in coming to earth (5:34–35;
7:31–35; 9:22, 31), they are still completely unable to comprehend
any of it. They are so controlled by Jewish expectations of the
Messiah coming to destroy the enemies of Israel and establish the
nation in the kingdom of God that they cannot accept Jesus as the
Isaianic Suffering Servant.[4]

---

4. We must remember also that the Jews understood the Servant Songs of Isa
52–54 of the nation rather than the Messiah.

Second, Luke tells us that "it was hidden from them, so that they did not grasp it." Again, we have a divine passive; God hid the knowledge from them, undoubtedly because they were not ready for it and had to be prepared by Christ to accept that difficult reality. This will also happen on the Emmaus road journey after the resurrection (24:16), when two disciples will be kept from recognizing the risen Lord until God opens their eyes with the breaking of bread and the opening of the word (24:31). God is orchestrating every detail of this scene.

The Twelve were also "afraid to ask him about it," continuing the fear motif (5:26; 7:16; 8:25, 35, 37; 9:34). To encounter Jesus is to experience theophany, and it produces of necessity both fear and awe. Jesus is the ineffable God-man, and we are overwhelmed by his very presence. There is the added mystery of the true destiny of Jesus. They could not handle what they knew down deep would involve them in ways for which they were not ready.

Rivalry over Greatness (9:46–48)

Luke in this episode abbreviates Mark 9:33–37 and so stresses even more the contrast between Jesus' self-sacrifice and the disciples' self-serving attitudes and desire for status. It is hard to imagine a greater polar opposite than Jesus' declaration of his future suffering and the disciples' quarrelling over future greatness. They did not just fail to understand. They failed even to listen or care about what Jesus was saying. What they were arguing about was their importance and rank in the apostolic band. Was Peter or John or Matthew the leader of the Twelve? Who was more important to Jesus? Worst of all, this will happen again at the Last Supper (22:23–30). They exemplify the "selfish ambition and vain conceit" of Philippians 2:3.

Jesus' response (9:47–48) is to have a small child stand before them as an example. Children had no status in the ancient world and were thought to be of little significance or value. Their lowly regard made them a perfect illustration for Jesus' purpose. They

were not really welcome in adult circles, so Jesus is calling for a
social revolution: "Whoever welcomes this little child in my name
welcomes me." At first glance this seems unrelated, but Christ is
centering on their "reception" and attitude toward the marginalized in society. How we receive children, the poor, and others
of low status constitutes how we receive Jesus and God. The way
children are treated is the way Jesus is treated (see Matt 25:31–46).
Greatness does not come by inherent superiority but by our servant attitudes. "In my name" is the key to discipleship and refers
to Christlikeness. To receive the child with love is to be like Christ.

Then Jesus turns this around: "Whoever welcomes me welcomes the one who sent me." Our openness to the poor and dis-
enfranchised in this world constitutes our relationship not only
with Jesus but also with God and will determine how God will treat
us. This is the principle of reciprocity and becomes the model for
ethics—what we do to others we do to God, and he will turn that
action back on our own heads. If we welcome others, God welcomes us; if we mistreat others, God will judge and condemn us. In
other words, there is no room for Christ followers to center on self;
we like our Lord and Master are servants and give our lives and
ministries in order to serve others, refusing to look down on them.

The concluding statement in verse 48 defines true greatness: "It
is the one who is least among you all who is the greatest." The true
leader will place herself and her needs last and live to help others,
as exemplified by Jesus in verse 44. Servanthood **Christology** is
the basis for discipleship, as in 22:27, "I am among you as one who
serves" (see also Mark 10:43–45). This is an essential principle for
kingdom ethics—the more we serve, the greater we are in God's
eyes. That doesn't say much for all too many Christian leaders
today. We so easily become dictators and people who live the high
life when we become famous. May each of us examine ourselves
very carefully in this light.

THE DISCIPLES ARE CONFLICTED
OVER RIVAL EXORCISTS (9:49-50)

This episode as well abbreviates Mark (9:38-40) and illustrates the problem over greatness. Note that their rivals were "driving out demons in your name," something the disciples in Luke had not yet done. These disciples did not just fight over their own greatness in the group but also believed greatness was exclusive to them. Apparently an anonymous exorcist was using Jesus' name (see Acts 3:16; 19:13 on the power of the name). We can also contrast this man's success to the disciples' failure in 9:40. He depended on Jesus; they were apparently centering on self. Luke is highlighting the self-centered sectarianism of the disciples. They actually have the gall to say, "He is not one of *us*" rather than of Jesus. This reminds me of many denominations and Christian movements today. It only takes a minor difference in theology or worship style to cause Christian groups to go to war against one another. Sometimes our petty doctrines have priority over God in our movements.

Jesus' response is critical: "Do not stop him ... for whoever is not against you is for you" (9:50). Those who are not opposed to the disciples (and Jesus) are on their side. Of course, that does not include false prophets and teachers, but Jesus is not talking about them. Jesus is saying that the problem was with the disciples, not the man. (See Rom 14:1-15:13 for a longer passage on a similar issue.) Casting out demons in the name of Jesus is God's work, even if the man was not part of the mission team itself. They had no right to "stop" someone doing God's work. The negative parallel is found in 11:23, where Jesus says, "Whoever is not with me is against me," speaking of those who connected him to Beelzebul. The message is this: those who in any way try to follow Jesus should not be rejected (see Phil 1:15-18). Workers of different stripes should support each other. Cooperation needs to replace rivalry.

———

Luke has a special emphasis on the training of the Twelve for the mission on which God is sending them. There are two major missions in his Gospel, those of the Twelve here and the seventy-two in 10:1–24, and both prepare for the mission of the whole church in the book of Acts. Here in verses 1–6 it is clear that on our mission we center entirely on our dependence on God and on the people to whom he has sent us. There is no room for seeking comfort or material luxuries, for we are envoys of God and represent him. The interest and perplexity of Herod remind us of two things— in mission there will always be opposition, and the primary question will always be, who is this Jesus? Our gospel message is clear. We proclaim Jesus, Lord and Savior of all. We do not proclaim ourselves and our own importance.

The feeding of the five thousand (vv. 10–17) is the perfect miracle following the mission, for it signifies God's provision for his people. Jesus took a simple meal for the poor and turned it into a sumptuous feast anticipating the messianic banquet of the last days. He also involved his disciples in every step to show them how they too could be the vehicle of the power of God in caring for his people.

Peter's confession (vv. 18–27) is the high point of this section and the turning point in Jesus' ministry, when he sets his face to the fulfillment of his messianic calling in Jerusalem. The disciples through Peter finally confess him as God's Messiah, and he clarifies that by teaching them that he has actually come to be the suffering Messiah of Isaiah, and through his suffering redemption will come to humankind.

This leads into a series of instructions on discipleship (vv. 23–26) in which Jesus demands that his followers die to self and embrace a Christlike life of sacrifice and service. Those who yield earthly comfort and become servants in this life will find great reward in eternity, while those who live for the things of this world will have nothing in eternity. What we receive at the final judgment will depend on what we do for Christ in this life.

The transfiguration (vv. 28-36) proves that with Christ God's kingdom has truly entered this world. He ascends the mountain like Moses at Sinai and this time takes his inner circle as witnesses. He shows himself to be the prophet like Moses as his inner glory shines through and his countenance and garments are transfigured—his preexistent glory radiates through his incarnate state, and the two messianic harbingers, Moses and Elijah, help him prepare for his glorious destiny, his "departure" or new "exodus" on the cross. The disciples fail to understand but become witnesses of the Shekinah glory of God, the cloud enveloping them as at Sinai, and are told that this One they know as Messiah is also his Son, the elect Chosen One who is to suffer. His glory is in his suffering.

The last two scenes of this section (the demon-possessed child in vv. 37-43a and the second passion prediction in vv. 43b-50) center on two related themes: Jesus' absolute sovereignty and authority now focused on the cross, and discipleship failure as his followers are powerless and unable to grasp what is coming. The sad plight of the boy is made worse by the inability of the disciples to do anything, but Christ once more has complete control over the powers of darkness and frees the child. Jesus embodies the greatness and mercy of God in all he does.

The second passion prediction (vv. 43b-48) demonstrates the extent to which his greatness is tied to his suffering, and it is accompanied by the amazing obsession of the disciples with themselves. As he is telling them of his coming sacrificial death, they are fighting over which of them is more important to their mission and to Jesus. All too many Christian leaders today are doing the same thing! The illustration of receiving the child is perfect, for while they want to be the greatest, Jesus is telling them that welcoming the least (the children) is actually a barometer of how great you are. This would be a great passage for a sermon on the children's ministry of the church.

The story of the "rival" exorcist (vv. 49-50) is a perfect example of the misbegotten delusions of grandeur these disciples had. Jesus'

authority had been virtually replaced with their own self-impor-
tance, and they had lost all perspective. The principle is essential—
when groups claim to be following Jesus and ministering in his
name, cooperate rather than condemn. This does not mean that
there are no heretics or cults who falsely claim such, just that our
initial reaction must be to accept them until we know better. All
truth and authority do not begin and end with our small group.

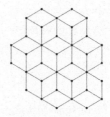

MISSION AND FURTHER TRAINING
(9:51–10:42)

This passage begins a long section (9:51-19:27) centering on Jesus' travel itinerary as he moves to Jerusalem to fulfill his destiny. Throughout the movement of the narrative there are frequent markers to tell us he is "going" on his "way to Jerusalem" (9:51-52, 57; 10:1, 38; 11:53; 13:22; 17:11; 18:31, 35; 19:1, 28). It is not a straight line, as he is an itinerant preacher still bringing the gospel to Galilee and Judea, but he is at all times "on the way." Jerusalem is the goal, and Jesus is on the move, but his teaching is central as he gradually reveals himself more thoroughly to his followers and trains them to be not only disciples but also leaders of his mission. As a result of all this, this section in Luke is much larger than the same section in Mark or Matthew.

On this journey, Jesus' primary goal is to train the Twelve, and the majority of the material is L material, gathered from eyewitnesses in Luke's "special sources."[1] Jesus still ministers to the crowds, but his followers are the focus. Luke follows the general contours of Mark and Matthew in the travel plan, but the stories are for the most part uniquely his. There are only a few miracles, and much of the material consists of parables (thirteen all told)

---

1. See "Sources" in the introduction.

and sayings as Jesus continues to prepare the disciples both for the passion events and their postresurrection mission to the world.

JESUS TRAINS HIS DISCIPLES FOR THE FUTURE (9:51–10:24)

Everything now points to Jerusalem. His whole focus has shifted, and here we see why. Luke tells us that "the time approached for him to be taken up to heaven," using the term for his ascension (*analēmpseōs*). This becomes almost a title for the next ten chapters, for the verb contains language of fulfillment, "the days fulfilled for the coming of his ascension." In 9:31 Moses and Elijah discuss with him his "exodus [NIV: 'departure'], which he was about to bring to fulfillment at Jerusalem," so the events to transpire are considered the culmination of God's plan of salvation, the central event of the ages.

Luke is the only evangelist to describe the ascension, and it is critical to his narrative, both concluding his Gospel (24:50–53) and introducing the book of Acts (1:9–11). The focus is not just on his death but also on his vindication and glory. Everything will change in Jerusalem, where Jesus will die for the sins of humankind and be exalted as he assumes his majesty and lordship in heaven. There the results of Jesus' passion will be realized as the mission to the world commences. So from this moment on, he "set out for Jerusalem," literally, "set his face," which indicates his single-minded goal or purpose.

MISSION IN SAMARIA (9:51–56)

Samaria stands between Galilee and Jerusalem, so when he "sent messengers on ahead," they naturally had to pass through Samaria (9:52). It is difficult to know if this means they were simply intending that the mission team spend the night there (they were likely arranging lodging) or to begin the world mission at that point. To some extent this latter point is correct, for they are following Jesus' principles for mission in the ensuing verses. Some link these messengers to the spies sent into Canaan to prepare for Moses and the rest of the Jewish people (Deut 1:22), but that may read too much into this verse. A better parallel would be John the Baptist preparing for Jesus' messianic arrival.

At any rate the townspeople rejected Jesus' messengers "because he was heading for Jerusalem." Actually, many Jews refused to pass through Samaria and went to the other side of the Jordan for this very reason. The centuries-old animosity between Jews and Samaritans (since the postexilic period four hundred years earlier) accounts for this. To the Samaritans the Jerusalem temple represented a false religion. So they wanted nothing to do with Jesus or his followers.

James and John are still ignorant of Jesus' purposes and focus on him as the conquering Messiah who will destroy their enemies. Jesus had told them to shake the dust from their feet as a warning to those who reject their gospel message (9:5; 10:11). This isn't good enough for them. They continue to have delusions of grandeur and want to be "the greatest" (9:46), as their brash suggestion shows. "Lord, do you want *us* to call fire down from heaven to destroy them?" (9:54). Some think their nickname "sons of thunder" (referring to their bad tempers) stems from this incident, but that is doubtful. Their request recalls Elijah's calling down fire from heaven on two different companies of Ahaziah's soldiers (2 Kgs 1:9-14). The disciples thought they, like Jesus, were modern Elijahs, prophets of God.

Jesus, needless to say, simply "turned and rebuked them" (9:55).[2] This reaction looks to the final judgment and has no place in the mission of the Twelve. Warnings of coming judgment, yes (9:5),

---

2. There are textual variants here. Some older texts like Sianiticus, Alexandrinus, and Vaticanus say simply, "Jesus rebuked them, and they went to another village." Many "wilder" Western texts like Codex Bezae add, "You do not know what manner of spirit you are." The NIV's reading is likely the better one.

but not destruction. This is the time for mercy, not judgment, for gospel promises rather than destruction. Opportunities must be given to reverse this opposition and repent. The disciples are not yet part of heaven's armies and the agents of retribution. That awaits another day when they will be taken up by Jesus to join the armies of heaven (Rev 17:14; 19:14) for the final battle.

They then follow Jesus' principle in 9:5; 10:10–11 that when rejected they simply go on to the next village (9:56). They like Jesus in all his mission journeys (4:43–44) are to go "from village to village, proclaiming the good news" (9:6).

The Cost of Discipleship (9:57–62)

Now several would-be followers of Jesus appear while he is "on the way" (NIV: "along the road") with his face set to Jerusalem. So the picture is of those willing to walk the path of suffering (Phil 3:10) with him and yet offering excuses to postpone starting the process. The emphasis is not on the excuses but on the principles that flow out of Jesus' responses. So this ends up being a primer for a discipleship program. It contains an all-important principle, for "the Way" will become the title for the Christian movement (9:2; 19:9, 23; 22:4; 24:14; 24:22). So we can label this "the way to becoming a disciple." There are three sets of qualifications here (Matt 8:19–22 has the first two).

The first offer promises: "I will follow you wherever you go." This is not yet an excuse and in fact leads into the other two. The man clearly wanted to be one of the Twelve, intimate followers rather than the wider circle of seventy-two in 10:1. Overall, this is a viable promise, but the question is how much this man understands what it truly means to follow Jesus all the way. If he is thinking of a comfortable life going from village to village making friends and learning Torah (the normal purpose of a rabbinic student), he is sadly mistaken. The way of Jesus is difficult and costly, demanding enormous sacrifice. He is not a mere rabbi, dispensing wisdom and Torah as his followers memorize what he is saying.

He makes this clear in his response (9:58). The man must realize the implications of becoming a Christ follower, that a comfortable or even a normal life will not be part of it. Jesus as an itinerant preacher had no home. Even wild animals have homes, but not Jesus and those who join his God-given mission. Peter says it right in 1 Peter 1:1, 17; 2:11: this world can never be our home, but we are called to be "foreigners" and "exiles" like Christ, strangers in a place to which we don't belong. Like him, we are homeless, for we are citizens of heaven (Phil 3:20). Many interpreters see even more meaning in "foxes have dens." Herod is a fox (13:32), so this means that the opponents of Christ and the church (Herod, Rome) have all the power, and those who follow Christ, the new Israel, are the marginalized and the captives in this world. We should never expect to be accepted by those who hold the reins of power and have turned their backs on Christ and his followers.

Jesus takes the initiative with the second and makes the standard invitation ("Follow me") also given to Levi (5:28). However, the man makes a qualification: "Lord, first let me go and bury my father" (9:59). This is certainly a reasonable request, for burying one's parents was a sacred duty that had precedence over everything, even the study of Torah (Gen 46:4; 50:5; Job 4:3; Tobit 4:3–4). To fail to fulfill this duty was an ultimate disgrace. However, the high priest and the Nazirite were called to avoid the corpse even of a parent (Lev 21:11; Num 6:6–8).

Jesus deliberately couches his reply in shocking language to make a very important point (9:60). "Let the dead bury their own dead" sounds unbelievably harsh and uncaring—let the (physically) dead be buried by the (spiritually) dead, namely, unbelievers. Some water this down somewhat by saying the request was actually to allow the son to postpone following Jesus while the parents are still alive, but that is unlikely. His point is that following him has priority over everything, even one's parents. To follow Jesus is a high and holy calling, a sacred position much like a Nazirite, for his followers obey a higher law, with precedence over other duties. His is the most solemn religious obligation.

However, Jesus is not saying that his followers are to jettison all obligations to parents or family in favor of him. Rather, they must make him their highest priority. There is a calculated hyperbole in the stark statement, as Peter's concern for his mother-in-law (and Jesus' healing of her) in 4:38–39 shows. The duties of discipleship have priority over all earthly obligations.

The third potential disciple is following the example of Elisha in 1 Kings 19:19–21, who promised to accept Elijah's mantle but after he bid farewell to his family. Elijah allowed him to do so, but Jesus does not. When he asks to "say goodbye to [his] family," Jesus responds again with a harsh warning: "No one who puts a hand to the plow and looks back is fit for service in the kingdom of God" (9:62). It is easy to miss the context of this in a society when commitment is often so shallow. To follow Jesus is lifelong and all-consuming, not a casual joining of a movement for a little while.

The metaphor is drawn from the Elisha story, for he was plowing a field when Elijah made his approach. This is a heavy iron plow drawn by an ox and easily shifts out of the line in a field. One hand is on the plow, the other guiding the ox. For a farmer to "look back" is to guarantee the plow will swerve out of its straight furrow. For a disciple, it means to keep one's attention firmly focused on Jesus and refuse to "look back" to the old way of life. Single-minded devotion to Christ and his teaching is mandated. The world and its ways have to be left behind. Christ demands our all.

THE MISSION OF THE SEVENTY-TWO (10:1–24)

From excuses for avoiding discipleship, Luke now turns to successful discipleship with a preview of the universal mission in Acts. This is the second successful mission and expands the first (9:1–6). Both prepare for the worldwide mission in Acts. Now Jesus involves all followers in what heretofore centered on the Twelve. Note the progression, from the Twelve to the seventy-two to all the church. This is a very positive section, culminating the preparation of the disciples thus far. Jesus makes salvation possible, but the disciples get the privilege of proclaiming this salvation and the arrival of the kingdom of God to a world that desperately needs everything they have to say.

Instructions for the Mission (10:1–12)

Jesus is Lord of the harvest, and his lordship is a feature of this Gospel (5:8; 7:6, 13, 19; 9:54, 59, 61; 10:39, 41) to stress the authority with which he conducts his God-given work. As sovereign he "appoints seventy-two."[3] It is difficult to know how recognized in the church these are as a group, for they are never mentioned again. Almost certainly they are not like "the Twelve" in their recognized status. Rather, they join the disciples as official envoys or "sent ones" (Aramaic: *shaluachim*) as they go from town to town in his name. In 6:13 Jesus chose the Twelve from a larger group of followers; now he may have organized the larger group. They are sent out in pairs as Deuteronomic witnesses (Deut 17:6; 19:15), and this became the practice in Acts (13:2; 15:27; 17:14). The number corresponds to the list of nations in Genesis 10:2–31, and the symbolism means that Christ has made provision for his universal mission to all the nations.

The great need in any mission is prayer, as Jesus himself proves throughout (see on 3:21). We cannot fulfill so important an obligation without bathing it and ourselves in prayer to God. In Jewish literature the idea of the final harvest centered on divine judgment involving the angelic harvesters (as in Matt 13:30, 39), but here as in 5:10 and Matthew 9:37–38 it is positive, building on the joy of the

---

3. The Greek manuscripts are almost equally divided between the readings "seventy" and "seventy-two," probably because the list of nations in Gen 10 has seventy in the Masoretic Text (Hebrew) and seventy-two in the **Septuagint** (Greek). The best explanation is that Luke wrote "seventy-two" from the Septuagint but later copyists wrote "seventy" from the Masoretic Text.

wheat harvest. Yet the need is great and "the harvest is plentiful," so abundant that there are not nearly enough harvesters for the task. Moreover, the harvesters cannot be chosen merely by putting out the word, for only "the Lord of the harvest" can find the right workers. Not anyone is up for the task, as all the training of the disciples thus far has shown. "The workers are few" for two reasons—few are able to do it, and few are willing to work in the difficult conditions of the harvest. So deep prayer is needed. The task needs divine intervention.

Jesus' words flow into a warning. In this mission they are not being sent into a comfortable and safe environment. As "lambs among wolves" (10:3) they will experience a great deal of danger from those who are opposed to everything they believe. This was a frequent image of Israel among the nations (Ezek 22:27; 34:25–28) and of danger from hostile enemies and false teachers (Matt 7:15; 10:16; John 10:12; Acts 20:29). This is a major reason why they must depend completely on the Lord, the major theme of this section. They are totally vulnerable, and the risk is great.

In light of this danger and in order to fulfill their mission, they are given instructions quite similar to those in 9:3. The items here—no purse, bag, or sandals (see 9:3; 22:35)—are quite extreme and would render them impoverished, virtual beggars, completely helpless from an earthly perspective and dependent on God's care. These commands are probably hyperbolic, intended to make the disciples center on their God-dependence. The same is true with the command, "Do not greet anyone on the road." This was demanded of travelers and considered common courtesy. Since greetings were often fairly lengthy, the message centers on the urgency of the task. They cannot afford to be distracted, because the situation of the nation without God is critical, and the message of repentance is desperately needed.

Verses 5–7 parallel Matthew 10:12–13 and tell them how to conduct themselves as they minister in town after town. They begin with the Jewish greeting. While such has just been prohibited on the road (v. 4b), here it is part of the gospel proclamation, for in a prophetic or apostolic visit the greeting imparts a sacramental "blessing" from God. The offer, "Peace to this house," builds on the Hebrew greeting *shalom*, or "peace," and is messianic, referring to the kingdom "peace" promised in the Old Testament (Isa 54:7–10; Ezek 34:25, 37:26). The greeting asks the people to respond to the offer of peace. As in Acts 10:36, their task is "announcing the good news of peace through Jesus Christ, who is Lord of all."

Among those who respond will be a few who promote peace (10:6), literally here "a son of peace," meaning they are characterized by peace and immediately respond to the promise of peace in the gospel presentation. The **eschatological** offer of God's peace will then "rest on them," meaning that conversion with God's peace will take residence in them. Jesus is saying that the gospel message is an offer of God's peace literally sent through the very greeting of the missionary. It becomes a tangible eschatological reality and can "rest on" a family or "return" to the disciple. Christ is indeed bestowing his authority on his followers as they take his message out on their mission to the nation and then the world. The idea of God's peace departing from a house and returning to the evangelist is a very serious warning.

Apparently, the home that accepts the offer of peace from verse 6 also becomes the host for the evangelists as they minister in the town. The rule here is to remain in that home for the whole time and not to "move around from house to house" (probably looking for better accommodations). They are not to care about the quality of the lodging or the keep they are offered. They must be satisfied with "whatever they give you." The gospel must be protected against upwardly mobile preachers who spend their time eating and sleeping in luxury. The purpose of eating with their hosts is table fellowship, not first-class meals. God's "workers" should never demand more than they are given and must be satisfied with whatever quality care their hosts can give them. This principle is so desperately needed yet so neglected in our time.

The reason for them to stay in the home that welcomes them is "the worker deserves his wages," a frequent principle (Matt 10:10; 1 Cor 9:14; 1 Tim 5:18), meaning that like all workers, God's ambassadors must earn what they receive and be satisfied with it. Here the wages are the room and board they are offered by those to whom they minister, and they must not allow themselves to be on the lookout for more. God will hold them accountable if they are greedy. I cannot help but apply this to Christian leaders today, especially to those who keep moving to bigger and better churches or ministries where they will be paid more. All too many of us in ministry will be experiencing the warning of 2 Timothy 2:15 and stand before God at our final accounting in shame because of our lifestyle. I have heard of well-known Christian musicians and speakers who have the same demands as the divas in the secular world; that is a disgrace!

Verses 8–12 expand on the last couple of verses and describe what to do when you are welcomed (vv. 8–9) and when you are not (vv. 10–12). Verse 8 virtually repeats verse 7: "eat what is offered to you." The missionary once more is not worldly, and the goal is always table fellowship with the people rather than lavish banquets. God is guiding their hosts, so to refuse what they offer is tantamount to refusing God. This may include the freedom to eat unclean food (in Gentile areas), but while that is clearly stated in Acts 10:9–16; 1 Cor 10:27, it is not indicated here, probably because this mission takes place in a Jewish context.

Their ministry will consist of both words and mighty deeds, healing the sick and proclaiming the entrance of God's kingdom into this world (10:9). The disciples have been given authority to heal and power over the cosmic powers (9:1), and they will exercise that on this mission. We will see in 10:17 that "even the demons submit to us in your name." The healings are signs of the in-breaking kingdom, and as in Acts the message follows and interprets the significance of the healings. The nearness (ēngiken) of the kingdom (4:43; Mark 1:15) is difficult to interpret. It is both near and at the same time has arrived (11:20). It is imminent and yet present, already here and not yet finalized. This means that the kingdom as the reign of God has arrived in this world with Jesus and is being proclaimed in the proclamation of the gospel, yet it is also in process of coming and will culminate in the second coming and arrival of the final kingdom.

The last three verses (10–12) center on what the believers in mission are to do when they are not "welcomed" or accepted by the people to whom they go. This develops 9:5, where they were to "shake the dust off your feet as a testimony against them." Here they turn this into a public condemnation of the town: "Even the dust of your town we wipe from our feet as a warning to you." Everything in their town has been rejected by God as unclean, even the dirt of their streets. The promise of peace is withdrawn and replaced with judgment. When Jesus preached Isaiah 61:1–2 in 4:18–19 he omitted the phrase, "and the day of vengeance of our God." The sense of what was omitted there (divine vengeance and judgment) is now present here for those who refuse God's gospel offer. Many interpreters think this was intentional on Luke's (and Jesus') part.

Still, they too are to be told, "The kingdom of God has come near to you." In verse 9 it was a positive promise that God's reign had begun, and those who had received his gospel peace were part of it. Here that is a negative proclamation, saying that for those who rejected his offer, the kingdom was coming in judgment. "Yet be sure of this" is literally, "Nevertheless, know this" and turns the imminent kingdom saying into a doom saying. God's reign will exalt those who turn to him, and it will destroy those who turn against him.

Verse 12 actually contrasts their judgment with that of the most notorious city of the Old Testament, Sodom, burned to ashes by God (Gen 19:24–29). The city became a constant symbol of judgment for sin (Matt 10:15; 11:24; Rom 9:29; 2 Pet 2:6; Jude 7). Their judgment is more severe because they have been given more than Sodom, namely, the kingdom truths of the gospel.

Woes on those who reject (10:13–15)

These verses parallel the woes of the Sermon on the Plain in 6:20–26 and, like them, do not just mean "I pity you," but rather "God's judgment has come on you." The first woe falls on two neighboring towns near to Capernaum—Chorazin (two miles away) and Bethsaida. The latter is probably not the home of Simon and Andrew on the northwestern side of the lake (John 1:44; 12:21) but a different town, Bethsaida Julius, which was closer to Chorazin. They are worse off than the pagan cities of Tyre and Sidon in Syria, two Phoenician cities doomed in prophecy (Isa 23; Ezek 26–28) and known for their rebellion against God. They were destroyed when Alexander the Great built a causeway out to the island fortress of Tyre and leveled it in 332 BC. Luke's point is that they would have repented "in sackcloth [coarse cloth of goat's hair worn in time of grief] and ashes [put on the head to signify mourning]" if Jesus' miracles had been done among them. These towns refused to do so, and so stand more guilty before God.

It will be "more bearable for Tyre and Sidon [and for Sodom] at the judgment than for you." Jesus' point is that these Galilean towns are more guilty, again because they have rejected so much more. Therefore, they will have more shame at the final judgment. Galilee, because Jesus and his apostolic team have been ministering there and brought the messianic kingdom with them, has been given a massive opportunity but has squandered it.

Capernaum (10:15) was Jesus' headquarters in Galilee and so had seen more than any other city. The people there had received more and therefore were responsible for more. If the other two towns are guilty, Capernaum is more so. Its people too have refused to repent. The question expects a negative answer: "Will you be lifted to the heavens?" They should have been exalted and proud of their accomplishments, but they rejected it all and as a result they will "go down to Hades," where they will have "torment" (16:23).

Three-stage authority of the missionary (10:16)

Those who engage in mission need not worry about the level of their authority, for they are the third stage of a three-level power from God to Jesus to them. We are the sent ones or envoys of Jesus, who is the Envoy of God. Thus the entire Godhead is behind us wherever we go. So those who are willing to listen and respond as well as those who refuse to do so are in reality responding to Jesus and the one who sent him when they respond to us. This is why we need not worry about how gifted we are or how much charisma we exude when we speak or lead a group. The Godhead is behind us.

Return of the seventy-two (10:17–24)

We weren't told whether the mission of the Twelve in 9:1–6 was successful, but that was the implication. This mission, however, ends quite well, as "the seventy-two returned with joy," not only the personal joy of a successful outcome but also the eschatological joy of the messianic kingdom, due to victory in the spiritual war against the powers of darkness. Jesus had passed on to them his authority over the demonic realm (9:1), and they have exercised it in exorcizing unclean spirits.

Moreover, they have finally done it right, depending entirely on him without trying to do so in their own strength. Two things show this: First, they recognize him as "Lord" and surrender totally to his power at work in them and through them. Second, the demons submit "in your name," and it is the power of his name that is the key, as we already saw (9:49) and will see even more so in Acts (3:16; 4:10; 16:18). The name of Jesus itself contains the power to accomplish wondrous things. In our time as well the dark world has no power over us. The darkness can defeat us only by deceiving us, not by overpowering us. Still, the battle is real, and our people desperately need to be made more aware of these realities.

Jesus' reply sums up the doctrine of spiritual warfare, defining the fall of Satan (v. 18) and its implications for the people of God (v. 19), then putting the matter into perspective (v. 20). When he says "I saw Satan fall like lightning from heaven," this is not just a metaphor symbolizing his defeat. He was present at the original rebellion in heaven when the great dragon Satan "swept a third of the stars out of the sky and flung them to the earth" (Rev 12:4), leading to the great rebellion and seducing a third of the angels to turn against God. He was then cast out of heaven and "hurled to the earth, and his angels with him" by Michael and the angels who remained faithful to God (Rev 12:7–9).[4]

So Jesus literally saw Satan fall from heaven to earth, which is now the prison house for these evil spirits (2 Pet 2:4; Jude 6). The language is reminiscent of Isaiah 14:12, describing the fall of Babylon as a satanic nation, "How you have fallen from heaven ... cast down to the earth." His point is that Satan is a fallen being, and that he remains so to this very day. In casting out demons, the disciples are continuing the reality of the fall of Satan. His minions are still "fallen angels," and when they are cast out, their true reality as fallen beings is exposed. Moreover, this is all a harbinger of the final downfall of the evil spirits when Christ returns. So the present exorcisms were reenacting the past defeat of Satan and at the same time looking forward to the future and final downfall. The final war had begun, and we in our day continue to participate in it.

Jesus had already given them authority over the demonic realm on the first mission (9:1), and he repeats that again and expands on what it means (10:19). Satan was the serpent in the garden in Genesis 3, and so the image is quite apt (see 2 Cor 11:1). By making this "snakes and scorpions" he is stressing the venomous nature of evil spirits; they exist to strike and harm all who are made in

---

4. Many scholars see Rev 12:4, 7–9, as simply a metaphor for the effects of the cross, but I do not think so (see my Revelation commentary in this series, pp. 209–11). I believe it was an actual "historical" (in heaven) event.

the image of God. In Acts 28:3-6 Paul survives a viper strike, and the point here is that with Christ we too will be safe from such demonic attacks. The idea of "trampling" these reptiles reminds us of Romans 16:20 (see also Gen 3:15), "The God of peace will soon crush Satan under your feet." It is an image often found in the Old Testament (Deut 8:15; Ps 91:13; Isa 11:8; T. Levi 18:12) and was taken literally in the second-century addition to Mark (Mark 16:18). The message is that the evil powers will not be able to harm us, and we will have power over them in Christ.

Christ puts it all in perspective in verse 20, where he reminds them that power over the satanic realm is an added privilege but not the main point. Exorcisms are proof of the binding of Satan and of the arrival of God's kingdom. However, the truly important truth and reason for rejoicing is "that your names are written in heaven." Temporary power over Satan is secondary to the fact of eternal life. Success in the war against Satan recedes into the background in the joy of the final victory. It is what we have in God and Christ, the heavenly reality, that truly counts. The salvation of the soul is far more important than acts of power.

Christ is referring to names written in the book of life. This book first appears in Exodus 32:32-33, where it is the register of the citizens of Israel (Pss 9:5; 87:6) and became the heavenly book containing the names of the righteous (Ps 69:28; Dan 12:1). The **Hellenistic** world contained similar ideas. In the New Testament the book guarantees the security of the believer as a citizen of heaven (Phil 4:3; Heb 12:23), and it is featured in Revelation, "the Lamb's book of life" (21:27), connected with predestination (13:8; 17:8), the record of one's deeds (20:12), and eternal reward or punishment (20:15). Christ wants his followers to realize the eternal realities behind their allegiance to him. It is not what authority we have here on earth that ultimately matters but what joyful life we will enjoy in heaven.

There are two sections in verses 21-24: praise to God for his revelation to Jesus and his followers (vv. 21-22), and blessing the disciples because of all they have seen (vv. 23–24). Luke describes Jesus as "full of joy through the Holy Spirit," providing the perfect conclusion to the mission with the emphasis on the disciples in their defeat of Satan and experience of victory for the sake of the kingdom. Christ is deeply thankful to his Father for the wisdom of the **apocalyptic** combination of hiddenness and revelation. The "wise and learned" are the Jewish leaders, particularly the legal experts, the scribes and Pharisees. The meaning and significance of Christ's ministry, his mission, and especially his messianic destiny have been "hidden" from them. They have rejected God's plan, so he has hidden its significance from them.

Then with the apocalyptic language of reversal, Jesus says that God has "revealed" these hidden truths "to little children," namely, the disciples and followers of Jesus. Their innocent, infant-like trust in God makes them open to divine revelation, so they are the liberated prisoners and the freed oppressed people of 4:18. The emphasis here is on divine sovereignty more than on human receptivity. God has chosen these marginalized to be the recipients of divine revelation. "Pleasing in your sight" (NIV: "pleased to do") is a rabbinic idiom for the divine will. The disciples are the elect focus of the truths of Christ.

The reason these truths have been revealed to these "little children" is because they belong to his Son, and the Father has committed all things to his Son (10:22). This is an astounding statement, for it turns this verse into a proclamation of Jesus' deity. "All things" is comprehensive and sounds very much like John's Gospel (see 1:1, 14, 18; 3:35; 10:15; 17:2), where Jesus is the living revealer of the Father and one with the Father (John 10:30). Here it is the revelation of divine knowledge that is especially handed down to the Son along with the transferal of power and authority in exercising that knowledge.

All of this is anchored in the mutual knowledge of both the Father and the Son—"no one knows who the Son is except the Father, and no one knows who the Father is except the Son."

There is a **chiasm** here: Son-Father: Father-Son. The way to one is through the other. The disciples truly understand the Father because Jesus has revealed the Father in all his glory to them. Theirs is the greatest privilege this world knows, because they are the "chosen," and the Son has elected to "reveal" the Father to them. The Son is sovereignly supreme, and the Christ followers are now part of the chain of revelation from Father to Son to them.

On that basis Jesus pours out his divine blessing (10:23-24) on them in another beatitude (see 1:45; 6:20-23; 7:23; 11:28). With 10:13-15 these verses replicate the blessings and woes of 6:20-26 but reverse the order. The woes fall on those who have refused Christ's offer of salvation; the blessings fall on those who not only accept the offer but also become committed followers. They are those who have eyes to see and therefore "see what you see," especially Jesus and the truths he has revealed to them about the Father in verse 22. By surrendering to Jesus, they not only see his mighty acts but also comprehend and obey them.

Their blessing is made clear in verse 24. Many of the "prophets and kings" of the Old Testament, the heroes of the past, would have given anything to be allowed by God to "see" and "hear" what they have been allowed to experience, but only the disciples were granted that privilege. As 1 Peter 1:10-12 says, the prophets "searched intently and with the greatest care" to "find out the time and circumstances to which the Spirit of Christ in them was pointing" regarding the "sufferings of the Messiah and the glories that would follow." The disciples are living in the time and fulfillment and get to experience the culmination of God's plan. What the prophets longed to see has been revealed as God's gift to them.

JESUS TELLS THE PARABLE OF THE GOOD SAMARITAN (10:25-37)

This parable continues the training of the Twelve and contains two lessons, teaching them about true love of neighbor (Lev 19:18) and at the same time a lesson on racial stereotypes. The true neighbor can be a member of a racial or ethnic group you despise. This parable has been the subject of countless poorly conceived sermons even by luminaries like Chrysostom or Luther. They and others engage in shallow allegorizing, as when they see this parable as Adam (the man) on his way to Paradise (Jericho) waylaid by temptation (the brigands) and led into sin (the wounds) but rescued by Christ (the Samaritan), who heals him (the oil = compassion, the wine = the blood of the Eucharist) and leads him to the church (the inn). It is critical that when dealing with parables we refuse to read into them any spiritual allegory we can devise but always ask instead what Jesus himself meant when he spoke them.

QUESTION REGARDING ETERNAL LIFE (10:25–28)

The "lawyer" is a legal expert in Torah, likely a scribe or Pharisee. Rabbis/teachers always sat, and students stood to ask questions, but this is not a rabbinic student, and he wants to "test" Jesus. Heretofore such tests have been negative, attempts to show Jesus' ignorance and prove him guilty of breaking Torah. In this case, his interlocutor does not seem so hostile, but he is nevertheless hardly looking to follow Jesus. This question will be asked again by the rich young ruler in 18:18, where it is more of an honest search for eternal life.

The "what must I do" assumes human ability to attain eternal life and falsifies the question. It is a question of Torah, as shown in the lawyer's reply from Deuteronomy 6:5 and Leviticus 19:18 in verse 27. Addressing Jesus as "teacher" implies that he is a rabbi addressing a legal issue from the Torah. "Eternal life" reflects Daniel 12:2 and refers in this Jewish setting to the kingdom life, assumed by most Jews to be an earthly reality linked to the inheritance of the land and further to keeping the Torah.

Jesus' reply (10:26) about "what is in the Law" turns it back to the lawyer and his legal perspective. Jesus is speaking as a rabbi and expects exactly the response he will get in the next verse, a recitation from the Law. So the lawyer cites what is called in

Matthew 22:36 "the greatest commandment." There it is Jesus who responds with these two passages. The combination of loving God and loving your neighbor makes perfect sense, because one cannot relate to God without relating to his creation. Redeemed humankind is part of God's family, and one cannot know him without relating to his people. Yet Jesus goes beyond that, for the "neighbor" includes those who are not followers of God. The Jewish perspective is vastly broadened, as is our responsibility.

There is both a vertical and a horizontal aspect to that responsibility. The vertical, from Deuteronomy 6:5, is "Love the Lord your God with all your heart ... soul ... strength and ... mind." The "mind" is added to the text here for greater comprehensiveness, referring to the total person. The four categories are not meant to have separate emphasis, as if loving God demands first the inner emotions, second the spiritual resources, third physical action, and fourth the intellectual side. Rather, our entire self must focus on our enjoyment of God.

The horizontal aspect stems from Leviticus 19:18, which refers to fellow Jews as well as aliens residing in the land. The lawyer meant it of just these groups, but Jesus intended it of all people. "As yourself" means "in the same way as you love yourself," thus showing others the same care and consideration you do yourself. Love of God and of neighbor are interdependent and inseparable. You cannot do the one without doing the other.

Jesus authenticates his response in verse 28, adding, "Do this and you will live." If he indeed follows this creed, he will be living life God's way and be headed for "eternal life." To the lawyer's assumption of life with God, Jesus is now making the "eternal" aspect evident.

THE TRUE NEIGHBOR: THE GOOD SAMARITAN (10:29–37)

Most Jewish people understood the term "neighbor" to apply only to their fellow Jews, so the lawyer's question, "And who is my neighbor?" is quite valid. Luke tells us he "wanted to justify himself" by continuing his minimalist understanding of obedience and thus regaining the initiative. He expected a Jewish answer, and he could then look good in the eyes of everyone there as he affirmed the complete fulfillment of his obligations. Jesus demands that this command embrace all people, but he doesn't want only that. In fact, he has upped the stakes by linking it to loving God. To restrict God's intention that love be universal, to fail to love the Gentile as well as the Jew, is to turn against God and refuse to love him as well.

Instead of answering the man directly, Jesus tells another parable that addresses the neighbor question with a powerful message. The setting of the story is the Jericho road, a grueling, seventeen-mile stretch that climbs thirty-six hundred feet from Jericho to Jerusalem and is part of the major route Jews would take when traveling from Galilee to Judea (Jesus will come that route quite soon on his way to his passion, 18:35; 19:1). The road was notorious for robber bands and thus quite dangerous. This unfortunate man is waylaid by thieves who "stripped him of his clothes, beat him and went away, leaving him half dead," a not uncommon occurrence. If he does not get help soon, he will die.

The issue is, who is the true neighbor who will give this seriously wounded man the aid he so desperately needs? Three people pass him by on the road. First, a priest comes (10:31), probably intended to be an upper-crust "chief priest" riding in a carriage or cart. Jericho housed a large number of priests, so he would be "going down" from his business in Jerusalem to his home there. As a servant of God whose whole life was lived for the people of the land, surely he would take care of the poor man. However, far from stopping to help, he deliberately "passed by on the other side," staying as far away as possible as he went on his way. Several have tried to give excuses for such behavior, like avoiding defilement from touching a corpse or a Gentile (the priest can't tell). Such an unclean state would last seven days (Lev 21:1–3). He also could have been afraid the robbers would return, but Luke gives no excuse. Clearly, in this story the man doesn't care enough to help.

The second person coming by on the road is a Levite (10:32), a lesser official who assisted the priest in his duties, performed the temple liturgy (especially the music), and policed the temple. Like the priest, he took one look at the wounded man and also "passed by on the other side." Neither Jewish official was willing to take the time to do what the Torah required in aiding the fallen. There was not even a modicum of compassion or mercy in either one.

The third man to come by (10:33) is the one no listener would ever think might come to the man's aid. This was a despised Samaritan, for centuries the enemies of the Jews (see on 9:52). In most stories they would have been the robbers who beat up the man (which often occurred when Jews passed through Samaria). A few years previously, a group had offended the Jews further by desecrating the Jerusalem temple by scattering human bones in the courtyard (Josephus, *Antiquities* 18.30). So it is a complete reversal of expectation for the Samaritan to be the one who shows compassion. He too risked defilement and overcame deep-seated prejudices, for he would certainly have assumed the other man was Jewish.

The extent of his pity and mercy is seen in the actions he takes (10:34). It may well be implied that he would have used strips of his own clothing, a real sacrifice in light of the absence of extensive wardrobes back then. Actually, he first would have poured wine on the wounds to clean them, using his own supply (wine was an ancient disinfectant), then used the olive oil (a medicine) for healing. After binding the wounds, the Samaritan put the man on his donkey and took him to an inn (10:35), undoubtedly walking the man there. He then paid the innkeeper two denarii—the equivalent of two days' wages and enough for two to three weeks—to "look after him." Finally, he promised to return and "reimburse [him] for any extra expense," guaranteeing the poor man would receive good care as he recovered. The kindness of this good Samaritan is unbounded.

As mentioned in the introduction to this passage, the parable of the good Samaritan should not be allegorized to speak of spiritual growth or the Eucharist and so on. It is clear that Jesus intends it to be a story about a true neighbor, as seen in the conclusion (10:36–37), when he asks, "Which of these three do you think was a neighbor to the man who fell into the hands of robbers?" The lawyer could only answer, "The one who had mercy on him." There are four aspects to its message: (1) There is no place for racial prejudice of any kind among God's people; (2) God uses everyone who is open to him, including the despised minorities in our world; (3) we must use everything we have, even our prized possessions, to serve God and others; (4) it is mercy and compassion that make a neighbor, not status in society or church.

JESUS SPENDS TIME WITH MARY AND MARTHA (10:38–42)

Mary and Martha are sisters of Lazarus who reside in Bethany, a suburb of Jerusalem (John 11). They were close friends and followers, and Jesus likely stayed in their home when he went there. It is difficult to know whether Jesus is already there this soon in his journey to Jerusalem, or whether they have a second home (or this is placed here for thematic reasons). Most take the latter on the basis of the unlikelihood that Jesus would come this early and then return to Galilee. Luke calls Bethany a "certain [omitted by NIV] village" to avoid this issue.

Martha was probably the older sister and served as host in her home. All the laws of hospitality were in play as she "opened her home to him." She was obviously very busy as she made sure everything was in place. Once more table fellowship is taking place, and she and her sister Mary are divided on the two aspects of it, with Martha centering on the table responsibilities and Mary enjoying the fellowship aspects, sitting "at the Lord's feet listening to what he said." It is interesting that Martha does all the talking in this section, and Mary never says a word, just centering on Jesus and his teaching. This is highly unusual, for there was debate in rabbinic circles as to whether women should be allowed to learn

Torah (most felt they could), and Mary has the posture of a disciple. Martha is the proper woman, Mary somewhat of an aberration. Jesus is redefining the place of women.

Martha's complaint (10:40) fits the circumstances and would be seen as completely valid. She is doing what women are supposed to do, working hard at preparing the meal and making everyone comfortable. Mary is doing what only male disciples are supposed to do. She has "left [Martha] to do the work" by herself, and so she wants Jesus to "tell her to help me." To her (and most Jews) Mary's true place is alongside Martha in the kitchen, not at Jesus' feet. Luke, however, shows he is aware of a higher duty, calling Martha "distracted" by her household chores and unaware of the more important duties of listening to the Lord. So once more Jesus has broken social conventions, this time in allowing Mary to act as a disciple rather than as a housemaid. Martha's problem is that she wants Jesus to accept her agenda and is not willing to consider his. He will correct that in the next two verses.

Jesus' response (10:41–42) would have been shocking. The double use of her name ("Martha, Martha") is not rebuke but affection as he corrects her. Instead of reproof and getting Mary back in her proper kitchen role, Jesus speaks entirely to Martha. She was the perfect hostess but allowed her duties to gain the upper hand, and she lost her sense of privilege as a follower of Jesus. The result is she became "worried and upset" about the "many things" she needed to get done. What was good in itself, serving Jesus, became a distraction when it became an end in itself. The things of lesser importance took over, and she forgot fellowship with Jesus.

Jesus is not denying the validity of Martha's concerns but wants to place them in proper perspective. Still, he uses strong terms for "worried" and "upset" ("troubled"), which connote a worldly attitude. She is placing the wrong thing first; her priorities are mixed up. Taking care of others is not wrong; after all, hospitality is a spiritual gift. But this must be submitted to discipleship and the truths of God.

The opening words of verse 42 are a major text-critical problem, with the older reading ("one thing is essential") supported by the manuscripts 𝔓45, 𝔓75, Codex Ephraemi, Byzantine, and many others, while the current NIV ("but few things are needed—or indeed only one") is supported by the manuscripts 𝔓3, Sinaiticus, Vaticanus, and several others. They are almost equally supported, and it is a difficult decision, but I cautiously opt for the NIV reading. Here Jesus recognizes that several things (like the meal) are valid, while the one—namely, time spent with him—is the main priority and dare not be neglected. Martha has chosen the "few" of lesser importance, while Mary has chosen "what is better, and it will not be taken away from her." Sitting at Jesus' feet is the higher good, and it has eternal consequences. The message is the importance of discipline, of living priorities. Earthly concerns like hospitality should not be ignored, but coming to know divine realities must always be top concern. Inheriting eternal life begins with imbibing eternal truths.

———

With this section, everything changes, for Jesus has in effect finished his mission to the Jewish people and now sets his face to Jerusalem to complete his destiny and bring God's salvation to sinful humankind. For the next ten-plus chapters he will be completing his earthly work and preparing his disciples to carry it on via the universal mission. This begins with a trip through Samaria (9:51–56), the first step in taking his gospel message to the nations. These people set the tone for this mission by rejecting his good news, which teaches the disciples that Jesus' sights are beyond the Jewish people to the world.

The cost of discipleship that Jesus outlines in verses 57–62 establishes what it entails to become a Christ follower. In this radical list Christ becomes the all-encompassing purpose of our existence. The homeless life of Christ is a metaphor rather than a demand (Peter owned his home), but the principle is still that we are citizens of heaven rather than earth and surrender everything for him. Second, Christ has priority over all earthly ties, even our parents. We are first members of God's family and only then part of an earthly family. This theme continues in the third principle. Discipleship demands that our consuming interest be Christ rather than earthly ties or past experiences. We center on him alone and refuse to look back.

The mission of the seventy-two (10:1-7) builds on 9:1-6 with much the same message: depend on God and be willing to accept whatever lodging and care people offer rather than focusing on earthly comforts and luxuries. Our task is to bring the world to God and enable them to find salvation, not to get rich through our ministry. Such a worldly goal will label us false prophets and teachers. For those who reject this gospel message, it turns into a doom saying (vv. 8-12), and they are to be told that they are now an unclean people in God's sight. They will be the Sodom of their time. Those cities that were the recipients of Jesus' Galilean ministry (vv. 13-15) were more responsible and therefore more guilty than Tyre and Sidon, for they rejected the kingdom truths of Jesus.

The seventy-two return from their mission rejoicing in their authority over Satan and their many successful bindings of the demonic forces. They have experienced God's power through them in a new way and have seen many freed from captivity and coming to Christ (vv. 17-20). The results of mission are found here—joy, thanksgiving, and divine blessing (vv. 21-24). To the disciples has been given the greatest gift imaginable: the revelation of the hidden truths of God. This would be a great theme for a Bible study—"the joy of discovery." God has given these incredible truths to us. It is our privilege to study them and uncover the treasures awaiting us in his word.

The well-known parable of the good Samaritan (vv. 29-37) is intended to define a true neighbor and break the racial prejudice that so dominated then as well as in our day. What God wants of us is a willingness to go out of our way to help others, even if they do not fit our preferred stereotypes. God demands that we accept the reality that every race is created in the image of God and equally loved by him. If that is so, we must welcome every kind of person and love them in the Lord. We must use our material resources to help them when they are struggling and do everything we can to alleviate their suffering. The church should become a smorgasbord of people groups who live together, love each other, and share everything.

The Mary and Martha incident (vv. 38–42) builds on the meaning of the true neighbor with an episode dealing with the laws of hospitality. This is an important passage that teaches us the priorities in the Christian life. Martha represents a traditional viewpoint in which serving others is the highest good, and she wants Jesus to rebuke her sister for failing to help her serve. Recognizing the place of hospitality and serving others, however, Jesus says the highest good is indeed sitting at his feet learning eternal truths. The heavenly has priority over the earthly. This is a correction for churches that are increasingly giving teaching the word low priority. Training God's people must always have the upper place in any list of the church's duties.

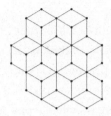

PRAYER AND CONFLICT
(11:1–54)

There is not a single geographical reference in this chapter, but clearly Jesus' sights are on his messianic destiny. One could title this chapter "The Power of Prayer in Light of Conflict and Opposition." The disciples, as they learn to place eternal realities first in their lives (10:38–42), must begin with their relationship to God, and prayer is a two-way conversation with the Father. The first major section was on discipleship (9:51–10:42), and that which provides strength and knowledge for all Christ followers is their prayer life. This is especially true in light of the opposition they will face from the powers of darkness (10:14–36) and from the evil Jewish leaders (10:37–54).

JESUS TEACHES ON PRAYER (11:1–13)

This is a trinitarian section, for prayer involves all three members of the Godhead. Jesus provides the model for prayer, the Father is the recipient of our prayers, and the Spirit is a gift from the Father to enhance our prayer life. In my opinion, this is the deepest single passage on prayer in all the New Testament. It contains not only the model prayer (vv. 2–4) but also a parable on prayer (vv. 5–8) and teaching on the incredible results of prayer (vv. 9–13). It has always been one of my favorite passages to preach from.

THE SETTING (11:1)

As throughout Luke (see on 3:21), at a key moment in his journey to his destiny in Jerusalem, Jesus is spending prayer time with his Father. He is not just providing the model prayer; he is the model pray-er for his followers. I am certain that for the rest of their lives, every day as they themselves prayed, they had a picture in their mind of Jesus standing and bowing or prostrate as he spoke to his Father.

When Jesus finished his time of prayer and looked up, he saw one of his disciples standing beside him, saying, "Lord,[1] teach us to pray, just as John taught his disciples." This is not a request for lessons on how to pray. Rabbinic groups and others had both liturgical prayers on specific themes (like the Eighteen Benedictions) but also particular formal prayers that groups uttered together. John the Baptist apparently had taught his followers one of those, and the disciples would like one for their apostolic band. Such a prayer would enable them to feel a distinctive group and enhance their fellowship.

THE LORD'S PRAYER (11:2-4)

This prayer does not correspond exactly to the prayer in Matthew 6:9-13. As an itinerant teacher, Jesus would have used the same or similar material on different occasions. Matthew's form stresses **eschatology** more, and Luke's emphasizes daily life. Jesus is using this to provide a pattern for true prayer, and many say the clauses of this also form a virtual summary of Jesus' teaching. This prayer is not just a model to emulate but also a theological masterpiece in its own right. There are two sections in it: "thou petitions" in verse 2, and "we petitions" in verses 3-4.

---

1. Jesus is not just the Lord of creation; he is the Lord of communication (with his Father).

There are three parts to the thou petitions (as opposed to four in Matthew[2]). There is immense theology behind this, for Jesus created a distinctive form using the Aramaic *Abba*, found at times (but rarely) in Jewish prayers.[3] Jewish prayers were more formal, while Jesus' contribution to Jewish prayer theology made it more intimate, with God as a "Father" who loved his people and held them in his arms, so to speak. *Abba* with *imma* were the first words a baby spoke and reflects the security children felt around their loving parents, stressing the centrality of relationship between God and his children. Pagan prayers spent an inordinate amount of time trying to mollify fickle gods who often did more harm than good, while Jesus introduces a God who deeply cares and can be approached directly.

"Hallowed be your name" calls for the sacredness of the name of God to be magnified in every area of life. His "name" was so holy that Jews would never utter it; the Targums would insert "Lord" for "Yahweh." In the Old Testament God will sanctify his own great name (Ezek 36:22–23), and it is to be "acknowledged" as such by his people (Lev 22:32) and "kept holy" (Isa 29:23). So there are two spheres in which this must take place. Jesus asks his Father to bring about a world in which his name will be universally glorified. So this petition is linked to the next as a prayer for the final kingdom to come when the sacredness of his name will be confessed everywhere. At the same time, it must be confessed by his followers by maintaining holiness in every area of life. We must honor his name in everything we do and proclaim his name everywhere we go.

"Your kingdom come" is connected to the previous petition in the Jewish *Qaddish* (holy) prayer that closed the synagogue service. The rabbis said that any prayer that fails to mention the kingdom of God is not a true prayer. All of the thou petitions are

---

2. Luke omits "your will be done, on earth as it is in heaven."

3. m. Sotah 9:15; t. Berakot 3:14.

inaugurated in thrust. They address the present spiritual walk of the believer and yet will not be fully realized until Christ returns and the eternal kingdom reign begins. It is only then that his true glory will be fully known among the nations (Ps 110:1). This request directly asks God to act in order to bring about his final reign. The earliest Christian prayer recorded is *Marana tha* in 1 Corinthians 16:22, "Come, Lord!" This prayer asks for the present reign of God to manifest itself in ever new ways but especially that God will end this present world order and bring his kingdom in its fullness.

The order, in which the we petitions follow the thou petitions, is an important spiritual point. Our prayers should reflect God's concerns first, and our own concerns should flow out of those. All too many of our prayers are entirely self-centered, with the things of God neglected in favor of a grocery list of the things we want him to do for us. Among the first words a baby learns are not just "Da-da" and "Ma-ma" but "I" and "me." And that never leaves us. This is reflected in the first we petition: "Give us each day our daily bread." "Bread" stands not just for food but for all our material needs. Many interpreters have understood this spiritually as the Eucharist or the eschatological bread of the messianic banquet, but that is quite unlikely. It is a metaphor for our daily needs.

There is extensive debate over whether the meaning of "daily" (*epiousion*) refers to the needs of today or of tomorrow or of the coming day, the final kingdom in heaven. I have already determined that the eschatological reading is unlikely. The best solution is to combine the first two. "Daily" meant "today" in the morning prayer of the temple service and "tomorrow" in the evening prayer of the temple. So this is best translated, "Give us our bread for today and for tomorrow"; in other words, "Lord, supply our needs now and in the future."

It is a prayer reflecting total dependence on God. Too many of us read this and start praying, "Lord give me this, give me that"— gimme, gimme, gimme! What it actually means is, "Lord, I rely on you for my needs." This fits the definition of faith in Hebrews

11:1: "Now faith is confidence in what we hope for and assurance about what we do not see." God must be in charge, and he takes care of each day as we put our trust in him. Luke 12:29, 31 sums up the issue: "And do not set your heart on what you will eat or drink. ... Seek his kingdom, and these things will be given to you as well."

"Forgive us our sins, for we also forgive everyone who sins against us" turns from physical to spiritual needs and shows that while the earthly side is important, the spiritual side is paramount. Both aspects are critical, God's forgiving us and our forgiving others. In fact, Matthew 6:14–15 emphasizes that until we are willing to forgive others, we cannot expect God to forgive us. This is implicit here but still implied. The two are interdependent. If we are bitter toward others, our own fellowship with God is broken (Matt 5:23–24). This is a critical need today, as so many people simply cannot forgive and reconcile with those who have hurt them. At the same time, experiencing forgiveness from God gives us the strength (and the model) for forgiving others. This is emphasized again in the parable of the unforgiving servant in Matthew 18:21–35. When *all* of our sins have been forgiven by God and Christ, that should enable us to forgive *individual* sins from others.

It is critical to note that Luke switches metaphors on the topic of sin, using the normal *hamartia* in the first clause and switching to "debts" (*opheilonti*) in the second clause. Debt to God and to those we wrong was a well-known image for sin in the first century. When we say, "You owe me," that should remind us of all we owe God.

Finally, "lead us not into temptation" might better be paraphrased, "do not let us yield to temptation." The term *peirasmos* means a "test/trial" or a temptation, and probably both aspects are intended here. As with Jesus in 4:1–13, when Satan's temptation of Jesus was used by God to test his Son, so we too are tested by being tempted to sin. James moves from the test (1:2–5) to the temptation (1:13–15). So this is not a request for God not to tempt us, for James 1:13 says, "God cannot be tempted by evil, nor does he tempt anyone." While God does not tempt, he does test all believers, as he did his Son in 4:1-13. So this is not asking that we not undergo the test or temptation. Rather, it is a prayer for strength and protection when we are tested or tempted.

THE PARABLE OF THE FRIEND AT MIDNIGHT (11:5-8)

In light of what the Lord's Prayer revels about the kind of God to whom we go in prayer, Jesus tells a parable intended to stress how open God is to our prayers and the tenacity with which we can therefore pray. The setting builds on the oriental laws of hospitality. A friend arrives unexpectedly at midnight. Because the days are so hot, they have had to travel after dark and so arrived very late. It was an emergency trip, so they couldn't let us know they were coming. Moreover, they were unable to eat an evening meal, and thus we are caught needing to feed them but have insufficient food. The problems just keep piling up.

There is an enormous amount of pressure on a host to provide for guests, and to be unable to do so is embarrassing and even disgraceful. In fact, the whole village is involved in the need for hospitality, so everyone is affected. If the host doesn't have enough food, the neighbors are responsible to find some. Moreover, it is midnight, so no stores are open. Bread is baked daily, but that doesn't help either. So what can we do? There is only one solution open, and that is to go next door and say, "Friend, lend me three loaves of bread; a friend of mine on a journey has come to me, and I have no food to offer him" (11:6). These are probably three small loaves, enough for one person. We would not want to wake an entire family just to borrow bread for one man unless it was an emergency; waking a person at that hour is a huge bother no matter what the situation. But the laws of hospitality demand that we do so, and everyone in the village knows that.

In this parable the "friend" likely lives in the average one-room home with the children in bed with the parents or right next to it, so to answer the door and comply with the request would disturb

the entire family. His initial unwillingness is completely understandable, and he responds, "Don't bother me. The door is already
locked, and my children and I are in bed. I can't get up and give you
anything" (11:7). While the whole village is involved in the responsibility, the friend feels it isn't worth it to wake the children. This
is a no-win situation.

The parable concludes with a very difficult saying (11:8), for
there are two opposite possible translations, each depending on
the translation of one word, *anaideia*. This in fact determines the
meaning of this entire parable. The NIV translates it "your shame-
less audacity," interpreting the parable as encouraging bold persistence in prayer (the traditional understanding). Yet the term itself
has to do with "shame," and so a second understanding takes it not
of "your" boldness but of "your friend's desire to avoid shame."

The actual Greek is "because of *his* shamelessness"; "his" could
be you the host or the friend with his children in bed. The NIV
approach sees it as the host's audacity in demanding his friend
provide the bread. However, I agree with those who say that "boldness" is an unusual meaning for the term, and the more regular
understanding would be "avoidance of shame" and refer to the
friend in the house. So the better translation of verse 8 is, "I tell
you, even though he will not get up and give you the bread because
of friendship, yet because of *his desire to avoid shame*, he will surely
get up and give you as much as you need." The neighbor will open
the door and get the bread because he is every bit as required as
the host to take care of the guest. If he refuses, his name will be
shamed in the entire village.

What is the meaning of the parable, and how does it apply to
prayer to God? The NIV understanding will lead into what follows (vv. 9-13) on tenacity in prayer and challenge the reader to an
audacious prayer life. The second understanding (the one I prefer)
looks back to the Lord's Prayer and says the very honor of God's
sacred name is at stake in God's answering prayer. We can pray
with absolute assurance that God is listening and will respond.

PROMISES REGARDING PRAYER (11:9-13)

We persist in prayer because God has promised to respond. That is the message here. The danger is expressed in James 4:2: "You do not have because you do not ask God." So Jesus himself encourages ongoing prayer.

This begins with a threefold challenge to tenacious prayer in verses 9-10, dealing with the *how* of prayer. These are present-tense commands telling us that we should at all times ask, seek, and knock. This ongoing persistence in prayer builds in intensity from bringing our requests to God to seeking God's response in faith to knocking for admission into God's presence. The motivation for this energetic prayer action comes from the three promises attached, all of which define the certainty of his response. This is commonly called "beggar's wisdom," the knowledge that it will get results. We have the assurance of a loving God whose very name is at stake in answering our prayers.

His promises are tremendously encouraging. When we come to him in persevering prayer, God will "give" us our requests, we will "find" the answers, and "the door will be opened" to the realization of his promises. Our needs will be met. This, however, is not prosperity theology, the promise that God wants to give us everything we want, keep us healthy and wealthy, if only we will ask and let him do it. That is false teaching. There are three possible answers to prayer, and God decides which is best in any and every situation—yes (giving what we ask for), no (refusing to give it because he knows it isn't for the best), and wait (giving the request but in his time, not in ours). God is sovereign, not us, but in everything we can be assured that "in all things God works for the good" (Rom 8:28) and responds in love and compassion to our prayers.

God in his compassionate giving is contrasted in verses 11-13 with a terrible father who plays a cruel and deadly practical joke on his child. The key is that in both instances what he gives looks like what the child is asking for. The child comes in for lunch and asks for some fish and an egg. Instead of the fish, the father gives a snake (obviously venomous) that resembles a fish somewhat, and instead of an egg he gives a scorpion that can curl into a ball to lure its prey. No true father would do anything that cruel, but that's the point.

The contrast is spelled out in verse 13. If you "evil" (sinful) people "know how to give good gifts" that will help rather than hurt others, how much more is that the case with your heavenly Father. The one thing we can be certain of is that God is a loving Father who watches over us and wants only what is best. That is proved in his greatest gift, the Holy Spirit.[4] Christ is predicting the coming of the Holy Spirit as the next great gift of the new era of salvation history (Luke 24:49; John 14:15-17; Acts 1:4-5), to be ful-filled at Pentecost (Acts 2:2-4).

JESUS' OPPONENTS ATTRIBUTE HIS POWER TO BEELZEBUL (11:14-28)

This incident occurs in different settings in the three **Synoptic** Gospels—in Jesus' opening ministry in Mark 3:22-27; in the second cycle of Jesus' ministry in Matthew 12:22-30; and here in a section on opposition in Luke 11:14-28. In all of them, however, the mes-sage is the same: Jesus has ultimate authority over the evil powers and the attempts of his human opponents to cast aspersion on his name. Scholars are in general agreement that all go back to an orig-inal event, with Matthew probably the original setting.

THE SETTING: CONFLICT OVER EXORCISM (11:14-16)

The miracle itself is told simply and quickly in order to prepare for the controversy it introduces. This time the demon has robbed the man of his ability to speak. The focus is on the amazement that ensues, the common result of miracles (4:36; 5:26; 7:16; 8:25, 56; 9:43). However, the wonder of many in the crowd produced the

---

4. The parallel Matt 7:11 has "good gifts," but Luke is thinking of the greatest of the good gifts, the Holy Spirit.

opposite reaction in others. Like the scribes and Pharisees, they had already rejected Jesus as a false prophet, so they had to find a rational reason for a blasphemer to be able to drive out demons.

The only other source of such power was Satan himself, and that fit their presumptions, so they spread the rumor that "by Beelzebul, the prince of demons, he is driving out demons" (11:15). There is general agreement that this stems from the name for the primary Canaanite deity, Baal, and could mean "Lord of the dung" but more likely "Lord of the heights,"[5] the pagan god who was a major opponent of the Israelites (1 Kgs 18:16-40). This became another name for Satan, the "prince" or "ruler" of the demonic realm. In Revelation 12:4, 7-9, it is Satan who has seduced one-third of the hosts of heaven and led them in rebellion against God, and he is at the head of the powers of darkness. By their logic Jesus could not have received his power from God, and they cannot deny his ability to cast out demons, so Satan himself as the origin became their best alternative.

Those who were more positive about Jesus (11:16) still would like further evidence that God is behind this, so they ask for "a sign from heaven." The term "sign" (sēmeion) becomes the word for miracles in the Gospel of John and refers to the spiritual meaning that is signified in the actual event. So they are wishing for a heavenly portent that would authenticate Jesus' claim that God is behind his miracles. They wanted **apocalyptic** proof like the sun standing still in Joshua 10 or the sun's shadow shifting in 2 Kings 20:8-11.

JESUS' COUNTERARGUMENTS (11:17-28)

Jesus responds in two stages—to the Beelzebul charge in 11:17-28 and to the demand for a sign in 11:29-32. He shows the ridiculous nature of their charge in verse 17. If he is truly casting out demons

---

5. Older versions like the KJV have "Beelzebub" from the Latin and from the chief god of Ekron (2 Kgs 1:2-6), but the Greek manuscripts have the form used here.

via Satan, the "kingdom" of the cosmic powers is undergoing civil war and in serious danger of being "ruined," actually "laid waste" or "made desolate," from the Greek *erēmoutai*, literally "made a desert." Divided kingdoms cannot stand and must end up in ruin. He adds the image of a "house divided against itself" for emphasis. A sad example of this would be the story of Absalom, David's son who murdered his brother Amnon (2 Sam 13) and formed a conspiracy to take the kingdom away from his father (2 Sam 15), dying for his efforts (2 Sam 17–18). David was heartbroken.

Jesus' conclusion is completely logical (11:18). If the rumor is true, Satan's kingdom is hopelessly divided and cannot possibly endure. He is driving out the very soldiers he uses in the war against God and his people, and internal discord will destroy everything he has built. No kingdom can survive internal strife. Therefore, the ridiculous rumor that Jesus' power came to him from Beelzebul is totally illogical and false.

If Jesus is guilty, what about their "followers" (v. 19; Greek "sons," referring to the "children" of Israel)? Jesus probably has in mind other Jewish exorcists of that day (as in 11:24), or perhaps the Jewish exorcists in 9:49–50. Some think he is referring to his own disciples, but that would not go very far with these people who are opposing not only Jesus but also his followers. The point is that they cannot accuse Jesus of anything without accusing their own exorcists. Jesus' words "they will be your judges" are difficult to interpret. Does "they will be" point to the last judgment? If so, it will refer to Jesus' followers who will join the angels when they "judge the world" (1 Cor 6:2). But there is likely a realized thrust here, meaning that their own people will judge them for their false rumor. My understanding is that their own Jewish exorcists will join Christ and his disciples in condemning this lie. The source of this power is God, not Satan.

Verse 20 begins with a condition of fact assuming the truth of the statement: "But if [as is indeed true] I drive out demons by the finger of God …" The "finger of God" alludes to Exodus 8:19, where the Egyptian magicians admit that Moses' miracles took place by "the finger of God"; and also to Exodus 31:18, where the two stone tablets with the Ten Commandments on them were written by "the finger of God." This verse is the clearest statement in the Gospels that God's kingdom is not just imminent in Jesus' ministry but "has [already] come upon you."

This is tantamount to saying that the messianic era, the time of salvation, is here. The saving power of God has arrived and can be grasped ("upon you"). The end-time realm and rule of God is not just a future reality but has been inaugurated in Jesus' coming. In the parallel Matthew 12:28 this takes place "by the Spirit of God," meaning that the Spirit is one of the primary signs of the new kingdom reign of God. There is an already/not-yet aspect of God's kingdom. It has already arrived but is still in process and not yet finalized. That finalization will take place at Christ's second coming. The defeat of the cosmic powers is proof positive that God's kingdom has begun in this world.

The plundering of the strong man's house in verses 21-22 refers to a common phenomenon in the ancient world in which a wealthy man with all his servants turns his home into a fortress and his servants into a private army, much like Abraham with his 318 servants/soldiers in Genesis 14:13-16. Jesus uses this to picture spiritual warfare against Satan and his fallen angels. This passage is more detailed than its parallel in Mark 3:27 and pictures Jesus as a stronger invader first defeating and then plundering Satan's realm, an incredible image for the battle against the powers of evil. The four verbs are progressive, as Jesus (by himself—he needs no army) first "attacks" then "overpowers" him, picturing exorcisms as acts of overpowering force that Satan and his army are helpless to stop. After completely defeating the cosmic powers, Jesus then "takes away the armor," a picture of stripping away all their weapons, as in Colossians 2:15, when at his ascension Jesus "disarmed the powers and authorities," making "a public spectacle of them, triumphing over them by the cross."

Finally, Jesus "divides up his plunder," a difficult concept to interpret. The image is easy to understand, as the "spoils" are all that the evil general has taken from the people he has conquered. But what is the "plunder" Satan has forcefully stolen from humankind? Jesus is clearly pictured here as able to enter Satan's cosmic household at will, bind Satan, and take his possessions by casting out demons and returning to God's people all he has stolen. Most recognize that the "plunder" refers to the release of captives (see 4:18–19) and the return of the blessings of salvation (forgiveness, redemption, eternal life) that the evil powers have tried to take away from God's people.

Jesus gives two warnings in verses 23–26. His saying in verse 23 is the opposite of 9:50, where he said, "whoever is not against you is for you." Here he is addressing spiritual warfare, so he states, "Whoever is not with me is against me." The message is that in the cosmic war no one can be neutral—there are no Switzerlands. You are either a follower of Jesus or of Satan. This is a challenge to make a commitment for Jesus, as there are eternal consequences at stake. The second image builds on the first—"whoever does not gather with me scatters," using the image of a shepherd who either gathers his flock around him or watches it scatter to the far hills. Some think this is harvest imagery as in Matthew 25:24–25 about sowing and scattering seed. The harvest is then lost. Either way the point is the gathering of Israel to God or seeing them scatter to the nations.

The second warning comes via the parable of the wandering spirit (vv. 24–26), and it concerns shallow exorcisms that do not display the true power of God along with a failure to follow up and help the person to grow spiritually. This is a warning to the disciples as well as the Jewish people, for the followers were unable to cast the demon out of the child in 9:37–43. When believers perform ministry in their own strength or to show off, it is guaranteed to fail in the long run. In order to be successful, spiritual warfare must be holistic and involve every area of the Christian life.

In this case the unclean spirit "comes out," probably as the result of an exorcism. For a time it "goes through arid places," namely, the desert, as the proper habitation for demons (Isa 13:21; 34:14). By returning to its "house," the demon is "seeking rest," after the apparently arduous task of possessing the person. However, demons are restless beings and incapable of finding rest.

The demon has been turned into a homeless traveler, and his only solution is to "return to the house I left," from which it was earlier cast out. Apparently, the person has insufficient strength to stop the demon from possessing him again. When it arrives, it "finds the house swept clean and put in order." The poor person is in even better shape than before and ready for occupancy, with nothing in it to resist the demon. The exorcist had cleaned house, but the person was not converted, or at best lacked spiritual depth. The attractive new dwelling place cries out for an inhabitant.

My view is that Jesus has both the disciples and the crowds in mind. Judaism had become neutral and even hostile to the things of Christ and so had become an empty religion, and the disciples too often failed spiritually in their ministries. So this applies to us as well as to unbelievers. The conclusion of the parable (11:26) shows how serious the issue is. The demon doesn't just return but comes accompanied with "seven other spirits more wicked than itself" in order to fill and completely occupy the now spotless but empty "house." The poor person will become another "Legion" (8:30), under the power of multiple demons. Seven demons is the perfect number of fellow soldiers to take control.

The result is that "the final condition of that person is worse than the first," in fact, eight times worse. This is an important message on spiritual growth. Jesus is clearly saying that half-measures are completely inadequate, and he demands that both new converts and those liberated from demons be deeply discipled and made firm in their walk with Christ.

Luke begins verse 27 with "as Jesus was saying these things," which makes this virtually a conclusion to the Beelzebul incident.

The way to disciple the new convert and the liberated former demoniac is to teach them to "hear the word of God and obey it." The scene begins with a woman emerging from the crowd who has obviously been deeply touched by Jesus and uttering a beatitude over Jesus' mother (and over Jesus through her): "Blessed is the mother who gave you birth and nursed you." She is clearly quite thankful for Jesus' authority over the demonic world and for his liberating those whom demons have enslaved. In the Jewish world the mothers who raised famous figures were understood to be somewhat responsible for their great deeds, and this becomes another incident where a woman breaks social conventions to show her appreciation for Jesus (see 7:36–50).

In verse 28 Jesus isn't really correcting her but rather using the rabbinic technique of the weightier and the lighter, providing his own beatitude, "Blessed rather are those who hear the word of God and obey it." The translation "but rather" sounds like Jesus is denying her blessing of his mother, but I don't think that is the case. He is saying that even "more blessed" are those who keep his word. We are at the very heart of discipleship here. The penultimate method of deepening someone's walk with Christ is to immerse them in the word and help them to "obey" it (see also 8:8, 15, 18, 21). This uses a strong verb for obeying, *phylassō*, to "watch over, guard," thus to "observe" and "follow" a teaching. So the idea is not just to obey but also to do so in order to guard and keep the teaching from being broken through disobedience.

JESUS GIVES THE SIGN OF JONAH (11:29–32)

Jesus in this section is responding to their demand for a sign in 11:16 (see on v. 17). He begins with a rebuke, calling them "a wicked generation" for demanding it. Because of the evil that dominates the land, they do not deserve a sign, and no such heavenly portent (see on v. 16) will be given it. Signs are for those with the eye of faith to accept and understand them. So if Christ were to give them a sign, it would do no good.

However, Christ will give them "the sign of Jonah." There are two meanings possible for this: On the one hand, it could refer to Jonah's preaching of repentance and judgment to Nineveh (3:4–10); his message of impending doom is the same as Jesus to the Israelites of his own day. On the other hand, it could be the sign of resurrection—Jonah's rescue from death would be an anticipation of Jesus' resurrection. With the emphasis on obeying "the word of God" in verse 28, the first makes best sense here. The second seems to be supported in Matthew 12:40, but there is no hint of resurrection in Luke. Jesus is calling here for repentance and warning his listeners of the coming judgment.

The reason for the sign of Jonah is that Jonah is a **typological** sign fulfilled in Jesus as Son of Man (11:30). When God sent Jonah to the Ninevites, his preaching brought repentance. God is now sending the Son of Man to the people of Israel, but his preaching unleashes only rejection and opposition. So the Son of Man is a sign of judgment to a nation that has turned against him, that has reversed the reaction of the Ninevites to Jonah.

Christ details two judges who will condemn Israel at the last judgment. Both are Gentiles, so this prepares for the universal mission in Luke. The Gentiles respond properly to Jesus' preaching, while the Jewish people do not. The first judge, "the Queen of the South" (11:31), also known as the queen of Sheba, "came from the ends of the earth [southern Arabia] to listen to Solomon's wisdom." In 1 Kings 10 and 2 Chronicles 9 she came with a huge caravan loaded with luxuries and quizzed Solomon with all the hard questions, then gave many wealthy items to him as gifts. As a Gentile who faithfully listens and responds to the wisdom of Solomon, she will stand at the last judgment and "condemn" the Jewish people of Jesus' day, because "now something greater than Solomon is here," and they have rejected him.

The second judge is the people of Nineveh (11:32), again Gentiles who responded and "repented at the preaching of Jonah." They responded properly to the lesser, Jonah, while the first-century

Jews refused to do so with the greater, Jesus and his gospel message. So they will join the queen of Sheba in standing up at the last judgment to condemn the apostate Israel of Jesus' day.

JESUS GIVES TWO "LIGHT" SAYINGS (11:33-36)

There are two sayings in this passage regarding the light of God in this world and the need to respond correctly. The image of light features the divine word proclaiming the hidden and now-revealed kingdom truths of Christ. Verse 33 is a doublet with 8:16 in the parable section, where it supports the disclosure of that which has been hidden. This was undoubtedly a favorite saying of Jesus, and he uses it again here to clarify further the "something greater" of verses 31 and 32. The light of God in Jesus must be "put ... on its stand" so it can be seen by everybody.

The Jewish people need no extra sign (11:16, 29-30), for the light is given and is visible in Jesus. His kingdom preaching is a light demanding response. However, they have hidden their light. With the image of a hidden place in the house, they have placed the light God gave them in the cellar or perhaps in the crevice of the wall; it is hidden from view and of no effect. Christ, on the other hand, has taken the light of God and put it in the open for all to see.

The next three verses (34-36) turn from the light in the house to the light in terms of the body. Clearly, the eye allows light to enter the body and so "is the lamp of your body." In other words, it is the source of light in your body and guides you in the direction you are to go. To do that, however, the light must be "healthy" (*haplous*) or sound, letting in the light (literally, "single" or single-minded). Here it is contrasted with the "evil" eye (*ponēros*, "unhealthy" in the NIV) and so has an ethical aspect to it, referring to spiritual integrity versus the "wicked generation" (11:29) under the control of sin. The Christ followers are "full of light," with the light of God illuminating their paths, while the Jewish people are "full of darkness" and have turned away from God and embraced evil.

The crowds as well as the disciples must be extremely careful, paying the closest possible attention to what they take in.
They must make absolutely sure that "the light within you is not
darkness" (11:35). Just as Satan "masquerades as an angel of light"
(2 Cor 11:14), so his lies are disguised as truths and can suck the
unwary in and destroy them. All of God's people must carefully
examine themselves and make sure what they are being taught. I
wonder how many believers in our churches know their theology
well enough to do that! In our age of the internet, it is remarkably
easy to disseminate "information" that has no substance whatsoever and to watch it be accepted in church after church. We must
help the people of our churches care about truth and as a result
become knowledgeable of Scripture and theology.

The concluding verse (11:36) provides an encouraging promise. When the "whole body is full of light," every area of our life
radiates the light of God in Christ; we glow with the glory of the
transfigured Christ. There is some debate as to whether Jesus is
speaking of our present life in Christ or the future glory we will
share with him when he returns. My understanding is that this is
another instance of "inaugurated eschatology," a both-and promise of the "already" or present glory as a guarantee of our final
or "not-yet" glory at the end of history. The truths of Christ in
the word of God illuminate our way and fill us completely to the
extent that we are aglow, since Christ is the "lamp" that "shines
[his] light" on us.

JESUS PRONOUNCES WOES ON THE
PHARISEES AND SCRIBES (11:37–54)

This material is quite similar to the woes of Matthew 23, but that
episode occurs in a different setting and is likely a separate occasion on which Christ castigated the Jewish leaders for their hypocrisy. It is common to think that Christ could not have made such
scathing comments, but studies have shown that every section can
be paralleled in rabbinic writings. Matthew and Luke both wish

for Christian leaders as well to read this and contemplate the areas where they too commit these sins.

In verses 37–38 Luke sets the scene at a meal. Luke prefers meal settings, for table fellowship is the perfect medium for messages like this (see 5:29; 10:38). Pharisees likely invited him often (7:36), trying to understand better what he was about. When Jesus does not follow tradition and "wash before the meal," the man is surprised. It was not required by the Torah but was part of the oral Torah, the practices developed by the Pharisees over the previous couple of centuries and practiced by many Jews. They believed that since every area of life should be undefiled, that included food and meals. So they would immerse their hands before meals if they had been in the home and immerse their whole arm if outside in the marketplace, where they could inadvertently come into contact with impure items or persons like Gentiles. Jesus probably did not follow this custom and had not thought to do so at this time. Most likely this "surprise" involved criticism, for Jesus goes on the offensive and castigates the customs they have developed to protect the Torah.

Jesus begins his woes on the Pharisees (vv. 39–44) with the hypocrisy of their traditions about eating (vv. 39–41) and then adds three woes on their oral traditions and practices in general. The first is the inside/outside antithesis that defines hypocrisy. The basic principle is found in Leviticus 11:33; 15:12, according to which unclean meat defiles a clay pot. This was then developed further in the oral tradition. They tried to keep the outside of cups and dishes spotless, but they were not so careful with the insides, where the food was found. Jesus uses this as an image of sin. They wanted to look pious on the surface, while "inside you are full of greed and wickedness." Appearances had priority over reality. So long as they appeared spiritual to others, it didn't matter overmuch how they really were on the inside.

The reality is that they are "foolish" (in Proverbs the fool is the person who ignores God), for God made the inside as well as the outside of the person and demands that both be clean. Failure to care for inward piety is just as ridiculous as washing the outside while ignoring the inside of a vessel. These people may be ritually clean on the surface, but inside they are filthy, filled with greed and wicked practices.

The only way to be clean in the eyes of God is to defeat greed, and Jesus suggests in 11:41 that this can only be accomplished by being "generous to the poor." The Pharisees were "foolish" to ignore this. The term behind "generous" is *eleēmosynē*, referring to "almsgiving." When one gives money or food to help the poor escape their destitution, it becomes a medicine for the soul and heals the greed that has consumed them.

The first woe (11:42) centers on their preference for the minor things that help them look good (tithing) while they ignore what God considers the major areas of life (love and justice). As I said at 6:24, woes are judgment oracles that mean God's wrath is coming. These Pharisees felt good about themselves because they were so assiduous in tithing even the smallest items like mint and rue and herbs. The legislation on tithing comes from Deuteronomy 12:11–19; 14:22–29; and Numbers 18:21–29, with each family sharing this harvest tithe in a sacred meal with the Levites (Deut 12:15–19). These tithes went to the Levites as their sacred "inheritance" (Num 18:21). Every third year the tithes were shared not just with the Levites but with the orphans and widows (Deut 14:28–29). The Pharisees were overly scrupulous in observing this, tithing every kind of food, not just major crops.

This practice was not wrong in itself. What was wrong was what they neglected, "justice and the love of God." By ignoring deeds of mercy, they become guilty before God. As Micah 6:8 says, God requires us "to act justly and to love mercy and to walk humbly with your God." Tithing is good but not without the greater duty of loving God and neighbor.

The second woe oracle (11:43) centers on the attention-grabbing practice of demanding "the most important seats in the synagogues and respectful greetings in the marketplaces." They don't want merely to look important. They want everyone around them to know how important they are. This ostentatious pride is a serious sin in every era. I know of many people who have gotten a Doctor of Ministry degree not so much for the ministry tools and knowledge they gained but so they can be called "doctor" and have greater authority in ministry settings (even get bigger churches to pastor). Seats in synagogues (and in many churches even today) were assigned to families and were points of prestige. To be greeted as "sir" or "Professor such-and-such" (some scholars demand this) tells everyone how much respect they should give you. All this is a sin—not to receive respect but to demand and live for such respect.

The third woe saying (11:44) spells out the indictment, not so much a sin they are committing as the loathsome beings they have become. When one comes into contact with a grave (and the body it contains), they become unclean for seven days. This is true even with "unmarked graves." The person who walks over them inadvertently is still unclean. These hypocritical Pharisees defile people by their very nature, for they are spiritually dead within and have become hidden graves, the same imagery as the "whitewashed tombs" in Matthew 23:27. So people who don't know their true nature are defiled by mere contact with their internal corruption. They think these Pharisees are models of piety and don't realize how empty these hypocrites actually are.

To the three woes on the Pharisees, Jesus in verses 45–52 delivers three corresponding woes on the scribes. One of these "experts in the law" complains that in indicting the Pharisees Jesus is condemning them as well. Jesus agrees and then adds three more that apply to them. Their guilt is proved, because Jesus' purpose is to bring them to repentance, but instead they only tell him, "you insult us also." They have assimilated nothing from the charges.

The first woe to the scribes (11:46) centers on the harsh burdens they heap on others while they do nothing to help them cope.

The image is of the yoke of the law (Matt 11:29; Acts 15:10), as they placed on the people a terrible weight constricting them to their minute laws. Spiritual depth via rules and regulations never works. Yet it is not just the number of rituals they make them keep. Just as bad is the complete failure to help the people learn how to keep these laws and draw near to God. In other words, they beat people down with weighty rules and at the same time force them to work out these burdens by themselves with no answers. There is absolutely no joy in the type of religion they have created, only a terrible weight of expectation.

The second woe here (11:47–48) is the fact that they have participated in the persecution and martyrdom of the prophets. Judaism in the first century was known for impressive monuments and tombs reverencing the prophets. Jesus is saying that they are building these tombs for the very prophets their ancestors had murdered. "They killed the prophets, and you build their tombs." Their building of tombs was giving passive assent to the very killings in which their ancestors were involved. They had a veneer of reverence but ignored their past actions against the prophets and their present actions against Jesus and his disciples. They are doing to Jesus and his followers exactly what the apostate nation had done to the prophets in the past, so they stand guilty.

In light of their guilt, he adds a judgment saying (11:49–51 = Matt 23:34–36) described as a wisdom saying. We have no evidence of such a saying, though some say it stems from a lost Book of Wisdom. In any case, it details the anti-prophet history of Judaism and the guilt of the nation as a result. God sent them prophets in the Old Testament and now is sending apostles in the New, and they treat both the same—"some ... they will kill and others they will persecute." The future tense means Jesus is thinking of their successors, probably preparing for events in the book of Acts. In this way the Jewish leaders continue the evil work of their ancestors.

The result is rather striking (11:50): "Therefore this generation will be held responsible for the blood of all the prophets that has been shed since the beginning of the world." That doesn't sound fair, but the parallel in 1 Thessalonians 2:15-16 states that they "killed the Lord Jesus and the prophets" and thus "they always heap up their sins to the limit." They are fulfilling or completing all the evil deeds of the nation from the beginning and so with them are guilty of it all. There is a difference of opinion as to whether the judgment this envisages is the destruction of Jerusalem in AD 70 or the final judgment. The apocalyptic air of this passage favors the latter.

Verse 51 amplifies what Jesus is talking about. The first murder of course was Abel in Genesis 4:1-6, and the last one here is "Zechariah, who was killed between the altar and the sanctuary" in 2 Chronicles 24:20-22. Zechariah was the son of the priest who proclaimed judgment on the nation and was "stoned … in the courtyard of the LORD's temple." Chronologically, 2 Chronicles is the last Old Testament book written, so this was the last death recorded.

The final woe oracle (11:52) condemns the scribes and Pharisees for restricting knowledge of God's truths. By their oral tradition they have taken over the interpretation of Torah and restricted its understanding to what they themselves come up with. The "key to knowledge" refers to the way they interpret Scripture, so their failure to give the people true knowledge is an extremely serious sin. They refused to "enter" the arena of divine truth and give the people only their false understandings. As such they "hinder" others from entering as well. To become an obstacle to truth is as grave an error as one can imagine.

In verses 53-54, the opposition intensifies further. The woes on the scribes and Pharisees, needless to say, enraged them and solidified their hostility. They began to pester Jesus constantly with questions, not to find out his thoughts on key issues but to "catch him in something he might say" that could turn the people of Israel against him. This is no different from what we have been seeing for some time, but it has now gotten worse. The language behind "catch him" refers to a hunting lure or trap that would draw the prey in and capture it. It is this attitude and atmosphere that will lead to the trials and death of Jesus. These two verses are important, for they set the tone of opposition that will govern the next several chapters.

———

Discipleship must take place in the midst of prayer, for our relationship with the Triune Godhead is the heart and soul of everything we do, and communication with the Godhead is absolutely essential. This is especially true in light of the serious conflict that ensues from our opposition with the powers of darkness (11:14-36) and with the secular powers arrayed against us (11:37-54).

The first area of emphasis in our prayer life is the things of God (the "thou petitions," v. 2). The center of our life is glorifying the name of God in everything we do and living the kingdom life in this world to such an extent that we help introduce his reign into this world. The second area is to relinquish control of our life to him and learn to depend on him (the "we petitions," vv. 3-4). We are consumer addicts, and we have been brainwashed by society never to be satisfied but always to want more. This prayer demands that we center on God first and then trust him for our physical needs, which demands that we gain control over luxury items. Many of those things we consider necessities would shock the ancient person, who would look in our homes and see wealth beyond their ken (and I am not thinking of modern technology). Also, as God-centered people, we learn to receive forgiveness from God and then to forgive those around us. We also pray for strength to turn our temptations into tests and rise above them, growing spiritually as we do so.

Does God answer prayer? Jesus addresses this in 11:5-8 in the parable of the friend at midnight. There we learn that God's very name and character are at stake in his answering our prayers. We are committed to prayer, and God our Father is committed to us when we pray. He answers prayer not only because he loves us but also because as Yahweh he is the covenant God who must show his glory by responding to our prayers and blessing us when we come to him in absolute dependence. Our part is to ask continuously, and God's part is to respond in love and give us what we need (vv. 9–10). This is proved by the greatest gift of all, the Holy Spirit to guide and empower his people (v. 13).

The reason for needing a deep prayer life is found in the rest of the chapter. Arrayed against God's people are three powers — their own selfish desires (vv. 1–13), the powers of darkness (vv. 14–36), and the secular powers in opposition to everything they stand for in Christ (vv. 37–54). With all this standing against them, they would not have a chance apart from the power of the Triune Godhead giving them strength and working behind the scenes.

The emphasis on spiritual warfare comes via the charge of the leaders that Jesus casts out demons under the power of Beelzebul or Satan as Baal, the "lord of the heights." Jesus shows how ridiculous this accusation is because it would constitute civil war and destroy Satan's own realm. Furthermore, if they are charging him they are turning against their own Jewish exorcists as well (vv. 17–19). This simply cannot be, and the reality of his power proves that the kingdom of God has indeed arrived. The fact is that Jesus as the Divine Warrior has entered into Satan's armed fortress, bound him in his house and disarmed his demonic army, and then returned his plunder to God's people (vv. 21–22).

So they are warned to center entirely on Jesus in spiritual battles and when either casting out demons or winning converts to give these cleansed individuals spiritual depth to fill their lives (vv. 23–26). When the exorcized demon returns with seven demons even worse than he is, the sad individual who is clean but spiritually empty will become worse than ever. This is a very important warning to all churches and organizations to help their followers walk deeply with Christ. Shallowness must never be allowed;

rather, people must be taught to "hear the word of God and obey it" (vv. 27–28).

The "sign of Jonah" (vv. 29–32) is given to the people of Jesus' day because they received the same evidence of God's call and their sins as did the Ninevites, but they refused to repent, unlike the Gentiles. So both the queen of Sheba and the Gentile Ninevites will witness against them for their obduracy at the last judgment (vv. 33–36).

The woes against the Pharisees are focused on their hypocrisy. They wish to look pious while being defiled by inner sin. Jesus mentions three areas for each of the Pharisees and scribes (vv. 42–44, 46–52). First, they tithe the smallest food but ignore justice and mercy, thereby deserving condemnation from God. Second, they demand the important seats and greetings that tell people how important they are. This lack of humility and servanthood shows them to be guilty of overwhelming pride in the eyes of God. Third, as a result they are walking "unmarked graves," defiling everyone they come in contact with because of the depth of their sin.

The three woes against the scribes (vv. 46–52) are similar. First, they place terrible legal burdens on their followers but do nothing to help them keep these difficult regulations. They are virtually the enemies of those who follow them. Second, they build beautiful tombs for the very prophets their ancestors have killed. Thus, they put them in the grave and then build a tomb over them. Third, their false views on the Old Testament mean that they restrict knowledge of God's word and have no truth to give in its place. They are purveyors of falsehood.

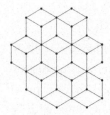

TRAINING TO TAKE OVER THE MISSION

(12:1–48)

This story line is firmly encased in the road to Jerusalem as Jesus has set his face toward his messianic destiny to provide salvation through the cross. The heart of this narrative is Jesus' training of the Twelve to take over his mission to the nations. In this chapter Jesus is passing on the tools and working on the spiritual attitudes necessary for that task. The first two-plus chapters (9:51-11:54) of the road to Jerusalem narrative ended with the crowd turning against Jesus and trying to trap him so they could arrest him. So this section begins with a warning to the disciples that they are included in that opposition and must be ready to proclaim boldly God's truths in this atmosphere of hostility (vv. 1-12). They can be assured of God's strengthening presence with them, but they must turn away from enslavement to material possessions (vv. 13-21) and not allow themselves to be anxious about earthly things (vv. 22-34). Instead, they are to trust God implicitly and live the time they have in readiness for the Lord's return rather than merely accumulating temporary possessions (vv. 35-48). In the end, we answer to him.

JESUS EXHORTS HIS DISCIPLES TO
FEARLESS CONFESSION (12:1–12)

In verses 1–3 Jesus warns against the yeast of the Pharisees, which provides a bridge from the woes against Pharisaic hypocrisy (11:37–54) to the need for the disciples to react with fearless proclamation of Christ. It is interesting that this section begins with "a crowd of many thousands" and then ignores the crowd and focuses on the disciples. The presence of "thousands" shows the increase of Jesus' popularity as it parallels a similar explosion of enmity from the leaders. Jesus takes no notice of the masses "trampling on one another" to hear him and turns to his disciples.

Wishing first to summarize the implications of his diatribe against the Pharisees, Jesus tells them, "Be on your guard against the yeast of the Pharisees, which is hypocrisy." Just as yeast causes the dough to rise, so Pharisaic hypocrisy (as seen in 11:37–54) breeds spiritual defilement. This is why the Passover bread had to be unleavened (Exod 12:14–20), and in fact all yeast had to be removed from the home, as it signified defilement. So the Pharisees and their hypocrisy were a defiling presence in Israel and were to be avoided at all cost.

The next two verses (2–3) repeat the "hidden/disclosed" imagery of 8:17. There it was the kingdom truths of Christ that were being revealed, but here interpreters differ over what it is that's being revealed. Some say that Christ is referring negatively to the Pharisees, whose hypocrisy will be revealed at the last judgment; others, that he refers to both the Pharisees' sin and the disciples' faithfulness. This second, a general promise that the heart of every person will be uncovered, is more likely. Those who are filled with evil and those who are characterized by goodness will receive their just rewards.

In verse 3 Jesus takes this general truth and applies it specifically to the disciples in their ministry of proclamation. This is both a promise and a warning that God is going to magnify everything they say. What is whispered in the dark will be shouted in full daylight, meaning things that are said privately will become public knowledge. Moreover, what is said in the inner rooms or private sanctuaries of the house will be shouted from the housetops. They are to become public figures, under the scrutiny of everyone around them, as Jesus is now. They dare not allow themselves to fall into the hypocrisy of the Pharisees, for that will become known. However, this is also a promise that their ministry and proclamation of the gospel will also be magnified by the Lord. They can be bold because God will bless everything they say.

In light of all the opposition they are facing, the disciples could be consumed by fear and unable to speak. Boldness is difficult and rendered nearly impossible when terror takes over. So Jesus addresses this in verse 4, telling them, "do not be afraid of those who kill the body and after that can do no more." It is critical to have a Christian perspective and know that this life is merely temporary, and that awaiting us is an eternity of absolute joy with God and Christ. It is wonderful to know that while we have little control over this life, our eternal existence is guaranteed when we know Christ as Savior and Lord. Paul in 1 Corinthians 15:26, 54, says it well: "The last enemy to be destroyed is death," and it will be "swallowed up in victory." For us death is grievous because we will not see our loved ones until they too come to heaven, but it is also a transition to our glorious future existence. For most of us, this is hard to understand because we have become so attached to this world's goods.

The only true basis for fear is God as Judge at the final judgment (12:5), the one who, "after your body has been killed, has authority to throw you into hell." Earthly death is temporary in its effects, while final judgment is eternal. "Hell" is actually "Gehenna," the trash dump in the Valley of Hinnom outside the Jerusalem walls where the fires burned night and day. This became a natural image for fiery judgment (Rev 19:20; 20:10, 14). Jesus' point is that the disciples don't have to be afraid of what they are about to endure. It is their opponents who should be filled with terror.

As the disciples go out and face persecution, they can be assured that they go out in the hands of their God. If we are martyred, does this mean God has forgotten us? In verse 6 Jesus uses the lowliest of birds, sparrows, as an example. They were the cheapest kind of food for the poor. An *assarion*, "penny" in the NIV, was the smallest copper Roman coin, and was worth one-sixteenth of a denarius (a day's wage). Sparrows are also small and common, and yet "not one of them is forgotten by God." If God cares that much for the smallest bird, how much does he care for us, his own people and family?

For his second example, Jesus turns in verse 7 to the fact that God knows what we could never know, how many hairs are on our head (unless we are bald!). My own body is quite frail, but I have a great head of hair, and I love it every time someone comments about it. But I have never tried to count my hairs. God watches over me so carefully that he knows every hair on my head. If he knows the smallest detail about our bodies, he is indeed watching over us with a care we cannot comprehend. As 1 Peter 5:7 states, "Cast all your anxiety on him because he cares for you." No wonder we don't need to be afraid; he knows the smallest thing about us, and we "are worth more than many sparrows."

Rather than be filled with terror, confess! Verses 8–9 form a kind of conclusion to verses 4–7 and use a double Son of Man saying centering on Jesus as **eschatological** Judge (Acts 10:42; 17:31) to make their point. The positive side states that whoever confesses (NIV: "acknowledges") Christ to others will be acknowledged before God's holy angels, undoubtedly the heavenly court at the last judgment. This is the reverse of 9:26, where Jesus uses the same formula of those "ashamed" of him.

The negative side (12:9) is similar to 9:26 and warns that those who deny (NIV: "disowns") Jesus will themselves be denied at the heavenly court and receive eternal punishment. This is not speaking of an unpardonable sin (12:10), where a single denial cannot be forgiven, but of a regular pattern of denials as liable to judgment.

A good example of what this refers to: not Peter's threefold denial (22:54–62) but Judas' rejection and betrayal (Matt 26:14–16; 27:1–10).

Elsewhere (Matt 12:31–32; Mark 3:28–29) Jesus' comments on the blasphemy of the Holy Spirit (vv. 10–12) are connected to the Beelzebul controversy, but here they follow the denial passage in the last two verses and describe an extreme form. The presence of "anyone" broadens this from the disciples to the crowds as well. The surprising element is the difference between speaking against the Son of Man and against the Spirit. Why can the former be forgiven but not the latter? The former refers to rejecting Jesus and denouncing him to others, much like Peter will do in 22:54–62 and like both leaders and crowds have done numerous times. This especially refers to the scurrilous attacks of the Pharisees. The blasphemy of the Holy Spirit is closely connected to the unpardonable sin, which in Jewish thought was "sin with a high hand" (Num 15:30–31; NIV: "sins defiantly"), especially profaning the name of God (m. Sanhedrin 7:5, building on Lev 24:15–16). In the New Testament this is linked with the question of apostasy in Hebrews 6:4–6 and 1 John 5:16.

The are several different understandings of this sin: (1) a post-Easter saying contrasting the earthly Jesus with the post-Easter Spirit; (2) rejection of Jesus by those who are not in the church versus by those who are members of the church; (3) rejecting Jesus during his earthly ministry versus rejecting him (and the Spirit) after receiving the gospel through apostolic preaching inspired by the Spirit; or (4) an ongoing refusal of the Spirit-infused gospel message. A combination of the latter three probably defines the doctrine.

There is a salvation-historical aspect to Jesus' words here that is critical: During his earthly ministry the glory of the Son of Man was incarnate and to some extent hidden, but after his ascension he was exalted to the right hand of God, and so what constituted blasphemy of the Holy Spirit here became extended to blasphemy of Jesus in Hebrews 6 and 1 John 5. It is characterized by a lifelong antipathy for all things Christian; the person will never again want anything to do with Christ (Heb 6:6). But it is also more than this. Mark 3:29 calls this an "eternal sin" that means God no longer wants them. They are beyond the pale of repentance and forgiveness.

Then in the next two verses (11–12) Jesus reveals the positive work of the Spirit among his followers. Christlikeness includes not just the spiritual attitudes and actions of Jesus but his treatment by others as well. So like him they will be "brought before synagogues, rulers and authorities," as shown in the book of Acts. They too will be arrested and some of them martyred, but when they stand before these hostile judges defending their right to live, they shouldn't worry about finding the proper words, for they won't be speaking in their own strength.

Spirit-inspired truth does not only encompass inspiration when writing Scripture or proclaiming the gospel. It also includes defending yourself and the cause of Christ in secular law courts (12:12 = Matt 10:19–20; Mark 13:11). I am thinking especially of the trials of Acts, where Stephen (Acts 7) and Paul (Acts 22; 26) make such impassioned speeches. Every word they said was inspired by the Spirit, and if we must go through a similar situation, what we say will be inspired as well. Boldness will be given to us, and the perfect words will come with the courage.

JESUS TELLS THE PARABLE OF
THE RICH FOOL (12:13–21)

Discipleship continues as we move from the issues of hypocrisy and fearless confession to the problem of possessions and materialism. If Christ's people are consumed by him, they cannot yield to consumerism.

This begins with a request from the crowd regarding a family issue: "Teacher, tell my brother to divide the inheritance with me." This is quite normal, for rabbis often went from town to town settling just such disputes. The rule was for the older brother to have two-thirds and the younger one-third of the inheritance. The Torah was clear on this (Num 27:10–11; Deut 21:17), but it is possible here that the older brother wants to keep the family estate intact to protect its standing in the community. To divide the wealth would be to diminish the family as a whole. This is likely the younger brother who like the prodigal son demands his share when he wishes.

Note that this (probably younger) brother is actually ordering Jesus to take his side. His interest isn't in justice but in material wealth. His problem is greed. Jesus' response is curt: "Man, who appointed me a judge or an arbiter between you?" (12:14). On the surface this seems to say, "I don't have the legal training or synagogue license to judge this," but as a rabbi he does. What he is really saying is, "It is not my place or calling to settle such material earthly disputes; I am here on kingdom business." His task is way beyond such legal disputes and materialistic desires.

But then he addresses the problematic attitude behind the dispute, warning, "Watch out! Be on your guard against all kinds of greed" (12:15). Paul calls greed "idolatry" (Eph 5:5; Col 3:5) because it places earthly possessions ahead of God in your life. In reality both brothers were focusing on their earthly wealth and consumed by greed, the one demanding the money, the other refusing to give it up. I know of an instance where two sisters turned their mother against their older sister so they could get the inheritance for themselves. It is too easy to be a wealthy parent and allow the inheritance to destroy the family. Jesus addresses both brothers but also the crowd as well, telling them, "Life does not consist in an abundance of possessions." True life must center on eternal realities, not temporary affluence.

Jesus then illustrates this with a parable (vv. 16–21), which again originates in the rich agricultural land of Galilee. This is not a tenant farmer but a wealthy landowner and farmer with a bumper crop. His debate with himself at first seems a prudent question, namely, finding a good place to store the extraordinary harvest of crops. He assumes his riches will last and continue and so develops plans for a much larger storage facility. However, implicit in this is the central place he holds in all his musings— everything is about "me, myself, and I," as we see in this and the ensuing verses. He ignores God and family in favor of himself.

In his plans, God is left out of the picture, and it is about him: "What shall I do ... I will tear down ... and build ... I will store ... I'll say to myself ..." He commits the sin of the shallow Christian businessman in James 4:13–17 who plans only to go from town to town making money and forgets God in the process. The elevation of self above God is the very definition of greed. Again, there is a certain prudence when the harvest demands bigger barns. The plural "barns" shows the productivity of the harvest. He seems to be a wise businessman until we notice the self-centered nature of it all.

His conclusion proves that our suspicion about his true motive was correct: "You have plenty of grain laid up for many years. Take life easy; eat, drink and be merry." His entire goal is self-indulgence rather than to use his largesse to help others or to serve God. His desire assumes the pleasure principle. In this story, no family or friends are mentioned, no one to share his plenty with or use it to help. He is all alone and wants it that way. "Eat, drink and be merry" stems from Ecclesiastes 8:15, where God's people are told to consider this world as a gift from God meant to produce "enjoyment of life." But he has turned it into selfish pleasure and polluted God's gift. "Be merry" is *euphrainomai*, "enjoy the good life," and that is all he lives for.

In verse 20 God actually calls him a "fool," *aphrōn*, a play on words with *euphrōn* above, "be merry." He thinks he has the good life but in reality is only another fool who has bought into the things of this world. He is about to die—"This very night your life will be demanded from you." He apparently has completed the huge new storage barns, and God is asking, "Who will get what you have prepared for yourself?" He has thought only of himself and his temporary pleasure in this world. He has no one to take advantage of his great wealth—no family, no friends. If there was any family, in fact, they would simply fight over the remains like the two brothers whose inheritance battle precipitated this issue in verses 13-14. He has lived only for the present and has nothing to take with him into the next life, and at the same time he has no family to leave his earthly wealth for. He has wasted his life and is truly a fool. This proves the old adage, "You can't take it with you," but it is also incredibly sad when you also can't leave it for anyone to enjoy.

The central question is whether we live our lives for self or for God. There is an empty eternity awaiting anyone who "stores up things for themselves but is not rich toward God" (v. 21). This seemingly successful man stored entirely the wrong thing and lost everything for all eternity. To store up treasure is incredibly important, but we must heed the warning of Matthew 6:19-21, "Do not store up for yourselves treasures on earth ... but store up for yourselves treasures in heaven. ... For where your treasure is, there your heart will be also." Wealth is not wrong, but it must be used for the glory of God and to help the needy. This is what Jesus means by becoming "rich toward God." When God blesses us with wealth, it means he is calling us to a ministry of sharing.

WORRY OVER POSSESSIONS (12:22-34)

This passage in a sense provides a **midrashic** (Jewish homily) commentary on the parable and tells how to overcome greed. It is in reverse order of the Sermon on the Mount: 12:22-32 = Matthew 6:25-34; 12:33-34 = Matthew 6:19-21. The message is that we must quit placing our faith in our possessions and start to trust God for our needs. He turns to nature for his examples—if God cares for the smallest elements of nature, how much more can we count on him to take care of us.

Thesis: Stop Worrying (12:22-23)

Jesus' words in these verses are called a "present-tense prohibition" and in a context like this are an indication to stop doing what you have been doing. Our worry over material things controls most of our lives. One thing I have discovered is that in our overly afflu-ent society, people can never have enough. People who can afford yachts never seem to have one big enough, and the new Toyota has to become the new BMW and then the new Porsche. I live in the north Chicago area, and I could not begin to count the number of mini-mansions in a twenty-mile radius (actually, the number of full-blown mansions!). The result is constant dissatisfaction and anxiety as whatever you have never seems to be enough.

In Jesus' day, the issue for most of the population was not the domicile or the family chariot; it was whether you and your family would have enough food to keep you from starvation. He would never have dreamed of saying, "Do not worry about your life, what kind of home you will live in or what kind of chariot you will have." That was not even an option. It was, "can we live on the amount of food we have, and will our clothing be sufficient for winter?" These are the essentials—there were never any extras. A man basically owned a robe and two tunics and would use the second for a blan-ket or pillow when traveling and sleeping on the ground (Luke 9:3: "no extra shirt").

The reason that one should not be filled with anxiety was because there is far more to life than food or clothes (12:23). Worry only takes over when we narrow our needs to the merely tempo-rary and material sides of life. The truth is that the excitement over the new car only lasts as long as it seems new. In a couple of months we start thinking about the next one, and within three years we have traded for it. Such is the life of the average mid-dle-class consumer addict. The answer here is simple: quit being anxious about necessities like food and clothes (and for us, about the extras), but learn to trust God for your needs and center on him. Jesus provided the answer in 4:4 from Deuteronomy 8:3; I will quote that verse: "Man does not live on bread alone but on every word that comes from the mouth of the LORD." The most important food is the spiritual food God supplies in his word. With that we begin to live eternally, not just for this particular day.

EXAMPLES FROM NATURE (12:24-30)

Jesus' two examples here relate to the sources of anxiety. The ravens in verses 24-26 were seen as unclean scavengers (Lev 11:15; Deut 14:14) and so the Jews avoided them. But God did not abandon them; he provided them food. Many ancients complained that ravens didn't even bother to return to their nest. Yet God even used them to provide food for Elijah in 1 Kings 17:3-6.

In 12:25-26, Jesus points out that worrying never helps you extend your life span. Medical studies back up this practical insight: people with more stressful jobs tend to have shorter life spans.[1] There is some debate about the translation here, since the term for "a single hour" is "cubit" (*pēchys*), and "life" could mean "stature" (*hēlikia*). So the question is whether Christ is talking about growing taller or living longer. While the former would be of interest to teenage boys who want to play basketball, the latter is more likely what Christ intended. The point is that worry shortens your life rather than extends it, so why let yourself do it? Be like the ravens and trust God to watch after your needs, then just go out and enjoy the life God allows you.

Therefore, since anxiety does absolutely nothing to help the necessities of life (food and clothes), why waste your energy worrying about your "guilty pleasures" as well? Verse 26 moves on from the necessities to the extras when it says, "why do you worry about the rest?" It does nothing to help either necessities or luxuries, so don't let yourself fall into what can never help but only hurt you.

---

1. See, for example, Bourree Lam, "Study: Stressful Jobs Make Life Shorter," *The Atlantic*, October 29, 2015, http://www.theatlantic.com/business/archive/2015/10/stressful-jobs-makes-life-shorter/412951/.

The power of clothes in our society never ceases to amaze me. It seems everyone craves designer clothes. From Air Jordans to haute couture, the materialist masses construe status as driven by the clothes you wear. This is true for the poor as well as the multi-millionaire jet-setting crowd. Here in Chicago, we have seen kids killed for their shoes, and former Chicago basketball star Michael Jordan himself has hundreds of shoes in his closet.

Jesus addresses this in verses 27–30 by means of flowers and grass, which clothe the fields of the world. The Greek *krina* (lilies; NIV: "wild flowers") could refer to the lily as we know it or the purple anemone. Either way, their beauty more than matches even the splendor of King Solomon (2 Chr 9:13–21), and there is no intensive labor or the spinning of cloth behind their majestic appearance. The amount spent by the super-rich on Paris fashions is shocking, and yet the red carpet of the Oscars cannot begin to match the tulip fields of Holland for beauty, for one example.

The same is true of "the grass of the field" (12:28). It is like the sparrows in its insignificance, here today and thrown into the fire and burned tomorrow. The image could either be of the Sirocco, the hot desert wind wilting grass and flowers in minutes, or perhaps the use of dried grass as fuel in the furnace along with wood. Either way, it describes what has only passing value and is transitory as a result. Yet God still "clothes" a field with it. This is followed by a key description of the shallow Christian—"you of little faith." In Matthew (6:30; 8:26; 14:31; 16:8), this is a primary phrase Jesus uses for his disciples: "little-faithed ones." Too often Jesus' followers are more tied to the world and its demands than they are to God, so material needs (like the right clothes) gain control of their lives.

Jesus sums up the problem in verse 29: "Do not set your heart on what you will eat or drink." Reversing the old adage, we become so earthly minded that we are of no heavenly good. We are so obsessed with these earthly concerns that we become consumed by worry. Our home isn't impressive enough, our meals not extravagant enough, so we refuse to have anyone over. Christ wants us to realize that if that is how we are, we have joined the "pagan world," which "runs after all such things" (12:30). All they have is this world, so they are consumed with it. That should not be true of us. We should know that we have a loving Father who knows our needs and cares deeply for us. That should free us for heavenly pursuits. We are secure in God and free from worldly anxiety. Now we need to live like that is true.

THE SOLUTION: KINGDOM LIVING (12:31–32)

The Christian perspective in the last verse, refusing to worry about material things, stands as the polar opposite of the pagan world, which "runs after all such things." What true believers "seek" are "kingdom" things (12:31); the present-tense *zēteite* means an ongoing pursuit of that life which reflects God's reign in this world. These are the spiritual aspects of our life, that which glorifies God and brings both peace and joy into our daily lives. This is the Christian "walk." In Colossians 1:10; 2:6 Paul urges his readers to "live a life worthy of the Lord and please him in every way" and to continue to "live your lives in him." When we live this way, Jesus promises that "these things [material needs] will be given to you as well" by the Father. Note that he is not promising wealth and prosperity but the basic things of life. In actuality, he is promising great wealth, but that will come when we reach heaven.

So Jesus concludes (12:32) that there is no reason whatsoever for fear or anxiety over either life's needs or over persecution by a hostile world, because they are God's "little flock." This is an Old Testament term of endearment (Ps 23:1; Isa 40:11; Jer 13:17; Zech 10:3) describing his people as the marginalized and vulnerable few at the mercy of powerful forces but under the protection of their divine Shepherd. While in this world we have little power, yet "your Father has been pleased to give you the kingdom." So in reality we fragile few are the possessors of the eternal kingdom, the richest people in the world. We are simply awaiting our inheritance, when we transform from paupers to princes. While the full inheritance is future, we can live now as kingdom people by refusing to center on the earthly and embracing the heavenly realities of life.

TRUE LIVING: TREASURE IN HEAVEN (12:33–34)

We are at the heart of one of Luke's primary themes—replacing earthly treasure with heavenly treasure (see introduction). Jesus states it with hyperbolic emphasis—"Sell your possessions and give to the poor." This is not meant as an absolute command—Zacchaeus in 19:8 gives half his possessions to the poor. But it is intended to establish priorities. Sharing with the needy is far more important than buying luxuries. This develops further the antithesis in 12:21 between storing up treasure for oneself and being "rich toward God." This has been misunderstood in past centuries in absolutist terms, resulting in vows of poverty and the belief that wealth in itself is a sin.

A biblical philosophy of wealth recognizes that earthly blessings include material prosperity, and that when God gives it he is calling that person to a ministry of sharing. As in the "eat, drink and be merry" of Ecclesiastes 8:15 (see 12:19 above), God wants us to enjoy the life he gives us on earth, but primarily he wants us to know that with wealth comes responsibility. He wants to use us to enhance the lives of the needy around us. We should consider wealth another spiritual gift like singing or speaking or working with our hands. It is a ministry to be used for the glory of God and the benefit of the saints.

Christ is using earthly images like purses and the monetary "treasures" in the purses as spiritual metaphors. Let me add the idea of bank accounts. Instead of banking our money on earth, we should give it away, and then it will be deposited in the bank of heaven, a "treasure in heaven that will never fail," never fall to inflation or bank closures. In heaven the interest continues to accumulate and can never fall. It will be "where no thief comes near and no moth destroys." The image of the moth relates to the fact that garments were passed down by inheritance, and moths could destroy expensive clothes. My wife and I are in retirement and occasionally check the stock market, hoping what we have accumulated will be enough and will not take a nose dive. What we have accumulated in heaven has no such pressure; it will grow for eternity.

Christ provides the basic principle in verse 34: "For where your treasure is, there your heart will be also." Your heart is under the control of your life's focus, and if that "treasure" is this-world-oriented, it will be controlled by the wrong things. The heart is the source of all nonmaterial aspects of life—the intellectual, the volitional, the emotional. So if the focus is wrong, everything in life is turned upside down. So don't pretend you are seeking God if you are centering on the things of this world—your priorities prove who you really are, and you are in serious trouble. Have we invested our resources in the earthly or the heavenly bank? That determines our destiny and our reward when we stand before God and answer for our life.

JESUS TELLS HIS DISCIPLES TO BE READY FOR THE COMING CRISIS (12:35-48)

We now turn from warnings about present possessions to warnings about future judgment. Christ is making a call to live expectantly and in readiness for his return. This is the time of eschatological crisis, and we are called to be faithful in light of these future events. As he has been saying, we must change our perspective from earthly to heavenly treasure and live accordingly. So this section expands on what it means to seek the kingdom realities by telling us how this world will end and be caught up into that heavenly reality.

PARABLE OF THE WAITING SERVANTS (12:35-40)

Jesus uses two metaphors on readiness for action in verse 35. The first, "Be dressed ready for service" (see 1 Pet 1:13), is literally, "gird up your loins," which involves tucking one's outer garment into one's belt in readiness for action. The perfect tense refers to a constant state of being, always ready to act. The second, "keep your lamps burning," refers to readiness also during the hours of darkness. So this demands a watchful, constant preparedness.

In reality, the parable of the waiting servants in verses 36–38 is a third illustration for readiness after the two in verse 35. These are servants waiting for their master to return from a wedding banquet, which could imply he is gone for the full seven days of the celebration. With verse 35, they are ready, and the lamps are lit for his return. They don't know exactly when he will arrive, just that it will be soon. Their task is simple—open the door and serve their master. The imagery of the master standing and knocking is also used in Revelation 3:20 of Jesus' coming.

The imagery of verse 37 is unusual, for the master promises those who are still watching for him that he will reverse their situation. He will dress as the servant, make them the special guests who "recline at the table," and then "will come and wait on them." Jesus did this when he washed the disciples' feet (John 13:4–5), but here it is a banquet he will be serving them. Masters serving the slaves was unheard of in the first century, and the reclining shows this is a special banquet, likely the messianic banquet (Rev 19:6–10).

The concluding verse is in the form of a beatitude, "It will be blessed [NIV: 'good'] for …" Those servants who have remained prepared and vigilant in the hours of waiting will experience a special blessing from the Lord "even if he comes in the middle of the night [the second watch] or toward daybreak [the third watch]." While the Romans had four night watches from six in the evening to six in the morning, the Jews had three (six to ten, ten to two, and two to six). Jesus likely is following Jewish practice here. The point is that it might be a long wait, and Jesus' followers must be ready for the long haul. It is important to realize that Jesus was not expecting a soon return but was preparing his disciples for an interim period, and spiritual vigilance is required of all God's servants.

The parable of the householder and the thief in verses 39-40 adds further warning. The parable comes in the form of a single-sentence truism: "If the owner of the house had known at what hour the thief was coming, he would not have let his house be broken into." This short little illustration is behind the "thief in the night" passages on Jesus' **parousia** or "coming" (Matt 24:43; 1 Thess 5:2; 2 Pet 3:10; Rev 3:3; 16:15), where shallow believers are warned of the unexpected nature of Jesus' return. "Broken into" is actually "broken through" and might picture the thief burrowing through the mud-brick walls of a Palestinian dwelling. This could be called a "parable of surprise" and is the opposite of the emphasis on readiness in previous verses. This householder was not "ready" for a thief breaking into his home.

So the moral of the story in 12:40 is critical: "You also must be ready, because the Son of Man will come at an hour when you do not expect him." Jesus will be Judge as well as conquering King at his second coming. At that time everyone will give an account for their lives (Heb 13:7), and those who are not ready will stand before him in shame (2 Tim 2:15). This is the heart of spiritual vigilance— always being on the lookout for Christ and ready for his return.

THE NEED FOR FAITHFUL STEWARDS (12:41-48)

In verse 41 Peter asks a question Luke wants us to ask as well. In reality, Jesus has primarily been speaking to his followers (12:1, 4, 22, 32, 42, 52), but he is also addressing the crowds (12:1, 13, 54). Peter is asking a hermeneutical question about interpreting the meaning of this material. In actuality, Jesus wants both groups to hear it all. It is intended to teach the disciples and make them ready for what is soon coming. As well, it is meant to help the crowds to realize what they are missing when they remain outside Jesus' (and God's) people.

Primarily addressing the disciples, Jesus in verse 42 asks whom he can count on to be "a faithful and wise steward" (NIV: "manager"; *oikonomos*). These are the leaders of Christ's messianic community. The steward was the slave placed in charge of the other slaves in managing the master's household and estate when he was away. He allotted the "food allowance" and other necessities to the other servants, a rare term for the "measure of grain," called by Romans the "grain dole" given to the poor to care for them. They made sure the slaves were taken care of properly. For the community of followers these people would be similar to the deacons and others who managed the care funds after the apostles handed over that duty (4:32–35; 6:3–6). These were to be faithful in discharging their responsibility and "wise" or "prudent" in the way they did so. This means they are "sensible" or steady as leaders.

Jesus in verses 43–44 uses another beatitude to describe the reward for faithful stewardship. As in 12:37–38 these are disciples who are not slack but faithful in discharging their office. The criterion for success is to be "that servant whom the master finds doing so when he returns." As throughout this section, Christ is referring to when he returns to set up his kingdom. Since that can be at any time in the future, this mandates that the leaders be found at all times faithful and wise as they guide and watch over God's flock.

The blessing itself is spelled out in verse 44. These stewards, given temporary authority as they were being examined by the Lord, are approved and "put ... in charge of all his possessions," now managing the entire estate of the master. This steward has complete authority over the household. Does this refer to authority over the church in the interim period or final authority in heaven? Since there is nowhere any indication of hierarchy in heaven, the former may be more likely. However, the context is describing the time following Christ's return, so it probably is also an image not describing a hierarchy of authority in heaven but rather the reward of faithful believers. Thus it indicates a special blessing and share in the glory of Christ.

In verse 45 there is a hyperbolic shift from the faithful to the evil steward. The master had given managerial authority over the other servants in verse 42, but this steward completely misuses that authority and, thinking the master will be gone for an extended period, "begins to beat the other servants, both men and women, and to eat and drink and get drunk" rather than give his fellow servants the food they need. In other words, he is power hungry and hedonistic, living for his own evil pleasures. His actions are the absolute antithesis of what Christ demands. Most likely, the description of his terrible behavior is meant to parallel the actions of false teachers who destroy their followers spiritually and use them to line their own pockets, living self-indulgently off them.

However, the master is not gone as long as the man thinks and returns at an unexpected time, seeing the wicked behavior for himself. The judgment is as terrible as his behavior was wicked: "He will cut him to pieces and assign him a place with the unbelievers." He beat the servants under his care, and now God will, as the Greek literally says, "dismember him" or "cut him in two." This, of course, is the final judgment and an image of eternal hellfire. His punishment fits his crime and the principle of reciprocity found throughout the book of Revelation. In fact, it is part of my definition of biblical ethics: what we do to others, whether good or bad, God will turn back on our own heads (= reward or punishment). In my Revelation commentary in this series, I argue that there will be degrees of punishment for those condemned to hell (p. 335 on 20:13–15), and these verses (45–48) would support such a view. Those who have done more terrible things will suffer a more terrible punishment. My fear is that more Christian leaders than we think will fall into this category, living for themselves and the earthly power and reward they can amass from their ministry. They will fall into this judgment.

Two further examples of degrees of punishment for unfaithful stewardship are provided in verses 47–48. The first is the slave who realizes what his master demands but deliberately refuses to do it (v. 47), and the second is one who does not know his master's will and inadvertently fails (v. 48). The first is "beaten with many blows" and the second with "few blows." This is describing Roman justice, though it seems extreme to us. The point is that each receives exactly the punishment their actions have earned.

So this deals with responsibility to live up to the level of knowledge you have. With the previous two verses there are three levels— deliberate sin (v. 45), sin of omission (v. 47), and ignorance (v. 48, still culpable, for he still should have known). The second (v. 47) is sin "with a high hand" or purposeful transgression (Num 15:30–31; Ps 19:13) and could be linked with the sin of omission of James 4:17: "knows the good they ought to do and doesn't do it." The "beating with many blows" would remind ancient readers of the synagogue punishment of beating with rods thirty-nine times.

In both instances the demand is that we know the master's will and obey it. The second servant (v. 48) is still culpable because he failed to follow this will. Ignorance is no excuse because the knowledge was there to be discovered, and so he is still guilty.

The lesson (12:48b) is clear: "From everyone who has been given much [all three levels], much will be demanded." This is every single one of us, for we have all been given the kingdom truths, and we are responsible to put them to good use in our lives. We all react differently to these wondrous truths (note the three levels above), but we are all responsible. Jesus is telling the disciples that they are required by God to be faithful to his calling. As he says here, we have been "entrusted with much," in fact, with the greatest truth this world will ever know: the gospel. The scientific discoveries that have gotten headlines of late are amazing, but they are nothing compared with the eternal gospel. A new phone or a cure for this or that disease is "good news" but not of eternal consequence. We have this knowledge; now it is time to live up to it.

———

Jesus in this chapter is training his followers for their future mission and summing up previous lessons. They must have nothing to do with the spreading evil of the Pharisees but realize that the words and deeds of both the wicked and the righteous are going to be made known to all, so they must make sure they are living and proclaiming the things of Christ (vv. 1-3). They need not worry about what people might do to them, for God watches over every hair on their head (vv. 4-7). They must simply acknowledge Christ in all they do, and their eternal future will be secure (vv. 8-9). They have the Holy Spirit. They are never to blaspheme his name but instead rely on him to tell them what to say in the crisis situations (vv. 10-12).

Jesus then turns from fearless confession to the problem of materialism. Two brothers fighting over their inheritance leads to the parable of the rich fool (vv. 13-21) addressing the issue of greed. The farmer with the huge crop ignores God and those around him in order to indulge himself. He shows himself to be a fool when he places possessions ahead of God and wastes his wealth all on himself.

The answer is to refuse to allow yourself to be consumed with worry over the quality of the food you eat or the clothes you wear or any other of the luxuries of life to which we become so addicted (vv. 22-34). If we truly know God and place our trust in him, we know he is watching over us and will supply our needs. That should allow us to pursue things of eternal value, not just the worldly goods of temporary worth. We need to discover the biblical view of wealth, that God gives us the things of this world partly to enjoy but mainly to use to glorify him and to better the lives of those around us, especially the poor and needy. So we must seek heavenly and not just earthly treasure and use our material possessions to serve God, thereby turning them into heavenly treasure.

Finally, Jesus turns from present possessions to being ready for his future return and the coming judgment (vv. 35-48). We are the servants waiting for the master's return, and if we are faithful we have the promise that he will reverse everything and serve us in the messianic banquet, rewarding us for our sacrifices (vv. 36–38). Then he turns from promise to warning (vv. 39–40). For those not ready, he comes like a thief and brings judgment with him. God's people must live in constant readiness.

Christ is calling for wise and faithful stewards who will serve the Lord in ministry and maintain his church in this interim period (vv. 41–44). Their reward will be great. But those who fail to serve the Lord and manage his church, turning their ministries into self-centered fiefdoms, will experience severe condemnation and be judged harshly when Christ returns (vv. 45–48). Every one of us, leaders and lay alike, must make sure we are living for the Lord and seeking his glory.

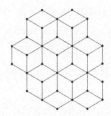

READINESS AND VIGILANCE
FOR THE COMING CRISIS
(12:49–13:35)

In Jesus' mind he is preparing his disciples for both the passion events in Jerusalem and for his **parousia** (coming) at the end of history. Division is the inevitable result of the kingdom preaching, for people will reject it, and his followers must be on the alert and read the signs of the times (12:49-59). The nation needs to repent, for the time is short (13:1-9). In the healing of 13:10-17 conflict continues, but healing and repentance are still present. Throughout the rest of chapter 13, Jesus centers on the presence and demands of the kingdom that have arrived with him. His followers must be ready for the coming crisis.

JESUS URGES HIS LISTENERS TO RECOGNIZE
THE SIGNS OF THE TIMES (12:49-59)

THE DIVISIVENESS OF JESUS (12:49-53)

The purpose of the incarnation is now expressed in startling fashion: "I have come to bring fire on the earth." Some think these are the fires of purification and cleansing through the coming of the Spirit, as in 3:16: "he will baptize with the Holy Spirit and fire," but this doesn't fit the context. It is more likely these are the fires of judgment, referenced not as much to the final judgment here as judgment via dividing the nation into believers and unbelievers, the good and the wicked (vv. 51–53). Division is a frequent motif (1:52–53; 2:34; 3:5; 6:20–26; 8:14–15), demanded by the leaders' obstinate opposition.

Jesus' wish fits every one of us: "How I wish it were already kindled" (note 11:2, "your kingdom come"). It must take place, and since that is true, let's get on with it! He came to bring God's final kingdom, but to do that the division of humankind and their judgment is necessary, and his fervent wish is that these final events be initiated (similar to Rev 22:20, "Amen. Come, Lord Jesus"; and 1 Cor 16:22, Marana tha [NIV: "Come, Lord!"]). This is a contrary-to-fact condition, meaning "I wish, but it cannot be." God is in control, and we must add (as is implicit here), "his will be done." Still, as I see the state of this world, Jesus' wish is my fervent wish as well.

For Jesus, however, there were necessary events that had to take place: "I have a baptism to undergo, and what constraint I am under until it is completed!" (12:50). This is not martyrdom (the view of Irenaeus) or Christian baptism, for neither actually fits here. This is Jesus' baptism, not ours. Rather, Jesus must be "immersed" (the meaning of "baptism") in his destiny, his passion on the cross. Jesus will be overwhelmed with catastrophe (the meaning of the baptism metaphor) when he becomes sin for us and undergoes our judgment on the cross on our behalf.

He clarifies the kind of judgment he brings by testifying that he has not come to "bring peace on earth" (as promised in Isa 9:5–7; Zech 9:9–10; as well as in Luke 2:14; 7:50; 8:48; 10:5–6) but "division." Before God's redemptive peace can be experienced, and long before his **eschatological** peace can come, the world of humanity must be divided along lines of accepting or rejecting God's salvation in Jesus. Christ has come to encounter sinful humankind, and this encounter demands decision, and that decision determines destiny. There will not be true unity among humankind until God's final heavenly kingdom is established and all evil destroyed.

Jesus exemplifies the extent of this division by describing the divided families that will result in the near future (12:52–53). He does so in considerable detail for effect. They will be divided on the basis of their responses to his gospel proclamation: in a family of five, three will believe and two reject, or two will believe and three reject. They are now hopelessly split into believer and unbeliever, and Jesus hints that the opposition and conflict will be total. He means the unsaved will reject the saved, as was his own experience (see Mark 3:20–21; John 7:2–5) and undoubtedly that of others among his disciples.

In verse 53 he turns from pure numbers to personal family relationships that will be disrupted between father and son, mother and daughter, and mother-in-law and daughter-in-law. This alludes to Micah 7:6, which describes the sinful conditions in Israel that brought God's judgment down on it. Even family life had disintegrated. Jesus' brothers did not believe in him at all during his life (John 7:5). It took resurrection appearances (1 Cor 15:7) to bring them to faith.

Reading the Signs of the Times (12:54–56)

He now turns and addresses the crowds, using the illustration of watching signs for weather patterns. A cloud arising in the west of Palestine stems from the rise of vapor from the Mediterranean and means rain is on the way. Southern winds come from the desert and herald the Sirocco, the hot wind that can wilt plants virtually in an instant. These were signs that could be counted on to tell a person the weather before it arrived.

He then applies this to the crowds, calling them "hypocrites," as shown in the woes of 11:39–52. They claim to know God and can know the weather but yet are unable to "know how to interpret this present time" (12:56). They are hypocrites because they can interpret the natural signs but cannot interpret the heavenly signs, meaning they have lost their relationship with God. They are unaware in this time of crisis that the time of fiery judgment

(12:49) has arrived. They should have seen the evidence of God's handiwork in Jesus' ministry and the divisions it caused. They should be ready but are not.

SETTLING ACCOUNTS WITH GOD (12:57–59)

Jesus now proceeds to tell them the true picture of the times and asks them to "judge for yourselves what is right." He is giving them the chance to do what they have failed to do until now, interpret the signs of the times. The story itself is pretty clear, as is its meaning. You are walking with an adversary on the way to see the magistrate. It is a financial issue involving debtor's court, as shown in "paid the last penny" in verse 59. You are probably guilty, as Jesus encourages you to "be reconciled on the way" rather than go to court. This is probably a **Hellenistic** court since in a Jewish setting a synagogue ruler or scribe would likely have made the decision.

Reconciliation is the only way to keep you out of prison. If you did go you would be in terrible trouble, for in jail you would probably be beaten regularly to get your family to pay more, and release at any time was rare, for the debt had to be paid in full before release would take place. People would sell themselves into slavery to avoid debtor's prison. A *lepton*, or "penny," was the smallest coin there was, worth 1/128 of a denarius, or less than a half hour of work.

The meaning of this is powerful. The accuser has been linked with Satan or earthly opponents or even God. Probably this scenario is not meant to be a symbol and is simply local color. The message centers on readiness for the last judgment, with God the Judge at the great white throne (Rev 20:11–15). The debt, as in the Lord's Prayer (11:4), refers to our sins as debts to God. We will give account to him for our lives, and many will stand before him in shame (Heb 13:7; 2 Tim 2:15). To reconcile with him clearly means to repent and receive forgiveness for sins. Otherwise, we will have to "pay the last penny" and receive eternal condemnation and judgment.

JESUS CALLS HIS LISTENERS TO REPENT (13:1–9)

Jesus has just been speaking of judgment, and so some members of the crowd ask about a recent atrocity perpetrated by the Romans when they slaughtered a group of Galilean pilgrims near the temple and "mixed" their blood "with their sacrifices" (possibly at Passover, when hundreds of animals were sacrificed). This particular event is not mentioned elsewhere by Josephus or anyone, but it is of a kind with similar tragedies in the past. In fact, it probably is like Herod's slaughter of the innocents in Matthew 2:16, just one of many such events. Similar events would be: (1) Many Jews murdered at the building of an aqueduct in Jerusalem (Josephus, *Jewish War* 2.175–77); (2) a massacre of Samaritans by Roman cavalry as they celebrated sacred vessels buried by Moses at Mount Gerizim (Josephus, *Antiquities* 18.85–87); (3) three thousand Jews killed by Herod Archelaus (son of Herod the Great) at Passover in 4 BC (Josephus, *Antiquities* 17.213–18). So this event was one of many. Undoubtedly, the man wanted commentary on the divine judgment on Rome this mandated.

Jesus responds by asking a question about guilt: "Do you think that these Galileans were worse sinners?" Most Jews assumed that such tragedies were the result of sin in the life of those who suffered (John 9:1). In the next verse (13:3) he answers his own question negatively, concluding, "But unless you repent, you too will all perish." While some interpret this as a reference to the destruction of Jerusalem, that is unlikely. This is certainly a reference to the last judgment and eternal punishment. No one can avoid death, but those who repent will not suffer the "second death" (Rev 20:6). It is eternal death we should fear, and the only way to avoid that is repentance and conversion. Tragedies like the massacre of the Galileans will happen in this world; it is for when our life in this world is over that we must be concerned.

In verses 4–5 Jesus adds another instance of human tragedy to make his point: when the tower of Siloam fell and killed eighteen people. Siloam was a reservoir near the southeastern wall of the city, and part of its tower apparently fell on a crowd. The same issue is raised: Were they shown to be "more guilty" than others by this incident? Jesus' response is the same: no, but it shows the fragility of life and the great importance of repenting while there is still time. The most important thing in the short life we have is getting right with God.

Jesus turns from universal judgment in verses 1–5 to universal mercy in verses 6–9, centering on the idea of a final chance, a period of grace so God's mercy might reach out. Fig trees normally bore fruit ten months of the year. Figs or fig trees in a vineyard are frequent metaphors for Israel (Isa 5:1–7; Jer 24:1–8; Mic 4:4; 7:1). The story is of a vineyard owner who discovers his fig tree is barren and has been unproductive for three years. This is the normal amount of time it is given to become mature, and then it is given three more years for the figs to become fully ripe. In the seventh year the fruit is first given to the Lord as firstfruits (Lev 19:23–24). The three years in the story are likely the three following this seventh year. The owner is ready to cut the tree down (13:7), but the vine keeper asks for one more year to dig around the roots and add manure to help it grow. Only after that year should it be cut down.

This is intended as a deliberate antithesis to Isaiah 5:1–7, where Israel as the unproductive vineyard was to be "destroyed" and made "a wasteland." The harsh indictment there is turned around here, with God offering the people (the fig tree) another opportunity to repent and bear fruit (figs). His listeners would have expected a similar ending to Isaiah, but surprisingly there is here a reversal of expectation. The thrust is that divine justice (vv. 1–5) is tempered by divine mercy (vv. 6–9).[1] Judgment is still on its way,

---

1. Some overly zealous interpreters have read all the details allegorically, like the three years being the length of Jesus' ministry or the fig tree being Jerusalem about to be destroyed or the fertilizer being the sacraments. Such details are local color, just part of the story itself, and not meant to be allegorized.

but Jesus is saying that the time of the present is an interim period where repentance is offered. In the same way as when Abraham pleaded for Sodom in Genesis 18:16–33, God will provide a time for the nation to turn around spiritually, but only for so long. Today is the day to repent (see Heb 4:6–7).

JESUS HEALS A WOMAN ON THE SABBATH (13:10–17)

This particular healing miracle is just the second one of the travel narrative (with 11:14) and centers on several principles endemic to this context. It is another encounter with the Jews and especially with the hypocrisy of the leaders (11:37–54). This becomes a sign of the times (12:54–56) calling for repentance (13:6–9) and continues the conflict, returning to the Sabbath controversies (4:31–37; 6:6–11).

This is Jesus' final time teaching in a synagogue, and as happened frequently, a crippled woman approached him there. As with the child in 9:37–43, the demon is using the woman's physical illness to torture her. She has been "crippled by a spirit for eighteen years," connecting her lengthy time of suffering with the eighteen who were killed in verse 4. The mention of the "spirit" is probably intended to add a note of cosmic conflict to the scene. Her condition likely involved a fusion and collapse of spinal bones, rendering her "bent over" and barely able to walk. Her sad condition may have lasted most of her life thus far.

Apparently while he was teaching, Jesus "saw her" there and decided to take care of her problem immediately. He interrupted his teaching (highly unusual) and called out in verse 12, "Woman, you are set free from your infirmity." Walking over, he laid hands on her (see 4:40), and her bones were instantly healed and straightened, a divine passive verb that stresses God healing her. Her "glorifying" (edoxazen; NIV: "praised") God is the natural response to God's healing touch in Jesus (2:20; 4:15; 5:25–26; 7:16). This shows her to be the antithesis of the synagogue ruler in the next verse who is caught up in legalities and cannot see the hand of God in Jesus.

The ruler of the synagogue (see 8:41) undoubtedly is the one who asked Jesus to speak and is upset that he has broken the oral tradition by healing on the Sabbath. He doesn't castigate Jesus but addresses the crowd in verse 14, probably to turn them against him. He argues that by healing Jesus has worked on the Sabbath, and that should only take place the other six days, drawing on Exodus 20:9–10, "six days you shall labor and do all your work." The woman should have come another day to be healed, not Saturday. She has disturbed the decorum of the synagogue service and caused him trouble, so he is indignant. He is far more concerned with his legalities than he is about her eighteen years of suffering.

Jesus once more calls them "hypocrites" (see 12:56), those who live false lives, pretending to be faithful to the law when in reality they are no friends of God, caring more for animals than for a suffering woman. The rabbis' oral tradition said an ox or donkey could be watered on the Sabbath only if it carried no burdens (so wasn't working). The animals also could be tethered so they wouldn't stray in spite of the rule against tying knots on the Sabbath (m. Shabbat 5:1–4). Jesus' point was that they were allowed to care for animals; why not people?

His argument is quite detailed (13:16). She is a "daughter of Abraham" and as such especially loved as a child of God. Satan has "kept [her] bound for eighteen long years," stressing the demonic war waged against her and her lengthy imprisonment. How dare they worry more about a donkey bound by a rope than Abraham's daughter bound by Satan! How dare they refuse to allow her to be "set free" from her bondage. Jesus' entire purpose in ministry is to fulfill Isaiah 61:1 and "set the oppressed free" (4:18), and the leaders wish to deny that.

As before, division results in verse 17: Jesus' "opponents were humiliated," but the people "were delighted with all the wonderful things he was doing." The shame of the leaders alludes to Isaiah

45:16 and the messianic humiliation of the idol makers there. The sins of the leaders who idolized their rules more than they had compassion for the hurting is the thrust. It is doubtful that they felt the shame, but those who were spiritually attuned were definitely aware of the truth. Meanwhile, the crowd rejoiced at the "wonderful things" Jesus performed in their midst. So now the true purpose of the Sabbath is realized, as Jesus performs wondrous deeds, the crowd rejoices, and God receives the glory.

JESUS TELLS TWO PARABLES ON THE KINGDOM OF GOD (13:18-21)

The healing of the crippled woman was another sign that God's kingdom reign had begun, so Jesus tells two parables that become his commentary on the significance of the healing. They show that in the ministry of Jesus God's rule is in process of growing and of demonstrating God's presence in the world. It will continue to grow in the ministry of the church in the world, both in the messianic community itself and in their mission to all humankind.

By healing and casting the demon from the woman, Christ showed that God's reign has begun, and so in verses 18-19 he describes its nature and character by likening it to a mustard seed, one of the smallest seeds (you can barely see it in your hand) but which produced a large tree, nine to ten feet high. So the mustard seed was proverbial for rapid, amazing growth. Jesus' point is exactly this: the kingdom seems insignificant in the present but has explosive potential for the future. There will not be the spectacular beginning the Jews expect (that will come with the second coming), but the future greatness will soon be evident.

The "birds perched in its branches" is stressed in all three **Synoptic** Gospels (Matt 13:32; Mark 4:32), and many see the image as simply stressing the size of the tree itself. However, it alludes to several passages (Ps 104:12; Dan 4:9-15; Ezek 17:23) that include the Gentiles (all humanity) among God's people. This is an emphasis throughout Luke-Acts but especially in 13:29-30 here. Christ is

likening the mustard tree to the cedar tree that is Israel shelter-
ing the nations in its branches, a picture of the universal mission
that is soon to be initiated in his disciples' ministry.

In a second illustration of the presence of the kingdom in verses
20–21, yeast in a huge amount of flour to make enough bread for a
village pictures the growth of the kingdom. In this case a woman
adds yeast to "three measures" (NIV: "sixty pounds") of flour, or
thirty-six dry quarts. The "leaven" itself (see 12:1) was older dough,
already fermented with yeast, added to the new batch of dough,
producing enough loaves to feed a couple hundred people.

Often yeast is used negatively of the growth of sin, but here
it is used positively rather than negatively, picturing the dough
rising and feeding this huge group. As such, it pictures the incredible results of the gospel as it permeates the world and produces
a wondrous number of converts. The kingdom has the power to
reach all the world with the salvation and kingdom truths brought
by Christ and his followers. Moreover, once the yeast is introduced
into the dough, its growth cannot be stopped. He is saying here that
the reign of God cannot be slowed and will indeed fill the world
with the reality of God in it.

JESUS TEACHES ON THE NARROW DOOR (13:22–30)

This passage establishes the theme for the ensuing material, centering on the great demands of the kingdom and the imminent
judgment. We are responsible, but on God's terms, not ours.

In verse 22 we are reminded once again that Jesus is on his
"way to Jerusalem" (see 9:51–52, 57; 10:1, 38; 11:53) to encounter his
final destiny, and once more he is teaching in all the villages he
passes through.

One of the most critical questions he will be asked comes in
verse 23: "Lord, are only a few people going to be saved?" This is the
question we all need to ask, for it provides the stimulus to mission.
Jesus has been warning them about this all along, and finally the
implications are beginning to infiltrate. Most Jews assumed they

would all make it into the kingdom, but a few Jewish writers discussed whether "few" would actually get in, speculating on reasons for rejection (Sabbath violations, blasphemy, etc.).[2]

Jesus stresses how stringent God's rule is for entering, and here he adds how brief the time is to respond. This is obviously entrance not just into God's kingdom but into God's very presence. The picture is probably that of a sumptuous banquet hall (the messianic banquet) with a narrow entrance and a time limit when the doors are open. Jesus has on numerous occasions stressed what is necessary: faith in him and acceptance of his message of salvation.

The narrowness of the entrance is because people cannot walk through it however they wish but must come in God's way by God's rules. The background stems from Deuteronomy 30:19 ("choose life"); Psalm 1:6 ("the way of the wicked"); and Jeremiah 21:8 ("the way of life and the way of death"). The "way of life" must be entered in God's time and is not easy. It will take "every effort," and one should not worry about how many will make it but about whether they themselves will make it. The "many" will not get in because they tried on their own terms and in their own time, only to discover it was too late. They waited too long. (See also the bridesmaids of Matt 25:8–12.) The emphasis is not just on "who" will make it but on "how" they can get into the messianic banquet.

The brevity of the time is because "the owner of the house" is going to get up and close the door (v. 25). This is a separate image, not just a narrow door but one that is shut to outsiders. Those who have waited too long are outside "knocking and pleading, 'Sir, open the door for us.'" But they clearly have not obeyed the owner's rules for entrance. They have missed both his instructions (the narrow way) and the time limit for entering (the closed door), so the owner replies, "I don't know you or where you come from" (so also Matt 7:23). They obviously have no relationship to the bride and groom and are not known, so they are not welcome. The "where you come

---

2. See 2 Apocalypse Baruch 18; 2 Esdras 8; m. Sanhedrin 10:1.

from" stems from the Jewish concern for family relationships and here means they are not part of God's family or invited guests to the wedding (see Rev 19:9).

They will keep trying to gain entrance (v. 26), coming up with further excuses. First, they claim to have had table fellowship with the owner ("ate and drank with you"), but clearly no relationship had ever been established. They also claimed to be followers of Jesus ("you taught in our streets"), but certainly they never committed to Jesus, just listened as he taught. So in reality neither was true.

Jesus refutes their claims by repeating, "I don't know you or where you come from" (v. 27). With the repetition the rejection is absolute. They are guilty and will never be accepted. He closes with a citation from Psalm 6:8, "Away from me, all you evildoers!" Psalm 6 deals with the righteous sufferer who puts his trust in Yahweh and commands his enemies to depart. So these people have not just become outsiders but have been shown to be evil, the enemies of God. Their exclusion from the messianic banquet is not just because they delayed their arrival too long but because their wickedness has been proved (as in Matt 7:23).

To clarify the implications of the "narrow door," Jesus specifies further beginning in verse 28 the destiny of those inside and those outside the banquet hall. Outside "there will be weeping there, and gnashing of teeth," indicating deep mourning and possibly anger in the grinding of teeth. They expected to be with the patriarchs and the prophets "in the kingdom of God," and when they are "thrown out" and excluded, they are filled with remorse and anger. They refused to feel the remorse earlier and repent from their sins, and now it is too late.

The insiders (v. 29) are the result of the universal mission, coming "from east and west and north and south," taken from Psalm 107:3, where they are "gathered from" all points of the compass to enjoy the goodness of God. The emphasis is on the inclusion of the Gentiles and prepares for the expansion of the gospel to

the nations in the book of Acts. This all recalls the identical promise in Matthew 8:11, where Jesus contrasts the Gentiles with the
apostate nation and speaks of the same reversal, as they enjoy the
messianic feast rather than the unfaithful nation.

This reversal is explained further in verse 30: "There are those
who are last who will be first, and first who will be last." As in
1:51–53 and 6:20–26, the downtrodden and marginalized (the last)
and those who view themselves as God's true people (the Jews)
will switch places. The rejection is not of all the Jewish people
but rather of those who refuse and oppose Christ, especially the
leaders. Christ is not denying his own people a place but rather is
saying that God's standards have now changed from a covenant-
based to a faith-based salvation. Both Jews and Gentiles now enter
the kingdom the same way, by repenting and turning to Christ.

JESUS LAMENTS FOR JERUSALEM (13:31–35)

One group of Pharisees has apparently not turned against Jesus,
for they warn him to "leave this place and go somewhere else.
Herod wants to kill you." Some have said this was an attempt to get
him to leave the area, but that is not likely. This is Herod Antipas,
tetrarch (ruler of "one-fourth" of a province) of Galilee (3:1; 9:7),
who had executed the Baptist (3:19–20; 9:9). This may have been
only a rumor, or it could have resulted from the fact that Jesus had
brought instability and conflict to the region. Herod and Pilate
appear in the same context (13:1), and they will work together at
the sentencing and mocking of Jesus. In 23:12 we are told that they
(who formerly were enemies) actually "became friends" over this
partnership in crime.

Jesus' reply shows his commitment to his God-given destiny (13:32). He calls Herod "that fox," which several interpreters think refers to an insignificant person but is better seen as
picturing him as sly and cunning, a conniver opposing God's will
for Jesus and trying to destroy him. The point is that such threats
won't work, for God is in charge, not Herod. Jesus, in spite of such

antagonism, will continue in his mission, "driving out demons and healing people."

The temporal markers are difficult to interpret. He will go on performing his messianic miracles "today and tomorrow, and on the third day I will reach my goal." This could not be meant literally, for it was going to be many days before he reached Jerusalem. Most likely it refers simply to a brief period of time before an event is reached and could be translated, "today, tomorrow, and the next day," just as in the next verse. It is used to stress God's control of events, stating that they will soon reach the intended goal.

Still, there is probably some intimation of the third-day motif for the resurrection; no Christian reader could read this without seeing this nuance (see Luke 9:22; 1 Cor 15:4). But it is not the main thrust. The verb for this is *teleioumai*, "complete, fulfill," as in 18:31, "everything that is written by the prophets about the Son of Man *will be fulfilled*." It is almost the time for God's plan to come to completion, and nothing Herod can do will be able to stop it. Most agree that this becomes another of the passion predictions in Luke (with 9:22, 44; 17:25; 18:31–33).

So Jesus will carry on with his messianic mission as he proceeds on the road to Jerusalem, as has often been indicated (9:51–52, 57; 10:1, 38; 11:53; 13:22). This in fact is divine necessity—"I *must* [*dei*] press on" (13:33). This could be called the high-water mark of the passion predictions—the "must" refers to his death in Jerusalem; only there can he realize his prophetic fate and find his destiny. He explains this carefully: "No prophet can die outside Jerusalem!" This does not mean that every prophet died in Jerusalem, for that clearly was not the case. Rather, this is hyperbole for the necessity of Jerusalem for the prophetic death of Jesus, thus rendering it in effect, "This prophet cannot die outside Jerusalem." Jesus is committed to his messianic destiny.

This fills Jesus with sorrow, not over his own fate but for the fate of what should still be "the city of God." In verses 33–34 the name "Jerusalem" appears three times in a row, but it is in sorrow as it has become a city of people "who kill the prophets and stone those sent to you." It is the city of Jesus' unrequited love, the place of his destiny, and the murderer of God's ambassadors (1 Sam 30:6; 1 Kgs 12:18; 21:13) and of Jesus himself (v. 33).

Jesus uses a wisdom saying on the rejection of wisdom's messengers to express his longing.[3] He depicts himself as a mother hen protecting her young under her wings (Deut 32:11; Ruth 2:12; Pss 17:8; 36:7), frustrated when the chicks (Jerusalem) run around the pen and refuse to gather under them. He longed to shelter his Jewish people under his messianic care and came to earth in order to bring them salvation, but they have summarily rejected his offer of love and protection. The city that throughout its history spurned God and his prophetic messengers again and again is now repeating its sordid history with God's Son.

In light of Jerusalem's obduracy, all that remains is a prophecy of judgment (13:35): "Look, your house is left to you desolate," an allusion to Jeremiah 12:7; 22:5, where Yahweh abandons his rebellious, sinful people. While "house" could refer to the temple, it more likely is a euphemism for the city of Jerusalem and its people. The idea of God "abandoning" the city is a prophecy of the coming destruction of Jerusalem in AD 68–70 (see 19:42–44; 21:6).

He concludes by telling them, "You will not see me again until you say, 'Blessed is he who comes in the name of the Lord,'" a citation from Psalm 118:26 sung by pilgrims as they came for a Jewish festival. Here it refers partly to the triumphal entry but mainly to the parousia, or second coming of Christ. (In Matt 23:39 it is said *after* Palm Sunday.) There is a strong irony in this judgment setting, for these Jewish people have rejected Jesus as the "Blessed One" and will not be caught up when he returns. So this is what they will miss in their desolate state. They will recognize him, but as their Judge rather than as their Savior.

---

3. For other examples of this from ancient Jewish writings, see 1 Enoch 42; Wisdom 7.

———

The purpose of the material in this section is preparation. As Jesus and his disciples near Jerusalem and the finalization of Jesus' purpose in coming to earth, he wants his followers to be ready both for the immediate crisis of the cross and for the final events of his return at the parousia. The first section warns the disciples that there will be little peace in their lives for Christ has divided humanity over belief in him, and they must expect opposition and rejection even from their own families (12:49–53). He then turns to the crowds and warns them to read the signs of the times (vv. 54–59). The time of judgment has arrived, and they must reconcile with God while there is still time or face eternal judgment for their sins. It is time to get right with him, and the final crisis is near.

Jesus in 13:1–9 expands on the need to repent. There are two examples of the fragility of life (vv. 1–5), the slaughter of Galilean pilgrims and a tower falling and killing several. The point is that life only has a few opportunities for us to get right with God and escape eternal punishment, and the time to repent is now. The parable of the fig tree stresses God's grace and mercy (vv. 6–9), and it is time to take advantage of this and repent.

A perfect example of the divisiveness Jesus causes is seen in his healing of the crippled woman in verses 10–17. She is released from eighteen years of imprisonment by an evil spirit, and she and others in the crowd are thrilled and glorify God. But this is a Sabbath miracle, and so the legalists, caring more for their rules than for the woman, are incensed that the miracle broke their precious regulations. Animals were treated better on the Sabbath than were people.

Two parables illustrate the significance of Jesus' ministry and of the miracle he has just performed. The mustard seed (vv. 18–19) demonstrates the explosive growth of the kingdom that is taking place, and the yeast in the bread dough (vv. 20–21) describes how powerful that process of growth is going to be. The two together tell the disciples that while their ministry may seem insignificant at present, its future greatness is guaranteed.

These divisions are further demonstrated in his teaching on the narrow door (vv. 22–30). The Jewish people in this teaching are outside seeking entrance into the messianic banquet, but they delayed too long and have shown themselves to be outside the true covenant people and so are denied entrance. The rules for getting in have changed and are no longer on the basis of keeping the Torah but on commitment to Jesus, God's Son. The old covenant people have been replaced by believing Jews and Gentiles, and these people Jesus is addressing have no place among God's kingdom people.

Finally, Jesus expresses his commitment to his destiny (vv. 31–33) and at the same time his sorrow for Jerusalem (vv. 34–35). Herod has now turned his malevolent gaze toward Jesus, but that is irrelevant to him. What matters is the divine necessity that he give his life as an atoning sacrifice for our sins. Yet that is Jesus' great sorrow as well, for Jerusalem, the city he loves and longs to protect, has become the city of rejection and the place where he is to die. The city that killed the prophets is now to become the city that killed *the* Prophet, God's Son and Messiah.

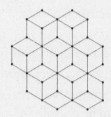

LESSONS FROM MEALS
(14:1–35)

There are two aspects to this chapter: first a series of meal scenes taking place at a Pharisee's home (vv. 1-24), and then teaching on the cost of discipleship (vv. 25-35). Several themes dominate. The chapter begins with a Sabbath miracle (vv. 1-6), and the theme of Jesus as the final interpreter of the law with authority over it. During the meal Jesus again rebukes his hosts, the Pharisees, and reiterates the principles for pleasing God and being his disciples—humility rather than self-seeking (vv. 7-11), concern for the poor and the outcasts (vv. 12-14), and a willingness to accept God's kingdom invitation (vv. 15-24). The surrender of all one has to the Lord (vv. 15-24) provides a fitting end to the chapter.

JESUS HEALS AGAIN ON THE SABBATH (14:1-6)

This is the final of three Sabbath healings (with 6:6-11; 13:10-17), and again the Jewish leaders make no attempt to get at the truth. Jesus is at the home of a leading (*archontōn*, "ruler," possibly a member of the Sanhedrin) Pharisee, being "carefully watched" by them, not to hear what he is saying but to trap him and turn the people against him. Instead, Jesus turns the tables on them and not only heals the man but once more exposes their own hypocrisy.

One of those sharing the meal was quite ill with edema, described in the NIV as "abnormal swelling of his body," another disease that to most was viewed as the result of sin in a person's life, often linked with gluttony or greed for money. So there is a strong metaphorical and spiritual component to this particular healing miracle.

Jesus takes the bait, but very soon it is the Pharisees who are on the defensive. They may have set a trap, but Jesus is willing and able to take them on. There are not only Pharisees present but also scribes, "experts in the law" who are in on the trap. So he addresses them both: "Is it lawful to heal on the Sabbath or not?" (14:3; repeating 6:9). The best defense is a good offense, and they should be aware that he has healed on the Sabbath three times (4:35; 6:10; 13:13).

It is remarkable that "they remained silent" (14:4), for they could have answered him. Their oral tradition allowed certain exceptions when healing on the Sabbath would be permissible, for if it was a life-threatening situation, healing was allowed. They could have said, "Bring him back tomorrow," and known the man and his family would have been happy to wait a day (as is said in 13:14). However, Jesus' point is that even a day is too long to suffer with a debilitating illness. They were not silenced by the legal issue but by Jesus' moral authority. Jesus, not they, occupied the moral high ground. So Jesus takes three rapid actions: "taking hold of the man, he healed him and sent him on his way." The emphasis is not on the healing itself but on Jesus' authority over the Sabbath and over disease. One could say in fact that failure to heal on a Sabbath would constitute a sin of omission (Jas 4:17).

Their inability to act or answer Jesus continues to the very end (14:5-6). Jesus turns the tables on them and asks about another Sabbath exception their oral tradition allows: "If one of you has a child or an ox that falls into a well on the Sabbath day, will you not immediately pull it out?" They should have responded with a yes, but that would be admitting that Jesus could be right, so they "had nothing to say." Their silence in both instances was eloquent testimony in itself. Score: Jesus 2, Pharisees 0.

JESUS TELLS THE PARABLE OF THE PLACE OF HONOR AT THE FEAST (14:7-11)

Jesus at the banquet takes notice "how the guests picked the places of honor at the table." This is common in every age. They had been watching him in verse 1, and now he is watching them. These would be the seats closest to the host, and they may have been "first come, first served" rather than assigned, for he observed the people jockeying for position. Couches would usually be arranged in a V shape, with the host at the point of the V. In the first century, status in society determined place at table; in later centuries age would become the determining factor.

Jesus addresses this situation with another "parable." In doing so, he changes simple advice on etiquette (the Jews called this "worldly wisdom") into a parable on behavior before God. In the first two verses (14:8–9) he advises them not to take the "place of honor," for it was common practice for the honored guest to enter last, and if you have their seat, you will be "humiliated" when you are banished to the "least important place," for it is the only seat left at that late time. Jesus is addressing both Jewish and Christian leaders who are playing the status game, and the theme is that of complete reversal: the first will be last and the last first (see 13:30). Humility must replace pride in our lives.

Instead of seeking the higher seats, "take the lowest place" (14:10), for then you will be told, "move up to a better place," and yours will be the place of "honor" or greater prestige. Jesus is likely adapting Proverbs 25:6–7, advising people not to exalt themselves before the king so that he will not "humiliate you before his nobles." There is a twofold application here, relating both to earthly and heavenly relationships. We should not allow our pride to make us upwardly mobile people who always seek to be known and respected by others. I have seen many pastors change churches several times in their career, always to a bigger church with a higher salary. I remember the secretary of a Christian leader once telling me of her boss, "He always has to be first." When such arrive in heaven, they will stand before God in shame (2 Tim 2:15). The key to greatness is servanthood (Mark 10:43–45).

This principle of reversal (1:52–53; 6:20–26; 13:30; 18:14) concludes the parable in 14:11: "For all those who exalt themselves will be humbled, and those who humble themselves will be exalted." These are divine passives, and it is God, not people, who will decide between the exalted and the humble. Jesus has in mind the last judgment, when believers as well as unbelievers will stand before God and "give an account" to him (Heb 13:17).

JESUS TELLS THE PARABLE ON
CHOOSING GUESTS (14:12–14)

The previous parable centered on the guests; this one focuses on the host. Yet again it is about social etiquette as a means of teaching a spiritual truth, this time about performing good deeds not for the sake of personal gain or temporary reward but for the sake of God and eternal reward. Jesus' point is that hospitality should not just be shown to friends, family, and neighbors, because they will "invite you back and so you will be repaid." You will have earthly reward, and that will be it. As Jesus said in 6:24, "you have already received your comfort."

Instead, he goes on to say, you should "invite the poor, the crippled, the lame, the blind" (the same four categories as in v. 21) to your banquet. Then "you will be blessed," another divine passive meaning you will receive eternal blessing from God because these poor will never be able to repay you. The message is that reward from God in heaven is vastly superior to being reciprocated from people on earth because it is eternal and never-ending. The marginalized and outcasts would never be invited to banquets hosted by either Jew or Gentile, but they will be featured at the messianic banquet

(14:21). Needless to say, it is much better to be "repaid at the resurrection of the righteous," a Jewish phrase (2 Maccabees 7:9; Luke 20:35) for the return of Christ when the rewards will be given to the just.

JESUS TELLS THE PARABLE OF THE GREAT BANQUET (14:15-24)

Now Jesus turns and centers on the invitation to the banquet itself, so he has in turn moved from the guests (vv. 7-11) to the host (vv. 12-14) and now to the invitation (vv. 15-24). A similar parable appears in Matthew 22:1-14 with quite a few variations. Critical scholars believe these are redactional (editorial) changes introduced by the later church, but I think Jesus gave both these variations at different times in his ministry. This is a very personal parable, for Jesus clearly is the host who is inviting the Jewish people to his messianic banquet, only to have them make all kinds of excuses for turning him down. He will then turn to the Gentiles, who will flock into his banquet hall.

A pious participant among the Pharisees' dinner guests in verse 15 blurts out a typical Jewish hope: "Blessed is the one who will eat at the feast in the kingdom of God." The beatitude has its typical Jewish meaning here: "True bliss is ..." To partake in the messianic banquet was the hope of every Jew (Ps 22:26; Isa 25:6-9). This of course means the Messiah has come, the Romans and all other enemies have been destroyed, God's reign on earth has become a full reality, and the Israelis have taken their rightful place in God's earthly kingdom. The banquet is a symbol of the initiation of that reign.

Jesus seizes the moment in verse 16, taking the opportunity to challenge those assembled about whether they will truly be a part of that banquet. A "great banquet" would only be held by an important, powerful host, and an invitation would be as close to a command performance as one could get. The common practice was to send two invitations, the first one (v. 16) to ascertain the number who accept and are coming, for that determines what kind of meal will be served: a young goat if under twenty, a sheep if in between twenty and forty, and a calf for more than that. They had no refrigeration or storage, so it was important to consume the whole animal at the banquet.

The second invitation (v. 17) occurs as servants are sent out to call those who have accepted to the meal itself. It was expected that refusals would take place at the first invitation, not the second. Common courtesy demanded that guests fulfill their obligation to attend. Only serious emergencies would suffice for rejecting at the second level.

Apparently everyone accepts at the first stage, and at the last minute "all alike," every single person who had said they would come, begins turning the invitation down and making flimsy excuses. It almost sounds like a conspiracy to reject and humiliate the host, but that is never said. The reason they are poor excuses is that each of the guests should have known earlier, and they insult and shame the host in front of the whole community. The three excuses here parallel the three discipleship excuses of 9:57-62 and possibly also the three in Deuteronomy 20:5-7 for refusing to participate in the holy war. The point is that they are not truly valid and are intended to disgrace him.

The first excuse (v. 18) is the purchase of property (a field) and the need to see it before buying it. This is possible but highly unusual because the actual inspection would normally have been before it was bought, not afterward. At the very least, this material concern is more important than the obligation to attend the banquet. It would have been considered a pretty lame excuse, for even if it were true they could put the inspection off for one day.

The second excuse (v. 19) is again a financial purchase, this time of "five yoke of oxen," indicating a large landowner (the average farmer would own a couple of yokes at best), and again it would be a simple thing to test the oxen the next day. This too would have seemed a poor excuse in the first century, a calculated reason not to come. Once more, financial concerns are to them a much greater priority than attending the banquet, and they don't care.

The third excuse (v. 20) seems more concrete, with the person having just gotten married. However, this would certainly have been known before the first invitation was accepted. It was common for such meals to be for men only, and the Torah allowed marriage to excuse a man from war (Deut 20:7). Everyone would assume that the reason was to procreate, and again this would be taken as an extremely flimsy excuse. In fact, men were not to speak of such things publicly, and this would be seen as the most brazen excuse yet. Men would scarcely talk about their wives, and to use them as an excuse like this was contemptible.

All three excuses would have come across as a rude and deliberate attempt to insult their host. The host's forthcoming reaction would have been understandable and appropriate. Jesus is clearly portraying the Jewish reaction to his gospel invitation, with similar studied rejections and insults coming from the leaders and the crowds.

The anger of "the owner of the house [oikodespotēs]" (to stress his authority) in verse 21 is to be expected. Their obvious snubs have put him to shame in front of the entire community. His honor demands quick action, and he takes it. Those he invites are the very ones named in 14:13, the poor who cannot pay you back. There are two groups—those unfortunates in the streets and alleys of the community (v. 21) and then those outside the community (v. 23). So there is a reversal of fortune here, and the "great banquet" will be populated by those who would normally never expect to be invited. The social order of society has been turned on its head. The attempt of the master's enemies to thwart and destroy the banquet has been for naught, and the only actual result is the rejection of those now shown to be unworthy from the great meal. The basic theme from Luke continues—God's concern for the downtrodden and the reversal of roles with the community leaders.

The spiritual symbolism is also clear: those from within the community (v. 21) are those Jewish converts who commit to Christ, and those outside the community (v. 23) are the Gentiles who become followers. The "roads and country lanes" would have been understood as the roads leaving the city for outlying areas and would refer to the universal mission of the book of Acts, the "gospel roads," so to speak, taken by Paul and others to the nations. So this section follows the contours of salvation history, with the gospel reaching out within the Jewish lands to the old covenant people (= Luke and Acts 1-7), and then the gospel moving out to all the nations (= Acts 8-28).

In verse 24 Jesus stops and addresses the people at the meal directly, providing his devastating conclusion to the parable. There are two positive lessons and one negative lesson. The two positive have just been discussed: (1) the concern of God and the church to help the needy and (2) the movement of the gospel and of the makeup of the people of God to the righteous remnant of the Jews and the Gentiles. Behind both of these is the grace and mercy of a loving God who opens up his kingdom to those who don't deserve it. The final, negative message is (3) the rejection of those who were formerly the covenant people and now have become the opponents of Jesus and the gospel.

Jesus states it quite strongly here: "Not one of those who were invited will get a taste of my banquet." There is a certain rabbinic hyperbole behind "not one," for we have already seen that some Pharisees and other Jews did indeed become followers of Christ. This is a kingdom parable, and Jesus is telling these Pharisees and others that unless they commit themselves to him they have no part in God's kingdom reign. There is still hope for a few of them, for he is announcing with this parable that the invitation is going out anew, and all they have to do is accept. Their choice will determine their eternal destiny.

JESUS TEACHES ON THE COST OF DISCIPLESHIP (14:25-35)

Interestingly, Jesus addresses the crowds rather than his disciples with this powerful section on the demands of God on those who

become his followers. Clearly, the primary barrier is still material possessions and the pride that comes with them. The grace of
God in the invitation of the previous parable now leads into the
demands of God here.

RELATIONSHIPS AND ACTIONS (14:25–27)

"Large crowds" are often the setting for teaching (4:42; 6:17; 8:4;
9:37; 12:1). Jesus continues to be as popular as ever, and people are
willing to accompany him almost anywhere to hear him lecture
and observe his miraculous power. In a sense discipleship is here
pictured as a journey of following Jesus. Here that journey is the
road to Jerusalem, and this is Jesus' response as he feels his messianic destiny pressing on him and meditates on its implications
for his followers. Such a destiny demands incredible sacrifice and
a willingness to jettison everything this world has to offer in order
to embrace the path God demands.

Family must be secondary to Christ in true discipleship (14:26).
The parallel in Matthew 10:37 has "anyone who loves their father
or mother more than me," but this is much stronger, with "hate
father and mother, wife and children, brothers and sisters—yes,
even their own life." Of course, we have another example of rabbinic hyperbole, meaning that we love Jesus so much that our natural love for family and even for self is as if it were hate in comparison. In other words, this is strong imagery for a total commitment
to Jesus and a desire to serve him completely. The normal interpretation of this as "love less than" is too weak. We are to be obsessed,
consumed with Jesus. We don't love our family less; we love Jesus
more. A parallel is found in 9:23: "deny themselves and take up
their cross daily." Hatred and denial are sister metaphors for total
surrender to Christ.

So 14:27 belongs with hatred of family and self on the basis of
9:23—"whoever does not carry their cross and follow me cannot
be my disciple." I said earlier that bearing your own cross means
that we become like Jesus on the road to Golgotha, who bore the

crossbeam to his execution site, signifying he was already dead. So this means that we die spiritually to self and the things of this world. In addition, it signifies a willingness to actually die for the name of Christ if need be. The verbs are present tense, meaning it is the continuous, "daily" (9:23) practice of our lives. Christlikeness involves "participation in his sufferings" (Phil 3:10) as we go all the way with Jesus.

PARABLES ON COUNTING THE COST (14:28–33)

There are two parables (vv. 28–30, 31–32) followed by an application (v. 33) that adds a third cost—possessions. In the first parable Jesus uses a construction metaphor on building a tower. This is a watchtower, a type of fortification designed to protect a large building or vineyard (like the tower of Antonia with the temple in Jerusalem). While it could be military, there is no indication of that in the text. It needs a foundation and so is quite large. First, the builder has to figure the expense of construction and decide if he has the resources to finish the project. Otherwise, everyone around would "ridicule" his foolish attempt to take on a project he "wasn't able to finish."

The point is that discipleship involves the same careful assessment of both your resources and your willingness to go all the way with Jesus. God demands a great deal of those who become Christ followers, and they must carefully count the cost and be sure they are willing to make the needed sacrifices to accept these demands. The consequences are stated very well in 2 Timothy 2:15: "Do your best to present yourself to God as one approved, a worker who does not need to be ashamed and who correctly handles the word of truth." When we fail in discipleship, we are not shamed before others but before God, and this will take place at the final judgment, when we stand before him and give account for our lives. This is as serious as it gets.

The second parable (14:31–32) centers on a king about to go to war. No military mind worth its salt would ever go into battle without

first carefully scouting the enemy to ascertain his strength and
how he has arrayed his forces. Every decision made is based on that
assessment. "Consider" (NIV) or "take counsel" refers to the command post where his top aides deliberate whether he has a chance
with just ten thousand men (two legions) against an army of twenty
thousand (four legions). It must be said that the Roman army often
did just that, for their battle array was vastly superior to the rag-
tag Gauls and others. But still, a very careful strategy was essential.

If it is a hopeless situation and the enemy is on the doorstep
prepared for battle, a wise king will have no recourse but to sue
for peace. Better surrender than destruction. Christ is clearly not
intending to picture spiritual warfare and the cosmic battle against
Satan. He is hardly talking about surrender to the powers of darkness. This is entirely about discipleship and surrendering to God.
The point in both parables is counting the cost and following Christ
with your eyes wide open and understanding what you are getting
into. Christ does not want half-hearted disciples.

In the two parables Christ has addressed both family relationships and bearing the cross. Now he addresses a third area of consideration, personal possessions (14:33). This is the negative side
of discipleship—not only commitment to Jesus but also renuncia-
tion of the things of this world. Again, Jesus states it quite strongly:
"those of you who do not give up everything you have cannot be my
disciples." The price of membership in the community of Christ
is everything you possess, a major Lukan theme (3:11–12; 5:11, 28;
8:3; 11:21; 12:15, 21, 33; 16:1–13, 19–31; 19:1–10; Acts 2:44–45; 4:32–34).
The verb "give up" means to "renounce" or "bid farewell" to something formerly precious (9:61: "say goodbye to my family"). This
was acted out in 5:11, 28, when the fishermen and Levi "left everything" to follow Jesus. As I have said frequently, wealth in itself is
not wrong and in fact can be a gift from God (see on 12:21, 33). It is
what you do with it that matters. Matthew the tax collector probably used his to help support the band of disciples.

SAYINGS ON SALT (14:34–35)

Salt was a precious commodity in the ancient world, not nearly as accessible as it is today, and used in a wide variety of areas—to flavor food, to preserve foods, as a fertilizer, and with grain offerings when sacrificing them as firstfruits (Lev 2:13). Yet how could it lose its saltiness? It does not really lose its properties as salt. Several solutions present themselves: Salt from the Dead Sea was often found to be insipid when it was found mixed with a substance called "carnalite" (does this have sermonic potential or what?) or gypsum. Also, unscrupulous sellers would sometimes mix it with fillers that would diminish its taste. At the same time, salt was used in ovens as a catalyst for fuel, and after several times it lost its usefulness and had to be replaced.

Jesus' point is that when disciples allow the world to intrude and diminish their effectiveness for Christ, they have lost their "saltiness," or value to the Lord. Verse 35 uses the image that such salt is "fit neither for the soil" (as a fertilizer) "nor for the manure pile" (as a preservative). The only thing left is to throw it away. How far do we take this image? There are three possibilities: expelled from the congregation, physical death (as in 1 Cor 11:30), or eternal punishment at the last judgment. Jesus does not explain further, and he may mean that God will decide which is appropriate given the circumstances. This is the most extreme form of discipleship failure, but Judas remains the primary example, and in a sense all three took place with him.

Jesus closes with his customary injunction to listen carefully (see 8:8 as well as Matt 11:15; 13:9, 43; Mark 4:23). It means in effect, "If you are willing to listen, you had better do so carefully" and emphasizes the importance of these key truths. We are certainly quite aware of the danger of half-hearted discipleship, for we see it in every church. All too many Christians want to get to heaven and yet live for the things of earth in the meantime. They are perfectly willing to "get in by the skin of their teeth" and wish to sacrifice very little for Christ. We must warn them regularly of the danger of playing games with their eternal destiny.

———

This chapter centers on meal scenes in which Jesus demonstrates serious spiritual and moral truths. At a banquet where the authorities are trying to trap him, he heals a person with abnormal swelling and demonstrates that compassion and mercy have priority over rigid legal rules. Those trying to trap Jesus are silenced by his moral authority (vv. 1-6). He then challenges these leaders with examples drawn from meal scenes, first to live lives of humility rather than pride, to seek the lower rather than the higher place so that you will be lifted up rather than lowered in status before those around you. The principle of reversal predominates, and those who serve will be deemed great in God's kingdom (vv. 7-11). Second, in our service God's people should center on the poor and lowly and receive not a temporary earthly reward that won't last but a heavenly reward that will be theirs for eternity (vv. 12-14).

The parable of the great banquet (vv. 15-24) is systemic in the sense that it describes the results of Jesus' ministry thus far. His words and deeds in Galilee have been an invitation to the Jewish people to come to him, but they have not only refused the invitation but also insulted Jesus and his Father in the process. As a result, God has withdrawn his offer to the nation and invited only the righteous remnant who have responded to his Son and the Gentiles to participate in his messianic banquet in his new kingdom. The Jewish people are now unbelievers and outsiders to the family of God.

The final section (vv. 25-35) centers on counting the cost, that is, understanding what it means to follow Jesus as his disciples. He has absolute priority over family and self, consuming us in our commitment to going all the way with him (vv. 25-27). This is followed by two parables from construction (vv. 28-30) and going to war (vv. 31-32) that together say that we in joining Jesus must be fully aware of what we're getting into and the sacrifices that we will be called to make in order to be successful servants of God. We must be willing to "give up everything" (v. 33) so as to follow him.

The salt sayings that close this section (vv. 34-35) warn us not to allow self and the things of this world to diminish and remove our effectiveness as Christ followers. We are called by God to stand out from the rabble and make a difference in this world for him, and we must work very hard to remain change agents in the church and in the world. We must listen carefully to his word and to the kingdom truths it gives us and remain effective for Christ.

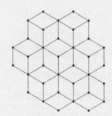

PARABLES ON THE JOY OF
FINDING LOST THINGS
(15:1–32)

J esus turns from negative warnings of judgment to positive
pronouncements of forgiveness and encounters of God's kingdom mercy, in particular the joy of finding the lost and returning them to God. The theme is God's great love and rejoicing over
bringing sinners to himself (5:32; 19:10). Three successive parables
carry this message. The first two center on the search for the lost,
and the third on forgiving the lost. All three present God's wondrous mercy, compassion, and love for the lost and his desire to
bring them to himself. The Pharisees and other leaders ignored
the impious and the secular members among the Jewish people
and spent all their time with people of their own kind, looking
down on Jesus for hobnobbing with the "sinners." Jesus is showing that God cares deeply for these disreputable people, and that
he is justified in putting them at the center.

JESUS TELLS THE PARABLE OF
THE LOST SHEEP (15:1-7)

The "tax collectors and sinners" appear often (3:12; 5:30; 7:34; 18:13).
"Sinners" probably refers not just to the truly wicked but includes
Jews who did not follow the rules of the Torah (ritual cleanliness,

and so on). The Pharisees shunned them as unclean and treated them with contempt. These outcasts were drawn to Jesus because he had time for them and made them welcome. They were a focal point of his ministry and formed those invited to the banquet in 14:21–23. It is they who respond to Jesus' call to hear in 14:35 and have gathered around for that very purpose.

The scribes and Pharisees as usual are upset at this and castigate him: "This man welcomes sinners and eats with them" (compare 5:30; 7:39). They are offended and consider Jesus unclean by virtue of association with such people. Table fellowship with people involves participation in their lives. He was removing boundaries that the Pharisees had spent a couple of centuries building, and so to them he cast aspersion on their entire system of religion. The three parables that follow form Jesus' reply to this rebuke, saying that God himself is behind Jesus' acceptance and time with these people. For us the message is that God loves everyone equally, and we must make everyone, especially those we are uncomfortable around like the homeless and the destitute, feel loved and accepted. The gospel is for them in a very special way.

Jesus chooses a shepherd for the first parable, possibly because they were looked down on as unclean (handling sheep carcasses and hides) by Pharisees, but because of David they became messianic figures. In Ezekiel 34:11–16 Yahweh pictures himself as a shepherd searching for his scattered flock and rescuing them, perfect background for this parable. When Jesus pictures the Pharisees as shepherds ("Suppose one of you has a hundred sheep"), it is a subtle correction of their self-righteous biases. The emphasis is on their total concern for the one that is missing, causing them to "leave the ninety-nine in the open country" in order to search for it. Shepherds would lead their flocks rather than drive them from the rear, and it would be easy for one in the back to stray off. They would count the sheep each night as they bedded down, and they would immediately know that one was missing.

This is a decently sized flock. (Three hundred was considered large.) No mention is made of a guard or assistant watching over the ninety-nine. Perhaps we are meant to assume this to be the case, but probably Jesus deliberately left this part out to emphasize the extraordinary dedication of the shepherd to the lost one.

There would have been no hope for this lost sheep without the careful search of the shepherd, and it is successful. The picture of the shepherd striding back with the sheep over his shoulders is justly famous. The emphasis is not just on searching and finding it but also on the loving effort to restore it to the flock. This is a perfect picture of the work of redemption: God not only seeks the lost but also brings them back to the flock. Christ paid the price to make salvation possible, the Spirit searches for and convicts the sinner, and God forgives them and declares them righteous (justifies them). It is a trinitarian act.

All three parables end with strong rejoicing, and there are two different times of joy. The shepherd rejoices as he brings the lost sheep back into the fold, and his friends and neighbors join in the rejoicing as they celebrate the return. The primary theme of the second half of the story is joy, and it typifies the joy of God and his people over every convert who comes into the church. Some believe the joy of the shepherd is that in finding the lost sheep he has avoided the disgrace he would have had if the sheep were to disappear, but that doesn't fit the story. The joy is entirely due to the return of the sheep to the flock. As we will see stressed twice (15:24, 32) in the parable of the prodigal son, that which was lost has been found.

There is a question as to whether the friends and neighbors are the members of the church or the angels in heaven. Do verses 6 and 7 refer to different groups (the saints and the angels) or one and the same group (the angels in heaven)? I believe the former is more likely. The movement is from God (v. 5) to the community of believers (v. 6) to the angels in heaven (v. 7). All are filled with joy at every person who finds Christ. There is a community celebration (this detail is found in all three parables) at the return of the lost, and then all of heaven participates in that celebration.

So heaven itself joins the people of God in the expression of joy (15:7) and becomes a third joyous group. Note another interesting movement from verses 6 to 7. The saints are the "friends and neighbors" in verse 6 and the "ninety-nine righteous persons who do not need to repent" in verse 7. There is no need to celebrate the latter because they repented long before and have remained faithful to the Lord. This hardly means there is no joy in heaven over the righteous, who continue to walk with the Lord. It is simply part of the story form. The celebration is to welcome new members into the family of God.

JESUS TELLS THE PARABLE OF THE LOST COIN (15:8–10)

This parable has the same message as the first one. A woman has ten silver drachmae or denarii, equivalent to ten days' wages. This may well be a peasant scene and refer to a small dowry. Some think of it as part of a wealthy woman's headdress, but that had as many as fifty coins on it, and it is hard to see why Jesus would single out just ten coins of that. More likely this was all the savings she could muster. She lives in the normal peasant one-room house with hard-packed dirt floors that have to be swept to see where the missing coin has fallen. She must have discovered the loss at night, for she also needs to light a lamp in order to see what the sweeping uncovers.

The emphasis is on the great effort she expends to find the single lost coin. Her joy in finding it is just as great as the shepherd's in verses 5–6. She too calls her "friends and neighbors" to a celebration in honor of finding the lost coin. This is certainly hyperbolic, but the parallels with the previous story are fully intentional. This is shown in verse 10, where "the angels of God" are overjoyed with every repentant sinner. Angels gather the harvest for the final judgment (Matt 13:41, 49) and form the heavenly court at that final event (Ps 89:7; Rev 4:4; 11:16), so this is a natural picture.

JESUS TELLS THE PARABLE OF
THE LOST SON (15:11–32)

One of the best known of the parables, this passage presents the gospel in embryo, as it is all about repentance and forgiveness. All the details of the story are not meant to be given allegorical meaning, and most are simply part of the story. It is generally agreed there are three main aspects that should be given meaning—the father, who is a forgiving God; the younger son, who represents the repentant sinner; and the older brother, who represents the mercy-less leadership of Israel. The main theme is the contrast between the boundless mercy of God and the repressive refusal of the Pharisees and others to accept sinners. The main thrust is the father's waiting and willingness to forgive in order to reconcile with his lost son; the subthemes are the repentance and return of the younger son, the joy of the community at that return, and the unwillingness of the older brother to welcome his prodigal brother back into the family.

SETTING: THE GREEDY SON (15:11–12)

The key figure is the father, who relates to each of his two sons in turn. The younger son repents and accepts his forgiveness and reinstatement to the family, but the older son refuses the father's offer to reconcile with his brother. So the parable starts with the younger brother leaving the family and ends with the older brother leaving the family.

The story begins, however, with the issue of inheritance. The younger son, probably about eighteen years old, the age young men normally got married and entered their occupations, decides that he wants to strike out on his own. According to the Torah, the older son should receive two-thirds of the estate, and the younger son one-third (Deut 21:15–17) in order to preserve the financial standing of the family in the community. However, they were not to get it until the father died, and the patriarch was to have the use of his estate as long as he lived.

So when the younger suddenly demanded, "Father, give me my share of the estate" and forced him to divide his property right then, he was depriving his father of his standard of living. Even worse, he was bringing shame on his father before the whole community. The brash young man was telling all around that to him his father was as good as dead, and he no longer cared about him. In fact, he was destroying his family's social status in the community, for he was taking away a third of its wealth. As in a similar demand in 12:13-15, this showed the greed that consumed this young man, and both Jewish and Roman readers would have been aghast at the insult this meant to the rest of the family.

The father is a complete contrast to both the sons in his gracious decision to grant the request. The term used for the "property" he distributed to his sons is *bios*, "life." He was giving away his very life, and in the story he becomes virtually destitute, with everything he would have "lived" on given away to his sons.

THE SON'S PROFLIGATE LIFE (15:13-16)

The life of sin that ensues proves how greedy and dissolute the kid really is. After virtually stealing his father's living from him, he proceeds to waste it all on immoral living. Every step he takes moves downward deeper and deeper into a wasted life. When he "got together all he had," it means he sold off the property that had given his family status for generations and converted it all to cash. He then takes it to "a distant country," the first-century equivalent of Las Vegas, and "squandered his wealth in wild living" (v. 30 adds, "with prostitutes"). In one fell swoop it is all gone, with nothing to show for it but a hangover and bankruptcy. He throws it all away in a matter of days.

He has not yet hit rock bottom. There are three stages left to his downward spiral. First, a "severe famine" strikes "that whole country" (15:14), and he is caught with no resources to fall back on. He has no home or family, no finances, and no one to care what happens to him. His destitution is now total.

The second stage takes place when he is forced to take employment with a pig farmer (15:15), so he is doubly unclean, his life under the control of a Gentile and then mucking around with pigs, as unclean an animal as you can get. There is strong language here, saying he "hired himself out," literally "associate with" or "join himself to" the Gentile pig farmer. There could not be a more disreputable job for a Jew, but he has no choice.

There is one final step downward (15:16), for he is starving and willing to eat (*epethymei*, connoting an intense desire) the food he gives to the pigs, possibly a carob pod, the fruit of a Palestinian tree used for animal fodder and consumed only by the very poor. However, the Gentile farmer is unwilling to allow him to do so, undoubtedly saying to himself that the pigs were worth far more to him than this Jewish kid. So his descent into the abyss is now complete; he is worth less than the pigs, shamed and starving.

REPENTANCE AND RETURN (15:17–20A)

After weeks of sinful slumber, he finally wakes up and comes to his senses. He realizes he is starving and will soon die if he stays there. There is some debate as to whether this constitutes repentance or he is simply waking up to his serious dilemma. His actions might simply indicate he doesn't want to do it but has no other options. However, I agree with those who see repentance in this. There is a later tradition that stated, "When Israel is forced to eat carob pods, then they will repent" (Leviticus Rabbah 35.6), and the young man's reactions are all about repenting, such as realizing his dilemma, returning to his father, and confessing to him that he had "sinned against heaven and against you."

His actions in verses 18–19 are all about reconciliation. Jesus actually says this twice for emphasis, when the son states his intentions (vv. 18–19) and again when he actually meets his father

(v. 21). So this is a key part of the story. The details picture a repentant sinner—getting up, returning to his father (see Isa 55:7; Jer 3:12), and confessing his sins. It is implied that he is asking for forgiveness. He admits he has sinned not only against his father but also against "heaven," or God himself. He needs forgiveness from both. However, he is "no longer worthy" (15:19), an essential aspect of the gospel to depict God's unmerited grace in forgiving sin. Every detail of the prodigal son's actions describes the process of repentance and forgiveness, so essential in Luke-Acts. This parable could be considered a paradigmatic narration for the process of the church's mission in Luke's writings.

The son knows he deserves nothing after the way he disgraced his father, but he also knows how gracious and forgiving his father is. He cannot expect to be received back as a son, but his father is too merciful to let him starve, and so he intends to ask to be allowed to be a "hired servant," at the bottom of the social scale but no longer starving. Note he is not trying to excuse his scandalous behavior or ask for reinstatement. He has committed too egregious an act to hope for that. He is just throwing himself on the mercy of his gracious father, soon to be his employer (he hopes).

THE FATHER'S LOVING RESPONSE (15:20B-24)

His father, though humiliated by his son, has apparently been waiting and hoping for the young man to return. No more beautiful picture of a father's love could be imagined. The father's reaction would be shocking to all Near Eastern people. Deuteronomy 21:18-21 states that the parents of a rebellious, disobedient son who is a glutton and a drunkard have the right to have him stoned so as to purge the evil from the community. This son had done all that and more. This punishment rarely happened, but it would have been expected for the father to have written him off. Instead, his father has obviously been watching for him all along.

Throwing off all dignity (patriarchs did not hike up their robes and run), he rushed to his son while he was "still a long way off"

and compassionately "threw his arms around him and kissed him."
The intense longing is even greater here than for the lost sheep
and lost coin. Embracing and kissing are Near Eastern signs of
reconciliation with forgiveness a natural extension (2 Sam 14:33).

The son fulfills his intention and confesses that he has "sinned
against heaven and against you" (15:21). Every first-century reader
would have expected the father to concur and reject the wayward
child, but he does just the opposite. He interrupts before the boy
has a chance to say, "make me like one of your hired servants"
(v. 19) and reinstates his son. His grace takes over, and he will have
none of his son earning the right to be forgiven.

In fact, he makes full restitution, ordering four things the son
would never have received before he had run away (15:22–23). Two
come from the household servants, and two from the farm workers. Each is a symbol of status and authority. "The best robe" is
not the robe the son would have originally worn but a finer one,
some think the robe the father himself would wear. At the least it
would signify restitution and perhaps a return of authority. The
ring would mean his sonship is returned to him, and many think
it would have contained the family seal (see Gen 41:42; Esth 6:6–11).
The sandals mean a return of his former wealth. He had returned
with nothing (in effect barefoot) and now is once more a valued
member of the family.

This also called for a celebratory banquet to welcome the son
back into the family (15:23). As was said at 14:16, calves were used
for large banquets of forty or more, and so this was to be a lavish
affair. A "fattened calf" was fed a special diet and kept ready for
just such a splendid occasion. Probably the entire village is being
invited to attend, and the reconciliation is extended to the whole
community. It was to be a momentous event. This son who had
been forced to eat the most menial diet of carob pods is now being
treated to the best banquet imaginable.

The reason is given in verse 24: "This son of mine was dead
and is alive again; he was lost and is found." Once more we have

language of the gospel reality. This "sinner" was a lost soul and through repentance and the father's forgiveness has found true life. The key phrase, "this son of mine," states the full restitution of sonship (compare Rom 8:14–17). The sinner was spiritually dead and lost in his sins but is now "found" and has been raised to new life.

THE OLDER BROTHER'S JEALOUSY (15:25–32)

Now we come to the remaining theme: the older brother, who symbolizes the Pharisees and other Jewish leaders in his antipathy toward his repentant younger brother. He has not been present until now because he was out in the field caring for the animals and so was unaware his brother had returned. As he drew near the house, he "heard music and dancing" and was naturally curious, for his father had earlier been subdued and still filled with sadness, watching for his estranged son to return home. The celebration would naturally puzzle this sibling.

Asking a household slave what was going on, he learned the (to him) shocking news that "your brother has come … and your father has killed the fattened calf because he has him back safe and sound" (15:27). He had thought he was free of his brother and had the rest of the estate all to himself. This worthless younger rebel had received his just deserts and was out of the picture. Yet the calf has been on the spit and is probably close to finished in preparation for the celebration. The older sibling's suspicious behavior tells us something is wrong. Brothers would normally run in the house excited, eager to join in the joyous occasion. The slave is speaking from the father's perspective, overjoyed at the reconciliation, and the sibling's negative response is very troubling.

His anger in verse 28 is difficult to understand at first, for one would think he would be just as happy as his father at having his brother back. But he is like the two brothers squabbling over their inheritance rights in 12:13–15, filled with avarice and thinking only of himself. Some think his anger justified because the kid had insulted the whole family and set them back financially, but in Jesus' story it is clearly the result of jealousy rather than righteous indignation. This older brother refuses to go in the house. This is a perfect depiction of the Pharisees in terms of their rejection of "sinners."

The result is that his father comes out to him and pleads for understanding. The response of the older brother would have been seen by first-century listeners as just as disrespectful as the younger brother had been. It omits the respectful address a son should make to his father in direct contrast to the younger man in verses 12, 18, 21. There is a self-centered attitude filled with complaints rather than compliance.

There is a complete reversal of status; the younger brother is now the insider and the older brother the outsider. By going outside and pleading with him, the father surrenders his dignity and authority and lowers himself out of love for his angry son. Unlike the younger man, he spurns his father's compassion and spits out a barrage of complaints over the injustice of it all. While his hedonistic brother was living the high life, he had been "slaving for you and never disobeyed your orders." This is ironic because he is presently being highly disobedient and disrespectful to his father. In this he is the perfect symbol of the hypocritical Pharisees, who gave the appearance of obedience but were just the opposite in reality (11:37–54).

He also has strong complaints about what he perceives as his father's favoritism to the younger man (15:29b–30). His father had never given him even a small banquet with a limited number of guests (a "young goat" or kid would be for a group of ten to fifteen people), while he was now hosting a huge celebration in honor of his formerly rebellious brother (a "fattened calf" would be for a huge meal of thirty-five to forty guests). So even though the one had squandered his inheritance on "prostitutes" and wild living (v. 13), the father welcomes him back with a celebration normally provided only for a marriage, while he had never done anything for the dutiful older brother.

It is clear this son has begrudged his relationship with his father for some time. Such hostility is not the result merely of his brother's return; rather, it is the last straw of a bitterness that has been a long time coming. He has felt used and unappreciated by his father for years, and it is now coming out. In a very real sense, the older brother is doing what the younger one did earlier, cutting himself off from his father and brother, rejecting them both. He refuses to accept either his brother's repentance or his father's compassion. Again, he is a perfect symbol of the Pharisees in their refusal to accept sinners.

The father shows the same compassion and mercy to the older brother as he had given to the younger. He corrects his false understanding of his father's attitude toward him in verse 31 and then regarding his brother in verse 32. He begins with a great deal more affection than his older son had shown when he calls him "child" (*teknon*, NIV: "my son"), acknowledging how dear he is to him. He is completely aware of his faithful service and wants him to know how much he appreciates it ("you are always with me"). He then assures him that the inheritance is indeed his and he will receive it ("everything I have is yours"). The return of the prodigal will not diminish what is legally and morally the elder brother's, and he needn't worry and shouldn't complain. There is no favoritism.

However, he is wrong about his brother. The Greek behind the NIV's "we had to" should be translated more strongly: "it is an absolute necessity [*edei*] that we celebrate and be glad." The community banquet is not an option; it must take place, and everyone in the region should share in the joy of reconciliation. The reason repeats the language of verse 24—the dead have arisen, and the lost have been found. Resurrection has taken place, and joy must be shown. We are at the true "moral of the story"—the joy of new life and of resurrection from the dead. This is the conclusion of all three parables.

———

This chapter centers on God's loving concern for the lost. These three completely synonymous parables show how deeply God cares and how thoroughly we must join him in reaching out and seeking to bring the lost to him. The progression of each details the process by which the gospel reaches out to sinners, and tells both how it rescues them and the resultant celebration that must take place on earth and in heaven whenever a person comes to Christ.

Let us trace the process by which this takes place according to these parables. God is always aware of every sinner and vigilant over humanity. The God who counts every hair on a person's head (12:7) also counts every person he has created and is watching over them. He knows every single sinner and loves each one. Therefore he is at all times mounting a rescue operation, using his Spirit to convict each one and draw them to himself (John 16:8–11), and using the church to reach out to them with the gospel.

When one of his sheep is "found," a double celebration takes place. They are returned to God's flock through repentance, conversion, and forgiveness of sins, and both all of heaven and the church on earth are filled with joy and celebrate the return of one of those created in God's image to him.

Each parable traces this picture. The shepherd (vv. 1–7) leaves the ninety-nine as an intact flock (= the church) in order to focus on searching for and finding the one that had wandered away. When he finds that hopeless sheep, he carries it back in joy and rejoices with the entire village for its return. The woman (vv. 8–10) who lost one of the silver coins of her dowry does the same, sweeping every inch of her dirt floor until she finds the missing coin and deeply rejoices at its return.

The parable of the lost son (vv. 11–32) dominates the chapter and provides by far the greatest detail on the conversion of the lost. The early part (vv. 13–16) provides an incredible picture of the descent into total depravity, with the foolish young man sinking deeper and deeper into the abyss as he takes one-third of his father's estate, converts it into cash, and quickly throws it all away on a hedonistic lifestyle. He becomes not only destitute but also doubly unclean, working under a Gentile and caring for pigs. When he ends up starving and begging to be allowed to eat pig food, he reaches rock bottom, considered more worthless than pigs. In a step necessary for all sinners, he realizes his unworthiness and throws himself on the mercy of his father.

The single primary theme comes next, the unmerited grace and mercy of the father, whose boundless love and compassion lead him to not only forgive but also to reinstate the unworthy son as a valued member of his family (vv. 17-22). Each step—the hugging and kissing, the bestowal of the robe, the ring, and the sandals—would have been shocking to ancient listeners but typifies our loving and forgiving heavenly Father. The celebratory banquet (vv. 23-24) includes the entire village in the joyous response.

The final aspect is the picture of the unforgiving older brother (vv. 25-32), who castigates the father and insults him anew, rendering this mercy-less brother as much of an outsider as the younger sibling had been. All the despicable actions of the younger toward his father are repeated now by the elder sibling, rejecting and insulting his father in the name of his own selfish pride. He shows he cares nothing for his father in actuality and is concerned solely for his inheritance. Yet in contrast the father still loves him (vv. 31-32) and wants his family to be whole and intact. However, this is not to be, for this jealous brother has placed himself outside the family.

SAYINGS ON WEALTH
AND POSSESSIONS

(16:1–31)

J esus continues to prepare his disciples to take over his mission to the world. He has shown them what sacrifices are necessary and how they need to center on the poor and the marginalized in their ministry, and now he addresses what part possessions
should play in their lives. The two parables of this chapter center
on a wise use of wealth for the kingdom rather than for self, and
in between them a rebuke of the Pharisees for their love of money.
The issue of wealth dominates, as seen in the intro to each unit:
"there was a rich man" (v. 1); "the Pharisees, who loved money"
(v. 14); "there was a rich man" (v. 19). Jesus is both warning his
followers of the dangers of wealth and encouraging them to use
whatever wealth they may accrue wisely. As Paul so carefully says,
money is not evil in itself but can easily become "a root of all kinds
of evil" (1 Tim 6:10).

JESUS TELLS THE PARABLE OF THE
SHREWD MANAGER (16:1-13)

This is probably the most confusing of all Jesus' parables and certainly is the one that has generated the most divergent theories
as to what it means. Three issues will help greatly.

1. There is a question as to whether this is primarily a business setting centering on interest accrued on a loan (the laws of usury), or whether it is an agricultural setting centering on crops paid by tenant farmers to an owner. The latter is a far more plausible scenario for Galilee, an agricultural province, and more in keeping with Jesus' usual parables, so often set in farming situations. Moreover, the fact that the payments are in farm goods (16:5-7) is evidence for an agriculture setting.

2. Is the dishonesty stated in verse 8 referring to the entire story, so that he was fired for dishonest actions in verses 1-2, or is it restricted to verses 5-7? As I will be saying, the latter is more likely. The opening centers on incompetence rather than dishonesty.

3. Does the story end at the end of verse 7 (1-7, 8-9, 10-13), at verse 8a (1-8a, 8b-9, 10-13), or at verse 9 (1-9, 10-13)? The tone of verses 8b-9 fits the conclusion that it is Jesus' explanation of the parable and makes the second option the best of the three.

THE PARABLE PROPER (16:1-8A)

This particular "rich man" is one of the many absentee landlords who owned huge tracts of land in Galilee and broke them into tenant farms of fifty to a hundred acres. The farmer kept half the produce, and the other half belonged to the landlord. This steward or manager was in charge of collecting and investing the profits for the wealthy owner. We don't know who the accuser was, but apparently he was entirely correct. "Wasting his possessions" was not dishonesty but incompetence. It is the same term (*diaskorpizō*) as in 15:13, when the prodigal son "squandered his wealth." It probably means he invested the profits very poorly and lost his master huge amounts of money.

So his master calls him to account and gives him the ultimatum. He now needs to get the books in order and "give an account of your management, because you cannot be manager any longer." He is fired. All that was left was giving an inventory of the financial situation for his successor. The manager can make no reply, for he is clearly guilty of all charges.

At the outset, we see the manager's mind as he wrestles with what to do to extricate himself from this desperate plight. He acknowledges that he is out of a job and doesn't know what to do. No job opportunities are available, and like all middle-level managers, there are two things he will not do. He is too weak to work as a common laborer ("not strong enough to dig") and too proud to become a lowly beggar ("ashamed to beg"). He is committed to only one thing—finding a job that allows him to maintain his status in society. He would like a parallel move to the same kind of job. The question is how to accomplish that given the situation.

Eureka! It finally hits him. He realizes what he has to do so that "when I lose my job here, people will welcome me into their houses" (16:4). He still controls the books, and all he has to do is make a couple of subtle changes to make himself look good to prospective bosses (possibly the debtors themselves). This is where the dishonesty takes place. On the surface, "welcome ... into their homes" makes him seem like a freeloader who just wants somewhere nice to live with no responsibilities. But that is not what the context implies. With the job came a place to live, and his main desire is for employment, which will automatically include a home. The wording Jesus uses here undoubtedly comes from the standpoint of verse 9 and the goal of being "welcomed into eternal dwellings" in heaven. He is willing to commit fraud to ensure a temporary home on earth, while we should seek eternal homes in heaven.

His plan involves cooking the books for the debtors one by one and significantly changing the amounts they owe. They will then be indebted to him for saving them so much money, and one of them may give him the job he craves. This is where one of the major debates occurs. Traditionally, it has been thought that he lowered the amount of their debts. Some believe his purpose was to make the master look generous so that the man would allow the change, but more likely he just hoped his act of fraud would not be noticed.

Others surmise that he did not change the bill but removed the interest (or perhaps his own commission). Since the Torah prohibited charging interest (the laws of usury, Deut 23:19), this would have made the master look pious to others. But the problem is that there is no hint of this in the story itself, and in addition no owner would prefer piety over profit. Interest was accepted back then, and it is far better to see here an act of dishonesty. The traditional view is best—he juggled the books.

The first creditor owed a hundred measures (about 875 gallons) of olive oil, and the second owed a hundred measures (about 1,100 bushels) of wheat. The olive oil's amount was cut in half, while only 20 percent was removed from the wheat, probably because olive oil could easily be watered down. It has been estimated that the amount saved for each of them was close to 500 denarii, or about sixteen months' wages. It has also been thought it would take about 150 trees and a couple hundred acres of land to produce that much, so these were large tenant farms and fairly wealthy tenant farmers. They were saved a small fortune and would have owed a great deal of gratitude to the manager.

Note also that he had the debtors change their own bills and so made them complicit in the fraud. He probably believed that in so doing they would have to pay him back in kind and give him a job.

In verse 8 we see the strangest conclusion of any of Jesus' parables. The owner certainly discovers the fraud, but instead of having the crooked manager arrested and thrown in jail, which is what would happen in any normal society, he praises the man "because he had acted shrewdly." I must have meditated on the meaning of this for a couple of decades before figuring it out to my satisfaction. The key is that the master (*kyrios*) is neither God nor Jesus, as some have supposed. This is a parable about the secular world and the way it operates. The phrase "dishonest manager" in the NIV literally means "unrighteous steward" in the Greek, meaning he is the perfect representative of this unrighteous world in his actions. This is a parable about worldliness.

No owner in all of history has ever commended a man who has defrauded him of a small fortune. Many point out that he praises the shrewdness, not the act of dishonesty, but they are one and the same act. You cannot separate them so easily. This is the supreme example of the reversal of expectation. It is the very shock of this that is Jesus' point. He is describing the illogical ways of the secular world. It is like the "golden rule" of Wall Street, "Do unto others *before* they can do unto you." In other words, get ahead at any cost. This is a parable about worldly shrewdness and the absolute dichotomy between the financial ways of the world and that of the kingdom people. The manager did find the solution and was able to solve his dilemma, but he did so at the cost of his moral values. The flip side, the way to get ahead with God, is the subject of 16:8b–9.

FIRST APPLICATION: GIVE IT AWAY (16:8B–9)

God's people are the polar opposite of the world. People get ahead in the world by taking everything they can for themselves. The saints get ahead with God by using what they have to help others. Christ followers repudiate the manipulative techniques of the world and so are the opposite of both the manager and the owner. Jesus is interpreting his own parable and applying it to his listeners. The key is the great contrast between "the people of this world" and "the people of the light," namely, the secular person and the Christian. There is a lesson to be learned: the shrewd act of the manager showed that he as an "unrighteous" agent of this world knew how to use his resources for his advantage. He and other worldly people are "more shrewd" than believers who belong to "the light" of God. They know how to get ahead in this world ("dealing with their own kind"), while believers don't know how to get ahead with God, namely, how to use their resources wisely.

In verse 9 Jesus proceeds to answer the dilemma and tell his followers how to be "shrewd" with their "worldly wealth." It is exactly opposite from what the manager did. He stole his master's resources for his own needs, but he did it to "gain friends" (the debtors) and get a job that would provide an earthly, temporary home for himself. Most likely it didn't last long. The one thing that didn't change was his incompetence, so it is doubtful that his new job lasted much longer than his first one had. Jesus is telling his followers that they too need to use their worldly wealth to "gain friends for yourselves," but in this case it could actually be seen as an idiom for almsgiving. We are shrewd when we use our resources to help others and to benefit the kingdom. As in 6:20–26; 12:13–21, 33–34, possessions should be seen as a divinely bestowed treasure to be used to benefit others more than self. This is the primary difference between followers of Christ and the shrewd manager.

Jesus here turns to the **eschatological** reality in which the saints use this life to prepare for the next. He concludes (in the Greek) with "they will welcome you into eternal dwellings." Most see the third plural "they" as passive in thrust, "you will be," a reference to God welcoming us to heaven. This could well be, but I prefer to keep the "they," with it meaning that the people we have helped will be in heaven to welcome us there. They will be our heavenly reward, all the good we have done with our resources. Everything we spend helping others is immediately banked in heaven waiting for us to arrive to collect the rewards we have earned. The manager had only temporary rewards and a temporary home, but ours is eternal.

Second Application: Faithful with Earthly Resources (16:10–13)

Jesus now uses a series of contrasts between the unfaithfulness of the manager and the trustworthiness expected of his disciples. The first is at the heart of stewardship—if we can be trusted in the small things of life (money), we can be trusted with the great things (kingdom resources). The manager showed this with respect to his "shrewd" use of dishonesty, but God wants to know if similar prudence will be exercised in us as well. God wants faithful stewards, and that means an absence of self-centered behavior.

Turning to specifics, good stewardship means trustworthiness in handling "worldly wealth" (16:11). This is what the parable was all about. The "little" would be day-to-day use of our physical resources, and the "true riches" would be the kingdom resources God has made available to us. If we are unfaithful with the earthly possessions he has given us, he can never trust us with kingdom riches. The point is that God has made us stewards in the arena of our earthly lives and ministries, and if we cannot handle that, then we will also misuse heavenly treasures. Many think the future tense here refers especially to the age to come, referring to an absence of heavenly reward for those who fail to use their resources for his glory.

In this light our earthly possessions are called "someone else's property," namely, God's (16:12). All we have actually belongs to him, and he has placed it under our care to manage. This would include spiritual realities, for it more literally reads "what belongs to another," broadening the field from material possessions to everything we have from God. These three verses look at this life as a proving ground for heaven. God is seeing where our priorities are and with what he can trust us. Our wealth, our possessions, and our ministry to others and the church must demonstrate faithful stewardship, and that will determine what is ours in heaven. These verses actually provide important material for a biblical doctrine of rewards.

The conclusion summarizes the issue (16:13). The question is who we will serve with allegiance and commitment. We must make a conscious choice, for "no one can serve two masters." It was not impossible for a Roman slave to have two owners, but if that extremely rare event ever happened, the slave could not be equally divided between them. The slave in the final analysis would have to "hate the one and love the other" or "be devoted to the one and despise the other."

Jesus here assumes the two masters are at opposite ends and opposed to one another. The one you reject of necessity will receive your contempt. This is especially true of the two masters here: "you cannot serve both God and money" (Greek: "mammon"). By its very nature money is an enslaving force, and let us all be honest. Every one of us is a materialist and to an extent enslaved by our possessions (Rom 6:19-22; 1 Tim 6:9-10, 17). We should realize that our money too easily becomes a demonic power trying to possess us and gain total control over us. God demands we switch our loyalty entirely over to him.

JESUS TEACHES ON WEALTH
AND THE LAW (16:14-18)

This brief interlude between the two parables provides a transition. The key is found in verse 15: We must carefully make ourselves aware of what we truly value the most in life, God or the things of this world. Our actions will always be the result of these choices. At the outset (vv. 14-15) the focus is on the Pharisees' greed and how it led to them to start "sneering at Jesus" in contempt. They were the perfect example of 16:13, as their devotion to money made them despise Jesus and the true things of God. Some have said the Sadducees were more known for their avarice, but studies show the Pharisees were also widely known for it (see 11:39; 20:46-47; Matt 23:25; Mark 12:40). Their open scorn for Jesus (15:2) intensified their opposition.

Jesus responds in 16:15 and once more hammers them for their hypocrisy: "You ... justify yourselves in the eyes of others, but God knows your hearts" (see 7:29; 11:37-54; 18:9-12; 20:20). The proof of this was also obvious—"what people value highly is detestable in God's sight," and greed at the top of the list. No one can escape the all-seeing eye of God (1 Sam 16:7; 1 Kgs 8:39; Ps 7:10).

The Pharisees may claim that mammon did not control them, but God knew where their values truly lay. Their pride and greed were an abomination ("detestable," Deut 7:25–26; Isa 1:13; 44:19) to God. Their hypocrisy was internal as well as external, allowing them even to fool themselves.

He now turns to a salvation-historical discussion of the place of the law in light of the arrival of God's kingdom in his ministry. He makes two points. First, the God-appointed time when the law functioned was "until John" came as the messianic forerunner to introduce the messianic age. While some think the Baptist was part of the old economy, this is saying he was the instigator of the new-covenant age and belonged to it. In a very real sense he belonged to both covenants, bringing the old to a close and introducing the new. Still, as the first preacher of the gospel (3:18; 7:27) and the one who prepared for the Messiah, he belonged more to the new era of salvation history. With the Baptist, the transition to the new era took place, and it is typified by carrying on his proclamation of the "good news of the kingdom."

The second issue is the meaning of the last line, specifying the results of preaching the good news of God's kingdom—"everyone is forcing their way into it." The verb is *biazetai*, meaning to "forcibly enter" a thing. The question is whether it is passive or middle in force. If passive, it means people are "urged/forced to enter it" by the gospel proclamation. If middle, everyone tries to "force" their way into it. Both are viable readings, and the question is whether Jesus is making a positive (the success of the gospel preaching) or negative (the battle against the gospel) statement. The parallel in Matthew 11:12–13 favors the negative thrust, centering on the opposition to the gospel from the powers of darkness and the opponents of Jesus. However, Luke seems to stress the positive side, focusing on the forceful decision the gospel preaching demands. As the disciples carry on this proclamation, Jesus is assuring them that their mission will be successful, and people will respond to the urgent demands of the gospel.

While the new age has come and its gospel message is going
forth, this does not mean the Torah or law has ceased to have any
place or relevance (16:17). The law still remains. It has eternal relevance and will never go away, so "it is easier for heaven and earth
to disappear than for the least stroke of a pen to drop out of the
Law." In fact, that is exactly what will happen, for at the end of history this world will disappear in fire (2 Pet 3:7, 10) and be replaced
by "a new heaven and a new earth" (2 Pet 3:13; Rev 21:1), while the
law and the gospel will be part of eternity.

The "least stroke of a pen" refers to the smallest strokes of the
Hebrew alphabet, called the "jot and tittle" in Matthew 5:18 KJV,
referring to the letter ' (yod) and the dot above the letter ש (shin),
which turns it from an s to an sh sound. The smallest part of the
law will remain intact for eternity. The question is how the law
can only be in force until John and yet last for eternity. There are
five options: (1) It refers to the moral rather than the ceremonial
law, but there is no hint of this in the text; (2) the law is indeed
meant to be eternally valid, but this goes against Matthew 5:17–20;
(3) it is not the Mosaic law that is still valid but the law as principle—this moves somewhat in the right direction but needs more
(namely in the next two), for the Mosaic law is definitely a part of
this; (4) it is the law as fulfilled in Jesus that has continuing validity; (5) the law as reinterpreted by Jesus becomes the "Torah of the
Messiah" (as in the Sermon on the Mount) and has eternal force.
These latter two capture the essence of Jesus' teaching here. Jesus'
kingdom preaching is the truly abiding aspect of Torah, for he has
brought the messianic Torah into this world.

In one sense, Jesus adds this saying on divorce (16:18) as an
illustration of the continuing validity of the law. In another it
goes beyond it and exemplifies the new kingdom relationships,
transcending Jewish expectations. The Torah was explicit in
Deuteronomy 24:1, with a certificate of divorce written only for
"something indecent," and the rabbinic school of Shammai interpreted it only of adultery. The more influential school of Hillel,

however, turned it into a "no fault" clause, namely, of anything that displeased a husband.

Jesus here allows no ground at all, saying, "Anyone who divorces his wife and marries another woman commits adultery," and then extends it by adding, "and the man who marries a divorced woman commits adultery." Jesus is saying that marriage is a covenant of both husband and wife not only with each other but also with God, and to break that covenant for any reason at all constitutes adultery in the eyes of God. He states it both ways for emphasis: both the one who divorces and remarries and the one who marries that person commit adultery. He does not mention any exceptions, stating only the basic principle. Elsewhere two exceptions are found—divorce caused by adultery (Matt 5:32; 19:9) and divorce initiated by an unbeliever (1 Cor 7:12–16). His emphasis here is that the continuing validity of the law is reflected in his teaching on divorce and remarriage. He is building on the principles of Torah in developing the new ethics of the kingdom.

JESUS TELLS THE PARABLE OF THE RICH MAN AND LAZARUS (16:19–31)

Some have thought that this is a historical story rather than a parable, but it has all the earmarks of the latter, including the introductory "there was a rich man who ..." (also in 16:1). In keeping with the tone of the rest of this chapter, it develops further the connection of mammon to salvation. The allegorical elements are pretty clear: the rich man typifies the Pharisees with their love of money, and the poverty-stricken Lazarus symbolizes the downtrodden sinners who are neglected and looked down on by the Pharisees. The theme of reversal, seen so often (1:50–53; 6:20–26; 16:13–15), continues here. The wealthy man who has everything in this life has nothing in the next, and Lazarus, the poorest beggar imaginable, has the most extravagant funeral in the Bible. The call is for a wise use of resources now, building on the parable of 16:1–13.

THE SOCIAL SETTING (16:19–21)

The rich man is described lavishly, with "purple and fine linen" and living in luxury. These kinds of garments were worn by royalty and the very rich. The "purple" was a very expensive wool mantle dyed in Phoenician purple derived from hundreds of small snails, and the "linen" was fancy undergarments. The description would have reminded first-century readers of the lives of the Herods or the Caesars. "Lived in luxury" is actually "ate sumptuously" and refers to the incredible banquets and eating habits of the super-rich.

In contrast, on a pallet at the gate of this ultra-rich snob was an undoubtedly crippled (lying there) beggar who was also covered with the type of sores that would brand him an unclean leper[1] at that time. The name Lazarus means "one whom God helps." The rich man needs no help, but Lazarus must depend completely on God. This is the central point of the whole story. No other character in any parable is ever named, so this is extremely significant. Names show a person's significance, and this multimillionaire has no individual significance (unnamed), while Lazarus is the one with true worth.

Covered from head to foot with ulcerous sores, he longs for the crumbs that "fell from the rich man's table" (16:21). Some think the "crumbs" were pieces of bread the wealthy used to wipe their hands and table of grease from the meal and then threw to the dogs. The dogs were filled, and the beggar received nothing. Likely this means he didn't receive any and was virtually starving. As the super-rich guy was eating the most expensive food money could buy, just outside his gate poor Lazarus was dying of starvation. The rich man did nothing whatsoever for Lazarus, and these very dogs (unclean wild animals, not pets) then "came and licked his sores." He suffered one degradation after another. The disparity

---

1. The fact that dogs licked the sores (16:21) shows that they were oozing fluid, which indicated leprosy.

is as great as it can get, from the wealthiest man to the poorest beggar in all of Palestine.

DEATH AND AFTERLIFE (16:22–23)

Time passed and both died, probably Lazarus fairly soon due to his deplorable situation. But here the scene experiences an incredible reversal. Most likely he was just thrown into a common grave for such beggars, but the reaction of heaven is remarkable. Enoch was translated to heaven, and Elijah ascended in a fiery chariot. Lazarus now joins them as "angels carried him to Abraham's side," as great an honor as any of the others. This recalls Jude 9, where Michael fights with Satan for the body of Moses. So the most despised of human beings on earth becomes one of the most majestic figures in heaven. The Jews believed that Abraham, as the father of the nation, would welcome his family (down through the generations) into heaven, as seen in the Hebrew phrase "gathered to your fathers" (NIV: "go to your ancestors," Gen 15:15; Deut 31:16). This unfortunate man, who had no one during his earthly life, has a massive family welcoming him into heaven.

In total contrast, the rich man died and just had a human burial—no big deal! Certainly he would have had a lavish earthly ceremony and been placed in an expensive tomb, but he was nothing more than another human corpse in this story. He has no mansion in the afterlife and is consigned to Hades, the place of the dead (16:23). Lazarus is in the place of blessing in Abraham's bosom, while he who had everything this world had to offer was consigned to the place of "torment" in Hades. Here Hades is more than the place of the dead. There were several ideas about Hades back then. For some it is simply the grave, or the place where the dead reside, the righteous and the sinners, aware of one another, in separate compartments (4 Ezra 7:85; 1 Enoch 22). Here Jesus links it with Gehenna, the place of fiery punishment (v. 24; see Matt 5:22, 29–30; NIV: "hell").

There the rich man looks up to the compartment of the righteous and sees "Abraham far away, with Lazarus by his side." Here we need to realize Jesus is not describing the way things are, for nowhere else in Scripture are the unrighteous dead in this kind of conscious intermediate state with a foretaste of the lake of fire. In Scripture this torment takes place after the final judgment, not as part of the intermediate state. Jesus is using the Jewish thinking of his day as part of the story rather than describing the way the afterlife will be (as in 1 Enoch 22; Wisdom 3:1; 4 Maccabees 13:15).

THE RICH MAN'S FIRST REQUEST (16:24–26)

As "Father Abraham," the patriarch has a certain authority over this realm, so the rich man's first plea is to him, begging him to "have pity on me" in the midst of his fiery torment. But notice that he still considers Lazarus to be his servant and therefore the one to "dip the tip of his finger in water and cool my tongue, because I am in agony in this fire." He had never given Lazarus even the table scraps fed to his dogs (16:21), but he wants Lazarus to serve him and his needs in Hades. His completely self-centered outlook continues even into the afterlife. He is sadly mistaken and does not seem to realize that his torment will be everlasting. He had his chance to repent and was too busy in his hedonistic pursuits to bother himself with getting right with God. Now he will have to pay for his folly.

Abraham interprets his plight from the standpoint of the principles of reciprocity and reversal (16:25). When he says to the ultra-rich guy "in your lifetime you received your good things," he means that he lived for his pleasures, was consumed by them to the extent that he ignored God and others entirely. He is getting his just deserts now. Lazarus, on the other hand, "received bad things." His earthly life was a day-to-day nightmare of deprivation. Now God's judgment on them both is to reverse how they had lived formerly, so that "he is comforted here and you are in agony." Their place in eternity is now set, and there is to be no change. As Revelation 14:10–11 says, "God's fury" is then "poured full strength into the cup of his wrath," and "the smoke of their torment will rise for ever and ever," with "no rest day or night."

The biblical principle behind this picture is both clear and sobering for every one of us—how we live our life on earth has a direct bearing on how God will treat us in eternity! I believe in the doctrine of degrees of reward and degrees of punishment. I see the latter in Revelation 20:13-15 (see my commentary on this) and the former throughout Luke, for instance in 16:8b-9 above, that everything we do to serve God with our resources and help others is banked in heaven, to be repaid to us by God when we arrive there. God's demand, as I have been saying, is to consider ourselves stewards of his riches with our wealth and share it both with others and for Christian pursuits.

Abraham then adds (16:26) that in spite of the fact that they can see each other, "between us and you a great chasm has been set in place," so great a gulf that it cannot be bridged. No one can cross that chasm from either side. Jesus uses this picture to depict the finality of eternity. With repentance, one can change the situation in this life. But once a person has died, nothing can be altered. Final judgment is just that—final! The saved and the lost will have no contact with each other for all of eternity, nor will their situations change. What we do in this life determines how we will spend eternity, and once this life is over, our eternal destiny is fixed.

THE RICH MAN'S SECOND REQUEST (16:27-31)

The rich man realizes it is too late for him and so turns to the situation of his family still on earth, asking Abraham to send Lazarus (whom he still considers to be his servant) to his five brothers (16:27-28), hoping to spare them his terrible fate. This is the first time he has ever cared for another person, so in some ways it is a step upward. They apparently are immersed in the same self-centered, hedonistic lifestyle he had been, and he wants them to be warned. The language the man uses actually translates literally as "testify" (*diamartyrētai*) to them, perhaps as an official "witness" to the doctrine of retribution for sins and to the reversal that was also awaiting them. He believes that as soon as they realize the torment awaiting them, they will repent. Most likely, these brothers embody the outlook of the Pharisees that their descent from Abraham is sufficient and they will never face judgment.

This is a common tactic in evangelism, in a sense frightening people into the kingdom. Undoubtedly, quite a few of us originally became believers in order to escape eternal hellfire. This is completely valid, but the fact is that most unbelievers already know of this doctrine and have chosen either to ignore it or to refuse to believe it. Abraham says it correctly in verse 29: "They have Moses and the Prophets; let them listen to them." In other words, Scripture already testifies to God's plan of salvation, and they must respond to that. Warnings from the departed are unnecessary, as they already have God's warnings in his word and have chosen to ignore them.

The man has one final argument (16:30): "If someone from the dead goes to them, they will repent." Most of us would agree with that. If my mother or brother, who have died, would suddenly appear before me, that would get my attention immediately. This actually happened in 1 Samuel 28, when Saul, who had stopped consulting God in his decisions, went to a medium at Endor and had her call up the spirit of Samuel for advice when facing the Philistine army. However, it did him no good, for Samuel simply told him of God's judgment and his impending death. Calling up the dead never accomplishes anything good. These brothers had already made their decision.

The truth of it all is stated in the concluding verse (31): "If they do not listen to Moses and the Prophets, they will not be convinced even if someone rises from the dead." The truth of this is seen when Jesus rose from the dead. While some became believers, like James and probably Jesus' other brothers (1 Cor 15:7), very few were converted. At Pentecost and the coming of the Spirit, three thousand more turned to Christ (Acts 2:41), but that is out of a city of about seventy thousand, with at least a quarter million pilgrims present for the festival. This rich man's five brothers had rejected the witness of Moses and the Prophets all their lives and chose to live purely for pleasure, and that would not change even if Lazarus were to come back from the dead. Moreover, everything Lazarus could tell them is already found in God's word, so they have all the official witness they need.

This principle is so important: God has witnessed to himself in his living word. Our task is to proclaim that witness by preaching the word, and that is more than enough.

———

This is a truly powerful chapter, one of the most important in Scripture, for it tells us clearly what to do about our earthly resources and treasures. The two parables are mind-blowing when understood properly. The shrewd manager (vv. 1–8a) is the secular person in embryo. As a manager of tenant farms for a wealthy owner, he invests the profits. However, he is incompetent, and he is fired, with just a couple of days to get the books in order. That is his salvation. He doctors the books, cheating his master but saving a couple of the biggest debtors a fortune, figuring they would owe him big time and give him both a job and a new home. The parable ends with the strangest conclusion ever, with the defrauded owner commending him for his shrewdness.

It seems to make no sense until Jesus tells the moral of the story and applies it (vv. 8b–9). The parable tells how the secular manager shrewdly gets ahead by taking everything he can for himself in order to make temporary profit. But we belong to the light and must do the exact opposite with our resources, giving it away to help others and glorify God. As we do that, God banks everything we have done for others in heaven, so that it comes back to us as eternal profit. This becomes a wonderful statement of the doctrine of rewards. The message (vv. 10–13) is that our earthly possessions are a test by which God is seeing whether he can trust us with true kingdom riches. All we have belongs to him, and he is checking to see if we will be good stewards. Which master will we serve?

The transition passage (vv. 14–18) focuses on both the problem of greed and the question of the law. In both areas Jesus sums up the law of God and demands absolute allegiance and obedience. He has given us the Torah of the Messiah, the final form of the law, and we must surrender all to him and his kingdom teaching.

The second parable (vv. 19–31) shows the true significance of coming to grips with our earthly possessions. What we do with our situation in life will determine our rewards in heaven. Those who live for worldly wealth will have nothing in heaven, and those who have little now will have everything in eternity. This does not mean that all poor people will be saved, but that those poor people who are saved will have special rewards (what they will be is never explained) that will make up for all that they have sacrificed. The reversal is absolute, and the parable makes the principle of 16:13 all the more critical—the master we serve now will determine our place in heaven. When I think of the number of members in our church who are obsessed with luxuries, this parable becomes all the more important.

The final request (vv. 27–31) is also quite critical for us to hear. We all want friends and loved ones to hear this message and repent, and the point here is that they have all the witness they need. Our God-given task is to proclaim the gospel to the lost and help them to understand, first, the truth of this, and second, how important the message is for them. Their eternal destiny is at stake.

FAITH, FORGIVENESS, AND THE KINGDOM
(17:1–37)

In this passage Jesus addresses the disciples on a series of topics that at first glance seem somewhat helter-skelter, but they all relate to attitudes and actions God demands of believers. The messianic community must keep itself distinct from the hypocritical Pharisees, who are false teachers and become stumbling blocks to God's people (vv. 1–4). The answer is to exercise faith and proper stewardship (vv. 5–10). The centrality of faith is seen in the healing of the ten lepers (vv. 11–14) and the faith of the Samaritan (vv. 15–19).

The second half of the chapter (vv. 20–37) centers on the events that will lead to the coming of the Son of Man and the final kingdom of God. Luke has taken the material in the Olivet Discourse of Matthew 24–25 and Mark 13 and placed it in two discourses, 17:20–37 and 21:5–33. This chapter is more **apocalyptic**, centering on the second coming, and chapter 21 deals more with the destruction of Jerusalem. This section also contains quite a bit of L material, which is drawn from Luke's special sources rather than from Mark or Q,[1] but there is no reason to doubt its basic historical veracity.

---

1. See "Sources" in the introduction.

JESUS TEACHES ON STUMBLING BLOCKS, FORGIVENESS, AND FAITH (17:1-10)

FALSE TEACHING AND STUMBLING BLOCKS (17:1-3A)

Recognizing the inevitability of the arrival of false teachers who "cause people to stumble," Jesus warns his listeners, "woe to anyone through whom they come." Both the shrewd manager and the rich man in the parables of chapter 16 would fit that category, but Jesus especially has the Pharisees in mind, the rabbis or teachers of his day causing the nation to turn from him and embrace their false legal system (which goes way beyond the Torah of Moses). A "stumbling block" is a trap that lures people in and then ensnares them and leads them into sin and apostasy. Such things are "bound to come" because Satan is behind them and the world is filled with such charlatans.

So Jesus warns them, saying "woe to anyone through whom they come." As in 6:24-26, "woe" does not mean "I feel sorry for you" but rather that God's judgment is coming down on your head. Those who trap God's people in lies that lead to sin and turning away from the faith deserve only his wrath. A "millstone" was the upper stone of a mill for grinding grain. This was undoubtedly the large mill turned by a donkey or ox, which weighed a couple of tons. Needless to say, you would drown. Jesus is saying that drowning would be eminently preferable to standing before an angry God while guilty of such a despicable crime. The "little ones" would refer to both disciples and the marginalized like Lazarus and the poor. Both groups should receive help in material things and instruction in spiritual things. Instead, they are led astray by manipulative deceivers.

The answer, Jesus says, is spiritual vigilance: "Watch yourselves." It is present tense and plural, calling for constant care on the part of the community. As a transition verse, it looks back at the need for watchfulness in the light of false teachers, and it also looks forward to the need for forgiveness in the community.

Still, its primary thrust is guarding the gospel truths of the kingdom. It enjoins every church to be steeped in doctrinal truth and to teach believers how to identify false teaching. I am honestly amazed at how much drivel is proclaimed every Sunday morning in some churches. There are people passing as "pastors" who don't even want to teach God's word or guide people into the deep doctrines of the faith. We are in a "feel-good" era with way too much shallowness.

Rebuke and Forgiveness (17:3b-4)

When vigilance is done properly, wrongs committed will be uncovered. Some call this a commentary on the prodigal son, but that is about forgiveness from God while this is forgiveness for a fellow disciple who has wronged you. As in the programmatic passage in Matthew 18:15-18, when a fellow believer "sins against" or hurts you, you begin with personal confrontation. Rather than harboring a grudge or seeking vengeance, you should admonish and correct the guilty party and get things right between you. In the Matthew passage, you may need to take with you a leader in the church or someone the guilty person respects. The key is that you refuse to judge them (Matt 7:1-5) but instead correct them in love (Gal 6:1; 1 Thess 5:14-15; 2 Thess 3:14-15; Titus 3:10; Heb 3:13).

The goal of the confrontation is not personal satisfaction but spiritual repentance. You desire reconciliation not just between yourselves but even more with God. If the person repents (to you and to God), Jesus enjoins you to forgive the person (God will be doing so as well). This is then stated very strongly—even if they continue to repeat that sin seven times in the same day and after each one ask for forgiveness, you grant it. This is not a limit on how often you forgive. Seven is a complete number; the number of times is boundless (Matt 18:22: "seventy-seven times"). This hardly calls for a naive failure to note shallow or even false repentance. Rather, it means a constant willingness to forgive (as with Peter's three denials, 22:54-62).

THE CALL FOR FAITH (17:5-6)

Still in the arena of discipleship, the Twelve (called "apostles" as in 6:13 to highlight their status as official "envoys" or agents of Christ) ask him to "increase our faith," not give them a gift of faith but help the faith they have to grow. It is possible this relates to the demand for forgiveness in verses 3b-4 and their feeling that they didn't have enough faith to do so. That may be part of it, but this likely is more general, the realization that they needed greater faith in every area of their lives. On the Christward journey—which Jesus emphasizes frequently on the "way to Jerusalem"—they realized the need for a deep faith that empowered them constantly.

Jesus answers (17:6) that it is not the quantity of faith but the quality of faith that counts. The mustard seed was one of the smallest of seeds, so tiny one could hardly see it in the palm of the hand. So his point is that even a tiny amount of faith can produce miracles like uprooting a mulberry tree—a very large tree, up to thirty-five feet high and with deep roots—and throwing it into the sea (the parallel in Matt 17:20; 21:21 is a mountain).

He hardly means this literally. It is a hyperbolic example to demonstrate the power of faith to accomplish wondrous things. Nor does it support prosperity theology, the view that all we need do is tell God what we want in faith and he has to give us whatever we ask. That is a materialistic Christianity and constitutes heresy, since it tells us we can control God. James 4:3 disallows such requests, since in them "you ask with wrong motives, that you may spend what you get on your pleasures."

PARABLE OF THE DUTIFUL SERVANT (17:7-10)

We are all God's "slaves" (*doulos*; NIV: "servant") and serve him. The message of this parable is that we serve him without thought of reward and simply want to do "our duty." This is a corollary to the teaching on rewards in 12:35-37, 42-48, and tells us that servanthood is the only means of achieving greatness before God.

In this parable a farmer has a small field and can afford only one slave who has to serve as both field hand and household servant. The slave finishes his fieldwork (plowing and tending the sheep) but is still not finished with his duties. When that slave comes back to the house, he is not allowed to sit down to his own meal until he has prepared the meal and fed his master. Only then is the slave allowed to eat his own supper. "Get yourself ready" is literally, "put on your apron and wait on me." This slave shifts from plowman to shepherd and then to cook and butler, doing it all to serve his master with no thought of reward. He is in a sense just "doing his job."

Jesus then asks, "Will he thank the servant because he did what he was told to do?" (17:9). The master does not owe anything, even thanks, to a slave when he performs his assigned task. This question expects a negative answer—"no, he doesn't have to do so." Clearly, in this parable all disciples are slaves of God, an image Paul looked on with joy in the opening of every epistle—"Paul, a slave of Christ Jesus." In Romans 6, Paul tells us that Christ has liberated us from the enslavement of sin and made us slaves of God. We serve him for the joy and privilege of being part of his family as slaves as well as his heirs. The message here is that we are not in a patron-client relationship where God is obliged to help us when we serve him. Rather, it is a master-slave relationship; we serve him with no expectation of return.

The point in verses 9–10 is that we do not do it for the payback we will receive but for the privilege of serving him. We deserve nothing from God and so serve him without demands. We serve God; he does not have to serve us. He is under no obligation when we simply do our assigned tasks. Our response is to be, "We are unworthy servants; we have only done our duty." We obey his commands without saying, "What's in it for me?" (contra the Pharisee in 18:12). We bring nothing worthy to the table. God loved us and saved us while we were still sinners and his enemies. This is the other side of 16:8b–9. That showed us God's side, who does indeed reward our acts of charity, but he does so out of love, not out of obligation. Here we see it from the perspective of those who serve him entirely for the privilege of doing so with no thought of reward.

JESUS HEALS TEN LEPERS (17:11–19)

Flowing out of the call for faith (vv. 5–6) and the note on grateful hearts serving God (vv. 7–10), this miracle centers on the faith and gratitude of the Samaritan leper who came back to thank Jesus. There is another reversal of expectation as the one who returns is a Samaritan, while the Jewish lepers never show repentance or gratitude.

In verse 11 Jesus is still "on his way to Jerusalem" (see 9:51; 13:22) to fulfill his God-given destiny, and he is now "along the border between Samaria and Galilee." As we have noticed, he did not make a straight line but crisscrossed the area for the sake of ministry. At this time he seems to be going east to west. We must remember that the "journey" format is theological more than it is geographical, with Jesus moving nearer and nearer to his divinely set purpose more than just to the city itself.

Somewhere in that region (we don't know whether in Galilee or Samaria) he enters a village and meets ten lepers. As one would expect, they stand "at a distance" from him; no one drew near a leper for fear of becoming unclean (see 4:27; 5:12). The fact of "ten" lepers does not have any significance; it is undoubtedly a historical note.

Their cry to Jesus as "Master" is common to Luke (5:5; 8:24, 45; 9:33, 49—alone among the Gospels) and looks on him not only as a rabbi but as the Lord who controls nature (as in other miracles). The plea for "mercy" or compassion is of course a cry for healing (18:38). They know Jesus is master of all disease and even of nature itself. The only question is whether he will have compassion on them.

In verse 14 Jesus makes an unusual move. In 5:12-14 he healed a leper and then told him to go to the priests, who would certify that he had been healed and could return home. Jesus does not do that here. He tells them, "Go, show yourselves to the priests" before healing them, most likely to test their faith. They are healed from a distance while on the way. This called for a great amount of faith on their part, to leave without being healed and yet with the expectation of being healed like Naaman, who was healed while washing in the Jordan (2 Kgs 5:10-14).

Of the ten, only one had the faith to return with praise and gratitude in his heart. His loud praise and prostration at Jesus' feet in verses 15-16 showed great piety as well as joy. The other nine (implied to be Jews) apparently felt no special gratitude but just accepted the healing and went on their way. The surprising thing, of course, is the revelation at the end of this small section that the one grateful person was a Samaritan. So this joins the parable of the good Samaritan as precursors of the universal mission, which itself will begin with Philip in Samaria in Acts 8:4-8. The other nine symbolize the Jewish people who are closed to Jesus, and God will turn to the nations, starting with the Samaritans, as implied in the parable of the great banquet (14:21-23).

The message of this episode is found in the three questions of verses 17-18. The first expects a positive answer: "Were not all ten cleansed?" Jesus had indeed shown mercy to every single one of the ten, and all were both healed of the leprosy and cleansed of the defilement with which the leprosy had cursed them. They were whole and could return home. Yet if all were cleansed, "where are the other nine?" They should have returned to praise God and thank Jesus for their healing. This is the central point, the ingratitude of these other nine. Refusing to respond to God's healing touch obviates the real purpose of a miracle—the physical healing remains, but the spiritual healing never takes place.

The third question (17:18) flows out of the second and carries the other major emphasis: "Has no one returned to give praise to

God except this foreigner?" The famous sign at the steps up to the inner courtyard of the temple prohibited "foreigners," or non-Jews, from entering that sacred space on penalty of death. So this was a negative term to all Jews. Yet this looks forward to a major salvation-historical switch that was to occur in Acts 7–8 and the beginning of the universal mission—the movement of the gospel to all the nations. The nine typified the majority of the nation who in Romans 11:17 are the branches of the olive tree (= true Israel) that have been "broken off" and are no longer part of the people of God, to be replaced by the "wild shoots," or Gentiles like this lone Samaritan.

So Jesus reiterates the promise he has made to others he has healed, this time to a Samaritan: "Rise and go; your faith has made you well" (literally, "saved you"; compare 7:50; 8:48). He has now experienced both physical healing and spiritual salvation. The nine refused to respond in faith to the God who had healed them and so missed out on the far more important healing. The praise and thanksgiving of the Samaritan were actually far more than gratitude. They constituted his faith decision; he was now a member of God's family and Christ's messianic community.

JESUS TEACHES ON THE COMING OF GOD'S KINGDOM (17:20–37)

The Pharisees represented the rest of Judaism in their assumption that the coming of God's kingdom was still future, linked with the arrival of the Messiah. They were right in their belief in the law but tragically wrong when they rejected Jesus as God's Messiah. By refusing to become new covenant followers, they placed themselves outside God's kingdom, which had arrived with Jesus. The kingdom had already been inaugurated on earth and was moving to its final, full appearance at the second coming. These two issues—the present kingdom (vv. 20–21) and the future, final kingdom (vv. 22–37)—are the subjects of this passage.

THE QUESTION REGARDING THE KINGDOM'S ARRIVAL (17:20-21)

The Pharisees, as did all of Judaism, believed the kingdom would not come until the Messiah arrived with heaven's armies to defeat the nations, especially the Romans, and instigate God's kingdom on earth. Since the Pharisees rejected Jesus as Messiah, that by necessity was a future event. Thus, they ask Jesus when it will come. Jesus' reply (centering on what "can be observed") shows he understood it to be a demand for a sign from heaven (as in 11:16). This is a standalone passage, for in the rest of the section (vv. 22–37) he is teaching the disciples, not the Pharisees. The reason is that this question deals with the kingdom in the present, while the rest centers on the final coming of the kingdom at the end of history. The Pharisees needed to understand the presence of the kingdom in Jesus, and so this is the passage for them.

This is where "inaugurated **eschatology**" is important. In verses 20-21 Jesus emphasizes the "already," while in verses 22-37 he focuses on the "not-yet" aspect of the kingdom. With Jesus' incarnation and first coming, God's kingdom was inaugurated, and at present God's reign is established in this world, yet at the same time it is in process. The final reign of God will come at the second coming, and then Christ and the saints will reign in heaven for eternity.

So Jesus answers, "The coming of the kingdom of God is not something that can be observed." It will not come via heavenly signs or by human efforts (for example, keeping the law). It will do no good to watch the heavens and wait for some supernatural sign that will enable people to say, "Here it is" or "There it is."

The last part of verse 21 is a critical statement for Luke's view of the end-time events. Interpreters have generally understood Jesus' statement "the kingdom of God is in your midst" in three different ways:

1. God's kingdom is "within/inside" his people, an internal reality. However, Jesus is addressing the Pharisees, not his

disciples, and this would hardly be appropriate. Also, God's kingdom is always an external force in this world and not just a spiritual entity. It is the Spirit who lives within us (Rom 8:11-17), not the kingdom.

2. Others see it as meaning "in your grasp or reach"; that is, it is in your ability to attain via repentance and conversion. However, this places it too much under human control and does not capture the essence of the kingdom as an active force in this world.

3. Best is to see it as the NIV, NASB, ESV, NET, and LEB: "in your midst" or "among you" (NRSV, NLT). In other words, the kingdom is already present and operative in this world if you only had eyes to see and ears to hear. God is on his throne, and the kingdom has entered this world. The messianic community exists for those who are open to Jesus.

THE COMING OF THE SON OF MAN (17:22-37)

Now Jesus turns to his disciples and addresses the future event. We must remember that there are two comings of Jesus in Scripture. In his first advent he has come to be suffering Messiah à la Isaiah 52-53 and inaugurate the kingdom or messianic age, and in his second advent he will come as conquering King to destroy the powers of evil and establish his final kingdom. He addressed the first in verses 20-21 and now turns to the second. This is the Old Testament Day of Yahweh, the time when the nations will be judged and the wrath of God assuaged (Isa 39:6; Jer 9:25; Dan 7:22; Amos 4:2; Mal 3:5).

The swiftness and power of the coming (17:22-25)

As his followers experience the powers of evil arrayed against them and the hatred they will face, they will long to see "the days of the Son of Man." Some see this as referring to the future troubles and opposition Jesus' followers will face, but while this is part of the meaning here, the context makes it far more likely that this here and in 17:26 speaks of the **parousia**, the return of the Son of Man / Messiah at the end of days. When Jesus says "you will not see it," he is referring to its unexpected nature. In the midst of the distress and troubles they will have to endure, they will often pray the Lord's Prayer, "May your kingdom come." But it will come in God's time, not theirs.

In fact, Jesus goes on to say, there will be constant rumors and sightings of signs (17:23), as already stated in verse 21—"'There he is!' or 'Here he is!'"—and while some may simply be rumor-mongers, he probably has in mind messianic pretenders and false teachers who will use such to lead many of God's people astray (Mark 13:21; Matt 24:23). The disciples are not to chase after false predictions. This is a warning that should caution us in our day as well, for all kinds of "prophecy preachers" are hawking their latest theories predicting exactly when Jesus is to come. I grew up in this camp, and it seems every year there are several rumors exactly like Jesus says. We must be careful not to let speculation replace content when preaching about the Lord's return.

Instead, when Christ returns, he will "be like the lightning, which flashes and lights up the sky from one end to the other." When the second coming takes place, it will not be in secret, known only to a few and told in rumors to be "here" or "there" as in verse 23. Like lightning it will be sudden yet public and visible to all, and no one will be unaware of what has happened. Lightning is a common symbol for a theophany, an appearance of God (Exod 19:16; 2 Sam 22:15; Pss 18:14; 97:3–4), and stresses his glory and majesty. As stated in 1 Thessalonians 4:16 (and 1 Cor 15:52), his return will be accompanied "with a loud command, with the voice of the archangel and with the trumpet call of God." I grew up being taught that there would be a "secret rapture," and that could not be farther from the truth.

Jesus provides another reason not to listen to the rumors in verse 25, for he could not return yet—"first he must suffer many things and be rejected by this generation." This is actually another passion prediction (9:22, 44; 12:50; 13:32-33; 18:32-33; Luke has more than any Gospel). The point here is not to listen to such false rumors, for the second coming is the distant future, not the immediate future. Jesus' purpose and destiny in the here and now is suffering and rejection, giving his life as the atoning sacrifice for our sins. He will be opposed and martyred by "this generation" (also 7:31; 9:41), but his followers will continue to suffer for generations to come until his final return. Jesus' glory will become visible afterward, at his resurrection, and the glory of his people will come at their final resurrection at his parousia.

Two examples for the nature of his coming (17:26-30)

"The days of Noah" (vv. 26-27) and "the days of Lot" (vv. 28-29) are meant to demonstrate the suddenness and unexpected nature of Christ's return. Noah and Lot are often used together to show God's judgment of the wicked and his deliverance of the saints. In the days of Noah right before the flood, people were going about their lives just as they are today and as they will be just before the Lord returns—"eating, drinking, marrying and being given in marriage." In other words, everything was normal until the cataclysm arrived.

When "Noah entered the ark" and "the flood came and destroyed them all," no one was ready. The emphasis here is on the sudden coming and the fact that it was too late for the people to do anything. In Genesis 6:4, 11, the stress is on the heedless and corrupt activities of Noah's contemporaries, and that is implicit here. The parallel in Matthew 24:37-39 highlights the need for constant vigilance and readiness, and that too is implicit here.

When Jesus speaks of "the days of Lot" (17:28-29, only in Luke) he adds a few details—buying, selling, planting, building (see Gen 19:15-23)—with the depravity of Sodom conspicuously absent and all the stronger for that. Even the terribly wicked people of Sodom engaged in normal pursuits and were not ready at all for judgment to fall on them. Like those who have turned

against Jesus, they were unprepared for the fate they had brought
on themselves.

The "revelation" of the Son of Man will be the same (17:30).
Jesus is coming like a thief (12:39), unexpectedly and frighteningly,
and the people of this world will not be ready. God's people had
better be ready. "Revealed" means that at that moment the whole
world, the unsaved as well as the saved, will be made aware of his
glory and power. It will be "manifested" to all, but it will be too
late for the unprepared.

Warnings regarding the day (17:31–36)

As in the previous two examples, Jesus emphasizes everyday activities rather than depraved actions. Everyone must choose between
an orientation to earthly things or to heavenly realities, and that
determines one's final destiny. The first warning is to flee earthly
possessions (17:31–32 = Matt 24:17–18; Mark 13:15–16). In Mark and
Matthew, this is part of the section on the destruction of Jerusalem,
but here the focus is on the parousia. The catastrophe hits with
no time to spare, and those who take the time to grab possessions
will be overtaken.

"Housetops" in first-century Palestine were flat roofs that
served as a combination dining and living room, and people regularly ate meals on them. When they descended, they took back
stairs down the side of the house, and went around to the front
to go in and get possessions. They will have no time for that, and
those so tied to earthly things as to try will perish. The same is
true of those in the fields. The armies are almost there, and to
return home is to die. Even when Lot's wife looked back (Gen 19:17,
26), probably unwilling to leave her possessions, she was turned
to salt and gone.

The great reversal dominates 17:33–35. The basic theme is the
need to choose whether to keep their life or lose it (v. 33) and then
two illustrations of that motif are provided (vv. 34–35). The key to
eternity is one's priorities in life, whether one seeks to preserve the

things of this life or to surrender them for Christ. To "keep their life" is to focus entirely on preserving the earthly side of life, and to "lose it" means to center on preserving the spiritual side of life over the earthly. In the latter, we choose the way of Christ, involving the world's hatred and "participation in his sufferings" (Phil 3:10).

The two illustrations portray the divisions in family (two in bed) and work (two at the mill) this great reversal will cause. In both cases "one will be taken and the other left." Those taken will be resurrected to life; those left will face fiery judgment. The two in bed would be husband and wife in the average one-room peasant home, so families will be torn asunder. The two at the mill were necessary to grind grain with a hand mill (about a foot in diameter on the average). One would sit on the ground and steady the bottom half while the other turned the upper stone (via the peg near its edge). Again, division results, as the one is ready (centering on the heavenly) while the other is not (centering on the earthly).

Verse 36 was almost certainly added by later scribes. It is missing in the better manuscripts ($\mathfrak{P}$75, ℵ, A, B, the Byzantine manuscripts) and was likely added in assimilation to Matthew 24:40.

Conclusion (17:37)

Both halves of this verse are somewhat confusing. In fact, the disciples' question shows that they are somewhat bewildered by all Jesus has said. Clearly, Jesus was going to return at some future date, so their question, "Where, Lord?" is a natural follow-up. In Zechariah 14:4 the Lord lands on the Mount of Olives and splits it in two, and this could be in their minds. They rightly see this as the day of the Lord, when God's judgment will fall on the nations.

Jesus' response is equally enigmatic. The picture of vultures circling over a dead body certainly connotes judgment, but with what emphasis? It might emphasize (1) the swiftness or (2) the suddenness and unexpected nature of the vultures appearing, or (3) the finality of the destruction. Some think of it as (4) an eagle rather than a vulture, thus stressing the Roman army (with an eagle as its emblem), but that doesn't fit here. A few have taken this as (5) an eagle that symbolizes the gathering of the righteous to Christ in heaven. This is interesting and possible, but the language seems to indicate these carrion birds circling the dead more than catching them up. So I agree with those who see this as (6) stressing the visible nature and universal effect of the parousia, building on the lightning flashing in the sky in verse 24. Jesus is saying to be ready at all times, for when it comes, it will be unavoidable.

———

This chapter moves into a theme that will dominate the rest of the travel narrative (chapters 17–19), the place of faith in the Christian life. The theme of this chapter is introduced in the first verses (vv. 1–10), the danger of false teachers overcome by forgiveness and faith in the community. Even the smallest amount of faith can bring about the greatest of results, for we serve a truly great God. Moreover, it is our privilege and joy to serve him. In reality, servanthood in itself is greatness, for we get to minister to and on behalf of the God of the universe. We have no thought of what we can get out of it; it is a wondrous honor to be chosen to be his slave.

The healing of the ten lepers (vv. 11–19) exemplifies what should constitute faith. There are two aspects of true faith—belief and trust in the healing presence of God (which all ten exemplify), and praise and gratitude to the healing God (seen only in the one). This meant that nine experienced physical healing, but only the one had spiritual healing as well. Moreover, that one was a foreigner, a Samaritan, and so this also became a harbinger of the universal mission in which the gospel went to the nations.

The rest of the chapter (vv. 20–37) centers on eschatology, beginning with the realized side (vv. 20–21) and the fact that the Jewish people had to realize that the kingdom was not a future reality but was first an actual presence in this world with Jesus and his new covenant community. God has sent his kingdom, and it is here. Yet at the same time, it is in process now and will not be finalized until the second coming. False teachers tried to make it a present thing to lead people astray (vv. 22–23), but when it does come no one will need to have it pointed out, for it will be visible to all (v. 24). In the present will come his suffering and rejection (v. 25).

The key is to be ready at all times, for the truth is that at his return life will be proceeding normally, as in the days of Noah or Lot (vv. 26–30), when destruction came suddenly and without warning. God's people must be vigilant and faithful, for it can come at any time. The first step to being ready is to eschew earthly possessions, for such an obsession will lead to their destruction. We must realize the great reversal that is awaiting us. Those who live for the things of this world will lose everything, and those who seek nothing in this world will have everything in eternity (vv. 33–35). Families and friends will be separated at the parousia, and those who are heaven-centered rather than earth-obsessed will be the ones who enjoy the rewards of heaven.

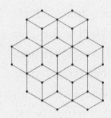

KINGDOM, PRAYER, AND FAITH
(18:1–43)

I n the last chapter Jesus centered on discipleship, with the two primary themes being faith and the coming of the kingdom. Here he builds on that, especially focusing on realized **eschatology** (the presence of the kingdom in the present age) and the need to place our complete trust in God and Jesus as we walk with Christ. The parable of the persistent widow (vv. 1–8) is an example of the prayer warrior who will not take no for an answer in bringing her need to God, and then we have the model of the tax collector (vv. 9–14) and later the blind beggar (vv. 35–43) who throw themselves entirely on the mercy of God. The little children are models of God-centered living (vv. 15–17), and following that (vv. 18–30) we are told that like these children we must eschew possessions and focus entirely on kingdom realities. We must learn to depend entirely on our merciful God.

JESUS TELLS THE PARABLE OF THE PERSISTENT WIDOW (18:1–8)

Again Jesus focuses on the disciples, and Luke tells us the theme right in verse 1—"to show them that they should always pray and not give up." Needless to say, this was an extremely difficult time for them, and the pressure was only going to increase. "Give up" is literally "grow weary" and addresses serious depression in the midst of trying times. Discipleship demands endurance and an unwavering trust and dependence on our gracious God. This is prayer that never gives up in hard times. Moreover, the NIV's "should always pray" is too weak. The particle is actually *dei*, used throughout Luke (eighteen times) and Acts (twenty-three times) for divine necessity (see on 2:49). It should read "that God deems it necessary for them to pray at all times." Prayer becomes the distinguishing characteristic of the believer, an active trust in God rather than self.

The characters are introduced in verses 2–3. This is a stern, uncompromising judge who was so caught up in himself that he "neither feared God nor cared what people thought." He was undoubtedly Jewish, for the Romans stayed away from civil concerns and left their subjects to themselves on local matters. Some think him a corrupt judge as in Amos 2:6–7; 5:10–13, but there isn't much indication of that. He is a wealthy, powerful leader in the community who cares only for his own upper strata and nothing for the poor and defenseless like this widow. He is the antithesis of what a judge should be. "Nor cared what people thought" here is *entrepō*, "feels no shame," an image for a person with no conscience (Jer 8:9, 12). Scripture mandates that judges defend widows (Exod 22:22–24; Deut 24:17; Ps 68:5; Isa 1:17; 54:4; Jer 22:3; Jas 1:27), but this one is completely cold-hearted. He is almost as bad as the scribes in Mark 12:40 who "devour widows' houses."

We don't know the situation of this widow, whether her dowry or husband's estate was being withheld or whether it was another type of (probably financial) situation, but she had not found justice. She has no recourse but to go before this judge and seek help, but his lack of concern meant she "kept coming" again and again and pleading for "justice against my adversary." Clearly, every time she is turned away with no help whatsoever.

The judge finally responds in verses 4–5. The first several times he flatly refused even to acknowledge her and her need. She outlasted him and forced a reply. He was well-known and proud of his reputation as a godless and hard-bitten judge (twice in vv. 2, 4, for emphasis) and didn't want to pay her any attention whatsoever. But she left him little choice. It was easier to give in and get it over with than to let her bother all his other clients with her constant pleas.

Note he says this only to himself and not publicly; he doesn't want his capitulation widely known. His reasoning is sound: "because this widow keeps bothering me, I will see that she gets justice, so that she won't eventually come and attack me." "Attack me" doesn't mean physical violence but public denunciation. He doesn't want his name vilified before others. The verb *hypōpiazē* means to "beat down," literally "give a black eye" (a boxing metaphor), to "wear out" with her constant appeals. A good paraphrase might be "lest she give me a headache with her continual yammering."

Jesus has two ideas in mind. Mainly, he is calling for persistent prayer. If a cold, uncaring judge can be moved, how much more a loving Father. Unlike the judge, our compassionate Lord does not have to be forced to grant our needs. Moreover, it is not God who needs our continual prayers; it is we who need to come before him regularly. The single necessary ingredient for spiritual growth is constant dependence and surrender to him. The second idea is that of justice. The disciples are soon to be beaten down and savaged by a world turned against them. The church must learn to use all its resources to help the poor find justice.

The message of the parable lies in the reaction of this judge to her persistence. Jesus calls him an "unjust judge" in verse 6, literally "judge of unrighteousness" (*adikias*), likely meaning that the man is both "unjust" in the total absence of concern for the widow's desperate situation and "unrighteous" in his disdain for God. He is truly a man of the world and speaks here as a completely secular person.

This is another "lesser to greater" message. If this wicked judge who has no compassion for anyone can react this way, how much more a loving God: "Will not God bring about justice for his chosen ones?" If even a cold, calculating judge will provide earthly justice, our heavenly Father will act for his people, his "elect" whom he has chosen out of this world. As those who belong to God, they are also the hated and the downtrodden, for the world has turned against them, and so they must turn to God for vindication. This is the absolute promise that they will receive that justice due them.

The elect, like the widow, cannot find justice in this world and must "cry out to him day and night." The point of the parable is the divine promise of his intervention and their exoneration. However, they must also realize that God will answer their cries in his time and not their own, as seen in Jesus' further question, "Will he keep putting them off?" The verb (*makrothymei*) means to "delay" or "wait patiently"; God will determine his timing.

The question of God delaying has several differing interpretations: (1) God shows patience with their prayers and in his own time responding (too weak); (2a, b) God delays or postpones his wrath against either his enemies or the elect (not in the context); (3) God vindicates the saints even though he delays his answer (but the emphasis in 8a is on swift justice); (4) God does not delay but vindicates the saints in his time; (5) God is patient in watching over the saints and protecting them until the **parousia**. A combination of the last two makes best sense here.

The promise jars a bit with all the discussion of delay, for he promises, "he will see that they get justice, and quickly" (18:8a). While *en tachei* can mean "suddenly" or "quickly," in this context the idea of "soon" is best. But how does that fit all the material in Luke-Acts on the lengthy delay before the Lord returns? Probably Luke is writing this on the basis of his view of salvation history, looking at the whole issue of God and time. Second Peter 3:8, 10, still says it best: "With the Lord a day is like a thousand years, and a thousand years are like a day," for "*he is patient with you*, not wanting anyone to perish, but everyone to come to repentance."

Truly "in all things God works for the good" (Rom 8:28), but we must remember the message of Hebrews 11 and the faith of the heroes of the past who did not receive their release until they left this world (especially Heb 11:39–40). The already and the not-yet govern this promise. God is already giving us justice, but final vindication will not come until Christ returns and eternity is launched.

Finally, Jesus turns to the question of his parousia, asking, "However, when the Son of Man comes, will he find faith on the earth?" (18:8b). This probably has two levels of meaning. On one level, the question is whether at the end of history conditions will be like the flood of Genesis 6, where Noah and his family were the only righteous people left. The second and related level relates to the saints, asking what kind of persevering and vigilant prayer will characterize his followers. Will they be ready for his return, trusting God in the midst of trying times and truly praying, "Your kingdom come"?

JESUS TELLS THE PARABLE OF THE PHARISEE AND THE TAX COLLECTOR (18:9-14)

This passage begins a section (18:9-43) that contrasts the legalistic self-righteousness and materialism of the Jewish leaders with the simple humility and trust demanded of true disciples. The Christ followers must learn to depend on God rather than self. Those who surrender everything in order to follow Jesus are the true leaders.

This is not a historical story but another parable. Jesus is not addressing only one sect of the Jews, the Pharisees, but using the Pharisee as an example of all self-righteous people. Likewise, the tax collector represents all sinners who realize their dilemma and throw themselves on the mercy of God. Luke spells out their basic problem at the outset. They were too "confident of their own righteousness and looked down on everyone else." This is the two-way street of self-centeredness: focusing entirely on yourself and disdaining others around you. Outwardly these people seem to live righteous lives, but inwardly they trust self rather than God. This leads naturally into contempt for others, as the superiority of self produces arrogance.

In verse 10 both men ascend to the temple to pray; the setting serves to contrast the two. Public prayers were uttered at nine in the morning and three in the afternoon, during the morning and evening sacrifices. These were primarily corporate prayers, but people would go up to utter personal prayers as well. Standing for prayer with hands upraised was the normal prayer posture (1 Tim 2:8) and signified reaching up to the heavens via prayer. Jewish people normally prayed out loud, but ostentatious prayers were looked down on (Matt 6:5, 6). The phrase "stood by himself" is actually "prayed to himself" (*pros heauton*) and could be taken to mean "about himself," highlighting the basic problem behind his prayer.

The prayer itself uses the first person five times (like the rich fool in 12:16-20). While thanksgiving was common in prayer, all Jews would notice the complete absence of confession and petition in his prayer. The Pharisee is only concerned about himself and his self-righteousness. He is "not like other people," showing he does indeed fit the description of verse 9, "looked down on everyone else." The three categories—robbers, evildoers, adulterers—likely stem from a common vice list and sum up the *hoi polloi*, lawbreakers who stand condemned. The middle category, evildoers, probably includes everyone but himself. He is another of those who think God is pretty lucky to have him around to look out for his affairs.

He singles out the tax collector as the worst of a bad lot (see on 3:12). Jesus has chosen polar opposites—the highest and the lowest of groups in the eyes of the common people. The contempt of the leaders is seen in 5:30, where they can't believe Jesus would share meals (and himself) with tax collectors like Levi.

The Pharisee's pride is especially seen in his fasting and tithing (18:12). Pharisees fasted on Mondays and Thursdays, the days tradition said Moses ascended and then descended Sinai when he received the Torah (Exod 19, 32). They felt more pious for going beyond what the Torah required for fasting, but the fact is they were required to do so by their oral tradition (see 5:33). The same is true of their tithing. They went beyond the norm (see 11:42) and tended to tithe everything, including "a tenth of all I get," meaning every item purchased, normally not required because the person who made the items had already paid tithes on the materials.

In contrast, the despised tax collector is forthright, honest, and humble in verse 13. He stands "at a distance," probably the outer court of the Gentiles, undoubtedly reflecting his sense of unworthiness to approach God. He raises neither his hands nor his eyes but "beat his breast" in sorrow and mourning for his sins. His abject humility and deep repentance could not be more opposite from the Pharisee.

All he can do is cry out from the depths of his misery, "God, have mercy on me, a sinner." There is no more apt cry leading to conversion in Scripture. "Have mercy" is *hilakesthai*, "make atonement" for sins, the primary New Testament term for Christ's death as an atoning sacrifice for our sins (Rom 3:24; Heb 2:17; 1 John 2:12), powerfully portraying God's incredible mercy in forgiving our sins. This man goes to God with no pretenses of self-worth or deeds to parade before him.

The terms of salvation, later used by Paul in Romans 3:22–24, are on full display in verse 14 as justification is added to propitiation/atonement. It is the tax collector, not the self-righteous Pharisee, who "went home justified before God." The term *dedikaiōmenos* has its full forensic sense (as in Rom 3:20, 24) of one who is "declared righteous" or right before God. The tax collector has repented and prayed for mercy, and now he stands acquitted and forgiven of his sins. The two terms here, "propitiation" and "justification," stand side by side in Paul's justly famous definition of salvation in Romans 3:20–24. So this is the primary statement of salvation in Luke. I disagree with those who say "justified" is too strong a translation and should read, "found favor" or "viewed as more upright." This is all about what kind of person is declared right by God.

Another statement of reversal completes the picture (see 1:51–53; 14:11), alluding to Ezekiel 21:26, "The lowly will be exalted and the exalted will be brought low." The attitude of one's heart is just as important to God as the works that result from it. Self-pride vitiates good deeds. This principle is a dominating theme in Luke—it is servanthood that is the true path to greatness, and humility will lead to God exalting us both now and in the final kingdom. This is the curse of talent; it so easily leads to that pride that negates in God's eyes what one is accomplishing with it.

CHILDREN ARE MODELS OF FAITH (18:15–17)

Luke has been using his own special material (L, stories not found in Matthew or Mark), but now he returns to Markan material (last used in Luke 9:40, now paralleling Mark 10:13–16). As we move to the finish of Luke's travel narrative in 19:27, the twin themes of discipleship and faith will continue to be the primary emphases. This is true here in this short passage on the place of children in the church. The tax collector in the immediately preceding section exemplified humility and dependence on the mercy of God and Christ. These are key characteristics of faith as well, and so the theme continues. To be a member of God's kingdom demands humble trust in God.

This episode begins with parents trying to bring their small children ("babies" here, referring to children up to three or four) to Jesus to receive his blessing, a practice often followed in Judaism with rabbis, elders, and scribes. This became a ritual on the evening of the Day of Atonement, though there is no indication that was the case here.

Jesus' disciples, probably because they thought him too busy for such things, "rebuked" the parents to keep them from bothering their Lord. This is an imperfect tense, meaning they "tried to rebuke" them. Some interpret this as an act of pride—Jesus and the disciples were too important to be bothered by such insignificant things as small infants.

Jesus saw their intentions and quickly responded (18:16), "Let the little children come to me, and do not hinder them, for the kingdom of God belongs to such as these." His disciples had no right to exclude anyone from "coming to" Jesus, especially children. Note that Jesus says it both ways (allow them, do not hinder them) to emphasize their right to be in his presence. Some take this as an allusion to infant baptism, but there is no hint of this, and it does not fit. This is part of Luke's central motif that the kingdom is especially open to the marginalized in society (the poor, women, children) and elevates them to important levels in the presence of God.

When he says God's reign especially "belongs to" these children, he goes beyond the previous episode on children (9:46–48): he stresses how valuable they are in the kingdom and their importance to the church. They are not only models of kingdom receptivity, with their humility and openness to the things of God; they are worthy candidates for the kingdom themselves, as they show that selfless trust and total dependence on their heavenly Father that they show their earthly parents.

He concludes with another *amēn* saying (see 4:24) stressing the absolute truth and importance of the point: "Anyone who will not receive the kingdom of God like a little child will never enter it" (18:17). The teachability and receptivity of children to what their parents tell them is a requirement for kingdom people. Every person who desires to join the kingdom community must exercise the same level of welcoming faith and trust in the Lord as exemplified by a child. In other words, we cannot bargain with God, "Lord, I will follow you if I can _____, so long as you don't ask me to _____." My wife was an elementary school teacher, and during the first parent-teacher conference every year, she always knew when she saw parents walk in who their child was, because the kids copied everything their parent did. That must be us—surrendering everything to follow and imitate the Lord completely.

JESUS MEETS THE RICH (YOUNG) RULER (18:18-30)

It is Luke who tells us the man was wealthy and Matthew (19:16-29) who tells us he was young. There are two parts to the story, the encounter with the rich ruler (vv. 18-23) and a series of sayings on materialism and salvation (vv. 24-30). The story illustrates the type of ties to this life that make it extremely difficult for those who (unlike children) cannot accept kingdom realities and so fail to enter the kingdom. Jesus' demand is itself quite difficult—sell all in order to follow him. In this section on receptive faith this wealthy ruler is the prime example of a person who cannot find such faith and so must remain an outsider. The message is that every would-be follower must choose between Christ and money (as in 16:13); you cannot serve them both.

ENCOUNTER WITH THE RICH RULER (18:18-23)

This "ruler" may have been a ruler of the synagogue like Jairus (8:41) or a member of the Sanhedrin. Whichever, he was an influential Jewish leader who was not opposed to Jesus and open to his teaching. His question is at the heart of everything and reiterates the lawyer in 10:25, "Good teacher, what must I do to inherit eternal life?" His is a question about good works. What must he do to guarantee eternity? The Jews were people of the covenant, right with God on the basis of their being the children of Abraham. But theirs was also an ethical religion centered on works, especially in the Pharisaic era with their elaborate oral tradition.

There is an interesting difference between the **Synoptic** accounts. Mark (10:17) and Luke have "good teacher," but Matthew (19:16) alters Mark from a **christological** statement to an ethical statement ("What good thing must I do?"). Some see a contradiction in the versions, but that is unnecessary. Both contain virtually the same message: Jesus is a respected rabbi being asked about good works and salvation.

Jesus' reply (18:19) turns the attention from himself to God: "Why do you call me good? ... No one is good—except God alone."

Jesus is deflecting the man's casual compliment and stressing the goodness of God as the first step to salvation. While some think he is admitting his own sinfulness, that is definitely not the case. We can tell by the way the ruler addresses Jesus that he believes he is one good man consulting another. Jesus lets him know that no one focuses on his or her own goodness when seeking to be right with God. Only one is truly good, God, and salvation comes only from him. So Jesus is telling the man to focus only on God, not on himself. Matthew 19:17 says it slightly differently but gets at the same point: "Why do you ask me about what is good?" This is implicit in Mark and Luke. Salvation does not come by good works but only through the good God.

Having set the theological scene in verses 18–19, Jesus in verse 20 begins to address the question of the ruler. As to what the man must do, Jesus responds, "You know the commandments," then names the second table (the ethical side) of the Decalogue, with the actual order slightly altered—numbers 7, 6, 8, 9, 5 (adultery, murder, stealing, false witness, honoring parents), placing the parents last possibly to end with a positive (thou shalt) rather than negative (thou shalt not) command. The lawyer in 10:27 responded to this issue that we should love the Lord and one's neighbor. Jesus here focuses only on love for neighbor. The reason for centering only on the ethical side may well be that the ruler's question dealt with good works, so Jesus does the same. To have a proper relationship with God you must relate properly to your fellow human beings.

The man proudly comments, "All these I have kept since I was a boy" (a further link to 18:15–17). This extravagant claim is similar to that of the Pharisee in 18:11. He is saying he has faithfully observed the Torah from the time he reached the age of legal responsibility (thirteen years). He assumes that he stands right with God and expects Jesus now to say he has done all he needs to do. He is waiting for his merit badge of salvation.

It had to come as a shock to learn there was an insurmountable obstacle that must be dealt with before he could be right with God. Jewish people assumed that wealth was a sign of divine blessing and pleasure and never a barrier to God. Moreover, Jesus says it so starkly that the man's mouth must have fallen open: "You still lack one thing. Sell everything you have and give to the poor, and you will have treasure in heaven." This is exactly the point of 16:8b-9, but here it is even stronger since he demands, "sell *everything*." His possessions had become his idol, and so he had to rid himself of this force that had enslaved him. These are the things that will keep him from eternal life, so he must divest himself of them. Nothing could have been more shocking to the average Jewish person, who assumed this very thing meant God favored them.

Some monastic movements (primarily in the Middle Ages) have taken this as an absolute rule for proper ministry and demanded vows of poverty. However, this is not mandated elsewhere. Zacchaeus in 19:8 gives away only half his possessions. The problem is most likely that this particular man was completely controlled by his wealth, and so he had to get away from it entirely. The radical demands of Jesus regarding mammon throughout Luke (6:20-26; 9:3; 16:13) and the centrality of caring for the poor are essential aspects of discipleship. It doesn't mean every Christian must rid herself of all possessions, but it does mean that all of us must live for God and Christ completely and allow nothing to come between us and our Lord.

When this ruler has done this, he can begin his discipleship: "*Then* come, follow me." To be a Christ follower demands radical surrender, and the shallow levels of commitment we so often see today just will not cut it. Christlikeness is a mandate in every New Testament book (see Eph 4:13, "the whole measure of the fullness of Christ"). The extent to which we depend on ourselves and our earthly resources will determine success or failure in our Christward walk.

At this point the ruler was filled with sadness "because he was very wealthy" (18:23). Jesus had truly hit on his insurmountable barrier—his possessions—and he felt unable to comply. He was not willing to divest himself of his riches, and they meant more to him than being right with God. He forsook eternity for the sake of temporary luxuries. In contrast, the inner circle of disciples in 5:11 "left everything and followed" Jesus. This man exemplified true addiction, what in our time has been labeled "affluenza." One wonders what would happen if Jesus got up in our churches and made the demand he made on this man. How many people would walk away from salvation?

SAYINGS ON WEALTH AND MATERIALISM (18:24–30)

Jesus responds to the ruler's unwillingness to part with his wealth by commenting, "How hard it is for the rich to enter the kingdom of God!" Riches so tie people to this world that they cannot leave their wealth for the sake of the next world. Entering the kingdom is another way to describe salvation. There is an inaugurated sense here, for we have "already" entered the kingdom when we became Christians but have "not yet" consummated our new life by entering heaven. Putting the picture together, this depicts a person's being rescued from the heavy chains that possessions have become and being transported to God's realm. Those who have overcome their ties to this world are the liberated captives of 4:18. The wealthy have so much power over this life that they perceive little need for God or the heavenly realm. They are their own gods and go to eternal damnation thinking they are in charge.

In verse 25 Jesus tells just how difficult it is to relinquish earthly possessions in order to attain salvation. "Indeed, it is easier for a camel to go through the eye of a needle" than for the rich to become children of the kingdom. The metaphor has been long misunderstood. You often still hear it said that there was a gate called the Needle's Eye in Jerusalem, a low opening that was difficult for a camel to pass through. However, no such gate existed in Jesus' day.

Others think it was originally a "rope" (*kamilon*) rather than a "camel" (*kamēlon*). But there is no need to alter the image, for it is simply rabbinic hyperbole: the largest animal in Palestine passing through the smallest possible hole. Jesus was simply colorfully picturing the extraordinary difficulty of converting the rich.

The natural response in verse 26 is astonishment: "Who then can be saved?" If the wealthy who are especially blessed by God cannot find eternal salvation, what chance does anyone else have? "Can" is *dynatai*, and in this context it asks "by what power is anyone able to find salvation?" Jesus responds that it is impossible from a human perspective but not for God. In reality the salvation of any of us is a total impossibility, but that is why God sent his Son to die on the cross as the atoning sacrifice for our sins. The idolatry of wealth, like any other sin, can be overcome by God. Humanly speaking, materialists cannot be moved away from their security and dependence on the world's goods, but by the grace and mercy of God that can take place. There is an echo here of Genesis 18:4 ("Is anything too hard for the LORD?") and Job 42:2 ("I know that you can do all things").

Peter, as usual, has been thinking of the situation of the disciples and wants to know where they fit in to all this. The negative tone has him worried, so he asks abruptly in verse 28, "We have left all we had to follow you." He is reminding Jesus that they have already passed the test that the wealthy ruler failed and left their possessions behind. Two things found in Matthew 19:27 are implied here: "to follow you" (they have entered their discipleship journey) and "What then will there be for us?" This is Peter's major question, and it shows they have not left their ambitions behind. Their desire for greatness and glory has long been evident (9:46; 22:24). Still, they have come far, and Jesus treats his comment seriously. The requirements for following Jesus have been clear (9:23; 11:9–10; 12:22, 40; 14:26, 27, 33), and he will build on that here.

Jesus' response (vv. 29–30) is another *amēn* saying (18:17) stressing the absolute truth and importance of the message. God will more than make up for every personal sacrifice. We are back to the issue of rewards in heaven (16:9). Following Jesus will indeed mean for many the loss of home and family "for the sake of the kingdom of God." This builds on Jesus' earlier teaching in which he stressed that his followers must put him above their family (9:60, 61), and that households would be divided as a result (12:52–53). Self-sacrifice is at the very heart of discipleship. Surrendering "all" does not just mean possessions (present in Matt 19:29) but family as well. Jesus probably has in mind here some family members who reject their stance for Christ, and others who join them but then are martyred. As his disciples suffer these losses, they need comfort and reassurance, and Jesus lets them know that God is not only aware of their sacrifice but will both vindicate and reward them for it as well.

He then spells out the divine recompense for such losses, which is twofold, referring to the already and the not-yet. First, we will "receive many times as much in this age" (Mark 10:30, "a hundred-fold"). The loss of our nuclear family will be replaced by our spiritual family in the messianic community (see 5:10; 8:21). Second, "in the age to come [we will receive] eternal life" (looking back to the question in v. 18). The reception of eternal life is the key concept, beginning and ending the whole unit here. The temporary (possessions and homes) is completely eclipsed by the eternal (life in heaven).

JESUS MAKES HIS THIRD PASSION PREDICTION (19:31-34)

The disciples may have to sacrifice home and possessions for Jesus; Jesus is sacrificing his very life for them on the cross. This might be called the third "official" prediction (with 9:22, 44), with several other allusions (5:35; 12:50; 13:32-33; 17:25). Luke replaces the accompanying selfish request by James and John for the key places of honor in the kingdom (Mark 10:35-37) with a twofold emphasis:

the lack of understanding on the part of the Twelve, and the connection of that with the divine plan of salvation history.

The prediction itself (vv. 31–33) defines the purpose of the road to Jerusalem and stands in absolute contrast with the ruler's unwillingness to sacrifice even his possessions (18:23). In the first verse here (31) Jesus tells them what will happen when they are "going up to Jerusalem." At that time "everything that is written by the prophets about the Son of Man will be fulfilled." All the rest of the chapter has led up to this point. All that has been said—the power of persistent prayer, a life of humility before God, a life of following Jesus, the gift of eternal life—is made possible by Jesus' passion in Jerusalem and its fulfillment of messianic prophecy.

This prediction contains the greatest detail of the three (18:32–33). He will not just be given over to the leaders of Israel but also "delivered over to the Gentiles." The entire world of humankind will be complicit in his death, as all turn against him. Jesus then lists five things they will do to him: (1) mockery, as seen in the guards in 22:63, Herod and his soldiers in 23:11, the rulers in 23:35, and the malefactor in 23:39; (2) insults, as with the soldiers of Herod in 23:11 and those at the cross in 23:36; (3) spitting on him, not in Luke but in Mark 14:65; 15:19; (4) flogging or beating him, referring to the guards in 22:63 and the scourging of Matthew 27:26; (5) putting him to death on the cross, done by the Jews (Acts 3:15) and the Gentiles (here). Then he will be raised on the third day, also stressed in the prediction of 9:22. We don't know how early in his life he became aware that all this was his God-given destiny, but it could have been from the very start.

The disciples' lack of comprehension (18:34) is given in detail via three synonymously parallel clauses in an ABA pattern, with their dullness (A) framing the divine hiddenness (B). Their Jewish background meant they looked at the Messiah entirely as the conquering King who would destroy the Romans and establish his kingdom on the earth with the Jews ruling the nations. The idea of a suffering Messiah was not part of that, and they understood Isaiah 52–53 of themselves as a suffering nation rather than of the Messiah.

The statement that "its meaning was hidden from them" is a divine passive. God has hidden this from them, an emphasis seen also in 9:45 (also a passion prediction), 19:42 (hidden from the Pharisees), and 24:16 (the disciples on the road to Emmaus). The disciples did not have the comprehensive perspective on God's plan and could not put the pieces together. The means of doing so would not be there until after the resurrection, so God kept the full reality from them. For now God wanted them to focus entirely on Jesus and their place in the unfolding events that would all too soon come to fruition. That would be more than enough for them. Only after the events have transpired can they understand God's whole purpose and the Old Testament prophecies that will be fulfilled in it.

JESUS HEALS A BLIND MAN IN JERICHO (18:35-43)

The two Jericho events (18:35-43; 19:1-10) in effect close the ministry portion of Luke and prepare directly for the passion events to follow. Luke adds the Zacchaeus incident and the parable of the money to Mark and Matthew, reiterating the Lukan theme of Jesus' messianic ("Son of David") compassion for the outcasts (a blind man and a tax collector). In so doing Luke combines Christology and social concern with the need for persistent faith. As in other healing miracles, the physical and spiritual components are united in a single act of "salvation." Salvation continues to be the consuming thread of the narrative, and we see it from the perspective of the cry for mercy (the blind man) and the results of salvation, the dispersal of money to help the poor (Zacchaeus). Zacchaeus provides the opposite response of the wealthy ruler in 18:23 and demonstrates true discipleship.

The travel narrative continues in verse 35 "as Jesus approached Jericho" (9:51-52, 57; 10:1, 38; 11:53; 13:22; 17:11; 18:31, 35; 19:1, 28).

Jericho is seventeen miles northeast of Jerusalem, close to the border of Judea. It is six miles from the Jordan and north of the Dead Sea. It consists of two cities: the old city, which had deteriorated over the centuries and was probably uninhabited at this point; and the Roman new city just south of it, built by Herod the Great around his winter palace and famed for its beauty. As Jesus is entering the city, he passes a blind beggar (named Bartimaeus in Mark 10:46), rendered destitute by his blindness and forced to beg to stay alive.

Passover was drawing near, and Jesus and his followers were probably part of a group of pilgrims heading up the road, as this was the normal route from Galilee to Judea. Hearing the commotion as Jesus is drawing near, the beggar asks a passerby what is going on and is told, "Jesus of Nazareth is passing by." Some see a double meaning in "of Nazareth," inferring that he is the Messiah, "the shoot/Branch from the stump of Jesse" (Isa 11:1, where the word translated "Branch" is Hebrew *netser*). However, this was a normal way of naming a person in the first century, and there is no hint here of such a symbolic use.

However, the blind man had heard a great deal about Jesus and seems to have become a believer, for he immediately cries out, probably at the top of his voice (18:38), "Jesus, Son of David, have mercy on me!" This is the only use of this title in a healing miracle in Luke, but it is often found in Matthew (9:27; 12:23; 15:22; 20:30, 31) and shows Jesus as the messianic Shepherd who heals the nation. Jesus as Davidic Messiah is found in 1:27, 32; 2:4; 3:31; 20:41; and on the lips of this blind man it is another example of the tremendous faith of the "little people" in Luke, as Jesus will acknowledge in verse 42. This messianic aura surrounding Jesus will increase as we move closer to Jerusalem. "Have mercy" is frequent in the Psalms as the cry of the afflicted to God for help (for example, 2:4; 6:2; 41:4).

Pilgrims in the crowd apparently tried to shield Jesus from this bothersome beggar and sternly rebuked his efforts (as the

disciples in 18:15). They stand in opposition to the mercy of God
in this scene and to Jesus' messianic ministry to the blind, preparing for the opposition Jesus will face in Jerusalem. They also
make it evident that the man is of no consequence, not worthy of
Jesus' time and effort. However, the more they rebuked him, the
louder he cried for mercy. He, like the persistent widow of 18:1-8,
was not to be denied.

Instead, it is the crowd that is implicitly rebuked by Jesus, who
has come into this world to "set the oppressed free" (see 4:18-19).
Luke simplifies Mark's dramatic detail (10:49-51) in order to center
on the conversation with the beggar. Jesus' concern for his plight is
clear, but he also wants to challenge his faith, so instead of healing
him immediately, he involves him in the faith process by asking,
"What do you want me to do for you?" He wants him to vocalize
his faith, and that is exactly what he does when he replies, "Lord,
I want to see." He has no doubt that Jesus can heal him. No blind
man had ever been healed before Jesus came, and it was widely
believed that would not take place until the Messiah arrived. The
blind man knew that this is exactly who this Son of David was. At
the start Jesus had used Isaiah 61:1-2 to state that his messianic
ministry would involve "recovery of sight for the blind" (4:18), and
it was a critical part of his ministry (7:21-22).

The miracle itself is prefaced by Jesus' own confession, "Receive
your sight; your faith has healed you" (v. 42; see also 5:20; 7:50; 8:48;
17:19). "Healed" is *sesōken*, with a double meaning, connoting both
physical healing and spiritual salvation. The man's faith-response
has brought God's spiritual presence into his life.

This is another miracle that does not require physical contact. Jesus proclaims; healing takes place. The fact that the man
became a believer is attested in the fact that he immediately began
to "follow" Jesus, initiating his life of discipleship. As in most other
times of contact and miracle, the result is also his "praising," or
"glorifying" (*doxazōn*), God (2:20; 5:25-26; 7:16; 13:13; 17:15). This further enhances the messianic aura of the scene, especially as the

people join in the refrain, with "all" of them praising God. This is a harbinger of the triumphal entry, where again all the bystanders will join in the praise (19:37). This will be short-lived, however, for at the trial just a few days from now they will be calling for Jesus to be crucified (23:18, 21, 23).

———

This is a wonderful chapter on the power of prayer, the importance of an active faith, and the kind of compassionate Father to whom we pray. The passage on the persistent widow and persevering prayer (vv. 1–8) emphasizes the merciful Lord to whom we go in prayer. If we can trust that justice takes place in this world, how much more can we be certain that justice reigns in heaven? Ongoing faith in trying times is critical for God's people.

What follows is a series of examples of the proper attitude behind prayer. In the first, the self-righteous prayer of the Pharisee is contrasted with the humble prayer of a lowly tax collector (vv. 9–14). In prayer we cast ourselves entirely on the mercy and compassion of God, and he rewards our surrender to him and declares us right before him. Then Jesus emphasizes the example and importance of children to the kingdom (vv. 15–17). Children are not just critical models of kingdom faith; they are important resources to the kingdom community. Children are essential to the life of the church.

The wealthy ruler (vv. 18–23) is a further negative example of what Jesus is talking about in this chapter. He wanted to follow Christ and was a serious "seeker," but he was addicted to material things and could not give them up in order to be a Christ follower. So he lost it all for earthly things. It sounds like no one who is rich can ever be saved, and the disciples despair, but Jesus assures them that his Father is the God of the impossible, and people can indeed overcome their materialism to find salvation (vv. 24–27). Jesus promises the disciples that God will more than repay us for everything we sacrifice in him, and those rewards will be eternal, not just temporary like earthly things (vv. 28–30).

An important example of such sacrifice is Jesus himself, as seen in the third passion prediction (vv. 31–34). They have surrendered earthly things, even family, but Jesus gives up his life for their salvation. Moreover, the reality and meaning of this has been hidden from them by God until the resurrection, when they would be able to understand it.

The healing of the blind man (vv. 35–43) concludes the miracle-working part of Jesus' public ministry that has dominated Luke (passion week begins two episodes later, 19:28). This man is the final person who shows true faith by throwing himself completely on Jesus' mercy and depending on him. This persistent faith results in both physical and spiritual healing, and he becomes a devoted follower of Jesus.

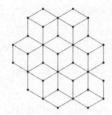

END OF JESUS' MINISTRY AND START OF PASSION WEEK
(19:1–48)

This chapter has to be divided in half. Jesus remains in Jericho for the first two parts (vv. 1-10, 11-27), and then he arrives in the environs of Jerusalem and begins passion week with the triumphal entry (vv. 28-44) and opening events at the temple (vv. 45-48). Jesus' time of destiny has arrived, and we are swiftly moving to the central event of human history, the cross and resurrection (which are a single event). Death is the path to life.

ZACCHAEUS IS CONVERTED (19:1-10)

Jericho was a major tax center for the region, and Zacchaeus was one of the administrators, which means he organized the taxes as well as the collectors and received a percentage of all the taxes collected (see further on 3:12). The result is that he was a very wealthy and powerful man. Like Levi/Matthew he was Jewish. Tradition says he later became bishop of Caesarea (*Apostolic Constitutions* 7.46), but we don't know how reliable that is. His name is the Greek form of Hebrew *zakkai*, "righteous/innocent one."

He had heard a great deal about Jesus but had never actually seen him, so he wishes to do so but can't see over the crowds since he is a short man. Also, being a despised tax collector and probably well known himself, he doesn't want to buck the crowds and face their contempt. So he takes the initiative, runs ahead a ways, and climbs up a "sycamore-fig tree," plenteous because Jericho contained many such trees. This was a large fig tree similar to an oak and easy to climb, with wide, low branches.

Zacchaeus just wants a look at Jesus, but he quickly finds out Jesus knows all about him. We don't know how, through omniscience (as in John 1:47–48) or simply asking about him. In the story, Jesus completely takes the initiative and calls Zacchaeus to salvation. He calls him by name and tells him, "Come down immediately. I must stay at your house today." The "must" is the frequent *dei*, which throughout Luke-Acts speaks of divine necessity (2:49; 4:43; 9:22; 17:25; Acts 1:16; 3:21; 6:12). Moreover, "today" is also filled with meaning, referring to the immediacy of divine salvation (2:11; 4:21; 23:43). God is truly making Zacchaeus one of the elect.

So he welcomes Jesus into his home and into his life with great joy (19:6: "gladly"). In the Near East a guest brought honor into a home, and this would have been especially true for a famous rabbi and miracle worker like Jesus. In fact, this would have been especially joyous because as a tax collector Zacchaeus would have been vilified by all around, so Jesus may have been the first Jewish leader ever to set foot in that home. His acceptance and love for Zacchaeus and his family must have astounded them.

In fact, the Jewish reaction becomes evident in verse 7 when they "began to mutter, 'He has gone to be the guest of a sinner,'" the same reaction as in 5:30, 15:2. To have table fellowship (share a meal) with a person in the ancient world meant to accept them and share their life. So Jesus by staying with him partook of his bad reputation in the town. He is tarred with the same brush, a common result of ministry to outcasts in our day as well. Jesus shares the bad with the good and truly takes the sorrows of his followers on himself.

We don't know where the conversation took place, whether under the tree or during the meal, though the latter is more likely since it is doubtful that Zacchaeus had made all these surprising decisions in just the moments it took him to climb down the tree. Tithing in the Old Testament added up to about 15 percent, and rabbis asked for 20 percent, so Zacchaeus in verse 8 is going way beyond the norm by giving "half of my possessions to the poor." Many think that the present-tense "here and now I give" means this was his current practice, but I agree with those who see it more as his present decision in the light of the impact Jesus and God's salvation have made on his life. This is favored by verse 9, for it seems part of his present faith-decision. So it represents his resolve for his future ethical actions. As the Baptist had told tax collectors to do in 3:8, Zacchaeus is producing "fruit in keeping with repentance."

Tax collectors were infamous frauds and constantly embezzled money. He admits this and then states, "If I have cheated anybody out of anything [which he obviously has], I will pay back four times the amount." The normal amount expected was the amount stolen plus 20 percent more (Lev 5:16; Num 5:6–7), although rustlers of cattle repaid four times the amount (Exod 22:1; 2 Sam 12:6). So he promises to more than repay all past wrongs. All of this shows not only that he has become a follower of Christ but also that he is more than compensating for past sins and establishing a pattern of social concern for all future dealings. He is a model of discipleship, clearly the opposite of the wealthy ruler in 18:22–23.

Jesus' reply (19:9–10) focuses on the promise of "today" in verse 5: "Today salvation has come to this house." Could there be a more joyous declaration? The "now-ness" of salvation is a frequent emphasis in Luke-Acts (2:11; 4:21; Acts 4:9; 26:29). Rejected as a tax collector, Zacchaeus is now part of the new Israel, a true "son of Abraham." His "house" is now part of the messianic community, and as in Acts (10:2; 11:14; 16:15; 18:8), this may mean that his extended family turned to Christ along with him. The determining factor is faith-decision and its ethical results in turning to the poor and emulating Jesus as his disciple.

Jesus explains this pronouncement regarding salvation in verse 10. Jesus' mission as Son of Man is "to seek and to save the lost." The Son of Man imagery recalls the glorified figure of Daniel 7:13-14 and presents him as the Shepherd of Yahweh seeking his scattered sheep that are not yet part of his fold (Ezek 34:16). Jesus is taking over God's mission to the world and will carry it to its final conclusion when this age comes to an end. As in 5:24, the Son of Man has come to earth with "authority ... to forgive sins," and his mission is to bring God's salvation to humankind. This is why it is the Son of Man who will be delivered to the cross (9:22, 44; 18:31-32). His atoning sacrifice is the basis for salvation. So Zacchaeus is the focus of Jesus' mission of salvation and now will join him in taking this salvation to the world.

JESUS TELLS THE PARABLE OF THE TEN MINAS (19:11-27)

This is the final episode in the travel narrative of Luke (9:51-19:27), as Jesus is "near Jerusalem" and about to begin passion week. It flows naturally out of the Zacchaeus episode, with its emphasis on wise use of money, and becomes a natural conclusion to the stress on possessions throughout Luke.[1] There is some question regarding its connection with the parable of the pounds in Matthew 25:14-30. Many think they are one and the same parable, but the details differ quite a bit, and it is more likely that Jesus used this story form and changed details to fit the different occasions.

THE SETTING: ARRIVAL OF THE KINGDOM (19:11)

Jesus' teaching has focused more and more on kingdom issues as he draws near Jerusalem, and so the people following him are wondering if "the kingdom of God was going to appear at once." Jesus had earlier said the kingdom had already arrived (11:20-23), and

---

1. See "Major Theological Themes" in the introduction.

they were interpreting this as the approach of heaven's armies and the day of the Lord, in which their enemies would be defeated.

Two questions arise: (1) Are "the people" (the Greek is literally translated "they") the disciples or the crowds? In light of the context (moving from Zacchaeus to the triumphal entry) it is likely a combination of both groups. (2) Does this center on the second coming or the events of passion week? Most likely, the latter is the focus. The people are thinking of a conquering king who will destroy the Romans, but Jesus is countering that set of expectations by stating that he has come to serve and give his life for humankind and that he is establishing an interim period before the final kingdom arrives.

A Noble Departs to Be Named King (19:12–14)

This parable is about a nobleman who sets out to "be appointed king." The background is the trip Archelaus took to Rome in 4 BC to be named king by Emperor Augustus after the death of his father Herod the Great, placing his officers in charge of his money and property. Jesus undoubtedly intends the interim period between the nobleman's departure and return to represent the period between his first and second advents. This period, in fact, is what this parable is all about.

The nobleman does not wish to leave his fortune unattended, so before he goes he calls ten key servants and gives them responsibility to watch over his treasures. These ten servants do not represent the twelve disciples. Rather, they represent all the followers ("servants") of Jesus. At any rate, they are each given a single "mina," a coin equivalent to one hundred Jewish drachmas or Roman denarii, and told to "put this money to work" and earn profit for him while he is gone.

A drachma is one day's wage for the average worker, so this would be equivalent to four months' wages. This is much less than Matthew's "talent" in his version of this parable (Matt 25:14–30), as a mina is one-sixtieth of a talent, and it is difficult to know why this future king gives so little to his servants. Most likely, the point is like that of 16:10, "Whoever can be trusted with very little can also be trusted with much," when the successful investors are given charge of ten and five cities in verses 17, 19. Here they are to take their master's money and use it to gain more, and then he will evaluate their success and give them even greater responsibility and honor after he returns.

After he leaves, it turns out that the people of his realm are opposed to him and send a delegation protesting against him, "We don't want this man to be our king." In the case of Archelaus, a Jewish delegation opposed his becoming king on the grounds of his massacre of three thousand people at Passover time (Josephus, *Antiquities* 17.9.3). The result was that he was not named king but ethnarch (ruler of half the province) of Judea and Samaria. In Jesus' case, the Jewish leaders will soon reject his kingship and demand his death at his trial before Pilate (23:18-23).

SETTLING ACCOUNTS (19:15-27)

Unlike Archelaus, this nobleman was crowned king and returns to his land in charge of everything. The first thing he does is call for his servants to see how they handled their responsibilities and determine how much authority he could give them in his new kingdom. The criterion for success is simple—the amount of profit they earned from their investments. Jesus chooses only three of the ten to make his point.

The first had terrific results, multiplying his mina tenfold, or 1,000 percent profit. He has not only been faithful but also very successful, proving he can be "trusted with much" (16:10, noted above). The true purpose of verse 13 in giving him the mina is now shown—it was a test of faithfulness to demonstrate the worthiness of the servant to rule over a portion of the master's/king's new kingdom. Having proved both resourceful and aggressive, he can now receive his reward. It seems incredibly disproportional, but it makes sense as a test in the area of a "very small matter" to see how worthy he is. His reward is to be made a nobleman and given rule over a large portion of the kingdom—ten cities, matching the profit of ten minas. This would remind Jesus' listeners of the Decapolis, the region with ten major cities in Gentile territory just north of them (Mark 5:20; 7:31).

The second servant also had excellent results, multiplying his mina fivefold, or 500 percent profit (19:18). The reward is also commensurate, as he is placed in rule over a region of five cities. The principle of reciprocity continues, as the reward matches the profit earned exactly. In the book of Revelation this is linked with **lex talionis**, the "law of retribution," and it covers both good deeds and bad deeds. It is the key rule for biblical ethics—what we do to those around us we are actually doing to the Lord (whether good or bad), and he will return it on our heads as a completely just reward or punishment.[2]

The third servant is emphasized as a very important warning to Jesus' followers. He has done nothing with his mina but instead "kept it laid away in a piece of cloth." This is a *soudarion*, a sweat cloth or handkerchief used to protect the head from the sun. This is a foolish method even compared to the third servant in Matthew's version of the parable; there the servant buried his talent (Matt 25:25), which was far safer than just putting it into a cloth in a drawer. In both versions, though, the final servant refuses to take the risk of investing the money.

The reason (19:21) is his fear of the nobleman, whom he perceived (an important point) as "a hard man," stern or strict, saying to him, "You take out what you did not put in and reap what you did not sow." The first is a commercial metaphor and the second an agricultural metaphor for the type of tough investor who exploits what belongs to others for his own advantage. His servants do all the work, and he takes all the profit for himself. This fearful

---

2. See the discussion of Rev 6:9–11; 16:5–7 in my Revelation commentary in this series.

servant is thinking that anything he earns will be taken from him, and he will be blamed for anything he fails to accomplish. So he hides the money and does nothing.

The king responds to this charge in verses 22–23 and shows how tragically wrong he is: "I will judge you by your own words, you wicked servant!" Actually, he was correct on one thing, that the king is stern and tough—but only with those who fully deserve it. This foolish man has not earned the response he wanted. He knew the king demanded profit, so if he was afraid to invest the mina, he could at least have deposited it in the bank to earn interest. If he was right about his master's hard demands, that should have spurred him to action. To do nothing was inexcusable. This foolish servant represents those followers who fail to live for Christ or serve him in the period between his two advents.

In verses 24–27 the king deals with this foolish servant and the enemies who opposed him in verse 14. In doing so, he demonstrates how tough and stern a judge he is.

First, the servant has forfeited the right to participate in the king's economic council, and so the mina is taken from him and given to the one who has best shown the ingenuity to invest it properly. He has shown he can handle the responsibility and make up for the waste caused by the lazy servant.

Several in the king's entourage (probably a few of the other servants who had been given a mina) protest this, perhaps wanting it to be divided up and given to them. Their reason is that he is already the best off of any of them and has received an incredible reward. Why not help the others? Yet their reasoning is wrongheaded. The purpose of giving the servants money in the first place was not to make them rich but to give them a job to do: making profit and showing how they could handle responsibility. The response to their protest proclaims the moral of the story and a very important **eschatological** principle that repeats 8:18. There it relates to knowledge of the kingdom mysteries, while here it relates to the rewards earned for faithfully serving the Lord. There is debate over who is speaking here, whether it is the king in the parable or Jesus applying the parable. The difference is overblown, though, for while it is certainly the master (note v. 27, "those enemies of mine," showing the parable continuing), the principle provided also comes from Jesus and is addressed to us.

Each of the two parts of the response to the servant is critical. First, "to everyone who has, more will be given," referring to the two servants who showed initiative and could be trusted with more responsibility. This builds on 16:10–13 and the concept of kingdom responsibility. Our earthly resources are given to us as a test to see if God can entrust his treasures to us. If we can prove ourselves good stewards of God's earthly treasures (our possessions), he will give us "true riches" (16:11), namely, the treasures of the kingdom and eternal rewards.

The second is that "the one who has nothing, even what they have will be taken away." This is confusing, for what can be "taken away" from "nothing"? In the parable the third servant loses his place of authority in the council and is stripped of his former status. Its meaning for us is more difficult, but its thrust relates to the issue of responsibility and rewards in the kingdom. All who belong to Jesus are given tasks and required to use their talents for the glory of God and to both enhance the kingdom and help those around us. If we take our God-given earthly resources and live for earthly pleasure rather than God, we will lose both our place in the church and our rewards in heaven.

One other issue needs to be discussed. Is what is "taken away" our rewards (but we will be "saved … as one escaping through the flames," 1 Cor 3:15) or our very salvation (constituting apostasy à la Heb 6:4–6; 1 John 5:16)? Is such a person a carnal Christian or an apostate or perhaps a non-Christian as in Matthew 7:22–23? Here the parallel in Matthew 25:30 is important: "Throw that worthless servant outside, into the darkness, where there will be weeping and gnashing of teeth." This punishment is not only loss of rewards but loss of everything. However we interpret the passages on apostasy, we know that those who don't care enough to live for Christ and waste away all that God has given them will end up with absolutely *nothing*.

Second, as for the "enemies" of the king (19:27) from verse 14, the verdict is very harsh—"Bring them here and kill them in front of me." This wholesale slaughter of enemies calls to mind the Old Testament mandate of holy war, where evil is seen as so serious that those who indulge in it dare not be allowed to live (Deut 7:1-2; 20:16-18). Joshua (Josh 10:16-27) and Samuel (1 Sam 16:33) did this to Israel's enemies. The difference is that here these "enemies" are Jewish, and some have seen this as a prediction of the destruction of Jerusalem by the Romans. That may well be, but the primary emphasis is on the day of the Lord and final judgment. The overall theme is the absolute justice of God, who repays all according to their deeds (Rev 20:13, "judged according to what they had done")— reward for the faithful servants, rejection for the unfaithful servants, destruction for enemies.

PASSION WEEK BEGINS (19:28-48)

The journey to Jerusalem is now finished, and passion week, the final seven days of Jesus' earthly life, is beginning. The events of 19:28-22:38 cover Sunday through Thursday, with the arrest and trial during the night of Thursday into Friday at dawn. Luke's order differs from Mark and Matthew slightly, but here is a précis of what transpires after Jesus arrives in Bethany on Friday:

- *Saturday*: Mary anoints Jesus (Matt 26:6-13 [placed later]; John 12:2-8).
- *Sunday*: Triumphal entry (Luke 19:28-40); weeps over Jerusalem (Luke 19:41-44).
- *Monday*: Cleansing the temple (Luke 19:45-46); cursing the fig tree (Matt 21:18-22).
- *Tuesday*: Controversies in the temple (Luke 19:47-20:44); woes against the scribes and Pharisees (Matt 23; Luke 20:45-47); Olivet Discourse (Matt 24-25; Luke 21:5-38).

- *Wednesday*: Jesus and his disciples apparently remain in Bethany (with Jesus teaching in the temple, 21:37); Judas arranges for his betrayal (Matt 26:14–16; Luke 22:3–6).
- *Thursday*: Preparations for Passover (Luke 22:7–14); Passover meal and events after sundown (Luke 22:15–38); Farewell Discourse (John 13–17); arrest at midnight (Luke 22:47–53).
- *Friday*: Peter's denials and mockery (Luke 22:54–65); trials before the Sanhedrin (Luke 22:66–71) and Pilate and Herod (Luke 23:1–25); crucifixion (Luke 23:26–49).

THE TRIUMPHAL ENTRY (19:28–40)

The seventeen miles from Jericho up to Jerusalem is a rugged walk, ascending thirty-five hundred feet. Bethphage and Bethany were on the southeastern side of the Mount of Olives, just a couple of miles from Jerusalem. The mountain consisted of three peaks, with the highest at three thousand feet. It is disputed whether Jesus sent the two disciples to Bethany or Bethphage. His purpose in the arrangements is definitely to show messianic fulfillment, centering on three passages: Zechariah 14:4, which prophesies that Yahweh will stand on the Mount of Olives on the day of Yahweh; Genesis 49:10–11, stating that the lion of the tribe of Judah will tether his donkey and colt to a branch; and 2 Samuel 15:30–31, when David returned to Jerusalem (after Absalom had forced him to flee) on a donkey.

Jesus' purpose here is to show that he will not be the conquering messiah they are expecting who will bring the armies of heaven to destroy Israel's enemies. Rather, he is the Suffering Servant, who is coming to defeat a different enemy, the sinfulness of humankind, and bring messianic peace, as symbolized by the donkey.

He instructs the two (v. 30) to enter the village and "find a colt tied there, which no one has ever ridden. Untie it and bring it here." Thoughts differ on whether Jesus had made prior arrangements for the donkeys or whether this is due to omniscience.

Whichever is the case (I prefer the latter), the emphasis is on the divine control of events. Matthew 21:2 has a donkey and a colt, fulfilling Zechariah 9:9, and this is Jesus' purpose, to show that he is indeed the long-awaited Messiah and fulfill the prophetic expectations. This is a symbolic action much like those done by Elijah and Jeremiah. Jesus is going to enter Jerusalem in abject humility on the colt of a donkey rather than a white warhorse. As the crowds cheer his messianic entry, they have no idea they are acclaiming the Suffering Servant who is the king of peace rather than war and will defeat not the Romans but the powers of darkness and bring spiritual salvation rather than political liberation.

It is possible that "the Lord needs it" (19:31) is a prearranged signal. However, there is no indication that this is the case in any of the Gospels that narrate this episode. It has the aura of the Roman practice of requisitioning, in which soldiers required people to perform tasks for them (like Simon bearing Jesus' cross in 23:26). This makes much better sense here. Jesus is acting like the messianic king, the "Lord" of the Old Testament, and this is his divine foreknowledge taking control of the events. This control is proved when the disciples arrive at the village and find everything "just as he had told them." Again, this is evidence of his foreknowledge rather than prior arrangements. Luke, in fact, takes the time to show in detail that the instructions came to pass perfectly (19:33–34), and that the owners of the colt complied with Jesus' command to requisition the animal. Once more, Jesus' control of every detail is emphasized.

As in Zechariah 9:9 (quoted in John 12:15), the humble king enters riding a donkey, the emblem of peace. Throughout the passage, Luke highlights the involvement of the disciples in seating Jesus, accompanying him, and leading the acclamation. (The other Gospels add the acclamation by the pilgrims as well.) The act of placing their cloaks on the colt and seating Jesus on it depicts homage to royalty, as with Solomon on David's mule in 1 Kings 1:33.

The people[3] spreading their cloaks on the road (the palm branches are found in John 12:13) recalls Jehu's acclamation as king in 2 Kings 9:13. All the Gospels depict this as a "red carpet ride" into the city. The royal Messiah is in procession into the city of God, but not for the purpose the people think.

They arrive at that spot where the path on the Mount of Olives makes a steep decline to the city gates, and the "whole crowd of disciples" erupts in joyful praise to God (19:37). Luke has a great deal of emphasis throughout his Gospel on praise and worship, as in the infancy narratives (1:10, 41–44, 46–47, 64, 68; 2:13–14, 20, 28–32, 38). This stress on worship will continue through the passion and resurrection narratives. Luke links this loud praise with "all the miracles they had seen," looking at Jesus' miracles as proof that God's kingdom has truly arrived (7:22; 11:20–23). Both the disciples and the pilgrims are rejoicing that now at last this miracle-working prophet, the one they believe to be the expected Messiah, is finally declaring himself.

The acclamation itself (19:38) celebrates this hope. Luke omits "Hosanna" from the other Gospels, probably because his Gentile readers would have trouble understanding it. He centers on the Hallel praise of Psalm 118:26, a cry used to greet pilgrims in the psalm. Here the emphasis is on the entry of the royal Messiah, the king who leads the pilgrims to the temple and receives royal acclamation, "Blessed is the king who comes in the name of the Lord." This was used earlier in 13:35, where Jesus in his lament over Jerusalem said they would see him no more until this psalm came to pass. That promise is partially fulfilled here as Jesus' messianic purpose comes to fulfillment. (It will be fulfilled completely at the second coming.) The humble King is entering God's city and temple "in the name of the Lord" to complete his messianic destiny.

---

3. Here the emphasis is on the actions of the disciples, but Matt 21:8 has "a very large crowd" of pilgrims joining in this accompaniment of Jesus into Jerusalem.

In 2:14 the angels prophesied that the coming of the Messiah would bring peace on earth. Now it is "peace in heaven," not the type of false peace promised and never provided in the *Pax Romana* ("Roman peace") but the true heavenly peace promised by God and now provided in the gift of his Son. Jerusalem will have no peace and will soon be destroyed by Rome, but for all who turn to Christ there will be an inexplicable peace from God that will come with his gift of salvation and the new age Christ is inaugurating.

The proper conclusion is "glory in the highest." In the Greek this takes **chiastic** form, "In heaven [A] peace [B] and glory [B′] in the highest [A′]," emphasizing the heavenly origin of the peace and glory. God has brought peace in his salvation, and all who receive that peace must praise and glorify him. The pilgrims who shouted this praise were thinking of earthly peace and praise, but Luke wants us to catch the heavenly origin of it all.

The final rebuke by the Pharisees occurs in verse 39 (only in Luke) as they demand that Jesus "rebuke [his] disciples." This shows they understood the messianic nature of their acclamation and, as we would expect, are offended by it. We have seen this often, with the crowd praising him and the leaders opposing him. They still consider him to be a rabbi and call him "teacher," another name for a rabbi. They don't want the common people stirred up during this highly emotional Passover season with such ideas.

Jesus responds (v. 40) that silence is completely impossible. The idea that "the stones will cry out" echoes Genesis 4:10 (Abel's blood crying out from the ground) and especially Habakkuk 2:11, where the stones cry out in protest of Israel's injustice. There are two possibilities here: crying out against the evil of the Jews in rejecting the Messiah; or crying out in witness to Jesus as Messiah. It is possible that both aspects are intended, but in this context the latter has priority. The triumphal entry is intended by God to unlock the reality of Jesus' true nature and messianic purpose, and it cannot be checked.

Lament over Jerusalem (19:41–44)

As he descended the hill and "approached Jerusalem," grief over the apostate city overwhelmed him and he cried out his sorrow. He knew what was about to overtake it, and his tears began to flow. His weeping echoes the prophets who also faced an apostate Holy City that is no longer holy (Jer 9:1; 14:17). Jesus' mention of "what would bring you peace" is likely a play on words, as the name Jerusalem means "city of peace." The very name of their city has now been "hidden from [their] eyes," for they have rejected their Messiah, and God has rejected them. They have blinded themselves to truth; God has blinded them to the path of peace.

The indictment and its resultant condemnation (19:43–44) mean God has removed his protection from Israel. Five actions against Jerusalem by her enemies depict the prophesied siege of Jerusalem by Rome in AD 68–70: (1) They "will build an embankment against you," a structure for breaching the wall (Isa 29:3; 37:33; Ezek 4:1–3). (2) They will "encircle" or surround her, a total siege blocking off all avenues of help or escape. (3) They will "hem you in on every side," exerting terrible pressure and a sense of helplessness. (4) They will "dash" the city "to the ground, you and the children," total destruction of both property and people. (5) They will "not leave one stone on another," also stated in Matthew 24:2. Some scholars claim that this is a "prophecy after the event," and on this basis argue that this Gospel had to have been written after AD 70.[4] However, there is not the detail that such would envisage, and the language is all taken from the Old Testament rather than from the future event.

The reason for such total devastation is that the Jewish people "did not recognize the time of God's coming to you." God in Jesus gave them opportunity after opportunity to recognize his hand in Jesus and the presence of the kingdom in his words and deeds,

---

4. See "Date" in the introduction.

but they rejected every sign. Virtually every detail in Luke's Gospel describes how the new era of God's salvation had arrived in the person of his Son Jesus Christ. So they stand before God completely guilty.

CLEANSING THE TEMPLE (19:45-46)

Luke is highly selective here, omitting the cursing of the fig tree and many of the details in order to focus on the greed of those selling sacrificial animals who have turned the temple into a merchandise mart. The other Gospels tell us how soon after Jesus arrived he went and observed the temple activities and then spent the night in Bethany (Mark 11:11-12). Monday morning he returned and cast out the money changers and sellers of animals. Here only the sellers are mentioned, and Luke mentions neither the entry into Jerusalem nor the night's stay in Bethany. The cleansing of the temple is directly linked to the aftermath of the triumphal entry itself and thus is presented as a further messianic event. Jesus acts as prophet and Messiah in purifying God's temple.

The court of the Gentiles, a huge area (twenty-five acres) that made up the outer precincts of Herod's temple, was home to various merchants selling both sacrificial animals (oxen and sheep for the wealthy, doves for the poor) and other sacrificial items like wine, oil, and salt as well as others exchanging pagan currencies for Tyrian silver for the temple tax. Both groups are probably included in "those who were selling," and they made exorbitant profits on these items. Jesus, highly offended, "began to drive [them] out," proclaiming his prophetic denunciation.

Jesus doesn't just show his own anger at such greed. He anchors it in what stands written in the prophets, referring first to the "house of prayer" in Isaiah 56:7. The core of temple worship was the morning and evening prayer, and Isaiah stresses that it is "for all nations," omitted by Luke probably to make the contrast with "den of robbers" more stark. The profit motive and the noise of the sellers and animals ruined the prayer time in the temple. Material greed had replaced temple worship.

Jeremiah 7:11 addresses the apostate nation of his day, decrying the fact that the temple, which "bears [God's] Name" has been turned into a "den of robbers" due to the idolatry and greed of the people. Jesus is saying this has been reenacted in his day. Several scholars believe this is unhistorical, since the term *lēstēs* came to denote revolutionary bandits in the 60s AD, and so they believe this reflects a later time. However, the term was used of thieves in Jesus' day, and that describes perfectly his charges against the activities in the temple. They were desecrating God's temple with their commercial interests.

Teaching and Opposition in the Temple (19:47-48)

Luke shows that at the outset of passion week the two opposing sides were very active. "Every day" (Monday through Wednesday, perhaps Thursday morning as well), Jesus spends teaching in the temple courts, as he has done whenever he was in Jerusalem. (His many trips are chronicled in John.) In absolute contrast, three groups are arrayed against him, not interested whatsoever in God's truth but only "trying to kill him." Obviously, Jesus is proclaiming the gospel every day in the temple as he nears the end of his life, preparing for the witness of his followers in the early chapters of Acts. His enemies are the leaders of Israel—the chief priests, the scribes, and other leaders (probably Pharisees and elders). The stage is now set for what follows.

Their dilemma is presented in verse 48, and it sets the tone for the rest of the week. They want to see Jesus executed, but they cannot "find any way to do it" due to his immense popularity with "all the people" (nineteen times in chapters 18-24). Luke tells us they "hung on his words," meaning they flocked after him and his teaching in the temple. If they tried to arrest him, the people would riot, and the Romans would intervene. They were totally stymied and didn't know what to do. They had to do two things—arrest Jesus quietly, outside the crowds, and turn the people against him. The first will be accomplished by the betrayal of Judas, the second at the trial before Pilate.

————

We have reached one of the major turning points in Jesus' life with the end of his public ministry (vv. 1–27) and the onset of passion week (vv. 29–48). Jesus is in Jericho just seventeen miles from his destiny, and two events end his lengthy journey to Jerusalem. Zacchaeus (vv. 1–10) is the final disciple to join him and typifies his ministry to the marginalized and his liberation of the outcast. (As a tax collector he was, while wealthy, despised by all.) He also shows what it means to be saved, to turn his back on the wealth that has dominated his life and use his money to minister to the poor and serve God. The social implications of salvation are very evident in this intriguing little story.

The parable of the ten minas (vv. 11–27) is a perfectly apt conclusion to Jesus' ministry because it demonstrates what will happen to all who have reacted to him, his followers, the crowds, and the leaders. The basic premise is that of *lex talionis*, the "law of retribution," which means that God is an absolutely just Judge who will give to all people exactly what they have brought on their own heads by virtue of their reactions to Jesus. The servants were given a fair amount of money (four months' wages) to invest and make a profit for the master as he went away to become king. This represents Jesus in heaven, who has tested us by giving each of us earthly resources and spiritual gifts to use for his glory and to help others. Our reward is based on our success in using all we have for ministry. At the same time, his enemies who oppose him (the Jewish leaders and others) will be destroyed and pay the price for rejecting him.

The rest of the chapter centers on the opening events of passion week. Jesus begins with his triumphal entry into Jerusalem

(vv. 28–40), and the preparatory actions are the perfect lead-in, as they demonstrate his foreknowledge and divine control of every detail. The stress is exactly on his divine sovereignty and jurisdiction over every aspect, as Zechariah 9:9 is fulfilled and Jesus rides in on a donkey, signifying the peace (rather than war) he will accomplish in the coming events. Then the entry itself is truly triumphal as the messianic king is acclaimed by his disciples and the crowds and celebrated as the glorious sovereign he is. They, of course, are thinking of him as Conqueror, and he is, but at this time he will conquer sin and death on the cross. It is peace in heaven rather than political peace on earth that will be achieved by this humble King. Still, the acclamation is well deserved and the cries of joy are greater even than they think, as heaven is undoubtedly joining them.

Two events conclude these opening scenes: Jesus' lament over Jerusalem (vv. 41–44), which has rejected their Messiah and brought the destruction of the city on her head; and the cleansing of the temple (vv. 45–46), where Jesus acts as prophet and Messiah in cleansing the temple of the greed of the leaders. They have used the temple courts as a marketplace to make money for themselves, thereby desecrating the sacred space that should have been used for prayer and converting it into a "den of robbers" who cared only for the illegal profits they could make.

Luke sets the tone for the whole of passion week in verses 47–48. Every morning and afternoon Jesus will be found in the temple courts teaching the people, undoubtedly giving them a final opportunity to repent and come to him. His great love is seen in this, for he knew his life was very soon to be over, yet he spent all his free time extolling the people with gospel truth. In contrast, the leaders were desperately looking for a way to end his life and get rid of this troublemaker. They were to find it with one of his so-called followers.

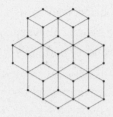

TEACHING AND CONTROVERSY
IN THE TEMPLE
(20:1–21:4)

The daily teaching (19:47) is now described and set in the midst of the opposition of the leaders via three sets of inquisitions (20:1, 20, 27) that try to trap Jesus and turn the people against him. Luke follows Mark's five controversies (20:1–44 = Mark 11:27–12:37) in which Jesus proves his greater wisdom as the true interpreter of Torah. He is in control, and his authority over God's truth contrasts the false claims of the leaders. Their trap is turned against them, and they are the ones who are shown to be ignorant of Torah.

JEWISH LEADERS QUESTION
JESUS' AUTHORITY (20:1–8)

The five temple debates extend his teaching ministry and in a very real sense carry further, via teaching, his prophetic act of cleansing the temple. The primary theme Luke establishes here is Jesus' messianic authority; throughout, Jesus uses the question-and-answer format, which was the rabbinic method for solving controversies. In each episode Jesus demonstrates his superiority to the legal experts as he decimates them in his handling of God's word. He is the final, authoritative interpreter of Torah.

Jesus cleansed the temple on Monday, and this is probably Tuesday morning when Jesus is teaching in the court of the Gentiles. These chief priests, scribes, and elders are probably an official delegation of the Sanhedrin, the ruling council of the Jews (also 9:22). We know from 19:47 that their goal is not to discover truth, for they have already decided that Jesus is a false prophet who must die.

Both questions arise from the authority Jesus had exercised the two previous days: the "what" (*poia*) focuses on the type of authority; the "who" (*tis*), on the person who was its source. To them Jesus is a rabbinic pretender with no official training or backer. They want to prove to the people that he has no pedigree and no authority behind his claims. They believe they have effectively entrapped him. If he answers "human authority" he will contradict his actions and claims, and if "divine authority" he will be guilty of blasphemy. The second question is similar, for they assume he could not have come from God and are daring him to incriminate himself by answering.

Jesus takes the offensive in verses 3–4 and traps the leaders in turn. This stylistic device is common in rabbinic dialogue and is brilliantly timed and adroitly put before them. Moreover, the question about Jesus' forerunner, John, is completely valid, since Jesus' claims are directly linked to those of the Baptist. The same questions often arose about John. So he turns the tables and asks the same loaded question of them: "Tell me: John's baptism—was it from heaven, or of human origin?" John preached "a baptism of repentance for the forgiveness of sins" (3:3), introducing the new age of salvation. So now the leaders are on the spot.

Their quandary is evident from their reasoning in verses 5–7. Luke pictures their frantic deliberations as they try to figure a way out. If they admit it is heavenly in origin, their own rejection of John is proved to have been false, and they should "believe him" and repent. The people also thought him to be a prophet, and to accept him mandates that they accept Jesus as well. If they say,

"Of human origin," those ("all the people," stressing the virtually universal following he received) who believe in John will stone them as false prophets (Deut 13:10; see Acts 5:26; 7:58). So they are caught on the horns of a dilemma and dare not answer either way.

So they can only reply, "We don't know where it was from" (20:7). They are virtually silenced by Jesus' brilliant riposte. Jesus' response is perfect: "Neither will I tell you by what authority I am doing these things." Jesus takes the lead in this contest. He will score four more times, and they won't even make a first down. They have shown themselves unworthy of God's kingdom truths, so they will be hidden from them (see 19:41). God's truths demand the eye of faith to be open to them. Those who blind themselves to these kingdom realities may find that God is no longer open to them.

JESUS TELLS THE PARABLE OF THE
WICKED TENANTS (20:9–19)

After besting the Jewish leaders, Jesus now shows why they stand guilty and condemned before God. This is an allegorical parable built on Isaiah 5:1–7, the Song of the Vineyard, which also decried the spiritual failure of the nation. It is prophetic in telling the people that the leaders not only oppose him but also are going to take his life. They realize he is speaking of them, but instead of warning them it hardens their resolve to do just that. There is difference of opinion on the thrust, as some take the vineyard to be Israel while others believe the tenant farmers are Israel. I think the vineyard is indeed Israel, as in Isaiah, and the farmers are the leaders of Israel. Then the servants are the prophets and apostles, the owner is God, and the Son is Jesus. It used to be thought that the extensive allegory meant this parable originated late and did not come from Jesus, but scholarship has moved on from such narrow views, and most agree that Jesus often used allegory in his parables.

The vineyard was one of the best-known images for Israel (see Isa 5:1–7). Over the doors to the sanctuary in the temple was a huge embroidered golden vine with large clusters of grapes hanging from it; the Jewish historian Josephus said this sight amazed onlookers (Josephus, *Antiquities* 15.394–95). As in the parable of the shrewd manager, this vineyard was leased to tenant farmers, after which the owner departed for a long time. This is not an unusual detail, as Galilee was largely made up of tenant farms with wealthy owners living far away. This situation depicts the covenant relationship God had with Israel after settling them in the promised land. It took four years for grape vineyards to be productive, and the owner would have subsidized the farmers for that time (= "for a long time") and then shared in the profits afterward.

Due to Herod's unfortunate economic policies of favoring absentee landlords, Galilee was a place of constant social unrest, and at times the picture given here of tenant farmers rebelling and trying to seize a farm would take place. Here the owner sends three different sets of servants to collect the profits due him. It is difficult to know whether this is three sets during the same year or three successive years. Either could make sense, but I find it difficult to think that an owner would let them get away with refusing to pay their rent for three years.

Whichever we prefer, the owner is unbelievably patient when the first servant is beaten and thrown out empty-handed, the second is "treated shamefully" and again given nothing, and the third is wounded and evicted. The mistreatment keeps escalating. The tenants not only refuse to honor the contract but also insult the owner by beating his servants and throwing them off the land. It is not realistic but depicts the patience of God in dealing with Israel. This graphically portrays Israel's treatment of the prophets and in Acts of the apostles sent by Jesus. The prophets are servants of Yahweh (1 Kgs 18:36; Jer 7:25; Amos 3:7). The shameful treatment of prophets echoes Hebrews 11:32–38. The prophets are mocked in 2 Chronicles 36:14–16; Jeremiah is beaten in Jeremiah 20:2; Zechariah is stoned in 2 Chronicles 24:21; Uriah is killed in Jeremiah 26:21–23.

On the surface, the owner's sending his son in verse 13 seems foolish. Why would his son be treated any better, and why wouldn't he be accompanied by armed mercenaries to protect him? Obviously, this is because Jesus is describing his own Father's love not only for him but also for the nation in sending his Son. Divine mercy and compassion are incomprehensible from a purely human perspective.

The owner reasons that his "son, whom I love," will receive the respect his servants did not and decides to send him to the tenant farmers. Jesus as beloved of his Father is highlighted at both the baptism (3:22) and transfiguration (9:35), and in the story this is intended to show the farmers how important it is that he be treated well.

The deliberation of the tenant farmers is rather shocking. It is all so illogical, thinking that murdering the heir will cause the inheritance of the land to go to the murderers themselves. In light of this difficulty, some interpreters have attempted various "legal" explanations—for instance, that if all the heirs were dead, the property would go to those who have taken residence of the land; or perhaps that the landowner was dead (sending the son and not coming himself) and had deeded the property over to the son; or perhaps that the owner might give up in light of the constant trouble the tenants have caused him. None of these work, however; the whole point is that sin is illogical. People who give themselves over to rebellion against God are not in their right minds, and Jesus wants his listeners to realize this.

Like sinners throughout history, the tenants/leaders of Israel are not reckoning with the reaction of the father after they kill his son. Criminals regularly fail to consider all the contingencies, and the facts often come to light rather easily. The parallels between this parable and the actions of the leaders over the next few days will prove this hypothesis. Every point here will take place over the next three days of passion week. As in verse 15, they will take Jesus outside the city and have him killed (John 19:17; Heb 13:12).

Jesus then involves the crowd and asks them, "What then will the owner of the vineyard do to them?" He then answers the question himself: "He will come and kill those tenants and give the vineyard to others." He wants everyone to think about it but wishes to make certain they find the correct answer. Whether the vengeance is accomplished through a legal trial or by armed intervention is not part of the story. Either is viable, and the point is that the murderers are destroyed. While this could point to final judgment, it is more likely that he means the destruction of Jerusalem and the temple in AD 70. The primary thrust is actually the loss of the covenant status of the nation as depicted in Romans 11:11-21, the breaking off of unbelieving Israel from the vine and their replacement by both the righteous remnant (believing Israel) and the Gentiles. These constitute the "others" who inherit the vineyard.

Three further responses conclude the parable—those of the crowd, Jesus, and the leaders themselves. The crowd (v. 16b) is shocked and utters the cry Paul uses ten times in Romans, "God forbid" or "May this never come to pass" (Rom 3:4, 6, 31; 6:2, 15; 7:7, 13; 9:14; 11:1, 11). They cannot believe this is the future of their nation. It is possible that the entire parable is in view and they don't want Jesus to be betrayed and put to death, but in the context it likely relates to the destruction of the nation.

Jesus then responds (vv. 17-18) with prophetic warning. He looks them (the crowds and the leaders) right in the eyes to get their undivided attention and asks a second question, this time regarding the meaning of the stone prophecy from Psalm 118:22. This is a thanksgiving hymn for Yahweh's having delivered the nation by supernatural intervention, and in the psalm Israel is the cornerstone. Jesus and the early church (Acts 4:11; Rom 9:33; 1 Pet 2:6-7) understood "the stone the builders rejected" **typologically** as fulfilled in Jesus' rejection by the leaders of Israel and vindication by God. Here the rejection as typified by the wicked tenants in the parable is paramount.

The second half, "has become the cornerstone," is not portrayed in the parable but is prophesied as part of the owner/father's response to the rejection. The cornerstone is the foundation stone at the bottom corner of a building. Some interpreters think it is the keystone at the top of the arch. I prefer the former, but the main thing is that it bears the weight of the building and is the focus of its purpose. The emphasis is on the restoration and vindication of the rejected Son, who now becomes the focal point of the action. Jesus as rejected is stressed in the passion predictions (9:22) and sums up all the Jews and Romans would do to him. The cornerstone imagery is fulfilled in his resurrection and glorification as Lord of all.

The following verse (18) draws on the other stone passages, from Isaiah 8:14–15: "a stone that causes people to stumble and a rock that makes them fall." Note the two ways this destruction is accomplished—they fall on the stone and are broken; it falls on them, and they are crushed. This elaborates the destruction of the wicked tenants. The crushing result stems from Daniel 2:34–35, 44–45, in the interpretation of Nebuchadnezzar's dream of the enormous idolatrous statue shattered by the rock. Now the leaders and the apostate nation will share Babylon's fate. They will reject and kill their Messiah, but he and his Father will utterly destroy them. Again, this is both the destruction of AD 70 and the final judgment.

The leaders add their reaction in 20:19. They know these dire predictions are addressed to them and "looked for a way to arrest him," now even more "immediately" than before. If they could, they would put him in chains at that very moment, but they cannot, for they are "afraid of the people," who are still on Jesus' side and would cause a riot.

JESUS IS QUESTIONED REGARDING PAYING TAXES TO CAESAR (20:20–26)

Now the leaders get really devious, sending "spies, who pretended to be sincere," in order to entrap Jesus and arrest him. They are hoping they can catch him in either a seditious statement and hand him over to the Romans or a pro-Roman statement that will turn the Jewish people against him. They figure a question about taxes will fit the bill perfectly, especially since they have duped Jesus into thinking they are followers.

The issue of tribute money to Rome was an incredibly emotional one. To introduce it, they try flattery to loosen Jesus up (20:21). There is great irony in this, for everything they say is exactly correct, but they don't know that. There are three emphases: (1) No one in human history has ever spoken and taught "what is right" more deeply than Jesus, who is himself the Word of God. The emphasis is on the correctness and accuracy (*orthōs*) of the truth he presents. (2) His impartiality or lack of favoritism is evident throughout Luke, for he fights for the outcasts and marginalized everywhere he goes. The true answer to racism and human prejudice is very simple: Jesus. We truly have heaven on earth when all of us, whatever color or national origin, love and share together in Christ. (3) He teaches "the way of God in accordance with the truth," which sums up the other two. The early church called itself "the Way" (Acts 9:2; 16:17; 19:9), and the message of the entire New Testament is that Jesus alone is the way to God. So the spies were trying to disarm him with flattery but were actually stating the simple truth.

Their question, they believe, can finally help them get rid of this troublemaker: "Is it right for us to pay taxes to Caesar or not?" (20:22). This was the one-denarius poll tax, the tribute money every adult (women as well as men) in a subject nation had to pay directly to Caesar. This was one of three taxes Jewish people had to pay with the temple tax and indirect taxes like customs/duties and sales taxes. The Jews were highly opposed, and several revolts had taken place over it (like that of Judas the Galilean in AD 6). So they have a right to expect Jesus will get in trouble however he answers (see above).

We see in verse 23 that Jesus was not fooled in the least but "saw through their duplicity" from the start. His response is to ask for a denarius, the basic coin worth one day's wage, undoubtedly a silver denarius with a head of Caesar and the inscription "Tiberius Caesar, Son of the Divine Augustus" on the one side, and on the other an image of his mother Livia in the guise of the goddess Pax (peace) with the inscription "High Priest." This demonstrates their hypocrisy, that they regularly carry and use such idolatrous coins, showing that they "loved money" (16:14). This was the coin Rome demanded for paying these taxes and was blasphemous to the Jews, claiming Caesar was a god.

So Jesus asks in verse 24, "Whose image and inscription are on it?" He is drawing the answer to their own question out of them. When they reply, "Caesar's," he responds, "Then give back to Caesar what is Caesar's, and to God what is God's." At first glance it sounds like he is making the two equal, with both Caesar and God given what is their due. However, that is not the case, as Caesar has his limited area while God's is unlimited.

There are a few possible interpretations of its implications: (1) Jesus could be implying a separation of church and state into two kingdoms: the political realm is Caesar's bailiwick and the spiritual realm God's. But this does not fit the context or other biblical teaching on the issue (for example, 1 Pet 2:17, "fear God, honor the emperor"). (2) It could be irony, with "give back to Caesar" set in contrast to total allegiance to God. But this too does not fit the context. (3) It might be a statement against the radical anti-Roman Zealots, with the coin and what it represents belonging to Caesar and worthy of recognition. But while this group may have existed in Jesus' day (one of the disciples, Simon, had been a "zealot"; see 6:15), it is questionable how powerful a force it was at the time. This option could be part of the background, but the primary thrust is that (4) God has given Caesar his proper place in the world order (clearing the way for Rom 13 on submission to government), while God is in control of every sphere of life. God's realm transcends yet includes that of Caesar's, so submitting to Caesar is part of submitting to God.

Three points in verse 26 virtually sum up not just this incident but the first half of passion week. The leaders, who hoped to be able to arrest Jesus at this moment, are first "unable to trap him" in their feeble attempt here, but they are both "astonished by his answer" and forced into silence by the brilliance of his reasoning. He once again has turned the tide and put them on the defensive.

JESUS IS QUESTIONED REGARDING THE RESURRECTION OF THE DEAD (20:27-40)

Now a third delegation arrives on the same day (Tuesday) to ensnare Jesus. His enemies are busy in their little plots, each of them wanting bragging rights as the ones who bring him down. These delegates are the Sadducees, who emerged in the second century BC (we don't know their exact origins for sure) and likely derived their name from Zadok, the high priest in the times of David and Solomon (1 Kgs 1:8; 1 Chr 29:22). They consisted of lay and priestly aristocrats who followed only the Torah and did not believe in the afterlife. This is the only time they appear in Luke (though see Acts 4:1; 5:17; 23:6).

They employ a riddle that had probably often worked in debates with the Pharisees, and they thought Jesus would be stymied as well. It intends to demonstrate how foolish a notion resurrection from the dead actually is. Since they accept only the Pentateuch as Scripture, they approach the topic through the teaching of Moses (v. 28) regarding the principle of levirate marriage (Gen 38:8; Deut 25:5). When a man dies childless, his brother will marry his wife and bear children in his name so it is not lost forever. "Levirate" means "brother's brother," and the belief is that the childless brother who dies can have progeny through his living brother. The family seed then continues.

So they posit the following scenario as described in verses 29-32. Seven successive brothers marry the same woman under this levirate law, but none of them produce any children before they die. Finally, the wife dies as well. The quandary is seven husbands and a single wife married to all of them, with no children to provide an heir. The issue, however, is not the children or the heirs but the question of marriage and family in the afterlife. You can almost see their knowing smiles as they ask Jesus, "At the resurrection [ha ha] whose wife will she be, since the seven were married to her?" (20:33). Note what they are taking for granted: that the afterlife will be exactly like this life, and that marriage in heaven must be monogamous. So in their thinking they have shown how ridiculous the idea of resurrection and afterlife really are.

The problem with the Sadducees, Jesus points out in verse 34, is their assumption that the age to come resembles this age. Those who are resurrected are like the angels, not like humans on earth. They no longer have earthly restrictions like marriage and family. Jesus, whose preexistence meant he knew of the next life personally, corrected their serious error: "Those who are considered worthy [by God] of taking part in the age to come and in the resurrection from the dead will neither marry nor be given in marriage" (20:35). The purpose of marriage was to bear children and "fill the earth" (Gen 1:28) with those made in the image of God. That is no longer needed in the new heavens and earth.

There God's elect will be "like the angels ... children of the resurrection" (20:36). Angels were immortal beings and so did not need to procreate; there was never a need to replenish the earth.[1] In heaven we will join the angels in worshipping the Triune Godhead. Like them, we will have no need of marriage, and in fact in heaven I believe I will know and love my wife infinitely more than I do now.

---

1. It is often said that the Sadducees rejected the existence of angels, yet they are numerous in the Pentateuch. The basis of this is a misunderstanding of Acts 23:8, "The Sadducees say that there is no resurrection, and that there are neither angels nor spirits." However, there is a growing consensus that this does not mean that they denied the existence of angels, but rather that they said there will be no resurrected people who resemble angels or spirits. This makes more sense.

Then Jesus corrects their error about resurrection from the dead (20:37–38). He takes their argument against resurrection from Moses (v. 28) and turns it against them. He could have used a more direct passage on the afterlife like Job 19:8 or Daniel 12:2, but for them only the five books of Moses (the Pentateuch) were Scripture, so he turned to an indirect passage from there.

He argues that in the "burning bush" passage of Exodus 3:6, Moses "revealed" (*mēnyō*; NIV: "showed") the reality of resurrection when he called the Lord "the God of Abraham, and the God of Isaac, and the God of Jacob." In the grammar of the passage these are present tenses, so Jesus is saying that at the time of Moses the patriarchs must have been still alive. This grammatical approach would have been a valid argument in the first century, based on God's saying, "*I am* the God of ..." Therefore, "He is not the God of the dead, but of the living" (v. 38) is based on the fact that Exodus 3:6 was said after the patriarchs had died on earth, meaning they were still living in heaven.

Then he adds, "to him all are alive," not just in terms of the immortality of the soul but in terms of actual physical resurrection. The patriarchs, Jesus is saying, are physically alive in the presence of God, as stated by Jewish writers in 4 Maccabees 7:19; b. Sanhedrin 90b–91a. Since the patriarchs are alive in heaven, God is the God of the living.

Matthew describes the astonishment of the crowd (Matt 22:33), but in verse 39 Luke records the accolades of the scribes, "Well said, teacher!" The scribes and Pharisees agreed with Jesus about the afterlife and were pleased to see this perfect answer to what had undoubtedly been an age-old debate between them and the Sadducees. In other words, they believe Jesus has proved his point from the Pentateuch, so there is no rejoinder.

Luke takes it further in verse 40. Jesus had won the battle of wits from the Torah over all the Jewish groups, and now "no one [scribe, Pharisee, or Sadducee] dared to ask him any more questions." They had begun the day with high hopes that what they assumed was their greater knowledge of Torah would prove to the people that Jesus was a charlatan. They are ending the day in abject defeat, forced to acknowledge Jesus as the victor. Each group in turn has taken a shot at Jesus and gone down in flames due to his superior knowledge of Torah. They cannot take a chance on being shown up again, so they withdraw and try to find another way. They will do so the next day when Judas comes to them.

JESUS TEACHES ON HIS MESSIANIC OFFICE (20:41–44)

No further questions come his way, so Jesus takes the initiative and clarifies his own understanding regarding his messianic office (vv. 41–44) and then concludes with a diatribe against the scribes (vv. 45–47). He has shown his vast knowledge of God's revealed word, and now he asks that they listen to what Scripture has to say about him.

He begins with a question that almost contains its own answer: "Why is it said that the Messiah is the son of David?" The question is not whether this is true but how this fact can be reconciled with Psalm 110:1, which states that the Messiah is David's Lord. Let me clarify by citing the quotation from 20:42, "The Lord [Yahweh] said to my Lord [David's Messiah]; 'Sit at my right hand' [the place of exaltation and power]." How can the Messiah at one and the same time be David's son and David's Lord?

Scholars debate whether Psalm 110 was a messianic psalm, though more and more recognize the likelihood of this. It makes perfect sense that Jesus would apply it to himself as the ideal royal Messiah of David. Jewish hope in a Davidic royal messiah centered on the use of 2 Samuel 7:11–16 in Psalms of Solomon 17:21–23 and **Qumran**'s 4Q Florilegium (see also Testament of Levi 18). Still, it is Jesus himself who put it all together, and New Testament emphases build directly on his insights.

The main thing is that Jesus emphasizes his role as Davidic Messiah (see 1:32–33; 3:23–28, 31) and then adds here that at the same time he is also David's Lord. He is handing himself over to his enemies, both Jews and Romans, in order to die on the cross as our atoning sacrifice. But that seeming defeat is actually the greatest cosmic victory in all of human history, and in it God will elevate him to the place of universal power (Dan 7:13-14) and "make your enemies a footstool for your feet." His death will be his great victory, both for him and for those who put their trust in him.

He asks a final question in 20:44: "David calls him 'Lord.' How then can he be his son?" The stress here is on Jesus' lordship. Since both sides are correct and yet seem to contradict one another, how do we reconcile them? The Jews separated this into a priestly and a royal messiah, but Jesus combined them into one. The answer is in Psalm 110 itself. Jesus was born son of David, and at the cross and resurrection God proclaimed him as exalted Messiah, the Lord of all. He is indeed both at the same time, and his extravagant claims for himself are entirely justified.

JESUS WARNS ABOUT THE SCRIBES (20:45-47)

This takes up an entire chapter in Matthew 23, but Mark 12:38-40 and Luke here both abbreviate the material and prefer to set the avarice of the scribes in contrast with the widow who gives what little she has to God (21:1-4). Luke has already provided material on their hypocrisy in 11:37-54, and Jesus makes his remarks to "all the people" who have gathered here in the court of the Gentiles for the debate with the leaders. He centers on their hypocrisy (v. 46) and greed (v. 47).

Their pride is seen in four observations, all related to the desire to be noticed and considered important: (1) To "walk around in flowing robes" refers to expensive cloaks that reach down to the feet, similar to priestly robes and those belonging to high officials. They signify high social status (as in 15:22). (2) To be "greeted with respect in the marketplace" repeats 11:43 (also 6:23) and refers to recognition by others as a community leader. When a rabbi passed, people were expected to rise to their feet. (3) The "most important

seats in the synagogues" refers to the bench in front of the ark
facing the congregation, reserved for synagogue officials. (4) The
"places of honor at banquets" are seats near the host at the center of
the V formed by the couches, as in 14:7-8. Such pride and demand
for attention are directly counter to the humility demanded by
God of those who would be great in the kingdom (9:48; 22:24-27).

Their avarice is demonstrated by a devastating comment that they
"devour widows' houses." There are several possible interpretations
of this comment, including abusing the widows' hospitality, defraud-
ing them of property, stealing their dowries, taking their homes as
pledges of loans they could not repay, or overcharging for legal services. We cannot know, and any or all of them could be intended.

Even while the scribes are cheating widows out of their due,
they "make lengthy prayers" in synagogues and other occasions to
show people how pious they are. None of it is real, and all of it is
for show. After committing social injustice of the worst kind, they
can still render ostentatious prayers to impress those around. No
wonder God's anger is kindled and they are to be "punished most
severely." Greater judgment (Rom 13:2; Heb 13:17; Jas 3:1) is the only
proper response from a holy God.

JESUS LAUDS THE WIDOW'S
TOTAL SACRIFICE (21:1-4)

In complete contrast to the scribes who cheat poor people like her,
the widow in this passage gives all her small savings to God. What
better proof can there be of her total trust in the Lord! The scene is
still in the temple courts, and Jesus is watching the wealthy place
their monetary gifts in thirteen trumpet-like receptacles placed
against the wall in the court of women. Each one was labeled, for
instance, "shekel dues," "bird offerings," and so on. You could
hear people announce to the priest in attendance what they were
giving, and they made sure the coins made as much noise as possible so all around would know of their largesse. Then the lowly
widow comes by and gives a mere "two very small copper coins," or

lepta (12:59), the smallest coin minted, worth one-eighth of a cent, or one-sixty-fourth of a denarius (a day's wage).

Jesus immediately tells those near him, "This poor widow has put in more than all the others" (21:3). He is not saying that their gifts are invalid, only that hers is the greater sacrifice and thus the higher gift. This is clear in the following verse. The true measure of a gift is how much sacrifice it involves. Their gift had little sacrifice, for they "gave their gifts out of their wealth." It is not the amount given but the heart behind it that matters. These wealthy people hardly thought about it as they gave, while she "out of her poverty put in all she had to live on." Only love could have produced such self-sacrifice.

As I have said, this does not mean God refuses to accept the gifts of the wealthy. The key is to give not out of a sense of duty or so people know you are pious but to give out of gratitude for all God has given you. Moreover, don't give as little as possible but as much as you can. The statistics on giving in the average church are totally embarrassing. Many churches in affluent areas have almost no one even tithing—that is, giving 10 percent of their income. They are all spending what they have on themselves. They are all the rich fool of 12:13–21.

———

This chapter traces the conflict between Jesus and the leaders to its bitter conclusion, as they believe their superior knowledge of Torah will enable them to trap him and turn the people against him. The very first foray (vv. 1–8) hits at his authority to speak as a rabbi, when in their minds his claims are blasphemous. Instead, he takes them at their own game with a question about John the Baptist that demonstrates their own lack of authority and true expertise.

In the parable of the wicked tenants (vv. 9–19), Jesus takes the fight to the leaders, showing how they are flaunting God's covenant mercies toward them by rejecting his servants the prophets

and now the apostles, and how they will bring God's wrath down
on their heads when they kill his Son, Jesus himself. Jesus defines
himself as the chief cornerstone (vv. 17-18), rejected by the builders (Israel) but now the focal point of God's plan of salvation and
a rock that will crush God's enemies.

The question about paying taxes to Caesar (vv. 20-26) was
another attempt to trap Jesus and turn the people against him, but
once more he turns the tables on them. What we learn from this is
that Caesar and secular government have their place in God's economy and deserve our respect and support. God rules over them
but uses them in this world, and so they deserve our tax support
and submission.

The Sadducees' story of the woman married to seven childless brothers in a row (vv. 27-40) was a further attempt to thwart
Jesus, this time his belief in the resurrection of the dead. To them
the thought of a woman married to seven men at the same time
in heaven was ridiculous and showed how illogical the doctrine of
an afterlife was. Jesus, however, showed their own lack of knowledge of scriptural truth, showing that in heaven we will be like
the angels and will not be married or bear children. Once again
he prevailed, and this time the scribes capitulated and recognized
his superior knowledge (vv. 39-40).

Jesus then addresses the group about two further issues, his
own exalted status and the sins of the scribes. Using Psalm 110:1, he
shows them that at his exaltation by God he will become not only
David's Son but also David's Lord at one and the same time. He is
indeed the glorified One (vv. 41-44). In contrast to that, he warns of
the hypocrisy of the scribes (vv. 45-47), who live for human accolades and care only for the attention they can receive and at the
same time are filled with avarice and greed. In complete contrast,
the poor widow gives all she has to God and trusts him implicitly
(21:1-4). That is a huge lesson for us all.

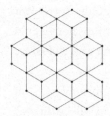

THE COMING DESTRUCTION
OF JERUSALEM
(21:5–38)

As I discussed in the introduction to 17:1-37, Luke has divided the Olivet Discourse into two segments, the first in 17:20-37 centering on the **apocalyptic** aspects, particularly the return of Christ, and the second here centering more on the destruction of Jerusalem. After the initial questions (vv. 5-7), the discourse is organized around the destruction of the temple (vv. 8-24) and the coming of the Son of Man (vv. 25-33) followed by a series of admonitions (vv. 34-38).

THE DISCIPLES ASK QUESTIONS ABOUT
THE TEMPLE'S DESTRUCTION (21:5-7)

If the Jerusalem temple had not been built by the Jews, it would have been one of the seven wonders of the world. It was larger than even the Temple of Diana in Ephesus and more beautifully adorned than any comparable building. It took eighty-three years for Herod to build it (20 BC to AD 63), and it was completed only seven years before it was destroyed by the Romans. He doubled its size and turned it into a truly magnificent structure. Many of the pure white marble stones were massive, sixty-seven by twelve feet in size, and when the sun hit the facade and the gold plates on it in the morning, it was blinding in its brilliance (Josephus, *Jewish War* 5.222–23). The "gifts dedicated to God" Jesus mentions here would have included the linen tapestries and the woven grape clusters at the entrance to the temple.

Jesus shocks his disciples with a devastating prophecy: "Not one stone will be left on another; every one of them will be thrown down." Jesus here repeats his prophecy from 19:44. The phrase is a metaphor for total destruction. Obviously, it came to pass: in AD 70, after fire raged through the temple, Titus ordered the entire structure to be leveled.

The disciples' question (v. 7) contains two parts: "when" will this destruction take place, and "what" sign will tell us it is imminent? They assume that both events, the temple's destruction and Jesus' return, will occur at the same time. The desire for a sign parallels the Pharisees in 11:16, but here there is a much more positive atmosphere, and Jesus treats it seriously. Jesus will answer them with four signs sayings: False signs that will come from false teachers and deceive many (vv. 8–11), the persecution of the disciples (vv. 12–19), the destruction of Jerusalem (vv. 20–25), and the coming of the Son of Man (vv. 25–28). The stress throughout is on the necessity of vigilance and readiness for God to act on behalf of his people.

JESUS WARNS OF FALSE SIGNS AND UPHEAVALS (21:8–11)

Vigilance (*blepete*, "watch out") is an absolute necessity, for false messiahs and prophets will be everywhere. These are messianic pretenders who "will come in my name" claiming to be God's messiah. There were many counterfeit messiahs in the first century (Josephus, *Antiquities* 18.4.1), and these could be multiplied by the false teachers of Paul's and John's writings (called "antichrists" in 1 John 2:18; 4:3). In our day hundreds of cults have sprung up teaching terrible falsehoods. We need to be on our guard constantly and make certain our people know their theology, lest they too be "led astray."

The example of people saying "the time is near" is particularly apropos for our day. I grew up with what we called "prophecy preachers," who had huge multicolored charts that filled the fronts of our churches. They wrote books on all the events that fulfilled prophecy and proved the Lord would return in the next few weeks or months. It all began to change for me in my twenties as I began to realize that none of the "prophecies" I had grown up with had ever come to pass and that new ones had taken their place. Now several decades later, that has morphed into an entire series of failed predictions. I have learned to let go of such speculative approaches and let the Lord come when he deems it the right time. I now try to preach his soon return according to the text and not play games with so-called signs that are not actually signs.

The primary example Jesus notes is political upheavals (21:9–10). There are always portents of divine judgments in history (Isa 13:6–8; Jer 4:19–21), and people will continue to link these with the approaching **eschaton** (end of history). Jesus is saying that these "wars and uprisings" are not signs. When he says that "these things must happen first, but the end will not come right away," he means the end will not follow immediately and be brought about by such events. The divine "must" (*dei*) states that world chaos is a constant rather than special judgment God has placed on this world. He has allowed this to characterize human history as a result of sin, but it does not follow that such upheavals are portents of Christ's return. I constantly hear how things have got so bad that the Lord has to return, but that was also said by Tertullian and Augustine and Luther and D. L. Moody and Billy Graham—in other words, by believers in every age. It will always be true that "nation will rise against nation," and we dare not allow any leaders to frighten us into joining their movement by such dire predictions.

To these can be added the cosmic disasters and natural upheavals (21:11). As I write, this particular year (2017) is one of the worst on record; terrible earthquakes, hurricanes, and forest fires have dominated the news for months. These "pestilences" and "fearful events" will also come on a regular basis, but I must admit that I have frequently said during these months (I am writing in October, just after an unbelievable series of catastrophes) that it seems nature may be signaling something special. Nevertheless, Matthew calls these "the beginning of birth pains" (Matt 24:8), meaning they are merely the harbinger of the final events, and they could be false labor—soon, but not now.

THE DISCIPLES WILL BE PERSECUTED (21:12-19)

Jesus now turns from the cosmic stage to the disciples' own personal situation. Apocalyptic situations are highly personal in nature, involving not just the world as a whole but each person individually.

ARREST AND WITNESS (21:12-13)

Jesus has faced a great deal of persecution, and now he reveals that his followers will face arrest and punishment with him in his name. Synagogues served as civic courts for minor offenses and had authority to beat offenders with rods (Matt 10:17; Acts 4:18-21; 5:20; 2 Cor 11:25). Imprisonment was a frequent occurrence for early Christians (Acts 3, 5, 12, 16). Jesus was brought before Herod and Pilate, and Paul before Felix, Festus, Agrippa, and Nero himself. Herod and Caesar could render the death penalty, as James, Paul, and Peter experienced.

All this was to take place "on account of [Jesus'] name," a phrase that dominates Acts (seventeen times) and occurs throughout the New Testament (Matt 10:22; 24:9; John 15:21; 1 Pet 4:14, 16; Rev 2:3). Philippians 3:10 calls this a "participation in his sufferings," and it is a critical part of the Christlike life. We share not only his calling and glory; we share in his rejection by the world of darkness.

In all the suffering and opposition God's people face, they have immense opportunities to "bear testimony to" Christ (21:13) in the midst of those difficult experiences. In nearly every chapter of Acts, this proves true (see 4:33; 22:18; 23:11). The powerful defenses of Stephen in Acts 7 and of Paul in Acts 26 are actually lengthy witness to the power of Christ in them.

WISDOM FOR THE DEFENSE (21:14–15)

The thought of what to say when dragged before synagogue councils and civic governors in a trial situation is quite daunting, and so Jesus addresses the worry that every saint must have in such difficult situations. Lawyers in the Roman world were known for their flattering speech and flowery phrases (much like today), and most of us just do not have that ability. Jesus, however, repeats 12:11–12 and strongly advises not to worry or prepare beforehand (unlike high-stakes trials today, where they do profiles on every juror). There he promised the Spirit would give his disciples the words to say; here he promises that he will inspire their defense and "give you words and wisdom" in the time of need.

Moreover, the "adversaries" they face will be completely unable "to resist or contradict" what they say. Both verbs are important, and they relate to the two aspects of the defense. Primarily, their words are a "witness" to the gospel and to Christ, and the accusers will not be able to "resist" the convicting presence of the Spirit (John 16:8–11). Secondarily, this witness is an essential component of their defense during the trial, and the accusers will be unable to "contradict" the truth of their innocence (1 Pet 2:12). Jesus' opponents were often brought to silence (Mark 3:4; Luke 20:26), and the same will happen to them. Festus and Agrippa were amazed at what Paul said and forced to acknowledge the Spirit at work (Acts 26:24–28), concluding, "This man could have been set free if he had not appealed to Caesar" (26:32).

THE EXTENT OF THE PERSECUTION (21:16–19)

Jesus' family remained unbelievers until after the resurrection (John 7:5), and his followers will also experience rejection and persecution by members of their own family (repeating 12:53). There would be times they would even be put to death by parents or siblings. This is the reverse of 14:26, where he commanded that we "hate" our families; now they will hate us and turn against us. Too often Christ followers will have to choose between Jesus and their loved ones, and that is the ultimate sacrifice. Jesus was betrayed by Judas, and many of his followers would go through similar tragedies.

It may get even worse. We must be ready to face universal rejection, for "everyone" to hate us (21:17). Not many of us will have to experience this, for we will always be a part of a church and have Christian friends. But I remember one time when I was ministering in Pakistan, and a missionary came through telling the story of a convert whose wife put ground glass in his evening meal, which proceeded to tear out his insides, and she became a hero to the entire village, who celebrated the horrible murder of an apostate who had become an infidel.

The promise of 21:18 that "not a hair of your head will perish" appears to contradict the prediction in verse 16 that some disciples will be put to death. Some take this as a partial promise— some will die but most of them survive. More take this as referring to final judgment. Several will face martyrdom, but there will be no "second death" (Rev 2:11; 20:6). I would combine this with the promise of spiritual protection. They may harm the body but cannot destroy what really matters, one's spiritual being (Rev 3:10; 7:3; 11:1-2).

In light of this, believers are challenged to "stand firm," so that they may in the end "win life." In spite of all the opposition and affliction they will experience, God's eternal promises and power are with them. Their part in all this is simple; they are called to spiritual steadfastness, to persevere and remain strong. Matthew 10:22 is quite similar: "The one who stands firm to the end will be saved." "Win life" is literally "gain your souls." Their bodies may be destroyed, but their souls cannot be harmed. Matthew 10:28 provides the apt conclusion: "Do not be afraid of those who kill the body but *cannot kill the soul.*"

JERUSALEM WILL BE DESTROYED (21:20-24)

Luke omits much material found in Matthew 24 and Mark 13—the severe tribulation, the cutting short of the days, the abomination of desolation—in order to center entirely on the destruction of Jerusalem. While Matthew 24 and Mark 13 see the events of the destruction of Jerusalem as a **proleptic** anticipation of the return of Christ and great tribulation of those days (see my commentaries on those books), Luke centers entirely on the former. In this section he wishes to focus on what the disciples will experience in this life, the events of AD 69-70, rather than the end of history, beginning with the fear every Jew had, the thought of "Jerusalem being surrounded by [the Roman] armies." When this happened, it would truly mean "its desolation is near." The ancient invasions of Assyria and Babylon were about to be repeated and made infinitely worse, for this "desolation" would last much longer.

This was already predicted in 19:43-44, and now Jesus adds what they will be forced to do at that time (21:21)—flee for their lives. Jesus provides three examples, all related to the siege of Jerusalem by the Romans. First, those who will be trapped in the regions of Judea must "flee to the mountains" to the east, north, and south. This is the common reaction throughout Jewish history (Judg 6:2; 1 Kgs 22;17; Jer 16:16; Amos 5:19-20; Zech 14:5). The early church historian Eusebius (*Ecclesiastical History* 3.5) describes a Christian oracle telling those in Jerusalem to flee to Pella across the Jordan, and that could be connected to this prophecy. There they can hide in the rocks and crevices of the hills. Second, those who will be killed when the city is leveled must "get out" while they can, similar to 17:31-35. Third, those in the countryside should in no way try to "enter the city," for it will be a death zone and hardly anyone will live through it.

The reason for fleeing the city is provided in verse 22. It is to become the focus of God's judgment. "Time of punishment" is actually "days of vengeance," which in Scripture is God's penalty for apostasy, for total rejection of God and his messengers, the prophets and apostles (Deut 32:35; Jer 46:10; Hos 9:7; Rom 12:19; 2 Thess 1:8; Heb 10:30). Jerusalem has once more become a pagan place, and it will suffer the consequences.

This is a mandatory punishment "in fulfillment of all that has been written," meaning the prophetic judgments are now coming to culmination (1 Kgs 9:6-9; Jer 6:1-8; Dan 9:26; Zech 8:1-8). The cycle of sin and rejection is complete in a once-holy city that has all too often killed the prophets and now will put to death the Son of God. Jerusalem's time is thus over, and God is turning to the righteous remnant, consisting of believing Jews and Gentiles (Rom 11:17-21). God's holy people are now made up of those who have put their faith in Christ.

In light of this, Christ delivers a devastating woe (NIV: "how dreadful") regarding the destruction of the city (21:23-24). Note that the sorrow is not for the city or the temple. They have brought divine judgment on themselves. The sorrow is for the people who have been caught in the conflagration. Those who are pregnant or nursing children will be encumbered and unable to get away. They will be trapped and destroyed. Their unborn and infant children will die with them. The "great distress" and "wrath" visited on the innocent by the conquering hordes will be a calamity hard even to imagine. The time for repentance is past, and judgment is all that remains. They had their chance and threw it away.

Only two options will remain (21:24)—escape will not be one of them. The people will either "fall by the sword" or "be taken as prisoners" and sold into slavery "to all the nations." This came to pass as a result of the Babylonian captivity as well as Rome. Josephus describes 1.1 million dead and 97,000 taken captive during the Roman siege (*Jewish War* 6.420).

Luke omits that the time will be "cut short" (Matt 24:22) in order to further stress the horror of the time. Jerusalem "trampled on by the Gentiles" was a common theme (Isa 63:18; Zech 12:3; Dan 8:10). This was to continue "until the times of the Gentiles are fulfilled," which could refer to the Gentile mission but is at the same time a political and military image, with the Gentiles as God's tool for judging Israel. Still, the two are not mutually exclusive, and the period of the Gentiles would last until the return of Christ (Mark 13:10; Matt 24:14). The Jewish people have been "trampled on by the Gentiles" up to our day, seen in the terrible pogroms and holocausts they have suffered over the last two millennia. Sadly, the church has often been complicit in this terrible anti-Semitic behavior. Still, it is clear that Israel does have a future, and the final restoration will take place in accordance with Christ's return (Rom 11:25–32).

THE SON OF MAN WILL COME AGAIN (21:25–28)

Now Luke turns to the second coming. Jesus offers no temporal hints as to the timing of these two events and leaves it enigmatic. Still, throughout his parables there is implicitly a lengthy period between the two, with the Master gone and returning much later (12:36–40, 42–48; 14:24–30; 17:26–35; 19:12–27; 20:9–16).

Jesus begins with cosmic and earthly signs (21:25–26; compare the nonsigns of 21:8–11), showing that all creation joins in welcoming the eschaton, or end of history. The "sun, moon and stars" will now provide the signs presaging Christ's return, and the earth will pour out its panic as the universe begins to dissolve around it, resulting in the nations experiencing "anguish and perplexity." In recent years, it has seemed that each natural disaster that strikes has been the worst of its kind in living memory. If that final set of cataclysms are any worse, the dismay will be hard to imagine.

The terror will be beyond imagination as people "faint from terror," which certainly happens today when communities are hit with hurricanes, earthquakes, and wildfires. I can't imagine being woken up out of the blue at two in the morning and being told we have one hour to flee for our lives. In fact, Jesus' description of being "apprehensive of what is coming on the world" is actually a little soft, for the reaction will be mind-numbing horror, not just apprehension. To know beyond a shadow of a doubt that in the next minutes you will suffer a terrible death and lose everything you have ever accumulated is beyond imagining.

But in this case it is far worse, for at that time "the heavenly bodies will be shaken" (Isa 34:4; Joel 2:31; 3:15). With this, the world will know that there will be no future whatsoever for their grandchildren as well. Life as they know it is over. It is one thing to know you are going to die, quite another to know everyone you love is going to die with you and that your whole way of life is over forever.

Next, Jesus turns to the **parousia** (coming) itself, drawing from Daniel 7:13-14 and its description of the universal dominion of the Son of Man (21:27-28). He will come "in a cloud with power and great glory" (see Dan 7:13). Some have opined that the Son of Man in Daniel is an angelic figure (unlikely) or the Messiah (partly correct). He is not fully explained until Jesus in the Gospels but is seen in Daniel as a quasi-divine figure who will share the authority of Yahweh himself. He is a Divine Warrior who will lead the saints to victory over the little horn.

It is this figure who is now fulfilled in Jesus and coming in the "cloud," depicting Yahweh on the cloud and encased in his **Shekinah** presence (9:34), a major image in the parousia passages (1 Thess 4:17; Rev 11:2). "Power and great glory" pictures Jesus as Yahweh riding on the clouds of majesty (Pss 68:33-34; 104:3). The humble child in the manger and the one who rode on a donkey into Jerusalem now will arrive with the glory of the heavens in his wake.

When these "signs" take place, the time of the deliverance and vindication of the saints has arrived, and it is the moment to "stand up and lift up your heads" (21:28). "Lift up your heads" contains a double meaning, lifting up the eyes to see Christ coming and looking up in joy and encouragement as you realize the world of evil is about to end. "Redemption" (*apolytrōsis*) is not meant in its Pauline sense of being liberated from sin but rather delivered from oppression and hard times. To the unbeliever these are signs of dismay and terror, but to the believer they signify hope and freedom.

JESUS TELLS THE PARABLE OF
THE FIG TREE (21:29-33)

Jesus uses a brief illustration about figs in summer (vv. 29-31) and then applies it to the nearness of the end (vv. 32-33). Figs were a very popular fruit, and their trees were numerous on the Mount of Olives. They blossom in early spring and so are a perfect harbinger of spring and summer. His point is simple and obvious. When you see the bare branches flourishing and the leaves blossoming, you know springtime is on its way.

The point is that the signs of the end function in exactly the same way—when you see them, "you know that the kingdom of God is near." The one problem is that these signs don't differ greatly from the natural disasters that *are not signs* in verse 11, where you also have both earthly and cosmic disasters. How is it that geopolitical events and disasters like earthquakes, tornadoes, and tsunamis on the one hand can be birth pangs and not point to the end (vv. 8-11) and yet somehow are also signs of the end (vv. 25-31)? When do earthly events turn into apocalyptic signs? My own thought is that the difference will be in the intensity of the signs. We have these things regularly from May to September, but when they begin to grow in number and power, they become apocalyptic. That is what has had me wondering in recent years, as in my lifetime I have not seen so many in so short a time. We will see.

The idea of the nearness is elaborated in 21:32-33. In another *amēn* saying (see on 4:24), Jesus points to an important truth when he says, "This generation will certainly not pass away until all hurricanes and wildfires have happened." The difficulty is understanding "this generation," which has been variously understood as that current generation of disciples or of the Jewish people (then Jesus would have erred); the Jewish nation throughout history (= Rom 11:25-32); the generation of Luke's time (the early church); or "this" generation that will be alive for the end-time events. In this strongly apocalyptic material, this last option is definitely the best option. As in 9:27, a salvation-historical link exists between the generation of Jesus and his disciples and the last days. In the biblical world a "generation" can last several lifetimes. So Jesus is comforting them that God is at work and will end this evil world in his own time. He asks us to be ready at all times.

If his followers can depend on anything in this uncertain world, they can depend on Jesus' words: "Heaven and earth will pass away, but my words will never pass away" (21:33). This world order as we know it and the entire universe will one day be destroyed in the fires of the new order (2 Pet 3:10-13), but his teaching is the word of God and eternal in force. There is no reason to doubt any of the absolutely astounding things he has said. Every one of them will come to pass.

JESUS CALLS HIS DISCIPLES TO SPIRITUAL VIGILANCE (21:34-36)

The unexpected nature of Christ's return and the end of history has been shown as a public event with visible signs (vv. 29-31) but paradoxically will also come as a "thief" (12:39; see also 1 Thess 5:2; 2 Pet 3:10; Rev 3:3; 16:19). The key is the need for spiritual vigilance and readiness. Those whose eyes are on the Lord and who walk with him will be prepared for the signs, and Christ's return will not arrive for them like a thief. "Be careful" (*prosechete*) means "stay alert" and calls for a life of watchful readiness.

Jesus names three enemies of being prepared—carousing, drunkenness, and the anxieties of life. The first two describe a party lifestyle of the search for earthly pleasures. This could be expanded to a life in which every penny we earn is spent on ourselves. Statistics about giving to Christian ministries are appalling. I know of a fairly large church in an area with many young urban professionals where not one church member gave the equivalent of a tithe, and another where 85 percent of the members gave nothing for the year. These people will not be ready.

The same can be said for people who constantly worry about their earthly situations and spend far more time and energy on the cares of life than they do on serving and trusting the Lord. For them that day will "close on you suddenly like a trap," and they will face divine judgment. The parables of Matthew 24-25 address this: the wicked servant of 24:48-51 will suffer eternal punishment; the bridesmaids who have no oil in 25:10-12 are not allowed into the messianic banquet; the man who buried his talent in 25:24-30 is thrown into outer darkness. It is absolutely essential that we all be vigilant and ready for Christ's return.

The day of judgment "will come on all those who live on the face of the whole earth" (21:35). It will be universal—no one will escape (Jer 48:43; Rev 14:6). Believers as well as unbelievers will "give an account" to God (Heb 13:17). All will be saved on the basis of their faith in Christ, but they will be judged (or rewarded) on the basis of what they have done with their lives (Rev 20:13).

So the answer is clear: "Be always on the watch," similar to the Scout Motto, *Semper Paratus*, "Always Prepared." Constant spiritual vigilance is an essential characteristic of each and every Christ follower. The way we maintain that vigilance is the persevering prayer of 11:1-11 and 18:1-8—"Pray that you may be able to escape all that is about to happen, and that you may be able to stand before the Son of Man." Persistent prayer is critical, for we cannot face our trials and overcome the world's temptation without the empowering presence and help of Christ and the Holy Spirit. We are not strong enough in ourselves.

The prayer need is twofold. First, "escape" (*ekpheugō*) could mean "flee out of" (the literal) or miss the events of the last days (Rev 3:10), but it more likely means to "flee" the temptations of verse 35 and thus "escape" God's wrath. Christ is calling for a life anchored in the security he provides. Second, when the Son of Man returns, we will "stand" before him. The Son of Man is **eschatological** Judge in 17:24, 26, 30; 18:8; and all will either be judged or rewarded for eternity. This is prayer for a life of perseverance, so that we may be able to stand before him in victory and joy and receive the reward for faithful service.

LUKE SUMMARIZES JESUS' TEMPLE
TEACHING (21:37-38)

Jesus' final days were spent doing what he loved most—teaching in the temple and challenging "all the people" to come to him and receive life. This was virtually a 24/7 ministry, each day in the temple courts, and every evening and night sleeping on the Mount of Olives. Preparation for Passover required being in the near environs of Jerusalem,[1] and Jesus may have alternated between Bethany (two miles away, see Matt 21:17) and the Mount of Olives. He and the disciples probably slept in the very olive grove of Gethsemane they would be in that final Friday night (John 18:2). Thousands of pilgrims would have been joining them and sleeping under the stars on the mount each night (Josephus, *Antiquities* 17.217).

Jesus' popularity continues, seen in the fact that "all the people came early in the morning to hear him at the temple." He had certainly become the most famous rabbi in Palestine. It is this very fact that kept the leaders from arresting him. This vast popularity would have led to a riot if anyone were to attempt a public arrest. Only Judas made it possible, leading them to Jesus in the stillness of the night.

―――

It is hard to imagine the scene when Jesus gave his devastating prophecy to the disciples. There is no equivalent structure for us. If someone had made such a prediction about the destruction of the World Trade Center years before it happened, it would have been horrifying. Yet it would be nothing like this, for the temple was not just a famous structure—it was the heart of the Jewish religion. The closest modern equivalent I can think of is St. Peter's in Rome, or Mecca for Muslims. The horror of the

---

1. Pilgrims were supposed to arrive a week early and purify themselves that week in preparation for the Passover itself.

thought is unimaginable. Of course, it wasn't the first time, for the Babylonians had destroyed Solomon's temple in 586 BC. As with that earlier cataclysm, nothing would be the same ever again.

Christ's response to the "when" and the "what" of the disciples' question comes via four sign sayings. The first (vv. 8–11) deals with what does not presage the soon return of Christ, namely, political upheaval and natural disasters. Messianic pretenders and false teachers will use these so-called signs to deceive people into following them, but these wars and earthquakes and terrible storms are not necessarily signs, and we must be wary.

The second set of possible signs is increased persecution (vv. 12–19). The disciples (and we) will be dragged before councils and high officials and forced to defend both themselves and Christ. So Jesus promises that in the moment he and the Spirit will guide them as to how to both defend themselves and witness to the gospel, as Paul did in Acts 25–26 before Festus and Agrippa. Still, many believers will be rejected by their own family and some by every single person around them (vv. 16–19), but their very suffering will be their victory. If that happens to us, God will be with us in a very special way as he guides us through "the valley of the shadow of death" (Ps 23:4 KJV).

The third sign is the destruction of Jerusalem itself (vv. 20–24), as Luke shows the terrible effects of the apostasy of the nation and describes the absolute destruction of the city and its people, a reenactment of the Babylonian captivity. Ultimate sin must pay the ultimate price, and that will be seen as the people flee the Roman armies and run for their lives. For them there is no hope, for the nation has turned its back on God and his Sent One, his Son and Messiah. Judgment is certain.

Actually, there is hope, but it exists only for those who have turned to Jesus and accepted his divine mission. The future will culminate in the return of the Son of Man, and he will bring with him the glory of the heavens (vv. 25–28). God's people must be ready at all times, for like figs coming in spring, there will be signs, and Christ's followers must prepare themselves (vv. 29-33). Spiritual vigilance is a necessity for the saints. We dare not allow the things of the world to consume us, for we must remain focused on Christ and centered on the things of God (vv. 34-36).

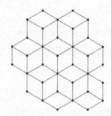

THE FINAL EVENTS OF
PASSION WEEK
(22:1–53)

We are now at Wednesday of this final week, and the pressure has mounted steadily on both Jesus and the leaders, who feel they have only a little more than twenty-four hours to accomplish their nefarious deed. Events now begin to move directly to the cross, and all eyes are on Jesus. The dilemma of the leaders is solved not by their own strategies but by one lone disciple who has never truly been a follower of Jesus but has been in it only for what he could get out of it. He apparently decides there is too little profit in continuing to follow and that the best recourse is to sell Jesus out to the leaders for money.

Judas' offer to the leaders to betray Jesus is almost the only event that took place on Wednesday that we know about. The Thursday events are dominated by Passover preparations during the day and then the meal itself, which we know as the Last Supper, at dusk. Like the triumphal entry, the emphasis in the preparations is on Jesus' sovereign control over every detail. He is orchestrating the message to his followers that he indeed fulfills the messianic implications of the Passover. This is even more true as they celebrate the meal itself, as the Passover liturgy points forward to its fulfillment in him.

There are two emphases in the Last Supper discourse: the explanation of how his coming death on the cross will fulfill the bread and the cup imagery of the Passover (vv. 14-20), and the prediction that the betrayal of Judas was prophesied long ago and in fact fulfills Jesus' messianic destiny (vv. 21-23). This leads into a discourse on discipleship (vv. 24-38) as demanding humility and perseverance in hard times.

The final events of this critical Thursday are Gethsemane and the arrest of Jesus. Jesus' submission to the Father's will as exemplified in his Gethsemane prayer demonstrates to the disciples what the God-centered life looks like (vv. 39-46). Personal vigilance and spiritual strength flow out of one's prayer life, and the critical challenge (emphasized twice in vv. 40, 46) is prayer as the antidote to being defeated by temptation. As a result, at his arrest, Jesus is in charge, not the Romans or the Jewish leaders (vv. 47-54).

JUDAS SELLS HIS SOUL (22:1-6)

Passover is an eight-day feast that actually comprises two festivals—Passover itself on the Friday, followed by the seven-day Festival of Unleavened Bread. Passover celebrated the angel of death "passing over" the firstborn sons of the Israelites, thus launching the exodus from Egypt. It signified the redemption/liberation of the nation from slavery. The celebration was on 14 Nisan, the Friday of passion week. The Feast of Unleavened Bread (15-21 Nisan) commemorated the deliverance from Egypt and from the bondage of sin. Leaven, a symbol of sin, was to be removed, and Exodus 12:19 commanded, "For seven days no yeast is to be found in your houses." The two feasts virtually became a single feast during which the people reflected on God's deliverance of the nation, as the numbers in Jerusalem swelled from a populace of about seventy thousand (Rev 11:13) to over a quarter million because of the pilgrims coming from all over the Jewish world.

This was just two days away, and the leaders were getting anxious, as no opportunity to arrest Jesus had yet presented itself.

They needed to find a way to "get rid of Jesus," for more and more of the people had begun to follow him. However, they "were afraid of" them (also 20:19) because any attempt to arrest Jesus could lead to a riot on his behalf by the people. Whatever the leaders did could lead to catastrophe, and they didn't know which way to turn.

Satan now enters the picture in the person of Judas (22:3 — on "Iscariot," see 6:16). It is this angel of darkness who orchestrates the events. We are told he "entered Judas" here and again at the Last Supper (John 13:27), a term for demon possession in the New Testament (Mark 4:33; 5:12–13; Luke 8:30; 11:26; Acts 5:3). In other words, Satan has seized control of Judas and is directing his actions. Still, Judas is completely open and receptive; it is not a hostile takeover.

According to Matthew 26:14–16 he did it for the money — thirty pieces of silver, the price of a slave according to Exodus 21:32. He was a thief who had been stealing money from the common purse of the Twelve (John 12:6). He was not a good person trying to force Jesus to fulfill his destiny, as some apocryphal gospels (like the Gospel of Judas) and the musical *Jesus Christ Superstar* have tried to say. Rather, he was a willing tool of Satan. In John 6:70, Jesus from the start labeled Judas as "a devil" — "Have I not chosen you, the Twelve? Yet one of you is a devil."

Judas took the initiative and went to the leaders (22:4), telling them how he could "betray Jesus" in such a way as not to cause a stir among the people. Knowing Jesus' intended schedule, he suggested a time for the arrest that would enable them to take him with a minimum of fuss. He provided insider information that would allow them the opportunity they wanted when no crowds would be around. The "officers of the temple guard" were the head Levites in the temple police who directed them in protecting the temple and maintaining order.

These Jewish leaders happily agreed to pay Judas his asking price (see above). He had taken the initiative here as well, as Matthew 26:14–16 makes evident. Their joy was evident, for the pressure was off. Judas would do all the work for them for a mere thirty pieces of silver. What could be simpler? With several ideas in his head, Judas began to look for the right "opportunity" and time when Jesus and his followers were alone with no crowd present. As we know, he found that time after the Last Supper in the garden of Gethsemane.

THE DISCIPLES PREPARE FOR THE PASSOVER MEAL (22:7-13)

The Passover lambs are slain between 2:30 and 5:30 p.m. on Thursday, just before the meal itself. As the evening meal approaches, every family spends the day getting ready. Before we can get into this, however, we must deal with a major discrepancy. In the **Synoptics**, it seems clear that this is a Passover celebration (Mark 14:12; Luke 22:7). However, John 19:14, 31, 42, seems to place the crucifixion on the "day of Preparation," and 18:28 has the Jewish leaders at the later trial wanting to avoid ceremonial uncleanness (seemingly from the Passover celebration). This seems an almost unsolvable discrepancy, and several recent scholars believe the Last Supper was not a Passover meal but a preparatory meal partaken on Wednesday rather than Thursday, with Jesus crucified on Thursday.

However, the evidence from Mark and Luke is crystal clear. Every detail—the reclining on couches, the meal after sunset rather than the normal time of late afternoon, the liturgical framework, Jesus' interpretations—all point to a Passover meal. So how do we reconcile this with John? Some have posited a sectarian calendar like the one followed at **Qumran**, but there is no evidence Jesus ever followed such, and it just doesn't solve the problem.

The best solution is to recognize that John's "day of Preparation" was oriented to the "special Sabbath" of Passover week rather than to that Friday. So the Passover meal mentioned in John 18:28 is not the actual Passover meal of Thursday night but the *chagigah* meal of Friday, also a Passover meal (launching the rest of the festival meals of the next seven days). The priests' fear of defilement in John 18:28; 19:14 refers to that second Passover meal on the morning of the first day (Friday) of the Feast of Unleavened Bread. Thus the "day of Preparation" referred to that Friday, resulting in the conclusion that John and the Synoptics are in agreement. They simply use different language for those same celebratory meals. For all four Gospels, the Last Supper was on Thursday night and the crucifixion was on Friday.

So that Thursday morning Jesus sends Peter and John to "make preparations for us to eat the Passover." A rabbi and his disciples were considered a family, with the rabbi the father of the family. In Mark and Matthew the disciples take the initiative, but Luke stresses Jesus taking sovereign control over the situation (as at the triumphal entry). It was important to get a room because Exodus 12:3–4 commanded a household setting, and the oral tradition demanded that the Passover meal be consumed within the city limits.

Jesus had to be careful since the leaders were watching and trying to arrest him, so there had to be some secrecy. In this case, there was a prearranged signal. A "man carrying a jar of water" (v. 10) was an unusual sight, for normally women carried the earthenware jars. He wanted to partake of the meal in peace and impart his instructions without any official interference. So the man with the water jar was to lead them to the upper room where Jesus had made arrangements for the Passover celebration.

The room itself would be "furnished" (21:12) with couches forming a V, following the **Hellenistic** custom for reclining at festive meals. This will become a virtual home base for the next several weeks, as the disciples will move back and forth from the crucifixion through Pentecost (Acts 1:13–14 is still this upper room).

The preparations were quite important (22:13). During the afternoon they would carry the lamb to the temple, where priests would slaughter the animal, catch the blood in bowls, and sacrifice it on the altar in the temple. Then the disciples would take the carcass and roast it for that evening's Passover meal. It had to be consumed entirely by the "family" present. The disciples would also prepare the herbs, wine, and unleavened bread for the meal.

JESUS AND THE DISCIPLES EAT THE PASSOVER MEAL / LAST SUPPER (22:14-20)

The real message in this scene is Jesus' reinterpretation of the Passover liturgy, which was normally read by the father with his family, as symbolizing his coming death on the cross. As Israel was given salvation and deliverance through the Passover, Jesus will provide eternal salvation through his atoning sacrifice. He and his disciples begin by reclining together in the V arrangement. They are a household, with him at the foot of the V as the head of the house.

It will be helpful to provide an order of events for this Passover meal:

1. It begins with the blessing and first cup of wine.
2. They bring in the food—the bread, herbs, greens, stewed fruit, and the lamb.
3. The eldest son asks about the night, and the father responds with the exodus story and praises God from the first half of the Hallel in Psalm 113-15.
4. The family partakes of the second cup.
5. The bread is blessed and distributed, eaten with the herbs and fruit, then explained by the father.
6. The meal itself is eaten, with the lamb completely consumed.
7. The third cup is shared and the second half of the Hallel sung, Psalm 116-18.
8. The fourth cup is shared, ending the celebration.

The disciples are thinking this will be the regular annual celebration, but Jesus wants them to know it is special, an event he has "eagerly desired" to both share and explain to them. He clearly believes this will help his followers understand better what is coming and be ready for the traumatic event. The Greek is very strong—literally, "with desire I desired"—expressing a deep-seated desire to share this Passover meal and all its implications with his disciples. Several scholars call this a "farewell speech" in which Jesus is showing how he will fulfill the exodus and Passover imagery in his coming "departure [literally, 'exodus']" (9:31) at his "suffering" on the cross.

There is some debate as to whether Jesus actually partook of the meal with his followers. The "again" in verse 16 ("I will not eat it again") is not in the Greek, and some read this as Jesus saying he will not partake of any food until his second coming. However, I agree with those who read verse 15 as saying Jesus intended to partake of the Passover meal with the disciples, so the "again" is justified as part of the translation.

What he is telling his followers is that this is his final Passover celebration until "it finds fulfillment in the kingdom of God." This in fact was a major thrust of the Passover festival, looking forward to the finalization of the redemption/salvation initiated in the original exodus, when the final kingdom of God will arrive. Jesus is saying that the true fulfillment of this expectation will come through the cross and then his **parousia**. His next meal will not be until the messianic banquet (Rev 19:6–10). This Passover meal is fulfilled first in his death and resurrection and then in his return, when he will establish God's final kingdom. Some find in "fulfillment" a reference to eucharistic celebration, but it makes better sense that this points to the parousia.

In verse 17 Jesus begins the cup and bread sayings. As we saw above, there are four cups during the meal. This is apparently the first cup and is unique to Luke. Mark begins with the third cup. Jesus refuses to partake of it but instead distributes it to the disciples. He would have begun with prayer and thanksgiving, "Blessed are you who created the fruit of the vine," then offered the disciples a common cup, "Take this and divide it among you." It was then distributed, and all partook of it after Jesus, the father of the "family," had first taken it.

Then in verse 18 Jesus makes a second vow of abstaining after verse 16. Many take this as meaning Jesus did not partake of the wine here but passed it to the others, but I agree with those who think he did so until the fourth cup at the end of the meal and then abstained. He states his intention twice at the outset to tell his followers that this is a unique Passover celebration pointing forward to his death and resurrection and then to his inauguration of the eternal kingdom at the consummation of the age. He wants them to realize his dedication to his messianic destiny. This meal is preparatory for his true twofold purpose, his final exodus and deliverance of his followers to God's salvation via the cross and his later coming to establish God's final reign over this world.

Before I can discuss verses 19–20, I have to solve a difficult and complex text-critical issue. The Western text tradition (Codex Bezae and some Old Latin manuscripts) omits verses 19b–20, and some accept it since it forms a more difficult, least likely reading as one of what has come to be labeled "western noninterpolations," meaning that later scribes more likely added extra material rather than deleted this important reading. However, there is such superior evidence for the longer reading ($\mathfrak{P}$75 א A B C W Byz etc.) that the majority of scholars accept the longer reading as the original one.

The greater problem is the possible presence of two traditions in the four scriptural passages, with Luke here and 1 Corinthians 11:24–25 adding "do this in remembrance of me" and "the new covenant in my blood" to what some deem the original tradition in Mark 14:24 and Matthew 26:28, "my blood of the covenant." Quite a few believe Luke and Paul added this material to introduce the effects of Jesus' blood sacrifice into the imagery. However, the differences are not as significant as they say and are due to the periphrastic nature of the Gospels. Everything here goes back to Jesus and is authentic.

These words occur later (steps 5–6 above) at the partaking of the paschal lamb, which has been served but not yet eaten. The father blesses the bread, breaks it, and passes it to the family members. This was usually done in silence, but Jesus interprets (the first saying, the bread) due to the critical nature of the imagery in light of his impending sacrificial death. Then the meal was consumed between the two sayings. After the meal the third cup is blessed (step 7), and again Jesus adds his **midrashic** interpretation (the second saying, the cup). Thus the two sayings were actually separated by the meal itself.

At the sharing of the bread (22:19) the four verbs (took, gave thanks, broke, gave) refer to that point in the meal (step 5) when the father/rabbi prepared for the meal itself. His reinterpretation introduces a new understanding in seeing the bread imagery fulfilled in his body. Far too much weight has been given to the verb "to be," *estin*, which becomes the basis for the transubstantiation view of Roman Catholics, so that the bread and cup literally become the actual body and blood of the Lord. Even some Jesuit scholars admit that Jesus did not utter the verb; he would have been speaking in Aramaic, where the verb "to be" is normally omitted in such sentences. Moreover, in the Greek the verb better means to "signify, represent, symbolize," so it is best translated, "This bread represents my body given for you." "Body" is best seen as the "whole person," referring to the paschal lamb that is to be wholly consumed.

There is a sacrificial flavor to the whole. "Given for you" is added to the Mark/Matthew version and lends a vicarious, substitutionary thrust reminiscent of Mark 10:45 / Matthew 20:28. Jesus views his coming death on the cross as an atoning sacrifice "for" sinners, resulting in forgiveness of sins. There could be a martyrdom thrust as well, as *hyper* (for) has that nuance in 2 Maccabees 7:9; 8:21.

"Do this in remembrance of me" stresses this as a memorial meal. As in 1 Corinthians 11, the details of the meal commemorate the body and blood of Jesus, given over for the salvation of each and every one of us. The broken bread memorializes his broken body, and the goal of eucharistic celebration in the church is to recall all that he accomplished on the cross on our behalf. This remembrance is twofold, first of God's deliverance in the exodus, and then in that greater deliverance on the cross.

Then "after the supper" (22:20) Jesus took the third "cup of thanksgiving" (1 Cor 10:16) and reinterpreted it as well. The "new covenant in my blood" alludes to the new covenant prophecy of Jeremiah 31:31–34, which itself reflects the old covenant ceremony of Exodus 24:8, when Moses took the sacrificial blood of twelve oxen and sprinkled it on the altar and on the people. Now Jesus' blood is the basis of the "new covenant," bringing God's salvation to the nations. This point has enormous significance, for this means the new covenant that inaugurates the new era is initiated at the death of Jesus, God's sacrificial Lamb.

This blood is "poured out for you," an allusion to Isaiah 53:12, "he poured out his life unto death ... and ... bore the sin of many." Again, the atoning nature of Jesus' sacrifice is stressed. Moreover, this is done as a sacrifice "for you," a point of enormous significance. Here we have the primary passage in Luke on Jesus' death as an atoning sacrifice for sin. Interestingly, only here and in Acts 20:28 are there passages in Luke stating the sacrificial nature of Jesus' death for the forgiveness of sins. Still, the stress is on the results of his death for the salvation of humankind.

JESUS PREDICTS HIS BETRAYAL (22:21–23)

To get a complete picture of how central this prophecy is, we need to put all four Gospels together. Luke has the one that takes place after the meal is over, but in actuality this theme permeates the supper scene. The first indication of betrayal actually occurred when they first reclined and before anything was served (Matt 26:21–23; Mark 14:18–20). At that time Jesus tells them the betrayer is one dipping bread with Jesus, so the issue carries into the meal itself. In John 13:18–30 the issue dominates the interaction, and Jesus gives a piece of the bread to Judas, at which time Satan enters him and he departs. It appears that John contradicts the Synoptic witness, with Judas leaving during the meal. This is unnecessary: as several scholars have pointed out, Luke arranges his material topically rather than chronologically and sets the betrayal aside until the meal has been covered, probably to connect it with the failure of the rest of the disciples in verses 24–30.

Judas' betrayal is a dominant theme, arising again and again throughout the meal. The reason is evident here. The work of Satan in Judas and the terrible series of events it unleashes actually prove God's complete control. On the surface it seems a devastating turn of events, but look carefully at how Luke tells the story. The horror of it is presented first, "the hand of him who is going to betray me is with mine on the table" of the bread, herbs, and fruit. In the midst of this symbol of liberation and exodus dwells total betrayal. The fact that Judas took part in this celebration of deliverance (his will be a terrible "deliverance") stresses the horror of the situation. Jesus' ultimate sacrifice directly contrasts Judas' ultimate treachery. The joy of table fellowship has been corrupted, for on the night Israel celebrated the deliverance of the nation in the exodus, Judas was plotting to "deliver" Jesus to his enemies.

However, in the very next breath Luke tells us what was really going on here: "The Son of Man will go as it has been decreed." Neither Satan nor Judas is in charge! God is in absolute control and has been for centuries. "Will go" is a futuristic present, "is going to proceed"; in other words, the future is secured by God. "As decreed" is the divine passive *hōrismenon*, "as God has ordained it." The betrayal was prophesied centuries earlier (see Matt 27:9; Mark 14:27, "as has been written"), and it is taking place not as Satan has planned it but as God has predestined it. Every decision Judas has made has been in accordance with God's will, and like Satan at Jesus' temptation (Luke 4), he is simply a tool used to accomplish the divine purpose.

At the same time, Judas made the decision to hand Jesus over to his enemies and stands guilty before God: "Woe to that man who betrays him." There is a wordplay between "Son of Man" and "man," establishing a bond between Jesus' destiny and that of his betrayer. Judas' destiny is eternal punishment. For "woe," see 6:24.

In typical fashion, the disciples, in total confusion, reflect their horror by bandying about which one of them Jesus could be talking about (22:23). It is amazing that Judas was able to hide his avarice so well from them. In all that time one would think someone would have noticed him stealing from the common purse he had looked after (John 12:6). Some of them even wondered if it could be them (Matt 26:22).

THE DISCIPLES ARE CONCERNED ABOUT GREATNESS (22:24–30)

For the second time (see 9:46), the disciples follow Jesus' discussion of his coming death with their own self-centered concerns about their future greatness. Since Jesus had pointed out the worst among them, this could have spurred speculation about who was the best among them. Thus two similar sins, betrayal and self-serving strife for greatness, are presented in successive scenes. Self-centeredness has always plagued the church, as pastors, musicians, and scholars alike vie to be viewed as the best.

DEFINITION OF GREATNESS (22:24–27)

As this passage begins, note the emphasis on "considered to be" in verse 24—it is all about other people's perception. The disciples weren't worried about who really was the most gifted but who people around them thought was the best of them. From the other Gospels we know that this was at least the third time this had arisen (Mark 9:33; 10:41), and every time it grates harshly in comparison with Jesus' servant heart.

Jesus' response (22:25–27) shows the secularity of such concerns. We should all strive to be the "best" we can be but never care that people perceive us as "better" than others around us. In Mark 10:35–45 it was James and John who wanted this, but now the virus has affected all of them. His first comment recalls Mark 10:42 and has two parts, as Jesus in both likens them to the pagan mindset. The Jews chafed under Roman rule, and so this was a devastating critique. Like the Roman kings, the disciples loved to "lord it over" and "exercise authority over" others. The lust for power over others is incredibly seductive, and the disciples have shown this tendency on several occasions (9:40, 49, 54; 18:15). The title "Benefactor" ironically was much sought after by these same tyrants like Augustus, Nero, or Vespasian. The wealthy would give huge gifts to cities and temples in order to be lauded by the people and given civic honors. The disciples reminded Jesus of such self-serving leaders.

The message is clear. Their leadership style is "not to be like that" (22:26). The pagans' idea of leadership is the absolute antithesis of God's and Christ's servant hearts. I have seen so many pastors and Christian leaders who were dictators of their own little fiefdoms; this sickens the mind of Christ. There are two reversals in Christ's words to his disciples. First, "the greatest among you should be like the youngest." The "elder" had all the status and prestige, so the "youngest" means to deliberately take the place of least position. Jesus is demanding a complete reappraisal of the world's ways among his followers. Clearly, this is a lesson that the church has still not learned.

In light of this, the second reversal takes place when the leader becomes the servant, definitely meant for Christian "leaders" (Heb 13:7, 17, 24), who should be known for their servanthood and compassion for others. I know of one famous preacher of many years ago who was not allowed to greet people at the door because of his rudeness and self-centered attitude. One wonders if he should even have been allowed to preach. This man filled the church but had no ministry skills or heart. In both of these examples humility is the norm. None of us dare allow ourselves to feel self-important. Every achievement is actually a gift from God for the sake of the church and for his glory.

For an illustration (22:27) Jesus uses the important person who is waited on at the table versus the one who serves the prestigious people. While in the world's order it is obviously the one "at the table," Jesus makes it clear that "I am among you as one who serves" (as in the footwashing of John 13:1–17). His query is clear—do we follow the world's way or God's way? The household servant or the wealthy guest? Jesus' model deliberately assumes that the servant role is the pattern for God's people, a distinct reversal of the societal norm and of the disciples' thinking in verse 24.

The Future Role of the Disciples (22:28–30)

Since his servants will be great, Jesus turns to the great future reserved for his servants. The basis of their greatness lies in whether they "have stood by me in my trials." Throughout his ministry (not just during passion week) they have remained at his side and supported him even when attacked by the Jewish leaders. Obviously, they have also failed him on many occasions, as they will very shortly do again when they desert him at his arrest. However, they have overall remained faithful, and he is pleased with them. This is an important reminder to us that failures can be forgiven. We must at all times strive to minimize such defeats.

Jesus identifies the reward for their faithfulness in 22:29: "a kingdom, just as my Father conferred one on me." This is an interesting way to put it, almost (but not quite) as if their kingdom was different yet similar to Jesus' kingdom. God has granted or assigned Jesus a kingdom, undoubtedly the future messianic kingdom, and Jesus now confers or assigns it in turn to his followers. Their apostolic authority and kingdom are an extension of his. The verb *diatithemai* is a cognate of *diathēkē*, "covenant," and introduces a new covenant theme (see 22:20). Jesus brings his disciples with him into the new era, the new covenant reality. He is Lord of the kingdom of God, which has arrived with him, and he now turns that earthly portion of his kingdom over to the disciples and gives them authority as his sent ones, or apostles (6:12–16).

Jesus stresses two results here (22:30): the Eleven (minus Judas) will share table fellowship at the messianic banquet with him in his kingdom, and they will sit as judges on thrones over the twelve tribes of Israel. They have been servants of the King, and now they sit in honor at his table (12:35-37; 14:15-24). With the parallel in Matthew 19:28, this teaches that they will share in Jesus' function as ruler and Judge in the new kingdom, paralleling the holy council of angels in heaven. There is a question whether this is reigning over new Israel or the millennial role of judgment over Israel in the **eschaton**. Both may well be intended (compare 1 Cor 6:2; Rev 3:21; 20:4). It reflects Psalm 122:4-5, which speaks of "thrones for judgment, the thrones of the house of David," when peace will be restored to Jerusalem. It is another case of the already and the not-yet, the already of ruling over the church as new Israel now and the not-yet of the eternal reign in God's kingdom.

JESUS FORETELLS PETER'S DENIAL (22:31-34)

The Synoptic Gospels highlight the coming desertion of the Twelve alongside the denial of Peter (Mark 14:27-31; Matt 26:31), but Luke doesn't even mention the former and turns Peter's coming failure into an instance of spiritual warfare. The use of the double name "Simon, Simon" brings out the personal nature of the attack. Satan has singled out Peter as the leader of the apostolic band, probably planning to reach the others through him. This is indicated by the plural "you," showing all of Jesus' followers are in mind.

The verb (*exaiteomai*) means not only to ask but also to receive what is requested. The critical thing here is that Satan does not have the right to sift Peter on his own. He has to receive permission from God. As with Jesus' temptation in 4:1-13, he is in reality a tool of God in testing Peter (and all the rest of us). The metaphor of sifting wheat pictures a violent shaking intended to dislodge the chaff, to break Peter apart spiritually. As Satan afflicted and tested Job in Job 2, he seeks to shake Peter up and defeat him.

However, while Satan has asked and received permission to tempt Peter, Jesus is interceding with God with far greater effect on Peter's behalf (22:32), praying "that your faith may not fail." Satan is a powerful being, a "roaring lion" wanting to "devour" him (1 Pet 5:8), but the prayers of Jesus nullify his nefarious activities and enable God's people to overcome, as will be the case with Simon Peter. This is an incredibly important passage and should be noted every time we deal with spiritual warfare issues. Satan does not have free access to us but is at all times under the control and power of the Triune Godhead. As the demonic powers try us, Christ intercedes for us, and we must surrender ourselves to the watchful care of Christ and the Spirit to be "more than conquerors" (Rom 8:37). The strength is there to enable us "not to fail," and we have only to partake of it.

When Simon has won through to the victory (see 22:54–62 and especially John 21:15–17), Jesus gives him an assignment: "When you have turned back, strengthen your brothers." The others will fail every bit as drastically as Simon and will need his help repenting and returning to their walk with Christ. The "turning back" means that through Christ's intercession, Peter will not fail utterly. He will experience defeat, but it will not be the complete spiritual failure and apostasy that Satan wants. As in James 5:19, he will "wander from the truth," but Christ will turn him "from the error of [his] way" and "cover over a multitude of sins." After he has returned to Christ, he must take that victory and share it with his fellow disciples, another important Christian principle. Our responsibility is at all times to take our life lessons and share them with others so that they may grow in Christ with us. Simon Peter indeed will do this and become the "rock" leading the church.

But Simon's braggadocio takes over, and he makes his typical rash promise: "Lord, I am ready to go with you to prison and to death" (22:33). Still, he now realizes what Jesus has been saying and the serious situation they are facing. This bold claim turns out to be untrue, but in a sense this is a prophecy for the apostolic band, who will face imprisonment and death often in the near future (Acts 4:3; 5:18; 12:1; 16:23; 22:4; 26:10). He wasn't able to fulfill this on this occasion, but Peter would be martyred by Nero. (Tradition says he was martyred upside down.)

Jesus responds with his famous prophecy: "Before the rooster crows today, you will deny three times that you know me" (22:34). This would take place mere hours later, as we will see in 22:54-62. The threefold denial stresses the extent of the failure. Only Luke adds "that you know me" to make the prophecy even more explicit and severe. Peter has been acting like a banty rooster crowing out his coming victory, so it is only fitting that a crowing rooster announce his failure to all.

THE DISCIPLES NEED TO BE PREPARED (22:35-38)

To encourage them, Jesus turns to their previous missions and reminds them how thoroughly God had taken care of them before. In both missions, they had been ordered not to take along purse, bag, or sandals (9:3; 10:4) and to rely entirely on God rather than themselves. They were watched over by God and cared for by the people they were sent to disciple, and both missions were quite successful. The same Lord who took care of them at that time will continue to do so in this crisis time.

The situation is desperate enough that Jesus is changing their previous instructions (22:36-37). "But now" stresses the changing situation when previous methods will no longer suffice. There will be no one to care for them, and they are on their own. Now they need to take a purse and bag with them, to watch over themselves in a hostile environment. Previously, the forces arrayed against them were occasional, but now they are organized and obsessed with destroying them. Jesus' followers will need all the help they can get.

Surprisingly, he adds, "If you don't have a sword, sell your cloak and buy one." Some have interpreted this to mean Jesus is a Zealot urging armed insurrection, but that goes against everything else about him and his spiritual ministry in the Gospels. In 22:49-51 he disallows the disciples' attempt to raise their swords, so this view is not possible. Others have said he intends the swords for defensive protection only, but the cutting off of the slave's ear in verse 50 is exactly that, so Jesus does not want any swordplay at all. Most likely the command to purchase swords is meant symbolically as a poignant sign to ready themselves for the terrible crisis ahead. The swords are a metaphor for the difficult and dangerous conditions they will face from that time on. This is proved in verse 38, when he says two swords are "enough"; he clearly does not have literal fighting against the Romans in mind. Rather, he is saying that they must be ready for all the hard times they are going to experience, not just in the days to come but in their future mission. Theirs would be a spiritual war, and as in Ephesians 6:10-17 they need "the full armor of God" to fight it.

To emphasize this further, Jesus anchors it in his own mission as fulfilling Isaiah 53:12: "And he was numbered with the transgressors" (22:37). He sees this prophecy as fulfilled in his coming passion and then as defining what his followers will share with him in a "participation in his sufferings" (Phil 3:10). Jesus will be the Suffering Servant of Yahweh. "Numbered with the transgressors" does not just picture his crucifixion between two criminals but defines the entire sequence of events from his arrest to his death on a cross. His point is that all this is now ready to be fulfilled, with Jesus' destiny "completed" (the meaning of "fulfilled") on the cross. Implicitly, he is also saying his followers will share in this ultimate rejection and must be ready.

The disciples misinterpret what he is saying literally and so report with glee, "See, Lord, here are two swords" (22:38). Their response shows how little they really understand. They probably are thinking that heaven's armies will soon erupt out of the sky to fight the final messianic war and destroy the Romans. Their minds almost have no spiritual component at this time, and they are locked into their false perceptions. Jesus' response is perfectly

translated in the NIV: "That's enough!" He could be understood by
the disciples as saying "two are enough," but he actually means it
as a rebuke: "Enough!" It is intended to put a stop to their erroneous perceptions (as in Deut 3:26).

JESUS PRAYS ON THE MOUNT
OF OLIVES (22:39–46)

It is Matthew who names the garden "Gethsemane" (26:36), and
John who tells us it was an olive grove (18:1). Luke also abbreviates the three cycles of Mark, giving us just one and adding the
point of an angel ministering to him (v. 43). The meal has ended,
and Jesus and the disciples have proceeded out of the city to the
Mount of Olives. That they "went out as usual" means that they
did this every evening and slept the night either at the home of
Lazarus in Bethany or in the olive grove. As stated in 21:37, he and
his team often spent the night there. Jesus spent whole nights in
prayer there.

EXHORTATION TO PRAY (22:39–40)

In Mark 14:34 Jesus' prayer is first; here his instructions to the disciples are first. As in the Lord's Prayer (11:4) they are to pray for
strength over temptation: "Pray that you will not fall into temptation" (22:40). This will be repeated in verse 46 and so is the primary emphasis in Luke's version. There is also a play on words, as
peirasmos means "trial, test," and the temptation that comes with
them (see Jas 1:3–5 [trial] and 13–15 [temptation]). Jesus' main concern is not for his own coming ordeal but for theirs. The phrase
he uses is "fall into temptation" and was also the subject in 8:13
and 11:4. Prayer is the antidote that turns temptation from a trial
to a test, in other words, that provides the strength to be victorious when Satan is trying to "sift all of you as wheat." This also
parallels 21:36: "Pray that you may be able to escape all that is
about to happen." With prayer we are grounded in God and find
the strength to endure the difficult tests we undergo.

JESUS' PERSONAL PRAYER (22:41-42)

Jesus goes a short distance away from the others to be somewhat alone and kneels on the ground (the others "falling to the ground") in humility to his Father. His opening, "Father, if you are willing" recognizes that what matters is not his desires but his Father's will, and he is submitting to it. If Jesus the Son of God so surrenders to his Father's predestined will, how much more must we. This is one of the major prayer lessons of Scripture. Note the incredible contrast with Peter's rash, "I am ready" (22:33).

Jesus' personal desire (how could it not be?) is that the Lord "take this cup from me." In the Old Testament the cup often refers to God's wrath and later became a euphemism for suffering. Some say this demonstrates a fear of the physical pain of the cross, but that is not as likely as a shrinking back from the alienation from God due to his becoming sin for us. This could be connected with the cry of dereliction, "My God, my God, why have you forsaken me" (Mark 15:4) and with "scorning its shame" in Hebrews 12:2. He would humanly prefer not to have to undergo this supreme trial. "Nevertheless" (*plēn*; NIV: "yet") is an important term here. In spite of Jesus' human desire, he surrenders to God's greater will.

Every one of us must pray regularly what I call the "Gethsemane prayer": "Yet not my will, but yours be done." Submission to God's greater wisdom and will is at the heart of spiritual commitment. Our prayer life should always be honest, but we must always be aware that while God listens to our honest requests, he always does what is best for us (Rom 8:28), and we must at the deepest level desire this more than our personal wants. This is a model prayer at the same level as the Lord's Prayer in 11:2-4.

STRENGTHENED FROM HEAVEN (22:43-44)

There is a major text-critical issue with 22:43-44, as a large number of ancient manuscripts have omitted this portion ($\mathfrak{P}$75 א1 B A T W and several others), with the result that many dismiss these verses as the shorter and least likely reading. However, א* D K L Byz and others include them, including a mixture of text families, and they fit Luke's style well. I agree with those who cautiously accept them and will proceed on that basis.

Thus Luke's is the Gospel that tells us that an angel came to Jesus in his distress and "strengthened him." That is deeply meaningful, for as Jesus prays for his followers and strengthens them (22:32), an angel has come to strengthen him in his time of need. This is clearly a turning point in the passion story, and all the powers of heaven are arrayed around it, with Satan and his minions very active (compare John 12:31; 14:30–31; 16:11), and they are countered by God and his angels. Again, Jesus is the model for us. If he needed heavenly strengthening, how much more do we?

Now we see his agony of soul (22:44). In spite of the presence of the angel, he is "in anguish" and prays "more earnestly, and his sweat was like drops of blood falling to the ground." The more intense the trial, the more intense should be the prayer placing it all in God's hands. Jesus' anxiety (*in agōnia*) has at times been interpreted as fear, but that is hardly likely in light of verses 42–43. This is anxiety in the midst of a serious trial. This pictures his intense exertion in prayer, a strong metaphor for deep-seated anxiety. His sweat is *like* drops of blood, so this does not indicate literal hematidrosis (the name for the condition in which blood exudes through the pores of the skin). There could be a further metaphor pointing to the shedding of his blood on the cross, but this can never be known for certain.

FURTHER WARNING TO PRAY (22:45–46)

In the very area that Christ has taught them at Gethsemane—persevering prayer—the disciples had failed. Jesus, after winning the victory over himself, returned to them, only to find them fast asleep, "exhausted from sorrow." In Matthew 26:40 he asks, "Couldn't you men keep watch with me for one hour?" It is Luke who tells us it was sorrow that had exhausted them. The impact of Jesus' own agony of heart transmitted itself to them, and while they only dimly realized the full implications, they knew he was soon to be arrested. The full extent of that realization was starting to wear them down. As we will soon see, this was a sorrow mingled with fear for their own safety.

Jesus concludes by repeating the major theme, "pray so that you will not fall into temptation." Without prayer there is no possibility of sufficient spiritual strength to overcome the pressures and anxieties of life. The disciples will prove that in the very next scene. Running away from the trial, as they will try to do, is no answer, for it is a defeat in itself. Rather, we must face our difficulties squarely and persevere due to the empowering presence of Christ and the Spirit in our lives, and this comes only through ongoing prayer.

JESUS IS ARRESTED (22:47–53)

Judas knew where Jesus and the other disciples would be, since they spent their nights there. It was an easy thing to lead the temple police there, and with them was a group of chief priests and elders, probably from the Sanhedrin. Only John mentions the Roman troops (18:3, 12) who were there to ensure no riot broke out. Since it was night, he had agreed that he would single out Jesus for them with the kiss of greeting. A rabbi would often be greeted with a kiss of respect on the hand. It is a tragic irony that the kiss of respect was turned that night into the kiss of betrayal. Mark 14:45 has Judas actually kiss Jesus. Luke has only the intention, possibly to highlight Jesus' challenge in the next verse.

Jesus of course knew exactly what Judas was doing and had predicted it at the Last Supper (22:21–22). So he identifies exactly what is happening, "Judas, are you betraying the Son of Man with a kiss?" (22:48). This oriental greeting signifying love and concern has been incongruously reversed into an act of treachery. The use of the Son of Man title links this with the passion predictions of 9:22, 44; 17:24–25; 18:31–33, demonstrating that this was not just an act of perfidy but part of God's sovereign plan.

Matthew 27:9-10 (Zech 11:12-13) and John 13:18 (Ps 41:9) show this betrayal is actually a fulfillment of prophecy, and God deemed it part of his divine purposes.

The rash question the disciples ask in verse 49 ("Lord, should we strike with our swords?") demonstrates their mindset. They likely believed the final messianic war was about to start and thought Jesus had told them to bring swords (22:36, 38) to prepare them for this very thing. In fact, their question in the Greek expects the answer yes ("We should, shouldn't we?"), meaning they were certain this was the case and that the angelic armies from heaven would soon arrive. It was allowed to carry swords for defensive purposes on the Sabbath and other festival days (1 Macc 2:34-36), and that is the case here.

Luke tells us that one of the disciples then "struck the servant of the high priest, cutting off his right ear" (22:50). John 18:10 tells us it was Simon Peter and that the slave was named Malchus. We don't know if the blow was intentional (Malchus may have been a member of the temple police) or accidental, but it was certainly effective. It is a miracle the police and Romans didn't immediately slaughter the disciples, but that was due to Jesus' quick action and most likely to God's direct intervention.

Jesus' immediate rebuke saves the day (and their lives) as he shouts, "No more of this!" (literally, "That's enough" as in verse 38).[1] The command was likely intended for the police and soldiers as well as for his disciples, and it defuses a very dangerous situation. Jesus needs no defense, and he knows the final war is millennia away. As we will see, he is in complete control of the entire situation, and the events will proceed as his divine destiny indicates. He wants no one hurt, so he touches the ear that had been cut off and reattaches and heals it. This is his final healing miracle. The Romans could clearly tell he was no danger, and his love

---

1. Some translate this, "Let them have their way" and see this as a surrender to the arresting forces, but that is not as likely as the version here.

for his enemies (6:27-31) was evident. The contrast between the violence of both the disciples and their enemies and Jesus' compassionate mercy is startling. Forgiveness and healing are Christ's way, and he reverses the evil done by both groups.

In verse 52 for the first time Luke mentions the official party—the chief priests, officers, and elders—undoubtedly an official arresting party from both the Sanhedrin and the temple authorities. This is a harbinger of the kind of powers that will be arrayed against Jesus at his trial. However, he had never given any reason for the implications of the arrest scene: "Am I leading a rebellion, that you have come with swords and clubs?" His use of *lēstēs* signifies a revolutionary brigand like Barabbas, and clearly he has no connections whatsoever with such people, as Pilate will realize in 23:18-22 (especially Matt 27:15-23). So the authorities need no weapons to arrest Jesus. He will surrender himself to them.

Jesus then notes all the opportunities for the whole week to arrest him while he was teaching in the temple courts (22:53). Of course, we know why they didn't, because they were afraid of how the crowds might react. His point is the hypocrisy of waiting for the cover of darkness. Then he concludes with a note of divine destiny: "This is your hour," which as in John refers to the appointed time that God had designated for Jesus to fulfill his destiny and give up his life (John 2:4; 7:30; 8:20; 12:23, 27, 31; 13:1; 17:1). They are only able to arrest Jesus because God has so willed this moment.

Moreover, this is also the hour "when darkness reigns," that time when God would allow Satan to exert his "authority" (*exousia*; translated as "reigns" in the NIV) over that realm that follows him as "the god of this age" (2 Cor 4:4). Again, John is the one who especially highlights Satan's involvement in the passion events (12:31; 13:27; 14:31; 16:11). The irony is that in orchestrating events that would lead Jesus to the cross, Satan participated in his own defeat. Still, the dominion of darkness had the joy of seeing the pain this brought all members of the Triune Godhead. The actions of the leaders here are portrayed as demonically inspired (compare 11:35;

Acts 26:18). For a time, under his control, God is allowing the forces of evil to act.

———

Events are moving to their climax, and the powers of evil, both human and cosmic, are gathering. The first to move is Judas (vv. 1-6), who has finally had enough and gives himself completely over to Satan. He has long stolen funds from the common purse of the apostolic band and decides the leaders out of their hatred for Jesus would be willing to pay well for a little help arresting Jesus in a quiet place where the crowds will not be around to mess it up.

The preparations for the Passover meal on Friday evening were critical (vv. 7-13). Jesus wanted everything to be perfect for what would become the Last Supper and demonstrate he was indeed the One who fulfilled the meaning of Passover and provided redemption. So the disciples made the room ready, gathered the foods and spices, and sacrificed the lamb for the meal.

As they partake of the meal, Jesus applies the imagery to himself as its fulfillment, beginning with the promise that it points to that time when he will share it with his followers in the final kingdom of God (vv. 15-16). At the first cup (vv. 17-18) he makes it clear that the entire meal points to its fulfillment in the cross as his sacrificial offering. Then in the words of institution (vv. 19-20), the bread and the cup become the central elements in the meaning of the meal. The bread represents his "body given" as a sacrifice for sinful humankind and becomes a "memorial" celebration making the cross the central event of salvation history. The cup looks to the blood as establishing the new covenant (Jer 31:31-34), which celebrates the atoning work of the cross for the salvation of the lost.

The betrayal seems to be a horrible downturn as the powers of evil seem to be victorious, but Luke shows (vv. 21-23) it is actually completely under God's control. Both Satan and Judas are tools of God and fulfill Scripture in proving that even the satanic realm is

under his greater power and acts to accomplish his greater purposes in the death of Jesus. The disciples add their part (vv. 24–27)
when they vie to be regarded as the "best" disciple of the lot. Jesus
makes it clear that this self-centered view of ministry is not of
God. The greatest are the true servants who minister to glorify
God and serve his people, a lesson all of us should ponder carefully.

The future of the disciples is incredibly great (vv. 28–30), for
they will share his authority and be judges and rulers over both
the new Israel on earth, his church, and the kingdom of God in
heaven as judges. They will in this sense parallel the council of
angels in heaven. Still, life in Christ is spiritual warfare, and Satan
is active in trying to defeat us. He will entice Simon Peter to fail
the Lord utterly (vv. 31–34), but it will not be a final defeat, and like
us he has Christ interceding for him and giving him the strength
to endure even in this.

The disciples need spiritual vigilance at the core (vv. 35–38) and
must be prepared for the difficult days that are not just immediately ahead but that will characterize the rest of their lives. When
Jesus tells them to purchase swords he doesn't mean to get ready
to fight the Romans but to be ready for the conflict that will define
their lives from that moment on. Theirs will be difficult but ultimately meaningful lives.

In the olive grove on the Mount of Olives (= Gethsemane) Jesus
prays first for them that strength from God will transform temptation to a test that will give them victory (vv. 39–40). He then prays
for himself (vv. 41–42) in his famous surrender to the will of his
Father in the terrible ordeal awaiting him. When we like Jesus
face overwhelming difficulties, it is absolutely essential that we
too surrender to his greater will. In his time of need, as he ago-
nizes in prayer, an angel comes from heaven and both encourages
and strengthens him (vv. 43–44). Again, he is the model for us. The
more earnestly we pray, the greater the divine strength that fills
us. So we must pray with all the energy we have, for the primary
source for spiritual strength we have is prayer (vv. 45–46).

Jesus' arrest (vv. 47–53) is the time when evil seems to triumph, and yet the entire scene shows God's (and Jesus') control over the situation. The disciples interpret this as the start of the final messianic war, and as Peter cuts off the ear of the high priest's slave, he undoubtedly thinks the angels, heaven's armies, are massing behind him. But Jesus is in charge and defuses the volatile situation, rebuking the leaders for treating him like a common brigand. He is in control, not them.

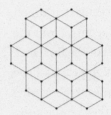

THE TRIALS OF JESUS
(22:54–23:25)

The final events are over. Jesus has spent his farewell meal, the Lord's Supper, with his disciples, gone to Gethsemane to pray, and been arrested there. Now the most negative chapter in Luke takes place, and it will lead directly to the cross. Simon Peter, that rash braggart who promised undying faithfulness, will fail utterly, and then the two trials—before the Jewish authorities and then the Roman authorities—will make it possible for Jesus to fulfill his divine appointment with his sacrificial death for humankind. The new era is on the cusp of history, and God's plan of salvation is about to come to completion.

PETER DENIES JESUS THREE TIMES (22:54-62)

In Mark 14 and Matthew 26 Peter's denials come after the Sanhedrin trial, but Luke places them at the forefront of the trial, possible to link them more closely with Jesus' prediction of them (v. 34). This is not a difficulty historically, for the others intersperse it with the ongoing trial while Luke simply narrates it first. In reality the three took place during the trial.

The main question lies in the three challenges themselves, as the four Gospels disagree with one another regarding the source of those who question Peter. All agree the first one is a servant girl; for the second Matthew and Mark have a maid while John has the crowd and Luke simply has "someone else"; for the third Mark and Matthew have bystanders, John a relative of Malchus, and Luke "another" person. How do we reconcile these disparate accounts? The key is that they took place at different times in the outer courtyard during the trial, and Peter was at all times in the midst of a milling crowd of people. Questions were coming at him from everywhere, and there were likely more than just the three challenges. The evangelists were following separate traditions about who asked what, so there is no real historical discrepancy.

The three challenges progress in intensity in Mark and Matthew but not so much in Luke, but in all the note of discipleship failure is paramount. Peter denies Jesus three times, while the others desert him completely and cower behind closed doors throughout the course of Christ's dying on the cross. Luke plays this down somewhat, removing the scene of the disciples running for their lives and deleting the note that Peter "began to call down curses" in Mark 14:71 and Matthew 26:74. Luke gives greater stress to the guilt of the leaders (v. 53) and focuses on that. For Luke, Simon Peter is corporately identified with the other disciples in his failure.

In verse 54, the arresting party takes Jesus to the high priest's palatial home, but there is minor disagreement among the Gospels. John 18:13 has him taken first to Annas, former high priest and patriarch of the family, while the others tell only of Caiaphas, current high priest. Most likely John has the whole picture, with Annas a preliminary interrogation to get evidence Caiaphas could use. There were actually three stages: a short time with Annas, a lengthier interrogation with Caiaphas, and then the Sanhedrin trial itself. It is possible that Annas and Caiaphas share the same palace, with Jesus taken briefly to the one and then to the other. The interrogation with Caiaphas took the first part of the night, and the Sanhedrin trial the hours before dawn. Peter's denials occurred during the time with Annas and Caiaphas.

It was a cold night in early spring, so the hangers-on "kindled a fire" in the courtyard, and everyone gathered around it. Large homes then were built around just such a courtyard, so this was a typical scene, with soldiers and servants together keeping warm and talking about what was going on inside. The servant girl had apparently seen Peter with Jesus earlier (perhaps in the temple) and recognized him. So when she saw him by the fire she exclaimed to the onlookers, "This man was with him." Luke reports his response as a denial, and the language is fairly strong, possibly reflecting a Jewish ban and strong rejection, "Woman, I don't know him." He is denying any connection with Jesus whatsoever.

In Mark 14:68 Peter leaves the fire and goes out to stand in the entryway, but Luke keeps the story simple, centering entirely on the drama of the confrontation. A short time later another unknown person becomes aware of him and challenges him directly, "You also are one of them" (v. 58). Undoubtedly everyone there turned to look at Peter, assuming the man was correct and that he was a member of the outlaw band. He is even more terrified by now, thinking he too is about to be arrested. The response is equally strong, "Man, I am not!" Now he denies any association not just with Jesus but with the other disciples as well. He wants nothing to do with any legal maneuverings against them. He is distinctly looking out for number one.

Another hour passes, likely to about the middle of the night. Now his Galilean accent betrays him (Matt 26:73), as one of the bystanders exclaims, "Certainly this fellow was with him, for he is a Galilean" (v. 59). The logic is totally valid, for why would a person from Galilee be warming himself by a fire in the high priest's home except because of a connection with Jesus? The same question will be addressed to Jesus in 23:5–6 but with quite different results (Jesus sent to Herod). Peter cannot get away from the queries that just keep coming.

This third denial is not as strong in Luke as it is in Mark 14:71, where he called down covenant curses on his own head. Yet still, it is quite vociferous, "Man, I don't know what you're talking about!" He just wants to be left alone (and safe from arrest). The irony is tragic. He is in the courtyard to support his Lord, and yet he is so scared he denies any connection whatsoever. He cannot deny his Galilean look and accent, but he is terrified of being linked with Jesus.

Luke alone tells us the rooster crows even as he is making his third denial (v. 60), thus immediately fulfilling verse 34. He also has Jesus turning at that moment and looking directly at Peter, further anchoring the man's guilt. The entire scene reeks of prophetic power and omniscience, for Jesus could hardly have heard the interchange. We cannot help but read the implicit message, "See, I told you so!" It is difficult to know where Jesus was at this time. We would expect he was inside the house being questioned by Caiaphas, but how could he have looked directly at Peter in the courtyard? He may have been in the process of being moved to another room, but we cannot know.

Due to Jesus' knowing look, Peter remembers the prophecy and weeps bitter tears at the extent of his failure and the hurt he had inflicted on his Lord. In 22:55 he had entered the courtyard, and now he leaves it in bitter sorrow at his capitulation to pressure from the onlookers. It is hard to imagine the impact on Peter when Jesus' eyes bored into his and he realized his utter foolishness and cowardice. He realizes how far he has fallen, yet at the same time his tears are the first step on the road to recovery. They are the opposite of Esau's bitter tears in Hebrews 12:17, which were merely sorrow for losing his birthright. Peter's are true repentance. One further contrast: Judas' remorse led to suicide (Matt 27:3-10), while Peter's leads eventually to reconciliation and reinstatement. It is often said that Jesus went to the cross utterly alone, with all of his companions having deserted him. However, we will see that the faithful women are there at every stage—the crucifixion (23:49), the burial (23:55-56), and the resurrection (24:1-8, 9-11).

JESUS IS MOCKED (22:63–65)

At the outset of the Sanhedrin trial and concurrent with Peter's denials, Jesus had to endure the mockery of the guards. This was commonplace after arrests, as the soldiers and temple police make sport and have a little fun at the expense of the criminal. The mocking and beating (Matt 26:67 adds that they "spit") were designed to break the will of the accused and get them to give up even before the crucifixion took place. They are intended by God to show the extent of the rejection (Job 30:10; Isa 50:5, 53:3), and Jesus had foretold this ridicule (Luke 13:33; 18:32).

The blindfolding and mocking questions were a version of the game "blind man's bluff." Blindfolded, the accused would be placed in the middle of a circle of soldiers, who would strike him from various angles and say, "Who hit you?" By challenging him to "prophesy," they mocked the claim that he was a prophet. Luke's comment that they were "insulting" him is actually *blasphēmountes*; they were "blaspheming" him and making fun of his religious heritage. They were not just mocking him but the God who sent him. The fact that most of them were Levites, temple police, illustrates the apostasy of the nation as it turned against the Son of God.

JESUS IS TRIED BEFORE THE
SANHEDRIN (22:66–71)

The historicity of this scene has occasioned fierce debate. According to the second-century rabbinic source the **Mishnah** (m. Sanhedrin 4–7), short night trials like this were outlawed. Capital trials were to take at least two days and take place during the daytime. Moreover, this seems more informal than an official trial. Thus many interpreters have decreed it unhistorical, a story made up to show Jewish guilt for the death of Jesus. Others argue that it happened but was not a trial, arguing instead that it was an interrogation to gather evidence to present to Pilate. However, the Gospel records have it ending with a declaration of guilt (Mark 14:64). Moreover, Luke has the decision made at dawn (22:66).

The proceedings likely took place during the night (Matthew and Mark's emphasis), with the final decision made at dawn (Luke) in time to send Jesus with the evidence and verdict to Pilate.

Moreover, there was precedence for bracketing such laws in an emergency situation, and we do not even know for sure that the second-century Mishnah represented the pre-AD 70 situation. Several interpreters have noted that the "illegalities" (if they were such at the time) were necessitated by the fact that the decision had to be made at dawn in order to take Jesus to Pilate, who did his business shortly after dawn. In short, I would conclude with many scholars that this was an official but informal "trial" setting where they did not need to reach an official verdict but only to find evidence that could convince Pilate to crucify Jesus. The Romans alone had the authority to execute a prisoner, so they had to go through Pilate.

Where was this "trial" held? Legally, it should have been in the inner courts of the temple, but the gates were closed at night, so it may have been at the home of Caiaphas, or Jesus may have been moved to a hall near the temple. That may be hinted at here, as Jesus is "led before them," probably the council chamber, but it is not clear, and we do not know. The fact that "the council of the elders of the people, both the chief priests and the teachers of the law"—that is, the members of the Sanhedrin—were present means that this was an official event.

The questioning is quite truncated in Luke. They ask Jesus only two **christological** questions, which echo the angelic testimony at his birth (1:32, 35), about whether he is Messiah and whether he is the Son of God. In his answer Jesus stresses his status as divine Son of Man to climax this highly theological scene. The first gets right to the main issue, "If you are the Messiah ... tell us" (22:67). The "if" is *ei*, the condition of fact, and means, "Since you claim to be Messiah, prove it." Luke clearly wants his readers to ask this question as well and enter into the reality of Jesus as God-sent Messiah. The Jewish leaders want to use this to prove that Jesus is a political threat to Rome, one of the messianic pretenders who stir up rebellion.

Jesus gives a twofold response. First (22:67b–68), he states that any reply on his part is useless, because "you will not believe me." The Greek is much stronger, "you will *never* [*ou mē*] believe" (no matter what I say). They have long ago decided he was a false prophet, and there was no use answering them. This is an allusion to Jeremiah 38:15, where the prophet makes this same response to the apostate king Zedekiah, so again Jewish guilt is uppermost. Moreover, Jesus adds, if he asked them anything in turn, they would refuse to answer him. This is a reference back to the debates in the temple, where their silence greeted his charges (20:7–8, 26, 40). Further discussion is pointless.

His second response is the key to this trial scene (22:69), where he takes the initiative and goes beyond their query. While he sits in the seat of the accused awaiting their judgment, in reality he will be the **eschatological** Judge over them. This declaration is not just a proclamation of his future glory; it is even more a statement of his future authority: "From now on, the Son of Man will be seated at the right hand of the mighty God." This is Psalm 110:1, the most powerful Old Testament prophecy on the exaltation of Christ. In it Yahweh promises he will "sit at my right hand until I make your enemies a footstool for your feet." When Jesus says "from now on" he means that this promise is set in motion with his death and resurrection; he will sit as a sovereign in heaven and rule over the final kingdom of God. So like Satan in 22:54, the leaders through this trial are participating in their own defeat. They will take Jesus' life and in doing so inaugurate the end-time events. The "power of God" (NIV: "mighty God") may well refer to the court of heaven, the counterpart to the Sanhedrin, where the real trial is taking place and where the leaders will be held accountable for their folly and rebellion. So the true judge is not the Jewish leadership but Jesus the exalted Lord, who will with his Father sit on the white throne of eternal judgment (Rev 20:11–15).

If Jesus will sit at the right hand of God, this must mean he claims to be the Son of God, a claim that forms the natural second query in verse 70. "Son of God" is at the core of Luke's Christology, but it is difficult to know exactly how the leaders understood it. Yet since it provides the basis for the charge of blasphemy, some exalted status, perhaps divinity, must be connoted.

Jesus likely meant his reply, "You say that I am," not as mere affirmation but to ironically mean, "It is as you say, but you cannot accept it." Jesus is saying they are right but do not deserve a reply. They take it as confirmation, saying there is no further need for testimony or evidence. Jesus has condemned himself. In the combination of verses 69 and 70b, he indeed has done just that, but in accord with his own destiny. This is where he delivers himself into their hands and accepts his Father's will. He, not they, is still in charge of the proceedings.

Scholars have presented several possibilities as the basis for the blasphemy charge: Messiah, Son of God, the statement about destroying the temple, the use of the divine name ("I Am"), and the claim to sit at the right hand of God. Probably the actual charge combined the Son of God title with the misuse of the divine name and the claim to sit at God's right hand. These would also allow the leaders to assert to Pilate that Jesus is a threat to Roman rule and wanted to usurp Rome's authority, making himself king.

JESUS IS TRIED BEFORE PILATE
AND HEROD (23:1-25)

Few deny the historicity of the trial before Pilate. It makes too much sense, for the Romans had to conduct any capital trial and execution. The leaders are certain Jesus is a false prophet (11:53–54; 19:47; 20:20) and believe they can now prove that he is a danger to Rome and so deliver him to Pilate for his morning civic session, held always just after dawn broke. Jesus is truly the innocent righteous sufferer of Isaiah, treated as a criminal when in reality he

is Messiah and Son of God. His innocence is stressed throughout
(23:4, 14, 15, 22, 41, 47).

JESUS BEFORE PILATE (23:1-5)

Jesus had to be brought before Pilate, as only he had the power of
life and death. This also fulfills the prophecy that Jesus would be
handed over to the Gentiles (9:22; 18:32). Pilate was the "prefect"
over Judea, responsible to maintain the Roman peace and generally govern the province. For trials such as this, he would listen
to the charges, interrogate the prisoner, and make his verdict.
There were three charges (23:2): (1) subverting or misleading the
nation, not much of an argument to the Romans because it didn't
involve them but was the major charge of the Jews themselves;
(2) opposing taxes to Caesar, a false charge, as Jesus demanded
such in 20:20-25, but this would be important to Pilate, whose
main duty was to collect these taxes (see on 3:1); (3) claiming to be
the anointed Messiah, or King of the Jews—this would constitute
sedition and be very serious; however, this was a religious office
for Jesus rather than political and again was actually no threat to
Roman rule.

In light of these charges, Pilate interrogates Jesus (23:3-4), getting immediately to the heart of the issue: "Are you the king of
the Jews?" Found in all four Gospels, this epithet is also made the
inscription on the cross by Pilate (23:38). He wants to see if Jesus'
accusers are right that he is a revolutionary who wishes to over-
throw Rome and make himself king. This happened often in the
first century, so it is a valid question. This was the one area Pilate
cared deeply about. Of course, he doesn't realize that in truth the
cross will become Jesus' throne, and he will ascend it to finalize
his anointing as royal Davidic Messiah.

Jesus responds, "You have said so [sy legeis]." He is separating
himself from the Jewish charge and refuses to bow to the pressure. The emphasis is on the "you," meaning Jesus recognizes
Pilate's query but is not that kind of king. Pilate actually seems

to understand his response and so renders a preliminary verdict, probably thinking that would settle the issue. Roman legal procedure was to interrogate the accused regarding the charges, listen to his response, then render a verdict. Having done so, he tells the Jewish leaders, "I find no basis for a charge against this man" (23:4). He saw no threat to Roman hegemony in Jesus.

However, if he thought that solved the problem, he was completely mistaken. The leaders repeat the charge that "he stirs up the people all over Judea by his teaching" (23:5). They are convinced this charge will work, for the Romans wanted nothing to do with Jewish riots of any kind. They add to the original charge that it is his "teaching," not something the Romans are concerned about (it is a Jewish problem), except for the unrest it is producing. They make another important point by saying that it "started in Galilee and has come all the way here." Galilee was the source of most of the revolutionary brigands and a hotbed of sedition to the Romans.

JESUS BEFORE HEROD ANTIPAS (23:6–12)

Many have doubted the historical worth of this scene as well, since it occurs only in Luke. However, it makes perfect sense, for Pilate could never understand the Jews and had no idea why his preliminary verdict was not accepted. So it was completely logical that he get the advice of the knowledgeable Herod Antipas, who had grown up in Jewish circles. In fact, it is exactly what the governor Festus did in consulting Herod Agrippa in Acts 25–26 at the trial of Paul. So there is no reason to doubt this event.

As soon as Pilate heard Jesus was from Galilee, he made sure that was true and realized he "was under Herod's jurisdiction" and that the man was in Jerusalem for a visit, probably for Passover (23:6–7). There is no hint that Pilate wanted to pass the buck, rather that Herod give him some insight into the situation. Pilate understood nothing about the Jews and was unsure how to proceed, so he wanted to see how Herod would handle the issue and thus sent Jesus to him. Antipas was the tetrarch (ruled a fourth of the whole province, see 3:1) in charge of Galilee and Perea. He was the one who had imprisoned John the Baptist in 3:19–20 and inquired about Jesus in 9:7–9. So it was quite natural for Pilate to bring him into the picture at this time. He would have been staying in the old Hasmonean palace just west of the temple, fairly close to Pilate's headquarters.

Herod's interrogation of Jesus was anticlimactic and disappointing (23:8–10). At the outset he was quite pleased at the opportunity, for he had long wanted to meet him, though his reason was not religious. He wanted to be entertained by seeing one of his famous and spectacular miracles. Herod had no interest in a search for truth or desire to learn about the claims that Jesus was the Messiah and Son of God. There was no hint of openness to God or Jesus, no search for faith as with Zacchaeus in 19:1–10, only an interest in a healing or a nature miracle.

When Herod queried him on several different issues, Luke tells us that Jesus "gave him no answer" to any of them. The indication is that the interrogation took some time but yielded no results. Matthew 27:12–14 indicates Jesus did the same later with Pilate, and the early church saw this as fulfilling Isaiah 53:7, according to which the Suffering Servant of Yahweh "did not open his mouth ... as a sheep before its shearers is silent, so he did not open his mouth." Jesus recognized Herod's actual intentions and refused to satisfy him.

Jesus' opponents, the chief priests and scribes, saw their opportunity and again began "vehemently accusing him" of blasphemy and sedition. They hoped they could get Herod to condemn Jesus and give them some leverage with Pilate. Herod had presided over the death of the Baptist, and they wanted a similar verdict against Jesus. They have no effect on Antipas, however, who apparently joins Pilate in giving tacit approval of Jesus but here is simply interested in making sport with his prisoner.

To Herod, Jesus with his total silence is not worthy of further effort, so he joins his soldiers in having some fun at his expense by ridiculing and mocking his so-called royal status (23:11). The contempt shown him fulfills Isaiah 53:3, "He was despised and rejected by mankind. ... He was despised, and we held him in low esteem." Dressing him "in an elegant robe" was part of the mockery, laughing at him as the lowly king. It is debated whether this is the white robe of the king-designate or the purple robe of royalty, but the latter is the more likely here. This is further irony, as the reader is aware that he will soon be the exalted one (22:69).

Former enemies now become friends (23:12), fulfilling Psalm 2:1-2 ("the rulers band together against the LORD and against his anointed"), also quoted in Acts 4:25-28. We don't know when Antipas and Pilate became enemies—perhaps the slaughter of Galilean pilgrims mentioned in 13:1 or perhaps the incident when Pilate brought his Roman auxiliaries and placed their shields in Herod's palace, causing his four sons to join in the appeal to Rome on behalf of the Jews, who were highly offended by the images on the shields.

JESUS SENTENCED AND DELIVERED (23:13-25)

After Jesus was returned to Pilate (probably halfway through his public time, about 7:30 or so), he had the Sanhedrin and the Jewish people reassemble to hear the results of his deliberations with Herod. The presence of the "people" is significant because they become witnesses of the official verdict and participants in the vendetta against Jesus. Until this point the common people have always sided with Jesus, but this is the time of the powers of darkness, and the people have mysteriously switched their allegiance and joined Jesus' enemies. The emphasis is on Jewish guilt, and now it is all of Judaism.

Nothing has changed in the verdict now of both Pilate and Herod. Several scholars have noted here the seven stages of the Roman trial: arrest (14a), charged (14b), *cognitio* or judgment (14c), verdict (14d), evidence supporting verdict (15a), acquittal (15b), and judicial warning (16). So Pilate recapitulates the process and announces the combined verdict, intending to punish Jesus for inciting the crowds (probably a beating) and then release him. Pilate's basic intention is expressed in verse 14—there is no basis for the Jewish charges. There is no evidence to support any danger of Jesus inciting the people to rebellion against Rome.

Then in 23:15 Pilate adds Herod's verdict, as he sent Jesus back as one who "has done nothing to deserve death." In returning Jesus, Herod was implicitly acknowledging his innocence, and Pilate uses this to cover his back and make it a combined verdict. There is no act of treason or sedition in anything Jesus has done. In 13:31 some Pharisees had told Jesus, "Herod wants to kill you." Either he had changed his mind or the rumor was exaggerated. At any rate, the combined Roman authorities want Jesus released.

Pilate's conclusion is his desire to "punish him and then release him" (23:16). The punishment (*paideuō*) refers to flogging. There were three levels: the *fustigatio*, a less severe beating for light offenses; the *flagellatio*, a severe beating for hardened criminals, and *verberatio*, the most severe form we know as scourging, accomplished with a whip made of strips of leather with pieces of bone or metal tied onto the strips. This would probably be the middle type of beating. Luke does not mention elsewhere the scourging of Jesus (see Mark 15:15-16 = Matt 27:26-27). So Pilate wished to placate the bloodthirsty Jews and thought this should suffice. He was wrong.

In verse 18, the Jews present began to clamor for what was called the "paschal amnesty" and demand that the prisoner released be Barabbas rather than Jesus.[1] The difficulty is the absence of evidence in any Roman record or Josephus for such an amnesty, so many critics doubt its veracity and consider it a literary creation meant to explain Jesus' guilty verdict. At the same time, much can

---

1. Verse 17, with its explanation of Pilate's obligation to free a prisoner at Passover, is omitted in several major manuscripts ($\mathfrak{P}$75 A B and others) and is most likely not original but a later assimilation to Mark 15:6 = Matthew 27:15.

be said on its behalf: (1) Roman law does show a magistrate has the authority to pardon prisoners to appease the crowds (Josephus, *Antiquities* 20.208–9). (2) A Jewish provision in the Mishnah ("they may slaughter for one ... whom they have promised to bring out of prison," m. Pesach 8:6a) is one of the oldest traditions in that work and points to just such a release of prisoners at a Passover in Jerusalem. (3) Roman law allowed two types of amnesty: *abolitio*, acquittal before trial, and *indulgentia*, acquittal after conviction. In other words, Pilate had the authority for this type of amnesty. It is common today to accept the likelihood that this was a true story. It makes perfect sense as a gesture of Roman goodwill.

The key is that Pilate wants this released prisoner to be Jesus, and the crowd follows the leaders in insisting it be Barabbas instead. The very name of Barabbas is supreme irony, as it means "son of the father." So the criminal "son of the father" will be released instead of the true "Son of the Father/God," Jesus. He was one of the insurrectionists rampant then and had led a riot in the very environs of Jerusalem and committed murder (Mark 15:7). He had actually committed the very crime Jesus is charged with in verses 5, 14, and they want to free the guilty party and crucify the innocent man. Probably the other two who were being crucified were associates of his. To many Jews he would have been a folk hero, an ancient Robin Hood, and so they would be in favor of him.

The more Pilate repeats his desire to free Jesus, the louder the crowds scream, "Crucify him! Crucify him!" (23:21). This is the first mention of crucifixion; and things are getting worse and worse, as the volume intensifies to free the guilty and put the innocent one on the cross. The insanity of mob action has won out, and justice has flown out the window. The normal Jewish penalty for blasphemy was stoning, but the Romans crucified people for sedition, and the Jews wanted this due to Deuteronomy 21:23, "anyone who is hung on a pole is under God's curse" (see also Gal 3:13). They wanted Jesus not only executed but under the covenant curse as well.

Pilate makes a third and final attempt to release Jesus in verse 22. He repeats the points of verses 14–16, asking them, "What crime [*kakon*, 'evil'] has this man committed?" We must remember he is asking this from a Roman perspective; from a Jewish standpoint Jesus is indeed a false Messiah and blasphemer. The leaders would have understood this, but the crowds would not have. Pilate's insistent decision to punish and then release Jesus has them livid with anger. As before, they respond with "loud shouts" and stridently "demanded that he be crucified." Luke makes Jewish guilt for the death of Jesus absolutely clear. The Romans carried out the penalty, but the Jewish people demanded it. Pilate would have set him free.

Finally, their screams prevail and Pilate surrenders (v. 24). He makes his final legal decision and decides a single death is preferable to a mass riot. Jesus is sacrificed on the altar of expediency. So the murderer is free. Jesus is dying in his place; and in fact he is dying to cover the sins of Pilate, of Caiaphas, and of Barabbas himself. In the final line of the passage, Pilate "surrendered Jesus to their will," ending on a note of Jewish guilt. The verb *paradidōmi* (delivered over) is used both ways. Jesus is "delivered over to the Gentiles" (18:32), and the Gentile Pilate delivers him over to the will of the Jews (here). Yet the final reality is that God has handed Jesus over to both. To the very end, God and Jesus are in total sovereign control of his destiny.

———

In this chapter events rush to their fulfillment in the cross. From the moment of Jesus' arrest to his death, he faces his destiny all alone. This is fitting, for he, not the Jews or the Romans, is in sovereign charge of these events. His solitary splendor at this end of his earthly sojourn takes place because he alone can pay the price for our sins. Luke omits the desertion of the Eleven and centers on Peter's three denials for dramatic purposes (vv. 54–62). Peter's total failure exemplifies the others and shows there are none on whom Jesus can depend at this terrible crisis. As you read the progression and total concern of Peter only for himself, think of yourself and how often you have done something similar—hidden your Christian allegiance so people wouldn't make fun of you. We can all see ourselves in Simon Peter on this occasion.

The mockery of Jesus at his trial (vv. 63-65) and on the cross is highly ironic, for the very thing they ridiculed him about—the claims that he is Messiah and King of the Jews—were in reality absolutely true. When the soldiers place the mock robe on him and the crown of thorns on his brow, they are in reality providing a prologue of the royal robe and crown he will wear shortly.

The Sanhedrin trial (vv. 66-71) does not just tell how the Jews were instrumental in Jesus' death. It is actually deeply christological and anchors the reality that Jesus is indeed Messiah and Son of God. The incredible irony continues, as Jesus reveals the true reality, that he is the eschatological Judge who will sit on the throne of God over his very persecutors. As Son of God, he transcends even the focus of their trial, for he is Yahweh himself, above earthly concerns, and yet he gives himself for the very sake of those placing him on the cross.

The trial before Herod and Pilate (23:1-25) highlights Jewish guilt, as Pilate several times tries to free Jesus, but the Jewish leaders won't let him do so. Still, the Romans stand equally guilty, and in fact all of us with our sinful acts have placed Jesus on the cross. It is clear in verses 1-5 that Pilate finds nothing anti-Roman in Jesus and realizes his innocence. But the Jews insist he is a danger to Rome. So Pilate involves Herod in the proceedings to take advantage of his knowledge of Jewish ways (vv. 6-12), but nothing of value transpires from it. Herod seeks entertainment rather than truth and ends up joining the Jews in mocking Jesus. For Luke this means that the world leaders join the Jews in condemning Jesus. Truly all humankind is involved and guilty before God.

The official verdict of Pilate and Herod (vv. 13–16) is to release Jesus with a beating. It doesn't work. Pilate then tries to release Jesus with his paschal amnesty, the liberation of a prisoner as a gift to the Jewish people. They will have none of it, and here the crowds join the leaders and change their minds, demanding the revolutionary brigand Barabbas be released rather than Jesus (vv. 18–23). In the end, Pilate does not have the moral fiber to do what is right and acquiesces to the crowd's demands, turning Jesus over to be crucified (vv. 24–25).

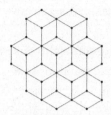

THE CRUCIFIXION AND
BURIAL OF JESUS
(23:26–56)

We have now reached the center point of salvation, indeed the center of human history, for with the cross and resurrection salvation has been rendered available for humankind. This is as true of the old covenant as it is of the new covenant age, for the effects of the cross reached back and are the basis of the salvation of Abraham and Moses in the same way as for Paul and Peter. The cross and resurrection (= the humiliation and exaltation of Christ in the creeds) form a single event in salvation history, the **eschatological** fulcrum removing the dividing wall between human beings and God.

We would think that if there is one story that is told the same in all four Gospels, it would be the crucifixion of Jesus, but in reality here too there are differing theological nuances, with Luke's the most unique. The other three focus on the cross becoming Jesus' throne, and Jesus exalted to royal Messiah by his death on the cross. So the crucifixion becomes a coronation scene. At the same time, Mark and Matthew are quite similar to each other, stressing the horror of putting to death the Son of God, while John is the opposite, removing all the negative elements (like the mocking, the earthquake, and the darkness) to present Jesus in all his sovereign majesty.

Luke has two emphases—Jesus as the innocent, righteous martyr and the crucifixion as a scene of awesome worship. This latter is seen in the three last words of Jesus in Luke 23:34, 43, 46, all centered on prayer. The omissions of Luke—the scourging, the wine and myrrh, the cry of dereliction, the Elijah taunt—are similar to John in highlighting the wonder of the cross as a salvific event.

These differences cause some critics to doubt the details of this crucifixion narrative, though nearly all accept the basic historicity of Jesus dying on the cross. For instance, the Jesus Seminar doubts the three last words. However, the majority are open to the likelihood that the unique elements of Luke 23 stem from L, the special material Luke discovered in his research (1:1-4) and used often in his narrative. All the Gospel writers selected from a vast store of details supplied by the countless eyewitnesses of the actual events (see 1:2). The choices, as here, come from the theological nuances the Spirit led Luke to bring out here.

JESUS PROCEEDS ALONG THE WAY TO THE CROSS (23:26-32)

The Romans required condemned criminals to carry the crossbeam to the point of execution, where it would be fastened to the pole. They did so to break the spirit of the condemned, to tell them that in effect they were already dead. Jesus carried his crossbeam as far as he could, but due to his weakened condition from the scourging (omitted by Luke), he was unable to go much past the city gates and was forced to quit.

In verse 26 Luke tells us the Romans conscripted a man coming into the city (Mark 15:21 says he was "passing by on his way in from the country") and forced him to bear the cross for Jesus. The soldiers would not sully themselves by bearing such a shameful cross piece. Such a requisitioning was a legal right of the Romans, so this was not unusual. Cyrene was a region in North Africa, modern Tripoli, and Simon may have been a pilgrim or a laborer working in the fields outside Jerusalem (the former seems more probable). Mark also tells us he was "the father of Alexander and Rufus," possibly the same Rufus of Romans 16:19, so it is likely the family became Christ followers after this event. By telling us that Simon bore the cross "behind Jesus," Luke may be implying discipleship, acting out Jesus' command in 9:23; 14:27 to "take up their cross and follow" him.

The large number following Jesus and Simon as they bore the cross included "women who mourned and wailed for him" (v. 27). These may be professional mourners who often followed parties to the execution site and offered up opiates (for instance, the drugged wine of Mark 15:23) and tears as acts of piety, fulfilling Zechariah 12:10-14, mourning for "the one they have pierced." Yet they also seem to be sympathizers who are sincerely filled with sorrow.

There are two contrasts and one parallel in this scene. The first is a threefold contrast. The crowds had acclaimed Jesus the triumphant messianic king as he entered Jerusalem (19:38), had demanded his death at the trial before Pilate (23:18-23), and now mourn his passing. Second, Jesus turns their sorrow for him into a lament and death knell over Jerusalem (23:28-31), repeating 13:34-35. The parallel is also in this area of the weeping for sorrow. Their weeping for Jesus' passing parallels his weeping upon entering Jerusalem (19:41-44 = 13:34-35; 21:20-24). The nation in rejecting the Son of God has brought divine judgment down on itself, and that provides much deeper grounds for sorrow. Jesus' death will result in universal salvation; their death results from apostasy against God.

So Jesus as he proceeds to the cross turns to those weeping and gives them a final opportunity to repent. Their sorrow should not be for him but for themselves and for the judgment the nation has brought on itself. They are the "daughters of Jerusalem" and so are intimately tied up with the fate of that onetime holy city.

His coming death is his divine destiny and eternal mission. It will bring salvation and joy to countless millions. They on the other hand will suffer a pointless fate occasioned by the refusal of their progeny to accept God's offer of life through their Messiah, whom they have refused to recognize as such.

He then predicts the near future, undoubtedly the events of AD 66–70 and the destruction of Jerusalem, already prophesied in 21:20–24. At that time these women themselves will cry out with a negative beatitude, stating that it would be better not to have been born, to be the nonliving results of "the childless women, the wombs that never bore and the breasts that never nursed." This is a powerful metaphor, for there was no greater blessing than for a woman to bear children, but at that time mothers will have to give up their children to death (compare Isa 54:1). The curse is no longer on the barren women but the fruitful women. So there is a complete reversal of all categories with the judgment that will fall on them.

Jesus then in 23:30 turns to Hosea 10:8, where the terror becomes so great that people prefer to be hidden under an avalanche, begging for the mountains and hills to "fall on us" (see Rev 6:16). It is more preferable to endure a swift death than to face a wrathful God. In both Hosea and here it is the apostasy of Israel that brings this divine judgment on their heads.

This closes with a proverb (23:31) contrasting his death with what awaits the nation. While some take this of humankind in general or of the Jews in particular, it is much more likely a contrast between the fate of the innocent Jesus and that of a guilty nation. Jesus is the "tree" that is "green," which should not be removed from the tree and burned, while Israel is the "dry" wood, which has died and is ready to be burned. The message is that if God has predestined his righteous Son to die, how much more do the unrepentant people of Israel deserve God's judgment.

The famous pictures of the crucifixion all show Jesus crucified between two other criminals, undoubtedly insurrectionists arrested alongside Barabbas (v. 32). This fulfilled Isaiah 53:12, "numbered with the transgressors," also noted in 22:37. These continue the contrasts, as their guilt is set alongside Jesus' innocence. However, the major emphasis will come in 23:39–43, as one of them will be the very first to experience the salvation his death would bring to humankind. They had spent their lives killing, but Jesus will now offer them life.

JESUS IS CRUCIFIED (23:33–43)

There are three emphases in Luke's treatment of the death of Jesus. First, three times he is taunted with some variation of "If you are the Messiah/king," then "save yourself" (vv. 35, 37, 39). This culminates in the addition of "and us" (v. 39), which becomes an unconscious prophecy of the salvific effects of the cross. The "people" (= the Jewish people) stand outside this as bystanders. Second, the three last sayings of Jesus (vv. 34, 43, 46) introduce the theme of prayer and worship as the true significance of the cross. Third, the three "save" passages (vv. 35, 37, 39) may have a double meaning, pointing to Jesus as "Savior." The one who refuses to save himself becomes the One who alone can save others (9:24; 19:10).

JESUS ON THE CROSS (23:33–34)

For Jews, crucifixion had to be outside the city (Lev 24:14), and the Romans always placed crosses on a major thoroughfare where everyone would see them as a deterrent to others. Mark 15:22 tells us the place was called "Golgotha," but Luke translates it for Gentile readers, "the Skull." It could have been named this because it was the Roman site for executions, but most assume the knoll resembled a skull. The popular site today called "Gordon's Cavalry" is probably not the correct place, and most archaeologists prefer the site inside the Church of the Holy Sepulchre as the best option.

There Jesus was crucified between the two other criminals by a Roman detail (usually four soldiers). There were four types of crosses: a stake in the ground, a cross in the shape of an X (now called St. Andrew's cross), one in the shape of a T (St. Anthony's cross), and the traditional one, used when they wanted to nail a tablet listing the crime for bystanders to see (23:37). Normally they would tie the condemned to the crossbeam, and it would take a couple of days for them to die in extreme agony as the arms slowly turned to gangrene. Since it was Passover, the condemned had to be dead and buried by sunset, so they nailed the hands and the feet so that blood loss would hasten their deaths (John 20:25; Col 2:14). They usually placed a small seat on the pole so the crucified could hoist himself up occasionally to catch a breath.

Luke omits the incident with the offer of the drugged wine (Matt 27:34). Instead, he provides the first of the "last sayings" of Jesus.[1] Jesus asks forgiveness on the very ones—primarily the Jewish leaders and people but also the Romans—who have placed him on the cross. As such it fulfills Isaiah 53:12, "made intercession for the transgressors," in an even more powerful way. It is likely Stephen in Acts 7:60 ("Lord, do not hold this sin against them") modeled his final prayer after Jesus' prayer for forgiveness here.

Jesus becomes the archetype of the righteous sufferer who loves his enemies (6:27–31) and reverses the norm for those mistreated seeking revenge. He is living out his model prayer to "forgive everyone who sins against us" (11:4). He is dying as the atoning sacrifice so that sinners can be forgiven by God, and so he asks for forgiveness even for his own murderers. So this prayer is a proper culmination for his life of compassion. In a very real sense this prayer lays the groundwork for the Jewish mission in Acts. Jesus prays for forgiveness for these very ones who have placed him on the cross, and his followers in Acts use this very fact to call

---

1. Several important manuscripts (𝔓75 B D* W and others) omit this prayer. It is difficult to account for its omission, and it may have been added in assimilation to Stephen's prayer in Acts 7:60. However, most tentatively accept it as original because Luke often includes doublets between Luke and Acts, and there is no good reason for later scribes to add such a saying here. So we will cautiously take it as original as well.

the Jewish people to repentance on the grounds of the cross (Acts 2:23–24, 36–39; 3:17–19; 4:10–12).

The basis of the prayer for forgiveness is "for they do not know what they are doing." They are ignorant of the fact that they are crucifying the One who is truly "King of the Jews" (v. 38) and Son of God. This ignorance will be the basis for the call to repentance in Acts 3:17; 13:27; 17:30. Of course, this forgiveness can only be obtained through repentance and faith-decision, and the nation still stands guilty before God. However, forgiveness is at all times available and is the basis for Paul's mandate in Romans 1:16 to bring the gospel "first to the Jew."

Luke provides only a brief comment that "they divided up his clothes by casting lots," a practice commonly done as the possessions of the criminal legally belonged to the soldiers who executed him. John 19:23–24 provides a lengthier narration and shows this fulfilled Psalm 22:18, "They divide my clothes among them and cast lots for my garment," David's cry of despair over the mockery inflicted on him by his enemies. The purpose is to show the external powerlessness of Jesus as the sacrificial Lamb before his enemies. Jesus died in ultimate shame, naked for all to see. Note the incredible contrast: as Jesus prays for God to forgive them, they are gambling for his very clothes and mocking him in front of everyone.

THE MOCKERY HE ENDURES (23:35–38)

Most of the crowd stood watching events unfold. As with the Wild West in the nineteenth century, executions became entertainment. The people in the crowd thus become passive witnesses of the mockery. Quite a few take the opportunity to scoff at Jesus, fulfilling Psalm 22:7, "All who see me mock me; they hurl insults, shaking their heads." There are two groups of taunts here (with a third in v. 39) and the inscription on the cross. The first taunt comes from the "rulers," the leaders of Israel. As in Psalm 22 and Isaiah 53, Jesus is scorned, despised, and mocked.

By "he saved others," they draw from the number of times he healed or "saved" the sick (6:9; 7:50; 8:36, 48, 50; 17:19; 18:42), laughingly calling on him to rescue himself from his own "affliction." Their challenge is that if he is really "God's Messiah, the Chosen One," he should prove it by saving himself. There is supreme irony in this full title; it is mockery on their part but absolute **christological** truth for Luke and the readers. By not saving himself, he will make it possible for them to be saved, though they will never recognize that. So the entire scene is ironic, as they put to death the very one who alone can give them life.

Then the soldiers add their taunts (23:36–37). They offer Jesus wine vinegar, a sour wine often drunk by the poor and by soldiers. While it could be an act of kindness, it is more likely part of the mockery and alludes to Psalm 69:21, "They put gall in my food and gave me vinegar for my thirst," scorning his helpless condition. They add to the leaders, scorning what to them was a laughable title, "king of the Jews," linked to Pilate's question (23:3), the purple robe they put on Jesus (23:11), and the inscription of 23:38. "Let this naked, skinny king 'save himself,'" they scornfully shouted.

The inscription was placed on the pole above the crossbeam and said, "THIS IS THE KING OF THE JEWS," which John 19:19–22 tells us was intended by Pilate to mock the leaders even more than Jesus. For all the Gospels this became a major christological emphasis, as the cross became Jesus' throne and the taunts became an ironic witness to the true effects of Jesus' sacrificial death. The people laughed at Jesus, but the words of their taunts were all true on the cosmic scale. This became a royal celebration, a coronation event.

THE TWO CRIMINALS (23:39–43)

The contrast between the two criminals here sums up the conflict, one aligning himself with the mockers and the other with Jesus' followers. The first malefactor "hurled insults," repeating the taunts of the leaders and soldiers, "Aren't you the Messiah? Save yourself and us!" The Messiah was supposed to come with the armies of heaven, destroy the Romans, and rescue the Jewish people. The added "and us" fits this expectation, but again it is hugely ironic, as that is exactly what Christ was doing in delivering himself up to the cross. Christ was in process of accomplishing this very redemption the criminal calls for and yet far more, for this would be eternal redemption, not just political liberation.

In fact, that is exactly what will happen to the other malefactor. He would be saved and join Jesus in paradise. He rebukes his partner in crime and is the lone supporter of Jesus, realizing and accepting his relationship with the Father. He challenges the man, "Don't you fear God?" The man is "under the same sentence" as Jesus—the death penalty—but under a far greater sentence, an eternal one, from God. Clearly the other criminal does indeed "fear God," the very heart of being a Jew living under covenant relationship with God. Here "fear" is not reverence but the terror of falling under the wrath and judgment of God the eternal Judge.

The second criminal recognizes and admits that they are guilty of the crimes for which they are being crucified (23:41) but goes one step further—he realizes his guilt before God as well. Yet while they are both guilty, Jesus is innocent, and the man acknowledges that and joins the voices protesting that righteous man's suffering and rejection, namely, Jesus' followers. In a very real sense, this is his repentance.

He finally throws himself on Jesus' mercy (23:42), asking, "Jesus, remember me when you come into your kingdom." If the previous verse represented his repentance, this becomes his conversion. He has complete faith not only that Jesus is the Messiah he claims to be but that he is also the Savior who has first inaugurated God's kingdom in this world and has the power to bring this former murderer into God's eternal kingdom. In this he realizes more than the disciples themselves do. This goes beyond earthly deliverance to heavenly salvation. We don't know where he got this great insight. Perhaps he had some prior contact with Jesus, or perhaps Jesus' prayer that his Father forgive his murderers touched the man's heart. It may be a combination of the two. The man wanted to experience that divine forgiveness for himself and believed Jesus could not only bring it about but also include him in his coming kingdom.

Jesus' response is perhaps the most beautiful promise in Scripture and comes in the form of a solemn *amēn* saying (see on 4:24), "Truly I tell you, today you will be with me in paradise" (23:43). This is far more than the man had been hoping, for he was thinking of the distant future, while Christ promises immediate results. "Paradise" is a Persian loanword for royal gardens, so this originally spoke of the garden of Eden and then became a metaphor for heaven as a new Eden, the beauty of the afterlife (Isa 51:3) as well as the heavenly abode (1 Enoch 17-19; Psalms of Solomon 14:3; 2 Cor 12:4; Rev 2:7). The promise is that as soon as he dies, he will join Jesus in paradise, a reference to the intermediate state (2 Cor 5:1-8; Phil 1:23). As such this is strong evidence for the deity of Christ. He controls the gateway to paradise, an authority only Yahweh possesses. This is also evidence that Jesus went to heaven after he died, not just at his ascension (24:50-53). The latter is a symbolic action to conclude his resurrection appearances, which were appearances from heaven.

JESUS DIES (23:44-46)

Luke omits the cry of dereliction (Mark 15:34), the Elijah comment (Mark 15:35-36), and the offer of sour wine (Mark 15:36) in order to center on the cosmic portents demonstrating the significance of Jesus' death. Luke tells us this took place at noon (the sixth hour), the midpoint of the crucifixion, three hours into the event (it began at nine in the morning, Mark 15:25). The darkness lasts three hours and summarizes the eschatological outpourings of the Old Testament signifying the day of the Lord (Amos 8:9; Joel 2:30-31; Zeph 1:15). The world has rejected the light of God and allowed evil to reign, taking the life not just of an innocent righteous sufferer, and not just of God's Messiah sent into this world. They have killed the Son of God, the Savior of the world. God's anger is kindled, and his wrath is evident. There is double meaning in this. In one sense the death of Jesus was predestined by God himself, who sent his Son to die on the cross as our atoning sacrifice, so our sins could be forgiven. In another sense, it is sinful humanity who put Christ on the cross, and God's wrath is kindled against those who have done so.

In this sense this is saying the day of the Lord has been initiated, and it will be seen right through the resurrection appearances and Pentecost. The further note that the sun stops shining does not indicate an eclipse or a Sirocco (the hot wind from the desert bringing a sandstorm), as some have said. This is a supernatural event that is part of divine judgment. It means the powers of darkness are still in charge, and God's wrath is coming.

The second portent is the splitting of the temple veil, in Matthew 27:51 caused by an earthquake. In Matthew 27:51 and Mark 15:38 this takes place after Jesus' death. Luke places it earlier for thematic reasons, seeing it as a cosmic portent. It is debated whether this is the outer veil that marked the entrance into the sanctuary, that is, the holy place, or the inner veil that separated the holy place from the holy of holies. The first would stress the public nature of the event, as that curtain (sixty by thirty feet in size) was incredibly ornate, made of Babylonian blue, scarlet, and purple. Many prefer the more public tearing, but I agree with those who say the tearing of either veil would be proclaimed throughout the land, and the inner veil has more theological significance.

Two primary themes flow out of the tearing of the inner veil. First, like the darkness, it signifies judgment on the temple and on Israel. The time of temple worship has now ended, and Christ is now the central figure in worship. In another sense this points to the destruction of the temple in AD 70. Second, it means access to God is now open to all; the holy of holies is now encased in every believer, as the Triune Godhead has entered our hearts (Heb 9:6–28; 10:19–22).

Jesus' final cry and death are presented in verse 46. His final prayer cry is, "Father, into your hands I commit my spirit" (23:46). This is drawn from Psalm 31:5, a psalm of commitment to God in the face of ones's enemies and used by Jews as part of their evening prayer before sleep. This evening prayer in the temple was uttered at three in the afternoon, and at that same hour Jesus yields his life to God in that final "sleep." At the end Jesus' trust is entirely in his Father, and he knows he will take him home. This is indeed our prayer as well, in general issues of life as well as when we are in "the valley of the shadow of death" (Ps 23:4 KJV). This is a prayer for resurrection, and it is at the heart of everything we are and do.

With this he "breathed his last," in control to the very end. The powers of darkness have not won but lost. In his death salvation was secured for humankind, and it came not when earthly or cosmic forces demanded but when God so willed. The greatest act of love humankind will ever know was now complete, and the powers of darkness were once for all conquered.

LUKE CALLS ATTENTION TO THE BYSTANDERS (23:47–49)

The centurion's cry has always been seen as a high point of the crucifixion narrative. As a centurion, he would have been head of the battalion at the site and overseeing the entire operation. He had been "seeing what had happened" throughout the three-plus hours and had seen firsthand Jesus' responses. This is his own interpretation of it all. In Mark 15:39 and Matthew 27:54 he provides the christological highpoint of their respective Gospels, saying, "Surely this man was the Son of God."

In Luke he provides the theological culmination of the death scene, confessing, "Surely this was a righteous [or 'innocent'] man." There is double meaning in "righteous/innocent," as both meanings of *dikaios* are intended. Jesus is the innocent, righteous sufferer. There is no real conflict with Mark and Matthew, for as a Roman the centurion would be referring especially to Jesus' righteous behavior, so Luke is translating the Son of God title in terms of its original intention. In Acts Jesus is often called "the Righteous One" (3:14–15; 7:52; 22:14).

Like the centurion the crowd also saw "what took place" (23:48) and returning home "they beat their breasts," indicating deepseated grief at the terrible event. They had seen many crucifixions and normally would not have been touched, but it was evident that Jesus was innocent and truly righteous. This hints strongly that they realized their error in demanding his death at the trial before Pilate. Luke stresses the reality of Christ as the innocent, righteous sufferer of Isaiah 52–53, shown in the acknowledgment of this even by the very crowds who demanded his death before Pilate.

Finally, many of Jesus' followers were present, especially the women "who had followed him from Galilee ... watching these things." These women are not named like they are in Mark and Matthew, but they still stand as official witnesses of the crucifixion and resurrection. Note that all three groups of bystanders are presented as witnesses who saw the events transpire. These would be the women listed in 8:1–3, and Luke refers to them as official witnesses of the death, burial, and resurrection.

We don't know who "all those who knew him" were, possibly John and Jesus' mother (John 19:26) as well as a few other relatives and unnamed followers from Galilee. They stood "at a distance," probably not out of fear of the Romans but out of reverence for Jesus. The Eleven were cowering behind closed doors (John 20:19) and apart from John never saw Jesus on the cross, so these were the more faithful followers.

JESUS IS BURIED (23:50–56)

It was Roman policy to take the bodies off the cross before sundown and throw them in a common grave, and this was especially mandated in light of the Passover celebration (Deut 21:22–23), for they had to be in a grave by sundown. Luke centers more on

Joseph of Arimathea's piety, while Mark and Matthew present his social standing. He was a member of the Sanhedrin and a wealthy leader who was a secret follower of Jesus (John 19:28) and dissented strongly from their actions.

He is described in verse 50 as "good and upright," or righteous (Greek: *dikaios*), linking him with Zechariah, Elizabeth, and Simeon (1:6–7; 2:25), and thus closely identified with "righteous" Jesus. He goes public with his faith when he oversees the burial of Jesus. He is from Arimathea, a town we cannot actually locate, noted here to separate him from other Josephs. Some interpret "waiting for the kingdom of God" in verse 51 as describing a faithful Jew rather than a Christian, but he is a believer (Matt 27:57; John 19:38) who with Simeon and Anna longed for God's final kingdom to arrive (2:25, 38). In this the birth and death of Jesus are inextricably brought together.

Normally Roman practice refused burial for executed criminals and put them in a common grave or left their bodies to be eaten by predators. As a member of the Sanhedrin, Joseph made an official request to Pilate for Jesus' body and was granted an exception to the rule (v. 52). Pilate would have thought this an acceptable thing due to Joseph's upstanding character.

He personally (with Nicodemus, John 19:39–40) removed Jesus from the cross (v. 53). The body had to be down and buried by sundown, and this is why the Romans broke the legs of the criminals beside Jesus in John 19:31–33: to hasten their death. He took the body, undoubtedly washed it and wrapped it in linen cloths,[2] and according to John 19:39 added one hundred pounds of burial spices, turning it into a royal burial. The royal aspect is also found in the note that this was a tomb cut out of rock, something only royalty or extremely wealthy families could afford.

---

2. Nearly all scholars today agree this is likely not the Shroud of Turin, since radiocarbon tests and others make it likely to have originated around the fourteenth century.

Jesus is buried with incredible honor in Joseph's own tomb. It was brand new (Matt 27:60; John 19:41), so no one had yet been buried there. The tomb, needless to say, was an essential part of the picture, for after the resurrection the "empty tomb" would become a byword for the risen Lord. In 1 Corinthians 15:4-8 the burial of Jesus is integral to the death-resurrection imagery.

Luke now provides a note on the time (23:54), telling us that this all took place on "Preparation Day," the day before the Sabbath as they got ready for the festivities. It would have been Thursday evening to Friday at sundown, and all the burial activities had to be finished when the "day" ended. He notes this to explain why the burial details were done as quickly as possible. Joseph was completely faithful to his Jewish roots in everything he did.

The women mentioned in verse 55 were the same women who witnessed Jesus' death on the cross (23:49), and now are official witnesses of the burial and of the resurrection (24:10). They are not named until verse 10—Mary Magdalene, Joanna, and Mary the mother of Jesus. They, not the disciples, are the God-chosen witnesses of the reality of these events. The fact that they followed Joseph and "saw the tomb" would enable them to return in 24:1 without difficulty. We are told they observed "how his body was laid in it," emphasizing the washing and wrapping of the body with its being laid in the tomb. In other words, Jesus had definitely died and was buried in the tomb, and they were witnesses of the reality of that crucial event.

Then we are told that these selfsame women returned to prepare "spices and perfumes" (v. 56). They were unable to return immediately to anoint the body, for it was the Passover Sabbath. They would return eighteen hours later, on Sunday morning, for that duty (24:1). Since the Jews refused to embalm bodies, it was necessary to use aromatic perfumes to assuage the smell of decay. It had become a religious rite. Mark 16:1 has the women purchase these perfumed oils after the Sabbath, but that may have been an extra amount to make certain they had enough. So they prepared one batch of ointments just after the burial Friday afternoon and then purchased more on the way to the tomb Sunday morning. Luke uses these activities to provide a transition from the burial to the resurrection, as we will see also in 24:1. They like the disciples expected nothing; they were attending to a corpse with love but had no further expectations.

———

The crucifixion of Jesus is at the center of salvation history, and every detail in Luke's narration looks to the meaning and effects of this great sacrifice for humanity Jesus will effect on the cross. Every aspect of the story emphasizes the abject humiliation he had to go through. At the outset he had to bear the crossbeam, signifying he was already dead. Then a bystander, Simon of Cyrene, had to bear it for him when he proved too weak. Several women wailing set the tone (vv. 27–31), more likely grieving followers than professional mourners. It was at one and the same time a tragic scene and a triumphant one, for eternal salvation was being made available to sinful humanity. As Jesus said, however, they should be weeping for themselves and for the nation that turned its back on its Messiah and brought God's wrath down on its head.

The first of the three last sayings occurs when Jesus is nailed to the cross, and instead of crying out for vengeance, he asks his Father to forgive the very ones who are crucifying him (24:34). In so doing he culminates his life of compassion and becomes the archetype of those who love their enemies. The true purpose of the cross is to make forgiveness possible, and Jesus exemplifies that.

In contrast, his enemies ridicule him. The soldiers divide his garments between themselves (v. 34b), and both the leaders and soldiers mock him (vv. 35–38), both fulfilling Scripture (Pss 22:7; 69:21) and providing further irony. They make fun of him for pretending to be King and Messiah, when in reality that is what he is. Thus the very taunts he endures are testimony to the truth about his real nature and office. So even the mockery here is a source of worship for us!

The second last saying stems from the two criminals crucified with Jesus (vv. 39–43). While the one joins in the taunts, the other repents and asks for forgiveness. Jesus not only forgives him but on the basis that he is indeed divine, part of the Trinity, promises that the man's prayers will be granted him that very day and that he will accompany Jesus to paradise. This is the greatest revelation of the entire scene, demonstrating that he is not just King and Messiah but God himself.

At Jesus' death, cosmic portents interpret the meaning of the cross for sinful humanity. While it makes salvation possible for those who believe, it also means divine wrath and judgment for those who refuse to believe. The darkness (vv. 44–45a) means that God has involved the powers of darkness to operate, signifying the unbeliever in sin. For three hours, a supernatural absence of light characterized the scene, meaning that these sinners were under divine judgment. Also, the veil of the temple, most likely the inner one, was torn in two (v. 45b), signifying both the coming destruction of the temple and the opening of access to God by the death of Christ. The cross brought all true believers into the very presence of God, and we have become temples, a virtual holy of holies, with God in Christ dwelling within us.

Jesus utters the final of the three prayer cries at his death (v. 46), as he commits his spirit and yields his life (he is in control to the very end) to his Father, ascending to his true heavenly home. His final cry comes from Psalm 31:5, uttered at the very time that passage was prayed in the afternoon prayers of the temple ceremony.

There were three groups of bystanders (vv. 47–49). The centurion confesses that Jesus is the "innocent" righteous martyr who deserves none of what has happened to him. The crowds in a sense repent of their sin of demanding Jesus' death before Pilate and weep in sorrow for their part in bringing about his death. Finally, several of his followers stand at a distance weeping and in a sense worshipping this one in whom they believe but whom they do not understand.

Jesus' burial (vv. 50–56) was remarkable in itself, as Joseph of Arimathea provided a tomb, a place of burial that would forever be known for being empty. Only Joseph could fulfill this need, for he was a wealthy Jew who had recently purchased a new tomb cut into the hillside. This becomes a royal event, as the true King of Israel is buried in it and carefully wrapped in a burial shroud and given a royal burial by Joseph, in preparation for fulfilling God's will. We can speak of the cross and the empty tomb because of what Joseph did. The faithful women become official witnesses of the death, burial, and resurrection of Jesus, and all four evangelists mention them to provide continuity between these eternity-shaping events. The women were there at each of the three parts— the cross, the burial, and the empty tomb—and could attest to the details found here.

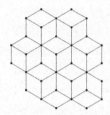

THE RESURRECTION OF JESUS
(24:1–53)

Every word in this commentary has pointed to this moment. The resurrection is the culmination of every theme in Luke. The humiliation of Jesus and emphasis on him as the lowly king have prepared now for his presentation as the exalted Lord. The death and resurrection of Jesus are a single event in salvation history. The death without the resurrection is just another tragic loss of innocent life—in fact the death of a megalomaniac who thought more of himself than he had a right to do. The resurrection without the cross is a military victory without a heart, domination without liberation. The result is the glory of God without the salvation of humanity. But the two did indeed occur together, and the result is both redemption and exaltation. As Paul said, if Jesus did not raise from the dead, the Christian faith is "useless" and "futile" (1 Cor 15:14, 17), robbed of any true significance. But we will see that Jesus was indeed raised, and the Christian truths we believe are proved right.

There have been many attempts through history to explain away the resurrection. These can be reduced to seven basic theories:

1. The Pharisees and leaders bribed the guards to say the disciples had stolen Jesus and hid the body, but the early church showed that that could not fit the actual events

(Matt 28:11–15). The disciples could hardly have overpowered the guards and accomplished such a nefarious deed.

2. The political theory of H. S. Reimarus in the seventeenth century said the disciples could not accept their defeat and made up a story about resurrection because they wanted to establish their own little kingdom, but the high moral content of their writings does not fit them as such political opportunists and frauds.

3. The swoon theory of Schleiermacher and others of the rational school in the eighteenth and nineteenth centuries said that Jesus fainted from his wounds on the cross, came to in the tomb, and snuck out of it. But the Romans were experts at death and would never have allowed this to happen. Jesus' death is stressed in every Gospel.

4. The mythological approach began with Frederick Strauss in the nineteenth century and says the early church combined themes from Greco-Roman myths to construct the story. However, 1 Corinthians 15 shows the developed story was propounded within five years of the event, and no myth has ever developed that quickly. It is tied up completely with belief in a supernatural God and fits the data perfectly.

5. Some believe in a subjective vision theory, that the disciples had dreams that convinced them Jesus was alive. They expressed this in their preaching and writings, convincing others as well. However, many of those to whom Jesus appeared were not believers (James, Paul), and a mass hallucination to "five hundred ... at the same time" (1 Cor 15:6) is hardly likely.

6. Others say Jesus did not actually appear physically but communicated his new life via God-sent visions from heaven that showed them the true reality. However, one wonders why God would do one and not the other (physical appearances), especially since all the Gospels and 1 Corinthians 15 unanimously present actual physical appearances.

7. The corporeal resurrection view, that Jesus bodily rose from the dead and appeared to his followers, makes by far the best sense. Jesus was literally raised as the firstfruits, guaranteeing our own future resurrections.

Luke 24 consists of four successive episodes taking place on the same day. We know from Acts 1:3 that Jesus actually appeared over a forty-day period and ascended to heaven ten days before Pentecost, when the Holy Spirit came on the believers. Luke presents it as a single-day drama for literary purposes. The first scene is the empty tomb (vv. 1–12), as the unsuspecting women and then the doubting disciples are confronted with the reality of the risen Lord. The second is the presence of Jesus as a stranger to two followers on the road to Emmaus (vv. 13–35), opening their eyes to the new reality. Third is the appearance to the Eleven in the upper room (vv. 36–49), proving his exaltation and commissioning them to their future Spirit-filled ministry. Fourth is his ascension to heaven (vv. 50–53), setting the scene for the church age.

Several important themes emerge from this remarkable chapter, the central theme being the movement from disbelief to belief, from possibility to probability to actuality: (1) a strong emphasis on salvation stresses the redemptive purposes, seeing them as the fulfillment of Scripture (vv. 17, 26, 46), with the **soteriological** effects of resurrection highlighted throughout Acts; (2) the church as the messianic community of resurrection provides a transition to Acts and the mission of the church to the world, beginning with Jerusalem and moving outward; (3) the witness theme is found in the place of the angels and women in the story as they prepare for the church's witness to the world; (4) fulfillment of Scripture is continued from the theme from the passion narrative, as in verses 19–21, 25–27, 44–46; the events are seen culminating Old Testament prophecy; (5) an apologetic motif progressively dispels disbelief, doubt, and all uncertainty as the factuality of the resurrection is proved again and again; (6) all of these combine to present Jesus as not only Messiah but as the exalted, risen Lord.

THE EMPTY TOMB IS DISCOVERED (24:1–12)

As the Torah commanded (Exod 20:10; Deut 5:14), the women spent the Sabbath as a day of rest, neither preparing spices nor coming to the tomb. They undoubtedly spent the day in absolute grief, but they did not come to anoint Jesus' body because no activity was allowed on the Sabbath. The following Sunday morning, however, they came to perform the sacred rite by anointing Jesus' corpse with spices. All the Gospels tell us this was "the first day of the week," for due to the resurrection making it "the Lord's day," it became the Christian day of worship. Luke stresses that it is dawn of the day ("very early in the morning"), and in fact John 20:1 states it is still dark. They left while it was still nighttime and arrived just after the sun came up. Bringing the prepared ointment, they had come to anoint a corpse, with no expectations stemming from the passion predictions of Christ (9:22; 18:32–33).

John 20:1–2 tells us that at this point, Mary Magdalene thinks Jesus' body was stolen from the tomb and returns to the disciples, which unleashes Peter and John for their race to the tomb. The other women remain, where they meet the angels and proceed to the next aspect of the **Synoptic** account. The two events— the race to the tomb and the women meeting the angels—occur simultaneously, with Peter and John arriving just after the women have left.

Luke's account of the events at the tomb in verses 2–3 abbreviates Mark and Matthew, focusing on the action leading to the climax in "Lord Jesus." There are no details on the stone rolled away, stressing the results, as the tomb is now open so the women can crawl in. There was normally a three-foot opening with a stone into a groove (to protect from grave robbers), but the stone had been removed. The women would have to crawl through the opening in order to enter with the spices.

When they enter, they find the tomb empty, without any body in the tomb. Note the progression—"they found the stone ... did not find the body." We are in the midst of the most remarkable set of events in human history, and the culminating miracle has already taken place without their knowledge. Even after all of Jesus' predictions that his death would lead to his resurrection, the women and the disciples are waiting for nothing, caught up in their grief. Angels rolled away the stone (Matt 28:2–4), and they are now awaiting the women.

Since they had seen Joseph place Jesus' body in the tomb, the women were completely "perplexed" (*aporeō*; NIV: "wondering") at what had happened (v. 4). As they were pondering the confusing situation, two figures appeared in the tomb and "stood beside them." While they look like men, Matthew and John call them what they actually are: angels (compare 24:23, where Luke clarifies this). Still, they are not normal men, for their clothes "gleamed like lightning," echoing both the transfigured Jesus (9:29; 10:18) and the two angels at the ascension (Acts 1:10). The presence of two men/angels recalls the demand for two witnesses in Deuteronomy 19:15 and shows that the angels join the women as official witnesses of the resurrection reality.

The sudden presence of these heavenly figures, as in all visible manifestations of heavenly beings, produces terror on the part of the women. Fear and prostration—they "bowed down with their faces to the ground" (v. 5)—are common responses to God's manifestation of himself via angelic beings. The women are filled with awe and wonder.

The angels will have none of that. They are here to correct an error of faith, a failure on the part of Jesus' followers to understand and accept his own prophetic witness to what would follow his death. They are focused on a corpse, but there is no corpse, so the angels rebuke their terrible error, "Why do you look for the living among the dead?" Jesus is alive, so the place to find him is not a tomb. They are seeking the completely wrong thing.

In language resembling Mark 6:6 the angels explicitly correct their error: "He is not here" (24:6). Get out of the tomb; that's not where Jesus is! This is not a time for sorrow but for joy. Then the remarkable truth is stated for the first time, "He has risen!"[1] This is a divine passive (*ēgerthē*), meaning "God has raised him from the dead." God has been at work at all times during Jesus' life, and now his mighty work has culminated in ultimate life.

What the women must do is "remember how [and what] he told you, while he was still with you in Galilee." These are the passion predictions of 9:22; 18:32–33, with several others in view as well (5:35; 9:44; 12:50; 13:32–33; 17:22, 25; 22:22). They should not have been preparing ointments to anoint Jesus' body and worrying how to get into the tomb. They should have been in breathless anticipation for his prophetic promises to be fulfilled. The angels sum them up in verse 7: "The Son of Man must be delivered over to the hands of sinners, be crucified and on the third day be raised again." The Son of Man title is found in most of Jesus' predictions and highlights the background of Daniel 7:13–14: Jesus as the glorified Son of Man with dominion and authority over God's creation.

The emphasis is on divine necessity, the "must" (*dei*) that dominates Jesus' death and resurrection. He would be delivered over to "sinful" humankind in order to die so their sins might be forgiven. The "third day" of course refers to the fact that Jesus was dead Friday (evening), Saturday, and Sunday (night), three days by Jewish reckoning. The third day is the day of new life (Hos 6:2; Jonah 1:17).

They finally "remembered his words" and woke up (24:8). The remembrance theme (see 22:61; Acts 11:18) is the key to spiritual growth throughout Scripture and guides both them and the reader into realizing the reality of the resurrection. Their minds made the switch to the greatest truth ever uttered. As they recalled how the past thirty-six hours had been prophesied by Jesus, joy could finally bubble to the surface. This is the basis for their report in the next verse. It is not commissioned by the angel but emerges

---

1. This is missing in several Western manuscripts (D it) but is found in many others (𝔓75 ℵ A B) and belongs here as part of Luke's text.

naturally from the bubbling joy in the new reality. They must tell the others.

Filled with excitement, the women ran back to the others who according to John 20:19 would still have been in the upper room where they had hidden from the authorities throughout the time when Jesus was on the cross and in the grave. They had to tell the others what the angels had imparted to them. "All the others" could be the 120 of Acts 1:15. This seems to contradict Mark 16:8, which has them saying "nothing to anyone, because they were afraid." However, when we combine the others, Matthew has the medium between Mark and Luke, with the women going forth "afraid yet filled with joy" to tell the disciples (Matt 28:8). Mark stresses the negative side, the fear they initially felt, and Luke the joy they felt after Jesus met them on the way (Matt 28:9–10), an appearance Luke omits, preferring to save that for the Emmaus journey.

It is here that we are told the names of the women, probably to stress their presence as official witnesses of the resurrection. They are the women who served as patrons and supporters of the apostolic band in 8:1–3. Mary the mother of James is the same as in Mark 15:40; 16:1. The "others with them" were other women from Galilee who were now with these three. Most of them were part of the entourage who journeyed with Jesus in his ministry and were now gathered together around these tumultuous events.

The results of the report are disappointing. The women do not have the authority of the angels, and the other followers do not believe them. In fact, "their words seemed to them like nonsense," a term (*lēros*) used to describe delirium. The disciples represent humanity's normal reaction to the resurrection tidings. This is a major motif in all four of the Gospel accounts (Matt 28:17; John 20:25, 27). Doubt and disbelief are the regular human responses to such news. It just is not normal and does not seem possible. Yet that is the point. What humans cannot conceive or do is the very place where God acts. This in fact is further evidence for the historical reliability of these reports. There is no attempt to play down or explain away the titanic struggle the disciples had with the truth of the resurrection. They found it as difficult to believe as the rest of us do. Yet it happened, and the world as a result will never be the same!

Peter's reaction in verse 12 recalls his race to the tomb with John in John 20:2-10 and probably stems from that event. He is the one inquisitive member and has to see for himself what the women are talking about and so runs to the tomb. Bending over to see into the small opening where the stone had been, he looks in and sees "the strips of linen lying by themselves."[2] The graveclothes are no longer around Jesus' body, signifying that he has risen.

The term translated "wondering to himself" (*thaumazō*) normally means "filled with wonder" or "amazed" and could mean he believed in the resurrection of Jesus. However, the context as well as the parallel in John 20:6-7 make it more likely that he was perplexed and uncertain like the women had been. So the NIV translation is justified. The state of tension is evident, with the women believing, nearly all the rest unable to do so, but Peter puzzled by the actual evidence at the tomb. The scene is set for the next stage, the Emmaus journey to faith.

JESUS APPEARS ON THE EMMAUS ROAD (24:13-35)

This is a recognition scene as the doubts and disbeliefs of Jesus' followers are finally overturned by the risen Lord himself. Luke has constructed his narrative to show how natural it is to struggle with the reality of the empty tomb, but that God himself will intervene to counter human doubt and make the truth of the resurrection known to us. God has deliberately closed their eyes because he wants the truth to become evident and recognition to come

---

2. As with verse 9, this verse is missing in Codex Bezae (D) and the Old Latin versions, and several consider it a late addition to Luke's text. However, once more, it is present in the majority of manuscripts ($\mathfrak{P}$75 ℵ A B L W and others) and belongs as a viable part of Luke's narrative.

through direct divine intervention in the opening of the word (vv. 26-27, 32) and the breaking of bread (vv. 30-31). The eye of faith is necessary to grasp this unbelievable truth, but God will provide. The struggle we all have with eternal truths is graphically and brilliantly portrayed in this wonderful story.

Some have doubted the historical veracity of this narrative since it is found only in Luke and involves supernatural revelation from God. However, it is very realistic, and it is far more likely that two discouraged disciples had this very experience and epitomized what the others went through as well. We can all identify with their odyssey from doubt to faith. To every one of us, Jesus often appears as a stranger whom we cannot quite recognize, but he progressively reveals himself to us.

TWO DISCOURAGED DISCIPLES MEET A STRANGER (24:13-16)

On that "same day" as the events were transpiring in the empty tomb and upper room, two of the disciples, Cleopas (v. 18) and an unnamed follower, likely from the 70 or the 120, were dejectedly walking home (?) to a small village called Emmaus. We do not know where it actually was, but Josephus (*Jewish War* 7.217) notes an Emmaus about a sixty-stadia, or seven-mile, round trip from Jerusalem, and that makes good sense.

Needless to say, their discussion centered on "everything that had happened" (24:14), meaning they had just left. The following verses show they were referring to the death, burial, and the report of the women about the empty tomb. So they typify the state of mind of all the followers apart from the women, totally discouraged about Jesus' death and confused about what the women had said and Peter had found. The main thing is they are confused and discouraged.

Suddenly their discussion is interrupted and a stranger joins them. We are told it is "Jesus himself" and are excited to see their reaction, but there isn't one. This is quite enigmatic, for they had undoubtedly been among the dedicated followers and knew him exceedingly well. To them he is just another pilgrim heading home from the festival. One thing this assures the reader of immediately is the physical nature of the resurrection. This is no apparition but a living person.

The key to this entire Emmaus story is seen in verse 16, where Luke tells us that "they were kept from recognizing him," with another divine passive meaning God has blinded their eyes from realizing this is Jesus. He is not so marred or changed that people could not know who he was. This is a divinely intended ignorance. We will see why as the story unfolds. This dramatic hiddenness is **apocalyptic**, part of the end-time intentions of God and similar to God's concealing understanding of the passion predictions in 9:45 and 18:34. God determines when understanding comes, and here the revelation of Jesus will be connected to the proclaimed word and the broken bread (24:31). These two thereby typify us, as we walk in ignorance and fail to realize the presence of Christ in our lives.

THE CONVERSATION OF THE JOURNEYMEN (24:17–27)

There is heavy irony in this scene, as the One who is asking for news is himself the news they are sharing. He takes the guise of an ignorant stranger and asks what they are discussing. There is a marvelous dramatic reversal in this, as we the readers know that the actual ignorance is theirs. Their stunned stillness and "downcast" looks are eloquent testimonials to their ignorance. They should be jumping for joy but instead are gloomy in their discouragement and defeat.

We know next to nothing about Cleopas, as he appears nowhere else (not the "Clopas" of John 19:25). He is incredulous and asks the obvious question, wondering how it could be possible for anyone to come from Jerusalem and know nothing about the recent events. It just does not seem possible for a pilgrim to have bypassed the events that so consumed all the people of Jerusalem. What happened to Jesus was so public and so well known that no one could be unaware. There is further irony in this, for Jesus is the only one there who actually *does* know exactly what happened.

In response to the stranger's leading question, "What things?" the pair together summarize the background. Luke includes this to focus the reader's mind on the setting behind the resurrection event. The response summarizes the events of the cross (vv. 19–21) and empty tomb (vv. 22–24), indicating that the hopes and dreams of the disciples have been crushed. At the outset, their inadequate understanding is presented. This man was Jesus who originated from Nazareth and to them had been "a prophet, powerful in word and deed before God and all the people." Jesus as prophet is certainly true, recalling 4:18–19, 24; 9:35. Likely they have in mind the prophet like Elijah, worker of miracles. They at the same time fail to understand fully, centering on his authoritative preaching and miraculous ministry but failing to recognize him as the suffering Messiah and Son of God. Jesus will correct this in verse 26. They should have realized his destiny as the Suffering Servant of Isaiah.

The "delivery" of Jesus to his enemies recapitulates the passion predictions of 9:22, 44; 18:32. Still, ultimately it was God who delivered Jesus into the hands of his enemies, and in that sense Jesus gave himself up as the atoning sacrifice for the very ones who put him on the cross. They then state the results of this for their own hopes, which were dashed by the terrible events (24:21). When they say they had hoped he "was the one who was going to redeem Israel," they were not thinking of redemption the way we do. They were thinking of messianic liberation, a political victory over Rome and the enemies of God's people. The followers of Jesus still do not understand the true meaning of the cross or of the events that have transpired. It will take them the entire forty days of appearances to come to any kind of full realization of what God has done in sending Jesus to die and be raised. In fact, it will be Paul who puts it all together.

Their statement that "it is the third day since all this took place" is supremely ironic. They are thinking entirely from a temporal perspective, that Jesus died on the cross three days earlier (Friday, Saturday, Sunday). For Luke and us the reader this is the third-day motif, the fulfillment of Jesus' passion prediction that he would rise on the third day (9:22; 13:32; 18:33).

Next their narration turns to the empty tomb as they report the visit of the women (24:22). It wasn't the fact that they went to the tomb to anoint the bodies that amazed the disciples; that was expected. It was the fact that they "didn't find his body." One would think this would have helped them recall the passion predictions, as it turned the tide for the women when the angels reminded them. But they too appeared blinded to the truth (like the two on the road to Emmaus). As we saw in verse 11 the report was seen as "nonsense." This was also the case of the appearance of the angels. Notice that the two disciples here report it as "a vision of angels, who said he was alive." To them the women must have dreamed it, for they were not ready to accept the truth of either the angels in the tomb or of the reality of Jesus' resurrection. This should have led them to belief, but it didn't. Again, the incredible irony is that they are telling this to the risen Lord himself.

Finally, they relate (24:24) the story of verse 12 and John 20:3-10. Note that now it is "some of our companions," not just Peter himself, reflecting the tradition from John 20 that it was Peter and John. So the empty tomb was now proved by some of their own number who corroborated the report of the women. The added note that "they did not see Jesus" refers to Peter and John rather than the women, who in Matthew 28:9-10 did encounter Jesus. Hearing about him is insufficient; they demand to see the risen Lord for themselves. Ironically, they were doing just that. As they gazed on the resurrected Jesus, they said in essence, "If only we could see him." So their doubt predominates over all this evidence, and they remain skeptical. Yet the tension is building and demands a resolution, which will soon be provided by God himself.

Jesus rebukes them first for failing to understand his passion and the scriptural fulfillment it represented. This is stronger than the angels' rebuke of the women in verse 5; they should have known better, for they had Scripture itself to guide them. He accuses them of being "foolish" and "slow to believe" in the truth staring them in the face from a thousand years of prophetic revelations and yet failing to understand what the prophets unanimously said, even after Jesus had on multiple occasions explained that prophetic witness to them. Note it is "*all* that the prophets have spoken," meaning the universal witness of the prophets. This does not mean every single prophecy pointed to Jesus, but rather that overall, the entire prophetic witness was intended to prepare for the coming of Jesus Messiah.

Jesus explains the primary prophetic witness in verse 26: "Did not the Messiah have to suffer these things and then enter his glory?" Of course, Jesus spoke of himself as the righteous suffering Messiah, the Servant of Yahweh from Isaiah 52-53, in his passion predictions (9:22, 44; 18:32-33). This is emphasized three times (vv. 7, 26, 44) and is one of the major themes of this chapter. The emphasis is on the divine "must" (*edei*) — he would "have to suffer." Behind this are the lament psalms (31, 69, 118) as well as Isaiah 52-53. Even though Judaism did not have this understanding in their messianic expectations, Jesus expected the disciples to have caught it from his teaching. The fact that they failed to do so proves how "foolish" and "slow" they had become.

The resurrection is seen in the added "enter his glory." His passion predictions (9:22; 18:33) ended with this promise, and he spoke of his future glory in 9:26; 21:27. They had already seen this in his transfiguration, and thus he expected his followers to have caught it as well. Christ's exaltation to the right hand of God from Psalm 110 had arrived, and he was eager to share this wondrous truth with his followers. The fact that they were not ready and able to receive it was exceedingly disappointing. The message of 1 Peter 1:10-11, that suffering is the path to glory, was unknown to them.

So the stranger / risen Lord took matters into his own hand: "Beginning with Moses and all the Prophets, he explained to them what was said in all the Scriptures concerning himself" (24:27). Don't we all wish we could be a fly on the wall and hear exactly what he said! All debates over the Old Testament in the New would be solved. So Jesus traced messianic fulfilment through the Old Testament and proved it all pointed to him. "All" appears three times in verses 25-27 to stress the comprehensive messianic portrait in Scripture (compare 24:25; Acts 17:2, 11; 18:24, 28). These were all "explained," and still the two failed to recognize Jesus. It was not quite time; one item needed to be added.

TABLE FELLOWSHIP AND THE BREAKING OF BREAD (24:28-31)

That item takes place now. God had determined that their eyes would be cleared through the opening of the word and the breaking of bread, that is, via Scripture and worship. As the party of travelers draws near to Emmaus, Jesus acts as if he intends to go past the town in order to get them to beg him to stay. Obviously they did not want him to leave and "urged him strongly" to stay with them, with the excuse that evening had arrived and it was too late for him to travel on. This is the way God wishes the event to transpire, with the men themselves strongly involved in the action. The table fellowship is made possible by this request. Jesus enters their home to stay with them.

Table fellowship in the Jewish world meant that all the participants shared not only their food but their lives as well. They became one by sharing a meal. Since God was present, this meant a union with him. It became the perfect venue for God to open their eyes to the reality of the stranger in their midst as the risen Lord. The description here is reminiscent of the feeding miracle (9:16) and especially the Last Supper (22:19): "He took bread, gave thanks, broke it and began to give it to them" (24:30). However, I do not believe this means they are taking the Eucharist, for there is no mention of wine (though many other interpreters disagree). In any case, it is a sacred celebration and signifies the church as the family of God sharing a meal with the resurrected Jesus. It becomes a transition from the table fellowship of Jesus and his disciples to that of the early church (the "breaking of bread" in Acts 2:42, 46; 20:7, 11; 27:35).

This is the moment God chooses to open their eyes (24:31), and they "recognized" the stranger as the risen Jesus. Almost certainly their eyes were bulging and their mouths gaping open as they realize finally who it is. This is the high point of the resurrection story thus far. The empty tomb has finally produced open eyes, and they are utterly astonished. In a reverse miracle, Jesus, just after he appears and reveals himself to them, disappears from them. It is difficult to know what to read into this. The emphasis here is on the reality of Jesus' resurrection as a stimulant to mission, to the duty of the two to tell the others and spread the good news of the ever-living Lord.

THE RESULTS OF THE ACTION (24:32–35)

Luke tells us first the internal result with the two (v. 32) and then the external results with the other disciples (vv. 33–35). Now that Cleopas and his partner know the identity of the risen Lord, they reflect on their emotions when he taught them from scriptural fulfillment: "Were not our hearts burning within us?" Their eyes had been closed, and their foolish minds had been slow, but now they remember that while the stranger spoke to them and taught them, their deepest emotions had been on fire all along. As with John Wesley much later, their hearts were "strangely warmed." Note that it is not only Jesus' exposition of scriptural truth but his general conversation as well. The risen Lord touched them deeply with his every word, but especially with the truths of scriptural fulfillment.

These two become a second set of witnesses after the women of the resurrection tidings as they "at once" leave Emmaus and return to Jerusalem in triumph. This is the journey motif of Luke, leaving Jerusalem in defeat and returning in joy with the knowledge that Christ is risen. They left in the dark (literally and figuratively) and return in glorious light. In fact, in verse 34 "Simon [Peter]" becomes a third witness as they learn the further report that "the Lord has risen and has appeared to Simon."[3] The apostolic band has been decimated by the loss of Judas Iscariot and will be "the Eleven" here and in Acts 1 until they add Matthias and become the Twelve once more.

The faith of the Eleven has greatly developed since Cleopas and the other disciple left, and they have already grasped the reality of the resurrection by the witness of Simon that the Lord appeared to him. This appearance is found in 1 Corinthians 15:5 but not recorded elsewhere in the Gospels. Most likely it occurred just after the tomb event in of verse 12 (= John 20:3–10), and Peter's joyous witness convinced the others. So the report of these two corroborated that great news. As to why no Gospel writer tells the story, we will have to ask them when we get to heaven!

The two add their report of Jesus appearing to them (24:35), and that undoubtedly caused even greater rejoicing. There have now been four appearances: To the women (Matt 28:9–10), to Mary (John 20:11–18), to Peter (here), and to the two on the road to Emmaus (here). The remarkable forty days of appearances by the risen One have begun with a vengeance. Note here the two elements in the opening of the eyes—the proclamation of the word (v. 32) and the breaking of bread (v. 35)—providing the two major lessons of the Emmaus road journey. The living Christ is mediated to us as well through the word and through living fellowship with him—either the Eucharist (Acts 2:42; 20:7, 11; 27:35) or more general fellowship with the Lord, most likely the latter.

---

3. A few manuscripts like Codex Bezae (D) have the report coming from the two Emmaus travelers, but there is no way they could have learned this, and that is very unlikely.

JESUS APPEARS TO THE ELEVEN
IN JERUSALEM (24:36–49)

This is the same appearance as in John 20:19-23 and 1 Corinthians 15:5. There are four items of great importance in this story, four theological truths that are highlighted: (1) The physical reality of the resurrection, seen first in the display of his physical body (vv. 39-40) and his eating the meal (vv. 42-43); (2) the third emphasis on the resurrection fulfilling Scripture (vv. 44-46); (3) the mission to the world that would flow out of this scene (vv. 47-48); and (4) the coming of the Spirit to inaugurate the new era (v. 49). The message of this incident is that the time for the new era to commence has now arrived, and they are to wait in Jerusalem for a short time as God initiates this new salvation-historical period.

THE APPEARANCE AND PHYSICAL PROOF (24:36–43)

The emphasis is on the sudden appearance of Jesus in their midst, a common theme in all the Gospels, as when he transported through the doors and walls in John 20:19. He disappeared in 24:31 and now reappears in the same way, through supernatural means. He is no longer held back by natural laws. His greeting turns everything around, as all the fear and doubt are wiped away in an instant. "While they were still talking" continues the same-day theme. Here and in John 20 this took place on the first day of the resurrection. The walk to Emmaus would have taken about three hours each way, so this was a late-afternoon gathering.

Picture the scene. The disciples have been filled with grief at the destruction of their dreams, but then reports began to filter in that gave them a glimmer of hope they were too crestfallen to accept at first. But disbelief and doubt slowly turned to perplexity and then hope. Still, everything was secondhand. Suddenly, Jesus is with them, but they are still too shocked and afraid to fully accept the reality. Jesus' promise of "peace" is messianic and is the counter to their fear of the next verse. There is double meaning in this. On one level it is the customary shalom of greeting. On the deeper level it fulfills Isaiah 9:6; 52:7, and means that God's messianic peace was now theirs to experience.

Their first reaction (24:37) is the normal response to a theophany, a manifestation of God and his messengers: fright. Their doubt and disbelief leads them to conclude that "they saw a ghost [*pneuma*]" similar to the apparition of Samuel in 1 Samuel 28:3–19. They are still not ready to find the faith to accept the truth. Their human nature is still in control. Think how much evidence they are discounting—Jesus' previous passion predictions, the women's witness, Peter's experience, the two from Emmaus, and now the appearance of Jesus himself. This is a must-read for everyone in our day who has serious doubts about the reality of Jesus' resurrection. The disciples are with you all the way!

The disciples needed a lot of help, and Jesus now proceeds to provide just that (24:38–39). He begins with a slight rebuke similar to the angels with the women in verses 5–6: Why the fear and doubt? There is no reason for such negative reactions; have a little faith. Still, he realizes they need further stimulus and so shows them the nail prints in his hands and feet to prove it really is the body of the crucified Jesus. Then he encourages them to touch him and feel he is not a "spirit." Doubt is met with empirical evidence, both sight and touch; the senses confirm the reality. It is really him. As he says, ghosts do not have physical substance. His is a glorified body, able to pass through walls. But it is also still a physical body of flesh. It is an eternal body but can be touched.

The disciples "still did not believe it," but their disbelief is mingled with "joy and amazement." They are incredulous, midway between doubt and joyous belief. In a sense, they are feeling that it is too good to be true. So he now adds a second proof of reality and eats a meal in front of his followers. This proves even further that he arose physically from the dead. The meal of fish is reminiscent of John 21:9, so some say this is a displaced Galilean tradition, since fish would have been unlikely in Jerusalem. However, there is indisputable evidence for the availability of fish in Jerusalem (see Neh 3:3; 13:16), and there is no reason for such a theory. Others see this as a eucharistic scene, but there is little evidence that fish were used in first-century eucharistic practice. The apologetic emphasis is primary, proving to the disciples (and us) that Jesus has indeed risen bodily from the dead. His eating the broiled fish "in their presence" was the second and final proof that gave them the faith in his resurrection that they needed.

THE COMMISSIONING SERVICE AND PROMISE OF THE SPIRIT (24:44–49)

The risen Jesus sums up his passion predictions that he had told them "while I was still with you" (9:22, 44; 17:25; 18:32–33; 22:37) in order to remind them why they should have realized these truths long before. Their ignorance was inexcusable. Jesus is emphasizing that he is the same person as he was before, the Jesus they had walked with in Galilee. In fact, this is the third time during the resurrection that the fulfillment theme has been presented (vv. 7, 26–27), proving that these events culminate not just the life of Jesus but the basic purpose of the Old Testament as a whole. This is stressed with the mention of all three sections of the Old Testament—the Law, the Prophets, and the Psalms (referring to all the Writings).

All of history has prepared for this moment, and the entire future of the human race rests on these three days from the cross to the empty tomb. Note that the divine "must" (*dei*) covers "everything … written about me." He is saying that every single iota of Scripture pointed to him, and the true purpose of the old covenant was to prepare Israel for the coming of Christ.

As the Father opened their eyes, Jesus now "opened their minds" to the Scripture truths (v. 45). In spite of all the times this had been addressed, none of his followers had been able to grasp the reality of what was coming. It was too far out of their religious experience and expectations, and so they misunderstood the God-intended meaning of the prophecies. Jesus now clears away the debris of false understandings and enables them to grasp the truth. The doubts that dominated their thinking are now over once and for all. Not only the reality of the cross and empty tomb but also the scriptural prophecies that foretold these events are now clearly perceived. There are two areas presented here—the passion and resurrection (v. 46) and the mission of the church (v. 47).

In verse 46 we have the third and final (after vv. 7, 25-27) presentation of how Jesus' suffering, death, and resurrection fulfilled Old Testament prophecy. These summarize Jesus' passion predictions (9:22, 44; 18:32-33) and show all of Scripture was meant to prepare for these as the culmination of God's plan of salvation. None of these three areas was part of Jewish messianic expectations, so this is what the disciples failed to grasp and what Jesus is opening their minds to comprehend.

Throughout the passion events the scriptural passages behind these themes (for instance Psalms 16, 22, 31, 69, 110, 118, and Isaiah 52-53) have been featured, showing that this was indeed the true intention of the old covenant. In fact, this truth will stimulate the mission of the next verse and give them the strength to persevere in the face of all the troubles they will encounter as they live out the life of Jesus in the future.

The proclamation of these truths to the world is an essential aspect of scriptural fulfillment according to verse 47, for "to preach" (*kēruchthēnai*; NIV: "will be preached") is actually the third infinitive of verses 46-47—for the Messiah to suffer and to die and for forgiveness and repentance to be proclaimed. These three encompass both the basis of salvation (death) and the results of salvation (proclamation). God provided from the start not only how salvation was to be secured but also how it was to be presented to a fallen world. The mission of the church is actually an essential part of the culmination of God's plan, for instance, of the Servant Songs (Isa 49:6, "a light for the Gentiles"), and the book of Acts specifically flows out of what Jesus says in verses 47-49.

Three items constitute the content of this mission:

1. Repentance, seen in 5:32 ("I have not come to call the righ-
    teous, but sinners to repentance") as pointing to Acts 13:3-4;
    15:7-8; 16:30; 17:3-4. This word group is found twenty-five
    times in Luke-Acts, referring both to a turning from sin
    and a turning to God as seen in righteous deeds (Acts
    2:38; 3:19; 11:18; 19:1-4). It is a changed heart leading to
    changed behavior.

2. Forgiveness of sins, God's response to repentance. This is
    frequent in these books (Luke 1:77; 3:18; 4:18; Acts 2:38; 5:31;
    10:43; 13:38; 26:18) and is absolutely necessary to experience
    salvation. Sin is the reason Christ died, and there can be no
    eternity without forgiveness.

3. Preaching, linked especially to Acts, where it is the prelude
    to conversion. The power behind this mission is the author-
    ity of his name, the source of the power behind the church
    (Acts 2:38; 3:6; 4:7, 10 and others). The recipient of the good
    news is "all nations" (Matt 28:19), preparing for Acts 1:8 and
    the whole book of Acts. The universal mission is the respon-
    sibility of God's people, expanding the missions of the dis-
    ciples in Galilee in Luke 9-10. Jesus' instructions for "begin-
    ning at Jerusalem" are also stressed in Acts 1:8. The Jews are
    a major focus of evangelism (Rom 1:16, "first to the Jew") and
    provide the base from which the mission is sent.

The message of the gospel is summed up at the end of the verse:
"repentance for the forgiveness of sins." Here we see the reason
why God sent his Son to die on the cross. It was the only way this
message could ever be proclaimed, for without Christ's atoning
sacrifice no repentance or forgiveness could ever be possible. No
sinful human being could ever attain eternal life by their own
efforts or by good works, for in our own strength we can never
stop sinning. Only the sinless sacrifice of Jesus the Christ could
effect salvation.

Witness is one of the primary themes of Luke 24, defining the work of Jesus' followers. Earlier it was the angels and the women, but now the official function of witnesses to the resurrection and the gospel becomes the purview of the whole church. The universal implications of the mission of the seventy in Luke 10 are developed further, preparing for Acts and the mission to the nations there. The apostles as witnesses is stressed in Acts 1:8, 22; 2:32; 3:15; 4:35; 5:32; 10:39; 13:31. Here it is especially Jesus as Suffering Servant and risen One, but in light of verse 47 it must include also the good news of salvation made available to the nations.

The Spirit was essential at Jesus' birth (1:35; 2:25–27), at the beginning of his ministry (3:22; 4:1), and in his ministry (4:14, 18; 5:17). However, the Spirit functioned as in the Old Testament, coming on a specific individual for a specific purpose. The promise here is far more sweeping and looks to the coming of the Spirit permanently on the church at Pentecost (Acts 1:8). An entirely new era is being inaugurated, and it is this that gives impetus to the universal mission to the world. This is the hallmark of the new covenant.

"What my Father has promised" refers both to the Old Testament promises (Joel 2:28–32; Isa 32:15; 44:3; Ezek 39:29) and to those of Jesus himself (12:12; Acts 1:4–5, see John 7:37–39). There is a strong trinitarian air to this, moving from Father to Son to Spirit, with all three active and constituting the new age of the Spirit. The promise is the new empowerment for life and ministry that the Spirit brings to the saints (John 16:12–15; Eph 1:14).

The disciples are to "stay in the city," obviously waiting for the Spirit to arrive at Pentecost (Acts 1:4–5, 8; 2:1–4). At that time the disciples will "be clothed with power from on high." Jerusalem is to be the launching pad (v. 47) for the mission, and the Spirit is to be the power behind the worldwide thrust of the gospel (Acts 1:8). The Spirit's power originating in heaven will envelop them, characteristic of the presence of the Spirit (1:17, 35; 4:14; 5:17; 9:1).

As the Spirit was essential to Jesus' ministry, so now he is God's gift to the church so they may continue that ministry. So the witness theme is connected to the idea of anointing or empowering for office. The last act of Jesus' ministry is inextricably linked with the first act of the new age.

JESUS ASCENDS (24:50-53)

Since the ascension is only recorded in Luke and Acts, some doubt its historical veracity, but it makes perfect sense as a proper conclusion to the resurrection appearances. If the resurrection happened, as I have strongly affirmed in this commentary, there is no reason to doubt the ascension. It has two distinct functions in the two books. It provides a doxological conclusion to Jesus' earthly ministry in the Gospel and an ecclesiological starting point launching the church's mission in the book of Acts. All of Luke from the transfiguration on has pointed forward to the "exodus" (9:31; NIV: "departure") and "ascension" (9:51) of Jesus to "the right hand of the mighty God" (22:69).

Bethany was the village where Lazarus and his sisters lived, a couple of miles from Jerusalem on the Mount of Olives. Jesus decided to end his earthly sojourn in that region, and he apparently took all who were there with him, perhaps the 120 of Acts 1:12-13. He ends his ministry with priestly blessing, lifting his hands as he blesses them. This is based on his new exalted status as risen Lord as he imparts a blessing, with the raised hands emphasizing the priestly nature as a fulfillment of messianic promise. In one sense this is modeled on the farewell scenes of Abraham (Gen 49) and Moses (Deut 32).

The ascension itself (24:51) parallels Acts 1:9-11 with stress on both the upward movement to the heavenly abode as well as the exaltation of Jesus. The primary thrust of the passage is worship. There may also be an Elijah theme here and in Acts 1:9-11 in Jesus' being "taken up into heaven." The whole scene presents the worship of the exalted Lord. Jesus fulfills his prediction of 22:69 that henceforth he would be at his Father's right hand by ascending to heaven. As heaven was rejoicing at his birth (2:13–14), so it does as he returns to his rightful home. The rest of the New Testament will present the current ministry of the exalted Lord as he rules all eternity as second person of the Trinity.

The worship scene continues, as the first thing the disciples do is to worship the ascended Lord after he has returned to his home in heaven. The entire Gospel has prepared for this moment, as for the first time Jesus is explicitly worshipped. Their misunderstanding has finally been fully overcome. The joy they feel as they return to Jerusalem is a worshipful joy, and the praise in the temple speaks for itself. Thomas had recognized the deity of Christ (John 20:28: "My Lord and my God!"), and now the group worships Jesus as God. While Luke presents this as a same-day event for dramatic purpose, we know from Acts 1:3 that he appeared to them for a period of forty days. During that time their understanding grew exponentially, and most of them would have been ready to worship him as they worshipped Yahweh.

In Jerusalem they followed Jesus' example from passion week and went to the temple every day. We need to remember that Pentecost took place fifty days after Passover, so there were only ten days between the ascension of Jesus and the coming of the Spirit at Pentecost. For that brief period the disciples were regularly in the temple, praising God publicly for all he had done in Jesus. I have no doubt that "praising God" should not be restricted to prayer and Christian worship but also included the witness Jesus mandated in verses 47–48. They praised God for Jesus publicly via witness in the temple. The Jesus story in Luke began with temple scenes (Zechariah: 1:5–25; Jesus: 2:21–52), and now it ends in the temple. The church's mission in Acts will also be initiated with temple ministry.

———

Luke has a unique presentation of the resurrection appearances, compressing the forty days of events into a single day for dramatic purposes. The result is a powerful and fast-moving series of events that very effectively grips readers and enables them to feel both the mighty power of God at work and the radical changes in the disciples as they slowly realize the truth about the risen Lord.

The opening event, the empty tomb (vv. 1–12), commences with the absolute ignorance of the women and the total doubt of the disciples. It is ironic that Jesus has already risen from the dead, but none of the participants are aware of this world-changing event even though Jesus had often told them what was coming. The turning point for the women comes with the angels (vv. 4–8), who rebuke their lack of realization and correct their misunderstanding. This turns everything around for the women but not for the men. When the women as official witnesses report the truth to the men, they are not believed. This is a very realistic scene, and Luke intends all of us to see ourselves in the participants in the story. Some of us believe, others are unable to do so and can only doubt their witness, and still others are like Peter (v. 12), confused by the evidence and wondering what to believe.

The Emmaus road journey (vv. 13–35) is meant to describe all of us as we encounter the evidence and are gradually given sight and insight into the truth about the resurrection. At the outset we like the disciples are puzzled and discouraged by the reports. Yet Jesus is soon walking with us, even if we fail to recognize him. The recapitulation of recent events by the two (vv. 19–24) shows the inadequacy of their understanding. They confess Jesus as a mighty prophet but not as Messiah and Son of God. They had hoped for redemption only as political liberation from the Romans but had no idea that Jesus was to die in order to bring salvation to sinners. They also believed the women's triumphal report was due to dreams rather than the reality of the empty tomb. They like so many of us expected very little from God at this point.

Jesus corrected these misunderstandings (vv. 25-27) and
explained once more how the prophetic witness of Scripture all
together pointed to his death and resurrection as the culmination
of their witness. Neither they nor we have any excuse in failing to
understand how Jesus fulfilled prophecy. The disciples' eyes are
finally opened in accordance with the opening of the word here
and the breaking of bread in 28-31. It is intended that Scripture
and worship lead us as well as them to faith and understanding.
This is God's way to find faith. This finally breaks the logjam of
faith (vv. 32-35), as the two run to add their witness to that of the
angels and the women. Finally, all the followers find the faith they
should have had from the beginning.

When Jesus finally appears to the Eleven (vv. 36-43), he first has
to prove it is really him, for they still cannot believe he has arisen
from the dead. So he provides twofold proof of his bodily resurrection—touch and eating a meal—proving their fears wrong (vv.
36-43). This is a great lesson for us, for we have the same incre-
dulity today, wondering how such an incomprehensible miracle
as physical resurrection could ever happen. We do not have Jesus'
body to touch, but we do have the numerous reports and proofs
from this and other New Testament texts to contemplate, and the
truth of Christ rising from the dead as firstfruits guaranteeing our
own future resurrections is too important to ignore. We too need
to experience this certainty of resurrection.

The narration now turns from what Christ has done for his
followers—namely, rise from the dead—to what they are to do
for him; namely, continue his mission to the world (vv. 44-49).
This appearance to the Eleven becomes a commissioning service,
launching the post-Pentecost mission of salvation to a lost world.
The Old Testament prophecies of the coming of the Messiah had as
an essential component the call to take the message to the nations,
and the disciples are to fulfill that call. The death and resurrection
of Christ are not a secret rite restricted only to followers. Jesus
died so the world of darkness could come into the light, and the

message must be shared with all in the world. Repentance leading to forgiveness of sins must be preached to all the nations.

To accomplish this mission, the disciples are promised (v. 49) the coming of the Spirit on them from heaven. Theirs is a superhuman task, and to fulfill that divine calling, God is sending the Spirit, who will come on the whole church at Pentecost and empower them in this universal mission. They must wait for that moment when the Spirit comes, and then they will have the God-given power to proclaim that world-changing truth.

The ascension of Jesus (vv. 50–53) provides the perfect culmination to his earthly ministry, as he reenacts Enoch and Elijah in being caught up to heaven in glory. The sight of Jesus rising to heaven enables his followers to realize the reality of Psalm 110:1, as he was raised to the right hand of God in exaltation. He is truly the risen Lord, no longer the Suffering Servant but the Lord of heaven and earth. The disciples recognize this and turn to praise and worship, both glorifying Jesus in their own collected worship and praising him as they witness in the temple, proclaiming the risen Lord to everyone they meet.

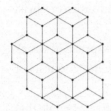

GLOSSARY

apocalyptic Refers to truths about God's plans for history that he has hidden in past generations but has revealed (the Greek *apokalypsis* means "unveiling") to his people. The name also describes a genre of ancient literature (including Revelation and parts of Daniel) that communicates these truths using vivid symbolism.

chiasm (n.), chiastic (adj.) A stylistic device in which a passage is organized into two sections, with the contents of the statements in the first half repeated in reverse order in the second half (ABC:C′B′A′).

christological (adj.), Christology (n.) Refers to the New Testament's presentation of the person and work of Christ, especially his identity as Messiah.

eschatological (adj.), eschatology (n.) Refers to the last things or the end times. Within this broad category, biblical scholars and theologians have identified more specific concepts. For instance, "realized eschatology" emphasizes the present work of Christ in the world as he prepares for the end of history. In "inaugurated eschatology," the last days have already begun but have not yet been consummated at the return of Christ.

eschaton Greek for "end" or "last," referring to the return of Christ and the end of history.

Hellenism (n.), Hellenistic (adj.) Relates to the spread of Greek culture in the Mediterranean world after the conquests of Alexander the Great (356–323 BC).

lex talionis Latin for "law of retaliation." This is the principle that those who have done some wrong will be punished in a similar degree and kind.

midrash (n.), midrashic (adj.) A Jewish exposition of a text using the techniques of ancient rabbis to give a detailed analysis of the meaning and theology of a text.

Mishnah An ancient Jewish source, compiled around AD 200, that contains the sayings of the rabbis. While it was not written down until later, it tells us about oral traditions that were in existence in Jesus' time.

parousia The event of Christ's second coming. The Greek word *parousia* means "arrival" or "presence."

proleptic Refers to the presentation of a future act as though it has already been accomplished.

Qumran A site near the northwestern corner of the Dead Sea where a collection of scrolls (called the Dead Sea Scrolls) was found beginning in the 1940s. The community that lived at this site and wrote these scrolls separated themselves from the rest of Jewish society. Many scholars believe they were a branch of the Essenes, one of the three major Jewish sects mentioned by Josephus (*Antiquities* 13.171–72). The Dead Sea Scrolls include manuscripts of Old Testament books as well as other writings that are not part of Scripture. They do not refer to Christianity, but do shed light on aspects of Judaism around the time of Jesus.

Septuagint An ancient Greek translation of the Old Testament that was used extensively in the early church. It is commonly abbreviated LXX.

Shekinah A word derived from the Hebrew *shakan* (to dwell), used
   to describe God's personal presence taking the form of a
   cloud, often in the context of the tabernacle or temple (e.g.,
   Exod 40:38; Num 9:15; 1 Kgs 8:10-11).

soteriological (adj.), soteriology (n.) Relating to the doctrine of
   salvation (Greek: *sōtēria*), including such subjects as atonement, justification, and sanctification.

Synoptic A term applied to the Gospels of Matthew, Mark, and
   Luke because of their many similarities and parallels, from
   the Greek meaning "having the same look."

typological (adj.), typology (n.) A literary device in which Old
   Testament persons or events are the types that correspond
   to and are fulfilled in New Testament realities.

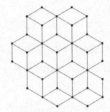

BIBLIOGRAPHY

Bock, Darrell L. *Luke*. Baker Exegetical Commentary on the New Testament. 2 vols. Grand Rapids: Baker, 1994–1996.

Caird, George B. *Saint Luke*. Penguin New Testament Commentary. London: Penguin, 1963.

Ellis, E. Earle. *The Gospel of Luke*. New Century Bible. Grand Rapids: Eerdmans, 1983.

Evans, Craig A. *Luke*. New International Biblical Commentary. Peabody, MA: Hendrickson, 1990.

Fitzmyer, Joseph A. *The Gospel According to Luke: A New Translation with Introduction and Commentary*. Anchor Bible 28, 28A. New York: Doubleday, 1981–1982.

France, R. T. *Luke*. Teach the Text Commentary Series. Grand Rapids: Baker, 2013.

Garland, David E. *Luke*. Zondervan Exegetical Commentary on the New Testament. Grand Rapids: Zondervan, 2011.

Godet, Frederic L. *A Commentary on the Gospel of St. Luke*. 2 vols. New York: I. K. Funk, 1881.

Green, Joel B. *The Gospel of Luke*. New International Commentary on the New Testament. Grand Rapids: Eerdmans, 1997.

Hughes, R. Kent. *Luke: That You May Know the Truth*. Preaching the Word. 2 vols. Wheaton, IL: Crossway, 1998.

Johnson, Luke Timothy. *The Gospel of Luke.* Sacra Pagina. Collegeville, MN: Liturgical Press, 1991.

Marshall, I. Howard. *The Gospel of Luke: A Commentary on the Greek Text.* New International Greek Testament Commentary. Grand Rapids: Eerdmans, 1978.

Nolland, John L. *Luke.* Word Biblical Commentary. 3 vols. Dallas: Word, 1989–1991.

Plummer, Alfred. *A Critical and Exegetical Commentary on the Gospel According to St. Luke.* International Critical Commentary. Edinburgh: T&T Clark, 1922.

Stein, Robert. *Luke.* New American Commentary. Nashville: Broadman, 1992.

Wilcock, Michael. *The Savior of the World: The Message of Luke's Gospel.* The Bible Speaks Today. Downers Grove, IL: InterVarsity Press, 1979.

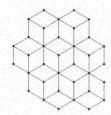

SUBJECT AND AUTHOR INDEX

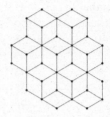

INDEX OF SCRIPTURE AND OTHER ANCIENT LITERATURE

Old Testament

New Testament

Deuterocanonical Works